HARD
JUDICIAL
CHOICES

HARD JUDICIAL CHOICES

Federal District Court Judges and State and Local Officials

Phillip J. Cooper

New York   Oxford
OXFORD UNIVERSITY PRESS
1988

Oxford University Press

Oxford   New York   Toronto
Delhi   Bombay   Calcutta   Madras   Karachi
Petaling Jaya   Singapore   Hong Kong   Tokyo
Nairobi   Dar es Saalam   Cape Town
Melbourne   Auckland

and associated companies in
Beirut   Berlin   Ibadan   Nicosia

Copyright © 1988 by Oxford University Press, Inc.

Published by Oxford University Press, Inc.
200 Madison Avenue, New York, New York 10016

Oxford is a registered trademark of Oxford University Press

Library of Congress Cataloging-in-Publication Data
Cooper, Phillip J.
Hard judicial choices.
Bibliography: p.
Includes index.
1. Judicial review of administrative acts—United
States.   2. District courts—United States.   3. Judicial
process—United States.   4. Remedies (Law)—United
States.   5. Abuse of administrative power—United
States—States.   6. Law and politics.   I. Title.
KF5425.C66   1988   347.73'5   87-7901
                         347.3075
ISBN 0-19-504191-7
ISBN 0-19-504192-5 (pbk.)

Printing (last digit): 9 8 7 6 5 4 3 2 1

Printed in the United States of America
on acid-free paper

For William Richardson, from whom I learned a great deal about the value of a first-rate colleague.

Preface

Judges make policy. That is a fact of American political life, and it will continue to be true whether judges are predominantly conservatives or liberals, Republicans or Democrats. Just how they make policy within several particularly complex fields and relate to other actors in the policy process is the subject of this book. In particular, it examines those situations in which judges issue complex remedial orders affecting education, housing, mental health, corrections, and police policy.

This book was written with several audiences in mind. They include students of the judicial process, public administration, the law, and policy analysis, as well as the educated lay public interested in the types of cases discussed here, about which they have read reports in newspapers and magazines or commentaries in journals of opinion. Some of the judges who have examined early drafts of this book have suggested that other judges, executive branch officials, and legislators would benefit from it as well.

Following the two introductory chapters, which consider critical concepts and provide a basic model of the remedial decree process, there are two chapters per policy area. Preceding each case study chapter is a policy survey chapter that sketches (and only sketches) the background of conflict in that policy area, as well as political and administrative problems and the role courts have played in the developments within the field. These chapters place the case studies in legal, administrative, and political context. The individual chapter conclusions do not attempt detailed analyses. That task is reserved for the final chapter. The policy survey and case study chapters are designed to stand independently. They can be read out of order.

In examining the case studies that follow, the reader will find a substantial number of rather lengthy quotations from trial and remedy hearing transcripts. There are also several fairly extensive descriptions of evidence presented. The intention is to give as much of the flavor of what the judge saw as possible and to indicate the context in which it was presented, since it is particularly important, for reasons discussed in the Introduction, to view the cases from the judges' perspective.

Albany, New York
September 1987

P.J.C.

Acknowledgments

This project involved more than five years of field work and analysis. As anyone who has ever undertaken such a project knows, it is impossible to give adequate recognition to the many people who have contributed to various aspects of the work since its inception, including all those who took valuable time from their busy schedules to submit to interviews and make their records available for inspection. Nevertheless, I would like to express special appreciation to a few of those who made particularly important contributions to the project.

A variety of academic colleagues provided both encouragement and assistance. They include: Howard Ball of the University of Utah; Dennis Dorin of North Carolina State University; Paula Eldot of California State University, Sacramento; Robert Gilmour of the University of Connecticut; Thomas Lauth of the University of Georgia; Tinsley Yarbrough of East Carolina University; and John Rohr of Virginia Polytechnic Institute. A number of my colleagues at the State University of New York at Albany have made contributions, including Carolyn Ban, David Bayley, Thomas Church, Roman Hedges, Todd Swanstrom, and Stephen Wasby. They performed the invaluable function of reading drafts and providing comments and suggestions in an effort to save this author from the most serious mistakes of substance and style. Unfortunately, it was not always possible to accept the recommendations, but this in no way detracts from their value. I am certain the volume could have been improved had I incorporated more of those ideas. Naturally, I absolve these kind colleagues of responsibility for any shortcomings in the present work.

In addition to academic contributors, there were many people in the various communities where research was conducted who took the time and effort to go well beyond simple cooperation in providing assistance. They include, among others; Allen Adler, Assistant Ohio Attorney General; Michael Barrett and Brian Heffernan of the Civil Rights Division, U.S. Department of Justice; Andrew Boyko, Law Officer for Parma, Ohio; Sheila Carnes, Office of the Clerk, United States District Court for the Middle District of Alabama; Peter Hearn of Pepper, Hamilton and Scheetz, Philadelphia; and Avery Friedman, Attorney at Law, Cleveland, Ohio.

I would also like to thank the staff at Oxford for their work on this manuscript. I am particularly grateful to Valerie Aubry, Susan Rabiner, Judith Mintz, Andrew Yockers, and Henry Krawitz.

Finally, let me publicly acknowledge my gratitude to my wife, Lynn, who endured my wanderings to research sites, the late-night scribbling, and the hours planted in front of the computer when I should have been doing other things. Her love and support mean more than she knows.

Contents

HARD
JUDICIAL
CHOICES

Introduction

The late Judge Stephen Roth was the federal district judge who, until his death in 1974, presided over the Detroit school busing controversy. Judge Roth was generally regarded as a conservative of impeccable credentials. Some time before what would come to be known as the *Milliken v. Bradley* case came to his court, Roth was quoted as opposing wide-ranging suits brought by "outsider" groups who sought court-ordered desegregation by busing and the inclusion of suburbs in city problems.[1] Yet upon his death three and a half years later, the *Detroit Free Press* story reporting his passing was headlined, "JUDGE ROTH DEAD AT 66: HE ORDERED AREA BUSING":

> He was one of the first judges anywhere to consider a metropolitan school integration plan. . . .
>
> The public controversy over the case has centered on Judge Roth, and not on the appeals court judges or any other participants.
>
> Not since the early days of the school integration movement in the South has a federal court judge presiding over a case become the focus of such abuse.
>
> The Detroit school case came to be called "the Roth case" even by the press and politicians. Bumper stickers with comments like "Roth is a four-letter word" and "Judge Roth is a child molester" appeared on cars throughout the Detroit area.[2]

A Hungarian immigrant who worked his way through Notre Dame and the University of Michigan School of Law and who had a successful political career in Michigan, Roth could hardly have underestimated the personal price he would pay for ordering cross-district busing between Detroit and its suburbs.

THE PROBLEM

A federal judge who is called upon to decide a case that concerns alleged discrimination in housing, employment, or schools; a dispute concerning conditions in prison or mental health facilities; or a challenge to local government administration in the area of police/community relations and who also has to render appropriate orders if the allegations are found accurate must perform one of the most difficult tasks in our system of government. The judge must stand as an officer of the national government against a local majority represented by state and local officials. The trial judge facing such a task does not enjoy the rarified and cloistered atmosphere of appellate courts. As one scholar has observed, trial judges must operate at the point where the political and legal systems meet.[3] And it is when a federal judge fashions a remedy following proof of a legal violation that the conflicts between law and politics and between federal courts and state and local officials become most intense. At that moment the difficulties that come in translating the principles involved in framing a government into the problems of running a government (such as protection of individual rights against rule by the majority) are felt most keenly. It is the realm of hard judicial choices.

In what has been said and written about this subject, no one has argued that the kind of intergovernmental conflict surrounding ongoing judicial involvement in administration (such as evaluating mental health services) is, in itself, desirable or that it is in some way good for a court. Well then, why does it occur? If one is to answer that question, it is necessary to see the cases as much as possible from the vantage point of a judge called upon to resolve a case in which a remedial decree is requested. How else can one comprehend why a judge submits himself or herself to what is sure to follow the issuance of such a remedial decree?

In addition to the problems encountered by Judge Roth, there is the now-familiar case of Judge Frank Johnson, formerly a district judge and presently a member of the Eleventh Circuit Court of Appeals. Judge Johnson's northern Alabama Republican background and his political career before coming to the federal bench hardly marked him as a liberal.[4] Yet his desegregation orders and his decrees requiring reform of state prisons[5] and mental health facilities[6] are generally regarded as the leading examples of judicial intervention in state and local administration. For his actions Johnson faced a cross burning on his lawn, copious quantities of hate mail and phone calls, and a dynamite attack on his mother's house.[7]

The difficulties encountered by Roth and Johnson are two of the more widely known and extreme cases, but it is not at all unusual for judges who issue detailed remedial orders to be objects of pressure, ridicule, and threats. Remedies continue to be criticized as frequently arbitrary, unilateral, overhead impositions that neither comprehend nor accommodate problems of cost, expertise, or the need for administrative and policy flexibility. Even so, judges continue to issue such orders. By 1981 "individual prisons or entire prison systems in at least 24 states had been declared unconstitutional,"[8] with many of these institutions still under remedial decrees.

For those who would understand the judicial process and the interaction between judges and the political and administrative institutions, a number of questions arise. Why do judges issue complex remedial decrees given the difficulties involved? How do these cases arise? How are they prosecuted and how are remedies fashioned where violations of rights are found? What lessons can be learned about the interactions of state and local officials and federal district judges that can be used to improve their relationships in the future? This book examines remedial decree litigation in search of answers to these questions as well as a better understanding of the process by which the cases develop and the problems and prospects of the judges called upon to develop a decree to remedy a violation of federally protected rights.

THE STUDY

Remedial decrees issued by federal courts in cases concerning schools, prisons, housing, employment, and mental health facilities have received considerable attention in recent years.[9] These decisions would have been controversial in any case, but that tension was exacerbated by the economic hard times of the past decade coupled with various anti-government and antitax movements which have had especially harsh impacts upon state and local government. The Supreme Court has been very much a part of the controversy, with the Burger Court moving to place limits on district court authority in the remedial decree area.[10]

A literature has developed in response to the controversy surrounding the complex decree cases, but it is far from complete. It consists largely of macrolevel debates about the appropriateness and feasibility of judges involving themselves in complex remedial decree cases and the problems this activity presents for the judiciary and the institutions which are the targets of the orders. This critical material is basically of two varieties: those works which proceed from certain assumptions about judicial role[11] and those which assert that the institutional capacity of the judiciary is exceeded in these institutional reform cases.[12] The judicial role critiques range from more analytic considerations of judicial behavior to jurisprudential theses making fervent normative arguments as to the proper role of the judge in the Anglo-American legal system and the appropriate nature and purpose of law within society.[13] The judicial capacity pieces argue that, even assuming judges should be involved in such cases, the courts lack the institutional ability in terms of resources and techniques for crafting the decrees and effectively implementing the judgments.[14] Cavanagh and Sarat refer to the latter as the court capacity model.[15]

There is, however, a less critical and more supportive literature that focuses on the remedial cases. Some of this work developed initially in law reviews as a number of lawyers and a few of the judges involved in litigating the most controversial of the cases argued that judges should and must render adequate and comprehensive remedies for proven violations of law, particularly in fields where state and local governments had been unwilling or unable to meet their responsibilities.[16] Part of this literature has been presented not so much to support the district judges as to criticize Burger Court rulings that limited the lower courts' remedial authority.[17]

Political scientists entered the lists, challenging the critics of federal court intervention. Several have rather convincingly demonstrated that much of the criticism of the judicial decree cases (and other types of cases on the new ''public law'' docket)[18] is a reformulation of the activism/restraint critique which, in turn, has a good deal more to do with the result of rulings than with the presumed proper role or capabilities of the judiciary.[19]

While much of the work has been very general discussion, there have been case study analyses of individual controversies, often in situations where the investigator wrote about a local conflict between a district court judge and state and local officials.[20] Most take a policy analysis approach to the cases, with particular interest in the always present question of judicial impact (as it is referred to in the law and judicial process literature) or implementation and evaluation (as it is described in the parlance of policy studies).[21]

In sum, the literature developed on remedial decrees thus far has focused primarily on whether judges can and should be involved in the preparation, issuance, and implementation of complex decrees. To the degree that this literature has addressed the process of remedial decree case development at all, it has been largely by way of pointing out important issues in the ongoing arguments for or against remedial orders.[22] Examples include the tendency to discuss the use of special masters in decree implementation or the complexity associated with the use of social science data in considering remedies.[23] This volume attempts to gain a more systematic understanding of the process by which remedial decree cases develop and operate.

This research began in an effort to learn more about the remedial decree process in a disciplined manner while avoiding the more obvious pitfalls of research in the field and retaining sensitivity for the complexity of the subject. A comparative case approach was employed. In-depth case studies were completed on five carefully selected remedial decree cases in five equitable decree policy areas: housing discrimination, school desegregation, mental health facilities and the right to treatment, prison conditions, and police/community relations. The remedy crafting portion of the cases served as the focal point, though not the only area, of analysis. Finally, preliminary analysis of the first cases provided a framework for further consideration of the full study. Each of these points requires brief explanation.

Much of the research on remedial decree cases has come in the form of case studies. Such studies, although not equally valuable or well done, are particularly useful for understanding remedial decree suits because of the complex nature, multiple parties, and lengthy procedures associated with this type of litigation.[24] Many of the case studies have been prepared either by those who participated, directly or indirectly, in the cases, which results in the obvious, and in some instances quite severe, problems of bias, or by scholars who are located at major universities near a community that is the subject of a remedial decree and who find such developments a kind of laboratory for observation. Both types of study have the virtue of on-site long-term access to documentary and interview sources as well as a perspective on local politics that cannot be equaled by an outside investigator in the absence of an extended visit to the community.[25] Moreover, such a vantage point can provide access to records that may soon be sent to central records depositories and interviews with participants who will likely decide they have had enough and wish no further approach from social scientists. These studies can be extremely interesting and provide a rich contribution to the literature, enhancing the data base on which further analysis can proceed.[26] In addition to problems of bias, there is often a serious question whether a particular case study was accomplished for analytical purposes or because, for one reason or another, it was handy.[27] The latter possibility increases the danger of encountering what Lowi referred to as the "one debilitating handicap of all case-studies, the problem of uniqueness."[28]

The approach taken in this research was to carefully select five cases from five different remedial decree policy areas in such a way as to minimize the weaknesses of the case study method and gain some of the advantages of comparative analysis.[29] The first step in identifying appropriate cases was to select the major policy areas in which courts have most often been called upon to issue complex decrees involving them directly in the operation of government institutions and public policy development: school desegregation, fair housing enforcement, prison conditions, mental health facilities reform, and local government administration. For each area a case was then chosen to reflect the changing national political context, to include changes from the Warren Court to the Burger Court, to span a significant period of time, and to reflect geographical diversity. Cases were divided between those which were upheld on appeal and those which were reversed. To guard against selection of cases that might trigger researcher bias, I avoided suits where I knew any of the actors or had any interest in a nearby community. Cases were also chosen to avoid prior knowledge beyond perhaps having read the Supreme Court's ruling or, as in the *Wyatt v. Stickney* study, having passing knowledge about the controversy surrounding Judge Frank Johnson.

The two racial discrimination cases were selected in part because they were northern cases, thus avoiding some of the special issues of southern desegregation and incorporating the difficulties of resolving cases where segregation was not mandated by statute.[30] The *Wyatt* case, on the other hand, involved a southern controversy, but a nonracial
one. The Philadelphia police and the Ohio prisons cases were selected partly because in
them the Burger Court overturned lower court remedies and issued warnings about excessive intervention into administration.

Milliken v. Bradley was chosen over *Keyes v. District No. 1, Denver*, the other
major northern school desegregation case of that period, because the latter was not
primarily a remedy case but more of an argument about the liability question.[31] *Milliken*
was also the most expansive of the school desegregation orders rendered by a federal
district court. It involved a metropolitan areawide remedy covering 53 school districts
affecting more than seven hundred thousand children, approximately three hundred
thousand of whom would have been transported to other schools, many across district
lines. Moreover, the Supreme Court rendered two full decisions in the case, first upholding the liability finding and striking down the remedy, then upholding a new remedy
developed in the trial court. One of the most significant features of the *Milliken* case
was that it came at the break point between the more expansive approach to judicial
interaction with states and localities of the Warren Court period and the narrowing of
district court remedial authority by the Court once the Burger majority was firmly established.

United States v. Parma, Ohio was also chosen because it concerned a northern
metropolitan area, in this case Cleveland. It focused on a city/suburban conflict over
open housing. The case was decided after the Burger Court cautioned district courts to
exercise more restraint in their approach to remedy crafting. It was litigated by the
Department of Justice (DOJ) rather than an established interest group like the NAACP,
which tried the *Milliken* case. The suit resulted in an order mandating a housing policy
for one suburban community. The decree was upheld on appeal and *certiorari* was
denied by the Supreme Court. *Parma* was chosen over *Hills v. Gautreaux*, the only
housing remedy case actually decided by the Court, although the latter would have been
easier to research.[32] Unlike *Milliken, Parma* was a case in which no previous research
had been conducted. For that reason, the *Parma* study was done first in an effort to get
a fresh view of the subject.

Wyatt was chosen over New York and Pennsylvania mental facilities cases partly
for reasons of geographical diversity and because it is considered the root of the controversy over remedial decree litigation. Even so, there has been little in-depth research on
the case except for law review pieces by participants and others, with the primary interest on implementation and impact rather than on the remedy crafting process.[33] The
case was also useful because it was an interaction involving state and federal governments without the local government dimension of the school and housing disputes.
Moreover, the decree, upheld on appeal by the Fifth Circuit Court of Appeals, has been
in place for a substantial period of time, thus allowing an opportunity to study the
relationship of the remedy development process and post decree proceedings. Finally,
while the case later became a focal point for mental health interest groups and the
Department of Justice, the principal parties prosecuting *Wyatt* were local private individuals. *Wyatt* is an example of a third type of litigation configuration in remedial decree
suits in addition to DOJ controlled litigation like *Parma*, and suits litigated by established interest groups, like the NAACP in *Milliken*.

Despite the fact that it presents many of the issues common to prison conditions suits, the *Rhodes v. Chapman* prison case offers a number of interesting features that make it a useful candidate for this study. Unlike many of the better known prison cases like the Arkansas and Alabama litigation, *Rhodes* involved a new prison built in the early 1970s with most of the state-of-the-art features. It opened just at the time of a shift from declining to increasing prison populations and of a political move toward more conservative public attitudes about corrections administration. Although the Court had ruled in *Bell v. Wolfish* on pretrial detention, the justices had specifically reserved questions about confinement conditions in regular imprisonment, so *Rhodes* was the first case in which the Supreme Court ruled upon prison conditions for long term confinement.

Finally, the field of police/community relations controversies was selected as a representative of a class of cases concerning problems of local administration. There are several other possible cases in this general policy area, the most visible of which is perhaps the matter of affirmative action hiring, but the police/community relations conflict offered greater contrast with the other cases explored in this study, and the school and housing cases already address the use of remedial decrees in racial discrimination claims. Within the field of police/community relations, the *Rizzo v. Goode* litigation was an important ruling by the Supreme Court that admonished district court judges to limit their use of remedial decrees. It was also a case that involved a challenge by interest groups to a tightly controlled government in one of the nation's oldest cities.

The Other Side of the Bench

The final methodological consideration is the fact that much of the remedial decree literature takes an external *post hoc* approach as opposed to an internal dynamic perspective. Little attempt has been made to see the remedial decree process from the perspective of the judge called upon to render such a ruling.[34] Instead the judge is often viewed as one of the players in a dispute that has been resolved. Commentators ask whether the judge's mandated reforms have worked. While external analysis that looks back at a decided case is useful and provides an interesting base, particularly for impact analysis and policy evaluation, it is neither the only nor the most useful approach for understanding the process. The judge's perspective cannot be ignored without distorting our understanding of the phenomenon. Unlike many studies of legislative or executive decisionmaking, we rarely ask what a judge saw at the time of decision, what options were available to the decisionmaker, and what forces constrained the judge's choice among options. Perhaps more can be learned about judicial policymaking in general and institutional reform rulings in particular by attempting to understand them from the perspective of the decisionmaker than by focusing on the reaction to a decree by groups who brought a suit or the responses of administrative officials called upon to implement court orders. In any case it is too important a perspective to be ignored. This research examines the complexities and pressures faced by Judges Frank Battisti, Stephen Roth, Robert DeMascio, Frank Johnson, Myron Thompson, Timothy Hogan, Robert Duncan, and John Fullam.

Moreover, the external perspective is often coupled with a rather static, *post hoc* view of the process. The environment within which the cases were decided has been frequently defined quite narrowly to include only the local political scene and to exclude such matters as changing patterns in Supreme Court rulings and developments in other district courts and courts of appeals. The environment does not remain static. Justice Department policies, federal grant programs, and statutory provisions change. That is particularly important for remedial decree cases where litigation frequently runs over several years.

THE NORMATIVE ARGUMENT

Several portions of this study have been presented at political science and public administration conferences. At some of these sessions, interested commentators insisted on my taking a position on whether judges should or should not issue complex remedial decrees. They said the findings of the papers were interesting and useful but where was the verdict on the judges? There are two answers and one caveat.

First, while this volume suggests some of the reasons why these cases develop and are handled as they are, I will not sit in judgment on the judges by declaring whether they should or should not have issued the orders in question. While I think that is an important and interesting question, I am not certain it is answerable in the very broad sense in which it is posed. Moreover, I do not think we have the kind of information on which to base such a conclusion at this point, unless the whole debate is to be largely ideological. This study suggests a number of problems in the existing literature of judicial process and behavior and of public administration, but it does not purport to either justify or condemn the judges involved. Furthermore, it reveals a number of reasons to believe the macrolevel question simply is not answerable in the manner in which it is often presented.

The caveat I would add is that I am somewhat concerned that we are once again swinging toward the extreme of the pendulum arc. Whereas there was an extended period during which all normative arguments were ruled illegitimate and only description, analysis, and prediction were permissible, we seem now to have traveled toward the other pole at which one must take a normative position—frequently with limited or highly selected empirical grounding—to which others often respond ideologically. As in most things, life at the extremes is not particularly constructive. There is more than enough room between them.

What I hope this study will accomplish is to provide a rather different view of the judicial process, one that attempts to integrate lower court and appellate court activity, provides a better understanding of the interactions of federal courts and state and local officials, and contributes a number of suggestions regarding ways in which administrators and judges can improve their relationships when litigants call upon courts to make these hard choices.

NOTES

1. William Serrin, "The Most Hated Man in Michigan," *Saturday Review,* Aug. 26, 1972, p. 14.

2. William Grant, "Judge Roth Dead at 66: He Ordered Area Busing," *Detroit Free Press,* Friday, July 12, 1974, p. 1A.

3. Kenneth M. Dolbeare, *Trial Courts in Urban Politics* (New York: Wiley, 1967).

4. *See generally* Tinsley Yarbrough, *Judge Frank M. Johnson and Human Rights in Alabama* (University: Univ. of Alabama Press, 1981).

5. *Pugh v. Locke,* 406 F. Supp. 318 (MDAL 1976), *aff'd as modified,* 559 F.2d 283 (5th Cir. 1977), *rev'd in part on other grounds* 438 U.S. 781 (1971); and *Newman v. Alabama,* 349 F. Supp. 278 (MDAL 1972).

6. *Wyatt v. Stickney,* 325 F. Supp. 781 (MDAL 1971) (liability opinion); 334 F. Supp. 1341 (EDAL 1971) (remedy guideline); 344 F. Supp. 373 (MDAL 1972) (Bryce and Searcy remedy order); 344 F. Supp. 387 (MDAL 1972) (Partlow remedy order), *aff'd* 503 F.2d 1305 (5th Cir. 1974).

7. Transcript, *Bill Moyer's Journal.* "Judge: The Law and Frank Johnson," (an interview with Judge Johnson), July 24, 1980, pp. 6–8. See also Yarbrough, *supra* note 4.

8. *Rhodes v. Chapman,* 425 U.S. 337, 353–54 (1981) (Brennan, J., concurring).

9. *See generally* Abram Chayes, "The Role of the Judge in Public Law Litigation," 89 *Harv. L. Rev.* 1281 (1976).

10. *Milliken v. Bradley,* 418 U.S. 717 (1974); *Rizzo v. Goode,* 423 U.S. 362 (1976); and *Pasadena Bd. of Ed. v. Spangler,* 427 U.S. 424 (1976).

11. *See, e.g.,* Colin S. Diver, "The Judge as Powerbroker: Superintending Change in Political Institutions," 65 *Va. L. Rev.* 43 (1979); Chayes, *supra* note 9; and Robert S. Gilmour, "Agency Administration by Judiciary," *Southern Review of Public Administration* 6 (Spring 1982): 26–42.

12. Donald Horowitz, *The Courts and Social Policy* (Wash., DC: Brookings, 1977). *See also* Roger C. Cramton, "Judicial Policy Making and Administration," *Public Administration Review* 31 (Sept./Oct. 1976): 551–54.

13. *See, e.g.,* Nathan Glazer, "Should Courts Administer Social Services?" *Public Interest* 50 (Winter 1978): 64–80; Raoul Berger, *Government by Judiciary* (Cambridge, MA: Harvard Univ. Press, 1977); Lon Fuller, "The Forms and Limits of Adjudication," 92 Harv. L. Rev. 353 (1978); and D.L. Kirp, "School Desegregation and the Limits of Legalism," *Public Interest* 47 (Spring 1977): 101–28.

14. Horowitz, *supra* note 12.

15. Ralph Cavanagh and Austin Sarat, "Thinking About Courts: Toward and Beyond a Jurisprudence of Judicial Competence," 14 *Law and Society Review* 371, 379 (1980).

16. For comments by lawyers, *see, e.g.,* J. Harold Flannery, *"De Jure* Desegregation: The Quest for Adequacy"; and, *id.* "An Anti-black Strategy and the Supreme Court," in R. Stephen Browning, ed., *From Brown to Bradley: School Desegregation, 1954–1974* (Cincinnati, OH: Jefferson Law Book Co., 1975); examples of judges' comments are Frank Johnson, "The Constitution and the Federal District Judge," 54 *Tex. L. Rev.* 903 (1976); and J. Skelly Wright, "Are Courts Abandoning the Cities?" in Browning, *supra.*

17. *See generally* Browning, *supra* note 16.

18. See Chayes, *supra* note 9, at 1292.

19. *See, e.g.,* Cavanagh and Sarat, *supra* note 15; Stephen L. Wasby, "Arrogation of Power or Accountability: 'Judicial Imperialism' Revisited," 65 *Judicature* 208 (1981); and Daniel J. Monti, "Administrative Foxes in Educational Chicken Coops: An Examination and Critique of Judicial Activism in School Desegregation Cases," 2 *Law and Politics Quarterly* 233 (1980).

20. *See, e.g.,* Anthony Champagne, "The Theory of Limited Judicial Impact: Reforming the Dallas Jail as a Case Study," in Stuart Nagel and Erika Fairchild, eds., *The Political Science of Criminal Justice* (Springfield, IL: Charles C. Thomas Pub., 1983). *See also* the case studies in Howard I. Kolodner and James J. Fishman, eds., *Limits of Justice: The Court's Role in School Desegregation* (Cambridge, MA: Ballinger, 1978).

21. *See* Monti, *supra* note 19, and Champagne, *supra* note 20. On impact, *see generally* Charles A. Johnson and Bradley C. Canon, *Judicial Policies: Implementation and Impact* (Wash., DC: Congressional Quarterly, 1984); and Stephen L. Wasby, *The Impact of the United States Supreme Court* (Homewood, IL: Dorsey, 1970). On implementation problems, *see* Robert K.

Nakamura and Frank Smallwood, *The Politics of Policy Implementation* (New York: St. Martins, 1980); and Charles S. Bullock III and Charles M. Lamb, eds., *Implementation of Civil Rights Policy* (Monterey, CA: Brooks/Cole, 1984).

22. *See* Diver, *supra* note 11; Gilmour, *supra* note 11, on one side, and Cavanagh and Sarat, *supra* note 15; Wasby, *supra* note 19, on the other.

23. Eleanor P. Wolf, "Social Science and the Courts: The Detroit Schools Case," *Public Interest* 4 (Winter 1976): 102–20.

24. Robert K. Yin, *Case Study Research: Design and Methods* (Beverly Hills, CA. Sage, 1984); Harry Eckstein, "Case Study and Theory in Political Science," in Fred I. Greenstein and Nelson W. Polsby, eds., *Handbook of Political Science,* Volume 7 (Reading, MA: Addison-Wesley, 1975); Arend Lijphart, "Comparative Politics and the Comparative Method," *American Political Science Review* 65 (Sept. 1971): 682–93; Theodore Lowi, "American Business, Public Policy, Case Studies, and Political Theory," *World Politics* 16 (July 1964): 677–715.

25. *See, e.g.,* Elwood Hain, "Sealing Off the City: School Desegregation in Detroit," in Kalodner and Fishman, *supra* note 20; and William R. Grant, "The Detroit School Case: An Historical Overview," 21 *Wayne L. Rev.* 851 (1975). *See generally,* Eckstein, *supra* note 24, at 121.

26. Lijphart, *supra* note 24, at 691–92.

27. Eckstein, *supra* note 24, at 106.

28. Lowi, *supra* note 24, at 686.

29. Eckstein, *supra* note 24, at 104–5. *See also* Sidney Verba, "Some Dilemmas in Comparative Research," *World Politics* 20 (Oct. 1967): 111–27.

30. Northern cases present a variety of interesting differences from problems presented in the southern cases. In some ways those cases are more complex since they do not generally evidence the kind of statutory segregation seen in the southern cases. On the other hand, there are features of southern social structure which differ markedly from the North and provide complexities of their own to those contemplating desegregation cases. See J.W. Peltason, *Fifty-eight Lonely Men: Southern Federal Judges and School Desegregation* (Urbana: Univ. of Illinois Press, 1971); and Robert Chafe, *Civil Liberties and Civilities* (New York: Oxford Univ. Press, 1978).

31. *Keyes v. School Dist. No. 1, Denver,* 413 U.S. 189 (1973).

32. *Hills v. Gautreaux,* 425 U.S. 284 (1976).

33. Tinsley Yarbrough's chapter on *Wyatt v. Stickney* in his *Judge Frank Johnson and Human Rights in Alabama, supra* note 4, is an exception, but that study was done primarily as a biography that focused on the judge rather than as an effort to understand the remedial decree process.

34. Most of what has been written in an attempt to understand the judge's situation has concerned the early desegregation cases—*e.g.,* Peltason, *supra* note 30. For more recent and slightly wider perspectives, *see* Yarbrough, *supra* note 4, and *Bill Moyers Journal, supra* note 7.

1

Judges Under the Microscope:
Remedial Decree Cases as a
Window on the Judicial Process

One of the ways social scientists study political institutions, actors, and processes is to determine how they operate on a day-to-day basis in accomplishing the assignments they are regularly asked to perform. There is, however, another way to study political institutions and processes, that is, by examining them when they are performing some of their most difficult tasks in the most stressful circumstances they encounter. These are often the situations in which judges and other officials must take their role as participants in the public policy process most seriously, testing their own notions of the obligations of their office and the limits of their ability and authority. A study of the so-called remedial decree cases, the decisions in which district judges have ordered desegregation and institutional reform, provides just such a perspective.

Judges called upon to issue a court order that will remedy racial discrimination or correct inhumane conditions in mental health facilities generally proceed by issuing what is known as an equitable decree. An examination of the process which produces equitable remedies provides an important perspective on the relationship of federal courts to state and local officials that is often considered in only the most cursory fashion by scholars of the judiciary or of public administration.

In order to comprehend the political and administrative importance of the hard judicial choices made by federal judges in the remedial decree litigation presented in the case studies that follow, however, one must begin with both a general understanding of the concepts underlying the use of equitable remedies and a basic model of the process by which they are fashioned. At a minimum, that requires a consideration of the nature of contemporary equitable decrees, the role of interest group claims for class remedies, and the remedial decree process itself.

THE NATURE OF EQUITABLE REMEDY

Without attempting to delve too deeply into matters of jurisprudence and civil procedure, one must consider some of the most important features of modern cases brought for equitable remedies, the kind of orders issued to remedy segregation or unconstitutional prison conditions. These include the differences between public law and private law contests, the problem of money damages, and the use of injunctions for negative and positive relief.

Judges are asked to resolve two kinds of disputes: private law cases and public law controversies.[1] Private law disputes involve suits by private citizens or organizations against one another. The government plays a more or less independent role by providing the rules for the resolution of the dispute (the law), a forum in which to decide the matter (a court), and an official to serve as an impartial decisionmaker (the judge). Public law contests, on the other hand, involve the government more directly. In these cases citizens or groups contend that some government institution or official has violated a right set forth in the state or federal constitution or statutes. Here, government is a direct party to the dispute and not merely an independent umpire in the suit. Government, though, is a special litigant. The laws, of course, grant to government special powers and limit it with a variety of citizens' rights and liberties. Public officers have only those powers granted to them by law and must exercise them in a manner compatible with the rights of its citizens.

Legal actions, whether public law or private law contests, may either be policy oriented or compensatory. The classic model of the private lawsuit is a situation in which two citizens go to court to resolve a dispute over a business contract, with the plaintiff hoping to win money damages to compensate his or her losses in the transaction. Public law contests may be of the same sort. A citizen may ask a judge to find that the government has injured him or her, for example, by providing inadequate payment for land taken for road construction by the power of eminent domain or by improperly deciding whether the litigant is eligible for Social Security disability benefits. The point of such suits is largely personal and not an attempt to change the policies of government or private industry. On the other hand, we have seen an increase in recent decades of policy oriented suits in private law cases. Hence, product liability suits and personal injury litigation have been used not merely to recompense persons hurt by industrial practices, but also in an attempt to change the business policy of these private firms. Recent examples include suits brought against the manufacturers of asbestos insulating materials used in homes and public buildings and others brought against the firms producing the chemical defoliant known during the Vietnam War as Agent Orange. Most often, however, policy oriented lawsuits are public law controversies: cases brought against the government not merely to recover damages, but to stop an allegedly illegal policy or practice. Hence, a suit brought to improve the conditions of confinement for those committed to mental hospitals is concerned with challenging policy. It is this kind of case, a policy oriented public lawsuit, that will be the focus of this book.

The use of money damages to remedy breaches of law has its limits. That is particularly true where government is the defendant. For one thing, government units, federal and state, as well as many officials enjoy immunity from damage claims. Judges, prosecutors, and in some instances legislators are virtually completely immune.[2] States are immune from damage suits under the Eleventh Amendment to the U.S. Constitution.[3] And even when they are not completely protected, all officials, at least in cases brought in federal courts, enjoy a form of limited immunity.[4] More important, however, is the fact that there are some situations in which an award of funds would not help the people who brought the suit a great deal even if they could collect a financial judgment. A patient in an unsafe mental institution deprived of care or a child in an illegally segregated school is far from fully recompensed by a monetary award.[5]

The way judges respond in situations where standard money damage claims are not adequate relief for the plaintiff is through the use of injunctive relief, orders that require the defendants to stop some current practice or direct them to eliminate the effects of their former illegal actions. These orders are generally referred to as equitable decrees. The concept of equity can be traced at least as far back as Aristotle, but it has undergone many changes since then. For present purposes, it is enough to trace the idea back to our English heritage.

When the king decided all major legal disputes, one could by definition be certain that absolute justice was done. After all, the king was annointed and presumed to embody justice. But as the number of judges in the law courts of the realm increased and since they were not, like the king, possessed of perfect justice, there arose the need to correct the mistakes of the judges and to deal with cases for which the law seemed to provide inadequate remedies. The lord high chancellor, known as the keeper of the king's conscience, took care of that need by issuing orders in equity. Later, equity courts were created, and, later still, judges in ordinary courts were given authority to act in both matters of law and equity. The principal tools of the trade in such courts is the use of prerogative writs, the most common of which for our purposes is the injunction. The term prerogative writ reminds us that these are orders issued as a matter of judicial discretion.

If a court has equity jurisdiction and concludes that the remedies at law are inadequate, the judge possesses a great deal of discretion in deciding whether and what kind of relief to order. Indeed, the Supreme Court has reminded us on numerous occasions that "[o]nce a right and a violation have been shown, the scope of a district court's equitable powers to remedy past wrongs is broad, for breadth and flexibility are inherent in equitable remedies."[6]

In many contemporary public law policy cases, the plaintiffs ask for both positive and negative relief. The plea for negative relief is generally a request that the judge declare past actions illegal and enjoin the government from any further such practices. If it has previously discriminated in housing practices, a government unit will be ordered to cease those illegal activities. The affirmative relief requested is for a decree with provisions which attempt, by directing changes in structure or practice, to undo the damage done to the plaintiffs and others similarly situated. Thus, a judge may order a city government to assist in the acquisition of low and moderate income housing if it is found guilty of past discrimination. Affirmative or positive relief is requested for other reasons beside the fact that money damages are inadequate to make the victims of some illegal actions whole again.

Another major rationale for mandating affirmative relief is the federal courts' experience of more than a quarter century with litigation in which legal declarations and general injunctive, but negative, relief were largely ignored.[7] The experience of political resistance to federal court rulings declaring racial discrimination illegal and others calling for an end to inhumane prison conditions indicated that more was needed if the remedial orders were to be more than mere empty statements. After all, in many of these cases the courts were ordering state and local officials to change policies in controversial areas in an atmosphere of public hostility, as in desegregation cases. In other situations, like prisons and mental hospitals, while there may have been no hostility, there certainly was no popular support for change. In effect, the courts have ordered remedies for particular groups which the majority had not been willing or able to provide through the normal legislative process.

GROUP CLAIMS FOR CLASS REMEDIES

Another significant feature of the remedial decree cases is the fact that they are often group claims brought to obtain class remedies. They are frequently not suits brought by individuals in order to obtain relief for their own personal situation. Instead, they are often class actions brought by interest groups. That fact requires clarification if one is to understand the circumstances confronting judges called upon to issue remedial decrees. In particular, it is important to think about what a class action is and then to note briefly the nature of interest group litigation giving rise to suits for complex remedies brought in federal district courts.

The Class Action Lawsuit

We often hear news stories these days about suits brought on behalf of all Vietnam veterans exposed to Agent Orange, all minority race children in a particular school district, all prisoners in a state prison system, or all patients in a specific mental health facility. These cases are class action lawsuits, litigation brought by one or a few people on behalf of a much larger group, of which the plaintiffs believe themselves to be representative. They seek a judicial consideration not only of the problem faced by the individuals bringing the suit, but of all members of the class.

The contemporary basis for class action suits brought in federal court is Rule 23 of the Federal Rules of Civil Procedure, which authorizes such lawsuits and specifies the requirements that must be met by those who wish to launch class action litigation. Would-be class action litigants must show that they are proper representatives for the class of persons they seek to champion, that the type of issues they wish to raise are common to the class, and they must be able to demonstrate how a remedy can be formed that will meet the needs of the class.

In order to understand the basis for these suits, one must look back to a much earlier time. Class action suits really developed in the sixteenth century for reasons of efficiency in judicial administration. At that time there were large numbers of tenants who wished to bring suits against their landlords. Many litigants were interested in obtaining an answer to the same legal question. If there were only a few claimants, then the court could join their cases and hear them together, but, if there were too many cases presenting the same question for all the parties to be brought into one court, a judge might solve the problem by allowing some of the parties to sue on behalf of everyone else in a similar circumstance and get one answer to be applied to all. Like so many other elements of our legal heritage, that notion came to the United States from England and has undergone a variety of modifications.

The class action device has been used as one of the very important tools in the kit of the many interest groups who have elected to use the courts as forums in which to seek their political goals. Although, as the brief history above makes clear, the class action suit is not really quite as new as some suggest, it is certainly true that interest group litigation has grown in frequency, scope, and sophistication following the lead of the civil rights organizations (specifically the NAACP Legal Defense and Education Fund) and their battles to end discrimination in schools and housing.[8] In fact, when one

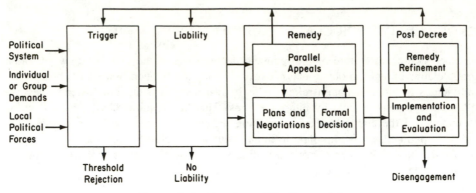

FIGURE 1–1. The decree litigation model.

thinks of interest group litigation, it is tempting to see the *Brown v. Board of Education* litigation achieving a declaration of an end to segregated schools as a kind of ideal/typical case.[9] When we do hear of that example, the description is often a picture of a well-organized, coherent strategy pursued by a group with careful coordination and control that is intent upon achieving its goals in a single key test case. In fact, as this study shows, policy oriented public law cases are launched by different kinds of parties, ranging from well-established groups with a long record of civil rights litigation, like the NAACP, to *ad hoc* groups of private parties (as in the *Wyatt v. Stickney* mental health case considered in Chapter 7, to the Civil Rights Division (CRD) of the U.S. Department of Justice (DOJ). Moreover, even where established interest groups do participate, the cases often do not fit the idealized *Brown v. Board* picture of careful planning, control, and coordination.[10] Even so, a sensitivity to the participation of a variety of interest groups bringing the suit is crucial to an understanding of the nature of the cases, the remedies sought, and the problems confronted by the judges in responding to the litigation.

THE REMEDIAL DECREE MODEL

The cases examined in this study suggest the outlines of a decree litigation model which provides a picture of the process by which remedial decree cases develop and are resolved. The presentation of cases in the remainder of this volume is considered in terms of this model. In general, it is an open system model consisting of trigger, liability, remedy, and post decree phases (see Figure 1–1). While these phases bear some relationship to the standard progression of a case, they are analytic categories and not primarily intended to present a chronology.

The Trigger Phase

Like most such models of the judicial process, this schema assumes that there are environmental inputs to the process in the form of political supports and demands aimed at or affecting courts. But the fact that these cases are so often multidirected conflicts that involve a number of levels of government (or differing agencies within a single level) suggests a need for enhanced sensitivity to these environmental influences. When we think of a major controversy over housing or schools in a particular city, it is quite normal to concentrate almost exclusively on what took place at the local level. There are indeed important local political forces at work, but one can miss critical political, economic, and legal forces operating at the state and national levels by focusing exclusively on local matters. Presidential politics, appointments to the U.S. Supreme Court, switches in litigation strategy by the DOJ, nationwide pressures on Congress, and a number of other factors played important roles in the development of the cases that are presented here. In sum, environmental influence from various levels of government must be examined in order to understand events that trigger remedial decree litigation.

It is also important to recognize the intergovernmental as well as the private-citizen-against-government nature of these conflicts. Remedial cases are multidirected controversies that involve a variety of players and are not simply cases of private citizens challenging government writ large. In some instances, like the housing case considered in Chapter 3, the suits are brought by the DOJ against a city. In others, like the Detroit schools case presented in Chapter 5, suits are launched by well organized interest groups against local governments on one set of grounds and against the state on others. In the mental health case examined in Chapter 7, we find a group of local individuals launching a suit against the state government, but later the DOJ and Department of Health, Education, and Welfare (HEW) (now known as Health and Human Services [HHS]) were invited into the litigation. Moreover, the parties often change and play different roles at different times during the litigation. Sometimes, in fact, the administrative agencies targeted in these cases benefit by having their superiors lose a suit that results in a decree, thus providing the agency with needed resources or program flexibility.[11] It is important to think about the different levels and directions of conflict in evaluating how decree litigation is launched and pursued.

In general, the equitable remedy cases are instituted as a reaction to a combination of historic policies or practices plus some triggering event. The cases tend to arise in situations where a number of controversial actions have been taken by one or more government units over time until a trigger level is reached. At that point, one critical action will engender a challenge not only to the most recent event, but to many of the past actions as well. In the Detroit case, for example, several educational practices by state and local governments could have prompted a suit, but the enactment of a statute blocking a desegregation plan sparked the litigation. Once launched, however, all past policies or practices became elements of the charge against the state and the school districts, which essentially expanded the scope of the conflict.

This picture of triggering suggests that remedial decree suits are often reactions and not carefully planned strategic moves by national interest groups, what we think of now as the *Brown v. Board* model. Because they are reactive and multidirected, the decree cases can be quite confusing in appearance. It is essential to understand the trigger stage in order to make sense of the litigation as it proceeds.

Once launched, these suits may meet threshold rejection for any of a number of reasons. The parties may, for example, be found to lack legal standing to bring the suit. That is, the trial court may conclude that the individual or group is not an appropriate litigant for the case presented.[12] Second, activity at the trigger phase is influenced by feedback from appellate court rulings. These higher court decisions may suggest to the would-be plaintiffs their chances of success given a particular form of litigation. How should the case be shaped? During the 1970s, for example, the changing trends of civil rights rulings in the U.S. Supreme Court had to be watched carefully by those who wanted to bring cases challenging government policies.

The Liability Phase

A case that survives pretrial disputes and comes to trial next enters the liability phase, the purpose of which is to determine whether there has been a violation of law justifying some sort of remedy and, if so, what is the extent of the injury suffered by the plaintiffs? There is a danger in thinking of these cases as involving a kind of black box machine into which one feeds a complaint and out of which emerges a complex remedial court order radically altering the operation of, say, a state prison. The liability stage is not merely a gatekeeping function for a remedy, but a set of actions intimately connected with any future remedy proceeding. If the party bringing the case cannot establish an adequate record and if the judge does not issue a strong opinion in the liability portion of the case, the chances for an adequate remedial order will be dramatically reduced. Any remedy that is issued may not survive on appeal to higher courts.

The development of the case at this stage is controlled largely by the lawyers for the plaintiffs, defendants, and any other organizations, government or private, that may be permitted to join the litigation. The groups bringing litigation must not only prove that their rights were violated but must also ensure the development of a strong record containing enough evidence of the right type that will assist the judge in crafting a strong liability opinion. That opinion and the record supporting it will serve as the basis for later remedy proceedings. And while the record established during the liability phase does not guarantee that the plaintiffs will get the remedy they seek, a complex remedy issued later without an adequate record is subject to reversal on appeal. If the defendants can cloud the record or the plaintiffs do not adequately construct it in the first instance, then the remedy crafting process is likely to be extremely difficult. To ensure an adequate record, plaintiff lawyers must be skilled in understanding what the appellate courts look for in reviewing lower court records; knowledgeable in the law in their field (*e.g.,* housing, education, or mental health); effective in locating and working with expert witnesses; and competent in the management ability needed to guide the case and relieve the judge of onerous case management details. As the cases in the following chapters demonstrate, however, government defendants have a variety of tools at their disposal to frustrate the plaintiffs' efforts and to make their own case. Groups who are allowed to enter the case after it is launched (called intervenors) may also be extremely important since they bring additional skills, interests, or resources. For example, when the DOJ intervenes in a case, it brings with it the investigatory resources of the FBI as well as the ability to call upon other federal agencies for expertise in housing, education, prisons, mental health, or the like.

If the trial court finds the defendant liable, meaning that the government did violate the plaintiffs' rights, the defendant may attempt to break out of the proceeding. That is generally done through an effort to obtain interlocutory appeals. These are requests that an appellate court review the trial court's conclusions even though the lower court has not yet completely finished with the case by issuing a remedy. While appeals courts, for a variety of reasons, tend to avoid this type of review, the attempt may buy time and prevent the trial court from launching a remedy. The Parma, Ohio, housing case and the Detroit schools litigation provide examples of this tactic.

The Remedy Phase

Once a liability opinion is issued, the remedy phase begins. It consists of a remedy crafting stage and, often, a parallel appeals process. The product of this remedy phase is a core remedy in the form of a decree or detailed remedy guideline. In many cases, including several of those discussed here, there are later interactions between the judge and the parties over requests for detailed modifications of the basic remedy, but these are really remedy refinements related to the implementation of the decrees in what is referred to here as the post decree phase rather than part of the remedy phase.

Remedy crafting consists of a plan development and negotiation stage and a formal decision stage. The judge often plays a facilitator role during the plan development stage, calling upon the parties to negotiate some kind of agreement on how to resolve the problems identified during the liability stage. In some instances the parties will agree on the means to remedy the offending conditions and submit that agreement to the court for legal ratification. In other cases, though, the parties may either not be willing to enter into negotiations at all or, if they do bargain, may be unable to produce a mutually acceptable remedial plan. When the plan development stage reaches its limits, the process becomes more formal and the judge becomes less a facilitator and more a validator, or ratifying official, placing the court's imprimatur on specific parts of the plans submitted by the parties without regard to voluntary acceptance by the parties.

The role the judge adopts may be limited by the role options afforded the court by the parties to the case. If those involved refuse to negotiate or provide significant positive reactions to the plans that are proposed, the judge's facilitator function is extremely narrow, pressing him or her to move to the ratifier/developer role. The polar opposite is the case in which the parties negotiate a consent decree before a formal liability finding is issued or before required remedy crafting processes are initiated. In that case the judge is simply a facilitator. A third role, that might be called the court-defender posture, may be played where a judge is presented with a negotiated remedy but thinks that the court is being used by the parties acting in collusion to leverage the government into taking action that is not remedial but goes far beyond what a remedy would provide or the political process would support.

If the parties are unable to negotiate an agreement, the formal process for remedy crafting begins, usually with the judge calling upon the defendants to work out some kind of plan. The remainder of the formal process often centers on a remedy hearing at which proposals made by the defendants and counterproposals submitted by the plaintiffs are presented and explained. Testimony is taken to determine the appropriateness and feasibility of the plans.

As was true of the liability stage, the abilities and tactics of the lawyers for the parties in the remedy stage are extremely important. The cases in the following chapters indicate the range of options and problems presented to the parties as they attempt to hammer out a final judgment. Especially critical is the role of expert testimony, usually a dominant element of any remedy hearing. The questioning of these witnesses by the plaintiffs, defendants, intervenors, and even the judge provides a way to test the boundaries and feasibility of proposed remedies.

The core remedies emerging from this formal decision process often contain similar elements. They (1) include a definition of the target agencies and beneficiaries; (2) provide procedures for further remedy refinement and implementation; (3) often establish some kind of forum for citizen participation, permitting discussion and providing a kind of watchdog role; (4) provide some kind of means for assessing and enhancing the institutional capabilities of the government organizations involved; (5) set some type of substantive standards for the remedy; and (6) frequently contain provisions concerning financial needs.

Remedial Adequacy Versus Discretion Limitation

At its core, of course, the decision about whether those bringing a suit have made a case that their rights have been violated and that they deserve a remedy is a decision to be made by the district court judge. An examination of the cases considered in this study indicates that the judges called upon to decide remedial decree cases are acutely aware of the core tension between the need to provide a remedy adequate to redress the injury suffered by deserving plaintiffs, on the one hand, and the importance of recognizing the appropriate limitations on judicial interference with government policy and practice on the other. There is ample evidence that the judges deciding these cases are very much aware of the dangers and difficulties, both legal and political, associated with their rulings. The fact that they choose to act despite the difficulties does not mean that they do not care about or are unaware of the consequences.

A judge faced with a request for a remedial decree has several factors to consider in formulating an adequate response. These elements of adequacy include the availability, nature, scope, and duration of relief for the situation presented by a case. The initial determination, of course, must be whether the alleged actions of the state or local government are proven; and, if so, whether they amount to a violation of statutory or constitutional provisions for which equitable relief is authorized.

If a remedy is available, the judge must determine the nature of the relief to be afforded. The judge's selection of remedial action is affected by what plaintiffs request, what the case law and statutes allow, and the degree to which proposed remedies actually redress the violation of legally protected rights. In most cases plaintiffs request negative relief in the form of an injunction against further illegal conduct and affirmative relief to redress the damage done to them. These affirmative remedies are (to recall the earlier discussions) often used because money damages are inadequate to make the victim whole again. The experience of the federal courts with state and local resistance to their orders is also important.

Judges may select from among a range of affirmative remedy options. These include process remedies, performance standards, or specified particular actions. Process remedies include such techniques as ordering formation of advisory committees, citizen participation requirements, educational programs, evaluation committees, dispute resolution procedures, or other devices that will operate to remedy past problems without mandating the particular form of action or the specific goals the government must pursue. Performance standards order specific quantities or types of remedial accomplishments, such as numbers or types of new housing units, racial attendance standards in schools, staffing levels at mental health institutions, or other targets, with the means of attainment left to the discretion of the officials who are the defendants in the suit. Specified remedial actions, such as school busing, modified school attendance zones, or required changes in the size and condition of hospital rooms or prison cells leave defendants with little or no flexibility concerning the remedial goals to be achieved or the means of attaining them.[13]

The scope of a remedy concerns the spatial dimensions of a decree. Those dimensions may be defined in terms of the programs affected, the people to be covered, or the political jurisdictions to be encompassed by the order. The duration of a remedy, by comparison, concerns the temporal dimension of court-ordered relief. It may be defined as time limits for formulation of plans, deadlines for accomplishment of particular elements of the decree, required sequential phasing of implementation, or the duration of the district court's retention of supervisory jurisdiction over an official or government unit to ensure compliance with the court's orders and evaluate results. Given the history of resistance to court-ordered relief and the political incentives to delay or avoid compliance, the court may well have to conduct some follow-up proceedings beyond mere announcement of an order. Taken far enough, though, unlimited duration of court involvement may place a judge in the position of administering institutions rather than remedying a legal violation.

Doctrinal Limits. There are limits to the intensely discretionary responses judges may make to demands for remedial orders. These constraints are products of doctrinal limits drawn from interpretations of the Constitution and statutes by appellate courts and self-imposed limits keyed to what might be termed *judicial policy range.* These two types of constraints pressure judges to consider problems with respect to each of the elements of remedial adequacy described above. The Burger Court has moved to limit the availability, scope, and duration of remedial decrees.[14]

With respect to the availability of a remedy, the doctrinal limits require the judge to ensure that appropriate allegations and proof are offered by the plaintiffs. Appropriate allegations are the sorts of charges that properly raise a justiciable dispute for which equitable relief is available. Most remedial decree cases brought under the Constitution assert a violation of equal protection of the law, due process, or cruel and unusual punishment provisions. Cases brought under federal statutes may be divided into those brought by private individuals or government officials authorized by the statute to sue and those cases brought by private parties who claim an implied right of action under a statute.[15] That is, they assert that Congress left them the option under a statute to sue for enforcement if government will not or cannot do so.

The nature of the remedy which a court may impose may be limited as well.[16] The Supreme Court has recently favored a standard which can be referred to as "incremental adverse effect."[17] In general, the nature of the remedy must reflect the nature of the violation. In some settings that means, according to the Court, that the task of a remedy is to eliminate the offending government conduct and restore those injured to the condition they would have enjoyed had the violation of law not occurred.[18] The problem for the judge is to determine the nature of the violation and what sorts of process, performance, or specified particular actions will redress the harm done.[19] While some appellate courts mandate the incremental adverse effect approach, they provide no guidance on how the judge is to determine just how much of one's current plight is directly attributable to past illegal action by government officials.

In addressing the permissible scope of a remedial order, the Supreme Court has recognized the need for breadth, but it has also reminded trial courts that they must give due consideration to the interests of states and localities in controlling their own land use policy, schools, and public institutions over which local control has usually been exercised.[20] The Court has been increasingly critical of remedial orders which cover more than those political jurisdictions specifically implicated in illegal conduct.

The question of the appropriate duration of a remedy and judicial supervision over implementation is always a difficult matter. Some have learned that by stalling long enough they can attract broad political support to end federal court involvement with state and local government without having actually carried out the provisions of a decree. The history of school desegregation presents the classic example.[21] On the other hand, there must be limits. Until the mid-1970s, the Court had consistently held that district courts were to retain jurisdiction over the implementation of remedial orders until the illegal conduct and its effects had been eliminated.[22] Lately, however, the Court has held that the district judges are to retain jurisdiction only until there is evidence of the onset of good faith implementation of an approved plan.[23] Just how one is to determine when good faith implementation has occurred has not been defined.

Judicial Policy Range. There are, then, several important, if ambiguous, formal limitations on judges issuing remedial decrees. But within the general doctrinal limits, trial judges still have a great deal of discretion. That area of flexibility presents a judge with a judicial policy range. It is the field of judicial options within constitutional limits. Like the doctrinal limits, one can think of judicial policy range in terms of the elements of remedial adequacy.

The availability of a remedy and its likely success on appeal both rest upon the quality of the record as well as the inferences drawn from that record and discussed in the opinion. Since the availability, nature, scope, and duration of any remedy are tied (in law if not always in practice) to the nature of the violation as described in the opinion of the trial court, it is obviously critical that the findings be carefully considered and explained. In order to support the findings, in turn, one must ensure the construction of a record adequate to support the necessary determinations and inferences.

The range of discretion the judge has in selecting the nature of relief is obviously broad. Whether he or she will employ process techniques which give the widest latitude to state and local governments regarding both the goals and the means of attaining them or use specified standards offering little flexibility as to either goals or means is an open matter. The key question, at least with respect to the political feasibility of a remedy, is to what degree do judges tend to acknowledge what might be termed *flexibility factors* of concern to state or local government?

The scope of a decree appears to be related to the capacity of the judge to engage in an effective analysis of linkages. How well can the judge interrelate the activities of the various actors and political jurisdictions involved in the course of conduct alleged to be illegal? Moreover, how well can the judge articulate those relationships in an opinion? The choices the trial judge makes in crafting both the liability findings and the remedial opinion become more than mere matters of form. Similarly, the ability to understand the relationships of the actions of subordinates to policy explicitly or implicitly pursued by superiors is critical to understanding whether a remedy is to be limited to a few individuals or is, in fact, a department or countywide problem. Finally, the ability to determine whether one is dealing with isolated incidents or a pattern and practice of conduct as well as to articulate the relationships among the elements of a pattern and practice is a determining factor in gauging the appropriate scope of a remedial decree.

Judicial policy range with respect to duration is wide. One may elect to establish time limits with respect to either the development of a decree after a finding of a violation or to the implementation and evaluation of a decree after it is developed. In the first instance, deadlines regarding negotiations or hearings conducted in an effort to craft a remedy may determine how well the plaintiffs or the defendants can prepare for, and participate in, the creation of a remedy. Further, the judge may elect time boundaries for implementation of various elements of the decree, for the evaluation of the effectiveness of the remedy, or both.

In sum, to understand the kinds of problems and opportunities facing a judge called upon to issue a remedial order, one must understand the nature of the relief requested and the applicable limiting factors. Of perhaps greatest interest to students of law, politics, and administration is the matter of how judges determine and utilize their judicial policy range.

Appeals

The appeals process is treated in the model as a parallel process within the remedy crafting stage. This study suggests that this is a far more accurate representation than picturing the appellate process as something later than, and apart from, decree crafting. The principal reason is that appeals are often launched while remedy crafting is under way. Moreover, stays of remedial orders are often obtained just after decree crafting, leading to changes in remedial orders prior to implementation. Even in cases in which the core remedy is upheld on appeal, the higher courts may require some modifications in the decree and provide specific direction for the role the lower court is to play during implementation of the remedy. Some judges even go so far as to impose stays on their own orders while they await comments and directions from appellate courts.

The Post Decree Phase

In a fashion rather like the relationship between remedy crafting and the appeals process, the post decree phase of a remedial decree litigation involves a parallel interactive relationship between remedy implementation and evaluation and remedy refinement. In many situations the parties in the case will return to the district judge while the decree is being carried out to ask for changes based upon implementation problems. Frequently, these suggested changes are accepted. It is not a situation in which a judge issues an order and, assuming it survives any appeals, never hears of the case again.

Just as the parties to the case can shape the remedy crafting role of the judge by affording or denying role options, so the role played by the judge in the post decree phase is shaped by the core remedy. A judge who orders a process remedy in which he or she specifies neither the precise targets to be met nor the means, but who provides some committee to make such decisions, may have an arm's-length relationship with the parties during implementation. A judge who orders specified particular actions, on the other hand, may find it necessary to play a much more active and specific role in implementing the ruling.

Finally, courts do, in fact, eventually disengage from the parties in the case when they actually remedy the situation that gave rise to the suit. However, it can be a very long time between the issuance of a remedial order and the determination by the court that the problem which gave rise to the suit has been resolved. In some cases more than a decade passes before the disengagement occurs.

CONCLUSION

Remedial decree cases provide us an opportunity to view the operation of the federal courts and their relationship to state and local administrators from a unique perspective. The attempt to see these very important policy oriented public law disputes from the judge's vantage point sharpens that focus. The remaining chapters present several revealing case studies of remedial decree litigation in such important policy areas as school and housing desegregation, mental health and prison reform, and police/community relations. In order to place the case study in context, recognizing the warnings issued earlier about the importance of the political, economic, and legal context, each of the major case treatments is preceded by a general discussion of the participation of courts in that area of policy. Let us turn first to the matter of open housing policy and the case of the *United States v. City of Parma, Ohio*. We begin that study with a survey of the role of federal courts in housing policy.

NOTES

1. This formulation is not the same as the approach to public law cases advanced in Abram Chayes, "The Role of the Judge in Public Law Litigation," 89 *Harv. L. Rev.* 1281 (1976).

2. On judges, *see Stump v. Sparkman,* 435 U.S. 349 (1978); on prosecutors, *Imbler v. Pachtman,* 424 U.S. 409 (1976); and on legislators, *Tenney v. Brandhove,* 341 U.S. 367 (1951).

3. *Edelman v. Jordan,* 415 U.S. 651 (1974).

4. *Harlow v. Fitzgerald,* 457 U.S. 800 (1982).

5. The complexity and problems associated with what is often thought to be the simple notion of money damages is outlined in a recent Supreme Court decision, *Smith v. Wade,* 75 L.Ed2d 623 (1983).

6. *Swann v. Charlotte-Mecklenburg Board of Education,* 402 U.S. 1, 15 (1971).

7. It is generally ignored, but the Supreme Court had been attempting to achieve compliance in the area of racial segregation through declaratory rulings long before *Brown v. Bd. of Ed.,* 347 U.S. 483 (1954). In these early cases, the Court found that it could not even get states and localities to obey the requirements of "separate but equal." *See, e.g., Missouri ex rel. Gaines v. Canada,* 305 U.S. 337 (1938); *Sweatt v. Painter,* 339 U.S. 629 (1950); and *McLaurin v. Oklahoma,* 339 U.S. 637 (1950). Rulings after *Brown v. Bd. of Ed.,* 349 U.S. 294 (1955) *(Brown II)* contained admonitions to states and localities to take action on their own or face federal court mandates. They warned that evasive schemes and attempts at intimidation would not be tolerated. *See, e.g., Cooper v. Aaron,* 358 U.S. 1 (1958); and *Green v. County School Bd.,* 391 U.S. 430 (1968).

8. *See, e.g.,* Clement Vose, *Caucasions Only: The Supreme Court, the NAACP, and the Restrictive Covenant Cases* (Berkeley: Univ. of California Press, 1959).

9. Richard Kluger, *Simple Justice* (New York: Knopf, 1976).

10. At the same time my research on this project produced this finding, Stephen L. Wasby presented a similar finding. See Wasby, "Is Planned Litigation Planned?" Unpublished paper delivered at the 1983 annual meeting of the American Political Science Association, Chicago, IL,

later published as Stephen L. Wasby, "How Planned Is 'Planned Litigation'?" *American Bar Foundation Research Journal 1984* (Winter 1984): 83–138.

11. Stephen L. Wasby, "Arrogation of Power or Accountability: 'Judicial Imperialism' Revisited," 65 *Judicature* 208, 213 (1981).

12. *See, e.g., Warth v. Seldin,* 422 U.S. 490 (1975).

13. For a general discussion of remedial options, see *Swann v. Charlotte-Mecklenburg Bd. of Ed., supra* note 6.

14. See *Milliken v. Bradley,* 418 U.S. 717 (1974); *Rizzo v. Goode,* 423 U.S. 362 (1976); and *Pasadena Bd. of Ed. v. Spangler,* 427 U.S. 424 (1976).

15. See *Middlesex County Sewage Auth. v. Nat'l Sea Clammers Ass'n.,* 453 U.S. 1 (1981); *California v. Sierra Club,* 451 U.S. 287 (1981); *Cannon v. Univ. of Chicago,* 441 U.S. 677 (1979).

16. Prior to relatively recent decisions, once a finding of a violation was made with regard to, say, racial discrimination in education, the judge was charged with eliminating the problem "root and branch." *Green v. County School Bd.,* 391 U.S. 430, 438 (1968). The Supreme Court has since that time, however, determined that such a sweeping charge to district court judges permits more intrusion into state and local government than is appropriate.

17. See *Dayton Bd. of Ed. v. Brinkman,* 433 U.S. 406 (1977).

18. But the Court has not applied this approach rigidly in all cases. *See Milliken v. Bradley,* 433 U.S. 267 (1977) *(Milliken II),* examined in Chapter 5.

19. The Court has allowed a bit more flexibility for the remedy where the legislature has made a specific finding in regard to the existence of widespread discrimination. *See, e.g., Fullilove v. Klutznick,* 488 U.S. 448 (1980).

20. *See generally San Antonio Indep. School Dist. v. Rodriguez,* 411 U.S. 1 (1973).

21. *See generally* Jack W. Peltason, *Fifty-eight Lonely Men: Southern Federal Judges and School Desegregation* (Urbana: Univ. of Illinois Press, 1971).

22. See *Green v. County School Bd., supra* note 16, and *Swann v. Charlottle-Mecklenburg Bd. of Ed., supra* note 6.

23. *Pasadena Bd. of Ed. v. Spangler, supra* note 14.

2

The Courts and Equal Housing

It is now more than thirty years since we declared that it is the policy of the United States that there should be "a decent home and suitable living environment for every American family."[1] Yet we are a long way from that goal. One of the reasons for this shortcoming is the difficulty of eliminating discrimination in the housing market. Federal courts have been called upon by individuals, interest groups, and the federal government to confront alleged discrimination in housing construction, sales, and leasing. Like school desegregation disputes, suits in which judges have ordered remedies for proven cases of housing discrimination have met with considerable criticism and resistance.

Housing policy, like the other areas in which federal courts have played important roles over the years, is far more complex than it may at first appear. Lawsuits, such as the *United States v. Parma, Ohio* case discussed in Chapter 3, that allege racial discrimination in housing are products of political, legal, and social dynamics. In order to come to grips with the difficult issues that courts are asked to address, one must have some sense of the forces at play in the field. This chapter provides an introduction to law and policy problems in the area of fair housing. Like the other law and policy chapters to follow, it is intended to provide an orientation to the kinds of problems and historical and political baggage encountered by a judge called upon to decide a difficult case and, if appropriate, to provide a remedy. These chapters also serve to relate the individual case study to the general position of litigation within each policy area. Finally, they are designed to provide a foundation for the five principal case studies. Each of these chapters presents a brief discussion of the evolution of the issues central to the policy space, describes the areas of primary federal judicial involvement, and considers the key political and administrative problems facing policymakers operating in the field.

DEVELOPING ISSUES OF LAW AND HOUSING POLICY

Contemporary housing patterns and the employment, education, and community services difficulties which have accompanied them did not emerge quickly and clearly in their present form. A judge hearing housing cases today faces the product of a variety of forces that have developed over the past century. These factors include a history of discrimination and early efforts to end it, economic collapse and the corresponding attempt to develop a sound housing market during the thirties, postwar suburban development and fair housing policy, the urban dilemma of the sixties, and the push for open housing thereafter.

A Legacy of Discrimination

Discrimination is nothing new in America. Even during our earliest years, we discriminated, sometimes violently, against others of different religious background, ethnic heritage, and social and economic class. This legacy of discrimination is no surprise to any student of American history, but it is important to recall nonetheless. Of course, the battle over slavery and the politics of post–Civil War reconstruction cast the issue of racial discrimination in high relief. Where blacks, orientals, and women were involved, discrimination was, until recently, overt and based upon observable characteristics. Although it was often less obvious, discrimination against religious minorities and immigrants was also widely practiced well into this century, particularly in the wake of post–World War I isolationism.

When most Americans lived with an extended family in rural settings, the question of open housing was not generally considered serious, but with urbanization came an intense need to confront the availability and condition of the nation's housing stock. Waves of immigrants brought to the industrial centers of the Northeast and Midwest needed immediate housing but had few resources to acquire it, even assuming an adequate supply. The supply was, in fact, woefully inadequate. Shortly after the European immigrants arrived, blacks began a migration from the rural South to the industrial centers.[2] As minorities developed the financial ability to enter the housing market, private groups and government units took direct action against them.

The most common techniques were zoning barriers and racially restrictive covenants. Zoning developed about 1910 in the form of local ordinances that regulated land use. The early notion was that zoning laws were rather like the law of nuisance in that they would protect residential and commercial property owners against inappropriate uses of neighboring property for industrial or other noxious purposes. In reality, zoning laws were used to exclude people who were presumably undesirable as well as businesses or activities.[3] The American Bar Association's (ABA) Advisory Commission on Housing and Urban Growth concluded:

> What is generally regarded as the first modern comprehensive zoning ordinance in the United States was enacted by New York City in 1916, and was an outgrowth of the desire of Fifth Avenue merchants to keep the women's garment industry from encroaching into their fashionable shopping district. The merchants feared that the presence on the streets of the large numbers of immigrants employed in the garment factories would repel their carriage-trade customers.[4]

The Supreme Court upheld local zoning laws in 1926 against the charge that they violated constitutionally protected property rights.[5] The zoning concept spread rapidly thereafter, with more than nine hundred municipalities adopting such ordinances by 1930.[6] Among the more common zoning prohibitions were provisions banning apartment houses, which effectively excluded from the community those who lacked resources to purchase property there. Some cities even went so far as to enact racially restrictive zoning laws, barring minorities from residence in specified areas of the community.

Racially restrictive covenants were parts of property sales contracts in which the buyer agreed not to sell the property to anyone but a Caucasion.[7] The penalties for violation of the agreement were twofold. The other signatories to the covenant, usually other property owners in the area, would petition the courts for an order evicting a minority purchaser and then sue the seller for violating the terms of the agreement.

The initial efforts to provide general protection against discrimination generally came much earlier in the Civil Rights Act of 1866 and the Fourteenth Amendment to the Constitution adopted in 1868. The former provided that ''[a]ll citizens of the United States shall have the same right, in every state and territory, as is enjoyed by white citizens thereof to inherit, purchase, lease, sell, hold and convey real and personal property.''[8] The Fourteenth Amendment, of course, prohibits government from depriving one of his or her property without due process of law and bars a state from denying ''to any person within its jurisdiction the equal protection of the laws.'' Citing these authorities, the Supreme Court struck down overt racial zoning in 1917.[9] Racially restrictive covenants survived for more than three decades thereafter.

Emerging National Housing Policy

No sooner had the battle over property regulation begun than the Great Depression hit. The failure of banks, the inability to repay loans, and the general economic emergency had a profound impact on the housing market. The federal government entered the field of housing policy in response, shaping the market in fundamentally new ways. While federal officials had been aware of a growing housing problem and there had been some federal involvement in limited housing construction during World War I, Washington was not an important participant in the housing market prior to the 1930s.[10]

The first step in the federal attack on housing problems was to stabilize and enhance the capital markets to provide mortgages. National bodies, including the Home Loan Bank Board and later the Federal Deposit Insurance Corporation (FDIC) and the Federal Savings and Loan Insurance Corporation (FSLIC), were created to support the banks.[11] With the passage of the Housing Act of 1934, the Federal Housing Administration (FHA) was born; the Act provided insured mortgages and thereby encouraged greater availability of mortgage capital. Another important element was added to the housing finance market with the development in 1938 of the Federal National Mortgage Association (later called Fannie Mae), which provided a vehicle for financial trading in mortgages. The other major piece of housing finance machinery came with enactment of the Servicemen's Readjustment Act of 1944 (now known as the G.I. Bill), which provided low-interest guaranteed mortgages for returning veterans. ''The VA and FHA programs enabled the production of enough housing to satisfy the enormous demand for new residences resulting from the Depression and World War II. Production jumped from 140,000 units in 1944 to a million in 1946, and was close to 2 million in 1950.''[12]

These federal housing policies had the effect of making more money available, extending the length of mortgages, and reducing interest rates. Another impact of the federal legislation was to increase the percentage of the full purchase price available in a mortgage from about half to ninety percent or more, reducing the down payment needed for the sale. More families could afford a house even with increasing prices, since the long payback, low interest, and tax advantages permitted a greater financial reach.

Still, many needed adequate shelter, let alone a new home. The Housing Act of 1937 created a program of federal loans for the development of public housing. It was an intergovernmental arrangement through which local public housing authorities (PHAs) planned the construction and operated the housing. The funds came from Washington to the PHAs. Of course, that meant that a community could avoid public housing if it wished by refusing to form a PHA.

While the federal government played an important role in providing a foundation for postwar housing development, it also participated with states and localities in the creation of a pattern of housing discrimination. The most direct features of that participation were the encouragement of the use of racially restrictive covenants and of discrimination in lending practices by financial institutions:

> From 1935 to 1950, the FHA Underwriting Manual warned of the "infiltration of inharmonious racial and national groups," "a lower class of inhabitants," or the "presence of incompatible racial elements" in new neighborhoods. Zoning was advocated as a device for exclusion, as was the use of racial covenants. A model restrictive covenant was prepared by FHA itself, with a space left blank for the prohibited races and religions, to be filled in by the builder. The Home Loan Bank System, the federal agency that regulates savings and loan institutions, as well as the VA, urged similar practices. This policy was in full effect during the first five years of the building boom after World War II, when over 900,000 units of FHA housing were produced. Even by 1948, federally approved racial covenants covered large portions of suburbia and established a pattern of suburban bias against blacks.[13]

Even though these agencies changed their policy at the end of 1949, the residential patterns were already established and unlikely to change in the foreseeable future. Moreover, the federal government did not take an active role in attempting to remedy discrimination. The fact that suburbs began and remained largely white was no accident of personal choice or financial effort.[14] Neither could the discriminatory pattern be laid solely at the feet of local governments. On the other hand, the federal government did begin a shift in policy in 1949 which, along with a variety of additional pieces of legislation and executive action in the next two decades, did take the nation in the direction of a national fair housing policy.

In Search of a "Decent Home": The Effort to Develop and Implement a Fair Housing Policy

The postwar demand for housing for returning veterans, the baby boom, the growth of metropolitan areas, and a slowly changing federal policy toward open housing compelled greater national attention to housing issues. The Housing Act of 1949 provided a comprehensive statement that said our goal was a "decent home and a suitable living environment for every American family," and it expanded federal efforts toward that end. That statute and the Housing Act of 1954 made urban renewal a priority. Programs like urban relocation funds for persons displaced by urban renewal and subsidies for senior citizen housing promised to spark new construction.[15] The various housing programs were consolidated under the aegis of a new cabinet-level department, the Department of Housing and Urban Development (HUD), in 1965.

By the mid-1960s, however, many had become impatient with the failure of the federal government to end discrimination in housing and disenchanted with the nation's inability to achieve its announced fair housing goals. President Kennedy issued Executive Order 11063 in 1962, which prohibited discrimination in federally financed housing, but the order was of limited scope and was interpreted essentially to include only public housing constructed after the date of the order's issuance.[16] Title VI of the Civil Rights Act of 1964 prohibited discrimination in any program receiving federal funds, but again it was late in coming and serious enforcement efforts seemed unlikely. Investigations of the urban violence of the mid-sixties found that a lack of adequate housing was one of the leading complaints among minorities in America's cities.[17] Beyond an awareness of the conditions, however, there was a resentment of the manner in which minority ghettos had been fostered by overt and covert discrimination. The Kerner Commission warned, "What white Americans have never fully understood—but what the Negro can never forget—is that white society is deeply implicated in the ghetto. White institutions created it, white institutions maintain it, and white society condones it."[18] The Commission concluded, "Our nation is moving toward two societies, one black, one white—separate and unequal."[19]

Reporting in 1968, the President's Commission on Urban Housing (the Kaiser Commission) observed that only by a massive effort to supply adequate housing and to remedy difficulties arising from earlier practices could the urban housing crisis be resolved. The Housing and Urban Development Act of 1968 was an attempt to move on the supply side, consolidating and improving several housing grants for new construction and rent subsidies. Two new funding devices—Section 235 grants for home ownership and Section 236 grants to fund low and moderate income rental housing—were established by the Act.[20] The 1968 statute reaffirmed the "decent home" policy set forth in the 1949 Act and added both a target date and a quantitative goal: the full housing policy was to be achieved by 1978 through construction of 6 million new units of low and moderate income housing and 20 million other housing units.[21]

Housing Problems: Race, Class, and the Urban Dilemma

The situation that confronted housing reformers of the late 1960s and early 1970s was extremely grave. There was a set of general urban problems, the adverse impact of existing federal programs, the barrier of exclusionary zoning, the dramatic shortcomings of public housing, and the presence of an unfair real estate market—all of which required attention.

At the heart of many urban problems was the basic mismatch between needs and resources. Past practices of discrimination, the increased cost of new housing construction in suburbs, the lack of transportation, and other factors concentrated minorities in the cities. Moreover, because of high service demands and relatively low resource bases, cities were unable to meet the social service needs of their residents. City tax rates escalated to obtain whatever revenue could be gleaned from the declining tax base. The needs and problems of urban citizens were often exacerbated by difficulties in city schools. Weak educational preparation decreased the chances for good jobs. That, in turn, reduced the likelihood of obtaining desirable housing.[22] The result is what Downs termed a "crisis ghetto" in which racial, social, and economic tensions interact.[23] The presence of these difficulties placed further strain on already overtaxed resources, even where services were limited to little more than police and fire protection. The more services declined, taxes increased, and schools deteriorated, the greater the exodus from the cities of those able to move to the suburbs. Indeed the suburbs were the primary centers of growth during the sixties.

Some of the same factors led businesses to leave for the suburbs as well. Jobs and shopping that used to be available in the cities were now located in suburban industrial parks and shopping centers. Unfortunately, many of the cities' unemployed lacked transportation to reach those suburban jobs. Danielson provides a useful summary of the problem:

> Especially in the larger metropolitan areas, the dispersal of jobs to the suburbs combines with restrictions which limit the supply of inexpensive housing to break the historical connection between urban growth and economic opportunity for the disadvantaged. Before the exodus of employment from the central city, housing available to the urban poor was close to the bulk of industrial and service jobs, and the unskilled worker usually could reach his job relatively quickly and cheaply by walking or riding on public transportation. In the decentralized metropolis, jobs increasingly are located far from the residences of the poor. More and more employment is situated in areas which lack moderately priced housing. Public transportation between the central city and these dispersed suburban job locations often is nonexistent. As a result, suburban job seekers and commuters from inner-city residences to employment in the suburbs must depend heavily on the private automobile. Many of the suburban jobs available to the lower-income groups denied access to housing in the suburbs, however, do not pay enough to make the long and expensive trip from inner city to suburb worthwhile.[24]

Residential patterns, jobs, and housing shortfalls may be metropolitan problems, but the solutions have generally not been attempted by the metropolis as a whole. Rather, metropolitan regions are themselves balkanized into dozens of local jurisdictions, each with independent zoning authority and building codes. Some major metropolitan areas have several hundred such local units making important land use, education, health, public safety, transportation, and government services decisions simultaneously, often with mutually harmful consequences.[25]

In addition to these general urban problems, several federal policies have had detrimental effects upon the metropolitan housing problem. Washington's participation in direct discrimination through its restrictive covenant and discriminatory mortgage policies as well as the failure to take action against lenders and real estate agents who engaged in various discriminatory practices played important roles in the growth of the white ring of suburbs surrounding cities with large minority concentrations. Those suburbs were made possible through the provision by the federal government of mortgage and tax policies which allowed dramatic increases in single-family housing construction on inexpensive land away from the problems of the city. Federally sponsored highway programs fostered the suburban sprawl by providing the roads necessary to permit rapid commuting for suburban residents. The federally funded interstate highway program became the major device for development of expressways. In addition to assisting in the exodus from the city, the highway programs had serious impacts upon existing housing stock within the cities. The superhighways were often constructed through areas of low income, often minority, housing, disrupting existing community relationships, displacing families, and imposing major geographical barriers between former friends and neighbors.[26] The urban renewal programs also severely affected the urban housing situation. The intention of the slum clearance and urban renewal efforts was to eliminate substandard buildings, both residential and commercial, and replace them with better quality housing stock and commercial space.[27] The assumption was that the families displaced in the process could move into the revitalized housing. In fact, those displaced by the program were overwhelmingly minority citizens who were compressed further into smaller areas of the city. A substantially higher percentage of the property involved was converted to commercial or high priced residential property than many anticipated, leaving less redeveloped property for low and moderate income residents. "At the end of 1971, approximately 600,000 housing units had been demolished on urban renewal sites, but only 201,000 new units had been completed, with an additional 43,000 units under construction, the majority of which were unsubsidized."[28] At that point, the Nixon administration declared a moratorium on further construction under the HUD Section 236 low and moderate income rental housing program.

The manifold shortcomings of public housing programs added to the problem of ensuring a "decent home." Many communities, in the North as well as the South, operated segregated public housing until well into the sixties, either under actual rules mandating race-based tenant assignments or under informal but long-standing practices. The racial polarization was exacerbated by the tendency to construct new public housing in existing ghetto areas. Zoning changes and technical resistance to building plans have been used to prevent construction in other parts of cities. Of course, among the reasons for resistance to public housing by middle class property owners and distaste for those units by the poor is the history of public housing problems. Because urban land is so expensive, public housing has often been constructed as high-rise, dense occupancy buildings. Those buildings were frequently difficult to maintain, lacking a sense of community, and they were insecure. Tales of such disastrous projects as St. Louis's Pruitt-Igoe have prompted many property owners to recoil at the very thought of public housing. For that and racial reasons, suburbs have resisted public housing even where plans are not at all like the kind of problem high-rise housing of the past.

A fourth major challenge in the search for adequate urban housing is the presence and carefully practiced use of exclusionary zoning. Modern zoning laws are extremely sophisticated, permitting a community by various exclusionary rules to control the type as well as the quantity of its residents. By requiring large lots (in some cases an acre or more minimum size); high minimum square-footage requirements for houses in the area; a low bedroom-per-house limit; height restrictions on all construction; open space of prescribed size on the front, sides, and back of a house within a lot, restricting multi-family dwellings; and barring mobile homes, many suburbs have been able to ensure relatively homogeneous middle class citizens.[29]

Presumably, these zoning practices would limit access to the community along class lines but not necessarily on racial grounds. That assumes that the real estate marketplace has been basically open and racially equal. It has not been. After the restrictive covenants and similar devices established racial patterns, real estate agents continued to reinforce the racial separation through such practices as blockbusting and racial steering. In the former case, agents would pass the word that a black family was about to move into the area and encourage whites to sell their homes quickly before the property values declined (which, of course, suggested that they do automatically decline, a fact many whites were prepared to believe without question). Steering is a long-standing process by which agents tend to show blacks property only in existing black or integrated communities while offering other property to white clients. In addition, banks and insurance companies during the 1950s and 1960s often engaged in what is known as redlining. They would simply refuse to grant mortgages or property insurance in certain areas of the community. Here again, race played a role.

The Effort to Make Basic Changes and the Shortcomings

In the face of these problems, the federal government created new tools to confront the housing dilemma. The Fair Housing Act, enacted as Title VIII of the Civil Rights Act of 1968, prohibited discrimination in housing sales or in rental by real estate firms or others (except for individual small property owners). The other major piece of legislation was the Housing and Community Development Act of 1974. The Nixon administration had been unhappy with several elements of the 1968 Housing and Community Development Act and its predecessors and imposed a moratorium on new housing grants. The White House sought a new bill that would convert money available to housing programs into special revenue sharing, an arrangement under which the funds would be returned to states and localities, with those units possessing extremely broad discretion in determining how the funds would be spent. Though Congress was willing to provide portions of federal housing and community development funds in the form of a block grant, allowing considerable flexibility to the local governments, they were not willing to remove all controls. Judging that the same local majority forces that had maintained existing residential patterns would be unlikely to use broad discretion to undo their own creation, the legislation mandated that communities wishing to receive Community Development Block Grant (CDBG) funds must provide a Housing Assistance Plan (HAP) that contained information on the level of need for low and moderate income housing in the community and set forth a so-called "expected to reside" figure indicating goals for responding to the need. The 1974 Act also eliminated the existing 235 and 236 programs and created a new low income housing subsidy known as Section 8 assistance (Section 8 of Title II of the Act). Under this provision, local governments were provided funds to be paid to owners of existing, rehabilitated, or new rental property. The subsidy made up the difference between the ability of the low income tenant to pay and reasonable market value. Section 8 could also be used in combination with other federal housing programs for new construction projects. The 1974 Act also extended protections against discrimination, such as its prohibition of sex discrimination in real estate and lending practices. Finally, the Act expanded HUD enforcement authority. Another potentially important fair housing tool is the Equal Credit Opportunity Act, which prohibits discriminatory lending practices and calls upon the Comptroller of the Currency, the Federal Reserve, the Department of the Treasury, the FDIC, FSLIC, and other federal financial agencies to play enforcement roles.[30]

The fair housing effort had to settle for limited successes. For one thing, the Nixon administration was not interested in alienating suburban voters by vigorous enforcement of the Fair Housing Act.[31] While the Housing and Credit Section of the Department of Justice (DOJ) attempted to move forcefully in its enforcement efforts, it faced conflicts within DOJ and restrictions from the White House.[32] Despite these difficulties, DOJ did manage an impressive string of victories in its fair housing cases during the 1970s, sometimes launching its own suits and on other occasions joining fair housing groups engaged in litigation around the country.

THE COURTS IN HOUSING POLICY

In attempting to decide the many types of housing cases brought to them during this century, federal courts have faced tensions among fundamental forces in the law. On the one hand, as lawyers, judges have been carefully trained in the importance of protecting the rights of property owners. Yet they have recognized from the earliest housing cases the fundamental constitutional authority possessed by local communities to regulate land use. Presumably such limitations as are placed on individual property use at the local level reflect the views of the majority of local citizens. However, for much of this century judges have also been faced with strong constitutional and statutory mandates to respond to charges of discrimination. In their efforts to meet this difficult responsibility, the courts have faced a complex admixture of constitutional and statutory issues, including zoning and restrictive covenant cases, questions of constitutional burdens and definition, issues of statutes and standing, specific low and moderate income housing development problems, and the puzzle of constructing remedies.

Zoning and Restrictive Covenants

While demonstrating its commitment to the right to acquire, use, and dispose of property, the Supreme Court has consistently held that property rights are not absolute and may be regulated for a number of purposes by states and localities. Well before the Court formally upheld zoning by local governments in *Euclid v. Ambler,*[33] it recognized the importance of the so-called police powers of local government which serve as the basis for zoning rules:

> True it is that dominion over property springing from ownership is not absolute and unqualified. The disposition and use of property may be controlled in the exercise of the police power in the interest of the public health, convenience, or welfare. Harmful occupations may be controlled and regulated. Legitimate business may also be regulated in the interest of the public. Certain uses of property may be confined to portions of the municipality other than the resident district, such as livery stables, brickyards and the like, because of the impairment of the health and comfort of the occupants of neighboring property.[34]

When the Court affirmed the zoning power in 1926, it not only recognized a formal regulatory authority, but also established a strong legal presumption in favor of the necessarily discretionary judgments that local communities would make about acceptable property uses. A zoning decision, the Court said, may concern "a right thing in the wrong place, like a pig in the parlor instead of a barnyard."[35] Doubts about the validity of a zoning classification ought to be resolved in favor of local legislative judgment. The Court ruled that, in order to strike down a zoning decision, a challenger must show that "such provisions are clearly arbitrary and unreasonable, having no substantial relation to the public health, safety, morals, or general welfare."[36] While it may be possible to demonstrate that a specific zoning decision about a particular piece of property was arbitrary, it would be much more difficult to make the same showing if the specific zoning ruling was based upon an existing comprehensive community zoning plan. Consequently, many communities adopted general zoning plans which favor the status quo, forcing anyone wishing to bring about substantial community changes to carry an extremely heavy burden to justify their plans. The *Euclid* Court did leave an escape clause, ruling that, ''It is not meant by this, however, to exclude the possibility of cases where the general public interest would so far outweigh the interest of the municipality that the municipality would not be allowed to stand in the way.''

The opinions authorizing zoning, however, also revealed substantial biases in housing and property uses. First, granting broad deference to zoning decisions favors a maintenance of the status quo and particularly supports the majority over traditionally disfavored minorities. Second, even when the Court appeared to be ruling in favor of racial or ethnic minorities, its language suggested an alternative explanation. For example, the *Buchanan v. Warley* decision prohibiting racial zoning was not primarily decided as a matter of equal protection of the law for the minority who wished to purchase a home in a white neighborhood of Louisville. Instead, it was held that the ordinance violated the due process rights of the white seller to alienate his property. Finally, some of the early rulings conveyed a strong bias against housing of the sort needed by low and moderate income citizens regardless of race. In *Euclid*, Justice Sutherland wrote:

> With particular reference to apartment houses, it is pointed out that the development of detached house sections is greatly retarded by the coming of apartment houses, which has sometimes resulted in destroying the entire section for private house purposes; that in such sections very often the apartment house is a mere parasite, constructed in order to take advantage of the open spaces and attractive surroundings created by the residential character of the district. Moreover, the coming of one apartment house is followed by others, interfering by their height and bulk with the free circulation of air and monopolizing the rays of the sun which otherwise would fall upon the smaller homes, and bringing, as their necessary accompaniments, the disturbing noises incident to increased traffic and business, and the occupation, by means of moving and parked automobiles, of larger portions of the street, thus detracting from their safety and depriving children of the privilege of quiet and open space for play, enjoyed by those in more favored localities—until, finally, the residential character of the neighborhood and its desirability as a place of detached residences are utterly destroyed.[37]

While government limited property uses by zoning, private individuals accomplished some of the same sorts of regulation by including sometimes complex sets of covenants in property deeds. Agreement to the covenants was a part of the sales contract. Private action, as opposed to government action, is not governed by constitutional provisions. The latter speak to the nature and limit of public, not private authority. Given that, the Supreme Court initially upheld racially restrictive covenants against their first challenge.[38] The NAACP, however, launched a concerted attack on racially restrictive covenants which brought the issue back to the Supreme Court in *Shelley v. Kraemer* decided in 1948.[39] The NAACP's strategy was to argue that the private agreements may not themselves have been barred, but that any effort to use the public courts to enforce them would be state action that discriminated in violation of the equal protection clause of the Fourteenth Amendment. The Court agreed.[40] Shortly thereafter, neighborhood associations attempted an end run around the *Shelley* decision by seeking to sue the white seller for breach of contract and thereby discourage others who might contemplate conveying their property to blacks. The Court ruled that whether the attempt was to oust a minority purchaser or punish a white seller, the effect was the same and courts were not permitted to support it.[41]

In later years, a variety of land use laws were tested. Of particular importance for open housing were urban renewal laws and lifestyle zoning issues. Under urban renewal statutes, local governments used their power of eminent domain to obtain property that they could redevelop directly or sell to private developers at low prices for new projects. Tenants of housing units and owners of existing businesses argued that it was one thing for local government to destroy a building because it was a safety hazard or to take one because it stood in the way of a needed public building like a hospital, but quite another to take large quantities of property in search of the possibility of general community improvement with the real result being enrichment of a private developer. The Court upheld the urban renewal efforts in a 1954 decision. In the process it read the police power as broad enough to extend to intangible public goals as well as specific health or safety considerations:

> We do not sit to determine whether a particular housing project is or is not desirable. The concept of the public welfare is broad and inclusive. . . . The values it repre- sents are spiritual as well as physical, aesthetic as well as monetary. It is within the power of the legislature to determine that the community should be beautiful as well as healthy, spacious as well as clean, well-balanced as well as carefully patrolled.[42]

In what are sometimes referred to as lifestyle zoning cases, the Court upheld the communities' attempts to limit the number of unrelated persons living together in resi- dential units. The leading case arose in the village of Belle Terre on Long Island, a town near a university campus. Belle Terre limited property to single-family residences and specifically excluded fraternity houses and apartment buildings. Single-family resi- dence was defined to include either persons related by blood or marriage or not more than two unrelated individuals living together as a family. A landlord renting to several students was challenged under the ordinance. Finding the maintenance of family values an adequate ground for zoning decisions, the Court rejected claims that the Belle Terre ordinance violated the students' or the landlord's right to privacy and was discrimina- tory, albeit on social rather than racial grounds.[43] The Court later balked, though, when it examined an East Cleveland ordinance which, according to some of the justices, attempted to eliminate the extended family and mandate a middle class suburban life- style by defining single family in terms that included the nuclear family but did not allow for family members beyond one's spouse and children.[44] In that case a grand- mother was found guilty of violating a single-family ordinance because her son and her two grandsons were living with her following a tragic fire in which the one boy's mother was killed. On this occasion, the broad zoning power of the community had run head- long into the fundamental constitutional protection for the family against intrusion by government.

Some issues have arisen where private action is at stake but where government is called upon for enforcement of private rental agreements or condominium governance. One of the currently unresolved but highly volatile challenges is to agreements common among renters and condominium purchasers to bring no children into the residence. A number of residents who later had children have argued that government could not interfere in a decision of a family to have a child or bar a family from residence in an area because of children. Therefore, they claim, for government to enforce the no-children rule by court ordered eviction or suits by other condominium residents is illegal state action in much the same sense as court enforcement of racially restrictive covenants. With large numbers of families frozen out of the single-family housing market by high prices and fewer family-oriented apartments available, these issues are likely to occupy judges for some time to come.

Who Sues Whom for What? Statutory and Constitutional Issues of Process and Substance

While there are constitutional grounds on which housing discrimination may be attacked, statutory challenges are more common and, for several reasons, more productive. First, the Supreme Court has held that the Constitution does not "guarantee access to dwellings of a particular quality."[45] So, at least at this time, there is no recognized right to housing under the Constitution.[46] As a practical matter, constitutional housing cases most often present claims to equal protection of the law. However, the Supreme Court altered the requirements needed to prove the existence of constitutionally illegal discrimination during the 1970s, making it extremely difficult for those charging violations of the equal protection clause to prevail. Prior to 1975 the Court had taken the position that a plaintiff needed to prove that official conduct produced a discriminatory effect.[47] If so, the burden shifted to the government to justify the action. The reason for this approach was twofold. For one thing, those who pursued a segregated society had long since become sufficiently sophisticated so as to avoid making any overt admissions that discrimination was their intention. Therefore, a requirement that those charging equal protection violations prove both that officials' decisions produced a segregative effect and that they were based upon segregative intent would make it extremely difficult, if not impossible, as a practical matter to prove discrimination and obtain relief. Another reason advanced by some judges is that officials should be judged by what they do, not by what they allegedly think, even assuming it is possible to know what a local government intended by any particular action. Nevertheless, the Court shifted its position on the requirements for proving discrimination, mandating that a plaintiff must demonstrate both intent and effect.[48] Moreover, the plaintiff must prove not merely that the legislature or some other official acted in spite of a knowledge that their decisions would have a discriminatory effect, but also that they acted at least in part *because* they would have a discriminatory impact.[49] Even assuming that one has evidence adequate to prove discrimination, he or she may be unable to meet the procedural requirements to present the case in federal court. In *Warth v. Seldin* in 1975, a badly divided Supreme Court defined the elements necessary to demonstrate that one has legal standing to sue so as to make it quite difficult to bring an equal protection based claim of housing discrimination.[50]

The principal statute used in open housing litigation is the Fair Housing Act of 1968 that prohibits discrimination by units of government or commercial real estate enterprises. The Supreme Court ruled later in 1968 that private noncommercial sellers and small renters not covered by the Fair Housing Act were prohibited from engaging in discriminatory practices by the Civil Rights Act of 1866. Justice Stewart writing for the Court in *Jones v. Alfred H. Mayer Co.* held that that statute "bars *all* racial discrimination, private as well as public, in the sale or rental of property, and that the statute thus construed, is a valid exercise of the power of Congress to enforce the Thirteenth

Amendment.''[51] When possible, though, most litigants choose the Fair Housing Act as the basis for their suits. That statute provides specific authority for the Justice Department to sue for enforcement of its provisions and contains a broad grant of standing to private citizens to litigate claims.[52] Moreover, while the Supreme Court has not addressed the question, those circuit courts of appeals which have considered the issue have held that it is not necessary to prove both discriminatory intent and effect under the Act.[53]

The Low and Moderate Income Housing Development Issues

The most common types of cases federal judges have been asked to address under these statutory and constitutional provisions during the seventies and eighties are issues concerning the construction and operation of public housing, interference with the development of planned low and moderate income housing projects, and refusal to provide (or discrimination in the availability of) public services to low income or predominantly minority housing. The challenges to public housing programs have been of two basic varieties. The first concerned the operation of segregated public housing either by formal rules or, more commonly, by the informal but closely followed custom of assigning applicants to housing according to race.[54] While judges have had no difficulty overturning such segregation, they have had considerable trouble attempting to fashion effective remedies for the problem. The reason for this dilemma involves the second challenge, cases that questioned the selection of sites for new construction by local public housing authorities and their support by HUD. Where it was common practice to construct most public housing in existing ghetto areas or in all white neighborhoods, it was difficult to encourage public housing residents to accept apartment assignments that would bring about desegregation. Several lower courts around the nation found that the selection of public housing sites that added to existing segregated housing patterns or perpetuated past segregation were violations of the statute and equal protection of the law.[55]

These public housing issues reached the U.S. Supreme Court in 1976 in a case originating in Chicago, *Hills v. Gautreaux*.[56] District Judge Austin found that the Chicago Housing Authority (CHA) had deliberately constructed new public housing in areas of high minority population and had used discriminatory housing assignments that ensured the perpetuation of segregation. Moreover, the city maintained a practice of permitting aldermen to veto public housing sites planned for their wards, a virtual guaranty that there would be no movement of public housing out of existing minority neighborhoods. The Seventh Circuit later found that HUD was aware of these practices but continued to fund the CHA, thus becoming a partner in the discrimination. The court ordered scattered-site housing outside existing black areas, not only in the city, but also in surrounding suburbs. The Supreme Court upheld the ruling, finding that since HUD was a defendant and its funding practices affected the pattern of housing within the metropolitan area, it could be required to take remedial steps outside the city proper. While this case was in its early stages, HUD declared a policy of promoting scattered-site housing to avoid problems of the sort found in the *Gautreaux* case. It was, however, a difficult policy to implement.

In addition to the public housing cases, federal judges have faced a variety of suits in which plaintiffs asserted that local governments attempted to block construction of low and moderate income housing because it was likely to include a substantial number of minority residents. Judge Marovitz of the Northern District of Illinois summarized the more or less standard categories in which such suits arise:

> There are three basic types of cases regarding zoning and housing problems that involve racial discrimination. The first deals with referendums that negate existent low and moderate income zoning or subject certain zoning to voter approval; the second involves those cases where the property as zoned accommodates low and moderate income housing but which is then rezoned by the city to exclude that housing; the third includes those cases where exclusion is accomplished by a refusal to rezone or a refusal to take affirmative action.[57]

There have been several different types of referenda used to block proposed housing projects. The Supreme Court has confronted such practices four times since 1967. In the first case, California repealed by referendum two fair housing laws and prohibited the state from making any law affecting a decision to sell or rent property related to race. The Court found that action amounted to state participation in the encouragement of racial discrimination and overturned the new law.[58] Similarly, the Court struck down an Akron, Ohio, amendment to its fair housing ordinance which required that any ordinance concerning the sale or lease of property involving decisions based upon "race, color, religion, national origin or ancestry" must be approved in a citywide referendum.[59] In 1971 and again in 1976, however, the Court upheld referendum requirements. In *James v. Valtierra,* California voters by initiative adopted a state constitutional provision requiring a local referendum before any low income housing could be constructed. The lower court struck down the enactment, but the Supreme Court reversed. In a 5–3 opinion by Justice Black, the Court concluded that, unlike the earlier referendum cases, this requirement did not single out race as a deciding factor and was not therefore discriminatory.[60] In 1976 the Court upheld an Eastlake, Ohio, ordinance requiring approval of fifty-five percent of the voters in a referendum in any case in which there was a request for a land use regulation change.[61] Unlike the earlier cases, *City of Eastlake v. Forest City Enterprises* did not involve alleged discrimination, but a claim that the ordinance violated the due process rights of landowners. While the Court has attempted to draw a distinction between local efforts to control low income housing as opposed to attempts at racial discrimination and while both class and race-based decisions are made with respect to low and moderate income housing, it is often impossible to know just how to evaluate any given community action.

Direct zoning decisions are somewhat more obvious and have been the basis for suits against local governments charging racial discrimination. As Judge Marovitz explained, these can be classified into situations in which zoning is changed to block low and moderate income housing and those in which a local government refuses to alter existing rules to permit development. One of the best known examples of the former occurred in an unincorporated area of suburban St. Louis. A church group, in cooperation with a number of individuals, proposed a project called Park View Heights to be constructed using HUD Section 236 funds. They purchased twelve acres of land and applied for construction finances. Residents of neighboring subdivisions mobilized to oppose the project, using mass meetings, letter-writing campaigns, and even a delegation to Washington to block the plan. After HUD issued a feasibility letter, the first step in approval of federal funding, the Black Jack Improvement Association petitioned the county government to be incorporated as the City of Black Jack, Missouri. Their petition was approved over the strenuous objection of the county planning office. Shortly thereafter, the newly created city adopted a zoning ordinance that, to all intents and purposes, blocked multiple-family housing. The litigation challenging the Black Jack action was originally launched by the Park View Heights group, but it was later taken up by DOJ. Judge Meredith dismissed the suit on grounds that the plaintiffs had not proven that the intent of the zoning ordinance was discriminatory. The Eighth Circuit reversed, finding that the Fair Housing Act does not require a demonstration of intent. It went on to hold the zoning ordinance in violation of the Act and ordered Meredith to issue an injunction against its use.[62]

In another such case, the City of Lackawanna, New York, responded to a proposed low and moderate income housing project that would be occupied primarily by black applicants by rezoning the area for recreational use only. Judge Curtin found the city in violation of both the equal protection clause and the Fair Housing Act.[63]

More common than zoning decisions to block development is the situation in which a community simply refuses to grant a variance or reclassification of property to accommodate a proposed housing project. Since the presumptions are generally in favor of an existing zoning plan, the burden imposed upon a group wishing to develop low and moderate housing projects in pursuit of open housing is substantial. Several federal courts have held, however, that a refusal to permit development may under some circumstances be discriminatory. Judge Marovitz explained that interpretation:

> The denial of a zoning petition though in a sense a negative process, when resulting in racial discrimination and part of a pattern that has perpetuated racial stratification is no less assertive conduct of a discriminatory nature than the more positive procedure of condemning or zoning out low and moderate income housing. Though the means may be different, they are both forms of zoning code manipulation whose effects are the same and the technical distinction between the degrees of activity involved is relevant only as to the burden of proof that the plaintiffs must bear rather than as to the question of whether a cause of action is sufficiently stated.[64]

One of the few fair housing cases to reach the Supreme Court originated from a refusal to grant a variance. Arlington Heights, a virtually all white northwestern suburb of Chicago, refused to grant a variance on property adjoining a Catholic high school for construction of a carefully designed low and moderate income housing project. The city argued that such housing could be built in the so-called buffer zone surrounding the area zoned for single-family construction, but the developer countered that no property was available that would accommodate the minimum requirements of HUD funding under the Section 236 program. The district judge found no intentional discrimination in the city's refusal to rezone, but the Seventh Circuit Court of Appeals reversed holding that the refusal to rezone had the discriminatory effect of maintaining the city's existing all white housing pattern.[65] The Supreme Court remanded the case after ruling that proof of both intent and effect was required to justify a finding of unconstitutional discrimination.[66] On remand, the Seventh Circuit found that there was a violation of the Fair Housing Act, which does not require proof of intent to discriminate.[67] On the other hand, courts have not automatically accepted complaints that all restrictive zoning ordinances are automatically illegal absent proof of discriminatory effect.[68]

Other decisions blocking development of low and moderate income housing have brought federal court reaction where there was a demonstrated discriminatory racial effect. Cases originating in Philadelphia; Lackawanna, New York; Parma, Ohio; and Atlanta resulted in rulings that building permits were refused, delayed, or revoked in an effort to block open housing plans.[69] In the Philadelphia case, Judge Broderick found that the city and several of its leading officials, including two mayors, had attempted to block completion of the Whitman Townhouse project by the Philadelphia Housing Authority, and, when it appeared unlikely that they could stop the project, they harassed the builder. He further determined that race was at the heart of this antagonism, as evidenced by the successful mayoral candidate's insistence that low income housing was the same as black housing and, as the judge summarized the mayor's comment, there "should not be any public housing placed in White neighborhoods because people in White neighborhoods did not want Black people moving in with them."[70] A number of federal courts have found as well that discriminatory provision of city services or a refusal to permit connections to water or sewer systems in an effort to block low and moderate income housing violates the equal protection clause, the Fair Housing Act, or both.[71]

Remedies

Where judges found violations, they have ordered a range of relief for victims of discrimination. Among the more common orders are requirements that (1) communities cease discrimination; (2) communities ensure completion of blocked projects; (3) violators publish notice that they no longer discriminate; (4) violators maintain records that can be checked to ensure compliance; and (5) violators provide financial support to make up for additional costs of projects that were delayed by discriminatory policies or practices. Others have been ordered to find either acceptable alternatives to permit construction of planned projects or to ease zoning barriers to allow completion of the project that had been originally proposed. But where there has been long-standing discriminatory housing practice, it has been extremely difficult for judges to enforce compliance with mandated remedies.

One of the clearer examples of difficulties in ensuring compliance is found in the Chicago case discussed earlier. In reviewing Judge Austin's efforts to obtain compliance, the Seventh Circuit Court of Appeals in an opinion by retired Supreme Court Justice Tom C. Clark found:

> Given the eight-year tortuous course of these cases, together with the findings and judgment orders of the District Court and the opinions of this Court (now numbering five), we believe the relief granted is not only much too little but also much too late in the proceedings. In effect appellants, having won the battle back in 1969, have now lost the war. We are fully aware of the many difficult and sensitive problems that the cases have presented to the able District Judge and we applaud the care, meticulous attention and the judicious manner in which he has approached them. With his orders being ignored and frustrated as they were, he kept his cool and courageously called the hand of the recalcitrant. . . .
>
> We shall not burden this opinion with the details of the eight-year delay that has thus far deprived the appellants of the fruits of the District Court's judgment entered on July 1, 1969. In addition the unconstitutional action of CHA has stripped thousands of residents of the City of Chicago of their Fifth and Fourteenth Amendment rights

for a score of years. Indeed, anyone reading the various opinions of the District Court and of this Court quickly discovers a callousness on the part of the appellees towards the rights of the black, underprivileged citizens of Chicago that is beyond comprehension.[72]

MONEY, POLITICS, AND FEAR: THE POLITICAL ENVIRONMENT OF FAIR HOUSING LITIGATION

The history of housing discrimination and the legislative, executive, and judicial responses to it have both affected and been conditioned by the political and economic environment within which they have developed and in which solutions have been pursued. Of particular importance during the period from the late 1960s into the 1980s are the politics of insularity, the dynamics of fear based on old mistakes, the money crunch, the changes in DOJ litigation policy, and the utility of the financial level for fair housing enforcement.

The movement of the middle class out of the city was not merely physical, nor was it a single action. It was in many ways a symbolic breaking of political and social connections, even though suburban economic interests often continued to depend on the city. An element of that division was a rejection by many suburban communities of responsibility for the problems of the city that spawned them. The worse the problems of the city became, the less the suburbs wished to deal with them. The movement did not, however, stop with a single ring of insular suburban communities but continued outward in many metropolitan areas to extended rings further out from the city than the earlier suburbs. Distance from the urban core and the buffering effect of the near suburbs added to the ability of the more distant communities to isolate themselves. The independence and insularity were manifest in politics as the suburbs became a dynamic political force.

At least three factors made the suburbs particularly significant political actors. First, the reapportionment decisions requiring that state legislatures and the seats in the U.S. House of Representatives be assigned on the basis of "one person, one vote" tended to place political power where the population was growing, in the suburbs. As a third force in the state legislature, suburbs were in a position to join with rural legislators against the cities when it was in their interest and with the cities against the rural representatives on other matters. Second, the types of citizens living in the suburbs are precisely the people most likely to turn out at the polls to defend their interests, real or imagined. Third, the intergovernmental aid system that provided direct project grants for essential services (like sewage-treatment plant construction), formula-based direct funding for education and community development, and general revenue sharing funds permitted sophisticated suburban communities to obtain direct financial support from the federal government and bypass some of the existing state and urban political control centers. All of these factors combined to make open housing efforts more difficult.

Further complicating the housing problem is the presence in many communities of fear based in part on mistakes of the past. Given what many suburbanites had seen of public housing in the cities, it is not surprising that they recoiled at the prospect of similar projects in their communities. Of course, it was in part the geographical, financial, and political situation in the cities which produced the high-rise, high-density projects which frightened the critics. Many assumed that low and moderate income housing was the same thing as the public housing they had seen elsewhere. Moreover, it was the cycle of housing problems, educational deficiencies, and the lack of jobs that bred some of the behavior that observers found so threatening. It had been in part the block-busting and racial steering tactics of unscrupulous real estate agents that had fostered the image of massive shift in neighborhoods and gave rise to myths about the results of integrated housing. The fear itself can bring about a self-fulfilling prophecy in which property owners panic over modest amounts of integration and, by panic selling, create the kind of picture they envisioned in the first place.

It would have been difficult enough to achieve the goals of the 1968 Housing Act if the real estate market had remained relatively stable through the 1970s. However, it was anything but stable, complicating the environment within which governments and private organizations were attempting to remedy earlier discrimination. First, property prices shot dramatically upward, taking rents up with them. Rising interest rates along with increasing prices froze substantial groups of first-time home buyers out of the market. The advent of variable interest rate mortgages added to the instability since a small rise in interest rates meant substantial increases in monthly payments. By the early 1980s mortgage foreclosure rates were climbing to dramatic new highs. Some areas were particularly hard hit when economic downturns resulted in dramatic increases in unemployment and underemployment. Within the cities the more desirable older resi-dential property values were driven significantly higher by gentrification, a process in which young professional couples purchased and renovated existing housing units. On the one hand, this process had a number of very positive consequences for the cities, but it simultaneously reduced the availability of low income housing and pushed general property values, and hence property taxes, even higher. Finally, the move to condomin-iums meant a further reduction in the availability of rental property. Conversion of existing apartment buildings to condominiums hit senior citizens particularly hard. Many communities have faced calls for creation of public or subsidized low and moderate income housing not only to end segregated housing patterns, but also to accommodate the elderly. At the same time rising property values, high interest rates, and substantial inflation rates made it difficult for local governments or private developers to plan and build new housing. Moreover, just as the need was increasing, federal assistance began declining both in terms of inflation and in absolute dollars as programs were cut back or eliminated.

Apart from the changes in the marketplace, there were also the dynamics of en-forcement of fair housing policies in DOJ and other federal agencies. The Nixon admin-istration resisted vigorous housing law enforcement where it appeared likely to anger suburban voters. The Housing and Credit section of the Civil Rights Division (CRD) had to debate superiors and the White House to file the cases they eventually pressed to successful conclusions. Similar pressures were placed on HUD enforcement officers that limited their ability to pursue complaints vigorously. The civil rights coalition which had been so important in enacting the statutes of the 1960s had broken down to the point where substantial effort was required even to ensure extensions of the Voting Rights Act. The effectiveness of some of the interest groups who had used litigation as an important tool in earlier years was limited as the complexity and cost of litigation increased.

For some years the financial lever to enforce compliance with fair housing require-ments has been available but it has been difficult to use. For one thing, while several agencies from the Treasury to the Federal Reserve have enforcement authority under various housing statutes and executive orders, it is not a priority for those organizations. Moreover, while funding cutoffs could be pursued under Title VI of the Civil Rights Act of 1964 by other agencies, recent history suggests that it is unlikely they will make good on the threat. Not only do they generate political conflict by a funding cut, but they seem to hurt themselves since the funding loss may mean reduced appropriations in the future and may signal a failure by the agency to congressional observers.

CONCLUSION

In sum, the cases presented to federal judges alleging discrimination in housing involve complex issues that must be resolved in a conflict ridden environment. It is an environment that has been shaped by choice and economic capacity, yes, but also by a variety of policies by both the national and state and local governments which intentionally and effectively discriminated in the development of metropolitan housing patterns. The effort to create open housing has been partially successful. The judge called upon to decide such an issue and devise an effective remedy has a difficult task indeed. Judge Frank Battisti was one judge asked to respond to such a suit, *United States v. City of Parma*. Chapter 3 examines that litigation.

NOTES

1. Housing Act of 1949, 42 U.S.C. Section 1441 (1978).
2. National Advisory Commission on Civil Disorders, *Report of the National Advisory Commission on Civil Disorders* (New York: Bantam, 1968), p. 12 [hereafter Kerner Commission Report].
3. Richard P. Fishman, ed., *Housing for All Under Law: New Directions in Housing and Land Use Planning Law* (Cambridge, MA: Ballinger, 1978), p. 41.
4. *Id.*
5. *Euclid v. Ambler Realty*, 272 U.S. 365 (1926).
6. Fishman, *supra* note 3, at 43.
7. *See generally* Clement Vose, *Caucasions Only: The Supreme Court, the NAACP, and the Restrictive Covenant Cases* (Berkeley: Univ. of California Press, 1959).
8. 14 Stat. 27 (1866).
9. *Buchanan v. Warley*, 245 U.S. 60 (1917).
10. President's Commission on Urban Housing, *A Decent Home*, (Wash., DC: Government Printing Office, 1968), p. 54 [hereafter Kaiser Commission Report].
11. For a further discussion of this historical development, *see generally* U.S. Commission on Civil Rights, *The Federal Fair Housing Enforcement Effort*, (Wash., DC: Government Printing Office, 1979); and, *id.*, *Twenty Years After Brown*, (Wash., DC: Government Printing Office, 1979).
12. Fishman, *supra* note 3, at 18.
13. *Id.*, at 19.
14. Charles M. Lamb, "Housing Discrimination and Segregation in America: Problematical Dimensions and the Federal Legal Response," 30 *Cath. U. L. Rev.* 363, 368 (1981).
15. *Twenty Years After Brown*, *supra* note 11, at 105.
16. Fishman, *supra* note 3, at 22.

17. Kerner Commission Report, *supra* note 2, at 8.

18. *Id.*, at 2.

19. *Id.*, at 1.

20. Kaiser Commission Report, *supra* note 10, at 13.

21. Anthony Downs, *Opening Up the Suburbs: An Urban Strategy for America*, (New Haven, CT: Yale Univ. Press, 1973), p. 36.

22. Lamb, *supra* note 14, at 391–92.

23. Downs, *supra* note 21, at 9.

24. Michael Danielson, *The Politics of Exclusion*, (New York: Columbia Univ. Press, 1976), p. 24.

25. *Id.*, at 17–18. *See also* Chester W. Hartman, *Housing and Social Policy*, (Englewood Cliffs, NJ: Prentice-Hall, 1974), p. 47; and *Southern Burlington County NAACP v. Township of Mt. Laurel*, 336 A.2d 713, 723 (NJ 1975).

26. Fishman, *supra* note 3, at 30.

27. *See generally* James Q. Wilson, *Urban Renewal: The Record and the Controversy*, (Cambridge, MA: MIT, 1966).

28. *Id.*, at 27.

29. *See generally* Danielson, *supra* note 24; Richard F. Babcock, *The Zoning Game*, (Madison: Univ. of Wisconsin Press, 1966); and Daniel R. Mandelker, *The Zoning Dilemma, a Legal Strategy for Urban Change*, (Indianapolis, IN: Bobbs-Merrill, 1971).

30. Equal Credit Opportunity Act, 15 U.S.C. Section 169 *et seq.*

31. Charles M. Lamb, "Equal Housing Opportunity," in Charles S. Bullock III and Charles M. Lamb, eds., *Implementation of Civil Rights Policy*, (Monterey, CA: Brooks/Cole, 1984), pp. 171–73.

32. *See generally Federal Fair Housing Enforcement Record*, *supra* note 11, at 66–74.

33. *Euclid v. Ambler*, *supra* note 5.

34. *Buchanan v. Warley*, *supra* note 9, at 74–75.

35. *Euclid v. Ambler*, *supra* note 5, at 388.

36. *Id.*, at 395.

37. *Id.*, at 394.

38. *Corrigan v. Buckley*, 271 U.S. 323 (1926).

39. Vose, *supra* note 7.

40. *Shelley v. Kraemer*, 334 U.S. 1 (1948).

41. *Barrows v. Jackson*, 346 U.S. 249 (1953).

42. *Berman v. Parker*, 348 U.S. 26, 32–33 (1954).

43. *Village of Belle Terre v. Boraas*, 416 U.S. 1 (1974).

44. *Moore v. East Cleveland*, 431 U.S. 494 (1977).

45. *Lindsey v. Normet*, 405 U.S. 56, 74 (1972).

46. Several commentators have argued, however, that there should be such a right. *See* Note: "Towards a Recognition of a Constitutional Right to Housing," 42 *U. Mo. Kan. City L. Rev.* 362 (1974).

47. *Wright v. Council of City of Emporia*, 407 U.S. 451, 461–62 (1972).

48. *Washington v. Davis*, 426 U.S. 229 (1976).

49. *Personnel Administrator v. Feeney*, 442 U.S. 256 (1979).

50. *Warth v. Seldin*, 422 U.S. 490 (1975).

51. *Jones v. Alfred H. Mayer Co.*, 392 U.S. 409, 413 (1968).

52. *See, e.g., Trafficante v. Metropolitan Life Ins. Co.*, 409 U.S. 205 (1972).

53. *Metro. Hous. Dev. Corp. v. Village of Arlington Heights*, 558 F.2d 1283 (7th Cir. 1977).

54. *See, e.g., Gautreaux v. Chicago Hous. Auth.* 296 F. Supp. 907, 909 (NDIL 1969).

55. See *Banks v. Perk*, 341 F. Supp. 1175 (NDOH 1972), *aff'd in part, rev'd in part*, 473 F.2d 910 (6th Cir. 1973); *Hicks v. Weaver*, 302 F. Supp. 610 (EDLA 1969); *El Cortez Heights*

Residents and Property Owners Ass'n. v. Tucson Hous. Auth., 457 F.2d 910 (6th Cir. 1973); and *Shannon v. Dept. of Housing and Urban Development*, 436 F.2d 809 (3rd Cir. 1970).

56. *Hills v. Gautreaux*, 425 U.S. 284 (1976).

57. *Sisters of Providence of St. Mary of the Woods v. City of Evanston*, 335 F. Supp. 396, 403 (NDIL 1971).

58. *Reitman v. Mulkey*, 387 U.S. 373 (1967).

59. *Hunter v. Erickson*, 393 U.S. 385 (1969). *See also S. Alameda Spanish Speaking Org. (SASSO) v. City of Union City, Cal.*, 424 F.2d 291 (9th Cir. 1970).

60. *James v. Valtierra*, 402 U.S. 137 (1971).

61. *City of Eastlake v. Forest City Enterprises*, 426 U.S. 668 (1976).

62. *United States v. City of Black Jack, Mo.*, 508 F.2d 1179 (8th Cir. 1974), *cert., denied* 422 U.S. 1042 (1975). Cities below are *Park View Heights Corp. v. City of Black Jack*, 355 F. Supp. 899 (EDMO 1972), *rev'd* 467 F.2d 1208 (8th Cir. 1972), *on remand sub nom. United States v. City of Black Jack, Mo.*, 372 F. Supp. 319 (EDMO 1974).

63. *Kennedy Park Homes Ass'n. v. City of Lackawanna*, 318 F. Supp. 669 (WDNY 1970), *aff'd* 436 F.2d 108 (2nd Cir. 1970), *cert. denied*, 401 U.S. 1010 (1971).

64. *Sisters of Providence v. Evanston*, *supra* note 57, at 403.

65. *Metro. Hous. Dev. Corp. v. Village of Arlington Heights*, 517 F.2d 409 (7th Cir. 1975), *reversing* 373 F. Supp. 208 (NDIL 1974).

66. *Village of Arlington Heights v. Metro. Hous. Dev. Corp.*, 429 U.S. 252 (1977).

67. *Metro. Hous. Dev. Corp. v. Village of Arlington Heights*, *supra* note 53.

68. *See, e.g., Yabarra v. Town of Los Altos Hills*, 370 F. Supp. 742 (NDCA 1973), upholding a zoning law requiring a minimum lot size of one acre; and *Construction Industry Ass'n. of Sonoma County v. City of Petaluma*, 522 F.2d 897 (9th Cir. 1975), limiting growth in a California community.

69. *Resident Advisory Bd. v. Rizzo*, 564 F.2d 126 (3rd Cir. 1977); *Kennedy Park v. City of Lackawanna*, *supra* note 63; *United States v. City of Parma, Ohio*, 494 F. Supp. 1049 (NDOH 1980); and *Crow v. Brown*, 332 F. Supp. 382 (NDGA 1971).

70. *Resident Advisory Bd. v. Rizzo*, 425 F. Supp. 987, 1001 (EDPA 1976).

71. *Kennedy Park v. Lackawanna*, *supra* note 63; *United Farmworkers of Florida Hous. Project Inc. v. City of Delray Beach*, 493 F.2d 799 (5th Cir. 1974); and *Hawkins v. Town of Shaw*, 461 F.2d 1171 (5th Cir. 1972).

72. *Gautreaux v. Chicago Hous. Auth.*, 503 F.2d 930, 932 (7th Cir. 1974).

3

United States v. City of Parma, Ohio: Open Housing Conflict in a Cleveland Suburb

Cleveland, like many northern and midwestern industrial cities, experienced burgeoning growth in the postwar years and again in the early 1960s. Like other such communities, it spawned a plethora of suburbs. Other towns, once seemingly isolated and independent, soon became a part of the expanding metropolis. In the early postwar years, when discrimination was still widely and legally practiced, those most able to take advantage of the new suburban lifestyle were members of the generally white, rising middle class. Conflict over racial discrimination in housing arose in Cleveland as it did in other cities around the nation.

This chapter investigates one of these open housing battles. An examination of *United States v. City of Parma, Ohio* provides a useful case study for understanding not only public law policy litigation, but also the problems of housing desegregation. The *Parma* suit, brought by the Civil Rights Division (CRD) of the Department of Justice (DOJ), charged Cleveland's largest suburb with intentional discrimination in housing on the basis of race. Several of the factual and legal issues presented in the Parma litigation have surfaced elsewhere, though it is important to understand the particular factors and personalities that affected the development of this particular case.

THE TRIGGER PHASE

The U.S. Civil Rights Commission (CRC) conducted hearings and investigations in Cleveland in 1966. The testimony from a range of public officials, community leaders, and private citizens along with reports prepared by CRC staff produced evidence that Cleveland was facing many of the same urban problems then surfacing in other American cities.[1] Depending upon which data source one examines, between ninety and ninety-five percent of blacks in Cleveland were concentrated in a few areas east of the Cuyahoga River.[2] Testimony at the CRC hearings indicated that while at one time blacks appeared to be moving westward into other parts of the city, a number of public and private actions were taken to block that movement. Some who were economically successful did migrate to suburbs, but most of these minority suburbanites clustered in communities on the east side of the city. Witnesses testified that they had sought housing on the west side or in western suburbs but had been met with a variety of subtle and not-so-subtle discriminatory housing practices.[3]

The hearings suggested that housing conditions for Cleveland's black citizens were declining. There was a deterioration of the housing stock attributable to age, lack of maintenance by owners, weak housing and building code enforcement, and an inability on the part of residents to rehabilitate the property for financial and other reasons. The economic climate grew worse as jobs moved to the suburbs where inexpensive land, tax advantages, and competition among communities for growth and development produced attractive business opportunities.[4] As jobs moved outward, transportation became a greater bar to employment for residents of Cleveland's east-side black community. That increasing unemployment, in turn, exacerbated existing housing conditions in minority neighborhoods.

Urban renewal was another major factor that contributed to growing tension over housing policy. Areas within the black community were designated as urban renewal zones. Testimony at the CRC hearings indicated that there were two immediate impacts from that urban renewal activity on minority residents. First, destruction of housing stock for urban renewal resulted in a concentration of the population in fewer housing units, which exacerbated maintenance problems and led to further deterioration of the housing stock. Second, those remaining units located within designated areas were not treated, for purposes of code enforcement, like residential units in other parts of the city. In fact, testimony by city housing officials established that these properties were essentially in an administrative limbo with virtually no significant code enforcement.[5]

Finally, Cleveland, like other communities, had deficiencies in its administration of public housing. Cleveland's Cuyahoga Metropolitan Housing Authority (CMHA) operated a number of facilities that were themselves not integrated. Siting for new projects tended to provide more units for low income minority families within existing economically depressed, primarily black, communities.[6] It would be the problems within the public housing authority and their relationship to Cleveland's overall housing patterns that would spark the first of several suits seeking the elimination of policies and practices that limited equal housing opportunities for blacks and called for enforcement of affirmative obligations for open housing in the communities making up the Cleveland metropolitan area.

Enter the Judges: The Banks and Mahaley Litigation

Judge Frank Battisti, Chief Judge of the U.S. District Court for the Northern District of Ohio, became an important figure in the housing policy controversy in greater Cleveland as early as 1972. It was then that Battisti rendered his decision in *Banks v. Perk*.[7] Maryann Banks, the NAACP, and the ACLU brought a class action suit against Mayor Ralph Perk of Cleveland, city housing officials, the CMHA, and CMHA's executive director alleging that city and CMHA practices discriminated in housing on the basis of race in violation of the Fourteenth Amendment. There were two parts to the charge.

In the first count, the city was charged with having illegally suspended construction permits previously granted for two public housing projects, Crest Drive and Green Valley, located west of the Cuyahoga River in Cleveland. The former was to have provided 18 units and the latter 132 units of low income housing. The CMHA, a defendant in count two, joined as plaintiff in this allegation against the city.

In count two, the plaintiffs charged CMHA with constructing low income housing projects for minority residents in already economically depressed black communities as well as discrimination in assignment of applicants to existing housing units. While the record indicated an improvement in CMHA practices since the CRC hearings had highlighted some of its most basic shortcomings, the plaintiffs sought court ordered elimination of all discriminatory practices and their effects.

Judge Battisti found that Cleveland was a segregated city:

> The City of Cleveland is a racially divided city. Except for a small pocket of Negroes on the west side of the Cuyahoga River, in the Bellaire section, almost all (96%) of the Negro citizens of the city live on the east side of the River. The Negro population of the City of Cleveland has grown dramatically since 1930 when Negroes constituted only 8% of the total population of the city. Today it is more than 38%. Since 1950 three neighborhoods on the east side of Cleveland, Hough, Glenville, and Lee-Seville, have changed from primarily White to almost entirely Negro. As a result, the schools in the City of Cleveland are quite badly segregated. . . . In addition, in the last six years more than 5,000 jobs have moved from Cleveland's inner city to the outskirts of the City and to nearby suburbs. Access to those jobs has decreased for those who live in the inner city.[8]

There had, he said, been specific actions taken to block desegregation, such as the suspension of building permits involved in the *Banks* case. The judge concluded that the record showed a city administration which had run on a platform of resisting public housing in any part of the city where residents did not wait it.[9] Two days after that new administration had taken office, and without consulting its legal department, without new evidence or findings, and without any provision in its ordinances authorizing suspension, Battisti wrote, the administration ordered suspension. Citing a series of similar cases decided in other circuits,[10] Battisti declared the city's actions violative of the Fourteenth Amendment and restrained city officials "from failing to issue all necessary building permits" for Green Valley and Crest Drive.[11]

Similarly, Battisti found CMHA's siting practices to be of the same type as those used by the City of Chicago, which found illegal in a case that had been recently decided by the District Court for the Northern District of Illinois.[12] The housing authority, he said, had an affirmative obligation to eliminate segregation by dispersal of housing units. He did not order construction of additional units but did rule that CMHA was "enjoined from planning any future public housing in Negro neighborhoods of the City of Cleveland. . . . CMHA shall consider only sites on the West side of the Cuyahoga River in its scattered site program and is enjoined from the consideration on any East side sites in the program."

Judge Battisti moved from one Cleveland housing dispute to another with the filing of *Mahaley v. Cuyahoga Metropolitan Housing Authority*.[13] This litigation was launched by Artie Mahaley, Dorothy Harrison, and the Path Association, a nonprofit fair housing interest group, on behalf of "all tenants and applicants for low income housing in the CMHA area" against CMHA and its board of directors and executive director; the Cleveland suburbs of Euclid, Garfield Heights, Parma, Solon, and Westlake as well as the mayors and council members of those municipalities; the Department of Housing and Urban Development (HUD) and its then Secretary, George Romney. The suit challenged the constitutionality of the 1949 Housing Act, which required federal authorities who wished to lend money or support to low income housing projects of any type to obtain agreement to the project from the local government unit involved, on grounds that the cooperative agreement requirement, as written, encouraged racial discrimination and had been used in a discriminatory manner.[14] Moreover, they charged that the failure of the suburbs to enter into housing agreements, despite repeated efforts to negotiate cooperative ventures, was discriminatory. Finally, the plaintiffs alleged that the failure of CMHA to negotiate for adequate numbers of public housing units in the greater Cleveland area and the city itself, along with its failure to obtain agreements from the suburbs, made it a participant in the perpetuation of discrimination. Because of the nature of the claim and the jurisdictional statutes in force at that time, *Mahaley* was argued before a three judge federal district court, of which Battisti was a member.[15]

It was Battisti who authored the opinion for the panel that rejected the challenge to the racial validity of the statutory cooperative agreement requirement and found no reason to hold the federal government guilty of an illegal application of this otherwise valid statute. "However," he wrote, "it may have been manipulated improperly." To make the determination whether the statute had, in fact, been used by communities to discriminate or perpetuate the effects of past discrimination, the three judge panel remanded the case to Judge Battisti sitting alone.[16]

Judge Lambros dissented, largely because he thought the three judge court had an adequate record on which to decide whether the communities had unconstitutionally applied the statutory cooperation mandate. In his view, "the situation presented is a clear case of housing discrimination":[17]

> Cuyahoga County is segregated racially with ninety-seven per cent of its black population residing in four municipalities. The defendant suburbs are examples of the more than fifty municipalities predominantly populated by whites which surround the black population. Four of the defendant suburbs are 99.1 to 99.8 per cent white, with the fifth suburb being 95.5 per cent white.

> Plaintiffs who are seeking to live in defendant suburbs, are predominantly black. In 1971, 86 per cent of the applicants for family units were black and 73 per cent of applicants for both elderly and family units were black.[18]

Lambros rejected the idea that this racially disproportionate impact was not due to any sort of affirmative act of discrimination and mentioned Parma specifically in his retort:

> The action required of the defendant suburbs was not actual spending and construction, as would be the case, for example, in the failure to build a school. All that was needed was the approval for the plans made by defendant CMHA and financed by the federal government. Furthermore, the defendant suburbs were pressed on numerous occasions for their decision in this regard. That they viewed their withholding of the Local Cooperation Agreement and negotiations related thereto as affirmative action is evident by remarks by officials in defendant Parma. There, both the Mayor and President of Council spoke of the need to exclude public housing and, in the case of the President of the City Council, to keep blacks from moving into the suburbs by way of public housing.

> In other words, *the refusals of defendant authorities to negotiate a Local Cooperation Agreement were not within the analogy of one who walks past a drowning person but were more akin to the analogy of one who holds a life preserver over a drowning person and, upon consideration, decides not to drop it.*[19] (emphasis added)

TABLE 3–1. Housing Need in Defendant Suburbs

	Family	Elderly
Euclid	1,545	252
Garfield Heights	931	151
Parma	1,873	232
Solon	145	13
Westlake	233	38

Source: Mahaley v. CMHA, 355 F. Supp. 1257, 1262 (ND OH 1973).

The suburbs had protested that, under the Supreme Court's 1971 ruling in *James v. Valtierra,* it was not illegal for communities to have referendum requirements or other approval devices for low and moderate income housing construction.[20] Lambros countered that *Valtierra* only stood for the proposition that there was no violation in merely having such a statute, but that under *Hunter v. Erickson* a clearance process would fall if it was employed openly or covertly to discriminate on the basis of race.[21]

There was, however, considerably less difference between Battisti and Lambros than the opinions from the three judge panel might have suggested. Only hours after issuing the panel opinion on February 22, 1973, Battisti handed down his opinion on remand. Battisti, too, thought the record very strong and the housing precedents from other circuits compelling.[22] First, there were the segregated housing patterns within the county to be considered. Second, there was the resistance to repeated CMHA efforts to work out agreements with the suburbs. Finally, there was the absence of any adequate alternative explanation for the resistance of the communities other than race.

Battisti began his *Mahaley* opinion almost exactly as he had his *Banks v. Perk* ruling, with a description of the racial pattern in the jurisdiction:

> Cuyahoga County is a racially segregated county. The population of Cuyahoga County in 1970 was 1,721,300; 328,419 of whom were Negro. 87% of these 328,419 Negroes reside in Cleveland. Of the 40,578 who reside outside of Cleveland but within Cuyahoga County, 80% live in three eastern suburbs: 23,196 in the City of East Cleveland; 5,250 in Shaker Heights; and 4,007 in Warrensville Heights. In 1970 the defendant city of Garfield Heights had 1,789 Negro (4.6%) residents. All but two resided in one area of Garfield Heights adjacent to the City of Cleveland. The other four defendant suburban cities' population in 1970 was from 99.1% to 99.8% Caucasion.[23]

He went on to outline the housing needs within the CMHA area, citing statistics that indicated the vast majority of those needing housing were black Cuyahoga County citizens, many of whom then lived in Cleveland. The judge concluded by reminding the parties of HUD's policy of housing dispersal in effect at that time as well as CMHA's support of that program.

Battisti found two CMHA activities of particular importance to the disposition of the case. The authority had conducted a study not only of the low and moderate income housing needs of the county, but of each of the suburbs within the county. The results appear in Table 3–1. Having identified the need, CMHA employed letters and meetings as means of communicating to the suburbs, including Parma, just what those shortages were and what CMHA was prepared to do to meet them with the cooperation of the communities.[24]

Finally, Battisti found it frustrating that the suburbs were unwilling to offer any justification for their refusal to cooperate with CMHA other than "bald allegations that their failure to act . . . was not motivated by racially discriminatory reasons. They offer only allegations of no need for low income housing and their fear of property tax loss. Neither reason was supported by the evidence, and the latter should not be considered adequate or compelling even if proof had been offered."[25] He found their actions in violation of the Thirteenth and Fourteenth Amendments, Title VI of the Civil Rights Act of 1964, the Fair Housing Act, the Housing Act of 1937 as amended, and HUD regulations.[26] The judge ordered CMHA to prepare basic requirements based on the need level for each suburban community and then to enter into negotiations with the communities on how to meet those levels. But Battisti's order was cut short when, in July 1974, his opinion was overturned by the Sixth Circuit Court of Appeals in an opinion for a divided panel written by Judge Weick.[27]

Weick's opinion chastized Battisti for misreading *James v. Valtierra* and attempting to provide a right to equal housing where none was provided by the Constitution. However, according to Weick, Battisti "made no findings of a prior pattern and practice of discrimination of the suburbs against racial minorities . . . [nor had he] pointed out any evidence of purposeful discrimination against racial minorities."[28] And in any case, Weick wrote, the case should never have gone that far since municipalities are immune from suit under the Civil Rights Act because they are not "persons" within the meaning of the act.[29]

Judge Edwards issued a strong dissent to Weick's opinion. In the first place, he insisted, the case should never have been accepted for interlocutory appeal since no final order had been issued and the district judge had not certified the appeal.[30] The question whether municipalities are "persons" is beside the point since the suit named the individual officials in each community and a civil rights complaint most assuredly does lie against them. But if the status of cities as persons is to be considered, the decision ought to be that the suits should be allowed. As to the allegations about Battisti's findings of fact, he asserted, it is not the business of the appeals court to examine the factual findings since no appellant asserted that the fact finding was "clearly erroneous."

What Edwards did not say, but could have noted, was that Weick avoided any mention of the nine major precedents employed in Battisti's ruling, citing only two precedents without differentiating them from the other case law. That became significant because Weick's *Mahaley* argument was to be the basis for his commentary in the *Joseph Skillken and Co. v. City of Toledo* case, which, in turn, was the primary precedent relied upon by Parma in its appeals of its case all the way to the U.S. Supreme Court.

This rather complex and detailed recitation of the housing controversies in Cleveland and Cuyahoga county provides both the legal and factual backdrop against which *Parma* arose. It was important as well because it gave rise to some of the strong sentiments exhibited by all parties involved. Battisti was already under criticism in Cleveland both because of the housing cases and school desegregation rulings.[31] He was now also coming to be seen as a foe of Parma. Another not inconsiderable adversary for Battisti in the area of housing law who was emerging on the scene was Judge Weick of the Sixth Circuit Court of Appeals, and Weick's views would be of continuing importance in the Parma litigation.

Parma Under Pressure

Parma, Ohio, is not the kind of place about which people are likely to have moderate sentiments. A postwar boom transformed it into Cleveland's largest suburb. A city populated by a large percentage of second generation Eastern European immigrants, Parma's pride shows. There is a pride in its ethnic heritage and in the community itself. There are a number of ethnic parishes with affiliated schools as well as a variety of businesses which boast a particular ethnic affiliation in their names or storefront displays. Signs remind residents and visitors of the Slavic Festival.

The community is proud, too, of its development locally. It is a stable place, seemingly missed by some of the tremors of the 1960s. Not one of the most affluent areas of northern Ohio, neither is Parma suffering quite as badly as some neighboring communities. Its machine tool industries, which support the Chevrolet plant and other local manufacturers, have provided substantial numbers of solid, steady jobs.

Parma's housing stock is extraordinarily well maintained as are its yards and public buildings. The city boasts recently developed parks, shopping centers, and a new historical society. There is a certain wariness about outsiders who make reference to Parma's manicured residential neighborhoods, since such comments have been used as a form of shorthand reference by some observers for a perceived community attitude.[32] Somehow it is not surprising to a visitor to find that Parma was recently the proud host of the National Softball Championship.

As one of the attorneys for Parma in the housing dispute put it, "We don't like to call ourselves a suburb because we're pretty self-contained."[33] Longtime Parma Mayor, John Petruska, has indicated on a number of occasions that Parma is an independent city that is, in fact, quite complete and self-contained.[34] At least one of those involved in the *Parma* case, speaking of Parma residents, insisted, "All they really want is to be left alone."[35] However, growth and change in the Cleveland area meant pressure on communities like Parma to change as well.

There was debate within Parma concerning just how the community should deal with its changing environment. Mayor Petruska proclaimed in a CBS interview aired in 1968 that Parma bore no responsibility to respond to the problems of Cleveland.[36] That was simply an untenable position given other forces than at work in the metropolitan area. The CRC began its hearings in Cleveland and disclosed housing discrimination in the city and its environs. The growing national support for what would become the Fair Housing Act of 1968 added to pressure for change in housing policy, and it was felt by Parma. One of the early examples of that pressure came with a visit by federal authorities to Parma to discuss a transfer of federal property, known as the Crile site, to Parma and neighboring Parma Heights.

The site, a 185-acre tract on the southwestern border between Parma and Parma Heights, was intended for defense purposes, but changing plans meant the property could be made available to the local communities. HUD expressed interest in having that land transferred with the understanding that it would be used for housing needs and not merely for general community development. Parma did not want any conditions attached to the land grant and, according to one of the HUD officials present, was not at all pleased that HUD was even involved in the discussions. In a memorandum reporting the meeting to Francis Fisher, HUD's Regional Administrator, Dean Swatzel, Assistant Regional Administrator for Renewal Assistance, wrote:

Mayor John Petruska of Parma and Mayor Paul Cassidy of Parma Heights were emphatic and adamant at the outset of the meeting that the land be used for the critical needs of their communities, i.e., school, public service, and recreational purposes. They stated they would relentlessly resist any housing (or industrial) development. . . . They recited their opposition to the development of housing for the Coast Guard in the past and their repeated requests to the Federal Government for the use of the land to meet local needs. There appeared to be irritation that HUD was involved in the matter for this presented a new and ominous "wrinkle" to the localities, and it was forcefully indicated that they were not concerned about the problems of others, i.e., Cleveland.[37]

After receiving this and other reports, Fisher wrote to Richard Steiner, Special Consultant to the Secretary of HUD, on January 30, 1968, warning of problems in Parma:

[I]t was the position of the field team members that no prospects exist for the development of varied income housing on the site because of resistance from citizens of Parma and Parma Heights.

I would hope that our procedures do not operate to make this land available for standard white residential suburban development as the leaders of these two towns hope.[38]

The land was made available and became the site of Cuyahoga Community College.

The conflict over pressure for change in Parma broke into the open later in 1968 with the debate over a fair housing resolution produced for the city council. Councilman John Sands introduced a general open community resolution welcoming "all persons of good will" to Parma. The motion was defeated, but more important, perhaps, than the vote itself for future events was the debate over the resolution and the reasons for its rejection.

Some of those speaking against the proposal, including Mayor Petruska, testified later that they opposed the resolution because it was unnecessary since there were already state fair housing laws. Parma attorneys argued that the defeat of the resolution had more to do with political rivalry among members of the city council than it did the question whether a welcome resolution was needed. The trial findings, however, maintained that it was during that period that Mayor Petruska was most adamant in his public statements and speeches delivered to community meetings that Cleveland should take care of its own problems and Parma should shoulder no responsibility for them.

Once the debate over housing became public and heated, there ensued a number of open statements by Parma officials that would be cited for the proposition that Parma authorities did not want any form of public housing, whether owned and operated by the CMHA or otherwise, and that opposition was directly related to the fact that most of the applicants would likely be blacks, many of whom now lived in neighborhoods on the east side of Cleveland. In the interim, several other important elements of the Parma housing dispute surfaced.

The CMHA began a campaign to enlist the cooperation of Parma and other suburbs in 1968. That program continued through 1972, with no favorable response from Parma and with a public statement of intent by Parma's Mayor Petruska to resist any effort to provide low income housing in that city.[39] After the HUD Section 236 low income housing program was eliminated and replaced by the Section 8 program under the Housing and Community Development Act of 1974, CMHA and HUD renewed the publicity program, notifying each of the area mayors by letter of the nature of the new program and hosting meetings at which its provisions were discussed. Parma neither attended the meetings nor responded to the letters.[40] There was one exception; it involved a meeting at Cleveland HUD offices in 1971 and concerned the Parmatown Woods apartment project, proposed by Forest City Enterprises, that was to be constructed using federal funds.

There were, in fact, a number of builders bringing development plans to Parma for a variety of commercial and residential projects on what little open land remained in the community, most of it on the western edge of Parma adjacent to Parma Heights. These proposals placed more pressure on Parma's generally calm and stable existence. Several of the plans engendered debate over whether, how much, and what kind of development should be permitted, but a number of the projects were eventually approved. Technical difficulties with zoning decisions, plans, and building permits were worked out informally and construction moved along. Some of those projects were developed by Forest City Enterprises.[41]

In the case of one such project, Forest City had unsuccessfully attempted to obtain a rezoning decision to allow construction of an apartment building in 1968, but it tried again in 1969, stressing the fact that the Parmatown Towers project was to be a luxury apartment building. In a brief filed later, the attorneys for the city recalled:

> Forest City . . . asked for rezoning of the area . . . based on a proposal to build five six-story, luxury-type, "Gold Coast" apartment buildings. . . . While there was still public opposition to the high rise expressed, the developer gave residents in the immediate area a buffer strip of 20–25 feet at the rear of their property and these people ceased their former vehement opposition to the rezoning. . . . Forest City also made a strong presentation concerning the tax benefits to the city from having the high income tenants the proposed luxury apartments would attract.[42]

The presentation must have been convincing, for the council voted 11–1 to allow the rezoning. Mayor Petruska, who had vetoed Forest City's request for that property a year earlier, now approved the decision, writing that the proposed apartment units "are not federally financed housing, are not low income and are not senior citizen housing. Rather they are high quality, high priced units."[43]

Some time later, the company applied for, and was granted, a building permit to construct Parmatown Towers as a *ten-story apartment building,* much taller than the original proposal, which, along with several exchanges between the company and Parma officials, led to a feeling on the part of city authorities that the company "was being deceitful."[44] Nevertheless, the city attorney concluded that under Parma's high-rise rules the firm was authorized to construct a ten-story building, and the matter moved along without further incident.

The troublesome pronouncements against low income housing and the dispute over Forest City and its high-rise construction came together in 1971. The resulting controversy would provide the basis for *United States v. City of Parma, Ohio.*

The community began consideration of its need for housing for Parma's elderly in early 1971. Forest City applied to HUD for funding to construct another ten-story apartment building to be called Parmatown Woods. The firm made two presentations to Parma officials, one in June to the Parma Planning Commission and a second on July 6 to the Parma City Council. The developer told the council that the project would be a building like Parmatown Towers but constructed with senior citizens in mind and that the rents charged would be set by HUD standards.

A July 13 meeting of the Parma Planning Commission, at which the consideration of Parmatown Woods was a leading agenda item, marked a turning point in Parma officials' approach to the project. A number of those present at the Commission meeting pressed representatives from the builder and the Regional Planning Commission concerning whether there could be any preference given to persons then living in Parma in rental of Parmatown Woods units. Councilwoman Evelyn Kopchak was given assurances by the builder representative that there was some flexibility in such matters without violating HUD regulations, but the spokesperson was sufficiently vague about that discretion that Kopchak followed up with research on Parma's options during the weeks following the meeting.[45] Others suggested the creation of a screening committee for Parmatown Woods tenants.[46]

What happened next is set out in the trial court findings. It summarizes the trial transcript, several government exhibits, and depositions of Parma City Council Chairman Kenneth Kuczma and Mayor John Petruska:

> Kuczma took the floor and stated, "I do not want Negroes in the City of Parma."
> . . . Kuczma felt that this was the real issue at stake in the construction of Parmatown Woods and his statement was meant to force everyone to face the issue realistically. . . . Kuczma stated that the people of Parma, all of whom he considered his constituents, were fearful of Negroes going into the City and that he himself had that fear. He thought many of the residents of Parma had moved there from the east side of Cleveland where they had suffered considerable losses in the sale of their real estate due to an influx of Negroes. He felt that a movement of Negroes into low cost housing in Parma would cause the community to deteriorate.

> Immediately after Kuczma's statement that he did not want Negroes in Parma, and after some people had gone off on "a tangent about black versus white" with regard to Parmatown Woods . . . , Mayor Petruska sought to assuage those present that even if Parmatown Woods were constructed, it would not mean that the doors of Parma would be open to the entire "East Side of Cleveland."[47]

Though they did not dispute the summary of what took place, Parma attorneys later argued that Kuczma's comments ought to be understood as the unfortunate remarks of one person who had been traumatized by a "sensitivity type" training session on race relations which he was required by his employer to attend in Washington, DC, in 1967.[48] Moreover, they said, Kuczma was on his way out as Council Chairman. He ran unsuccessfully in the primary against Mayor Petruska. Kuczma was later reelected Council Chairman. In any event, Parma officials argued, the Mayor did not oppose the project at the July 13 meeting, and it was approved pending a zoning commission study. The stipulation was, however, added that the parking variance reducing the number of spaces required from two and one half to one per unit should not be granted unless the variance stated that the project was for senior citizen use only.

Local media outlets interpreted Kuczma's statement as an overt comment that revealed the covert reason for opposition to low income housing. Moreover, Mayor Petruska's actions were viewed as considerably less than benign given the fact that he employed campaign literature in 1971 which plainly stated opposition to low income housing in Parma.[49] He would use similar campaign statements in 1975.[50]

The likelihood of final approval for Parmatown Woods disintegrated when two events transpired which made it clear that HUD would not allow Parma to ensure preference for Parma senior citizens or permit any form of control by the city over who could become tenants in the building. Forest City submitted plans and building permit requests on July 30, 1971. On August 26 the plans were returned as incomplete, whereupon Forest City resubmitted. Between the July 13 meeting and events that would reach a climax in the fall, local debate intensified. Community groups formed to oppose low income housing projects. On October 6, after concluding her research on the project, Kopchak wrote Mayor Petruska informing him that Parmatown Woods units would be available "to anyone who meets the income limitations imposed by the Federal Government and cannot be limited strictly to Senior Citizens" and it "is doubtful that any stipulations can be imposed whereby the apartments would be limited to Parma residents."[51] On October 7 the Building Commissioner returned the plans to the developer noting that he and the city engineer had concluded that the application could not be processed further because of a number of inadequacies in the proposal. Forest City reapplied on October 26, but there had been meetings and discussions in Parma in the interim that, along with the Kopchak letter, signaled an increase in tensions and reduced the chances of approval for the project.

At the time of the controversy over Parmatown Woods, Charles Lucas served as HUD's Deputy Director for the Cleveland Insurance Office. Lucas, a black, operated with considerable knowledge of minority and low income housing problems in the Cleveland area since he had sold real estate in and around the city for sixteen years. Lucas testified that some time prior to October 20 he received a number of calls from Parma officials requesting information about the HUD Section 236 housing program.[52] Lucas suggested a meeting at his office where HUD technical staff would be readily available to answer questions. The meeting was set for October 20. Lucas particularly remembers one call from a Parma councilwoman:

> [S]he called to inquire about the 236 program and did I know anything about Forest City's involvement and so forth.
> QUESTION: What else did she say?
> ANSWER: In the course of the conversation, I indicated to her that there was a meeting scheduled for the 20th of October, and I hoped that she would come to it. And as a final parting comment, she said to me something to this effect: "Do you know that we don't want blacks in Parma?"
> And I really ducked a response and said, "Don't we?" Then she hung up.[53]

When asked about the conversation later, the councilwoman testified that she could not recall any such conversation.[54]

Lucas later recounted the events of the meeting as follows:

> QUESTION: How would you describe the reaction of the group when you appeared?
> ANSWER: Well, I noticed some facial reactions when I came in because I think my impression was they didn't expect who they saw.
> QUESTION: Were there any black people at the meeting?

ANSWER: None. I was the only one.

QUESTION: What questions, if any, did the officials ask you concerning Parmatown Woods?

ANSWER: Well I opened with a few brief words and I had asked . . . experts in the field . . . to come in to respond to any question relative to the 236 program, and especially in regard to the proposed project of Parmatown Woods. And as I concluded, one of the . . . first question[s] was, "Under the 236 program can tenants from Parmatown Woods come exclusively from the City of Parma, could it be strictly and solely a project for the citizens of the residents of Parma?" And I answered that question myself. . . . My answer to that question triggered some conflicting comments as to what they had been told by the developers and the sponsors of the proposed project.

And my answer was at variance with what they had alleged they had been told and then there were several—just all at once, looks across the room. . . .

And after this subsided and I had hoped we would get into the nuts and bolts of the program rather than extraneous talk about who said what and so on, when I quieted it down . . . the question was "could blacks from Hough and Puerto Ricans from West 28th Street become tenants?"

And I answered that in the affirmative if they met the family size income limits and were eligible.

Again that triggered buzzing conversation all over the place. And each time after one of the questions we would have to settle down and try to get order and proceed in an orderly fashion.[55]

Following the Lucas meeting, public concern about the coming project within Parma increased with council members and others receiving frequent inquiries from Parma residents.

November 1971 was an important month in Parma both because it was on November 3 that Parma officials again rejected the Parmatown Woods building permit applications, citing a number of technical deficiencies, and because it was election time. Forest City abandoned its efforts to meet the objections posed by Parma officials, which was unusual because it had previously been able to obtain permits while construction got under way with informal resolutions of technical deficiencies following in due course.[56] The election was important to possible future housing projects for Parma because local citizen groups had qualified two initiative measures for consideration, both of which were approved. One set a 35-foot height limit for construction of buildings in the city.[57] The other mandated that

[n]o low rent housing project shall be developed, constructed or acquired in the city in any manner by any public body, or authority, nor shall approval be granted for participation in a federal rent supplement program, until a majority of the qualified electors of the city voting upon such issue, such project, or such participation approve by voting in favor thereof at an election to be held for that purpose or at the next primary or general election. Such elections shall be provided for by resolution of Council.[58]

Litigation would follow challenging Parma's efforts to block low income housing, the statements made by officials regarding race and low income housing, the city officials' behavior at the Lucas meeting, the uncharacteristic formality of the Parmatown

Woods application review process, and the enactment of the two land use ordinances. However, there was one more important round of the housing controversy in Parma which took place after the litigation had begun. It concerned Parma's application for funds under the Community Development Block Grant (CDBG) program created by the Housing and Community Development Act of 1974.[59]

Parma officials initiated an application for CDBG funds in late 1974, holding meetings on the matter until February 1975. Parma's City Council then approved the application. Parma's submission was one of a very few applications rejected at that time. The basis for the rejection was that it set a goal of meeting low income housing needs as zero and provided a zero "expected to reside" figure.[60] Parma's Mayor was not pleased with HUD's response. He wrote the HUD regional office in Chicago expressing his anger:

> I do not believe that the intent of Congress was to force down the throats of any community in this great nation decisions effecting [sic] their daily living as a blackmail or bargaining point for the acquisition of federal dollars rightfully theirs as their fair share of taxation paid by them to our government in Washington. . . .
>
> We in Parma will take care of those in Parma; and that, gentlemen, is our obligation. Under those circumstances, we feel that you would be stealing dollars rightfully due us if you turned down this grant application because of your bureaucratic regulation and determination of those regulations.[61]

The authority of HUD to approve any application for CDBG funds which did *not* contain a Housing Assistance Plan (HAP) that included appropriate need estimates and expected to reside figures was litigated not long after the Parma controversy in *City of Hartford v. Hills*.[62] In this case HUD was informed that the commitment to low income housing as an integral part of the Housing and Community Development Act could not be waived and applications which did not include adequate HAPs must be rejected. The CDBG episode became one of the important elements in the *Parma* case.

THE LIABILITY PHASE

Until relatively recently, the Civil Rights Division of the Justice Department did not have an established policy governing the decision whether to prosecute a case. However, there were clearance procedures within the department which must be met before formal action can be taken.[63] DOJ receives newspapers from various parts of the nation and occasionally gets word of incidents worthy of the Civil Rights Division attention from individuals and groups. In order to protect those sources against reprisals, it is the policy of the division not to reveal their identities.[64] There are two basic means by which the CRD enters a case: (1) by filing its own actions on behalf of the United States under various statutes, such as the Fair Housing Act, which authorize the Attorney General to sue or (2) by participation as *amicus curiae* in litigation brought by others. It has employed both avenues in fair housing enforcement.

A tentative decision was made to launch a suit against Parma in mid-1972, but politics within the Nixon administration created difficulties for civil rights enforcement. Frank Schwelb, then Chief of the CRD Housing and Credit Section, later explained:

As you probably know, President Nixon came out publicly against "forced integration of the suburbs." The Watergate tapes contain a conversation between Mr. Nixon and John Ehrlichman dated April 19, 1971, in which the *Black Jack* [Missouri, a St. Louis suburb] and *Lackawanna* cases were discussed. President Nixon called the issue a "can of worms" and asked Ehrlichman to "waffle it and keep us out of it." In June 1971, the *Black Jack* case was finally filed, three quarters of a year after we proposed it, amidst considerable fanfare, but it was made clear that such cases would be approved only upon a showing of discriminatory purpose. We developed a number of other possible suits during this period, including one against the City of Cleveland, Ohio [which was brought by private litigants as *Banks v. Perk*] and others in Lauderdale Lakes, Florida and Pascagoula, Mississippi. I do not recall the precise dates of these, but these cases were held up as a result of uncertainties as to policy. We would also probably have participated in *Crow v. Brown* [an Atlanta area dispute . . . and *SASSO v. Union City, California* . . . but for the policy restrictions. We proposed a suit against Parma, Ohio, in mid-72, and this one was not filed until April 27, 1973, by which time Mr. Pottinger was Assistant Attorney General, and Mr. Nixon and Mr. Ehrlichman had other preoccupations.[65]

Schwelb wrote Mayor Petruska in January 1973 to arrange a meeting with Parma officials regarding the action contemplated against the city. Schwelb and two other DOJ attorneys met with Parma officials in February, but it quickly became apparent that there was no basis for negotiation. It was also during February 1973 that Judge Battisti announced his decision for the three judge panel and his own opinion on remand in the *Mahaley* case. In April DOJ filed suit in district court for the Northern District of Ohio, alleging that the Parma had engaged in a pattern and practice of conduct with the purpose and effect of making equal housing opportunity unavailable because of race in violation of the Fair Housing Act. The case was assigned to Judge Battisti.

Parma's Reaction to the Suit

Asked why the litigation was instituted, Robert Soltis, Parma's Special Counsel, replied:

There was a pattern from previous cases. They [DOJ] thought they had a friendly forum. Neither HUD nor DOJ ever revealed who instituted the complaint. Parma sought discovery of that information but it was never revealed. Then there was the publicity about the one unfortunate remark [Mr. Kuczma's statement].

This being a cosmopolitan community (some people say ethnic) might have something to do with it. The case seems to be a reflection of inborn prejudices. The spirit of the punitive immigration act is still alive. There have been any number of ethnic jokes directed at Parma reflecting some prejudices.[66]

Andrew Boyko, City Law Director, considered that the impetus for the case "might have had something to do with Parma's size and development. . . . It had its greatest boom just after WWII, which brought the population over 100,000. When you do that, you're in the big league." Asked why Parma was sued instead of other neighboring metropolitan area suburbs, Boyko also thought, "It might be because of resources. Because they stay away from more affluent cities which have the resources to fight the federal government."

A number of those in Parma, including Petruska, were of the opinion that the suit was launched because Richard Nixon wanted to take revenge against the city for an incident during the 1972 presidential campaign when the Mayor refused to provide extra security to meet White House demands during a ride through the community by Mr. Nixon. They could not have known how incorrect that particular theory was.

Boyko had represented the city and its officials in the *Mahaley* litigation but brought in a special counsel, Robert Soltis, for the appellate work on the *Mahaley* case. When the *Parma* litigation was launched, Boyko "recommended Bob to the City Council to be special counsel for this case because he is not only qualified, but has the pulse and feel of the community. A feeling for your community, a sensitivity is very important." Asked why he took on such a case, Soltis answered, "Because it is an important matter. This is turning the concept of our government on its head. Here we have the unelected federal judiciary running the community."

Boyko remembers the meeting with DOJ officials, but he saw no opportunity for compromise, "It was a take it or leave it situation. They just said here's what we want and you can save yourself some money by agreeing and avoiding the expense of litigation. We had 101% support of the community. The community support is still strong; in fact, it is stronger."

Parma's strategy was to reject all aspects of the government's case and go on the offensive, filing a counterclaim alleging discrimination by the federal government on the basis of the Eastern European national origin of Parma's residents in violation of the same Fair Housing Act under which Parma itself was challenged. The community's reaction is a recurring phenomenon in remedial decree cases. It is a kind of conflict-conversion process in which defendants see themselves as the victims, the initial alleged victim as innocent pawn, and the federal government in the person of the federal judge or the DOJ as aggressor, usurper, even invader.

The anger of Parma's attorneys came through in their answer to the charges. The government's complaint contained a paragraph noting Parma's less than one percent black population in a community adjoining Cleveland with a thirty-eight percent black population, to which Parma responded "that the allegations contained therein are immaterial and impertinent."[67]

Parma challenged the jurisdiction of the court sitting as a single judge court, the standing of the Attorney General, the timeliness of the charge, the interpretation of the Fair Housing Act, and the authority of the government to call for an equitable decree in light of its early history of discrimination. The city argued that if the Fair Housing Act or any other federal authority were asserted to allow interference with Parma's ability to enact land use ordinances or to interfere with freedom of choice or natural ethnic migration patterns, it would constitute discrimination and a violation of freedom of association and the principles of federalism. On the federalism point, the city demanded a three judge district court panel to try its constitutional challenge to the Fair Housing Act. Asked why the city demanded a three judge court, Soltis replied, "At that time you could appeal directly to the Supreme Court. We wanted to get the constitutional issue of the housing act applied to cities to the Supreme Court."

By the time Parma answered the charges in the district court, Battisti had already ruled in the *Banks* and *Mahaley* cases. Asked whether there was any consideration of attempting to remove Battisti for possible bias given the fact that Parma had been a defendant in *Mahaley* and that a considerable amount of material had been presented in that case concerning housing in Parma, Soltis and Boyko responded in the negative.

Boyko indicated, "We felt there was tension. It's so hard to remove a judge. We felt it might create a difficulty."

The Department of Justice sought an order enjoining Parma, its agents, officers, and employees from:

a. interfering with any person or group of persons seeking to exercise the right to equal housing opportunity without regard to race, color, religion or national origin or the right to aid or encourage others in the exercise of these rights;

b. discriminating against any person or group of persons on account of race, color, religion, or national origin in the planning, development or implementation of any program or project relating to housing;

c. engaging in conduct which had the purpose or effect of perpetuating or promoting racial residential segregation; and

d. failing or refusing to take all necessary and appropriate steps to correct the effects of its past unlawful practices.[68]

In response, Parma asked that

the complaint be dismissed; that a three judge court be convened to declare 42 U.S.C. Section 3601 and the allegedly relevant regulations herein involved to be unconstitutional per se or as attempted to the applied to defendant city and its residents; and for an order enjoining plaintiffs, and any of its officers, employees, agents, or departments from interfering or attempting to interfere with defendant and its residents, and similarly situated communities, from developing by the free and unfettered choice of the people its own residential patterns without coercion, intimidation, or interference by the national governments.[69]

Pretrial Activity

The period between the filing of Parma's answer and counterclaim, in July 1973, and the trial, in November and December 1979, witnessed several important developments, including decisions by the U.S. Supreme Court and other federal appellate courts; the involvement of private litigants who wished to participate in the suit against Parma; and the interactions among attorneys for Parma, Judge Battisti, and DOJ lawyers. Supreme Court rulings were important because in a series of cases the Court held that in cases claiming unconstitutional racially discriminatory action, racially discriminatory effect of government actions does not automatically trigger strict judicial scrutiny and that proof of intentional discrimination was required.[70]

One of those cases, *Metropolitan Housing Development Corporation v. Village of Arlington Heights,* a dispute involving efforts to develop 236 housing in a dispersed manner in the Chicago metropolitan area, shared a number of similarities with the Cleveland and Parma situations.[71] The Seventh Circuit Court of Appeals had found Arlington Heights' refusal to rezone for 236 housing a violation of the Fourteenth Amendment's equal protection clause because its clear effect was to perpetuate the effects of past discrimination in a nearly all-white community located within an area with a large minority population in need of housing near suburban jobs. The Supreme Court decided that case on the basis of its recently announced requirement in *Washington v.*

Davis for proof of discriminatory intent, but it went on to describe a number of evidentiary standards by which to infer intentional discrimination. After all, it is unusual for those who discriminate in this day and time to openly state their intentions. As Judge Battisti would later summarize it, the Supreme Court held:

> [W]hether invidiously discriminatory purpose was a motivating factor demands a sensitive inquiry into such circumstantial and direct evidence of intent as may be available. . . . To find racial intent, a court must evaluate evidence derived from consideration of numerous factors, including: (1) the discriminatory impact of the policy or practice; (2) the historical background; (3) the "sequence of events leading up to the challenged decisions"; (4) departures from "normal procedural sequences"; (5) departures from normal substantive criteria; and legislative or administrative history of the challenged decisions.[72]

Of course, there are some statutes, particularly civil rights acts, which do not require a showing of intent, and the Seventh Circuit ruled on remand in *Arlington Heights* that the Fair Housing Act was such a statute.[73]

The Supreme Court also, however, handed down a number of decisions maintaining that while there were limits, district courts that do encounter intentional discrimination are empowered, and indeed required, to craft equitable remedies sufficient to respond to the nature of the injury.[74]

Finally, a number of other fair housing cases were decided in other circuits around the country. All but a few of those ran against the narrowing construction Parma wished to have given to the Fair Housing Act.[75]

Back in Parma, private citizens and public interest groups had acted following Parma's battle over low income housing by launching a suit against the city in the name of Jacqueline Cornelius.[76] The suit was brought by five black residents of the metropolitan area who desired to live in Parma but felt they were prevented from residing there because of racial discrimination; two white citizens of Parma who asserted, in the language of the Supreme Court's *Trafficante v. Metropolitan Life Insurance Co.* ruling (allowing whites to sue against racial discrimination aimed at blacks), that they were denied the benefits of living in an integrated community; the NAACP; the Housing Task Force; and the Ozane Construction Company.[77] The *Cornelius v. City of Parma* case was consolidated with *United States v. City of Parma* in September 1973.

Judge Battisti called for arguments regarding standing and other threshold questions, which took place in December. In February 1974 he dismissed the *Cornelius* suit for lack of standing. He also dismissed any direct challenge to the land use ordinances enacted by Parma but allowed that, if the pattern and practice case survived on the merits, the ordinances could become a factor in any effort to remedy proven discrimination. Apart from that, however, the ordinances had not as yet been employed to deny any particular housing project. Therefore, a challenge to the ordinances alone presented no ripe controversy. Battisti also rejected Parma's call for a three judge court and reminded Parma that it could assert as a defense anything the city perceived to be an unconstitutional application of statute.

Parma filed notice of appeal of the decision on the three judge court, but that appeal was rejected by the Sixth Circuit in September 1974 because there was neither a final appealable order nor a certification by the trial judge of a question for appeal under the governing statutes.

The city employed two additional strategies. It filed its own suit separately against the federal government, styled *Parma v. Levi,* in which it sought an injunction to block the Attorney General's litigation against the city. The community was unsuccessful in that suit and its appeal of the adverse ruling.[78] Second, Parma filed a motion for summary judgment in its favor in September 1975 and followed this with stacks of additional materials. If there was any doubt that Parma's defense attorneys saw the city as leading an important cause rather than concentrating strictly on the defense of their particular lawsuit, those documents removed that uncertainty.

Parma's written arguments accused the government of trying to avoid a legitimate challenge to its claimed authority by proposing a consent decree, of reverse discrimination because it referred to Parma as a virtually all-white community and challenged the voluntary gathering of compatible individuals of various types, and argued that the statements in the meeting in February 1973 between Frank Schwelb of CRD and Parma representatives constituted an effort to "coerce, intimidate, threaten or interfere with Parma's officials and residents in the exercise or enjoyment of right[s] granted or protected by . . . the Fair Housing Act." It claimed that the DOJ's "discrimination" against Parma was really discrimination on the basis of the fact that many Parma citizens were of an Eastern European national origin. Soltis and Boyko urged that the challenge to the land use ordinances adopted by initiative in November 1973 was an attempt to interfere with Parma citizens' right to vote. Parma's attorney charged, "Thus does the Department of Justice seek to perpetuate the badges and incidents of second class citizenship and implications of inferiority inherent in the notoriously immoral and insulting National Origins Quotas Immigration Act, enforced by the Department of Justice until it was amended to eliminate the discriminatory despised quota system only a decade ago."[79] Then Parma's attorneys stopped being measured in their use of language. Responding to the claims by the government, as a part of its pattern and practice allegation, that Parma had earned and perpetuated an antiblack image that worked to discourage potential black residents from moving to Parma, city lawyers wrote:

> "Images" of people are very dangerous. Hitler created an image of Jews as being traitors to the fatherland, and history had recorded what was the result. The blood of millions of Christians has been spilt because of their "image" in the minds of the Caesars of Rome, and of the Stalins, and of other present day totalitarians. Witches were burned in Salem and other places because of the unfavorable image they were said to project. . . . In a child's fantasy world, "image" and pretending often merge with reality, and children are very sensitive to what is said; they often confuse what is said with what is fact. Government decisions should be made by adults who are supposed to discriminate between reality and fantasy. Name-calling and labelling supposedly ended with the era of Joseph McCarthy, or so the media states. But maybe "McCarthyism" still lives at the Department of Justice, and if its employees hang a label of "segregation" on a city, then its "image" and its people may be punishable with an "integration" order. But words and labels and "images" are not facts, and plaintiff has adduced no facts to sustain its burden of proof.[80]

In addition to the fact that Parma itself in an ideological battle involving, in its view, the lack of authority of federal officials to interfere in its community, city lawyers also pursued their severe rhetoric because they totally rejected the concept of a pattern and practice case or the demonstration of discriminatory intent by inference from actions that in themselves did not necessarily illegally discriminate. Soltis argued that pattern and practice matters only to the degree that the suspected existence of a pattern and practice allows the Attorney General to proceed with a case, but he rejected the proposition that apart from individual actions, each of which is in itself discriminatory, there can be any such thing as a pattern and practice of discrimination.

The government was arguing two points with its references to Parma's character and image. First, it was asserting the existence of the kind of evidence necessary to establish a pattern and practice as the concept is generally understood in civil rights law. Second, it was establishing the evidence necessary to prove that there was not only a pattern and practice of behavior which had a disproportionately harmful effect on minorities, but also that those actions were intentionally discriminatory.

There then ensued what Battisti termed "a series of counter, reply, and supplementary briefs with affidavits," the last of which was ordered in late January 1979. Battisti ruled on July 13, 1979.[81] It was clear that the judge was fast losing patience with Parma's rhetoric:

> The pending summary judgment motion and briefs by defendant, though painstakingly loquacious and for the most part irrelevant, boil down to a singular proposition which, itself, defeats the defendant's motion because it involves a bona fide factual dispute. At the heart of the muck and mire of defendant's rhetoric is the bold contention that the building permit for the proposed Parmatown Woods development was denied solely on the basis that it failed to comply with the city's building code. . . .
>
> The plaintiff and amicus curiae argue that defendant has totally misconceived the legal nature of this action and, therefore, has failed to recognize that the factual controversies which they present and support by affidavits are highly relevant under the case law pertinent to a Title VIII law suit.[82]

This being the situation, there were clearly material issues of fact that had to proceed to trial. Specifically, the issues to be tried were whether Parma's "all-white character" occurred "adventitiously" or resulted from deliberate discrimination, whether Parma's actions had "the purpose or effect of making housing unavailable to persons because of race," and whether Parmatown Woods was rejected for neutral reasons or was "treated less favorably than other proposals, wholly or partially because of the actual or anticipated race of some of the prospective residents."[83]

The Liability Trial

Following another minor skirmish or two, the case proceeded to trial in November and December 1979. Apart from the development of the testimony by the principals in the actions described in the discussion of the trigger phase earlier, the parties concentrated on trading arguments over whether Parma's all-white character (it had about fifty black residents in a population of approximately one hundred thousand persons) was indeed the result of natural patterns of movement out from the city, as Parma argued, or was, as DOJ contended, the result of a deliberate pattern and practice of discrimination.

The argument over patterns of residence meant a confrontation among expert witnesses. Parma based its position on the theory, supported by its expert, Dr. Bonutti, that there are corridors of out-migration along which different racial and ethnic groups move as they become financially able to leave the city. The Justice Department argued that this was only partly correct since few blacks were able to leave the city because of economic and housing discrimination and those who could acquire sufficient funds were met with hostility when they attempted to move west of the Cuyahoga River. The key for the federal government was testimony by Dr. Campbell and the admission by Parma's witness, Dr. Bonutti, on cross-examination that all of the Caucasian ethnic groups were relatively evenly distributed throughout the metropolitan area, but not blacks. The most significant evidence in that regard was the testimony of Dr. John Kain, of Harvard's Kennedy School, reporting the findings of his econometric evaluation of housing patterns based on census data for 1970. Kain found that the actual and predicted percentage distributions of the various ethnic groups in the metropolitan area were quite close, except for racial minorities. Controlling for economic status, Kain concluded that blacks were still the only group whose actual residential patterns differed appreciably from the expected distribution.[84]

In March 1980 Battisti heard additional arguments on several points of the relationship between the law and the specific elements of evidence involved. He was particularly interested in determining whether the antiblack image of Parma was really relevant. Of greatest importance, however, was his attempt to determine whether there was, in fact, a clear discrimination on the basis of race at work in this case. He had, after all, rejected the idea that mere discrimination against low income housing without a showing that such discrimination was based upon race was illegal in his *Mahaley* decision for the three judge panel. He put the question to the government's lead attorney, Robert Reinstein:

> QUESTION: Do you feel that in this case, however, the inference, legitimate inference that can be made in this case is that it was race?
> ANSWER: I want to answer that question carefully. . . . Every time that Parma had to make a decision between doing something that would have a segregative effect, Parma chose . . . the segregative effect.[85]

The Liability Opinion

Battisti delivered his memorandum opinion and preliminary order on June 5, 1980, holding Parma had indeed intentionally engaged in a pattern and practice of discrimination in violation of the Fair Housing Act.[86] He ordered DOJ and lawyers for Parma to meet within thirty days to negotiate a proposed remedy.

The opinion was nearly a hundred pages long and contained a veritable catalog of Fair Housing Act case law. Battisti's experience with fair housing cases from his *Banks* and *Mahaley* opinions was augmented by the arguments presented by DOJ attorneys who, not surprisingly, had substantial knowledge of developing civil rights case law from around the nation.

The opinion was tightly structured. The initial discussion in the ruling framed the current standards for cases brought under the Fair Housing Act. Since the Justice Department argued both discriminatory intent and effect, it was unnecessary for Battisti to parse the cases that indicated that discriminatory intend need not be proven under this particular statute. The judge did use the constitutional law cases discussing the nature of discriminatory intent from the Supreme Court and circuit courts to explain what kinds of evidence can be used to infer intent. Specifically, he focused on the *Arlington Heights* ruling as the guideline.[87]

The second major portion of the opinion dealt with contentions that the racial housing patterns in the area could be explained apart from any discriminatory acts by local governments. Relying on the expert testimony presented at trial as well as his *Banks* and *Mahaley* opinions, Battisti concluded:

> Based on the record, the Court finds that the racial segregation in the Cleveland area cannot be attributed to either associational preferences or economics. The Court finds that a principal cause of the housing segregation is the past and present discrimination suffered by blacks.[88]

The opinion turned next to Parma's actions alleged to be a pattern and practice of housing discrimination. Battisti concentrated on analyzing each of the core elements of the pattern and practice case and on establishing the evidence that proved these actions were taken with the specific intent to exclude blacks. He held:

> The Court specifically finds that the rejection of the fair housing resolution, the consistent refusal to sign a cooperation agreement with CMHA, the adamant and longstanding opposition to any form of public housing, the denial of a building permit for Parmatown Woods, the passage of the 35-foot height restriction ordinance, the passage of the ordinance requiring voter approval for low-income housing, and the refusal to submit an adequate housing assistance plan in the Community Development Block Grant application, individually and collectively, were motivated by a racially discriminatory and exclusionary intent. The purpose of these actions, the Court finds, was to exclude blacks from residing in Parma and to maintain the segregated "character" of the City. These actions, individually and collectively, also violated the Fair Housing Act by denying to blacks, Parma residents, and prospective low-income housing developers rights secured by Sections 804(a) and 817.[89]

Three aspects of the record appeared particularly troublesome to Battisti. The most obvious difficulty was the list of public statements made by Parma officials, which suggested that race was a major consideration in the city's actions. Second, the departures from the apparently normally informal negotiated arrangements for the granting of building permits precisely fit the criteria for proving intent discussed by the Supreme Court and the Seventh Circuit on remand in the *Arlington Heights* case. Finally, Parma's rejection of CDBG funds meant a refusal of millions of dollars with relatively few administrative strings attached at a time when Parma claimed serious financial pressures. Moreover, the fact that this action was taken two years after the *Mahaley* opinion had been delivered and the present litigation commenced made it extremely difficult to believe Parma's claim that there was no continuing pattern and practice. That grant rejection also indicated that Parma had available to it resources to meet what CMHA's needs assessment found to be a very significant level of need for low and moderate income housing in the community.

One final aspect of Battisti's opinion is worthy of note. There was very little case law Parma could rely on in support of its interpretations of permissible state and local actions under the Fair Housing Act and the equal protection clause. Battisti's opinion directly confronted most of those cases on the simple ground that there had been a clear and specific finding of discriminatory intent in this case that had not been present in the contrary cases.[90] The two cases Judge Battisti did not find were on point, *Mahaley* and *Joseph Skillken*[91] would be seemingly but not really important to Parma's unsuccessful appeals strategy. Both opinions were written by Judge Weick, the only member of the Sixth Circuit Court of Appeals who found Parma's claim sufficiently worthy of an interlocutory review or an en banc reconsideration to dissent from the denial of review. But Parma's actions after the liability finding were not primarily directed at argument on the applicability of precedents.

THE REMEDY PHASE

Following the liability decision, the adversary relationship was as much focused on the interaction between attorneys for Parma and Judge Battisti as between Parma and DOJ. Parma, convinced it would ultimately prevail on appeal, sought, according to Soltis, to "stop the process . . . to maintain the status quo and move the appeal on the constitutional question along more expeditiously."[92] Battisti seemed just as intent upon moving the remedy crafting process along and avoiding delaying tactics. Each managed partial success. Judge Battisti did begin the development of the remedy. Judgment on that decree was entered in December 1980. Parma was able to obtain a stay on the decree for nearly a year and a half while the case wound its way through the appellate process, which ultimately upheld Battisti's decision and most of his remedial order.

Crafting the Remedy

Battisti concluded his liability opinion with the instructions to the parties to begin negotiations within thirty days aimed at producing a remedy or submit papers for further formal remedy proceedings if no agreement could be reached.[93]

On June 13, a week after the memorandum opinion was issued, Parma asked Battisti to certify the case for appeal. He refused. Even so, Parma filed notice of appeal on August 1, 1980. Parma's attorneys had legal and pragmatic reasons for their several attempts to take interlocutory appeals. Soltis maintained that he wanted to take the liability issues on appeal without the complication of a remedial order. Boyko added, "We did not want to wait to get the remedial orders. Once the money was spent for an expensive remedy, the harm would already be done."

Parma's attorneys met with DOJ representatives on August 4. The DOJ attorneys presented a proposal, but Parma refused to place anything on the table. Asked why they made no proposal of their own, Soltis answered, "If you come up with a compulsory remedy you're, in effect, admitting there is basis for liability." Boyko added, "Once you enter an agreed remedial aspect, you've waived the liability aspect." The attorneys were simply incorrect in that assessment as the discussion of the *Rizzo v. Goode* case in Chapter 11 demonstrates.

When Parma refused to enter a counterproposal, DOJ asked Battisti to schedule an evidentiary hearing on its suggested remedy. Parma argued that Battisti no longer had jurisdiction in the case, notwithstanding the fact that no final appealable order had been entered. Though it had been unwilling to suggest a remedy for fear of jeopardizing its appeal, Parma now did just that. It proposed that it would like to purchase the Westview

Apartments in Parma and operate them as public housing. In order to do that, however, the city needed money. Parma suggested avoiding a court order and having the federal government "cut through the bureaucratic red tape and . . . expedite full funding" without indicating any willingness to comply with CDBG requirements or any federal guidelines.[94] Mayor Petruska would later testify at the evidentiary hearing that the Westview area and the adjacent Knollwood are "not up to what I consider proper housing for people in the way of parking facilities, safety facilities. It's a high crime area, It's probably the worst area of our community."[95]

Battisti granted the DOJ request for a hearing. In its brief in response to that order, Parma continued its use of highly charged rhetoric, asserting that "the Government's Proposal has a Totalitarian, Not Democratic Orientation" and that DOJ was "more interested in making a point than in providing housing assistance."[96]

Evidentiary hearings were held from September 24 through 26. Brian Heffernan summarized the government's position in his opening statement:

> Our purpose here today is to present further and more expansive information to the court so that it has available to it the information necessary to formulate a comprehensive remedial plan to cure the violations that have been found in this case. . . . Traditionally, equity courts have broad powers to issue remedies designed to cure legal violations. That is especially true here where the court must be guided by the purposes of the Fair Housing Act to provide an equal choice of housing to promote integrated living patterns.
>
> At the same time the court must be careful not to intrude on the governmental functions of Parma. . . .
>
> The government's proposed remedy here is designed to do just that, to afford Parma the freedom and flexibility to formulate within certain guidelines a remedial plan which will give it some chance of success. Of course, Parma's efforts must be subject to court review for determining compliance at some point.[97]

The DOJ presented a series of witnesses who testified to the nature and basic requirements of a minimally adequate remedy and argued for its feasibility. The key government witness was Paul Davidoff, a consultant and researcher on matters of metropolitan housing desegregation with a substantial legal and academic background. He had at one time worked in Cleveland but was based in New York at the time of the hearing.

Davidoff premised his assessment of the situation to be remedied and his specific recommendations on his belief that the community should be given as much latitude and discretion as possible to make its own way toward desegregation within the broad limits which must be imposed to ensure that they do, in fact, desegregate.[98] He argued for establishment of a Fair Housing Committee (FHC) made up of a broad cross-section of Parma citizens who would set goals and make judgments as to the specifics of housing desegregation.[99] Their activities would then be monitored by an Evaluation Committee whose purpose was to ensure that the FHC was really making serious efforts to desegregate.[100]

Davidoff urged a series of other actions, two of which focused on ridding Parma of its antiblack image. That could be accomplished, he said, by passage of some type of open housing resolution and an outreach advertising program. He further suggested that Parma officials be required to undergo an educational process to better understand the problems of housing discrimination and the need for a remedy.[101]

The other key aspect of the ruling, in Davidoff's view, was the section of a decree that would mandate efforts to construct low income housing.[102] First, the community should be open to private sector efforts to develop new housing and refrain from obstructing such projects. Second, the community must seek to fill the minimum housing needs established by HUD through public efforts if private projects were not adequate. Parma should have a choice whether to cooperate in that effort with CMHA or establish its own housing authority.

The other government witnesses were HUD personnel from various offices dealing with housing needs and assistance.[103] They established the basis for housing needs calculations. The recommendation for Parma was for construction of 133 units per year moving toward the approximately 2000 units needed. Remaining DOJ witnesses testified on sources of federal funds available to support Parma's housing efforts.

Parma's posture was essentially that of defending itself against the imposition of any mandate. The city's attorneys cross-examined DOJ witnesses extensively. Since the scope of an equitable remedy is supposed to be determined by the nature of the violation, Parma's lawyers sought to use cross-examination to provide support for their claim that there really had been no violation. Battisti repeatedly admonished Soltis that the hearing was not for the purpose of retrying the liability issue. At one point, Battisti's dwindling patience showed as he indicated to Soltis:

> Oh, we are not going into the liability aspect of this case. We are here, as I said yesterday, hopefully to reason together, to assist and cooperate together in the development of the best, most reasonable, intelligent plan following from the liability orders. That is the purpose of this hearing.[104]

A second important aspect of Parma's defensiveness was the concern that once elements of a remedy were in place, it would be difficult to prevail on appeal.

Parma presented two types of witnesses for its own case, city officials and experts. The Mayor and Police Chief testified that any order would be an intolerably intrusive and expensive imposition on the community. The primary burden of expert testimony was carried by Harry Henshaw, a planner, who critiqued the government's proposed remedy. On cross-examination, Henshaw admitted that he had not been asked to propose a remedy or elements of a remedy for Parma but merely to challenge the government's proposal.[105] Battisti seemed particularly interested in the comments of Parma's experts and, in fact, modified those portions of the proposed decree dealing with Parma's land use ordinances in an attempt to accommodate some of their concerns. At the end of the day on September 26, Battisti called counsel into chambers. The next day he indicated that he had given instruction for modifications in the proposed remedy.

Battisti produced an order presenting the government's modified proposal as the court's remedy. That remedy was basically the recommendation presented by Paul Davidoff during the hearing. The primary modification was the requirement for a special master to administer the decree, a feature that Judge Battisti added himself. In calling for a special master, the judge added the requirement that the person chosen for the job must be an attorney with real estate experience who is familiar with the Cleveland metropolitan area and the ''political realities'' of Parma.

Parma particularly objected to the special master. Parma attorneys now employed some of the same kind of rhetoric on Battisti previously directed at DOJ. Referring to the order ''as outrageous as using a hydrogen bomb to dig a hole when a spade would do,''[106] the argument went on to quote extensively from a very controversial opinion Judge Weick had written in 1975 that stated in part, "Low cost public housing could move into the most exclusive neighborhoods of [Parma] and property values would be slaughtered."[107] Parma's angry reaction to the proposed order was promptly featured in local newspapers.

When the final remedial order was issued on December 4, 1980, Battisti observed:

> Parma never submitted a remedial proposal to the Court. Not only were Parma's submissions not helpful to the Court, but the briefs filed by Parma quoted inapposite cases and employed racially incendiary language. Such a use of documents within the public record could be expected to, and in fact did, reach the press. The Court has admonished the defendant's present lawyers both in chambers and from the bench, not to traumatize and incite those who may be affected by the delicate and necessary steps that the Court must take to remediate the statutory violation found in Parma.[108]

The DOJ order which Battisti modified was essentially a combination of remedial steps used in other cases. Recognizing that the order must be broad enough to ensure an adequate remedy, Battisti observed that "this Court should not order relief that is more intrusive on the governmental functions of Parma than is necessary." The order included the following elements

1. The injunction prayed for by the government at the outset of the litigation.

2. A requirement for an educational program of some type for Parma officials and employees calculated to make them aware of problems of housing discrimination and its remedies.

3. A requirement that Parma "enact a fair housing resolution welcoming persons of all races, creeds and colors to reside in Parma and setting forth Parma's policy of nondiscrimination in all aspects of housing in the city."[109]

4. An advertising program "promoting Parma as an equal housing opportunity community."[110]

5. A requirement to make copies of the opinions in United States v. Parma available to citizens upon request.

6. Limitations on the ordinances, including the holding that the low-income housing ordinance enacted on the basis of discriminatory intent is void and that the 35-foot ordinance, the two-and-one-half parking space ordinance, and Parma's zoning ordinance stand so long as they are not applied in such a manner as to block low and moderate income housing projects.

7. A plan to obtain by some means low income housing, including at a minimum a commitment on the part of Parma to develop the FHC and to participate in the operation of the Evaluation Committee.[111]

8. A requirement that Parma sign a cooperation agreement with the CMHA or that it develop its own public housing authority.

9. That Parma do what is necessary to make itself eligible to participate in the Section 8 Housing Program under the Housing and Community Development Act.

10. That Parma apply for the funds due it under the CDBG program.

11. A requirement that Parma must develop by public or private means at least 133 units of low income housing per year and that tenants for that housing must come in part from the CMHA waiting list.

12. A provision for a special master to administer the decree and monitor progress.

The Sixth Circuit Court of Appeals denied a rehearing *en banc* on Parma's interlocutory appeal on December 9, with Judge Weick dissenting. Parma entered a motion for a stay of the order, which Battisti rejected, terming Parma's request a "delaying tactic" and suggesting that, "Instead of seeking excuses or ways of avoiding its responsibilities, defendants must now put their efforts toward executing the tasks set forth in the December 5, 1980, remedial order."[112] Parma went directly to Judge Weick of the Sixth Circuit for a stay of Battisti's order. Despite strong opposition, the district court order was stayed pending appeal.

The Appeal

The appeals process was for Parma a complex matter, but it was unsuccessful. In the end Parma obtained only minor modifications of Battisti's order. The city's approach to the appeal was not helpful to its cause. Attorneys for the city perceived the constitutional question as the most important. Asked why their briefs made so little reference to Fair Housing Act details or equitable decree scope questions, Soltis indicated that time and space were limited. It was therefore necessary to press the most important issue. That was an unfortunate strategy for Parma since there was no reason to believe the appeals courts would provide the kind of wide-ranging protection against federal statutes or court orders that Parma was seeking.[113]

Second, Parma's counsel felt the need "to raise the consciousness of appellate judges" on issues they saw as critical by the use of very strong rhetoric. For example, Parma's briefs referred to Hans Christian Anderson's "The Emperor's New Clothes"[114] with respect to the perceived lack of substance in the government's case, repeated its charges of "McCarthyism,"[115] and insisted that the order was as bad as "Reconstruction," involving outsiders operating the city of Parma like "latter-day carpetbaggers."[116]

Though they preferred to concentrate on the federalism issue, Parma's lawyers still wanted to pursue all options. In their overall briefing strategy, they presented a range of issues, including such matters as the Attorney General's standing and the time restrictions arguments. Whether it was intended to or not, this combination of a wide range of issues, vehement rhetoric, and demands for fundamental reconsideration of constitutional doctrines against long odds appeared as an ideologically based outcry which carried along with it a variety of extraneous legal questions.

On October 14, 1981 the Sixth Circuit Court of Appeals affirmed Battisti's ruling.[117] Though Parma did not allege that the district court findings were clearly erroneous, the city, nevertheless, had argued that the court of appeals should not be bound by the lower court's factual findings. The Sixth Circuit rejected the claim but ruled in any event that the findings on the record before it were not clearly erroneous.[118] It also found the constitutional claim "unsubstantial, if not frivolous."[119] The panel rejected the assertion that the Fair Housing Act does not apply to municipalities based on rulings in four circuits with no countervailing precedents. It labeled Parma's standing challenge to DOJ "hard to understand" in light of the fact that "the Act clearly authorizes the Attorney General to sue." [120] The timeliness challenge simply does not fit a "continuing pattern and practice case." [121] Given the findings of intentional discrimination, the court could identify no grounds for the challenge to the order as a whole. It did, however, eliminate the 133-unit new construction requirement and the special master provision as premature, suggesting there would be time enough to use more specific measures if the FHC and city officials refused to move ahead. [122] While the court found the fair housing resolution and the advertising requirements novel, it saw no particular difficulty with them so long as the order was directed at the city and not individual Parma residents.

Parma sought rehearing en banc which was refused. It then filed a petition for a writ of *certiorari* in the U.S. Supreme Court, which was rejected early in 1982. City officials were frustrated and angered by the Court's refusal to take what they saw as a case of fundamental importance. In fact on June 9, 1982, the Parma City Council passed a resolution in the form of a petition for a redress of grievances to the U.S. Congress which read in part:

> That this council of the City of Parma, on behalf of the City and its Citizens hereby petitions the Congress of the United States for redress of its grievances. It is respectfully urged, requested, and demanded that the Congress entertain and hear an appeal from the City of Parma in the case entitled *United States v. City of Parma*, the Supreme Court having forfeited its right and failed in its obligation to hear said appeal.

Speaking for the House Judiciary Committee, Chairman Peter Rodino wrote Representative Ron Mottl, who represented Parma in the House, on August 12, 1982, indicating that Congress has no such power.

THE POST DECREE PHASE

Despite continuing opposition from some local political figures, Parma began taking preliminary steps to comply with Battisti's order in the summer of 1982. Though the principal participants in the remedy implementation effort disagree as to how close Parma has come to accomplishing the letter, spirit, and goals of the order, progress has been made. After two years of work, the parties moved to refine the remedy in light of their early experience in order to facilitate completion of the unfulfilled aspects of the remedy.

Implementation

Parma created a Community Development Department as a focal point for implementation efforts within the city administration, with its first task the application for CDBG funds as required by the court's mandate. The responsibility for creating the details of the remedy was to be vested in the FHC, made up of Parma citizens. The FHC was to be supervised by the Evaluation Committee, consisting of open housing experts from the Cleveland metropolitan area. The eight members of the FHC and the ten-member

Evaluation Committee were appointed in late 1982. After receiving suggestions from the attorneys involved, Battisti issued instructions to the committees to start them on their work. In particular, Parma had requested that it be permitted to work with the FHC. Battisti warmly endorsed that suggestion while warning that this support for a cooperative effort was not a signal that the Committee was to cede its responsibility for shaping the details of the remedy to the city. He wrote:

> [Parma's request] seeks to emphasize a point which the court now enthusiastically endorses and affirms: that, in Parma's words, "the duties assigned to city officials and to the Fair Housing Committee are in the nature of a team effort—not in the least to be considered antagonistic, but rather mutually supportive and harmonious." . . .

> However, it must be understood that the Committee is intended to function as an independent body accountable only to the court. Parma's participation will not entitle it, through its representative, to a voice in the actual deliberations of the Committee. . . .

> However, Parma need not fear becoming a "vassal" of the Committee. While the Committee is charged with being primarily responsible for developing a remedial plan, it would be inconsistent with both the Remedial Order and the decision of the Sixth Circuit not to permit Parma to take the initiative in developing proposals, and in offering to the Committee its views on the feasibility of proposed remedial action.[123]

But Parma was taking the initiative to such an extent that the FHC role was transformed from that of creating the plan for implementation of the remedy to providing oversight of the city's efforts. Paul Kirner, who became Chairperson of the FHC (following the resignation of the original Chairperson shortly after the Committee was formed) observed that the city had already done so much that the FHC "played catch up" for months.[124] The city, with FHC approval,

> applied for CDBG funds,
> developed a Parma Housing Agency,
> obtained certification for the city to administer federal housing subsidies under Section 8 of Title II of the 1974 Act,
> enacted a fair housing resolution,
> contracted with the Cuyahoga Plan of Ohio, a fair housing organization, to provide the education program on fair housing for Parma officials,
> had a fair housing guidebook prepared for officials, employees, and citizens of the community,
> asked the Regional Planning Commission to perform a site selection study for construction of public housing in the community,
> arranged for housing referral services through the Cuyahoga Plan,
> obtained approval of the site-selection study and purchased options on property identified in that survey,
> applied for federal funds to construct Parma public housing.

The Evaluation Committee played a generally limited role in the first year of implementation, both because the Committee considered that the Parma FHC had the primary responsibility for implementation, with the Evaluation Committee restricted to oversight, and because the Committee wanted to avoid interference or unnecessary conflict with the city or the FHC. The Evaluation Committee had only minor disagreements over some of the language in early drafts of the fair housing resolution and did not find it necessary to overrule a proposal advanced by the city or the FHC until the fall of 1984. At that point, the Committee overturned the proposed advertising program.

Battisti had ordered the city to develop some kind of advertising project to respond to the extremely negative image of the city among Cleveland area minorities. The Justice Department had argued vigorously that Parma would never be a truly open community so long as potential minority residents had reason to believe they would not be welcome there. The order indicated some of the elements that should be included in formulating such an advertising effort. Headed by a HUD equal housing logo, Parma's proposed ad read:

PARMA IS A GOOD COMMUNITY FOR ALL PERSONS TO RESIDE

Parma is seeking to become an open housing community

Parma is attempting to expand housing choice for minorities in the City

All persons are welcome in Parma

Discriminatory practices which have characterized Parma in the past no longer reflect the official attitude of the City (emphasis added)

Copies of the Remedial Order and Memorandum Opinion are available, free of charge, at Parma's City Hall

The Evaluation Committee observed that the discussions of Parma's past discrimination would have the effect of discouraging, not encouraging, minority residents. There were other disagreements, including the fact that Parma proposed to publish its ads in the *Parma Sun Post,* a suburban newspaper, and the *Call and Post,* a Cleveland area minority newspaper, but not in the *Cleveland Plain Dealer,* the city's leading general circulation paper. Apart from these relatively minor disagreements, the relationships between the Evaluation and Fair Housing committees were positive. Nancy Cronin, Evaluation Committee Chairperson, saw no evidence of resistance or efforts to undermine compliance with the court's order, though she recognized that there were varying opinions on the best way to make Parma a truly open community.[125]

Despite these positive relationships among the players in the implementation process, there were problems. In the early going, Parma met resistance from the CMHA when the city announced formation of its own housing authority. Battisti had given the city a choice of cooperating with CMHA (a prospect absolutely abhorrent to Parma leaders) or forming its own PHA. However, the statutes governing creation of authorities and federal funding programs left some question whether a new body could be created within an area already covered by an existing housing authority. After changing the name to Parma Housing Agency and presenting legal arguments on the question, Parma was authorized by Battisti to develop the office.

One of the most important problems facing the city was the likelihood that federal budget cuts in the eighties meant less available financial resources to support construction of new public housing and operation of other housing programs. Parma reported to Battisti that the city's CDBG awards declined from $774,000 in 1982 to $688,000 in 1983 and $544,000 in 1984.[126] Other efforts to obtain funding for low incoming housing were affected by budget cutbacks. The fact that there were fewer total dollars available

for housing construction grants meant much more intense competition for HUD support
by communities around the nation. Though Parma submitted proposals in cooperation
with some local builders, apart from its own public housing project, the efforts were
unsuccessful. Department of Justice lawyers recognized the effort and the financial
shortfalls.[127]

HUD processing time for public housing construction applications created difficulty
for Parma because of the existence of options the city had purchased on prospective
housing construction sites.[128] The options were purchased following approval by the
court of the site-selection study carried out for the city by the Regional Planning Commission.

The irony of the funding difficulty stems from the fact that Parma had been fighting
participation in federal programs during the years in which funds were most available.
It had, for example, forfeited CDBG dollars from 1975 through 1981 and had not availed
itself of any low income housing funding available under the Housing and Community
Development Act of 1974. Moreover, the refusal to settle the case in the early months,
to move quickly toward a remedy once the liability finding was made, to obtain stays,
and to appeal all the way to the Supreme Court kept Parma out of the competition for
financial resources when they were much more readily accessible.

There were other considerations which, while not presenting major hurdles for
implementation, did affect the process. Though the city was generally cooperative in
the implementation efforts, some local political figures continued to use caustic rhetoric
diverting energy and, to some extent at least, attention away from the positive aspects
of the fair housing program. One of the most visible of these was Councilman Ron
Mottl, Jr., who denounced the court's order and refused to participate in activities like
the equal housing training program which was part of the order. While the Parma FHC
had tried to avoid entanglement in unproductive squabbles with those engaged in such
posturing, the Committee considered Mottl's challenge to be too clearly a violation of
the order to be tolerated. In a June 1984 letter to Battisti, Chairman Kirner observed:

> While we have taken careful steps to safeguard the spirit of cooperation with your
> office, the Evaluation Committee, Council and the City Administration, we strongly
> believe Mr. Mottl's action [sic] undermine our progress and jeopardize this spirit of
> cooperation we have established. . . .
>
> Regardless of Mr. Mottl Jr.'s interpretation of the law, our Committee wants you to
> know that Mr. Mottl Jr.'s statements have cast aspersions on our Committee and all
> concerned. His public statements have aggravated a harmonious environment as evi-
> denced in Mr. [Avery] Friedman's letter to you.
>
> Please be advised that our Committee unanimously is on record that we cannot tol-
> erate such actions of a councilman and do not condone them.[129]

This matter was resolved following a meeting between Mottl and DOJ officials in Washington in which the Councilman was informed of DOJ's intention to press for enforcement of this portion of the remedial order. Mottl agreed to attend a special fair housing
education program.[130]

Remedy Refinement

Apart from these specific issues, Battisti determined that there was a need to address a
number of wider concerns with further proceedings in 1985 aimed at refinement of the

remedy so that implementation could be accomplished smoothly and effectively. Any thought that this refinement process could be completed quickly and informally was eliminated when Parma's counsel chose this occasion as another opportunity to escalate the level of conflict.

Battisti had asked Avery Friedman, a nationally recognized fair housing attorney, to continue to serve as *amicus curiae* during the implementation of the remedy. After the committees had been in operation for a year, Friedman submitted a report to the court on the progress of implementation. In his view, Parma had a great deal to do and there might be need to modify the remedy to help accomplish the overall goals of the remedy.[131] On the basis of Friedman's report and his own observations, Battisti wrote DOJ officials asking whether they thought it might not be appropriate to raise the question of a special master once again. Battisti wrote that while he did not wish to interfere in Parma's affairs more than necessary, he was concerned that a master would be useful "to coordinate the balance of the implementation of the Court's remedial order." Moreover, he was particularly concerned that there was a need to coordinate the flow of information among the city, the FHC, the Evaluation Committee, the Court and any public announcements that were necessary. Battisti thought a master could not only assist the court and the parties but also provide a solid source of reliable information to the public, which is important to minimize anxiety fueled by rumors.[132]

Parma's response was essentially an attack on Friedman's report that charged he had ignored Parma's many accomplishments and overstated what problems there were.[133] Part of the tension was a difference of perspective, but part of it had to do with a clear rejection of Friedman's role in the case. As early as March 1983, Parma had demanded that Battisti eliminate Friedman from the case, charging that he was attempting to use that role to "obtain leverage in another case in which he serves as counsel."[134] It would not be the last time Parma's counsel challenged the position of the court-appointed *amicus curiae*.

The Justice Department, while finding that Parma was "doing a commendable job of complying with the Remedial Order," agreed that there were communications difficulties to be dealt with and that there had been "some apparent confusion" over the proper role of the FHC.[135] It suggested that Parma should begin submitting monthly compliance reports, that communication should be increased among all the principal actors in the implementation process, and that both committees should adopt a more open, flexible, and dynamic posture. The court agreed and ordered Parma to begin the reporting process.

Shortly thereafter, however, when Parma submitted its problematic advertising proposal, more questions emerged. There were still information flow difficulties as well. On November 29, 1984, Battisti agreed with the Evaluation Committee that there were serious questions to be answered regarding the advertising program and other issues. He called for hearings at which all parties could attempt clarification. The hearing, held in Battisti's chambers on January 10, 1985, produced little agreement.[136] Heffernan, for DOJ, found the advertising proposal unacceptable but was generally pleased with Parma's progress. Soltis, for Parma, saw the discussion of the city's advertising program as a disruption of an exemplary compliance effort by the city. Battisti was still not satisfied that the communications were any clearer or more effective than they had been months before. Moreover, he was concerned that DOJ did not seem to be taking an active role in monitoring the implementation of the order it had requested.

Battisti asked Friedman to prepare a report summarizing his views and setting forth proposals for meeting the problems encountered to date. Friedman complied in late

March. His report determined that Parma's approach to implementation of the order was much too narrow and limited. To be effective, he suggested, the order should be approached with a more comprehensive perspective on housing problems within the larger Cleveland metropolitan community. The committees, particularly the Evaluation Committee, staffed with recognized and experienced fair housing experts in Cleveland, should take a more active approach and provide measurable goals toward which the implementation efforts could be directed. As to specific changes, Friedman suggested

1. A professional marketing campaign to correct the Parma image.

2. Meetings with minority groups and others who would be likely to actually convey the message to area minorities.

3. Development of a housing information office in Parma.

4. Enactment of a Parma Fair Housing Law to handle complaints.

5. Efforts to make builders and financial institutions more aware of Parma's new policies to encourage those who had been discouraged by their earlier encounters with the city.

6. Community meetings to educate Parma citizens on the benefits of an open housing community.

7. Development of construction incentives to encourage developers to consider Parma.

8. Provision of staff for the Evaluation Committee so that it could make a greater contribution to the effort.

Reactions to Friedman's submission were mixed, with some concerned that he had been too hard on the city and others observing that he was simply providing a candid and realistic appraisal with useful suggestions. Heffernan agreed that action should be taken to ensure that the advertising campaign was corrected but, apart from that, argued that no additional orders were necessary. Parma's reaction was immediate and hostile. Parma attorneys alleged that this was a whole new lawsuit brought by an improper party.[137] They charged that Friedman with "implacable hostility to Parma" and a "malicious and malevolent" attitude.

Battisti found on the basis of the January discussions, his own observations, the suggestions of the *amicus curiae,* and on other grounds that there should be formal hearings held to obtain answers to specific questions that needed to be addressed as Parma moved into the last stages of the implementation process. Some of these questions were those raised by Friedman, but others concerned issues like the feasibility of some of the features of the remedy in light of declining federal funding, the communications difficulties that remained, and whether the Evaluation Committee should take a more active role than it had to date. Those hearings were set for late August 1985.

There was another part to Battisti's July order, a response to Parma's counsel's attacks on Friedman. He held that "Parma's repeated, unwarranted and unprofessional attacks on Mr. Friedman in filings before this Court are intolerable."[138] It was quite clear that Battisti had simply reached the end of his patience with Parma counsel. He had admonished them during the remedy process and in writing in his remedy order that they should not persist in employing hostile rhetoric calculated to generate unnecessary conflict. Friedman was serving without pay at the request of the court, and while his views may or may not be used by the court, Battisti was simply not going to permit disrespect. In the particular incident in question, Battisti reminded the parties that it had been the court that had called upon Friedman during the January hearings to produce the document for which he was later attacked. He found that Parma's counsel had violated Rule 11 of the Federal Rules of Civil Procedure, deleted the objectionable material from the record before the court, and warned that any further similar actions would "result in appropriate monetary sanctions." [139]

Parma asked Battisti to delay the August hearings to permit them to appeal the proceedings, but he refused. Days before the scheduled appearance, Parma obtained an emergency stay order from the Sixth Circuit Court of Appeals to block the hearing pending an appeal of the order seeking further proceedings.

Apart from the tensions between one or more of Parma's lawyers and other participants in the case, the disagreements among the committees, DOJ, Avery Friedman, and the court, were calm, limited, and reasonably positive differences in perspective. Friedman saw the implementation process from the perspective of a fair housing lawyer who perceived an opportunity for a major change in the housing picture of the greater Cleveland area with Parma playing its proper role as a member of that wider community. Given history and based upon his experience around the nation, Friedman, when asked by the court for his opinion, saw little in Parma's fair housing efforts of the broad approach to open housing that would be needed if area minorities were to really believe the city was open and hospitable. [140] Without clarification of goals, participation by the minority community, and improved coordination of the remedial efforts, success would be limited at best. Members of the Evaluation Committee, however, were more optimistic, though they, too, would have been happy to play a wider role in a broader remedial effort. They were chosen because they were active in fair housing issues in the greater Cleveland area. The idea of merely acting as a check on the Parma FHC was a considerably less active role than several Evaluation Committee members were used to. On the other hand, as the Chairperson of the Evaluation Committee put it, the Committee was happy to play whatever constructive role it could in the implementation of the remedy in its current form or otherwise. Paul Kirner, FHC Chairperson, and other members of the FHC were anxious to complete the implementation process and return to their own personal and professional obligations convinced that Parma would be a better community because of the fair housing mandate. Kirner saw the city's progress as quite good, nearing "that point in time when your Honor can say that we have completed fully with the Remedial Order." [141] The Committee wanted to meet the letter and spirit of the order, but its view of the task was that of a group within Parma. Parma's attorneys, at the other end of the spectrum from Friedman and the Evaluation Committee, saw the order as the outside limit of what can be required of the city. [142] They contested the case from the outset on ideological grounds and were prepared to challenge any expansion of an order which they already considered unjustifiably intrusive.

From an outside perspective, Parma has come a considerable distance. Though some of the most difficult tasks (construction of the new housing units and implementation of an effective public relations campaign among other things) remain to be done, the city has already accomplished a range of activities that it earlier contended it could not or would not do. The relationships among most of the participants have remained amicable and constructive. There is little indication that major dislocations have occurred within the community as a result of the fair housing efforts.

CONCLUSION

The Justice Department was successful in the Parma case both in proving its allegations of housing discrimination and in obtaining a process remedy aimed at improving the availability of housing in the Cleveland metropolitan area on a nondiscriminatory basis. At the same time, the process remedy avoided imposition of a host of detailed requirements, leaving those decisions to a committee of Parma citizens.

Parma's heavily ideological and highly politicized posture did not serve the city well either in the liability stage or the remedy phase of the litigation. Notwithstanding the justification for reaching further, Battisti was content to escape DOJ's remedy plan. Evidence from the remedy hearing indicates that Parma could have won specific limitations on the plan had its representatives concentrated on remedy development when the opportunity was presented.

At the same time that federal courts were responding to demands by individuals and groups for enforcement of fair housing statutes and equal protection of the law, others were asking the judges to ensure implementation of the Supreme Court's two-decade-old ruling that segregated education was unconstitutional. It is to the set of hard judicial choices associated with school desegregation that we turn next.

NOTES

1. U.S. Commission on Civil Rights, *Hearings Before the United States Commission on Civil Rights: Hearings Held in Cleveland, Ohio, April 1–7, 1966* (Wash., DC: Government Printing Office,. 1966) [hereafter CRC Hearings].

2. *Banks v. Perk,* 341 F. Supp. 1175, 1178 (NDOH 1972); and CRC Hearings, *supra* note 1, at 95.

3. *See* testimony of Leonard Simmons in CRC Hearings, *supra* note 1, at 70–77. *See also* testimony of Morris Thorington, *id.,* at 37–42; and testimony of F. Barnard Sellers, *id.* at 96.

4. *See generally* Michael Danielson, *The Politics of Exclusion* (New York: Columbia Univ. Press, 1976); and CRC Hearings, *supra* note 1, at 102, 208–9.

5. Testimony of Charles Sheboy, Cleveland Commissioner of Housing, in CRC Hearings, *supra* note 1, at 126–36.

6. Testimony of Bayla White, in *id.,* at 156–58.

7. *Banks v. Perk, supra* note 2, *aff'd in part* 473 F.2d 910 (6th Cir. 1973).

8. *Id.,* at 1178.

9. *Id.*

10. Battisti particularly relied on *Kennedy Park Homes Ass'n. v. City of Lackawanna,* 436 F.2d 108 (2nd Cir. 1970), *cert. denied,* 401 U.S. 1010 (1971); *Daily v. City of Lawton,* 425 F.2d 1037 (10th Cir. 1970); *Crow v. Brown,* 332 F. Supp. 382 (NDGA 1971), *aff'd* 457 F.2d 788 (5th Cir. 1972); and *Shannon v. Dept. of Housing and Urban Development* 436 F.2d 809 (3rd Cir. 1970).

11. *Banks v. Perk, supra* note 2, at 1180.

12. *Gautreaux v. Chicago Hous. Auth.* 265 F. Supp. 582 (NDIL 1967); 296 F. Supp. 907 (NDIL 1969). The orders against CHA and HUD were eventually affirmed in *Hills v. Gautreaux,* 425 U.S. 284 (1976).

13. *Mahaley v. Cuyahoga Metro. Hous. Auth.,* 355 F. Supp. 1245 (NDOH 1973), 355 F. Supp. 1257 (NDOH 1973), *rev'd* 500 F.2d 1087 (6th Cir. 1974).

14. *See generally Mahaley, supra* note 13, at 1247.

15. The other judges were Lambros and Celebreeze.

16. *Mahaley, supra* note 13, at 1250. The reason given for not deciding the case as a panel was that its jurisdiction was based on the substantial constitutional challenge to the statute. Having upheld the statutes, the jurisdictional base no longer remained.

17. *Id.,* at 1253.

18. *Id.,* at 1252–53.

19. *Id.*

20. *James v. Valtierra,* 402 U.S. 137 (1971).

21. *Hunter v. Erickson* 393 U.S. 385 (1969).

22. Battisti relied on *Banks v. Perk, supra* note 2; *Hawkins v. Town of Shaw,* 461 F.2d 1171 (5th Cir. 1972); *Hobson v. Hansen,* 269 F. Supp. 401 (DDC 1967); *Shannon, Crow, Kennedy Park,* and *City of Lawton, supra* note 10; and *Gautreaux, supra* note 12. He also found support in *S. Alameda Spanish Speaking Org. (SASSO) v. City of Union City, Cal.,* 424 F.2d 291 (9th Cir. 1970). He focused particularly on the factual similarities between the present case and *Crow.*

23. Mahaley, *supra* note 13 at 1259.

24. *Id.,* at 1261.

25. *Id.,* at 1266.

26. *Id.,* at 1268.

27. *Mahaley v. Cuyahoga Metro. Hous. Dev. Auth.,* 500 F.2d 1087 (6th Cir. 1974).

28. *Id.,* at 1094.

29. *Id.,* at 1092, citing *City of Kenosha v. Bruno,* 412 U.S. 507 (1973); and *Monroe v. Pape,* 365 U.S. 167 (1961).

30. *Mahaley, supra* note 27, at 1096.

31. *Reed v. Roe,* 422 F. Supp. 706 (NDOH 1976).

32. Interview with Robert R. Soltis, Special Counsel, City of Parma, and Andrew Boyko, Law Director, City of Parma, Sept. 2, 1982 [hereafter Soltis interview and Boyko interview, respectively]. In particular, Soltis objected to references to flamingos on lawns and Parma citizens clad in white socks.

33. Boyko Interview.

34. CBS News, Special Report, "The City (Part I): A City Is to Live In," Monday, June 24, 1968, in Joint Appendix at 1903–4 [hereafter Joint Appendix].

35. Soltis interview, *supra* note 32.

36. Joint Appendix, *supra* note 34.

37. *Id.,* at 1912.

38. *Id.,* at 1911.

39. *United States v. City of Parma, Ohio,* 494 F. Supp. 1049, 1070 (NDOH 1980).

40. *Id.,* at 1071–72.

41. The projects are described in *Id.,* at 1074–76.

42. Brief of Defendant-City or Appellant City of Parma, Ohio, in Case No. 81–3031, *United States v. City of Parma, Ohio.* U.S. Court of Appeals for the Sixth Circuit, Apr. 20, 1981, p. 13 [hereafter Parma's 6th Circuit Brief].

43. *Parma, supra* note 39, at 1096.

44. *Parma's 6th Circuit Brief, supra* note 42, at 14.

45. *Parma, supra* note 39, at 1079–80.

46. *Id.*

47. *Id.*

48. Parma's 6th Circuit Brief, *supra* note 42, at 15; and Soltis interview, *supra* note 32.

49. *Parma, supra* note 39, at 1072.

50. *Id.*

51. *Id.,* at 1080.

52. Joint Appendix, *supra* note 34, at 527–28.

53. *Id.*, at 528–29.

54. *Id.*, at 1086.

55. *Id.*, at 526–31.

56. See *Parma, supra* note 39, at 1074–77.

57. "No building designed for and occupied in whole or in part as a residence including, but not limited to single-family houses, dwelling houses, multiple dwellings, lodging houses, apartment houses, hotels and condominiums, shall exceed 35 feet in height. (Initiative passed 11/2/71)." Ordinance 1529.37.

58. Joint Appendix, *supra* note 34, at 165; Ordinance 1528.02.

59. Housing and Community Development Act of 1974, 42 U.S.C. Sections 5301 *et seq.* For a thorough exploration of the program and its origins, see Advisory Commission on Intergovernmental Relations, *Community Development: The Workings of Federal-Local Block Grant,* (Wash., DC: ACIR, 1977).

60. *Parma, supra* note 39, at 1092.

61. Joint Appendix, *supra* note 34, at 2025–27.

62. *City of Hartford v. Hills,* 408 F. Supp. 889 (DCT. 1976), *rev'd sub nom. City of Hartford v. Town of Glastonbury,* 561 F.2d 1032 (2d Cir. 1977).

63. Interviews with Michael Barrett and Brian Heffernan, CRD, DOJ, Sept. 16, 1982.

64. *Id.*

65. Frank Schwelb, Chief Housing and Credit Section, CRD, DOJ, to Cynthia Graae, Office of Federal Evaluation, CRC, Feb. 22, 1978, pp. 6–7.

66. Soltis interview, *supra* note 32.

67. Joint Appendix, *supra* note 34, at 25.

68. *Id.*, at 23.

69. *Id.*, at 43–44.

70. *Washington v. Davis,* 426 U.S. 229 (1976).

71. *Metro. Hous. Dev. Corp. v. Village of Arlington Heights,* 373 F. Supp. 208 (NDIL 1974); 517 F.2d 409 (7th Cir. 1975) *(Arlington Heights I);* 558 F.2d 1283 (7th Cir. 1977) *(Arlington Heights II), cert. denied* 434 U.S. 1025 (1978).

72. *Parma, supra* note 39, at 1054.

73. *Arlington Heights II, supra* note 71.

74. *See e.g., Swann v. Charlotte-Mecklenburg, Bd. of Ed.* 402 U.S. 1 (1971); *Hills v. Gautreaux, supra* note 12; *Milliken v. Bradley,* 433 U.S. 267 (1977) *(Milliken II).*

75. *See supra* notes 10, 12, and 22. *See also Robinson v. 12 Lofts Realty Inc.,* 610 F.2d 1032 (2nd Cir. 1979); *Resident Advisory Bd. v. Rizzo,* 564 F.2d 126 (3rd Cir. 1977), *cert. denied,* 435 U.S. 908 (1978); and *United States v. City of Black Jack,* 508 F.2d 1179 (8th Cir. 1974), *cert. denied,* 422 U.S. 1042 (1975).

76. *Cornelius v. City of Parma,* 374 F. Supp. 730 (NDOH 1974), *vacated and remanded,* 506 F.2d 1400 (6th Cir. 1974), *vacated and remanded* 422 U.S. 1052, *remanded for dismissal,* 521 F.2d 1401 (6th Cir. 1975), *cert. denied,* 424 U.S. 955 (1976).

77. *Trafficante v. Metro. Life Ins. Co.,* 409 U.S. 205 (1972).

78. *Parma v. Levi,* P.H.E.O.H. Rep. 13,720 (NDOH 1975), *aff'd* 536 F.2d 133 (6th Cir. 1976).

79. Joint Appendix, *supra* note 34, at 91.

80. *Id.*, at 135.

81. *United States v. City of Parma, Ohio,* 471 F. Supp. 453 (NDOH 1979).

82. *Id.*, at 454.

83. *Id.*, at 454–55.

84. Summarized in *Parma, supra* note 39, at 1062–65.

85. Transcript of Hearings Before Chief Judge Frank Battisti, Mar. 25, 1980, at 15–16 [hereafter Remedy Hearing Transcript].

86. *Parma, supra* note 39, at 1049.

87. *Arlington Heights II, supra* note 71.

88. *Parma, supra* note 39, at 1065.

89. *Id.,* at 1096.

90. *Id.,* at 1098–99.

91. *John Skillden and Co. v. City of Toledo,* 528 F.2d 867 (6th Cir. 1975).

92. Soltis interview, *supra* note 32.

93. *Parma, supra* note 39, at 1101.

94. Joint Appendix, *supra* note 34, at 274–76.

95. Remedy Hearing Transcript, *supra* note 85, at 294–95.

96. Joint Appendix, *supra* note 34, at 288–89.

97. Remedy Hearing Transcript, *supra* note 85, at 3–5.

98. *Id.,* at 25.

99. *Id.,* at 29

100. *Id.,* at 31.

101. *Id.,* at 35.

102. *Id.,* at 35–36.

103. *Id.,* at 111–268.

104. *Id.,* at 236.

105. Soltis and Boyko confirmed this in their interviews, *supra* note 32.

106. Joint Appendix, *supra* note 34, at 355–57.

107. Parma quoting *Skillken, supra* note 91 at 880–81.

108. *United States v. City of Parma, Ohio,* 504 F. Supp. 913, 916 (NDOH 1980).

109. *Id.,* at 919.

110. *Id.*

111. *Id.,* at 920–22.

112. Joint Appendix, *supra* note 34, at 417.

113. Parma relied heavily, as did a number of other communities, on *Nat'l. League of Cities v. Usery,* 426 U.S. 833 (1976), but the Supreme Court had heard and rejected the claim that *Usery* barred federal intervention in matters significantly affecting state and local land-use regulations in *Hodel v. Virginia Surface Mining and Reclamation Ass'n,* 452 U.S. 264 (1981).

114. Parma's 6th Circuit Brief, *supra* note 42, at 52.

115. *Id.*

116. Parma Reply Brief in 6th Circuit, at 1.

117. *United States v. City of Parma, Ohio,* 661 F.2d 562 (6th Cir. 1981).

118. *Id.,* at 570.

119. *Id.,* at 571.

120. *Id.,* at 572.

121. *Id.,* at 573.

122. *Id.,* at 576–77.

123. *United States v. City of Parma, Ohio,* C73–439, Apr. 8, 1983, pp. 1–2.

124. Interview with Paul Kirner, Chairperson, FHC, Parma, Ohio, Aug. 22, 1985.

125. Interview with Nancy Cronin, Chairperson Evaluation Committee, Cleveland, Ohio, Aug. 22, 1985.

126. "First Monthly Report of Defendant City of Parma Detailing Status of the City's Efforts to Complete Each of the Tasks Required Under the Remedial Order," Aug. 31, 1984 [hereafter Parma Monthly Report].

127. Brian Heffernan to Judge Frank Battisti, Aug. 28, 1984, p. 4.

128. Parma Ninth Monthly Report, May 30, 1985.

129. Paul Kirner to Judge Frank Battisti, June 12, 1984, pp. 1–2.

130. Brian Heffernan, DOJ, to Ron Mottl, Jr., Oct. 5, 1984.

131. Avery Friedman to Judge Frank Battisti, May 22, 1984.

132. Judge Frank Battisti to Thomas Keeling, June 1, 1984, pp. 1–2.

133. "Response of City of Parma to Letter of 'Amicus Curiae' Dated May 22, 1984," June 5, 1984.

134. *See United States v. City of Parma, Ohio,* Memorandum and Order, Mar. 28, 1983, p. 4.

135. Brian Heffernan to Judge Frank Battisti, Aug. 28, 1984.

136. Transcript of Proceedings Had Before the Honorable Frank J. Battisti, Chief Judge, on Thursday, Jan. 10, 1985.

137. "Objections and Response of Defendant City of Parma to 'Submission of Proposal for Consideration by *Amicus Curiae,*' " May 10, 1985.

138. *United States v. City of Parma, Ohio,* Order, July 30, 1985, p. 4.

139. *Id.,* at 6.

140. Interview with Avery Friedman, court-appointed *amicus curiae,* Cleveland, Ohio, Aug. 19, 1985.

141. "Reply to Order of Court Fair Housing Committee's Outline," Aug. 14, 1985.

142. Interview with Avery Friedman, court-appointed *amicus curiae,* Cleveland, Ohio, Aug. 19, 1985.

4

Equal Educational Opportunity: Federal Courts and School Desegregation

There is a certain irony in the fact that the role played by federal courts in school desegregation has been the focus of some of the greatest praise ever accorded the judiciary and also much of the harshest criticism. The opinion in *Brown v. Board of Education* declaring segregation unconstitutional has been lauded as a second Emancipation Proclamation, yet the later rulings attempting to enforce the mandate to eliminate segregated schools "root and branch" have made the federal courts at all levels targets of vituperation.

This chapter, and the *Milliken v. Bradley* case study which follows, will explore the background, issues, and problems before judges in the field of school desegregation. It is an area of judicial activity marked by often loud and threatening rhetoric which has been a key public policy problem across the nation. Precisely because the judicial decisions involved in the effort to desegregate schools directly concern children, the level of fear and anger has been particularly high. It has often been said that we wish equal educational opportunity for all children, yet we insist that *our* children receive the *best* education. The blend of racial tensions, the press of social change, and the impact of all these factors on children make school desegregation truly a realm of hard judicial choices.

COURTS AND THE PRESS FOR EQUAL PROTECTION

The process by which the school desegregation cases have developed is one that can only be understood with at least a modicum of historical perspective. The steps have been varied, often halting, and generally incomplete in the movement to end and remedy a legacy of racial discrimination. It is a history in several parts, including the pre-*Brown* development of the "separate but equal doctrine," the *Brown v. Board* rulings, the post-*Brown* remedy cases, and the mid-seventies shift in Supreme Court rulings on the remedial authority of federal courts.

From Sarah Roberts to Linda Brown: The Rise and Fall of the "Separate but Equal Doctrine"

It is surprising how many Americans believe that questions of racial segregation in schools began with the 1954 *Brown* decision. In truth, a century before Linda Brown's parents and NAACP Legal Defense Fund lawyers launched the *Brown* case, the father of a girl named Sarah Roberts was engaged in a similar fight in Boston. The decision of the Massachusetts Supreme Court in the 1850 case established the so-called "separate but equal" doctrine that sustained segregated schools from that day until the Warren Court ruling in *Brown*.

The fact that the early segregation case, *Sarah C. Roberts v. City of Boston,* arose in a northern city has provided some southerners with a measure of satisfaction, but, of course, the issue of equal educational opportunity was not open to debate in the antebellum South.[1] The first separate black school in Boston was founded in 1798 at the request of minority parents because of prejudice in the white schools. The Smith School was annexed into the public system in 1815. By 1846 black parents had learned that discrimination was far easier when the black children were not merely a minority within a largely white student body, but were completely separated from the other students in an all-black school. The Special Committee of the Grammar School Board refused the request to integrate, concluding that segregated education "[is] not only legal and just, but is best adapted to promote the education of that class of our population."[2] Benjamin Roberts sued, challenging the Board's decision. Chief Justice Shaw, speaking for a unanimous Massachusetts Supreme Court, upheld separate but equal education.

The *Roberts* decision was cited as precedent in support of segregated schools by several state and a number of federal district courts. The Supreme Court later adopted the view that "equal and separate" educational facilities violated no constitutional protection in the *Plessy v. Ferguson* ruling in 1896.[3] In the interim, the Civil War and the creation of the Thirteenth, Fourteenth, and Fifteenth amendments presented a variety of new issues. The Court, however, found segregated facilities and services no violation of the equal protection clause of the Fourteenth Amendment.

The *Plessy* case came not from educational segregation, but as a challenge to a Louisiana railroad statute passed in 1890 called, "An Act to Promote the Comfort of Passengers."[4] A group of blacks, known as the Committee to Test the Constitutionality of the Separate Car Law, selected Homer Adolph Plessy, a man who appeared to be white but was seven-eighths white and one-eighth black, to provide a test case. Plessy was arrested for refusing to leave a rail car for whites only and the challenge was launched. With only Justice Harlan dissenting, the Supreme Court upheld the statute against claims that it violated the Fourteenth Amendment and was a "badge of servitude" prohibited by the Thirteenth Amendment. Justice Brown, writing for the Court observed:

> The argument also assumes social prejudices may be overcome by legislation, and that equal rights cannot be secured to the negro except by an enforced commingling of the two races. We cannot accept this proposition. If the two races are to meet upon terms of social equality, it must be the result of natural affinities, a mutual appreciation of each other's merits and a voluntary consent of individuals.[5]

Justice Harlan, in dissent, predicted the ruling would in future years be seen, along with the decision in *Dred Scott v. Sanford,* as one of the great tragedies in American judicial history. He insisted: "[I]n view of the Constitution, in the eyes of the law, there is in this country no superior, dominant, ruling class of citizens. There is no caste here. Our Constitution is colorblind, and neither knows nor tolerates classes among citizens."[6]

The separate but equal concept was later applied by the Court to schools as well as transportation.[7]

The demise of separate but equal was the result of changing political and social realities, an inherently unworkable as well as undesirable conceptualization, and the diligent efforts of civil rights activists. The NAACP realized that the separate but equal doctrine could be undermined without forcing an immediate, direct, and probably futile confrontation.[8] The strategy was to force the states to provide equal separate facilities, something the states would not do. Moreover, by pressing the battle at the level of graduate and professional schools in the early going, the challengers could avoid the emotional issues that would surely attend efforts to desegregate primary and secondary classrooms. Education was not the only active civil rights front. Challenges were also launched in the fields of voting rights and housing segregation.[9] The picture that emerged was a clear illustration of recalcitrance by the states, an unwillingness to meet their own claims to providing segregated equality, assuming such a condition were possible.

On the educational front, civil rights activists won an impressive series of victories in the Supreme Court, the beginning of the end of the "separate but equal" doctrine. The first of these, *Missouri ex rel. Gaines v. Canada*. struck down a Missouri policy under which qualified black law student applicants were denied admission to the state university law school but were given subsidies to complete professional studies elsewhere.[10] The Court held on a 7–2 vote that separate but equal meant what it said.

State governments scrambled to survive challenges to their graduate and professional school programs while retaining segregation. The responses came in two forms. The first was to establish what amounted to sham programs supposedly creating separate but equal facilities. The other approach was to admit black students but isolate them within the schools, a form of internal segregation. The Supreme Court struck down both efforts on the same day in 1950. In a Texas case, *Sweatt v. Painter,* the Court overturned an attempt to open a black law school as an alternative to desegregation of the University of Texas School of Law. In a unanimous opinion, Chief Justice Vinson found it absurd to seriously contend that the new law school was equal to the existing professional program at the University of Texas so that any reasonable person would choose to go to the black school if given an option between the two. More important to the future of "separate but equal," however, was the Court's judgment that even if the physical environment had been roughly equal, there would remain intangible factors, "qualities which are incapable of objective measurement but which make for greatness in a law school," such as "reputation of the faculty, experience of the administration, position and influence of the alumni, standing in the community, traditions and prestige" that rendered the black school unequal.[11] Perhaps as significant to the Court was the fact that a separate black law school would deny the students the opportunity to interact with whites they would encounter in the practice of law.

This inability to freely associate with whites was also important in the resolution of an internal segregation case, *McLaurin v. Oklahoma.* G.W. McLaurin was admitted to the University of Oklahoma to pursue graduate training in education. He was placed in a special area in the classroom where he could see and hear the instructor but could not be seen by or communicate with the other students. He was assigned an isolated desk in the library and a separate table in the dining room. Concluding that this program of internal segregation was unconstitutional, Justice Vinson held that McLaurin was denied an "ability to study, to engage in discussions and exchange views with other students, and, in general, to learn his profession."[12]

Brown and After: Pronouncing the Rule and Making It Happen

By the early fifties, the Court had seen continuous efforts to circumvent its prior rulings and a desire by the states to maintain segregated and unequal facilities and services. It was then that the NAACP brought appeals in cases challenging segregated schools in Kansas, South Carolina, Virginia, Delaware, and the District of Columbia. This time the Court was faced with a direct attack on "separate but equal" education. While the *Brown v. Board* ruling overturning *Plessy* was a momentous decision for the Court, the effort by the Justices and by lower federal court judges to ensure enforcement of the *Brown* mandate was even more challenging.

The five cases brought to the Court by the NAACP contesting *Plessy* were styled *Brown v. Board of Education of Topeka, Kansas.* In the lead case, the district court had made an explicit finding that the facilities for white and minority students were indeed equal, making it essential to address the more fundamental issue of the inherent inequality of segregated schools.

The Court heard arguments in *Brown* first in the 1952 term while Chief Justice Vinson presided. It was apparent that the Court was badly divided with Vinson one of strongest voices for retaining *Plessy*. Fortunately, the justices did not press for an early vote. Instead, at Justice Frankfurter's suggestion, the Court called for reargument in the 1953 term. By the time the case was reargued in December, Chief Justice Vinson had died, an event which Frankfurter was convinced proved that "there is a God."[13] Vinson was replaced by Earl Warren who played an important role in the development of a unanimous opinion overturning the separate but equal doctrine. Using a process of delay and careful sensitive persuasion, Warren was able to avoid a fragmented court, a condition that would have jeopardized the effectiveness of the ruling. The unanimity in the first *Brown* decision was assured when, at Justice Jackson's suggestion, the Court delayed prescribing a remedy for existing segregated schools, holding that issue over for further argument in the next term. That made it possible for some members of the Court to vote for the desegregation principle while taking more time to resolve their fears about how to enforce an end to racial discrimination in the schools. In a brief opinion the Court maintained, "In these days, it is doubtful that any child may reasonably be expected to succeed in life if he is denied the opportunity of an education. *Such an opportunity, where the state has undertaken to provide it, is a right which must be made available to all on equal terms.*"[14] (emphasis added). It concluded, "In the field of public education the doctrine of 'separate but equal' has no place. Separate educational facilities are inherently unequal."[15]

Claiming that they had already endured segregation for too long, the NAACP sought a decree from the Court mandating immediate desegregation. The defendants, however, responded that the justices should merely declare the law and permit the states to implement it. Given the history of discrimination, the Court was not prepared to rely on vague assurances by the states, nor was it willing to involve itself directly in a specific remedial decree. Instead, the Court in its *Brown II* ruling assigned the responsibility to dismantle the segregated system to state and local school officials and the task of over-sight of those efforts to the federal district courts. The school districts were required to "make a prompt and reasonable start toward full compliance" with the *Brown I* rul-ing.[16] While the district courts might find it necessary to permit some additional time to meet particular problems, the "burden rests upon the defendants to establish that such time is necessary in the public interest and is consistent with good faith compliance at the earliest practicable date."[17] Moreover, the district courts were to retain jurisdiction during the transition from segregated to unitary schools. With that, the Court "re-manded to the District Courts to take such proceedings and enter such orders and de-crees consistent with this opinion as are necessary and proper to admit to public schools on a racially nondiscriminatory basis with all deliberate speed the parties to these cases."[18]

As the Court would later observe, however, there was a great deal of deliberation and very little speed in the years following the two *Brown* decisions.[19] Almost imme-diately, the southern states launched a campaign of "massive resistance" to the school desegregation rulings, charging that the Supreme Court had abused its constitutional authority and vowing to fight the decisions in every way possible. A variety of means were indeed used to frustrate *Brown v. Board,* including refusal to respond without specific orders from district courts, appeals of every adverse decision regardless of the merits of the case, passage of a variety of state statutes that attempted to circumvent desegregation orders, enactment of so-called interposition laws that directly challenged the authority of the federal courts to rule on school desegregation, simple delaying tactics, the use of optional plans which permitted white children to escape assignment to predominantly black schools and intimidated black students from attendance at over-whelmingly white institutions, the closing of public schools, and public support for private segregated schools. The federal district courts and circuit courts of appeals, particularly the Fourth and Fifth circuits, faced these tactics and attempted to implement the *Brown* decisions.[20] The Supreme Court was generally content for most of the decade following *Brown* to leave the matter to the lower courts, often affirming their decisions with simple *per curiam* opinions. There were exceptions, however, and by the late sixties the Supreme Court assumed a more direct role in ordering action.

The first major confrontation following *Brown* occurred when a district court in Little Rock, Arkansas, facing a cooperative local school board but a recalcitrant state government, relented and allowed a substantial delay in school desegregation plans after early efforts produced violent confrontations. Governor Faubus had ordered out the Ar-kansas National Guard to block the desegregation of Little Rock Central High School, but President Eisenhower sent in federal troops in support of the integration plan. In the face of that confrontation, the school board sought and received a two-and-a-half-year delay of further action. The court of appeals reversed the district court and the Supreme Court affirmed that judgment. The state argued two points. First, the *Brown* decision did not apply to Arkansas, a state not a party to the 1954 case. Second, the appellate courts should uphold the delay since it was intended to protect the safety of the black children. The *Cooper v. Aaron* decision marked the only occasion in the history of the Supreme Court in which all members of the Court individually signed an opinion (ac-tually written by Justice Brennan), thus taking not only group, but individual responsi-bility for its authorship.[21] The Court rejected the state's first assertion, holding that the *Brown* decision applied to all states and adding, "State support of segregated schools through any arrangement, management, funds, or property cannot be squared with the [Fourteenth] Amendment's command that no State shall deny to any person within its jurisdiction the equal protection of the laws.''[22] The Court warned that it would not allow the minority childrens' rights ''to be sacrificed or yielded to the violence and disorder which have followed upon the actions of the Governor and the Legislature'' and declared that it would not permit their rights to be ''nullified openly and directly by state legislators or state executive or judicial officers, nor nullified indirectly by them through evasive schemes.''[23]

By 1964 the Court had lost its patience, not only with the fact that little desegregation had actually occurred in the decade following *Brown,* but also because state and local governments had engaged in so many disingenuous attempts to evade the law. Such efforts to avoid desegregation in Virginia prompted *Griffin v. School Board of Prince Edward County.*[24] The Prince Edward County School Board was under a court order to desegregate. To avoid integration the county refused to levy the property tax, forcing the closure of the public schools. The county legislature promptly enacted a series of measures providing financial support for the establishment of private segregated schools. The district court found that the closure of public schools to avoid desegregation was a patent violation of the Fourteenth Amendment and the Supreme Court agreed. Letting the Court's impatience show, Justice Black wrote that ''[t]he time for 'deliberate speed' has run out, and that phrase can no longer justify denying children their rights to equal educational opportunity.''[25]

The years 1964 and 1965 were important, too, on the legislative front. The Civil Rights Act of 1964 contained provisions that permitted the Justice Department (DOJ) to bring suit to enforce school desegregation (Title IV) and that prohibited federal funding of programs that were engaged in racial discrimination (Title VI). The latter provided authority for enforcement action by the Department of Health, Education, and Welfare (HEW). The funding incentive became even more important with enactment of the Elementary and Secondary Education Act of 1965 which provided substantially increased federal aid to education with large sums targeted for southern districts and other relatively poor areas.[26] The regulations governing funding issued by HEW made the fact that a district was under a court order to desegregate and agreement to comply with the order automatic grounds for funding. That caused many districts to seek mild, negotiated court orders producing little effective desegregation.[27] The most common of these was the ''freedom of choice'' plan under which students could attend any school they wished within their district. It was the widespread use of such plans that sparked a number of cases eventually resolved by the Supreme Court in 1968.

The Court's rulings in *Green v. County School Board of New Kent County, Virginia* and its companion cases from Arkansas and Alabama held that while ''freedom of choice'' plans might be part of a desegregation remedy, they would not likely be permissible as complete remedies in themselves because they simply were not effective.[28] White children had not chosen to attend predominantly black schools, which were generally inferior to their present institutions. Black students had not moved to predominantly white schools under such plans because of intimidation, inconvenience, or administrative burdens imposed by the districts.

These decisions were perhaps most important because of the general instructions they provided to school districts and to the district judges presiding over desegregation cases. As to the former, the Court warned that school boards had an ''affirmative duty to take whatever steps might be necessary to convert to a unitary system in which racial discrimination would be eliminated *root and branch*''[29] (emphasis added). Delays were no longer to be tolerated and officials were obligated to produce ''a plan that promises realistically to work, and promises realistically to work *now.*''[30] The test of any plan, said the Court, is its likely effectiveness. The availability of more effective means of desegregation places a heavy burden on local authorities to justify less rigorous action. For their part the district judges were to examine the proposals from local officials ''in light of the facts at hand and in light of any alternatives which may be shown as feasible and more promising in their effectiveness.''[31] They were also admonished to maintain supervisory jurisdiction ''until it is clear that the state imposed segregation *has been completely removed*''[32] (emphasis added).

While the Court had expressed an unwillingness to tolerate further delays in desegregation in the *Griffin* and *Green* cases, it flatly abandoned the ''all deliberate speed'' language of *Brown II* in 1969, terming it ''no longer constitutionally permissible.''[33] As of that date the Court held that ''the obligation of every district is to terminate dual school systems at once and to operate now and hereafter only unitary schools.''[34]

Still, the Court had avoided comprehensive and detailed discussions of the remedial options available to district courts in desegregation cases. It took on that task in a series of opinions rendered in 1971. Chief Justice Burger's opinion for the unanimous Court in *Swann v. Charlotte-Mecklenburg Board of Education* sought to clarify three types of issues, including the grounds for finding segregation and ordering a remedy, the kinds of tools that were available to judges in designing remedial decrees, and the limitations on district court remedial authority.[35] As to the first, the Court, citing *Green,* warned that the school administrators had a duty to eliminate dual school systems and that evidence of the continued existence of segregation shifted the burden to officials to justify the current conditions in their schools. Courts were instructed to consider such factors as racial composition of students, faculty, school location (indicating choices of construction sites which tend to exacerbate segregation), and segregation of extracurricular activities in judging the existence of a dual system:

> Independent of student assignment, where it is possible to identify a ''white school'' or a ''Negro School'' simply by reference to the racial composition of teachers and staff, the quality of school buildings and equipment, or the organization of sports activities, *a prima facie case of violation of substantive constitutional rights under the Equal Protection Clause is shown.*[36] (emphasis added)

Failure to adequately respond to such a prima facie case justified a remedy, and ''[o]nce a right and a violation have been shown, the scope of a district court's equitable powers are broad, for breadth and flexibility are inherent in equitable remedies.''[37] Permissible remedial tools include court ordered modification of attendance zones, reassignments using pairing or clustering of schools (including noncontiguous zones), restrictions on school construction and school closing decisions, the use of mathematical ratios as starting points for remedial decisionmaking, and the requirement of transportation of pupils—busing. After noting that nearly forty percent of the nation's schoolchildren already rode buses to school, the Court observed, ''Desegregation plans cannot be limited to the walk-in school.''[38]

Burger cautioned that courts were not required to eliminate all one-race schools, but they were to scrutinize carefully any facilities that remained racially identifiable after desegregation of the system. Neither were plaintiffs in a school desegregation case entitled to ''any particular degree of racial balance'' in the sense of a fixed numerical figure requiring a matching of ''racial composition of the school system as a whole.''[39] Where busing was used, the Court indicated that parents were entitled to question the assignment if ''the time or distance of travel is so great as to either risk the health of

the children or significantly impinge on the educational process."[40] While district courts
were not to continually require readjustments year-by-year of racial composition, they
were required to ensure that "the affirmative duty to desegregate has been accomplished
and racial discrimination through official action is eliminated from the system." The
Court admonished district judges that remedies could be applied only in proven cases
of violation of constitutional rights. The "nature of the violation determines the scope
of the remedy."[41]

In the end, however, the Court recognized that desegregation would be a difficult
and rending task:

> Absent a constitutional violation there would be no basis for judicially ordering as-
> signment of students on a racial basis. All things being equal, with no history of
> discrimination, it might well be desirable to assign pupils to schools nearest their
> homes. But all things are not equal in a system that has been deliberately constructed
> and maintained to enforce racial segregation. The remedy for such segregation may
> be administratively awkward, inconvenient, and even bizarre in some situations, and
> may impose burdens on some; but all awkwardness and inconvenience cannot be
> avoided in the interim period when remedial adjustments are being made to eliminate
> the dual school system.[42]

A Changing Court and a More Limited View of Judicial Discretion in Desegregation Cases

The unanimity found in *Swann* and many of the earlier desegregation cases was, however, about to end. The appointment by President Nixon of Justices Burger, Rehnquist,
Blackmun, and Powell was central to the significant changes that occurred in the school
cases decided from approximately 1973 on. More specifically, those rulings altered the
requirements to be met in order for plaintiffs to qualify for a judicial remedy, the permissible scope of any decree that was entered by district judges, and the proper duration
of supervision over implementation of an order by the lower courts.

The new members of the Court had been picked with Nixon's dislike for federal
court interference with state and local government in mind. By 1972, those concerns
surfaced in a vigorous four person dissenting opinion prepared by Chief Justice Burger.
The case involved a policy adopted by the city of Emporia, Virginia. Though the community attained city status under Virginia law in 1967, it continued to send its children
to county schools under a contractual arrangement. After the Supreme Court's decision
in *Green v. County School Board,* the district court issued a remedy, including school
pairing for the county. At that point Emporia, citing plans to provide better quality
education, sought to withdraw from the agreement with the county and establish its own
school district. The effect of the new arrangement was to remove nearly half the white
students from the county system and eliminate the only existing predominantly white
schools. The district court enjoined Emporia's plan, finding it would undermine the
desegregation effort. The court of appeals reversed, but the Supreme Court upheld the
district court, ruling that any changes made in a school district under a court ordered
remedy must be assessed in terms of whether they advance or hinder the desegregation
effort.[43] The dissenters argued that the remedial discretion of the district court should
be limited by the need for deference to the principle of local control of schools.[44] From
that point on, the desegregation rulings were often sharply divided, with the votes of

Justices Stewart or Blackmun most often crucial to determining the outcome. Once Justice Douglas left the Court, the traditional Warren Court majority was in the minority, needing two votes from the possible swing voters—Stevens, Stewart, or Blackmun—to carry close cases.

The determination of the need for a judicial remedy in a desegregation dispute had been relatively easy in southern cases, both because there were usually statutes that required segregation and since local political figures overtly employed segregationist rhetoric. If the school districts in such a setting failed in their affirmative obligation to dismantle the dual system, the plaintiffs were entitled to court ordered relief. The failure of the local government was assessed by an examination of the existing state of schools and educational services, as indicated in the discussion of *Swann* above. After all, *Brown I* had said that "education is a right which must be made available to all on equal terms."[45]

The decision by the Supreme Court in *San Antonio Independent School District v. Rodriguez* modified the approach to school cases in an important respect. The 5–4 opinion by Justice Powell reversed a three judge district court determination that the Texas property-tax-based system of school finance violated the equal protection clause. The case arose because of the increasingly common fiscal problems (mentioned in Chapter 2) encountered in the nation's cities. Despite the fact that city residents already faced much higher property tax rates than the suburbanites and received less state and federal aid per student, the Court determined that differences among districts were matters central to local control of schools and not appropriate to close judicial scrutiny. Critical to that judgment was Powell's determination that: "Education, of course, is not among the rights afforded explicit protection under our Federal Constitution. Nor do we find any basis for saying it is implicitly so protected."[46]

The Court also encountered increasing pressure to deal with northern cases, suits brought in states where legislation had not mandated segregated schools for decades. The Court decided the first of these, a Denver case, in 1973.[47] Until the mid-seventies, the requirement for plaintiffs was to show the existence of segregated and unequal schools, at which point the burden shifted to the schools; beginning in 1976 that changed. In a series of opinions, the Court held that a plaintiff in a race discrimination case must prove both the intent to discriminate and the effect of that discrimination in order to obtain relief.[48] Moreover, it was not enough to show that officials were informed that their decisions would have a discriminatory impact. It was necessary to demonstrate that they acted not merely in spite of, but at least in part because of, that anticipated discriminatory effect.[49] That was an extremely difficult burden for plaintiffs to meet.

Similarly, the sharply divided Court issued a series of rulings suggesting greater restraint by judges as to the scope of any relief that was ordered. Whereas the cases up to 1971 had spoken of effectiveness as the key, stressed the inherent breadth and flexibility of equitable remedies, and commanded the lower courts to assure the elimination of segregation "root and branch," the later rulings urged careful tailoring of relief, a respect for local control of schools, and commitment to interfere no more than necessary to correct the specific injuries done to victims of segregated schools. As the Court put it in a Dayton, Ohio case:

> If such violations are found, the District Court in the first instance . . . must determine how much incremental segregative effect these violations had on the racial distribution of the Dayton school population as presently constituted, when that dis-

tribution is compared to what it would have been in the absence of such constitutional violations. The remedy must be designed to redress that difference, and only if there has been a systemwide impact may there be a systemwide remedy.[50]

The instructions to district courts included admonitions to be careful about the scope of the relief they granted within school districts and to avoid multidistrict remedies unless the plaintiffs could prove that the outlying districts constructed or maintained their boundaries for the purpose of discrimination.[51] As the case study of *Milliken v. Bradley* to follow indicates, such restrictions made the task of the district judge extremely difficult.

A similarly subtle but important shift also emerged with respect to the duration of district court oversight over desegregation. Virtually all of the rulings since *Brown II* had commanded district courts to maintain supervisory jurisdiction over the school district until the desegregation "had been accomplished" and the vestiges of the dual school system "had been eliminated."[52] In 1976, however, the Court, again in a sharply divided decision, admonished the lower courts to exercise more restraint. A desegregation suit was launched against the Pasadena Unified School District (PUSD) in 1968. The district court ordered the PUSD to produce a desegregation plan to ensure by September 1970 that there would be no school which had a "majority of minority students" and retained jurisdiction over the remedy. While the plan was initially implemented, there ensued a hard fought battle over the remedy which Justice Marshall characterized as "a three year pattern of opposition." Elections for the School Board featured promises by candidates to seek termination of the desegregation order. In 1974 the new members of the PUSD Board petitioned for an end to the court order and proposed their own plan for the future. The court found that the district had not yet completed implementation of the earlier decree and its new proposal would result in resegregation. Justice Rehnquist described the district court action as an attempt to require year-by-year rebalancing of students. The *Swann* case had specifically indicated that year-by-year readjustments should not be required "once the affirmative duty to desegregate has been accomplished and racial discrimination through official action is eliminated from the system." Rehnquist observed that "[i]t may well be that petitioners have not yet totally achieved the unitary system contemplated by this quotation from *Swann*." Even so, "having once implemented a racially neutral attendance pattern in order to remedy the perceived constitutional violations . . . , the District Court had fully performed its function of providing the appropriate remedy for previous racially discriminatory attendance patterns."[53]

Though the majorities shifted from case to case on the specifics, with some rulings sustaining and others reversing district court actions, it was clear that the Supreme Court was taking a less expansive approach to remedial orders than its language in earlier cases required.[54]

PROBLEMS AND PRACTICES: ISSUES CONFRONTING DISTRICT JUDGES IN ENFORCING THE MANDATE OF BROWN II

While the Supreme Court moved through a variety of cases presenting a relatively few specific issues, the district courts were confronted with suits presenting a host of problems. District judges functioned under *Brown II* for a decade with little or no guidance from the Supreme Court. When the Court did begin to speak, its instructions to the lower courts were essentially to be thorough and diligent in the face of opposition, but specifics were often avoided. Finally, just when the lower courts thought they were receiving clearer instructions in the wake of *Swann,* the Supreme Court began its internal changes, appearing more divided and less certain of the proper guidelines for school desegregation cases. The Justice Department, which had been so helpful to district judges, was facing new orders to accommodate local governments, asking for more time and flexibility where it would previously have called for immediate action.[55]

The judges were left in the difficult position of attempting to implement their mandate to end segregation where it was proven to exist, on the one hand, while seeking to deal with local tensions and hostility on the other. Several specific issues were recurring problems. They included the debate over the application of the *Brown* rulings, the argument over desegregation versus integration, the effort to understand the distinction between *de jure* and *de facto* segregation, the ambiguity of the role of racial balance, the proper function of the neighborhood schools concept, and the issues of busing, white flight, and metropolitan remedies.

The Debate Over the Scope of Brown

The members of the Supreme Court were extremely concerned about the impact of the remedial opinion, *Brown II,* issued in 1955. Justice Black and other southern justices had warned of the tremendous difficulties that would be encountered in the effort to achieve what they all acknowledged was an essential goal.[56] Therefore, the Court spoke in positive but open textured language, leaving considerable room for accommodation to what the Court would later term "the practicalities."[57] Of course, the price of flexibility in the announcement of a policy is ambiguity and uncertainty in the implementation process. Indeed some members of the Court later regretted such vague constructions as "all deliberate speed."

During discussions of the *Brown II* opinion, the justices changed the wording of their concluding instructions to the district courts. The Court instructed the lower courts to provide necessary orders to "the parties to these cases." An earlier draft contained much broader language.[58] The interpretation given to the narrower construction was that *Brown* applied only to the specific parties to the five suits consolidated under that particular opinion. Many southern districts immediately adopted the position that their affirmative obligation to dismantle their dual system would not begin until they were found in violation of the equal protection clause. Northern districts argued that, since they were not operating statutorily mandated dual systems at the time of *Brown,* they were not covered by the decision.

The 1964 Civil Rights Act facilitated enforcement suits by private citizens and DOJ, but the delays between *Brown* and the legislation made the litigation difficult. It was argued that, precisely because so much time had elapsed, courts should move cautiously. Indeed, in two cases decided by the Supreme Court in 1979, the lower courts had determined that the districts had been segregated in 1954 and had not been desegregated. The majority accepted that as evidence of intentional discrimination but dissenters argued that the situation was so different than it had been at the time of *Brown* that the Court should not use that history as proof against the local governments.[59]

The Court found it necessary to argue at length in the Little Rock, Arkansas case that the substantive holding of *Brown* applied to all school officials, but by then the pattern of delay pending specific court rulings was established.[60]

Desegregation Versus Integration

Another issue that developed rapidly in the wake of *Brown II* was the argument by many that *Brown* required school districts to end forced segregation of minority students but did not mandate that existing schools be integrated by the assignment of white and minority students to the same schools. The effect of such an interpretation, of course, would be to freeze in place the existing segregated system of education.

The rejection of integration came almost immediately on the heels of the *Brown II* ruling. Judge Parker, writing for a three judge district court in one of the cases remanded in *Brown* for remedial action, explained what the Supreme Court had said and what it had not required.

> It has not decided that the federal courts are to take over or regulate the public schools of the states. It has not decided that the states must mix persons of different races in the schools or must require them to attend schools or must deprive them of the right of choosing the schools they attend. What it has decided, and all that it has decided, is that a state may not deny to any person on account of race the right to attend any school that it maintains. . . . The Constitution, in other words, does not require integration. It merely forbids [segregation].[61]

The notion that *Brown II* had required only a narrow remedy spread rapidly in the North as well as the South.[62] It endured until 1966 when the Fifth Circuit Court of Appeals rejected the idea in a comprehensive decision which, like the Supreme Court's later opinion in *Swann,* sought to clarify school desegregation law.[63] The Supreme Court's decisions from *Green* to *Swann* ended the debate nationally, rejecting the desegregation/integration dichotomy. Chief Justice Burger almost resurrected the debate in early drafts of *Swann.* In his March 4 draft, Burger had indicated, "The Constitution, of course, does not command integration; it forbids segregation." Justice Brennan responded, "That statement in almost *haec verba* was the rallying cry of the massive resistance movement in Virginia, and of die-hard segregationists for years after *Brown.* It calls to mind Judge Parker's opinion which caused so much trouble for so long a time. To revive it again would I think only rekindle vain hopes." The passage was removed.

The desegregation versus integration argument also influenced disputes over the use of the concept of racial balance. Opponents of integration argued that the real purpose behind many district court orders was not to remedy segregation but to achieve the judges' preferences as social engineers for racial balance. A similar attack was unsuccessfully launched against HEW regulations enforcing Title VI of the 1964 Civil Rights Act. Southern states contended that since the Constitution did not require integration, the federal government could not mandate administratively what it could not require by judicial decree.[64]

Lower courts were split on just how statistical measures of disparities between minority population figures in the community and racial patterns in schools, generally termed racial balance, ought to be used. The Supreme Court eventually indicated that while no particular degree of racial balance may be required as a matter of constitutional right, district judges may use statistical measures in two ways. First, dramatic disparities may be part of a pattern of evidence used to determine the existence of discrimination requiring a judicial remedy. For many lower courts, that type of evidence was often presented in school litigation and was frequently quite extreme with seventy-five percent or more of a district's children attending single-race schools.[65] The second permissible use of such data is as a starting point for the development of desegregation plans. Those are both still very open textured policies, with a range of interpretations in the district and circuit courts around the nation. Ironically, the requirement by the Supreme Court that district judges limit their remedial orders to the elimination of the incremental segregative effect of past government practices pressures the lower courts to try to parse the statistical issues in more, rather than less, detail. How else can they determine how much of the existing segregation is due to intentional government action and how much is accidental?

De Facto Versus De Jure Segregation

The language of intentional versus accidental racial isolation is at the heart of another key issue, the distinction between *de jure* and *de facto* segregation and how the courts should respond to both. District judges began to see school desegregation cases emerging in districts in which there had been no law mandating segregation for years, long before the Supreme Court had provided guidance on what to do with such cases. There was considerable disagreement regarding how to determine whether a district with racially identifiable schools was really entitled to federal judicial action. As one judge put the problem:

> As every student of the Constitution knows, the intense debate over racial segregation in the schools has clustered around two seminal concepts: *de jure* and *de facto* segregation. The first of these, as already indicated, adverts to segregation specifically mandated by law or by public policy pursued under color of law; this is the segregation unequivocally denounced by *Bolling* and *Brown*. School segregation is *de facto* when it results from the action of pupil assignment policies not based on race but upon social or other conditions for which government cannot be held responsible; whether segregation so occasioned does fall within *Brown's* proscription the Supreme Court has not yet [as of 1967] considered or decided.[66]

Some judges assumed that a showing that schools were segregated and that government actions had brought about that pattern or failed to dismantle existing segregation was adequate to trigger a remedial order.[67] Others concluded that in order to be considered *de jure*, the government action had to have been intentional. Most acknowledged, though, that the government's intent need not be proven directly, but could be inferred from its policies or its failure to act in the face of existing racial segregation. Many contended that "[a] standard requiring plaintiffs in a school desegregation case to adduce *direct* proof of a 'racial motive' on the part of the multiperson school board would border on the impossible."[68]

In *Wright v. Emporia*, the Supreme Court had argued that the proper focus was "upon the effect—not the purpose or motivation—of a school board's action."[69] A year later, the Court in *dicta* in its *Keyes* opinion concerning Denver schools, stressed that *de jure* segregation was intentional segregation. It did not require direct proof of intent, but supported the use of indirect evidence, such as the existing patterns of pupil assignment, historic policy decisions within a district, evidence of school construction or school closing decisions affecting racial patterns, and the like, to demonstrate intent. A number of the justices had been prepared to use the opportunity of the *Keyes* ruling to eliminate the *de jure/de facto* distinction. Indeed Justices Powell and Douglas wrote separate opinions arguing that the Court should have done just that. In later rulings, however, the Court called for more specific evidence of intentional discrimination, suggesting that the distinction was to be maintained and that only clearly demonstrated *de jure* segregation was to be afforded judicial response. In the wake of these varying interpretations, district courts have faced considerable uncertainty as to just how much of which types of evidence are adequate to demonstrate *de jure,* and therefore illegal, segregation.

Finally, in addition to all their other complexities, the district courts faced significant pressure where their remedial orders required busing to remedy proven cases of *de jure* segregation, even after—one might add particularly after—the Supreme Court supported the use of the busing remedy in *Swann.* The busing issue arose in a package with two related matters, the inability to employ metropolitan areawide remedies for segregated city schools in most cases and the debate over the relationship between busing and white flight from the city to the suburbs. After the Supreme Court's 1974 ruling in *Milliken v. Bradley,* it was unlikely that many plaintiffs would be able to provide the kind of evidence necessary to justify the use of suburban school districts to remedy segregation in the city. That led some to argue that district courts ought to limit the extent of their intracity remedies because to do otherwise would increase white flight to the suburbs. Busing became the symbol of complex city desegregation remedies and engendered immediate claims that of all tools to eliminate segregation, busing was the most likely to promote white flight. Probably nowhere was the conflict over the use of such remedies more rending than in Boston. Judge Garrity put the matter as follows:

> Toward lessening widespread misunderstanding on the point, it may be stated that the court does not favor forced busing. . . . If there were a way to accomplish desegregation in Boston without transporting students to schools beyond walking distance, the court and all parties would much prefer that alternative. . . . Boston is simply not a city that can provide its black school-children with a desegregated education absent considerable mandatory transportation. No party familiar with the requirements of the law and with the city has ever suggested otherwise.[70]

It has never been explained to district courts exactly how they would carry out the requirements of the Supreme Court's interpretation of the equal protection clause if they were not permitted to order reassignment and transportation of students for desegregation. The adversaries in the debate over the impact of busing on white flight never reached consensus. On the one hand, some, like Professor James S. Coleman, performed research they claimed demonstrated an increase in white flight resulting from the desegregation orders, whereas others found such studies flawed. The latter concluded that white flight to the suburbs had been going on since World War II for a variety of reasons and that the advent of desegregation orders did not seem to add significantly to the already high rate of out-migration.[71]

In sum, the legal issues and their evidentiary and remedial complexities made the task of any district judge, regardless of his or her political persuasion, extremely difficult. But to that mélange of hard choices was added the pressures of an extremely difficult political environment.

THE POLITICAL CONTEXT OF SCHOOL DESEGREGATION

The continuing fact of life for federal district judges in desegregation cases is that in order to effectively carry out their obligations they must deal with other policymakers at all levels of government on a more or less continuous basis. Where the political incentives are such that conflict with the courts pays at election time, as in school desegregation cases, the effort to establish and maintain effective working relationships is all the more difficult. In order to comprehend the environment within which such judges operate, it is important to consider issues of federalism, the relationship of the president to the judicial desegregation effort, the role of Congress, and the fiscal constraints on decisionmaking.

The States and Desegregation

It was clear to the justices of the Supreme Court at the time of the *Brown* decision that they could count on dramatic resistance from state and local governments to any desegregation orders issued by lower courts. Bernard Schwartz recounts an exchange between Chief Justice Earl Warren and S. Emory Rogers, attorney for the southern defendants, during the reargument on the remedy portion of *Brown:*

> [WARREN] "Is there any basis upon which we can assume that there will be an immediate attempt to comply with the decree of this Court, whatever it may be?"
>
> Rogers replied that the question of compliance should be left to the lower court. Warren insisted on the question of compliance, "But you are not willing to say here that there would be an honest attempt to conform to this decree, if we did leave it to the district court?"
>
> "No, I am not," answered Rogers. And, raising his forefinger toward the bench, he declared, "Let us get the word 'honest' out of there."
>
> "No," countered the Chief, by now quite flushed, "leave it in."
>
> The Southerner was not repressed, "No," he came back, "because I would have to tell you that right now we would not conform—we would not send our white children to the Negro schools." [72]

Perhaps even more than the Supreme Court justices, district court judges had a good idea of what they would likely face. District judges after all must live in the district where they sit, and not in Washington, D.C. They are by and large appointed by senatorial courtesy, which is often accorded to those who have served state political organizations well and faithfully. They are generally local people who are extremely sensitive to the issues of importance to their neighbors. They would not have long to wait for what they anticipated would come.

Soon after the *Brown II* ruling, several states passed interposition laws that attempted to nullify the Supreme Court's decision, adopted rigid pupil assignment laws, and, in the case of Arkansas, enacted a state constitutional amendment that mandated opposition by state officials to desegregation. Moreover, there was every reason to believe that there would be political rewards for those urging federalism as a bar to federal court desegregation orders and political costs for those who cooperated with district court remedial efforts.

The northern cases came later. Some northerners who were only too happy to see the South facing desegregation orders responded very differently when attention was turned to the northern states where discrimination was widely practiced, though not publicly proclaimed. The greatest populations of blacks in the North were found in the larger cities. The suburbanization movement was already well under way by the time the major northern desegregation cases came to court and many of the metropolitan problems discussed earlier had already begun to surface. The timing was also important because most of the northern suits came after the Supreme Court's reapportionment rulings of the early 1960s had made the suburbs important political actors in the state legislatures. Within the cities, many of the whites most directly affected by desegregation programs were working class or lower middle class families who were likely to resist the changes and could not as easily escape to the suburbs. During the 1970s these forces moved in state legislatures or by voter initiative to enact bans on busing and other desegregation tactics.

THE PRESIDENTIAL RESPONSE

There has been considerable speculation ever since the 1950s concerning whether the actions (or the lack of them) of the Eisenhower and Kennedy administrations allowed the states to mount an effective opposition to the federal courts. With the exception of the response to the Little Rock Central High School incident, President Eisenhower did little to support the *Brown* rulings. Even the Kennedy administration was not willing in its early months to actively support the civil rights movement. By 1963 the administration was advocating new civil rights legislation, initiatives pressed by Johnson following Kennedy's assassination. As of the mid-1960s, however, resistance was well entrenched. Johnson pushed for enforcement, but he was heavily occupied with other matters, most notably Vietnam.

President Nixon used his "southern strategy" to help win and hold the White House. The need to maintain southern support, his campaign against Warren Court activism, and his resistance to busing prompted directions to HEW and DOJ to moderate enforcement efforts. At the same time, Nixon pursued antibusing legislation and made judicial appointments calculated to reduce what he perceived to be excessive intrusions by the federal courts into state and local matters. Enforcement efforts have fluctuated since 1974 with Reagan Justice Department policymakers under continuous fire for their enforcement policies.

Congress and the Courts

From the perspective of a district judge attempting to implement the *Brown* mandate, the Congress has been a mixed political bag. Southern legislators generally joined the opposition. Approximately one hundred signed the Southern Manifesto challenging the legitimacy of the *Brown* decision and vowed to fight for its reversal.[73] The role of southern legislators became particularly important since, under the seniority system, a number of the opponents to *Brown* were in key committee chair and leadership positions. Later generations of southern legislators have been more supportive of civil rights than their predecessors.

Northern congressmen and senators were split. Many recoiled at the flagrant violations of the Constitution, the evasion of the Supreme Court's decisions, and the violence directed against blacks and white civil rights workers. They joined Presidents Kennedy and Johnson in supporting enactment of the Civil Rights Act of 1964, the Voting Rights Act of 1965, and the Fair Housing Act of 1968. On the other hand, the legislation, particularly the 1964 Act, encountered stiff opposition, some from northern legislators. And by the early 1970s, northern representatives were feeling the effects of desegregation cases in their own constituencies. Several responded with efforts to limit judicial remedial action, particularly school busing.[74]

Congress did add language to Section 407 of the 1964 Act that limited orders "requiring the transportation of pupils or students from one school to another or one school district to another in order to achieve racial balance, or otherwise enlarge the existing power of the courts to insure compliance with constitutional standards." The Supreme Court in *Swann* interpreted that language to mean the Congress intended to preclude busing for balance in *de facto* segregation cases, but did not intend to interfere with remedies for *de jure* segregation.[75] The legislature incorporated similar language in the Elementary and Secondary Education Act of 1965 and later appropriation bills and the courts have interpreted it in the same manner as *Swann*.[76] By limiting its action to date to busing for "balance" and not to the effort to desegregate *de jure* segregated districts, the Congress and the federal courts have avoided a head-on confrontation. Antibusing constitutional amendments have been introduced from time to time, but none has cleared the legislature.

The Financial Problem

The politics of school finance have been extremely important constraints on judges who are faced with desegregation rulings. The division of city and suburb, the declining tax base in many central cities, the concentration of the poor and unemployed in the city center, the use of the property tax as the principal vehicle for funding primary and secondary education, and the urban, rural, and suburban splits within state legislatures have all contributed to the difficulty. The availability of federal funding, particularly after 1965, provided an important tool to coerce, but also to assist compliance with the desegregation requirement. As the amount of federal assistance grew and Congress added greater enforcement authority for HEW, the funding tool became even more important.[77] In the final analysis, however, the federal government rarely actually cut off funding.

Despite the availability of federal assistance, though, district judges have often been called upon to enforce desegregation orders in communities facing severe financial stress. There is a certain irony in the fact that many northern cases emerged in the 1970s during a period of dramatic economic downturn just as the South was beginning what we now call Sun-Belt development.

In sum, financial issues have provided both leverage and limitations for federal district judges in their attempt to resolve school cases.

CONCLUSION

This chapter has provided a brief and broad overview of the history, issues, and political environment within which school desegregation litigation has developed. The fact that race and children have been at the center of the school desegregation controversy has made it a particularly volatile and difficult policy space for judges called upon to decide cases and fashion remedies where appropriate.

Despite the Supreme Court's effort (indeed perhaps partly because of those efforts) to be sensitive to the political and social tensions at the heart of desegregation, there were dramatic opposition and attempts at evasion. District court judges faced those efforts directly. The Supreme Court avoided for nearly a decade any detailed involvement in the process. Just as the Court waded into the fray, the conflict shifted as northern desegregation cases increased presenting new issues concerning how to deal with *de facto* versus *de jure* segregation and what the differences really were between them.

District courts grappled with the conflict, the ambiguity, and the complexity of the many cases arising around the country, and they continue to do so at the time of this writing. As they have attempted to make the hard choices presented in these cases, they have been both empowered and constrained by the changing political and fiscal environment within which schools cases arise. The only effective way to comprehend just how these various forces interact is to view a major piece of school desegregation litigation in depth. Chapter 5 provides an analysis of the *Milliken v. Bradley* cases concerning Detroit, one of the more complex and important of desegregation cases presented to a federal judge.

NOTES

1. *Sarah C. Roberts v. City of Boston,* 5 Cush. 198, 59 MA 198 (1850).

2. Leonard W. Levy, *The Law of the Commonwealth and Chief Justice Shaw* (Chicago: Univ. of Chicago Press, 1957), p. 110.

3. *Plessy v. Ferguson,* 163 U.S. 537 (1896). The language we now interpret as the "separate but equal" doctrine was presented in *Plessy* as "equal but separate." *See* Stephen L. Wasby, Anthony A. D'Amato, and Rosemary Metrailer, *Desegregation from Brown to Alexander,* (Carbondale: Southern Illinois Univ. Press, 1977), p. 28.

4. *See generally* Henry J. Abraham, *Freedom and the Court,* 3rd ed. (New York: Oxford Univ. Press, 1977), pp. 358–60.

5. *Plessy, supra* note 3, at 551.

6. *Id.,* at 562 (Harlan, J., dissenting).

7. *Gong Lum v. Rice,* 275 U.S. 78 (1927). *See also Cumming v. Bd. of Ed. of Richmond,* 175 U.S. 528 (1899); and *Berea College v. Ky.,* 211 U.S. 45 (1908).

8. Richard Kluger, *Simple Justice* (New York: Knopf, 1976). *See also* Loren Miller, *The Petitioners* (New York: Pantheon, 1966).

9. Wasby et al., *supra* note 3, at 26–50.

10. *Mo. ex rel. Gaines v. Canada,* 305 U.S. 337 (1938).

11. *Sweatt v. Painter,* 339 U.S. 629, 633–34 (1950).

12. *McLaurin v. Okla.,* 339 U.S. 637, 641 (1950). *See also Sipuel v. Okla.,* 332 U.S. 631 (1948).

13. Bernard Schwartz, *Super Chief* (New York: New York Univ. Press, 1983), p. 72.

14. *Brown v. Bd. of Ed. of Topeka, Kan.* 347 U.S. 483, 493 (1954). [Hereafter *Brown I*].

15. *Id.,* at 495.

16. *Brown v. Bd. of Ed.,* 349 U.S. 294, 299 (1955) [hereafter *Brown II*].

17. *Id.,* at 300.

18. *Id.,* at 301.

19. *Griffin v. School Bd. of Prince Edward County,* 377 U.S. 218, 229 (1964).

20. *See generally* Jack W. Peltason, *Fifty-eight Lonely Men* (Urbana: Univ. of Illinois, Press 1971); and Jack Bass, *Unlikely Heroes* (New York: Simon and Schuster, 1981). *See also* Charles S. Bullock III and Charles M. Lamb, eds., *Implementation of Civil Rights Policy* (Monterey, CA: Brooks/Cole, 1984); Harrell R. Rodgers, Jr., and Charles S. Bullock III, *Coercion to Compliance* (Lexington, MA: Lexington, 1976); and U.S. Commission on Civil Rights, *Twenty Years After Brown* (Wash., DC: Government Printing Office, 1979).

21. *Cooper v. Aaron,* 358 U.S. 1 (1958). Actually the full opinion came after the announcement of a *per curiam* opinion affirming the court of appeals ruling. For a complete discussion of the development of the case, *see* Schwartz, *supra* note 13, at 289–303.

22. *Cooper v. Aaron,* at 18–19.

23. *Id.,* at 16–17.

24. *Griffin, supera* note 19, at 218.

25. *Id.,* at 234.

26. *United States v. Jefferson County Bd. of Ed.,* 372 F.2d 836, 851, and 851 n. 5 (5th Cir. 1966), *aff'd en banc* 380 F.2d 385 (5th Cir. 1967), *cert. denied* 389 U.S. 840 (1967).

27. *Id.,* at 859.

28. *Green v. County School Bd. of New Kent County, Va.,* 391 U.S. 430 (1968); *Raney v. Bd. of Ed.,* 391 U.S. 443 (1968); and *Monroe v. Bd. of Commissioners,* 391 U.S. 450 (1968).

29. *Green v. County School Bd.* at 437–38.

30. *Id.,* at 439.

31. *Id.*

32. *Id.*

33. *Alexander v. Holmes County Bd. of Ed.,* 396 U.S. 19, 20 (1969). *See also Carter v. W. Feliciano Parish School Bd.,* 396 U.S. 290 (1970).

34. *Alexander.*

35. *Swann v. Charlotte-Mecklenburg Bd. of Ed.,* 402 U.S. 1 (1971). *See also N.C. State Bd. of Ed. v. Swann,* 402 U.S. 43 (1971); *McDaniel v. Barresi,* 402 U.S. 39 (1971); *Davis v. Bd. of School Comm's of Mobile County,* 402 U.S. 33 (1971); and *Moore v. Charlotte-Mecklenburg Bd. of Ed.,* 402 U.S. 47 (1971).

36. *Swann,* at 18.

37. *Id.,* at 15.

38. *Id.,* at 30.

39. *Id.,* at 24.

40. *Id.,* at 30–31.

41. *Id.,* at 16.

42. *Id.,* at 28.

43. *Wright v. Council of the City of Emporia,* 407 U.S. 451 (1972).

44. *Id.,* at 477–78.

45. *San Antonio Indep. School Dist. v. Rodriquez,* 411 U.S. 1 (1973).

46. *Id.,* at 35.

47. *Keyes v. School Dist. No. 1, Denver,* 413 U.S. 189 (1973).

48. *Washington v. Davis*, 426 U.S. 229 (1976). *See also Village of Arlington Heights v. Metro. Hous. Dev. Corp.*, 429 U.S. 252 (1977).

49. *Personnel Adm'r. v. Feeney*, 442 U.S. 256 (1979). *See also Memphis v. Green*, 451 U.S. 100 (1981).

50. *Dayton Bd. of Ed v. Brinkman*, 433 U.S. 406, 420 (1977).

51. *Milliken v. Bradley*, 418 U.S. 717 (1974).

52. *See e.g., Green v. County School Bd.* and *Raney v. Bd. of Ed., supra* note 28.

53. *Pasadena Bd. of Ed. v. Spangler*, 427 U.S. 424, 436–37 (1976).

54. *See, e.g., Columbus Bd. of Ed. v. Penick*, 443 U.S. 449 (1979); and *Dayton Bd. of Ed. v. Brinkman*, 443 U.S. 526 (1979).

55. *See Alexander v. Holmes County Bd. of Ed., supra* note 33.

56. Schwartz, *supra* note 13, at ch. 3.

57. *Davis v. Bd. of School Comm's of Mobile County*, 402 U.S. 33, 37 (1971).

58. Schwartz, *supra* note 13, at 120.

59. *Columbus Bd. of Ed. v. Penick*, 443 U.S. 449, 492–94 (1979) (Rehnquist, J., dissenting).

60. *Cooper v. Aaron, supra* note 21.

61. *Briggs v. Elliott*, 132 F. Supp. 776, 777 (EDSC 1955), cited in *United States v. Jefferson County Bd. of Ed.*, 372 F.2d 836, 862 (5th Cir. 1966).

62. *See, e.g., Bell v. School City of Gary, Ind.*, 324 F.2d 209, 212–13 (7th Cir. 1963); *Downs v. Bd. of Ed. of Kansas City*, 336 F.2d 988, 998 (10th Cir. 1964); and *Deal v. Cincinnati Bd. of Ed.*, 369 F.2d 55, 62 (6th Cir. 1966). *See also* cases cited *Blocker v. Bd. of Ed. of Manhasset, N.Y.*, 226 F. Supp. 208, 220 n. 11 (EDNY 1964); and *United States v. Jefferson County Bd. of Ed., supra* note 61, at 862 n. 57.

63. *See United States v. Jefferson County Bd. of Ed., supra* note 61.

64. *Id.*

65. *Id.*, at 903–05.

66. *Hobson v. Hansen*, 269 F.Supp. 401, 493 (DCDC 1967).

67. *Cisneros v. Corpus Christi Indep. School Dist.*, 467 F.2d 142, 148 (5th Cir. 1972). *See also Soria v. Oxnard School Dist. Bd. of Trustees*, 328 F. Supp. 155, 157 (CDCA 1971).

68. *Penick v. Columbus Bd. of Ed.*, 429 F. Supp. 229, 255 (SDOH 1977). *See generally, Johnson v. San Francisco Unified School Dist.*, 339 F. Supp. 1315 (NDCA 1971); *Oliver v. Kalamazoo Bd. of Ed.*, 368 F. Supp. 143 (WDMI 1973); and *Hart v. Community School Bd. of Brooklyn, NY, School Dist. No. 21*, 383 F. Supp. 699 (EDNY 1974).

69. *Wright v. Emporia, supra* note 43, at 461–62.

70. *Morgan v. Kerrigan*, 401 F. Supp. 216, 239 (DMA 1975). For an interesting alternative perspective on the Boston case, *see* J. Anthony Lukas, *Common Ground* (New York: Knopf, 1985).

71. See U.S. Commission on Civil Rights, *School Desegregation: The Courts and Suburban Migration* (Wash., DC: U.S. Commission on Civil Rights, 1975); and *id., Reviewing a Decade of School Desegregation 1966–1975* (Wash., DC: U.S. Commission on Civil Rights, 1977), p. 6.

72. Schwartz, *supra* note 13, at 124.

73. Wasby et al., *supra* note 3, at 167.

74. James Bolner and Robert Shanley, *Busing: The Political and Judicial Process* (New York: Praeger, 1974).

75. Robert McKay, "Court, Congress, and School Desegregation," in *School Desegregation, supra* note 71, at 67.

76. *See, e.g.,* Bullock and Lamb, *supra* note 20, at 67.

77. *Id.*, at 81.

5

Milliken v. Bradley: The Detroit Busing Case

Detroit has always been a dynamic city. Its problems of growth, development, and decline have been highly volatile and often, for good or ill, quite visible. By 1960 Detroit had been made aware that its schools were segregated, not by any statute mandating it, but as a result of a variety of government practices. A strong but difficult reform effort during the sixties led to a complex social and political confrontation that would spawn the *Bradley v. Milliken* litigation and, in the process, dramatically alter school board politics.[1]

The *Milliken* case would reach the U.S. Supreme Court twice. Its importance stems not merely from the fact that it presented complicated questions of how to remedy segregated schools in the northern states, but also from its strategic significance as a turning point in the development of Supreme Court guidance on school desegregation. Before *Milliken,* the Court provided generally consistent support for remedies as broad and potent as necessary to ensure that desegregation was, in fact, implemented. Beginning with the *Milliken* ruling, though, the Court served notice on district judges that they should exercise greater restraint when they interfered with the normal operations of school districts. Apart from these distinctive characteristics, the Detroit case presents a variety of issues that have been typical of school desegregation litigation.

THE TRIGGER PHASE

The city's population grew significantly in the early twentieth century as its industrial base developed, doubling its population each decade until about 1940. By 1950 the population began to drop off precipitously as suburbs grew.[2] Like many northern cities, different groups came to Detroit in waves, with substantial numbers of blacks arriving between 1920 and 1940.[3] The city experienced one of the early major outbreaks of racial violence in 1943 in which thirty-four were killed and over a thousand injured.[4] Tensions were not eased as the housing market expanded since, ''[of] 87,000 new housing units built between 1940 and 1950, only 2% were available to Negroes.''[5]

Between 1950 and 1970, Detroit, like so many other cities, felt the impact of the shift to the suburbs. ''In 1950, the city population constituted 61% of the total population of the standard metropolitan statistical area and in 1970 it was but 36% of the metropolitan population.''[6] As the out-migration continued, the age of the remaining

Caucasion population increased beyond childbearing years, whereas minorities in the younger age range increased as a percentage of the total city population. As a result, black children made up 45.8% of the 1961–62 school population in Detroit and 63.8% in 1970–71.[7]

Within the city during the late 1950s and into the 1960s, minority citizens were insisting upon their rightful place in the community. A series of human relations and education groups became increasingly active and were joined by city-appointed study commissions.[8] In 1959, the Citizens Advisory Committee on School Needs (known as the Romney Committee) reported, "Numerous public schools in Detroit are presently segregated by race. The allegation that purposeful devices have at times been used to perpetuate segregation in some schools in clearly warranted."[9] The next year the Citizens Association for Better Schools charged that city education officials were pursuing a "policy of containment of minority groups within specified boundaries."[10]

Several practices during the 1950s prompted such criticism. First, faculty assignments were made by race for most of the decade.[11] Second, optional attendance zones allowed white children in neighborhoods undergoing racial transition "to escape"[12] and school feeder patterns were changed in such a way as to maintain the segregation of the schools as residential patterns shifted.[13] Third, the designation of a new administrative subdivision, known as the Center District, as part of an experimental regionalization of the schools created an overwhelmingly minority inner city district and was seen as an effort to cordon off the central city area. The Center District matter created a strong and immediate outcry from black parents, many of whom had recently moved to the area and had supported the 1959 tax millage increase campaign to underwrite improvements in city schools.[14] Finally, where black children were bused because of school overcrowding, they were in several instances transported past white facilities with available space to other predominantly minority schools.[15]

The need to redress these problems led in the 1960s to tension between the desire to desegregate, on the one hand, and the growing insistence upon community control of schools, a major factor in the urban community power movement.[16] The 1964 elections resulted in changes on the Detroit Board of Education, producing a liberal majority headed by A. L. Zwerdling, a man committed to school integration.[17] School Superintendent Samuel Brownell was replaced by Norman Drachler who, like Zwerdling,was determined to desegregate.[18] Drachler, with Zwerdling's support, moved aggressively to increase minority hiring of both teachers and administrators. He required firms doing business with the district to give evidence of minority hiring efforts.[19] Changes were also instituted in student transfer policies. Any students wishing to use the voluntary transfer option available in the city were obligated to show that the transfer would aid desegregation. Where students were transferred because of school overcrowding, reassignments were to be made in a manner that would support integration.

The competing force to the measures adopted by the central school administration, however, was the move to decentralize the school district to permit community control of this important government function. A part of the civil rights conflict of the period concerned the suspicion in the minority community that large centralized political and administrative institutions were neither sensitive nor responsive to minority community wishes.[20] In Detroit, a number of local political leaders, like the Reverend Albert Cleage, Jr., organized to force decentralization. Among other things, Cleage's support aided Andrew Perdue in his election to the school board in 1968 on a community control platform. In the spring of 1969 the NAACP formally requested decentralization legislation which was sponsored in the state legislature by then Senator Coleman Young.[21] Enacted as Act 244, the statute did decentralize the system, but it did not draw the subunit boundaries.[22] When the details of how to decentralize were considered, it became clear that a number of black community control advocates wanted regions drawn on neighborhood lines to maximize minority voting strength.

Zwerdling, determined that decentralization would not interfere with desegregation,[23] worked with Drachler to produce a plan that decentralized, but also integrated. The plan, and the controversy surrounding it, were to trigger the *Bradley v. Milliken* case. The compromise plan captured the pivotal vote of Andrew Perdue (necessary because Remus Robinson, one of Zwerdling's supporters on the Board, was hospitalized at the time of the vote) and was adopted. The plan called for modification of the feeder patterns of about half of the city's twenty-two high schools. Perhaps more significant was the fact that it would have meant two-way integration, albeit on a relatively small scale, that would have resulted in integration of the existing white schools.[24] The agreement in principle among Board members was reached at a closed dinner session in the week before the formal meeting of the Board scheduled for April 7. Later in the week, when copies of the plan were provided to Board members, a Zwerdling opponent who had resisted the integration plan made the proposal available to reporters who, in turn, gave it wide publicity in the weekend papers.[25] Notwithstanding angry demonstrations, primarily involving white residents, the Board met and approved the proposal, which came to be known as the April 7 Plan.

Almost immediately, the nature of the political controversy over School Board policy shifted. Prior to that point, the conflict had been between advocates within the liberal group of community control and those committed to desegregation. From this point forward, the controversy was about school integration that pitted, for the most part, conservative white residents against minority spokespersons. The Concerned Citizens for Better Education (CCBE) was formed to oppose the April 7 Plan and the Board members who supported it. Patrick McDonald, the Board member who had released the plan to the press, mentioned the possibility of a recall election in a speech to protesters and the CCBE took the idea as a rallying point.[26] The formal recall effort began on May 4.

Legislation was introduced on April 8 to eliminate decentralization, curb the powers of the School Board, and block mandatory integration policies. Senator Coleman Young moved to minimize the damage, attempting to save decentralization and some School Board independence.[27] Governor Milliken notified legislators involved in the controversy that he would sign no legislation unless there was unified Detroit delegation support. Young did not fight language that would block desegregation on grounds that it would be eliminated in any court challenge, an argument accepted by other minority and liberal legislators.[28] A second mechanism of compromise in the legislation was agreement that the regions would be drawn by a commission to be appointed by the governor.[29] Finally, assurances, later disputed, were provided that the recall effort would be abandoned.[30] Act 48 passed nearly unanimously and was signed by Governor Milliken on July 7.

The most important provision of the legislation was Section 12, which concerned pupil assignment changes in "first class school districts."[31] Detroit was the only such district in the state. The legislation had essentially three consequences. It maintained a regionally decentralized Board of Education to be elected later in the year. The April 7 Plan was delayed pending the election of the new Board. The "free choice" and neighborhood school provisions of Act 48 repealed the two major pupil transfer policy reforms concerning voluntary transfers or reassignments to remedy overcrowding.[32]

The passage of Act 48 virtually guaranteed an NAACP suit, but the exact form and scope of the litigation was uncertain.[33] The expected abandonment of the recall drive did not materialize. In fact, on August 4, 1970, Zwerdling and the three other Board members who voted in favor of the April 7 Plan were removed from office by a substantial margin in an election clearly characterized by bloc voting. It was the first such recall in the history of the Detroit Board of Education.[34] On the same day the boundary commission announced its plan that created essentially four black controlled regions and four regions with clear white majorities. The NAACP filed suit in federal court for the Eastern District of Michigan on August 18 on behalf of a number of individual minority students in the city schools against Governor Milliken, Attorney General Kelley, the Superintendent of Public Instruction, the State Board of Education, the Detroit Board of Education, and the remaining members of the Detroit Board.

THE LIABILITY PHASE

The suit sparked a complex set of pretrial activities that resulted in a finding, six months before the full case was tried on the merits, that Act 48 was unconstitutional. Judge Stephen Roth, to whom the suit was assigned and who initially took a dim view of the plaintiff's case, would undergo a surprising change in his approach to desegregation litigation by the time the liability portion of the case ended. Moreover, the attorney for Denise Magdowski, et al., who intervened for the CCBE on behalf of parents of white Detroit school children, would formally call for a metropolitan desegregation plan involving all eighty-five suburban districts in the tri-county Detroit metropolitan area.

The assignment of the case to Judge Roth presented difficulties for the plaintiffs. Although he was a Democrat appointed by President Kennedy, Roth was by all accounts a man of redoubtable conservative credentials. During the first day of hearings, he responded to the NAACP attorneys' request for quick action by noting that they could not "expect push-button relief here. . . . I am not going to move hastily."[35] In the months prior to trial, Roth made clear his objection to "forced" integration plans and "outsider" groups who pressed demands for such remedies.[36]

After three days of hearings, Roth rejected NAACP requests for a preliminary injunction that would have required implementation of the April 7 Plan for the 1970–71 school year.[37] He dismissed the state officials as defendants and scheduled the remaining case against the Detroit Board for trial on November 2. Denise Magdowski, representing CCBE, was permitted to intervene as a defendant.

The plaintiffs immediately appealed Roth's denial of a preliminary injunction to the Sixth Circuit. Chief Judge Phillips heard arguments in Nashville on September 8, the day Detroit schools opened for the fall term, but refused to issue an injunction, pending consideration by the full Sixth Circuit panel. That panel heard arguments in less than a month and, recognizing the need for dispatch in the case, announced its ruling on October 13. The appeals court upheld Roth's refusal to grant the injunction.[38] However, it reversed Roth's dismissal of the state officials as defendants and held Act 48 unconstitutional on equal protection grounds because it interfered with Detroit voluntary desegregation efforts.[39]

The NAACP returned to Roth seeking an order mandating implementation of the April 7 Plan for the second semester of the 1970–71 school year on the basis of the Sixth Circuit rejection of Act 48. The judge called instead for the district to submit a proposal based on the April 7 Plan for consideration.

In the meantime, the new School Board was elected. Minority candidates did not do well either on the central board or the regional boards even in regions with a black voting majority.[40] Moreover, the Board became considerably more conservative, select- ing Patrick McDonald as its Chair. The interim Board members submitted three plans to Roth on November 16; the McDonald-Magnet School Plan, the Magnet-Curriculum Plan, and the April 7 Plan. While the April 7 Plan was a mandatory integration pro- gram, the other two were variations on freedom-of-choice programs with magnet schools to provide incentives for integration.

On December 3 Roth ordered implementation of the McDonald-Magnet Plan, in- volving magnet high schools and middle schools, but not until the fall of 1971. He wrote:

> Comparing the McDonald and April Plans, it appears to us that the April Plan's principal aim is to improve integration by the "numbers," as several witnesses de- scribed it. Whether in the long run it will do even that is a serious question. It is a plan which does not take into account the basics which we have heretofore men- tioned and it does not offer incentives to or provide motivation for the student him- self. Instead of offering a change of diet, it offers forced-feeding.[41]

In addition, Roth delayed the trial date.

Again the NAACP went to the Sixth Circuit. Responding on February 22, 1971, the appeals court remanded the case for a hearing on the merits "forthwith."[42] The opinion criticized Roth for having previously promised to deal with the case quickly only to delay the trial on the merits. The panel also rejected his remedy order for the McDonald Plan on the grounds that, while it is true that the state may not block vol- untary desegregation efforts, it is also clear that district courts may not impose a remedy without finding that the school district is illegally segregated.[43]

The trial began on April 6 and ran for more than forty trial days until July 22, 1971. The plaintiffs presented a two part case. They argued that individual actions by the School Board and its responsible state supervisors proved both city and state guilty of discrimination. In particular, they alleged that officials had used optional attendance zones in transitional neighborhoods; employed feeder patterns so as to maintain segre- gated schools; established school subdivisions, such as the Center District, to contain minority population; and bused black children past white schools to other predominantly black facilities. But the NAACP was also presenting a larger case, one that asserted a direct and causal relationship between government support for housing discrimination and school segregation.[44] They argued that the residential segregation of blacks in the city and their exclusion from the suburbs was unlike concentrations of other ethnic groups. It was not based upon free association or economics, though economics played a role, but on specific acts of housing discrimination by federal, state, and local govern- ments.[45] These ranged from federal government participation in loan discrimination and restrictive covenants to Detroit's practice of segregated public housing, terminated only after an adverse court ruling in the fifties.

Both the state and Detroit school district officials objected to the housing evidence as irrelevant, but Roth allowed it. In early testimony, though, Roth cautioned plaintiffs' attorneys that this was not a suit about the metropolitan area, but one concerning the city.[46] Efforts to get defendants to stipulate that there was housing segregation in Detroit were rebuffed, which meant that Roth and others received a lengthy explanation of the problem as the plaintiffs' proofs were considered one by one.[47]

The state defendants' strategy was quite simple. Such segregation as there was in Detroit presented a classic *de facto* case and not a question of *de jure* discrimination. In any event, they said, it was a suit against the Detroit Board, and not really against either the state or its officials. The Detroit Board accepted the fact that there had been discrimination in the early years but argued that the Board and school officials had aggressively worked to correct the deficiencies. Such problems as remained were *de facto* in nature.

Roth found a prima facie case of segregation. Alexander Ritchie, counsel for Magdowski, then pressed the need for a broad remedy, moving that all eighty-five school districts in the tri-county area be made defendants for purposes of the remedy.[48] Roth took that motion under advisement and ordered a halt to any new school construction pending his ruling on liability.

Judge Roth announced his decision on September 27, 1971. He found both the state officials and the Detroit Board guilty of fostering, operating, and maintaining segregated schools.[49] His opinion was in four parts: (1) the city and surrounding area were pervasively segregated, including its schools; (2) the community residential and educational segregation were mutually interdependent; (3) the state and Detroit School Board were guilty of a number of specific acts of *de jure* discrimination; and (4) even having found *de jure* violations, the *de facto/de jure* distinction was not a useful approach to the problem of segregated schools.

Reviewing the demographic evidence from 1940 on, Roth found that Detroit schools had 63.8% black students in 1970, which was likely to increase to 75% by 1975 and 80.7% by 1980.[50] "In 1961 there were eight schools in the system without white pupils and 73 schools with no negro students. In 1970 there were 30 schools with no white pupils and 11 students with no negro pupils."[51]

The condition of the schools, Roth observed, was in large part a reflection of the community:

> The City of Detroit is a community generally divided by racial lines. Residential segregation within the city and throughout the larger metropolitan area is substantial, pervasive and of long standing. Black citizens are located in separate and distinct areas within the city and are not generally to be found in the suburbs. While the racially unrestricted choice of black persons and economic factors may have played some part in the development of this pattern of residential segregation, it is, in the main, the result of past and present practices and customs of racial discrimination, both public and private, which have and do restrict the housing opportunities of black people. On the record there can be no other finding.

> Government actions and inaction at all levels, federal, state and local have combined, with those of private organizations, such as loaning institutions and real estate associations and brokerage firms, to establish and to maintain the pattern of residential segregation throughout the Detroit metropolitan area.[52]

Housing segregation and school desegregation in Detroit are, he wrote, "interdependent phenomena."[53] The school authorities have an obligation to "adopt and implement pupil assignment practices and policies that compensate for and avoid incorporation into the school system of the effects of residential racial segregation."[54]

Not only did he determine that the city had failed in that obligation, but he also found that school officials had intentionally used school construction, attendance zones, feeder patterns, and student transfers to foster a segregated system in violation of both the U.S. Constitution and the laws and policies of the state of Michigan.[55] Beyond that, the "State and its agencies, in addition to their general responsibility for and supervision of public education, have acted directly to control and maintain the pattern of segregation in the Detroit schools."[56] That finding stemmed from the passage of Act 48, the failure of the state to use its powers over local districts to remedy segregation, and the existence of financial programs and practices that exacerbated existing inequalities.

Finally, though he had found specific *de jure* violations, Roth added his reservations on the continuing *de facto/de jure* distinction. While he saw it as "unfair to charge the present defendants with what other governmental officers or agencies have done, it can be said that the actions or failure to act by the responsible school authorities, both city and state, were linked to that of these other governmental units. . . . Perhaps the most that can be said is that all of them . . . are in part responsible for the segregated condition which exists."[57] "It is," he said, "unfortunate that we cannot deal with public school segregation on a no fault basis, for if racial segregation in our public schools is an evil, then it should make no difference whether we classify it as *de jure* or *de facto*."[58]

THE REMEDY PHASE

Judge Roth would create a remedial decree in *Milliken*, but the reversal by the Supreme Court of the interdistrict elements of his remedy in the parallel appellate process required further consideration. Roth died in 1974 just before the Supreme Court's decision, which resulted in the delegation of responsibility for recreating the remedy to Judge Robert DeMascio. DeMascio's order did survive the parallel appellate process which took the case all the way back to the Supreme Court in 1977.

Crafting the *Milliken I* Remedy

Roth opened the remedy phase with a preliminary hearing on October 4, 1971, designed to establish the process by which a remedy would be crafted. From the bench, he directed the Detroit Board to submit a plan for Detroit-only desegregation within 60 days and simultaneously instructed the state defendants to prepare a metropolitan area-wide remedy for consideration within 120 days. An understanding of the remedy process that processed the first *Milliken* decree necessitates consideration of the political and legal context within which the remedy was crafted, the tactical positions adopted by the participants, the hearings on Detroit-only remedies and metropolitan relief, and the remedy guidelines that emerged in the summer of 1972.

In the period of nearly a year between his liability opinion and the announcement of his remedy guideline, Roth saw a variety of contextual forces at work. One such factor was the developing body of case law emanating from the substantial number of school desegregation cases litigated just prior to, and during, the pendency of the *Milliken* suit. From 1968 to April 1971 the Supreme Court handed down a series of desegregation opinions culminating in the *Swann v. Charlotte-Mecklenburg Board of Education* ruling, which was delivered while the *Milliken* trial was in progress.[59] These decisions were aimed primarily at forcing compliance with *Brown v. Board of Education* mandated desegregation. They placed the burden on school officials to desegregate and charged district judges with the authority and responsibility for producing desegregation plans "that worked," noting that such rulings may at times be "administratively awkward, inconvenient and even bizarre"[60] but concluding that segregation must be eliminated "root and branch."[61] While there had been some differences of opinion regarding the exact application of the rules for finding and remedying segregation among lower courts,[62] the 1970–71 period saw major findings against school districts in Pasadena, California;[63] San Francisco;[64] Indianapolis;[65] Richmond, Virginia;[66] and Pontiac, Michigan.[67]

School desegregation, and particularly busing as a remedy, was a major national issue during the period. The Nixon administration had enjoyed support from a variety of groups and individuals who felt the judiciary had gone too far in a number of areas. Following the *Swann* decision, the President escalated his criticism of the courts.[68] Just what the administration intended to do was unclear, although the busing issue was obviously going to be a significant factor in the 1972 campaigns. Nixon staked out his position in a televised address on the evening of March 16, 1972, two days after the remedy hearings began in Detroit.[69] He called for Congress to enact a moratorium on busing remedies and announced that he was directing Justice Department attorneys to intervene in pending litigation to oppose further use of such remedies in the interim. Not surprisingly, DOJ moved to intervene in the Detroit case almost immediately. In Congress, 1971 and 1972 saw debates over anti-busing constitutional and statutory amendments.[70] Michigan Senator Griffin was one of those who introduced anti-busing measures. William Broomfield, also of Michigan, introduced what came to be known as the Broomfield Amendment, which barred expenditures of federal education funds for busing "for the purposes of achieving racial balance . . . until all such appeals in connection with such orders have been exhausted."[71]

At the state and local levels, reactions varied. Response to Roth's ruling on segregation was mixed, in part because, until his October 4 order requiring the state to produce a metropolitan plan, it was unclear just how far he would go in search of a remedy. Later in October an organization known as the Tri-County Citizens for Intervention, a suburban group, was formed to contest any metropolitan relief. The Detroit Federation of Teachers (DFT) was obviously very much interested and active, as were several suburban teachers' groups, such as the Professional Personnel of Van Dyke. The suburban school districts refrained from intervention until February 10, 1972, claiming they were not officially on notice of their involvement in the case until the state informed them that their districts were part of the metropolitan plan the state would present to Roth. In Detroit, the changes under way on the School Board added to the confusion. There was, among other things, the problem of establishing the nature of School Board politics on the newly elected panel. One result of the changes on the board was a strain in relations between the Board and the attorney who had represented the city in the liability portion of the trial; he was replaced in December 1971. Beyond that, however, there was disagreement over the position the Board ought to take in the remedy proceedings. Some wanted to fight the decision on all fronts immediately, others suggested compliance, and some argued that, for a variety of reasons (not the least of which was the financial plight of the city), it would be in the city's best interest to bring the suburbs into the process.[72]

The complexities of this environment were important in shaping the tactical positions adopted by the various parties as the remedy crafting process got under way. The Detroit Board pressed the metropolitan remedy, becoming, somewhat ironically, the leading advocate for that position along with the CCBE intevenors. The NAACP was, as Louis Beer, one of the new attorneys for the Detroit Board, would later point out, in a difficult position.[73] On the one hand, a metropolitan remedy would certainly have achieved more than the plaintiffs had originally requested and would clearly be preferable to a Detroit-only remedy. On the other hand, the findings on the issue of segregation gave the NAACP a solid platform for a strong city remedy as well as clear precedent in a northern city for the use of housing discrimination allegations as a part of a school desegregation suit. Moreover, the NAACP was already involved in one interdistrict metropolitan remedy case in Richmond, Virginia, that was certain to be sharply challenged on appeal.[74] During the Detroit-only hearings, the NAACP would be the primary advocate for such a limited remedy, arguing that a Detroit-only plan should be developed at least as an interim approach to desegregation pending implementation of a metropolitan plan. If that strategy succeeded, any appeal of a wider long term remedy would not jeopardize the core case and the basic city-only remedy. The state sought to limit the scope of any remedy Roth might produce as much as possible, a strategy that would cause the state's attorney considerable difficulty in the remedy hearings.

The suburbs waited as long as possible to file for intervention and then requested delays in the proceedings to give them more time to prepare. Only forty of the districts asked permission to participate, and Roth did not rule on the Magdowski motion to make the others parties. Roth notified all parties and potential intervenors, including the suburban districts, on March 6 of the briefing and hearing schedules for the Detroit-only and metropolitan hearings. He asked them to submit proposed conditions for intervention, but the lead district, Grosse Pointe, did not submit its recommendations until March 14, the day the Detroit-only hearings were scheduled to begin. Roth granted intervention the next day, adopting almost verbatim the recommendations contained in the Grosse Pointe letter, but the suburban districts did not participate until the metropolitan remedy hearings.[75]

The Detroit-only remedy hearings, which ran from March 14 to March 21, were curious in that no one really advocated a Detroit-only remedy as the best way to desegregate Detroit schools. The Detroit School Board had been required by Roth to prepare a plan. They produced two, known as Plan A and Plan C. The former was essentially a freedom-of-choice plan based upon magnet schools that involved an estimated twenty thousand students. The second plan was a part-time variation in which students would be transported to other city schools for periods during the week to participate jointly in various special programs. Having announced its plans, however, the city promptly made the case against them with the assistance of NAACP attorneys, and Alexander Ritchie, counsel for CCBE. Patrick McDonald testified that he saw no likelihood that Plan C would be at all effective and that Plan A would be extremely expensive to implement.[76] Moreover, he could not refute evidence, submitted in the form of a progress report prepared by the Board at Roth's instruction, that asserted the effectiveness of the magnet schools the city had operated during the past year. The report demonstrated that no significant desegregation had been accomplished.[77] The only other person who had any positive testimony on Detroit programs was the principal of one of the magnet middle schools that had been launched during the past year. However, she promptly urged, under questioning by counsel for the Detroit Board, that a Detroit-only remedy should be abandoned in favor of a metropolitan plan.[78]

Plaintiffs had submitted a proposed remedy prepared by their lead expert, Gordon Foster of the University of Miami.[79] Foster had participated in the liability phase and had been involved with a variety of such cases in Memphis, Dayton, Pasadena, Norfolk, Richmond, Petersburg, Virginia, and Corpus Christi.[80] The plaintiffs' plan involved transfers and intracity transportation of students to achieve a rough sixty-five percent to thirty-five percent ratio in all schools. It involved two-way integration based upon five new high school clusters. The plan altered feeder patterns and used pairing and clustering of elementary schools, but it omitted kindergarten. Foster estimated transportation costs at $4.3 million.[81] He added, however, that he, too, favored a metropolitan area remedy, cautioning, "but I want to make it quite clear to the extent that the School Board is putting all of its eggs in the metropolitan basket and to some extent avoiding the current issue of intracity desegregation, I in no way go along with this."[82] Under cross-examination, Foster admitted that he had not done a census of the existing faculty distribution and skills, that the plan could be undermined by white flight, and, in the end, that the schools would remain clearly racially indentifiable.[83]

It was, however, Louis Beer and George Roumell for the Detroit Board who set the central theme of the hearings. Their witnesses testified that any Detroit-only remedy would be less effective, less feasible, and less stable than a metropolitan alternative. Eugene Kuthy, a transportation consultant, testified that the city would need as many as 750 buses and a complete administrative apparatus to operate them while the suburban districts already had substantial numbers of buses, drivers, and maintenance facilities.[84] In response to questioning by Judge Roth, Kuthy indicated that his studies showed there would be a substantial savings in a three-county consolidated transportation system over adding a new system in Detroit.[85] Alexander Ritchie elicited testimony from Kuthy on cross-examination that the state was, in fact, already funding some cross-district busing, albeit for other purposes, under what was known as the "In and Out exemption."[86]

Dr. Betsy Ritzenhein, the magnet middle school principal, and Dr. James Guthrie, an education expert, testified that the Detroit-only remedies under consideration were unlikely to be stable over time and suggested the likelihood of resegregation.[87] Ritzenhein spoke from her thirty years of teaching and administrative experience in Detroit. Guthrie's testimony, on the other hand, was directed at assessing the plan against national experience. He discussed the concept of racial isolation and associated terms, including the *tipping point*, that is, the point at which the increase in the number of minority students seems to be followed by large-scale white flight. He argued that sixty-five percent of minority schools were well beyond the generally accepted notions of the tipping point and would, for all practical purposes, result in as much racial isolation effect as if the schools were ninety percent or more minority.[88] Moreover, the white flight likely to follow would have a variety of unfortunate consequences, including student violence.[89]

The other dimension of Detroit's case was testimony by Professor Roger Marz who explained to Roth the meaning of a Standard Metropolian Statistical Area and argued that under each of the criteria used in mapping SMSAs, the tri-county Detroit area clearly qualified as a community.[90] In part for that reason, he said, a number of metropolitan areawide administrative units had been organized and operated, including Detroit

Metropolitan Water and Sewer, Southern Michigan Transit Authority, and others. Finally, Beer, noting Marz was a member of the Oakland County Planning Commission (one of the three metropolitan Detroit counties), elicited the latter's agreement that the suburban counties necessarily included considerations of Detroit in virtually all of their significant planning efforts.[91]

On March 28, Roth announced his ruling rejecting proposed Detroit-only remedies. Hearings on metropolitan areawide plans began the same day. Roth had approached the hearings with the intention of permitting a significant measure of participation to interested groups. The suburban school districts were intervenors, as were CCBE representatives, Tri-County Citizens for Intervention, and the DFT. While he denied motions for intervention by others, the judge simultaneously granted them *amicus curiae* status. His problem was not so much to exclude enough groups to keep the case manageable, but how to get adequate participation from some of those present. Roth was particularly unhappy with the state officials and the attorneys representing suburban schools districts.

The state had been ordered to produce a plan for metropolitan areawide desegregation. It produced six plans, with no recommendation as to which plan was preferable. The state's posture became a matter of controversy at the outset of the hearings. Louis Lucas, lead counsel for the NAACP, asked how the state intended to proceed given the fact that it was presenting no particular remedy proposal. Eugene Krasicky, the Assistant Attorney General representing the state, responded that the plans were submitted without recommendation and that his only intention was to present a witness who could explain them to the court. Roth had similar questions:

> THE COURT: That raises a point which has troubled me since the response of
> the Board by the filing of these several plans. The Board as you pointed out submitted these plans without recommendations. Perhaps you could enlighten me on what
> that means.
> MR. KRASICKY: Well, it means what it says. . . .
> THE COURT: See if I understand what that means. Does that mean the Board
> is opposed to desegregation?
> MR. KRASICKY: I don't believe so.
> THE COURT: Or does it mean that the Board is for desegregation but it cannot
> agree on a plan of desegregation?[92]

Krasicky indicated that the actual preference seemed to be for the April 7 Plan.

The state's position was that it lacked authority over local school districts of a sort that would permit restructuring or modification of the districts. Roth was particularly unhappy with that argument for a number of reasons, one of which was that the state was then arguing in a Texas case pending before the U.S. Supreme Court that the state, not the local districts, was the principal body constitutionally obligated to ensure equal educational opportunity.[93] He later characterized the state's role in the hearings as follows:

> At the hearings, moreover, the state defendants did not purport to present evidence
> in support, or even in opposition, to the State Proposal. The State, despite prodding
> by the court, presented only one witness, who merely explained what appeared in
> the face of the various State "Plans" submitted. The State's cross-examination of
> witnesses was of no assistance to the court in ascertaining any preference, legal or
> educational. Put bluntly, State defendants in this hearing deliberately chose not to

assist the court in choosing an appropriate area for effective desegregation of the Detroit public schools. Their resistance and abdication of responsibility throughout has been consistent with the other failures to meet their obligations noted in the court's earlier rulings. Indeed, some of the submissions spoke as clearly in opposition to desegregation as did the legislature in Sec. 12 of Act 48 of 1978 . . . ruled unconstitutional by the Sixth Circuit.[94]

He was similarly frustrated by the approach taken by the suburban districts. With the exception of raising questions about the impact of some of the plans on local government units and the estimated length of possible bus routes, their lawyers did not participate in the shaping of a metropolitan remedy. They argued against any such remedy by moving their cross-examination of the Detroit Board witnesses from the Board plan to the more general question whether to compel any integration. They insisted that forced integration did not benefit educational quality and was therefore to be avoided.[95] Roth replied:

> I understand your position and you have a perfect right to stand on that position. But you see I don't confuse one object with the other although I want to pursue both. You try to put it in the alternative that what we ought to be about is achieving educational excellence and I am for that but I am also under command to do something else and that is accomplish desegregation. Hopefully if you do one you will achieve the other. I know the test results differ and there are different philosophies and viewpoints on this.[96]

Lucas objected later when William Saxton, the lawyer for the suburbs, again argued through cross-examination that busing and other mandated measures were educationally inappropriate. Lucas accused Saxton of injecting "the new political curseword of busing" and attempting to "relitigate *Brown v. Board of Education.*"[97] The situation was not diffused by Saxton's reply that he was proceeding on his understanding of what desegregation was about, namely "desegregation means removing any legal or other barriers which preclude one from attending a school district on account of their *[sic]* race."[98] That, of course, was essentially the post *Brown v. Board* integration-versus-desegregtion argument discussed in Chapter 4.

Lucas again challenged the suburban district counsel in support of a motion to quash a subpoena issued by Saxton to Charles Wells, Assistant Superintendent for Pupil Personnel Services, which called upon him to produce all records of incidents of violence in the Detroit schools over the preceding two years. Lucas charged that this request was directed at "pandering to racial fears, propagandizing racial hatred and its just an attempt to inflame and stir up the community."[99] Saxton replied that the question of potential for violence was evidence relevant to the nature of a remedy. While his subpoena was extrememly broad, he did have a foundation for raising the issue given the fact that the Detroit Board had elicited testimony from James Guthrie in the Detroit-only hearings on the potential for instability, including possible violent incidents. In fact, school discipline issues would be among the more troublesme problems that Judge Roth's successors would encounter in later stages of the case.

The core of the suburban case was in three parts: (1) that based upon the findings of Professor David Armor, desegregation would produce no particular educational advantage for minority children; (2) that all of the suburban school district boundaries had been established before the incidents found to be discriminatory in the liability portion and that none had been formed with the intention to discriminate; and (3) that using the Wells testimony, a strong mandated desegregation plan would likely create safety risks, including potential violence.[100] Roth would later write:

> Similarly, the newly intervening defendant school districts did not attempt at the hearing to assist the court in determining which area was appropriate to accomplish effective desegregation. They were given the opportunity, by express written order and several admonitions during the course of the hearings, to assist the court in the task at hand but chose in their best judgment instead, in the main, to suggest their view that separate schools were preferable.[101]

The plans considered by the Court at the hearing were submitted by CCBE, the Detroit Board, and the NAACP. Most were variations on clustering, pairing, and feeder pattern modification within the metropolitan area by use of busing and other techniques. The remainder of the hearing was spent on determining which suburban districts to eliminate. The Detroit Board presented a range of testimony, including that of two fifteen-year-old boys, one black and the other white, who had been attending a private school in one of the suburbs but who lived in Detroit. They established that they had found no difficulty in riding the bus to school nor were they having any problem participating in extracurricular activities or ensuring parental involvement in their school programs.

Roth announced his ruling on the remedy on June 14, 1972.[102] Still seeking a participatory role for the suburban school districts and the state, Roth opted to mandate a process to develop a final plan within geographic and time limits. What follows is a summary of the elements of his order:

1. That there would be created a desegregation panel of nine (later expanded to eleven) members, including representatives of all the participating organizations and government units.

2. That within forty-five days from the order, the panel was to provide a plan to desegregate within the geographic boundaries and other guidelines provided by the court. Any transportation requirements were to be made within twenty days to permit time for acquisition of vehicles.

3. That "complete and final desegregation [was] to proceed in no event later than the fall 1973 term."[103]

4. The final plan should desegregate within the fifty-three suburban districts plus Detroit according to the fifteen cluster-modified Detroit School Board plan.

5. Within that area, the panel could use student reassignments, feeder-pattern changes, pairing, or other techniques provided that the integration was a two-way process having a roughly equal impact on white and minority students. And where students were transported, the rides should be limited to approximately forty-minutes one way.

6. "Consistent with the requirements of maximum actual desegregation, every effort should be made to minimize the numbers of pupils to be reassigned and requiring transportation, the time pupils spend in transit, and the number and cost of new transportation facilities to be acquired."[104]

7. "Within the limitations of reasonable travel time and distance factors pupil reassignments shall be effected within the clusters . . . so as to achieve the greatest

degree of actual desegregation to the end that, upon implementation, no school, grade or classroom be substantially disproportionate to the overall pupil racial composition." [105]

8. The State Superintendent of Public Instruction was to provide recommendations within forty-five days for any changes necessary in administrative, contractual, financial, or property management practices.

9. The state was responsible to provide financial and staff support to the desegregation panel along with access to whatever information was necessary to accomplish its task.

10. The state was henceforth to enforce its published guidelines in new school construction and disapprove school construction in those situations in which residential segregation would perpetuate the effects of discrimination.

11. Hearings were to be held within fifteen days after the reports of the panel and the state reports required in the order were filed in order to clarify final arrangements. Those hearings would entertain no argument that mandatory desegregation should be abandoned.

12. Faculty reassignments would be necessary to ensure that schools had at least a ten percent minority faculty composition.

13. Several educational component programs would be necessary for implementation of the decree, including biracial councils for each school; reevaluation of curriculum content and materials "to reflect the diversity of ethnic and cultural backgrounds of the children"; [106] in-service training for faculty and administrators in human relations; and the "entire grading, reporting, counselling, and testing program should be reviewed in light of desegregated schools compared to traditional schools and to avoid imposing the effects of past discrimination on the children." [107]

Roth began from the premise that previous testimony had established that "relief of segregation in the Detroit public schools cannot be accomplished within the corporate geographic limits of the city." [108] Given that the three-county metropolitan Detroit area was for many purposes a community, [109] that several cross-jurisdictional programs were already in place, [110] and that school district boundaries in the area were not drawn to conform to other local political jurisdictions, there was no realistic administrative or legal obstacle to a metropolitan areawide remedy. Where there appeared to be time or distance difficulties, Roth reduced the size of the proposed desegregation area. Moreover, the state as defendant did not show that district lines were "rationally related to any legitimate state purpose; and the . . . particular welter of existing boundaries for 86 school districts [was] necessary to the promotion of any compelling state interest." [111] Given Michigan's argument in *San Antonio Independent School District v. Rodriquez* that state's have responsibility for all equal educational opportunity issues, Roth rejected the assertion that the state was powerless to deal with suburban districts.

Roth did, however, note that he had heard no testimony on the reasons the suburban district lines were originally drawn, nor had he taken evidence or made findings regarding any discriminatory actions by the suburban school districts in the remedy.

The judge devoted a substantial portion of the opinion to his findings as to the scope of the remedy necessary to deal with the violation. The state, he wrote, was responsible for the fact that the metropolitan Detroit area was segregated and the state had not only failed to act to prevent that segregation but had, in fact, acted to promote it. The principal question regarding scope was a question of both the nature of the remedy and the scope of its application, namely, cross-district busing.

Given the fact that a large percentage of students were already regularly bused all over the state and in the Detroit suburbs, "for school authorities or private citizens to now object to such transportation practices raises the inference not of hostility to pupil transportation but rather racially motivated hostility to the desegregated school at the end of the ride." [112]

> In the rent past more than 300,000 pupils in the tri-county area regularly rode to school on some type of bus. . . . Throughout the state approximately 35–40% of all students arrive at school on a bus. In school districts eligible for state reimbursement on transportation costs in three affected counties, the percent of pupils transported in 1969–70 ranged from 42–52%.
>
> In comparison approximately 40% or 310,000, of the 780,000 children within the desegregation area will require transportation in order to accomplish maximum actual desegregation. [113]

Beyond that, Roth said, the testimony had clearly extablished that a metropolitan remedy was "physically easier and more practicable and more feasible than desegregation efforts limited to the corporate geographic limits of Detroit." [114]

Finally, Roth expressed reservations he felt at how deeply he had become involved in the educational process in Detroit, but argued that under the Constitution and given the facts in this case, he could do no less.

> [W]e remind the parties that this court's task is to enforce constitutional rights not to act as a schoolmaster; the court's task is to protect the constitutional rights here found violated with as little intrusion into the education process as possible. The court's objective is to establish the minimum constitutional framework within which the system of public schools may operate now and hereafter in a racially unified, non-discriminatory fashion. Within that framework the body politic, educators, parents and most particularly the children must be given the maximum opportunity to experiment and secure a high quality, and equal, educational opportunity. However, experience has proven that specific goals, deadlines and methods of reporting and review must be required in all desegregation cases to ensure compliance. [115]

Some weeks later, Roth, at the suggestion of the desegregation panel, ordered the state to purchase 295 buses for the desegregation process, adding the state treasurer to the case as a defendant in the process.

The reaction to Roth's ruling was extremely harsh in a number of Michigan communities. Reviled as a "child molester," Roth was hung in effigy after a mock trial in Wyandotte. But there were also moderating influences. The *Detroit Free Press* featured an editorial roundly condemning the personal attacks on the judge as showing "contempt for the law":

> Judge Roth did not seek the case, and Lord knows life has not been made easier for him since he took it. But it was the job assigned to him and it was the job he did. Whether he is right or wrong, no one can accuse him of failure to be conscientious. To attack him personally as a "child molester" or hang him in effigy for doing his job is scurrility beneath contempt. [116]

The president of the state bar association lauded the newspaper and reprinted the piece in the association's journal. The Michigan Bar Association unanimously adopted a resolution at its September meeting in which it paid "tribute to [Roth's] conscientious and courageous performance of his duty" and condemned those who attacked him personally. The American Bar Association (ABA) followed suit in October.[117]

The *Milliken I* Appeals

Efforts had been made to advance an interlucutory appeal against Roth's ruling on segregation a year earlier, but that attempt had failed. Following the presentation of his guidelines for the remedy, however, Roth did certify the case for appeal at the request of several of the parties. It would be two years before the Supreme Court ruling which struck down the cross-district remedy.[118]

In December 1972, a panel of the Sixth Circuit affirmed all the elements of Roth's ruling but required participation in remedy crafting by all affected suburbs. However, the court granted an *en banc* review, which was completed in June 1973. Three principal questions were raised. Were Roth's findings clearly erroneous? Was Roth in error in holding that on the record a Detroit-only remedy would be inadequate? Did Roth abuse his equity powers in granting a multidistrict remedy involving transportation of children in the larger metropolitan area? In a very lengthy and detailed opinion, the court supported Roth on all points, but vacated the remedy ordering him to join all of the suburban districts that might be directly involved in such a plan. They were to be allowed to participate in the metropolitan remedy plan development but were not to be permitted to argue against the initial finding of segregation or the findings on the Detroit-only remedy issue.[119]

Judge Phillips' opinion was far more detailed than either of Roth's prior rulings, reproducing substantial portions of testimony that showed the specific violations and the interconnected nature of the actions of the state and the Detroit Board. Though it acknowledged the appropriateness of Roth's findings on the relationship between residential and school segregation,[120] the Sixth Circuit chose to focus on specific *de jure* violations, such as the transportation of black suburban students from one district that had no high school to a black Detroit high school while passing available white suburban schools in the process.[121] The Sixth Circuit decision also reproduced several pages of findings on the inadequacy of the Detroit-only remedy. It then considered what it found to be the most important factor, the role of the state in establishing and maintaining the status quo:

> Thus, the record established that the state has committed *de jure* acts of segregation and that the State controls the instrumentalities whose action is necessary to remedy the harmful effects of the State acts. . . . *In the instant case, the only feasible desegregation plan involves the crossings of the boundary lines between the Detroit School District and adjacent or nearby school districts for the limited purpose of providing an effective desegregation plan.* The power to disregard such artificial barriers is all the more clear where, as here, the State has been guilty of discrimination which had the effect of creating and maintaining racial segregation along school district lines. . . .
>
> There exists, however, an even more compelling basis for the District Court's crossing artificial boundary lines to cure the State's constitutional violations. The instant

case calls up haunting memories of the now long overruled and discredited "separate
but equal doctrine." . . . If we hold that school district boundaries are absolute
barriers to a Detroit school desegregation plan, we would be opening a way to nullify
Brown v. Board of Education.[122] (emphasis added)

The Supreme Court heard the case in February 1974. It was a complex appeal
coming to the Court at a difficult time. The state argued that this was essentially a case
of *de facto* segregation in which a judge had become "preoccupied with the majority
Black character of the Detroit School district."[123] "Thus, the underlying premise of
both lower courts is the achievement of what they perceived as the desirable social goal
of racial balance among school districts, rather than the vindication of constitutional
rights to attend a school free from racial discrimination by public school authorities."[124]

The assertion that this was a case of social engineering by a district judge run
amuck was central to the arguments of both the state officials and the suburban districts.
Both state and suburb also asserted that involving them in a remedy was a form of
punishment for which the suburbs at least had not been accorded due process of law.[125]
The other major element in the petitioners' argument was that the state lacked authority
over the suburban districts. The judge could only reach those districts if they individually had committed intentionally discriminatory acts.

The Detroit Board filed a brief as a respondent supporting the lower court decisions
and the NAACP position, but no representative of the Board participated in the oral
argument. The NAACP argued that both lower courts had established *de jure* violations
against the state and the city that transcended city boundaries. J. Harold Flannery for
the NAACP argued that the interlocking relationship between state and local action on
housing and schools had been important elements in the case from the beginning and
that Judge Roth, who began the case thinking otherwise, came to agree by virtue of the
weight of the evidence presented.[126] The NAACP General Counsel, Nathaniel Jones,
also for the plaintiffs, observed that Roth had heard uncontroverted testimony about the
interconnected nature of the three-county metropolitan area during his consideration of
the remedy. The NAACP counsel reminded the Court that both lower courts had found
abundant evidence that no Detroit-only remedy would be meaningful. Finally, they argued that in a variety of cases, most notably reapportionment, the Court had frequently
required jurisdictions not defendants in the liability case into a remedy.

Solicitor General Robert Bork appeared for the United States as *amicus curiae*.
Bork simply argued that the scope of the remedy exceeded the scope of the violation.
In the absence of proof of an interdistrict violation, there could be no interdistrict relief.[127] Without some showing that the suburban districts were themselves involved in
de jure segregation or that the specific boundaries concerned had been drawn by the
state for that purpose, there could be no cross-district remedy.[128] The Court agreed.

Milliken I marked a turning point for the Supreme Court in its remedy cases. Any
number of reasons might be identified as the cause of this particular ruling.[129] Most
important was the fact that the Burger Court was coming into its own. Justices Powell
and Rehnquist had been appointed since the *Swann* decision, and there was little doubt
where their votes would be. Justice Stewart had voted with three members of the Court
to affirm by a tie vote (with Powell not participating) the court of appeals dicision in
the Richmond schools case, rejecting Judge Mehrige's cross-district remedy. That case,
as the Sixth Circuit opinion indicated, was quite unlike *Milliken* in several respects, but
the doctrinal point was not the primary factor here. Moreover, Chief Justice Burger had

substantially altered his approach from his opinion for the Court in *Swann*, reading as limiting language terms in *Swann* that had clearly been permissive in nature with respect to the authority of district judges. In addition, the period from 1971 to 1974 had been one of the most difficult times in the recent history of the Court as opposition to deseg-regation decisions, particularly *Swann*, had brought all manner of condemnation from the public, the White House, and the Congress.

Also of potential significance, at least with respect to the opinion itself, was the fact that *Milliken* was decided and the opinion prepared during the peak of the Watergate crisis. Judge Sirica had rendered his ruling on the tape disclosure question on May 20, 1974.[130] From that point on, the Court was faced with the task of resolving a constitu-tional clash of the first magnitude that involved two branches of the federal government.

Milliken was announced the day after the Court rendered its ruling in the Watergate tapes case. The Detroit suit had a complex record of some six volumes, but the decision shows quite clearly that the opinion was not based on a careful examination of the record. As Justices White and Marshall pointed out in their dissents, there were a num-ber of significant inaccuracies in the majority's presentation of the facts and rulings in the lower court. Justice Stewart concurred (making a fifth vote), suggesting that under some factual conditions he might be persuaded of the appropriateness of a cross-district remedy, but not on the *Milliken* findings.[131] Justices White, Marshall, Brennan, and Douglas dissented vigorously.

RECREATING THE REMEDY

The Supreme Court, striking only the cross-district portion of the lower court rulings and leaving all other elements intact, remanded the case. The question was where the lower courts would go from that point. Because Judge Roth had died, the case was assigned to Judge Robert E. DeMascio who found himself in the position of recreating a remedy in a case without have heard the liability portion. It was under his order that the Detroit School District launched an integration program in January of 1976. But it was a decree that made the judge a target of criticism from both the plaintiffs and the state, notwithstanding the fact that he began with what was acknowledged by many to be an impossible situation.[132]

Crafting the *Milliken II* Remedy

DeMascio was immediately faced with case management questions, changing condi-tions, and compelling elements of the prior record. He began by calling a pretrial con-ference for mid-February 1975, at which he ordered both the plaintiffs and the Detroit Board to produce remedy plans by April 1. The state defendants were to evaluate those plans after submission. As he began his own assessment of the proposals, DeMascio quickly concluded that he needed help. He appointed three experts to assist him.[133] The plans submitted by the plaintiffs and the district were very different in both strategy and tactics, leaving little room for a negotiated settlement.[134] Remedy hearings ran on and off between April 29 and June 27. DeMascio filed remedial guidelines for a final plan on August 15.[135] Following adjustments of various plans, he entered judgment on a desegregation order on November 4, 1975.[136]

The case management and remedy crafting were complicated by changing and interrelated political and economic conditions. When the case was decided in 1971, the Detroit Board of Education had ten white members and three blacks; but by the time the case came to DeMascio, the composition had changed to nine blacks and four whites.[137] Minority administrators also occupied more important posts. There was still tension as the 9–4 racially divided vote on the Board's 1975 desegregation proposal indicates, but the political environment had changed since the first remedy was crafted. As Hain notes, such groups as the Metropolitan Coalition for Peaceful Integration (formed in1972 in anticipation of the decree Judge Roth was then developing)[138] had worked diligently to reduce tensions. The larger political context had changed as well in that fewer major figures were openly exploiting the problems of desegregation than in 1972.

But if some aspects of the political landscape appeared more stable, the same certainly could not be said for the economy. The major economic stresses of the 1970s were felt quickly and severely in Detroit. In addition to the more general difficulties experienced nationally, Detroit suffered several specific problems. Business and industry left the city along with the general suburbanization, resulting in a dramatic decrease in the tax base.[139] At one point Detroit was running a $75-million deficit and "came . . . in 1973, within four days of being unable to meet a payroll."[140] Budget cuts were instituted to clear the debt and meet changing conditions. The tax burden ran very high:

> The total of all municipal taxes paid by Detroit citizens translates into a municipal millage equivalent of 84.83 mills. This is the highest tax burden in the state and is 55% higher than the state average. Only 16 cities in the State of Michigan levy an income tax; among them, Detroit's rate is the highest. However, Detroit's per capita income tax yield is substantially lower than the other 15 cities. Moreover, county taxes paid by Detroit citizens are 14.4% higher than the state average, and Detroit municipal taxes are 14.6% higher than the state average.[141]

The property tax rate of 24.76 mills in Detroit was just short of the 25 mills necessary to qualify for the full state "power equalizing" subsidy, but given the tax burden in the city it was all but impossible to increase the millage rate.[142] Finally, while the state had legislation to partially offset municipal overburden, it was only funded at a twenty-eight percent level.[143] In short, the city could not stand an increase in taxes to qualify for more state assistance, and even if it could, the actual dollars available from the state would not have been adequate to the needs.

The other major fact of life confronting DeMascio was the record developed in the Detroit-only and metropolitan phases of Roth's remedial process. The finding that no adequate Detroit-only remedy was feasible had stood throughout the appeals. The Detroit Board had built an excellent case that any intracity remedy would cost more, disrupt more students, and accomplish less than a metropolitan remedy. Moreover, uncontested testimony established the very high probability that an intracity remedy would be very unstable, leading to resegregation within a relatively short period of time. The NAACP had quite ably defended the necessity of the metropolitan remedy on appeal even though its lead expert, Gordon Foster, had cautioned Judge Roth against putting all of the remedial eggs in one metropolitan basket.

The plaintiffs' plan prepared by Foster was a modified form of the Detroit-only plan he had prepared for Roth. It sought to bring all schools within fifteen percent of the racial composition of the city, requiring transportation of 77,303 students.

The Detroit Board proposal concentrated on eliminating racially identifiable white schools (those with less than twenty-five percent black enrollment) and aimed for a forty percent to sixty percent black enrollment. The plan did not deal with Regions 1, 5, and 8, which were home for the overwhelmingly majority of black students in the city. Even so, the Board proposal would have required transportation of approximately 51,000 students. It did, however, call for a list of educational components far more extensive than those included in Roth's decree.

Based upon a stated awareness of these changes and his own views on desegregation, DeMascio established a set of decision principles he referred to as "the practicalities of the situation":

> One legitimate concern deserving of weight is the undesirability of forced reassignment of students achieving only negligible results. Another of the practicalities is the shifting demography occuring naturally in the school district together with the persistent increase in black student enrollment. Still another of the practicalities to be taken into account is the racial population of the district which is predominantly black by a wide margin. Further practicalities that must be considered by this court include the declining tax base of the City of Detroit, the depressed economy of the city, and the volatile atmosphere created by the highest rate of unemployment in the nation. Finally, the decree must consider the overriding community concern for the quality of educational services available in the school district.[144]

Working from these premises, DeMascio rejected both plans submitted by the parties and prepared guidelines establishing his own reassignment rules. He also adopted a modified form of the educational components program called for by the Detroit Board's plan.

DeMascio found plaintiffs' plan rigid and arbitrary, requiring a great deal of busing without achieving much actual desegregation. Furthermore, the kinds of changes recommended were likely to lead to resegregation:

> If such an extraordinary remedy as bussing is to be employed, it should be used to bus black children to white schools, not to schools that are predominantly black. The use of such a remedy in these circumstances contains all of the seeds for resegregation, which this court has stated must be avoided at all costs.[145]

Upon comparing the plaintiffs' plan with testimony in Roth's remedy hearings, DeMascio concluded that Foster had underestimated the scale, cost, and administrative feasibility of the transportation requirements in his present proposal.

The judge rejected portions of the Detroit Board's plan for similar reasons. He added, however, that the manner in which the plan was drawn suggested a political compromise among various regional representatives on the School Board rather than an independent attempt to develop a workable proposal.[146] When the authority over the schools was decentralized in response to the earlier community power movement in the city, it became possible for the regional representatives on the School Board to block action. The judge went further. He suggested that the political and organizational difficulties between the central and regional boards would make implementation of any remedy difficult because of the multiple layers of bureaucracy. In fact, DeMascio went so far as to suggest the legislature ought to consider eliminating the decentralized Detroit school structure.[147] Given the substantial quantity of supporting testimony on the point, the judge felt compelled to adopt the educational components proposals.

Even though DeMascio criticized the Detroit plan because it was not adequate in the reassignment area, he accepted the need to exclude Regions 1, 5, and 8 from his own guidelines, thus omitting many black students from the plan. He observed, "the racial composition of these regions precludes their inclusion in a desegregation plan."[148] Any plan adequate to deal with these core city regions, he said, would result in tremendous dislocation within the rest of the district with negligible results.[149]

The judge was trying to build a base of support and cooperation for his remedy. He took a number of actions toward that end while preparing his remedial guidelines. In April DeMascio asked one of his experts to meet with officials from Wayne State University and the University of Michigan to determine ways in which those institutions could work with the Detroit schools in the future.[150] Though he did not personally participate in the discussions, DeMascio made substantial use of the results of those talks in his guidelines. He employed the offers of help in his instructions to the Detroit Board, called upon officials to work with the universities, and invoked the participation of the universities in staking his claim to community support.[151] In another such effort, the judge attended a "luncheon meeting with various business, community and labor leaders to encourage them to support the Detroit Board's effort to deliver quality education."[152] Again, DeMascio avoided discussion of the remedy itself. Finally, on August 15, the day the remedy guideline opinion was filed, but before it was publicly announced, he met with representatives of the Detroit Board and the Detroit Federation of Teachers.[153] DeMascio was worried that a breakdown in talks might bring a strike that would disrupt the remedy implementation effort. He subsequently ordered the parties to conduct daily negotiations until a settlement was reached. In preparing his opinion, DeMascio made certain to include strong praise for the good faith efforts of Detroit school authorities and the local community.

Judge DeMascio's August remedy guidelines included the following provisions:

1. The board must produce a "plan that eliminates racially identifiable white schools in the district by reassigning black students, who are in the majority to schools throughout the city."[154]

2. Rezoning is to be used in preference to transportation, and regional lines need not be honored in the zoning process.

3. "The revised transportation plan should avoid bussing black children to black schools. A school that is 55% or more black is a predominantly black school." And "[n]either black nor white children should be bussed to schools that are desegregated according to these guidelines."[155]

4. "Elementary schools should not be paired when or both of the schools already satisfied the court's definition of a desegregated school."[156]

5. In pairing schools, "[t]he Board should, wherever possible, pair an identifiably white school with the nearest school exceeding 55% black enrollment."[157]

6. The Board should use uniform grade structures (K–5, 6–8, 9–12) for educational consistency and to facilitate monitoring.

7. "Schools with a resident population in the service area of between 30% and 55% black shall be considered desegregated. If a school is within this range, no change in pupil assignment is necessary." [158]

8. In some cases a school may exceed fifty-five percent minority, but no school may be more than seventy percent white.

9. In cases of pairing, "one-half of the pupils in each grade from each school will be bussed to the school or schools in the pair. The classes will be rotated annually or semi-annually so that each child will attend his neighborhood school at least every other year." [159]

10. The city shall use open enrollment (magnet) middle schools and zoned middle schools with a fifty percent black target enrollment and fifty-five to seventy percent black enrollment in magnet schools.

11. "Generally, no child should be bussed for more than five of his eight years. Any child that is bussed for desegregation at the elementary level for five years should not be bussed for desegregation to a middle school." [160]

12. The Board is to create four vocational high schools and two technical high schools.

13. The General Superintendent is to appoint a committee to develop and implement a remedial reading program.

14. A comprehensive in-service training program is to be instituted for faculty and staff dealing with "teacher expectations, human relations, minority culture, testing, the student code of conduct and the administration of discipline" as well as familiarization with the desegregation order. [161]

15. The Detroit Board and the state are required to develop an adequate testing program.

16. The Board is required to complete plans for, and vigorously administer, a Uniform Student Code of Conduct.

17. The Board must institute a comprehensive community relations program that offers wide participation.

18. The Board must submit a career guidance and counseling plan.

19. The court adopts the concept of a Detroit junior high school cocurricular consortium program in conjunction with a number of libraries, museums, and universities.

20. Bilingual programs are to be continued.

21. The Board and the DFT are required to prepare a student and faculty census.

22. There will be a broadly representative monitoring group which shall report directly to the court, with staff assistance and financial support to be provided by the State Superintendent of Public Instruction.

23. The state is to pay fifty percent of the costs of the remedy and the Detroit Board is to pay the remaining fifty percent, except for the transportation costs, in which the state shall pay seventy-five percent and the Detroit Board twenty-five percent.

With plans approved in November of 1975 and a great deal of human relations effort, the desegregation in January 1976 took place without major incident.

The Appeals of *Milliken II*

Both the NAACP and the state sought review of DeMascio's order. Plaintiffs challenged the decree primarily because it had not accomplished desegregation for the majority of black students in the city residing in Regions 1, 5, and 8. The state balked at the $5.8 million first payment for its share of the cost of the educational components (items 12 through 23 of the remedy guidelines).

Judge Phillips, writing for the Sixth Circuit, praised Detroit for its peaceful implementation of the remedy.[162] The court affirmed DeMascio's ruling but remanded the decision on Regions 1, 5, and 8, finding that, after years of litigation, the children in whose names the case was originally brought would be excluded from desegregation because they lived in the core districts. In so doing, however, the Sixth Circuit found "itself unable to give any direction to the District Court which would accomplish the desegregation of the Detroit school system in light of the realities of the present racial composition"[163] because *"genuine constitutional desegregation can not be accomplished within the school district boundaries of the Detroit School District"*[164] (emphasis added).

In June 1977 the Supreme Court announced its second *Milliken* opinion, this time rejecting the state's challenge to DeMascio's order.[165]

THE POST DECREE PHASE

A variety of questions remained for DeMascio to resolve after the appeals. Part of this unfinished business stemmed from his efforts to deal with criticism of his remedy. The remainder of his assignment was to fine-tune the remedy itself.

Implementation

There were critical reactions to the tenor and impact of the *Milliken II* remedy. Because of the specifications built into the decree restricting reassignment of many students, only approximately 21,000 children were available for substantial reassignments, far less than either the Board or plaintiffs had recommended. Moreover, because of the concern with community stability and its relationship to possible resegregation, more one-way desegregation was involved than was desirable, with black students carrying the heavier burden. Further, elements of the vocational high school program were not feasible and had to be scrapped.

Some of the rhetoric employed in DeMascio's decree conveyed to critics a less than adequate commitment to desegregation. References to a dislike for treating students as "pigmented pawns," concentration on "stability," and the overriding community interest in educational quality are all subject to a variety of interpretations whatever their original intent.

Manifesting frustration with their perception of DeMascio's approach to the case, plaintiffs brought a recusal motion arguing that the judge's off-the-record use of experts, his attendance at the community luncheon meeting, and his participation in the meeting with the Detroit Board and the DFT on August 15, 1975, indicated bias. DeMascio dismissed the motion as untimely but raised the appearance of bias question on his own motion. He requested that another judge be assigned to make an independent finding.[166] That task was given to Judge Churchill, who offered to take evidence on the question. No evidence was proffered, however, and Churchill found no bias. In fact, he praised DeMascio for exemplary conduct in the case.[167]

Remedy Refinement

Judge DeMascio issued a number of orders on faculty reassignment and attendance modifications. He had before him yet the question of what to do about Regions 1, 5, and 8. He attempted to resolve these remaining tasks in an August 7, 1978, opinion.[168] DeMascio began by indicating that he had agreed all along with Judge Roth's finding that "an adequate remedy based on pupil reassignments limited to the corporate limits of Detroit would be impossible.[169] He observed that the Supreme Court had not overturned that determination and the Sixth Circuit had reiterated the point even as it called upon him to deal with Regions 1, 5, and 8. He thought it important to observe that it was extremely difficult for him to respond to the court of appeals admonition, not only because of the large and increasing minority population, but also because the parties in the case were no longer taking the initiative. For that matter they were not even participating fully when he called for action.[170]

DeMascio interpreted the Sixth Circuit as having said that he must either include the three regions or carry the "heavy burden" of justifying the exception. He concluded he could meet that burden by explaining in more detail why he had excluded the three regions in the first instance. After an extensive discussion of the city's demographics, he found that Regions 1, 5, and 8 could not be included in the decree. He did, however, promise to adjust Region 2 slightly for more desegregation. The opinion also modified faculty reassignment limits and disbanded the monitoring commission.

The court of appeals ruled in April 1980 that DeMascio had not carried the burden of justifying the exemption of the three regions.[171] The other major element of the decision concerned the judge's refusal to recuse himself. Although the Sixth Circuit concluded he had not erred in refusing to step down, it suggested that "in view of the public interest in the instant school desegregation case, the challenge raised by the plaintiffs and the bitter feelings that have developed, this court suggests that, on remand, the Chief Judge of the District Court should reassign the case."[172]

The case was reassigned to a three judge district court panel. After a series of filings and hearings, the court approved amendments to the proposed pupil reassignment plan.

However, the actual placement of students was not the only area of debate remaining. In fact, since 1981 the principal disputes have concerned implementation and operation of the educational components that had been upheld by the Supreme Court, the funding of those programs, and the role of the court-created monitoring commission. The programs included in-service training, testing, counseling and guidance, remedial reading, bilingual/bicultural education, and school/community relations projects. All parties agreed to stipulations filed with the court—in effect, a consent decree—in August 1981 which estimated and apportioned the costs for the programs between the Detroit Board and the state, set the end of the 1987–88 school year as the termination date, and left the court-ordered monitoring commission in place until that time to ensure compliance.[173]

Conflict reemerged when the Detroit Board sought to modify the Uniform Student Code of Conduct developed by DeMascio and the school/community relations program. It also asked the court to terminate its jurisdiction over these two programs and transfer oversight from the monitoring commission well before the 1987–88 termination date established in the 1981 agreement.

The Uniform Student Code of Conduct has been a sensitive area all along. Judge DeMascio had admonished the city for delay in its implementation and the DFT had repeatedly sought judicial pressure to enforce full compliance. During 1983 both the court ordered monitoring commission and the state issued reports critical of disciplinary practices in Detroit schools.

The concern about the school/community relations program was a function of some disagreements over its operation, but there was a more important structural issue. The state had replaced the decentralized regional board arrangement in Detroit with a unified centralized structure. In the process, the state required development of a school/community relations program. The Board wanted to develop its own program in light of the change.

Judges Feikers, Churchill, and Cohn heard arguments in January 1984 on the state of implementation and the requested changes. The court wanted to avoid further interference in areas where the Board appeared to have state sanction to act, particularly in discipline and community relations matters. It was also concerned that the court should eliminate any interference caused by the monitoring commission in the normal political operation of the school district. The judges terminated the in-service training and testing programs.[174] They held that the student code of conduct and community relations programs would end as soon as the city had completed development of its own plans in those fields. Once that was accomplished, the court concluded, there would no longer be a need for the monitoring commission. Such oversight as remained should be transferred back to the state. The city Board adopted its discipline and community relations plans in August.

The plaintiffs and the DFT appealed the district court ruling. A Sixth Circuit panel vacated the lower court order on procedural grounds and sent the case back to the three judges.[175] In the fall of 1985, the case was assigned to one of the three judges, Avern Cohn.

The Detroit Board called upon the court to permit it to use its existing (1984) discipline and community relations programs and not to reconstitute the defunct monitoring commission. The state concurred but urged the court to retain jurisdiction until the termination date of the original agreement in 1988. The plaintiffs and the DFT protested that, under the circuit court ruling and the provisions of the 1981 agreement, they were entitled to have the situation restored to what it had been before the April 1984 district court ruling had turned over the discipline and community relations programs to the city. In particular, they insisted that the commission be reestablished, claiming that the monitoring board had played a crucial role in identifying areas of noncompliance by the city.

Following hearings in January and February 1986, Cohn required continuation of the code of conduct as stipulated in the 1981 agreement along with the community relations program, though he did indicate a willingness to consider changes that the Detroit Board might propose as the agreement moved toward its 1988 termination date.

Cohn has attempted to obtain agreement by the parties to the greatest extent possible in order to avoid any further judicial involvement in the city's schools during the relatively short period remaining until the scheduled termination of the order. While there remain a number of very limited disputes among the parties at the time of this writing, it appears likely that the court will terminate its jurisdiction as planned in 1988.

CONCLUSION

An examination of the Detroit school desegregation case provides not only a study of the true complexity of school desegregation litigation, but also a realistic understanding of remedial decree litigation in general. It began with a judge who stood opposed to the remedies sought by plaintiffs who nevertheless eventually issued one of the most sweeping desegregation orders in history. On the other hand, when the flexibility that Judge Roth had built into his order was lost on the appeal, an even more conservative jurist, Robert DeMascio, inherited the case and fashioned a more intensive, if narrower, order to deal with the situation of the city. In the end DeMascio's effort to ensure implementation of the remedy was not so much a function of dealing with contentious parties as it was an effort to get the parties to provide any help at all or even on some occasions to show appropriate attention to the issues.

The three judge panel that was given the case after DeMascio left pressed hard for early settlement, but was reversed on appeal. Though the termination date is in sight, Judge Cohn has been faced with conflict over the remaining elements of the order.

The problems confronting the judges who decided the racial discrimination cases considered to this point were in some ways similar to, but in others quite different from, those facing judges who rendered rulings in the so-called institutional reform cases. These are the suits in which conditions in state prisons and mental hospitals around the country have been challenged. It is to these issues that the next four chapters are directed.

NOTES

1. *Milliken v. Bradley,* 418 U.S. 717 (1974).

2. Testimony of Robert M. Frehse, Executive Director, Detroit Roundtable of the Michigan Region, National Conference of Christians and Jews, in U.S. Commission on Civil Rights, *Hearings Held in Detroit, Michigan, December 14–15 (1960)* (Wash., DC: Government Printing Office, 1961), pp. 25–38.

3. *Id.*

4. *Id.,* at 31.

5. *Id.,* at 34.

6. *Bradley v. Milliken,* 388 F. Supp. 582, 585 (EDMI 1971).

7. *Id.,* at 586

8. Elwood Hain, "Sealing Off the City: School Desegregation in Detroit," in Howard I. Kolodner and James J. Fishman, eds., *Limits of Justice: The Court's Role in School Desegregation* (Cambridge, MA: Ballinger, 1978), p. 228.

9. *Milliken v. Bradley*, 418 U.S. 717 (1974), Joint Appendix, IIa6 [hereafter as *Milliken I*, JA].

10. *Bradley v. Milliken*, 484 F.2d 215, 224 (6th Cir. 1973).

11. Hain, *supra* note 8, at 228.

12. *Bradley v. Milliken, supra* note 10, at 232–35.

13. *Id.,* at 226–27.

14. *Id.,* at 223.

15. *Bradley v. Milliken, supra* note 6, at 582, 588.

16. William Grant provides an excellent explanation of this tension in his "Community Control vs. School Integration—The Case of Detroit," *Public Interest* 24 (Summer 1971): 62–79. *See also* Grant, "The Detroit School Case: An Historical Overview," 21 *Wayne L. Rev.* 851 (1975).

17. Grant, "Historical Overview," *supra* note 16, at 856.

18. Hain, *supra* note 8, at 229–30.

19. Grant, "Community Control," *supra* note 16, at 65.

20. *Id.,* at 66.

21. *Id.,* at 68.

22. *See generally* Wolfgang Pindur, "Legislative and Judicial Roles in the Detroit School Decentralization Controversy," 50 *Journal of Urban Law* 53 (1972).

23. Grant, "Historical Overview," *supra* note 16, at 856.

24. Grant, "Community Control," *supra* note 16, at 71.

25. Hain, *supra* note 8, at 233.

26. *Id.,* at 234; and Grant, "Community Control," *supra* note 16, at 72.

27. Grant, "Historical Overview," *supra* note 16, at 857–58; and, *id.,* "Community Control," *supra* note 16, at 73. *See also* Hain, *supra* note 8, at 234–35.

28. Pindur, *supra* note 22, at 66–68; and "Brief for Respondents Board of Education for the School District of the City of Detroit, et al., in No. 73–434, *Milliken v. Bradley [Milliken II]*," in Philip B. Kurland and Gerhard Casper, eds., *Landmark Briefs and Arguments of the Supreme Court of the United States: Constitutional Law* (Arlington, VA: Univ. Publications of America, Inc., 1975), vol. 80, p. 1008 [hereafter *Landmark Briefs*].

29. Grant, "Community Control," *supra* note 16, at 73.

30. Pindur, *supra* note 22, at 68.

31. *Bradley v. Milliken*, 433 F.2d 897, 900 (6th Cir. 1970).

32. Pindur, *supra* note 22, at 68–69.

33. Hain, *supra* note 8, at 236–38.

34. Grant, "Community Control," *supra* note 16, at 75.

35. Grant, "Historical Overview," *supra* note 16, at 859.

36. *Id.,* at 851. *See also* William Serrin, "The Most Hated Man in Michigan," *Saturday Review,* Aug. 26, 1972, pp. 13–15; and Jerry M. Flint, "Judge in Busing Case: Stephen John Roth," *New York Times,* June 16, 1972.

37. Roth found, "Here the proofs are not convincing that there has been a course of action which can be characterized as directed toward the maintenance of a dual system of schools, either *de jure* or *de facto.* To the contrary the evidence before the court indicates that there has been a conscious, deliberative, progressive, and continuous attempt to promote and advance the integration of both pupils and faculty." *Milliken I,* JA, *supra* note 9, at Ia60.

38. *Bradley v. Milliken, supra* note 31, at 897.

39. *Id.,* at 902–3.

40. Grant, "Community Control," *supra* note 16, at 76.

41. *Milliken I,* JA, *supra* note 9, at Ia91.

42. *Bradley v. Milliken*, 438 F.2d 945 (6th Cir. 1971).

43. *Id.,* at 946–47.

44. Grant, "Historical Overview," *supra* note 16, at 862.

45. Particularly interesting was the testimony of Richard Marks, *Milliken I, supra* note 9, JA, Ia16–18; and the testimony of Karl Taeuber, *Milliken I*, JA, *supra* note 9, Ia23. The essentials of the housing case are in William L. Taylor, "The Supreme Court and Urban Reality: A Tactical Analysis of Milliken v. Bradley," 21 *Wayne L. Rev.* 751, 765–68 (1975).

46. Brief for Petitioners, in *Milliken v. Bradley (Milliken I),* in 80 *Landmark Briefs, supra* note 28, at 696 n. 9.

47. *See* Paul R. Dimond, *Beyond Busing* (Ann Arbor: Univ. of Michigan Press, 1985), pp. 42–56. *See also* Grant, "Historical Overview," *supra* note 16, at 862–63.

48. *Milliken I,* JA, *supra* note 9, at Ia119–20.

49. *Bradley v. Milliken, supra* note 6, at 582.

50. *Id.,* at 585–86.

51. *Id.*

52. *Id.,* at 586–87.

53. *Id.,* at 593.

54. *Id.*

55. *Id.,* at 588.

56. *Id.,* at 589.

57. *Id.,* at 587.

58. *Id.,* at 592.

59. *Green v. County School Bd., of New Kent County, Va.* 391 U.S. 430 (1968); *Raney v. Bd. of Ed.,* 391 U.S. 443 (1968); *Monroe v. Bd. of Commissioners,* 391 U.S. 450 (1968); *Alexander v. Holmes County Bd. of Ed.,* 396 U.S. 19 (1969); *Carter v. West Feliciano Parish School Board,* 396 U.S. 226 (1969); *Swann v. Charlotte-Mecklenburg Bd. of Ed.,* 402 U.S. 33 (1971).

60. *Swann v. Charlotte-Mecklenburg, supra* note 59, at 28.

61. *Green v. County School Bd., supra* note 59, at 437–38.

62. *See e.g.,* James Bolner and Robert Shanley, *Busing: The Political and Judicial Process* (New York: Praeger, 1974), ch. 1.

63. *Spangler v. Pasadena,* 311 F. Supp. 501 (SDCA 1970).

64. *Johnson v. San Francisco Unified School Dist.,* 339 F. Supp. 1315 (NDCA 1971).

65. *United States v. Bd. of Comm'rs of Indianapolis,* 332 F. Supp. 655 (SDIN 1971).

66. *Bradley v. Richmond,* 325 F. Supp. 828 (EDVA 1971).

67. *Davis v. School Dist. of Pontiac,* 390 F. Supp. 734 (EDMI 1970).

68. Bolner and Shanley, *supra* note 62, at 148–50.

69. The text of the speech is reprinted in the *New York Times,* Mar. 17, 1972, p. 22.

70. Bolner and Shanley, *supra* note 62, ch. 2.

71. Broomfield Amendment, P.L. 92–311, Section 803.

72. Louis D. Beer, "The Nature of the Violation and the Scope of the Remedy: An Analysis of Milliken v. Bradley in Terms of the Evolution of the Theory of the Violation," 21 *Wayne L. Rev.* 903, 909 (1975).

73. It is Beer's position that *Milliken* ended as it did because tactical difficulties caused the case to get out of hand. He concluded that the NAACP really wanted to try this case to establish the linkage between past housing discrimination and school segregation and not as a metropolitan remedy case. For the NAACP perspective, see Dimond, *supra* note 47, chs. 2–3.

74. *Bradley v. Richmond, supra* note 66. The interdistrict remedy ordered by Judge Mehrige in Richmond was struck down by the Fourth Circuit, 462 F.2d 1058 (4th Cir. 1972), *aff'd by an equally divided court,* 412 U.S. 92 (1973).

75. *Milliken I,* JA, *supra* note 9, at Ia206–7.

76. *Id.,* at IVa1.

77. *Id.*

78. Testimony of Dr. Betsy Ritzenhein, *supra* note 9, at IVa44 *et seq.*

79. Testimony of Dr. Gordon Foster, *supra* note 9, at IVa63 *et seq.*

80. *Id.,* at IVa64.

81. *Id.*, at IVa74–77.

82. *Id.*, at IVa70.

83. "Q. Mr. Krasicky asked you a hypothetical question with regard I believe to the constitutionality of the plan, making the assumption that Detroit was an educational island, self-contained surrounded by a sea and you said it would be a sound plan. Now I ask you to look at it realistically as an educational island surrounded by a sea whose suburban community is basically white. Without addressing yourself to the problem of correcting the obligations of the Detroit school system but going up a level in our responsibility to the problems of the state itself, taking your plan and assuming that it is completely effective and results in a school district as you have proposed, would you not have looking at your plan with suburban communities, the State of Michigan maintaining a plenary school system, namely a school system in Detroit which is identifiable as racially black surrounded by others which are identifiable as racially white? . . .

A. Well, I think I have inferred already that Detroit taken in the context of the metropolitan area, at least technically would be racially indentifiable." *Id.*, at IVa103.

84. *Id.*, at IVa11.

85. *Id.*, at IVa23.

86. *Id.*, at IVa22–23.

87. *Id.*, at IVa58.

88. *Id.*, at Va112–14.

89. "Not only would you not be able to have the social and economic advantages of racial desegregation in that instance, you are also stirring a pot which has substantially more volatility to it. You are putting students together for whom racial intolerance is typically the highest and you are running the risk at least in the initial years of such desegregation of increased student violence in such schools, increased over that which it would be if you could desegregate across social economic status boundaries." *Id.*, at IVa114.

90. *Id.*, at IVa32–44.

91. *Id.*, at IVa39.

92. *Id.*, at IVa144–45.

93. *Bradley v. Milliken*, 345 F. Supp. 914, 934, n. 22 (EDMI 1972).

94. *Id.*, at 923–24.

95. *Milliken I*, JA, *supra* note 9, at IVa207, 224–26.

96. *Id.*, at IVa207.

97. *Id.*, at IVa224.

98. *Id.*, at IVa225.

99. *Id.*, at IVa234.

100. *Id.*, at IVa235–37.

101. *Bradley v. Milliken*, *supra* note 93, at 924.

102. *Id.*

103. *Id.*, at 917.

104. *Id.*, at 918.

105. *Id.*

106. *Id.*, at 936.

107. *Id.*

108. *Id.*, at 916.

109. *Id.*, at 935.

110. *Id.*

111. *Id.*

112. *Id.*

113. *Id.*, at 929.

114. *Id.*, at 930.

115. *Id.*, at 936.

116. "Attacks on Judge Roth Show Contempt for Law," *Detroit Free Press*, Aug. 1, 1972; reproduced in 51 *Mich. St. Bar J.* 481 (1972).

117. "Attacks on Judge Roth Condemned," 51 *Mich. St. Bar J.* 716 (1972).

118. *Milliken v. Bradley, supra* note 1.

119. *Bradley v. Milliken, supra* note 10, at 215, 252.

120. *Id.,* at 242.

121. *Id.,* at 231.

122. *Id.,* at 249.

123. Transcript of Oral Argument in the Supreme Court of the United States in Nos. 73–434, 73–435, 73–436, *Milliken v. Bradley* (Wash., DC: Hoover Reporting Co., p. 1974), at 6 [hereafter *Milliken I* argument].

124. Brief of Petitioners, in *Milliken v. Bradley,* 80 *Landmark Briefs, supra* note 28, at 709.

125. Saxton, in *Milliken I* argument, *supra* note 123, at 25.

126. Flannery, in *Milliken I* argument, *supra* note 123, at 51–53, 59.

127. *See* Robert Bork, in *Milliken I* argument, *supra* note 123, at 33–39.

128. Memorandum for the United States as Amicus Curiae, 80 *Landmark Briefs, supra* note 28, at 1095–1124.

129. See Taylor, *supra* note 45.

130. *See generally* Leon Friedman, ed., *United States v. Nixon: The President Before the Supreme Court* (New York: Chelsea House, 1974).

131. *See* Taylor, *supra* note 45. *See also* Thomas F. Pettigrew, "A Sociological View of the Post Bradley Era," 21 *Wayne L. Rev.* 813 (1975).

132. For a summary of the criticism, *see* Hain, *supra* note 8, at 277–306.

133. *Id.,* at 274 n. 276. DeMascio found Judge Weinstein's discussion of the use of experts in *Hart v. Community School Bd., of Brooklyn, N.Y., School Dist. No. 21* 383 F. Supp. 699, 764–67 (EDNY 1974) useful. *Bradley v. Milliken,* 426 F. Supp. 929, 939 (EDMI 1977).

134. *Bradley v. Milliken,* 411 F. Supp. 943, 944 (EDMI 1975).

135. *Bradley v. Milliken,* 402 F. Supp. 1096 (EDMI 1975).

136. *Bradley v. Milliken, supra* note 134, at 943.

137. *Bradley v. Milliken, supra* note 135 at 1105.

138. Hain, *supra* note 8, at 300.

139. Testimony of Charles Wolfe, in *Milliken II*, Milliken v. Bradley, 433 U.S. 267 (1977), Joint Appendix at 10. [hereafter cited as Milliken II, JA]

140. *Id.,* at 9.

141. *Bradley v. Milliken, supra* note 135, at 1119.

142. *Id.,* at 1120. *See also* testimony of Alfred Pelham, in *Milliken II,* JA, *supra* note 139, at 15–22; and testimony of Detroit School Board President Cornelius Golightly, in *id.,* at 12–14.

143. *Bradley v. Milliken, supra* note 135, at 1120.

144. *Id.,* at 1101.

145. *Id.,* at 1125.

146. *Id.,* at 1116.

147. *Id.,* at 1128.

148. *Id.,* at 1129.

149. *Id.*

150. *Bradley v. Milliken, supra* note 133, at 929, 936.

151. *Bradley v. Milliken, supra* note 134, at 1125–26.

152. *Bradley v. Milliken, supra* note 133, at 937.

153. *Id.,* at 935–36.

154. *Bradley v. Milliken, supra* note 134, at 1134.

155. *Id.*

156. *Id.,* at 1135.

157. *Id.*

158. *Id.*

159. *Id.,* at 1136.

160. *Id.*

161. *Id.,* at 1139.

162. *Bradley v. Milliken,* 540 F.2d 229 (6th Cir. 1976).

163. *Id.,* at 239.

164. *Id.,* at 240.

165. *Milliken v. Bradley,* 433 U.S. 267 (1977) *(Milliken II).*

166. *Bradley v. Milliken, supra* note 133, at 929.

167. *Id.,* at 943–44.

168. *Bradley v. Milliken,* 460 F. Supp. 299 (EDMI 1978).

169. *Id.,* at 301.

170. *Id.,* at 302–3.

171. *Bradley v. Milliken,* 620 F.2d 1143 (6th Cir. 1980).

172. *Id.,* at 1150.

173. *Bradley v. Milliken,* Civ. Action No. 35257, "Stipulation of the Parties Regrading Funding and Implementation of the Court-Ordered Educational Components, Attorney Fees, and Costs," June 29, 1981.

174. *Bradley v. Milliken,* Civ. Action No. 35257, "Memorandum and Opinion," Apr. 24, 1984.

175. *Bradley v. Milliken,* Nos. 84–1364 and 84–1365, Sixth Circuit, Sept. 16, 1985.

6

Politics and Pathos: Federal Courts and the Right to Treatment in Mental Health Facilities

"Before medicine, there was magic."[1] Albert Deutsch began his important work *The Mentally Ill in America* with these words. He could just as well have added, "and after medicine, there was controversy." This chapter is about the role of the courts in mental health policy. Conditions in mental health facilities and demands for adequate treatment for people committed to those institutions have been the subjects of some of the most often criticized federal district court rulings.

Issues in these cases differ markedly from the housing and schools cases considered in previous chapters. Unlike those controversies, policy contests over mental health facilities involve life in what are generally referred to as total institutions. Patients are totally dependent upon the administrators of these facilities to provide for all of their physical needs as well as their actual treatment. Their lives are, in turn, completely controlled by the rules and organizational routines those administrators establish.

Those who administer mental health institutions are, however, politically and financially constrained in their ability to meet the needs of patients charged to their care. Like the school desegregation and housing cases, the development and implementation of mental health policies are the products of a variety of government and private actors and processes. Unlike the administrators in those highly visible education and housing cases, though, mental health administrators face different political and managerial problems because theirs is a much less politically visible clientele.

In order to fully comprehend the dynamics of complex mental health remedial decrees, like the *Wyatt v. Stickney* litigation that will be the focal case study for this policy area, one must address: (1) the significant features of mental health policy development; (2) the law and policy issues of greatest concern to mental health; and (3) the political and legal tensions affecting the administrative and judicial responses to those issues.

THE DEVELOPING MENTAL HEALTH PICTURE

In ancient civilizations mental illness and retardation were considered manifestations of demonic possession. Not surprisingly, priests were called upon to meet mental health needs.[2] Various techniques were employed over the centuries to drive out the presumed demons, ranging from physical torture to religious ceremonies of exorcism.

Greece and Rome departed from the earlier approach regarding those afflicted as ill, and Rome established guardianship laws for their protection.[3] Progress was, however, exceedingly uneven. Indeed, the "cures" utilized in the Middle Ages of Europe were "a superstitious mixture of astrology, alchemy, and a retreat to theology, magic rites and exorcism, with the accompanying belief in demoniacal possession."[4]

Monasteries, hospitals, prisons, and poorhouses were variously employed to house the mentally ill and mentally retarded in later-day Europe. Facilities in Paris and the Bethlehem (later known as Bedlam) and York asylums in England produced tales of neglect and abuse that provided future generations of mental health professionals with a zeal for reform.

In the American colonies, families were primarily responsible for the mentally ill. They often hid the sick or retarded from public view. As early as 1676 some families prevailed upon their communities for assistance in providing subsistence for their mentally ill dependents.[5] By and large, though, mentally ill or retarded Americans, like their European counterparts, were often committed to workhouses, jails, and almshouses. Some were even auctioned off as farm laborers.[6] Public efforts to develop hospitals for the mentally ill were led by Benjamin Franklin in Pennsylvania in 1751 and members of the Virginia House of Burgesses in 1773. The first facility dedicated entirely to mental health was constructed in Williamsburg, Virginia, but such hospitals were not replicated elsewhere until the Eastern Lunatic Asylum was constructed in Lexington, Kentucky, in 1824.[7]

A Century of Reform

Efforts to provide decent facilities and improved treatment for the mentally ill produced a century of reform, the beginnings of which can be traced to 1844. It was then that a group of hospital superintendents led by Dr. Benjamin Rush (often called "the father of American psychiatry") formed the American Psychiatric Association (APA), a major force in mental health reform from that time on. In addition to organized reform activity, individual practitioners contributed their clinical efforts toward development of more humane and efficacious treatment procedures.[8]

Of nearly equal importance to the clinical developments, though, were the reform efforts of a number of social activists, most notably Dorothea Lynde Dix. Dix quickly discovered the difficulty of representing the mentally ill as a political constituency. Her memorial to the Massachusetts legislature began, "I come to present the strong claims of suffering humanity. I come to place before the Legislature of Massachusetts the condition of the miserable, the desolate, the outcast. I come as the advocate of helpless, forgotten, insane and idiotic men and women . . . of beings wretched in our prisons, and more wretched in our Alms-Houses."[9]

Dix learned another lesson in her early work, the importance of careful, systematic research and the methods of using that research to best political advantage. The visit to the East Cambridge, Massachusetts, jail, which first made her aware of the conditions under which the mentally ill were confined, happened by accident. She had gone as a substitute Sunday-school teacher. Before issuing her political demands for reform, however, Dix completed a two-year survey of Massachusetts jails and other facilities where the mentally ill were kept. Her documentation of numerous cases of abuse in various jurisdictions proved unanswerable. After winning her crusade in Massachusetts, Dix carried the fight from one state to another, using her political skills and data to best advantage. By the time of her retirement in 1881, after forty years of crusading for mental health reform, she had fostered development of mental health facilities in twenty states, the District of Columbia, Canada, Scotland, and England.

A somewhat different but also important part of the reform movement was the effort to prevent improper commitments. The legal basis for commitment of the mentally ill was not firmly established until 1845.[10] Standards and procedures varied widely in different jurisdictions. Several authors published tales of improper commitments accomplished by malevolent relatives or business competitors. In later years there would be tension between the attention paid to the commitment questions and the lack of concern for hospital conditions. Albert Deutsch expressed this frustration:

> Of all the social problems arising out of the phenomenon of mental disease, perhaps none has captured the popular imagination during the past century as the possibility of confining sane persons in "insane asylums." Let thousands of mental patients in the public hospitals of a state exist under terrible conditions of overcrowding; let them be fed with bad food; let them be placed under all sorts of restraints; let them lack adequate medical care due to poor therapeutic equipment or an understaffed personnel; let them be housed in dangerous firetraps; let them suffer a thousand and one unnecessary indignities and humiliations, and more likely than not, their plight will attract but little attention. The newspapers will maintain a respectful silence. But once let rumor spread about a man or woman illegally committed to a mental hospital, and newspaper headlines will scream; the public will seethe with indignation; investigations and punitive expeditions will be demanded.[11]

One other impetus for reform combined with the work of clinical professionals and the campaigns of the social reformers: the psychological effects of war. World War I and II increased the need for education in, and research on, psychiatry. In fact, psychiatry was first fully recognized by the military with the establishment of a position on the staff of the Surgeon General during World War II. The impact of the war on psychiatry in federal institutions carried over into the postwar years with requests for psychiatric services at Veterans Administration hospitals.

Postwar Criticism

There had indeed been areas of improvement in American mental health treatment, but it was painfully clear by the early postwar years that "[o]ver-optimistic historical accounts . . . tended to concentrate on the peaks of progress that arise here and there, overlooking the lowlands and the valleys which still comprise the general level."[12] Albert Deutsch led criticism of American mental health treatment with his study of the conditions in state hospitals in the 1930s, when the effects of economic depression were particularly severe for mental health facilities. After World War II Deutsch conducted another survey. He found:

> In some of the wards, there were scenes that rivaled the horrors of the Nazi concentration camps—hundreds of naked mental patients herded into huge, barnlike, filth-

infested wards, in all degrees of deterioration, untended and untreated, stripped of every vestige of human decency, many in stages of semi-starvation.

The writer heard state hospital doctors frankly admit that the animals of near-by piggeries were better fed, housed and treated than many of the patients in their wards.[13]

The APA was alarmed as well. It began studies leading to the publication in 1945 of standards detailing basic physical plant and staffing minimums required to ensure essential care and treatment of mental patients. The organization launched a program of inspections and ratings for mental hospitals patterned after the American Medical Association's (AMA's) evaluations of medical facilities.

Lawyers also became involved, working with psychiatrists in an effort to improve cooperation between the two professions.[14] Tensions between the two groups had been increasing and there was little communication between them even though their work was necessarily interrelated. The American Bar Association (ABA) launched more formal efforts to determine whether a standing committee on mental health and the law should be established and statutory reform efforts promoted. Earlier, the bar had dealt with mental health matters through its committees on property, trusts, and estates, but questions of criminal law and psychiatry, commitment, and contested forms of care and treatment required an expanded view. After extensive preliminary work dating from 1945, the American Bar Foundation launched a wide-ranging study on the mentally disabled and the law that was published in 1961.[15]

At about this time, Morton Birnbaum, a New York physician and lawyer, pulled the various arguments for reform together into a case for a "legal right of a mentally ill inmate of a public mental institution to adequate medical treatment for his mental illness."[16] Birnbaum's thesis was that medicine and its various psychiatric specialties could, and should, help the many people committed by law to public mental health facilities but that a lack of political support prevented it.[17] He argued that the basis for the right to treatment is the due process clause of the Fourteenth Amendment to the U.S. Constitution. One who is committed for treatment and does not receive it is deprived of due process of law because treatment is the only legitimate basis for depriving one of his or her liberty. The lack of treatment eliminates the grounds for commitment. The *American Bar Association Journal* promptly supported Birnbaum's thesis in an editorial.[18]

The Legislative Push

Congress responded to the growing concern about mental health care with hearings in Senator Sam Ervin's Subcommittee on Constitutional Rights of the Senate Judiciary Committee in 1961 and 1963.[19] The Ervin Committee's activities were important for a number of reasons. The immediate fruit of the investigation was new District of Columbia mental health legislation with a variety of reform provisions. The hearings served as a focal point for discussions of the need for reform that had been in progress in various professional and social groups. The resulting legislation provided additional support for reformers in the states. Ten states approved substantial changes in their mental health laws between 1964 and 1969.[20] The District of Columbia law itself would be of major importance not only because of its local impact, but because it would serve as the basis for Judge David L. Bazelon's opinion in *Rouse v. Cameron* announcing a statutory "right to treatment" in the District of Columbia and suggesting a constitutional right to treatment as well.[21]

Five years after its adoption of the 1964 reform bill, the Committee reopened hearings on the rights of the mentally ill to determine the success of the District of Columbia legislation and take up a variety of issues not contemplated in that statute. It quickly became apparent that there was an entire collection of mental health issues to be addressed beyond questions about commitment procedures. In introducing the hearings, Ervin observed:

> The nation wide study that unfolded during those 1961 hearings was shocking and chilling. Witnesses presented reports of archaic, cumbersome laws and procedures, and of judicial machinery geared to problems of a century ago. Lack of funds, of personnel and facilities added to the complex of legal problems. . . .
>
> There were few laws or policies recognizing that a patient had any rights after the hospital door had closed upon him. The concept of a legal right to treatment as an essential part of constitutional due process was only a gleam in the eye of a few legal scholars. . . .
>
> Hospitalized patients are not politically important; they are voiceless. They lack the large, heavily financed organization to lobby for protections of their rights.[22]

The growing awareness of the numbers of citizens who would at one time or another need mental health treatment, the aftermath of the *Rouse v. Cameron* decision, the increasing litigation brought by developing mental health interest groups, the litany of cases presenting tales of grotesque, and in some cases brutal, conditions in the institutions spawned a continuing series of congressional inquiries and legislative responses throughout the 1970s.[23] Congress reacted to a number of the mental health issues with legislation keyed to federal funding. The Education for All Handicapped Children Act mandated a free appropriate public education for all children, including the physically or mentally handicapped.[24] The Developmental Disabilities Act was another important product, with its Bill of Rights for the Developmentally Disabled that insisted, "Persons with developmental disabilities have a right to appropriate treatment, services, and habilitation for such disabilities."[25]

Judicial Participation in the Reform Movement

The courts have been involved in mental health issues for centuries. One of the earliest judicial attempts at synthesizing the law on mental health was Lord Coke's opinion in *Beverly's Case* in 1603.[26] Much of the historic litigation concerned property rights and the obligations of guardians of the mentally ill or retarded. The recognition of a power to commit patients to mental health facilities reaches back to *In the Matter of Josiah Oakes,* an opinion by Chief Justice Shaw of the Massachusetts Supreme Court in 1845.[27] The insanity defense can be tracked back beyond *Beverly's Case,* but it came to this country largely through the British *McNaghten's Case* rendered in 1843.[28] *McNaghten* was applied in state courts in 1844, and by 1897 the U.S. Supreme Court had applied that doctrine nationally.[29]

As the mental health reform movement gathered momentum in the mid-twentieth century, courts at all levels were asked to address a wider range of issues, including complaints regarding institutional conditions, claims to a right to treatment, and challenges to commitment procedures. Most of these cases were petitions for writs of habeas corpus brought by patients seeking release. Judges were finding it extremely difficult to maintain the fiction that mental patients were being held for their own good rather than simply being punished by imprisonment, as in the case of a man tried for a misdemeanor who was committed as mentally ill to San Quentin. The court wrote:

> The emphasis that appellant places on the fact that he was originally convicted of a misdemeanor and now finds himself in San Quentin, possibly for life, is misplaced. *This argument would be sound only were his confinement punishment.*[30] (emphasis added)

Many judges, while attempting to avoid a direct confrontation over precisely what constituted minimally adequate treatment, were clearly moving in the direction of requiring some kind of care for patients who were ostensibly committed for the purpose of treatment.[31]

The Massachusetts Supreme Court confronted that question in 1959 in a case involving a man who had served his sentence in prison for a sex offense but was recommitted as a sexual psychopath on the motion of the district attorney. He objected that he could not be held unless he was to be treated and that the state had no such program except for the same kind of psychiatric counseling available to all prisoners. The court warned:

> But to be sustained as a nonpenal statute, in its application to the defendant, it is necessary that the remedial aspect of confinement thereunder have foundations in fact. It is not sufficient that the Legislature announce a remedial purpose if the consequences to the individual are penal. While we are not now called upon to state the standards which such a center must observe to fulfill its remedial purpose, we hold that a confinement in a prison which is undifferentiated from the incarceration of convicted criminals is not so remedial as to escape requirements of due process.[32]

Federal courts also appeared to be moving inexorably toward the declaration of a right to treatment. The Fourth Circuit went out of its way to avoid forcing Maryland to take any particular actions to improve its juvenile facilities, but admonished the state:

> [A] statute "fair on its face and impartial in appearance" may be fraught with the possibility of abuse in that if not administered in the spirit in which it is conceived it can be a mere device for warehousing the obnoxious and antisocial elements of society. . . . Deficiencies in staff, facilities, and finances would undermine the efficacy of the Institution and the justification for the law, and ultimately the constitutionality of its application.[33]

Judge Fahy's comment in another case that without treatment a hospital is transformed "into a penitentiary where one could be held indefinitely for no convicted offense" anticipated the developing legal trend in the District of Columbia Circuit.[34]

Judge Bazelon brought the growing case law, the legislative activity, and the suggestions of the mental health reform movement together in his opinion in *Rouse v. Cameron* in 1966. Relying primarily upon the 1964 Hospitalization of the Mentally Ill

Act, the court announced a right to treatment. Rouse had been committed to St. Elizabeth's Hospital in November 1962 after he was found not guilty, by reason of insanity, of carrying a deadly weapon, a misdemeanor normally punishable by a maximum of one year in jail. He filed an unsuccessful petition in the district court for a writ of habeas corpus alleging that he was being illegally confined since he was receiving no treatment. The appeals court reversed the district court dismissal of the petition.

Bazelon quoted the Ervin Committee hearings extensively, but not merely to underscore the congressional intention to create a statutory right to treatment in the 1964 legislation. He wrote, "Because we hold that the right to treatment provision [in the statute] applies to appellant, we need not resolve the serious constitutional questions that Congress avoided by prescribing this right."[35] But Bazelon left little question as to his conclusion on the constitutional issue for anyone who reads the opinion. He cited the case law holding that, absent additional explanation, commitment to a mental hospital was presumed to be for purposes of treatment. Quoting Birnbaum, he suggested that a failure to render treatment might be a violation of due process. He found possible equal protection or cruel and unusual punishment issues as well.[36]

In attempting to define the right, Bazelon accepted the need for flexibility in determining the appropriate types of treatment. He wrote, "The hospital need not show that the treatment will cure or improve him but only that there is a bona fide effort to do so. This requires the hospital to show that initial and periodic inquiries are made into the needs and conditions of the patient with a view to providing suitable treatment for him, and that the program provided is suited to his particular needs."[37]

Though he acknowledged the medical, political, and financial complexities involved in providing adequate staffs and facilities, he refused to accept shortages in those areas as reasons for inaction.[38] In the case of the District of Columbia statute, Congress had rejected a proposed provision that would have limited the need to provide treatment to "the extent that facilities, equipment, and personnel are available.[39] Bazelon went on to make a wider observation based upon civil rights precedent: "[I]ndefinite delay cannot be approved. 'The rights here asserted are . . . present rights . . . and, unless there is an overwhelmingly compelling reason, they are to be promptly fulfilled.' "[40]

The *Rouse* ruling not only provided grounds for a number of applications of the statutory right in the District of Columbia, but it established a further basis for broad constitutional rulings in other courts. It also prompted a wide-ranging discussion within the legal community about the right to treatment, its bases, application, and limits.[41] If there had been any question remaining as to Bazelon's commitment to a wider right to treatment, it was eliminated in his contribution to the *Georgetown Law Journal* symposium on the subject.[42] Acknowledging his support for the right, the judge went on to indicate that courts could decide cases brought under such a doctrine without interfering with mental health professionals' judgments about what types and quantities of treatment were best. Bazelon suggested that criteria, such as evidence of adequate staffing levels, acceptable maintenance of facilities, and indications that efforts were being made to design and deliver individualized treatment, expressed in the form of patient records should be sufficient to make the necessary findings. The Georgetown collection and a similar symposium prepared by the *University of Chicago Law Review* brought together a group of mental health law practitioners who were the leading characters in the battle for expanded rights for the mentally ill and mentally retarded.[43]

The constitutional development of the right-to-treatment principle continued with the Massachusetts Supreme Court arguing the existence of equal protection and due process grounds for the right.[44] The District of Columbia Circuit held that confinement must be in the least restrictive alternative situation available to avoid due process difficulty in light of the "drastic curtailment of rights" associated with commitment.[45] Finally, in 1971, Judge Frank Johnson found in *Wyatt v. Stickney* that there is a constitutional right to treatment for those committed to state mental health facilities protected by the due process clause of the Fourteenth Amendment. Following that decision "approximately 14 States . . . enacted legislation establishing 'bills of rights' for psychiatric patients and 12 have promulgated similar legislation for mentally retarded persons."[46]

Another change was in progress as well. Prior to the establishment of the right to treatment, most litigation was brought as habeas corpus petitions seeking a guarantee that the patient would be provided with treatment or be released. Of course, for many of those involved, the point was not to have persons who should be helped released because no help was available, but to force the government units concerned to provide the treatment and minimal living conditions necessary to all patients in their care. In order to achieve that end, attorneys used lessons learned from the civil rights movement and sought remedial orders that required adequate staff and facilities, acceptable basic living conditions, and individualized treatment programs.

Litigation continued around the country after *Wyatt,* with many courts accepting the right-to-treatment argument and crafting remedial decrees to rectify inadequacies.[47] In some instances judges were able to avoid mandating remedies because the parties to the case entered into consent decrees having negotiated an appropriate response for their situation.[48]

The Supreme Court was inevitably drawn into this reform discussion. In 1972 the Court struck down an Indiana application of its statutes concerning confinement of persons unable to stand trial by reason of mental deficiency.[49] The case arose when a twenty-seven-year-old man who had "the mental level of a pre-school child" and was speech and hearing impaired was charged with two robberies netting $9.00. He was found unable to stand trial by reason of his mental and physical condition and committed indefinitely to a mental health institution. The procedures for that type of commitment were considerably less stringent and the release possibilities much more limited than if he had been committed under standard state commitment procedures. The Court found violations of both the equal protection and due process clauses of the Fourteenth Amendment. In the process, the Court said, "[D]ue process requires that the nature and duration of commitment bear some reasonable relation to the purpose for which the individual is committed."[50] Clearly, if that purpose was treatment, the implication of the court's comment was plain.

In 1975 the Court held that the due process clause prohibited states from holding against his will "a nondangerous individual who is capable of surviving safely in freedom by himself or with the help of willing and responsible family members or friends.[51] The record showed that Kenneth Donaldson had been detained for fifteen years without treatment. Donaldson was one of the plaintiffs represented by Morton Birnbaum. Birnbaum reported extensively on that case while the litigation was in progress to the 1969–70 Ervin Committee hearings.

Addington v. Texas, like the two cases before it, was primarily concerned with providing protections against unlawful commitment or unlawful refusal to terminate custody.[52] In this case, the Court required something more than a preponderance-of-the-evidence standard for commitment to prevent abuses of commitment laws. In the process the Court recognized that commitment involves not only a curtailment of liberty, but also carries a social stigma that remains after the commitment has ended.

In 1982 the Court went well beyond its commitment rulings to reach the conditions of confinement, freedom from excessive use of restraints, and right to training or habilitation issues. Nicholas Romeo was a profoundly mentally retarded man who was committed to Pennhurst State School and Hospital when his mother was no longer able to care for him. Pennhurst had been under legal challenge for some years because of institutional conditions, staffing, and lack of treatment.[53] On visiting him at Pennhurst, Ms. Romeo found that her son suffered repeated injuries, some sixty-four incidents between July 1974 and November 1976. He was placed in the medical hospital section of Pennhurst and was physically restrained for substantial periods. His mother sued, charging violations of the Eighth Amendment bar against cruel and unusual punishment and the due process clause of the Fourteenth Amendment on the grounds that the state had an obligation to protect his physical safety, to avoid excessive use of bodily restraints, and to provide him with adequate habilitation and training to permit him to function as well as possible. The Court agreed with Eighth and Fourteenth Amendment claims, concluding:

> We repeat that the state concedes a duty to provide adequate food, shelter, clothing and medical care. These are the essentials of the care that the state must provide. The state also has the unquestioned duty to provide reasonable safety for all residents and personnel within the institution. And it may not restrain residents except when and to the extent professional judgment deems this necessary to assure such safety or to provide needed training. In this case, therefore, the state is under a duty to provide respondent with such training as an appropriate professional would consider reasonable to ensure his safety and to facilitate his ability to function free from bodily restraints. It may well be unreasonable not to provide training when training could significantly reduce the need for restraints or the likelihood of violence.[54]

The Court, however, chose not to answer some of the questions put to it and suggested the need for deference to the judgment of mental health professionals on others. While the Court recognized a right to training or habilitation, it drew narrow limits around just what would be included in that right, at least in the *Youngberg* case. It refused to address a wider concept of the right to treatment for the mentally ill or habilitation for the mentally retarded. The freedom from excessive bodily restraint is, according to the Court, to be assessed by a balancing test with the interests of the individual, on the one side, and the interests of the state, including administrative and financial burdens, on the other. Individuals have difficulty overcoming that kind of balancing formula. Since all parties accepted the need to provide adequate food, clothing, and shelter, the Court found it unnecessary to indicate what minimum standards might be. On the same day as its *Youngberg* ruling, the Court issued its opinion in a Massachusetts case that presented the question of whether there is a right to refuse behavior-modifying drugs.[55] The Court vacated a lower court ruling in favor of such a right in order to permit state courts to determine whether the right to refuse the drugs exists under state law. Thus, it avoided, for a time at least, several of the most difficult law and policy issues in mental health.

LAW AND POLICY ISSUES IN MENTAL
HEALTH AND RETARDATION

Like the other policy spaces investigated in earlier chapters, mental health and mental retardation policy is not concerned with one or two questions, but with a collection of issues that have made their way onto the public policy agenda. Cases in which courts are asked to address mental health policy may present one, a few, or many of these issues. The *Wyatt v. Stickney* case presents many, indeed most, of the recurring issues in this policy space. Historically, the central issues in mental health and retardation have included questions of commitment, conditions of institutionalization, the right to treatment, the right to refuse treatment, deinstitutionalization and community treatment, and legal protection for institutionalized citizens.

Commitment

The fear of wrongful commitment has been a continuing (and until recently predominating) focus of law and mental health policy debate. As Deutsch and Birnbaum observed, there is a certain irony in the fact that so much anxiety has been expressed about the possibility of commitment to a mental institution, on the one hand, while so little concern has been given to the reasons the institutions are deemed so undesirable.[56] The legal basis for civil commitment in the United States can be traced back to an 1845 Massachusetts Supreme Court decision concerning the commitment of one Josiah Oakes. Oakes sought a habeas corpus release from the McLean Asylum to which he had been committed at the request of his son. Chief Justice Shaw wrote:

> The right to restrain an insane person of his liberty, is found in that great law of humanity, which makes it necessary to confine those whose going at large would be dangerous to themselves or others. In the delirium of a fever, or in the case of a person seized with a fit, unless this were the law, no one could be restrained against his will. . . .

> The question must then arise, in each particular case, whether a person's own safety or that of others requires that he should be restrained for a certain time, and whether restraint is necessary for his restoration, or will be conducive thereto.[57]

Clearly, commitment to institution represents "a massive curtailment of liberty" that requires the protection of due process of law under the Fourteenth Amendment.[58] Placement in such an institution can mean more than a loss of the ability to come and go at will. It can mean tight control on freedom of action and movement within the hospital. It can also result in a loss of such other "rights as those of association, privacy, movement, and interstate travel."[59] Depending upon the circumstances and the particular state involved, "commitment may result in loss of custody of one's children, and loss of the rights to vote, to be a candidate for or retain public office, serve on a jury, practice a profession, obtain a driver's license, and make a contract or will."[60] Of almost equal concern to some, however, is the totally inappropriate, but nevertheless real, stigmatizing effect of having been committed to a mental hospital. "[T]he stigma attached, though in theory less severe than the stigma attached to criminal conviction, may in reality be as severe, or more so."[61]

Despite the obvious need for due process protection, different jurisdictions have historically varied widely in the kinds of procedural protections available to those facing commitment, ranging from very informal hearings largely predicated on recommendations by family or physicians to full-blown trial-type hearings before juries. Traditionally, those involved have not been afforded the minimal protections available to a person accused of criminal offenses. Though the Supreme Court has ruled that involuntary commitment is a deprivation of liberty requiring due process,[62] it has not specifically determined "whether, when, or by what procedures, a mentally ill person may be confined by the State on any of the grounds which . . . are generally advanced to justify involuntary commitment."[63] Summarizing the Court's holdings on the subject, Justice Brennan observed:

> In the absence of a voluntary waiver, adults facing commitment to mental institutions are entitled to full and fair adversary hearings in which the necessity for their commitment is established to the satisfaction of a neutral tribunal. At such hearings they must be accorded the right to "be present with counsel, have an opportunity to be heard, be confronted with witnesses against [them], have the right to cross-examine, and to offer evidence of [their] own."[64]

The problem identified in the Ervin hearings associated with increased procedural complexity, though, is that it may increase the traumatic effect of institutionalization to the patient and his or her family. It may also delay needed treatment while courtlike procedures are carried out. In fact, the complexity of the commitment process may even discourage family members from seeking treatment for those in need.

Judgments regarding the proper procedural guidelines are merely one part of the commitment process. There must be a set of standards for commitment to guide the substantive decision in individual cases. Again courts have been key actors, often leading legislative decisionmaking. The standards employed now are modern versions of the basic grounds for commitment mentioned in *Oakes*.

Nonemergency commitments occur either by voluntary admission to a facility or by involuntary civil commitment launched by the government, physicians, or concerned family members. Obviously, the most desirable option is for the patient to be convinced of the need to seek help and simply enter a facility. Indeed voluntary admissions have been steadily rising for years. Some have questioned the voluntary nature of these admissions on grounds that patients are often talked, coerced, or deceived into signing things they do not understand.[65] Involuntary nonemergency commitments are generally justified on the basis of what is referred to as the *parens patriae* authority of the state. Under this doctrine the state is the "general guardian of all infants, idiots, and lunatics."[66] *Parens patriae* commitments occur where a person is either unable to care for himself or is unable to understand the need for mental treatment.[67] As a general guardian, the state assumes the obligation of providing minimally safe and healthful living conditions and treatment. It is this kind of commitment that most clearly supports the case for a right to treatment. The Supreme Court has served notice that the judgment about one's ability to provide for one's self is a decision not to be taken lightly:

> That the state has a proper interest in providing care and assistance to the unfortunate goes without saying. But the mere presence of mental illness does not disqualify a

person from preferring his home to the comforts of an institution. Moreover, while the State may arguably confine a person to save him from harm, incarceration is rarely if ever a necessary condition for raising the living standards of those capable of surviving safely in freedom, on their own or with the help of family or friends. . . .

May the State fence in the harmless mentally ill solely to save its citizens from exposure to those whose ways are different? One might as well ask if the State, to avoid public unease could incarcerate all who are physically unattractive or socially eccentric. Mere public intolerance or animosity cannot constitutionally justify the deprivation of a person's physical liberty. . . .

In short, a State cannot constitutionally confine without more a nondangerous individual who is capable of surviving in freedom by himself or with the help of willing and responsible family members or friends.[68]

Criticisms of *parens patriae* commitments run in two quite different directions. Some physicians argue that these legal protections do not protect, they inhibit. They sap time, energy, and resources that ought to be dedicated to treatment, and they make it difficult to obtain treatment for those who need it. Some charge that the federal court rulings mean that patients must be released regardless of their ability to care for themselves. Others argue, however, that under conditions of fiscal scarcity, there is a tendency to use the kind of judicial comments cited earlier to justify dumping patients whose ability to care for themselves is questionable at best into a community ill equipped to assist them. The rapid release notion assumes community support programs, such as outpatient services or group homes that are often not available. Judges have been less than eager to accept blame for abuses of the effort to guard against inappropriate commitments. One judge insisted:

Finally, we wish to emphasize that our purpose is not to impose unnecessary restrictions upon the authorities charged with the care and treatment of [this state's] mentally ill. It is not our intention that the treatment of any mentally ill resident of [this state's] mental institutions be disrupted. And, contrary to the assumption made by [some], we neither contemplate nor order that the state release from its care and custody any persons presently confined in state mental hospitals who are unable to care and provide for themselves.[69]

Emergency commitments occur when patients are dangerous to themselves or to others. The basis for this kind of commitment is the state's police power, the power to regulate in matters of health, safety, and public welfare.[70] But the definition of an emergency situation may be less than clear. Legislators, judges, physicians, and other actors in the mental health policy arena have disagreed on the nature of psychiatric emergencies and what to do about them. For example, just how dangerous must one be to justify commitment? How immediate must the danger be? How great a harm must be threatened? Does danger to property rather than a person suffice? Perhaps one of the most difficult of all is the question how certain must the danger be?

One difficulty is that in situations of moderate or even slight risk of any harm, commitment can be used as preventive detention. That sort of detention can become an indefinite sentence without the protections normally available to a criminal defendant.[71] How much evidence ought to suffice to support such a commitment? How about the burden of proof? The Supreme Court has said that any commitment requires clear and convincing evidence, which is more than a mere preponderance of the evidence, but something less than the beyond a reasonable doubt standard.[72] Courts and legislatures have generally been willing to allow at least short term preventive detention with minimum procedural requirements in emergency situations so long as more complete procedures are available at some later time.

In addition to these general issues of commitment law and policy, there are several more specific, but broadly significant, special commitment problems. Two of the most widespread difficulties are the peculiarities of juvenile commitment and the problem of the relationship between commitment and competency.

Juvenile commitment presents somewhat different policy issues, depending upon whether the parents are the key decisionmakers or the government is acting for a ward of the state or limiting the choices of parents in state-operated programs. A number of states have voluntary admissions procedures by which parents can have their children committed to a mental hospital or retardation center on their signature and a diagnosis by an admitting physician. Unfortunately, as one mental health administrator observed, "There are a lot of people who still treat [mental hospitals] as dumping grounds."[73] The Supreme Court has held that "a child in common with adults, has a substantial liberty interest in not being confined unnecessarily for medical treatment."[74] Even so, parental decisions about treatment usually limit the liberty of the child. The Court has ruled that so long as there is an independent person, such as a diagnosing physician, involved in the commitment decision, the minor does not have a right to a hearing on his or her commitment, either at the time of commitment or thereafter.[75] In some states the effect of that approach has been that minors remained institutionalized even though staff members indicated they should not be in the hospitals because the state was unable or unwilling to shoulder the financial burden of creating alternative placement facilities, such as specialized foster care.[76] The problem becomes more acute where the child is the ward of the state and there is no parental involvement. The question arises whether the child was committed because of psychological need or because he or she was unlikely to be adopted and there seemed no suitable alternative placement.[77] Writing for the majority, Chief Justice Burger has said there is no special problem with wards of the state since it must be assumed that the state acts in the best interests of the child. One of the dissenters replied, "With equal logic, it could be argued that criminal trials are unnecessary since prosecutors are not supposed to prosecute innocent persons."[78]

Another issue of commitment that has important implications for such questions as the right to refuse treatment and other aspects of mental health care concerns the distinction between competency and commitment. It is often assumed that one who suffers from mental illness that requires treatment is by definition legally incompetent to make wills, enter contracts, control property, and the like. Testifying before the Senate Subcommittee on Constitutional Rights in 1969, Dr. Mildred Bateman cautioned, "While this may be true of many patients, it is not true of all."[79] The observation that many mental illnesses are specific and not completely debilitating and that patients may have prolonged lucid periods interrupted by psychiatric episodes is not a particularly new or novel notion. Indeed, Justinian's Code, the Visigothic Code, and early British law all recognized competence at least for some periods in otherwise mentally ill persons.[80] Thus, where questions arise about decisions that might be made by mental patients, one must take some care in determining whether the patient is, in fact, incompetent.[81]

Conditions of Institutionalization

Attention to criminal or civil mechanisms by which people are committed has oversha-dowed questions of the conditions within those institutions. Yet judicial and legislative activity in the late 1960s and after forced a consideration of law and policy questions associated with institutional conditions. This general question presents a cluster of spe-cific issues, including constitutional questions of a right to minimally adequate condi-tions; description of the specific kinds of minimal conditions required; the demand for the least restrictive conditions of confinement; and the problem of institutional peonage.

Most of the discussion of constitutional rights to treatment presented earlier focused on a claim to protection under the due process clause of the Fourteenth Amendment. Failure to provide treatment for those originally committed on grounds that they required treatment has been held by a variety of courts to be a deprivation of liberty without due process. But other constitutional issues have been raised concerning institutional condi-tions and right to treatment. The most frequent of these are assertions that institutional conditions are so bad as to constitute cruel and unusual punishment within the meaning of the Eighth Amendment and that arbitrary treatment of the mentally ill or retarded purely on the basis of their mental condition violates the Fourteenth Amendment re-quirement of equal protection of the law.[82]

The Eighth Amendment argument is made on two grounds. The Supreme Court ruled in 1962 that punishing a person for a physical condition, such as drug addiction, is cruel and unusual punishment.[83] A variety of courts have held that while punishment is generally a function of legislative intention, keeping someone confined within an institution without reason or basic physical necessities of health and human decency is, in fact, cruel and unusual punishment.[84] The Supreme Court has said, "If it is cruel and unusual punishment to hold convicted criminals in unsafe conditions, it must be unconstitutional to confine the involuntarily committed—who may not be punished at all—in unsafe conditions."[85]

Equal protection arguments contend that when the state treats the mentally ill dif-ferently from others within the society so as to deprive them of fundamental liberties, there is a form of discrimination that can be allowed only if the state can show compel-ling justification.[86] There can be no compelling reasons for locking mentally ill or re-tarded persons up in inhumane conditions.

There is one additional constitutional argument made repeatedly in the past decade, namely, that even if the state has adequate authority to institutionalize a person for nonpenal reasons, it must use the least restrictive means of accommodating the state purposes consistent with the maintenance of individual freedom and dignity. This least-restrictive-treatment theory is based upon cases in which the Supreme Court has held that "even though the governmental purpose be legitimate and substantial, that purpose cannot be pursued by means that broadly stifle fundamental liberties when the end can be more narrowly achieved."[87] There must be, then, some notion of liberty even inside a mental health or retardation institution.[88]

There have been surprisingly few disagreements about the minimum institutional conditions needed to provide safe and humane care. They generally include reasonable space to avoid overcrowding, a healthful climate that avoids extremes of temperature, basic cleanliness, decent repair of buildings, and surroundings free of rodents and ex-cessive insect infestation (a problem often accompanying inadequate sanitation and poor

climate control). For the patients, minimum standards have entailed protections of physical safety from abuse by staff members or other patients, elementary fire and emergency safeguards (including evacuation plans), adequate medical care provided by qualified medical practitioners, and access to adequate hygiene facilities. While there have
been differences of opinion over how much space is necessary per patient and how large
a support staff is needed, few disagree about the types of services required. The lack of
public attention and competing political and financial tensions, however, have meant
that demands for these minimum conditions were often forced into judicial forums.

The concept of treatment and habilitation (the type of training provided to the
mentally retarded) in the least restrictive environment took on specific requirements over
time. These include proper placement in the right kind of institution for the type of
assistance the patient or mentally retarded person requires; freedom from unnecessary
physical restraints; protection against excessive use of psychotropic (behavior-modifying)
drugs; freedom from the unnecessary use of isolation rooms; minimum protections of
privacy and private property; access to recreation and outdoor activity; opportunities to
communicate with friends, family, and legal counsel through the mails or over the
telephone; visitation rights; opportunities to request release from confinement; and protection against arbitrary sterilization or experimentation.

Here, there was resistance from some administrators and psychiatrists. The former
felt caught in a squeeze between the lack of adequate staff and facilities and demands
for more service and better protection for patients. How does one assure the safety of
patients without excessive use of physical restraints, isolation, or chemical restraints
when there are not nearly enough mental health professionals, paraprofessionals, or even
ward assistants? Some members of the psychiatric community rebelled against judicial
rulings in this area because judgments about least restrictive conditions deprived physicians of absolute control over their patients' care. On the one hand, conditions and
treatment suits meant that overburdened professionals would have to divert time and
energy from patients to satisfying potential challengers regarding their treatment of patients. How does one explain to nonprofessionals the bases of all forms of treatment
employed? Perhaps of equal importance, however, was a sort of professional self-doubt:
It was difficult to retreat to a claim to professional knowledge when there was so much
disagreement within the profession itself about mental retardation and mental disease
and treatment.

A frequent rejoinder to the claim that outsiders, and particularly judges, ought to
stay out of professional decisionmaking was that in many cases the evidence clearly
established that patients were not in their current institutional conditions because of
professional judgment but by virtue of neglect and understaffing. The lower court in
Donaldson v. O'Connor, for example, found that Donaldson saw his psychiatrist six
times in eighteen months for a total of one hour; and in eight-and-a-half years with a
second psychiatrist, he "did not speak with [this psychiatrist] more than a total of two
hours—an average of about fourteen minutes a year."[89] When the Supreme Court reviewed the case it concluded:

> The evidence showed that Donaldson's confinement was a simple regime of enforced
> custodial care, not a program designed to alleviate or cure his supposed illness.
> Numerous witnesses, including one of O'Connor's codefendants, testified that Don-
> aldson received nothing but custodial care while at the hospital. O'Connor described
> Donaldson's treatment as "milieu therapy." But witnesses from the hospital staff

conceded that, in the context of this case, "milieu therapy" was a euphemism for confinement in the "milieu" of a mental hospital. For substantial periods, Donaldson was simply kept in a large room that housed 60 patients, many of whom were under criminal commitment. Donaldson's requests for grounds privileges, occupational training, and an opportunity to discuss his case with O'Connor or other staff members were repeatedly denied.[90]

Judges consistently argued that they had no interest in second-guessing the judgments of mental health professionals, but they were required to ensure that someone had, in fact, made a professional judgment about a patient's needs or freedoms and was guiding his care.[91]

The final conditions of confinement issue that provided continued controversy was the practice of institutional peonage, the use of patients or mentally retarded residents to perform labor, ranging from menial housekeeping chores to participating in patient care without compensation and without the protections of maximum hours and minimum working conditions that apply outside the institution.[92] The Task Panel of Legal and Ethical Issues of the President's Commission on Mental Health reported in 1978:

> A 1972 study of 154 institutions in 47 States, which represents 76 percent of existing public facilities for the mentally handicapped, found that 32,180 of 150,000 residents were participating in work programs. Thirty percent were receiving no payment at all and an additional 50 percent were receiving less than $10 per week.[93]

Dr. F. Lewis Bartlett of the National Medical Committee for Human Rights testified before the Ervin Subcommittee that "unpaid patient labor" had become an integral part of the operation of state mental facilities though it was generally referred to by the euphemism, "work therapy."[94]

Challenges have been brought to institutional peonage on grounds that it represents involuntary servitude in violation of the Thirteenth Amendment, but judges have generally avoided that charge, finding in most instances that the patient was not absolutely compelled to perform the labor and, in others, that the labor was at least arguably within the realm of legitimate work therapy.[95] Some lower courts have, however, held that institutional patient labor is covered by the provisions of the Fair Labor Standards Act that govern minimum wages and working conditions.[96]

The Right to Treatment

Whether emanating from a statutory protection or based upon one of several constitutional grounds, the right to treatment seems relatively well established. Its parameters are, however, far from clear. In the case of mentally retarded persons, the phrase used is *a right to habilitation*. Retarded persons are not suffering from a mental illness, but a developmental disability. Under proper conditions and with proper services, retarded persons may be helped to maximize their capabilities within the limits of their disability. Those services and supportive conditions are referred to as elements of habilitation, as distinguished from treatment. While many lower courts have recognized rather sophisticated formulations of the right to treatment and habilitation, the Supreme Court has supported the basic concept but has avoided defining it and has cautioned that the starting point for any discussion of the topic must be deference to the expertise of mental health professionals.[97]

Many of the right-to-treatment opinions and legislative innovations have started from the basic treatment factors outlined in the *Rouse v. Cameron* decision, including provision of a humane physical environment, adequate staff and facilities, and a specific and individualized treatment or habilitation program for each patient or resident that is supported by adequate recordkeeping.

Some mental health professionals have resisted the notion of a right to treatment from the time of the *Rouse* ruling. The APA took a position against that ruling almost at once.[98] Their principal concern remained interference with treatment of patients by imposition of various legal standards and usurpation of professional medical judgment. Moreover, the attempt to apply staffing minimums came to be rejected by many psychiatric professionals because there were so many types and sizes of mental health facilities. Standard setting, they said, was impossible. Critics argued that the real reason for the APA resistance was that many facilities were in such dire straits that there was a vested interest in preventing outsiders from really understanding how bad things were.

In any case evaluations of the compliance with the right to treatment have raised two issues. First, most courts concur with Bazelon's view that right-to-treatment assessments must include both institutionwide conditions and examination of delivery of treatment to individual patients as evidenced by medical records.[99] Second, courts have refused to accept arguments that patients are entitled to the best available treatment rather than some minimally adequate treatment.[100]

The Right to Refuse Treatment

One of the most controversial of the issues in mental health policy presented to courts is related to the right to treatment but distinct from it.[101] If the state has an obligation to provide treatment, does the patient have a duty to accept it? This question has arisen in connection with two general kinds of clinical practices. The most prevalent cases have been those in which patients have been administered psychotropic (mind-altering) drugs. The other class of challenged practices has been the use of aversion therapy, electroshock therapy, or lobotomy. A number of federal and state courts have found that there is indeed a right to refuse treatment under some circumstances.[102]

Advocates of a right to refuse treatment have argued that the Constitution provides a number of bases for this, including the right to privacy based upon one's ability to maintain one's bodily integrity; the due process clause protection against deprivation of liberty without due process when drugs that chemically restrain patients are administered without notice or opportunity to object; the First Amendment protection of free speech and thought; and Eighth Amendment restrictions on cruel and unusual punishment.[103] Physicians and others have objected on several grounds. Their first claim is interference with medical judgment. Delays from procedural requirements and mandatory record-keeping are already burdensome. More specifically, they object that patients are in no position to know what treatment is best for them. That is in part why they are in a mental hospital.

The response has been that historically many facilities have given too many drugs too often without informing those being medicated what they were going to experience or notifying them of the possibility of long-term side effects. Drug have been one way to chemically handcuff patients in situations where shortages of staff made a quiet population easier to handle. These difficulties have been compounded by a lack of careful recordkeeping. Moreover, to argue the *parens patriae* notion that the patients must be medicated for their own good even though they do not understand it, assumes that commitment to a mental institution and mental incompetency are identical. The typical remedy has been to order the use of a consent form that sets forth the information about the drugs and their effects and the patient's right to refuse.[104] Even advocates of the right to refuse, however, do recognize that many patients will not be able to understand or give informed consent about the use of such treatment. The case law has established a system by which a refusal to accept treatment can be overcome where it is necessary to permit treatment of incompetent patients or is required for the safety of the patients or those around them.[105] One of the judges who issued such an order found it interesting that a year after his decision, the expenditures for medication at one New Jersey facility dropped from $191,000 to $98,000.[106]

Deinstitutionalization and Community Treatment

A fundamental thrust within mental health policy in the postwar years has been a move toward decentralized community-based treatment and away from large residential institutions. Two arguments supported the move. First, patients could avoid the detrimental effects of life in a large institution:

> One of the problems of institutionalization is clearly that it doesn't matter whether the institution is a prison institution or welfare institution but that if it is a total kind of institution, there are certain administrative procedures and processes which take over which act to condition the lives of the people within them, and then it becomes very difficult to speak meaningfully of releasing people from these institutions because they readjust their lives to the routine of the institution.[107]

Decentralized programs include halfway houses, group homes, community-based outpatient care, counseling centers, and vocational rehabilitation programs. Judges have, among other things, been asked to compel deinstitutionalization on the basis of least-restrictive-placement arguments.[108] The other deinstitutionalization argument has been a feasibility case, suggesting that it is administratively and financially better to have local centers not only because they are closer to the patients' homes but also because more federal funding sources are available to provide support.

There have, however, been counterpressures. Deinstitutionalization has sometimes resulted in discharge of patients into the community who were not yet ready to be returned. It has not always been accompanied by adequate support for community-based programs nor have officials watched those programs carefully. Moreover, some communities have fought establishment of group homes and halfway houses in their areas, meaning that some of those facilities have been placed in some of the least desirable parts of the community.[109] Finally, resources provided to community facilities often had to be taken away from large state facilities, which exacerbated conditions there and led to internecine warfare among administrators.

FINANCIAL AND POLITICAL TENSIONS

In addition to the specific issues that shape mental health policy, there have been important underlying political and financial tensions. Morton Birnbaum quite accurately asserted that many aspects of the mental health debate are as concerned with political dynamics and economic scarcity as they are about the most appropriate forms of treatment for the mentally ill.[110]

Political Dynamics of Mental Health Policy

Mental health policy has been shaped by several different types of political conflict. Professional politics within the mental health community has been an important element of this controversy. Conflict within these professional organizations spilled over into the wider political arena in the wake of the *Rouse* right-to-treatment ruling and in the Ervin Committee hearings of 1969–70. Dr. Zigmond M. Lebensohn of Georgetown University, representing the APA before the Committee, challenged the right-to-treatment decisions. He said, "The association holds that every patient has the inalienable right to receive treatment appropriate to his illness under conditions that protect his privacy and with essential humanity."[111] That view of patient rights was somewhat different from Birnbaum's. For Lebensohn, the danger to patient rights was not hospital conditions, indeed the APA had repudiated its own earlier standards for staff/patient ratios. Instead, the right the APA worried about was freedom from government interference in the form of burdensome procedures for getting patients into hospitals or care centers and in making treatment decisions thereafter.[112]

Birnbaum argued that the APA was abusing the concept of the right to treatment. In fact, he went so far as to charge that "one of the most effective barriers to the recognition and enforcement of the concept of a right to treatment is the official opposition of the American Psychiatric Association."[113] They kept trying, he said, to equate the right to some form of medically recognized treatment in minimally safe and decent conditions with a need for doctors to argue with judges about diagnoses and treatment, and the creation of roadblocks to voluntary admission to mental treatment.[114] Other organizations supported the right to treatment and disagreed with the APA. Dr. F. Lewis Bartlett testified on behalf of the National Medical Committee on Human Rights and issued the most direct challenge to the APA position:

> Although the indigent welfare State hospital model has denigrated State hospital employment through low salary scales, low standards, low demands, and unrealistically low professional status, the American Psychiatric Association bears the major responsibility for this state of affairs. It has, from time to time, deplored State hospital conditions, but it has never shown leadership in raising State hospital professional standards. . . . Its silence smothers criticism and it has left the public, the legislatures and the judiciary to believe that State hospital conditions are unfortunate, but acceptable.
>
> Prior to the Second World War, the association was largely hospital oriented. However, immediately following the war it was taken over politically by a small, organized group of psychoanalytically oriented psychiatrists who championed "dynamic

psychiatry.'' Because of the dynamism of their own personalities, this group was able to lead American psychiatrists out of the hospitals to the greener pastures of the less disturbed. Their organization, The Group for the Advancement of Psychiatry (GAP) maintains a membership of 200 and an additional 100 former members. Since 1948 it has annually effected the elections from its own ranks of all but three of the presidents of the American Psychiatric Association and three of the chairmen of the Nominating Committee. For practical purposes, it dominates all prestgous [sic] psychiatric activities, whether misguided or not. Furthermore, its self-serving aspects have been made possible by financial support since its inception from foundations and drug houses. . . .

The reason for this diatribe is that what conditions exist, good and bad, in State hospitals have been of little effective concern on the part the American Psychiatric Association. Unfortunately it has exercised its leadership in attempting to set up a federally financed, separate mental health system of community health centers. Although these are needed in conjunction with State hospitals, their separateness is creating devastating strains on both systems.[115]

The lack of mental health professionals who were willing to practice in state hospitals, the movement by some toward complete abandonment of large state facilities, the reaction to judicial right-to-treatment decisions, and other internal tensions produced a politically complex policy environment.

In addition to the internal politics of the mental health professions, there was a history of poor communications and general tension between lawyers and physicians.[116] And if physicians did not appreciate what they perceived to be the meddling of lawyers, many were absolutely adamant about the intrusion into their activities of court orders. Lawyers often reciprocated the antagonism, rejecting the validity of psychiatric testimony and claims to knowledge.

When physicians charged that courts should not be involved in evaluating medical matters, lawyers responded that courts had been doing so for years in a variety of areas of law.[117] Mere complexity was no bar to legal accountability. When mental health professionals charged that judges were making intrusive rulings with inadequate attention to medical opinion, lawyers countered that, if anything, judges had been too cautious in protecting patients and families against arbitrary and unacceptable mental health practices. Charles Halpern insisted, ''In particular, the psychiatrists' concern that judges will attempt to make psychiatric decisions, such as selection among competing therapies, has proved totally baseless. Instead, the courts apparently have been too willing to accept at face value the assertions of adequacy of treatment made by the treating institutions.''[118] The situation, he said, would have been much better had the psychiatric profession chosen to cooperate with courts instead of engaging in turf protection.[119] Speaking as a judge, Bazelon claimed that courts can deal with practices in mental health agencies the way they do in other administrative agencies: with deference to the professional practitioners' acknowledged expertise but with an insistence upon protecting patients against arbitrariness and illegal conduct.[120]

There have also been wider political factors affecting the ongoing mental health policy discussion. In particular, tensions between administrators and elected officials who nodded in the direction of improved mental health policy by creating new statutes but then refused to appropriate funds for their implementation has been an ongoing problem. Another major political dynamic is federalism. While many state officials resent federal direction, the picture is at worst mixed. For one thing, the external pressure for reform has been leverage to assist state officials in obtaining needed resources. The expertise available from the federal government is also useful. Moreover, there simply is not much of a constitutional basis for claims that federal statutes and court orders in the field of mental health illegally invade the province of the states.[121]

The National Association of State Attorneys General opposed legislation authorizing the Justice Department to bring suit on behalf of institutionalized persons.[122] The DOJ had initially become involved in those suits at the request of judges.[123] Assistant Attorney General Drew Days, testifying on one version of DOJ access legislation, stressed the need to ensure that state and local officials were given an opportunity to correct problems before the federal government intervened.[124] That, he hoped, would reduce some of the tension over the federalism issue.

Financial Tensions

At the root of some of the political conflicts, however, has been fiscal scarcity. If adequate funding were available to develop alternative treatment centers, construct modern safe and spacious hospitals, hire adequate professional and nonprofessional staffs, acquire modern patient-records systems, and staff transition centers for patients leaving treatment facilities, many of the issues of confinement, institutional conditions, right to treatment, and right to refuse treatment would be ameliorated if not solved. However, there has never been a likelihood that sufficient funds could be found to accomplish all these goals. Since courts have held that states cannot refuse to protect basic civil rights because of a claimed lack of resources, the financial pressures have been one source of antagonism between state and local officials and federal courts.[125]

One of the first problems encountered in attempts to assess financial needs and efficient use of existing resources is determining appropriate measures. The two traditional measures used in mental health administration are per patient expenditure and average duration of hospitalization. Presumably, a low average duration of hospitalization suggests successful treatment and release of patients. These measures can be troublesome. Administrators wishing to present a favorable picture of their hospitals have an incentive to reduce duration, but if patients are released prematurely, the decrease in average duration is a meaningless figure and may have detrimental consequences. Few professionals would intentionally release patients known to be ill, but if staff resources are stretched to the limit, there may not be time or personnel to make adequate assessments. Alternatively, one may transfer patients to decentralized programs or facilities, but while that will reduce average patient duration, it does not, in fact, reflect anything like a "cure" rate. Since many of those facilities are underfunded, transfers may produce unfortunate results.

The per patient expenditure measure is also troublesome. If one has a new facility with adequate numbers of well trained staff and a moderate patient load to begin with, the per patient cost may very well be lower than in an older facility that requires extensive maintenance, lacks adequate staff, and is overloaded with patients. The per patient figure may also vary in significance where one has a patient load with illnesses relatively less serious than another facility or where medical illnesses are few and most resources can be concentrated on direct psychiatric care. Some hospitals have very well supported volunteer programs and others may have large numbers of student volunteers from various kinds of health programs. In short, while extremely low per patient figures are likely to reflect poor quality care, at higher levels the figures may be poor management tools.

There are a number of demands for funds which make it difficult to acquire adequate support. Old facilities require high maintenance expenditures which legislators may be unwilling to cover as bad investments, yet new facilities generally require increased bonded indebtedness in a period of high interest rates. Political pressures to reduce indebtedness make that a difficult option. There are multiple demands in such fields as corrections or education that are often direct competitors for state dollars. Then, of course, there is the contest for the mental health dollar between centralized mental health institutions and decentralized community programs. In purely budgetary terms, decentralized treatment, can, under some circumstances, be much less expensive than centralized hospitalization, though the type and level of care may or may not be adequate to the needs of all patients.[126] There is a further complexity in determining the nature of personnel expenditures. Should one suffer a loss in numbers of positions in order to hire highly qualified mental health professionals or try to provide more institutional services by hiring fewer professionals but more paraprofessionals or nonprofessionals? Should patient labor, in the form of work therapy, be considered in assessing budgetary needs? If not, how does one accommodate prevailing practice?

Resources for mental health come from the federal government, states, and counties. Federal funds have come in the form of categorical grants, education funds, revenue sharing, some block grant money, and social security programs, including Medicare/Medicaid. Some of those resources, like Medicaid and education funds, are administered through the state government, but others, like revenue sharing and some categorical or project grants, go directly to local government. The federal funds generate a number of political, administrative, and financial difficulties even though they provide a very important revenue source for mental health. First, they create intergovernmental tension because the funds carry with them a variety of federal requirements for programs receiving the assistance. The Developmental Disabilities Act and the Education for All Handicapped Children Act, for example, contain substantial requirements for service delivery. Second, there is often a need to qualify for the funds through what may be a complex application process. This complexity brings about the need to acquire someone usually referred to as a *grantsman,* a person who has skill and experience in obtaining and administering grants. That process may involve high overhead and reporting costs. There may be matching fund requirements under which the states and localities must fund a portion of the program up front to receive assistance. Finally, there may be tension between the state and local governments as each attempts to control the use of grant funds.

CONCLUSION

Like other issue areas, mental health policy litigation must be understood in proper context. This chapter has presented a sketch of the development of the relationship between courts and mental health policy. It is a history of reform cycles that never really succeeded. While there have been active mental health professionals and committed state mental health providers, it is a field about which the public wishes to know or do little, and it succeeds.

The chapter examined the specific problems courts have been called upon to resolve most often, including commitment, conditions of institutionalization, the right to treatment, and the right to refuse treatment. As with the other fields considered here, the various specific legal issues overlap. The effort to deal with these problems has been greatly affected by conflict between the mental health community and the legal profession and within the professional organizations in mental health. The intricacies of budgetary politics and intergovernmental relations have also played a key role.

Once again, to understand the interaction of judges and public officials in this field, let us turn to an in-depth analysis of these problems in a particular case, the case of *Wyatt v. Stickney* that has been so important to mental health policy development.

NOTES

1. Albert Deutsch, *The Mentally Ill in America: A History of Their Care and Treatment from Colonial Times, 2nd ed.* (New York: Columbia Univ. Press, 1949), p. 3.

2. *Id.*, ch. 1.

3. Frank T. Lindman and Donald McIntyre, Jr., eds., *The Mentally Disabled and the Law: Report of the American Bar Foundation on the Rights of the Mentally Ill* (Chicago: Univ. of Chicago Press, 1961), p. 7.

4. Deutsch, *supra* note 1, at 12.

5. *Id.*, at 42.

6. *Id.*, at 53.

7. Lindman and McIntyre, *supra* note 3, at 10.

8. *See, e.g.*, Deutsch, *supra* note 1 , at 213–15.

9. *Id.*, at 165.

10. *In the Matter of Josiah Oakes,* 8 Law Reporter 123 (1845–46).

11. Deutsch, *supra* note 1, at 419.

12. *Id.*, at 442.

13. *Id.*, at 449.

14. Manfred S. Guttmacher and Henry Weihofen, *Psychiatry and the Law,* (New York: Norton, 1952).

15. Lindman and McIntyre, *supra* note 3.

16. Morton Birnbaum, "The Right to Treatment," 46 *A.B.A. J.* 499 (1960).

17. *Id.*, at 499.

18. "Editorial: A New Right," 46 *A.B.A. J.* 516 (1960).

19. U.S. Senate, Hearings Before the Subcommittee on Constitutional Rights of the Committee on the Judiciary, *Constitutional Rights of the Mentally Ill,* 87th Cong., 1st Sess. (1961), Parts I and II. *See also* U.S. Senate, Hearings Before the Subcommittee on Constitutional Rights of the Committee on the Judiciary, *To Protect the Constitutional Right of the Mentally Ill,* 88th Cong., 1st Sess. (1963).

20. U.S. Senate, Hearings Before the Subcommittee on Constitutional Rights of the Committee on the Judiciary, *Constitutional Rights of the Mentally Ill,* 91st Cong., 1st and 2d Sess. (1969–70), pp. 86–90 [hereafter 1970 Hearings].

21. *Rouse v. Cameron,* 373 F.2d 541 (DCC 1966).

22. 1970 Hearings, *supra* note 20, at 2.

23. *See, e.g.,* U.S. House of Representatives, Hearings Before the Subcommittee on Courts, Civil Liberties, and the Administration of Justice, *Civil Rights for Institutionalized Persons,* 95th Cong., 1st Sess. (1977); U.S. Senate, Hearings Before the Subcommittee on the Constitution of the Committee on the Judiciary, *Civil Rights of Institutionalized Persons,* 95th Cong., 1st Sess. (1977); and U.S. House of Representatives, Hearings Before the Subcommittee on Courts, Civil Liberties, and the Administration of Justice of the Committee on the Judiciary, *Civil Rights of Institutionalized Persons* 96th Cong., 1st Sess. (1979).

24. The Education for All Handicapped Children Act, P.L. 94–142, 20 U.S.C. 1401.

25. The Developmental Disabilities Act, 42 U.S.C. 6010.

26. *Beverly's Case,* 4 Co. 123b, 76 Eng. Rep. 1118 (KB, 1603).

27. *In the Matter of Oakes, supra* note 10.

28. *McNaghten's Case,* 10 Clark and F 199 (1843).

29. *Davis v. United States,* 165 U.S. 373 (1897). *See also Davis v. United States,* 160 U.S. 469 (1895).

30. *People v. Levy,* 151 Cal. App. 2d 460, 311 P.2d 897 (1st Dist. Ct. App. 1957).

31. *See, e.g., Benton v. Reid,* 231 F.2d 780 (DCC 1956).

32. *Commonwealth v. Page,* 339 MA 313, 159 NE 2d 82 (1959). *See also People v. Jackson,* 245 NYS 2d 534 (1963).

33. *Sas v. Maryland,* 334 F.2d 506 (4th Cir. 1964). *But see Director of Patuxent Inst. v. Daniels,* 243 MD 16, 221 A.2d 397 (1966).

34. *Ragsdale v. Overholser,* 281 F.2d 943, 950 (DCC 1960) (Fahy, concurring).

35. *Rouse v. Cameron, supra* note 21, at 455.

36. *Id.,* at 457.

37. *Id.,* at 453.

38. *Id.,* at 456.

39. *Id.,* at 457.

40. *Id.,* at 458. *And see* Note: "Implementing the Right to Treatment for Involuntarily Confined Mental Patients: Wyatt v. Stickney," 3 *N.M. L. Rev.* 338, 339–40 (1973).

41. *See, e.g.,* Note: "The Nascent Right to Treatment," 53 *Va. L. Rev.* 1134 (1967); Note: "Civil Restraint, Mental Illness, and the Right to Treatment," 77 *Yale L.J.* 87 (1967); Council of the American Psychiatric Association, "Position Statement on the Question of Adequacy of Treatment," 123 *American Journal of Psychiatry* 1458 (1967); Note: "Rouse v. Cameron," 80 *Harv. L. Rev.* 898 (1967).

42. Symposium: "Observations on the Right to Treatment," 57 *Geo. L.J.* 673 (1969).

43. Symposium: "The Mentally Ill and the Right to Treatment," 36 *U. Chi. L. Rev.* 742 (1969).

44. *Nason v. Superintendent of Bridgewater State Hospital,* 233 NE 2d 908 (1968).

45. *Covington v. Harris,* 419 F.2d 617 (DCC 1969).

46. Task Panel on Legal and Ethical Issues of the President's Commission on Mental Health, "Mental Health and Human Rights," 20 *Ariz. L. Rev.* 49, 133 (1978) [hereafter Task Panel Report].

47. *See, e.g., Stachulak v. Coughlin,* 364 F. Supp. 686 (NDIL 1973); *Davis v. Watkins,* 384 F. Supp. 1196 (NDOH 1974); *Donaldson v. O'Connor,* 493 F.2d 507 (5th Cir. 1974); *Gary W. v. State of Louisiana,* 437 F. Supp. 1209 (EDLA 1976). *But see Burnham v. Dep't of Public Health of the State of Georgia,* 349 F. Supp. 1335 (NDGA 1972), *rev'd* 503 F.2d 1319 (5th Cir. 1094).

48. *See, e.g., New York State Ass'n for Retarded Children v. Carey,* 393 F. Supp. 715 (EDNY 1975) approving the consent decree. The full story of this litigation is told in a variety of reported opinions, including *New York State Ass'n for Retarded Children v. Carey,* 357 F. Supp. 752 (EDNY 1973); 393 F. Supp. 715 (EDNY 1975); 409 F. Supp. 606 (EDNY 1976); 438 F. Supp. 440 (EDNY 1977); 456 F. Supp. 85 (EDNY 1978); 466 F. Supp. 479 (EDNY 1978), *aff'd,* 612 F.2d 644 (2nd Cir. 1979); 466 F. Supp. 487 (EDNY 1979); 596 F.2d 27 (2nd Cir.

1979), *cert. denied,* 444 U.S. 836 (1979); F. Supp. 1099 (EDNY 1980); 492 F. Supp. 1110 (EDNY 1980), *rev'd,* 631 F.2d 162 (2nd Cir. 1980); 544 F. Supp. 330 (EDNY 1982), *aff'd* 706 F.2d 956 (2nd Cir. 1983). *See also* David J. Rothman and Sheila M. Rothman, *The Willowbrook Wars,* (New York: Harper and Row, 1984).

49. *Jackson v. Indiana,* 406 U.S. 715 (1972).

50. *Id.,* at 738.

51. *O'Connor v. Donaldson,* 422 U.S. 563, 576 (1975).

52. *Addington v. Texas,* 439 U.S. 908 (1979).

53. *Halderman v. Pennhurst State School and Hospital,* 446 F. Supp. 1295 (EDPA 1977); *aff'd in part, rev'd in part* 612 F.2d 84 (3rd Cir. 1979) *(en banc); rev'd* 67 L.Ed2d 694 (1981); 673 F.2d 647 (3rd Cir. 1982); *rev'd* 79 L.Ed2d 67 (1984).

54. *Youngberg v. Romeo,* 457 U.S. 307, 324 (1982).

55. *Mills v. Rogers,* 457 U.S. 29 (1982). The decision below is *Rogers v. Okin,* 478 F. Supp. 1342 (DMA 1979), *aff'd in part, rev'd in part,* 634 F.2d 650 (1st Cir. 1980).

56. Deutsch, *supra* note 1, at 419. See also Birnbaum, *supra* note 16, at 502.

57. *In the Matter of Oakes, supra* note 10, at 122, 124–25 (1846).

58. *Humphrey v. Cady,* 405 U.S. 504, 509 (1972).

59. Comment: "Wyatt v. Stickney and the Right of the Civilly Committed Patients to Adequate Treatment," 86 *Harv. L. Rev.* 1282, 1287 (1973).

60. Developments in the Law: "Civil Commitment of the Mentally Ill," 87 *Harv. L. Rev.* 1190, 1198–99 (1974) [hereafter "Civil Commitment"].

61. *Donaldson v. O'Connor,* 493 F.2d 507, 520 (5th Cir. 1974). *See also* "Civil Commitment," *supra* note 60, at 1200 *et seq.*

62. *Specht v. Patterson,* 368 U.S. 605, 608 (1967).

63. *O'Connor v. Donaldson, supra* note 51, at 563, 574.

64. *Parham v. J.R.,* 442 U.S. 584, 627 (1979) (Brennan, J., concurring in part, dissenting in part). *See* Judge Johnson decision for a three-judge panel in *Lynch v. Baxley,* 386 F. Supp. 378 (MDAL 1974), a complete discussion of the various elements of due process in a commitment proceeding.

65. Forms of coercion can be quite subtle and complex. *See Doe v. Public Health Trust of Dade County,* 696 F.2d 901 (11th Cir. 1983).

66. *Hawaii v. Standard Oil,* 405 U.S. 251, 257 (1972).

67. *See generally* "Civil Commitment," *supra* note 60, at 1207–22.

68. *O'Connor v. Donaldson, supra* note 51, at 575–76.

69. *Lynch v. Baxley, supra* note 64, at 396.

70. "Civil Commitment," *supra* note 60, at 1222–45.

71. On the dangers of overcautious judgments, *see id.,* at 1242–43.

72. *Addington v. Texas, supra* note 52.

73. Dr. John P. Filley, Director, Georgia Child and Adolescent Mental Health Services, deposition at 48, in *J.L. v. Parham,* 412 F. Supp. 112, 133 (MDGA 1976). *See also* Ellis, "Volunteering Children: Parental Commitment of Minors to Mental Institutions," 62 *Calif. L. Rev.* 840 (1974).

74. *Parham v. J.R., supra* note 64, at 600.

75. *Id.,* at 126–27.

76. In Georgia a Study Commission on Mental Health Services for Children and Youth after a six-month investigation found that "more than half of the hospitalized children and youth would not need hospitalization if other forms of care were available in communities." *J.L. v. Parham, supra* note 73, at 122. It also determined, "The mental health laws of Georgia should be reviewed with specific reference to the rights of children and youth." *Id.,* at 123. The legislature and governor concluded care was adequate and no further improvements could be made without increasing taxes. *Id.,* at 126.

77. *J.L. v. Parham, supra* note 73.

78. *Parham v. J.R., supra* note 64, at 637, (Brennan, J., concurring in part, dissenting in part).

79. 1970 Hearings, *supra* note 20, at 33. *See also* "Civil Commitment," *supra* note 60, at 1214.

80. Lindman and McIntyre, *supra* note 3, at 7–8.

81. *Rogers v. Okin,* 634 F.2d 650 (1st Cir. 1980), *vacated and remanded on other grounds sub nom., Mills v. Rogers, supra* note 55.

82. *See generally,* Comment: "Wyatt v. Stickney . . . ," *supra* note 59, at 1282, 1291–94; and "Civil Commitment," *supra* note 60, at 1259–60.

83. *Robinson v. Cal.,* 370 U.S. 660 (1962).

84. *See, e.g.,* Task Panel Report, *supra* note 46 at 49, 98–103.

85. *Youngberg v. Romeo, supra* note 54, at 315–16.

86. *Jackson v. Indiana, supra* note 49.

87. *See, e.g., Shelton v. Tucker,* 364 U.S. 479 (1960). *See also* Task Panel Report, *supra* note 46, at 103–6.

88. *Youngberg v. Romeo, supra* note 54.

89. *Donaldson v. O'Connor, supra* note 61, at 507, 514.

90. *O'Connor v. Donaldson, supra* note 63, at 563, 569.

91. David L. Bazelon, "Implementing the Right to Treatment," 36 *U. Chi. L. Rev.* 742, 745 (1969). *See also* Charles R. Halpern, "A Practicing Lawyer Views the Right to Treatment," 57 *Geo. L.J.* 782, 790 (1969).

92. Dr. F. Lewis Bartlett, "Institutional Peonage—Our Exploitation of Mental Patients," *Atlantic Monthly* July 1964, in 1970 Hearings, *supra* note 20, at 339–43. *See also* Paul R. Friedman, "The Mentally Handicapped Citizen and Institutional Labor," 87 *Harv. L. Rev.* 567 (1975).

93. Task Panel Report, *supra* note 46, at 69–72.

94. Bartlett, in 1970 Hearings, *supra* note 20, at 195–96.

95. "Civil Commitment," *supra* note 60, at 1372–76.

96. *See, e.g., Souder v. Brennan,* 367 F. Supp., 808 (DDC 1973).

97. *Youngberg v. Romeo,* 457 U.S. at 323.

98. Council of the APA, *supra* note 41, at 1458.

99. Bazelon, *supra* note 91, at 746. *See also* Halpern, *supra* note 91, at 790.

100. Halpern, *supra* note 91, at 790. See also *Youngberg v. Romeo, supra* note 54.

101. *See generally* A. Edward Doudera and Judith P. Swazey, eds., *Refusing Treatment in Mental Health Institutions—Values in Conflict,* (Ann Arbor, MI: AUPHA Press, 1982).

102. *Rogers v. Okin, supra* note 81; *Mills v. Rogers, supra* note 55 (1982); *Rennie v. Klein,* 462 F. Supp. 1131 (DNJ 1978), *aff'd* 653 F.2d 836 (3rd Cir. 1981); *Davis v. Hubbard,* 506 F. Supp. 915 (NDOH 1980); *Scott v. Plante,* 532 F.2d 939 (3rd Cir. 1976); *Knecht v. Gillman,* 488 F.2d 1136 (8th Cir. 1973); *Mackey v. Procunier,* 477 F.2d (9th Cir. 1973); *In the Matter of Guardianship of Richard Roe III,* 421 NE2d 40 (MA 1981); *Halderman v. Pennhurst, supra* note 53, at 1295, 1328–29.

103. Task Panel Report, *supra* note 46, at 106–7.

104. Stanley S. Brotman, "Behind the Bench in Rennie v. Klein," in Doudera and Sawzey, *supra* note 101, at 36.

105. *See e.g., Rogers v. Okin, supra* note 81.

106. Brotman, *supra* note 104, at 39.

107. Testimony of Arthur Cohen, in 1970 Hearings, *supra* note 20, at 214.

108. *Halderman v. Pennhurst, supra* note 53.

109. *But see Cleburne v. Cleburne Living Center,* 87 L.Ed2d 313 (1985).

110. Birnbaum, *supra* note 16, at 499.

111. 1970 Hearings, *supra* note 20, at 17.

112. *Id.,* at 16–17, 29–30.

113. *Id.*, at 50–51.

114. *See* the debate between Birnbaum and Twerski in Symposium: "Observations on the Right to Treatment," 10 *Duq. L. Rev.* 553 (1972).

115. 1970 Hearings, *supra* note 20, at 200–210.

116. Guttmacher and Weihofen, *supra* note 14, at 3–4.

117. Comment: "Wyatt v. Stickney . . . ," *supra* note 59, at 1297.

118. Halpern, *supra* note 91, at 709.

119. *Id.*, at 802–5.

120. Bazelon, *supra* note 91.

121. Comment: "Wyatt v. Stickney . . . ," *supra* note 59, at 1299–1304. *See also* testimony of Abram Chayes, in U.S. Senate, Hearings, *Civil Rights of Institutionalized Persons*, 95th Cong., 1st Sess., *supra* note 23, at 161 *et seq.*

122. *Id.*, at 6

123. *Id.*, at 8

124. *Id.*, at 5

125. *Hamilton v. Love*, 328 F. Supp. 1182, 1194 (EDAR 1971); *Swann v. Charlotte Mechlenburg Bd. of Ed.*, 311 F. Supp. 265, 268 (WDNC 1970); *Inmates of Suffolk County Jail v. Eisenstadt*, 360 F. Supp. 676, 687 (DMA 1973).

126. *See e.g., Halderman v. Pennhurst*, *supra* note 53, at 1311–12; and *J.L. v. Parham*, *supra* note 73, at 112, 125–26.

7

Wyatt v. Stickney: Judge Frank Johnson and Mental Health in Alabama

Alabama was a leading state in mental health reform in the nineteenth century. By the 1960s, however, its facilities were considered some of the most dramatic examples of the decline in the quality of mental health care in the nation. The controversy surrounding conditions at the state's three major facilities resulted in a lawsuit now regarded as the classic case of federal court intervention in state and local administration, *Wyatt v. Stickney*.[1] The judge who decided it, Judge Frank Johnson, is viewed as the best (or worst, depending upon one's perspective) example of an interventionist federal jurist. Yet this study suggests a considerably different reality behind the popular caricature. It provides an opportunity to examine the interaction of a federal judge and state government in a policy space quite different from the two previous cases.

TRIGGER PHASE

The litigation brought in 1970 against Mental Health Commissioner Stonewall Stickney, challenging conditions at Bryce State Mental Hospital, like so many of these cases, traces its origins back into the state's past. Alabama's mental health policy history, the crucial events of the 1960s, and the immediate factors that triggered the litigation in 1970 all shaped the relationship between the federal district court in Montgomery and the state.

Alabama Mental Health History

Alabama was one of the states affected by Dorothea Dix's reform pressures. It began construction of its first mental hospital in 1853.[2] The new Alabama Insane Hospital was, according to the legislation creating it, to "command cheerful views" and be constructed so that it "shall open such aspects as will admit the sun's rays a portion of the day into every suite of the building apartments."[3] That project, though, was nearly halted when Governor Winston vetoed the appropriations bill. Only a veto override move led by Senator Robert Jemison saved it.[4] Dr. Peter Bryce, a South Carolina physician, was chosen as the hospital's first superintendent at the suggestion of Dorothea Dix.

Bryce was a progressive in the mental health field, committed to four clinical principles, "(1) Early treatment (2) Tender loving care (3) Occupational therapy, and (4) Non-restraint."[5] He was upset that patients were often brought to him only after they were so physically and mentally ill that they could not be hidden away by their families any longer. Some died en route to the hospital or soon after arrival. He objected to punishment of patients and insisted that their care be humane. Bryce, who was a strong advocate of work therapy, believed "If there is one thing more than another calculated to destroy the peace and tranquility of the patients, and the orderly quiet of the wards in which they reside it is a life of enforced idleness."[6] He absolutely rejected the use of patient restraints. He included a comment on his view of restraints in an 1890 report to his Board:

> During this long period, with a house averaging nearly a thousand patients, there has been no resort whatever to any species of mechanical restraint. . . . Not a vestige of restraining apparatus of any kind is to be found about the premises, nor has there occurred a single case in the wards of the hospital during this long period, which seemed to justify or require its use. Instances have occasionally occurred which to others might have appeared to call for such applications; but in no single case have they failed, in our hands, to yield to milder measures.[7]

He instituted basic rules for hospital personnel with fines for violators. These included absolute bars against "[1] [d]iscourteous treatment, or impolite language to a patient; [and 2] [n]ot keeping patients clean, neatly dressed, and properly nursed at all times."[8]

However, as Alabama's first mental health administrator, Bryce faced a variety of difficulties as well as opportunities for clinical innovation. For one thing, Bryce complained in 1875 that the hospital was becoming a dumping ground for "paupers, the mentally defective [mentally retarded], and harmless eccentrics or vagrants."[9] He wanted to end immediately the practice of committing criminals to serve sentences at the hospital. Money was a continuing problem. The Board of Directors initially set $3.00 per week per patient as the appropriate funding level, with the finances to be provided by the counties, but the local governments frequently did not pay. In 1865, in the wake of the war, the Board went so far as to authorize Bryce to borrow money from the federal government in the form of a mortgage against the hospital property.[10]

Dr. James Searcy, a former Chairman of the Bryce Hospital Board of Trustees, succeeded Bryce. Searcy developed the second of the state's hospitals at Mt. Vernon, near Mobile. The facility was a slightly renovated military reservation given to the state by the federal government in 1895. The state, in turn, dedicated the property for mental health in 1900, and what would later be known as Searcy State Hospital opened the following year. The impetus for the expansion stemmed from the number of freed blacks who came to Bryce for help during reconstruction. The Mt. Vernon facility became the mental hospital for Alabama's black citizens.

Like Bryce before him, Searcy faced administrative challenges. A full examination of the state's two mental health facilities in 1900 led to unification of the hospitals under one board of directors. State legislators called for an investigation into alleged patient abuse and poor conditions at Bryce. The commission created to study the situation concluded that Bryce was functioning well but needed two important changes. First, it recommended that aged patients who were not actually mentally ill should be moved to another facility. Second, it called for an increase in funding from $3.00 to $4.00 per week per patient.[11] Neither suggestion was implemented. In fact, the funding level did not reach $4.00 until 1940, by which time many other states were expending $7.00 or more per week per patient.[12]

The third major element in Alabama's mental health complex was a facility for the mentally retarded developed by Dr. W.D. Partlow, who succeeded Searcy as state mental health director. Founded in 1923 as the Alabama Home for Mental Defectives, the facility would later be known as the Partlow State School and Hospital.[13] Within a month of its opening, Partlow was already faced with a waiting list.

Partlow was replaced as the state's mental health administrator in 1950 by James S. Tarwater. The new director found a "total population of 6,045 at Bryce and Searcy, and 1,188 at the Partlow State School."[14] Tarwater headed the Alabama mental health programs until the reorganization of the entire mental health administration in the late 1960s.

The Attempt at Mental Health Reform

The debate concerning the declining state of mental health support addressed in the legislative study of 1900, and raised again in the 1940s, resurfaced with the release in 1958 of the *Report on the State Mental Hospitals of Alabama* prepared by the Central Inspection Board of the American Psychiatric Association (APA). The report indicted the state's facilities and particularly its lack of funding, the lowest in the nation. Among other suggestions for improvement, the APA provided recommended staffing levels for the state's hospitals. The legislature soon launched its own study of the mental health program. The Legislative Interim Committee on Mental Health and Retardation issued its report in 1963, advising a complete reorganization of the mental health system. Citing overcrowding and improper admission of patients who were committed simply because there seemed nowhere else to put them, the Committee also called for changes in commitment and admission practices:

> [Aged patients] over the years have been admitted to the State Hospitals when actually they could in little or no way benefit from the treatment program at the State Hospitals. . . . These patients, for the most part, are not mentally ill.
>
> No additional elderly patients [should] be admitted to either Bryce Hospital or Searcy Hospital unless it has been clearly established that they are psychotic or mentally ill.
>
> A State Nursing Home [should] be built to care for and treat those elderly, senile and obstreperous patients who cannot be cared for in private nursing homes.[15]

The legislative product of the Committee's work was a complete reformulation of the Alabama mental health system under what was known as the Alabama Mental Health Plan of 1965. The centerpiece of the reform program was a newly constituted State Mental Health Board and the designation of a new chief administrative officer for the system to be known as the State Mental Health Commissioner.[16] Full implementation of the program awaited the recruitment of the Commissioner. Dr. Stonewall Stickney assumed that office in 1968. By the time he took over, however, Stickney found his program already in the midst of major legal and financial difficulties.

Alabama Politics, Money, and Federal Civil Rights

Obviously, the key to any major reform would be development of funds which had to that point not been located. The legislative committee had urged state administrators to make a major effort to acquire federal grants to assist in the reform project. Yet conditions in Alabama in the mid-1960s suggested that not only would the state be unlikely to acquire more federal help, but it could very easily lose some of the support it was already receiving. The reasons for this threat came from within the mental health system itself, the political posture of the governors, and legal action launched under newly created federal civil rights statutes.

Before Stickney took office, Mental Health Administrator James Tarwater was having difficulty funding current service levels without considering any major improvements in existing facilities let alone development of new programs. He wrote, "By 1960, the appropriation was $2.50 per patient, per day. . . . Today [1964], the Bryce and Searcy Hospitals operate on a $3.00 per day, per patient appropriation. The Partlow State School and Hospital operates on a $3.05 per patient, per day basis." [17] Tarwater reassured Alabamians that the state Board understood the need to dramatically improve the care at existing facilities and had accepted the necessity of developing additional facilities, including new hospitals, day care centers, and outpatient clinics. At the same time, he warned that none of those projects could be undertaken without dramatic increases in funds.

Given the historical lack of state financial support for mental health, Tarwater stressed the need to obtain federal assistance. The Board, for example, proposed to construct several new facilities, using federal money under the Hill-Burton Act even though that required state matching funds. But Alabama was about to lose some of its existing federal help. The mental health department applied for certified Medicare provider status when the Medicare regulations were issued in 1965, but the Alabama Bureau of Licensure and Certification refused to recommend it since Bryce, Searcy, and Partlow clearly did not meet minimum standards. A second major blow came in 1967 when the American Association on Mental Deficiency Institutional Evaluation Project published its *Final Report for Partlow State School and Hospital*. The inspection and subsequent report were key elements in the growing image of Alabama mental health institutions within the national mental health community as the example of how bad such facilities could be. The image compounded the state's problems because few mental health professionals were willing to consider accepting positions at Alabama hospitals.

With all of its problems, Alabama was already heavily dependent upon federal dollars for many of its programs:

> In 1967, as has been true over the past 10 years, federal funds were the largest single source of revenue for the state from any source. In 1967 Alabama received almost $246,000,000 or 30.8 per cent of all its revenue from the federal government. [18]

> In the field of education about 16 per cent of the money spent was federal money. In highways the amount was up to about 46 per cent, while in public welfare it was up to 75 per cent. [19]

Even though the state's mental health agency had not fared particularly well in its search to obtain and keep federal dollars, it was receiving several grants. In 1966 the state garnered about $200,000 in Public Health Service funds, a roughly equivalent amount in contributions from the surplus commodities program administered by the Department of Agriculture, surplus property and equipment conveyed to the state under the Federal Property and Administrative Services Act, and support from the Elementary and Secondary Education Act of 1965.[20] Alabama gubernatorial politics, however, placed the federal assistance in immediate jeopardy.

The more or less continuous battle between George Wallace and the federal government and the federal courts across the range of civil rights issues, from voting rights to school desegregation, has often been chronicled.[21] Wallace came to the statehouse in 1963 and immediately began to encourage resistance to desegregation efforts. The passage of the Civil Rights Act of 1964 provided a financial enforcement lever for the federal government. Title VI of the Act prohibited discrimination in programs funded by the federal government. As soon as its regulations implementing the statute had been prepared, the Department of Health, Education, and Welfare (HEW) (now the Department of Health and Human Services [HHS]) and other federal agencies served notice of their intent to enforce the law. Various Alabama officials responded by February 1965 and indicated their willingness to comply. In fact, the state provided "eight written assurances" between 1965 and 1967 of its good faith.[22]

The state mental health system began desegregating in early 1966, but that progress was cut short when the governor's office informed Tarwater that Wallace opposed the change. The facilities were then resegregated. Tarwater officially notified the Public Health Service that the state did not intend to take further action.[23] Soon thereafter HEW responded by instituting administrative proceedings to revoke federal funding. In October 1967 a HEW administrative law judge found Alabama in violation of Title VI and called for HEW and the Department of Agriculture to terminate financial aid.[24]

Alabama filed suit in November, charging that HEW had exceeded its authority and abused what legitimate authority it possessed. Civil rights attorneys led by Jack Greenberg entered the case on behalf of Loveman Marable and other Alabama mental health patients, charging not only that the state was discriminating under the statutes, but also was in violation of the Constitution's equal protection clause.[25] There were no meaningful factual disagreements since the segregation of facilities was required by statute and by the clear policy the governor had instituted after passage of the Civil Rights Act. The facilities that did have both black and white patients were officially segregated internally and the facilities or programs serving minority patients were clearly inferior to those available to white residents. The general conditions at state hospitals were not at issue in the case. In fact, in their efforts to highlight the relative deprivations of black patients, counsel indirectly suggested to the court that conditions for white patients were adequate.[26]

In a February 1969 ruling, a three judge federal district court found a violation of the equal protection clause and ordered the state to desegregate Bryce and Searcy within a year and Partlow within three months. It was therefore unnecessary for the court to reach the question raised by Alabama concerning the statutory authority of federal agencies.[27]

The author of the *Marable* opinion was Judge Frank Johnson, the man who would later preside in the challenge to conditions in Alabama's three mental health facilities. A northwestern Alabama Republican, Johnson had graduated from the University of Alabama School of Law. Following service abroad during World War II, he returned to a general law practice in northern Alabama and later served as city attorney for the

town of Jasper. An Eisenhower delegate in 1952, Johnson received a patronage appointment as U.S. Attorney for the Northern District of Alabama after the new administration
took office. Despite some opposition from down-state partisans, Johnson was appointed
in 1955 to a seat on the U.S. District Court for the Middle District of Alabama head-
quartered in Montgomery.

A moderate conservative known as a no-nonsense jurist and efficient judicial administrator, Frank Johnson's seat in the Alabama capital during the late 1950s and 1960s
virtually guaranteed he would face some of the most difficult and contentious civil rights
battles in modern history. And it was in the field of civil rights that Johnson gained the
most notoriety. He either sat as a single judge or participated as a member of a three-
judge panel in desegregation cases that involved schools, colleges, transportation systems and facilities, and prisons. He presided as well in several major cases presented
by the federal government in its attempt to enforce voting rights for Alabama's minority
citizens.

Several of these cases brought Johnson into direct confrontation with Governor
George Wallace. In fact, Wallace used Johnson as a campaign issue in his bid for the
governorship, referring to him as an "integrating, scalawagging, carpet-bagging, race-
mixing, bald-faced liar."[28] There is a particular irony in all this since Johnson and
Wallace had been friends and law school classmates during a time when Wallace was
known as a New Deal liberal. Wallace took office in 1963 but was forced to leave at
the end of his term since Alabama law set a one term limit.

He managed to retain power by successfully running his wife, Lurleen, as his
successor, with the public understanding that he would continue to make the key decisions. She did indeed maintain the segregationist rhetoric and defiance of the federal
government that became a Wallace trademark. Lurleen Wallace died of cancer in 1968,
however, and was succeeded by then Lieutenant Governor Albert Brewer. Brewer, in
turn, was defeated by George Wallace in a bitterly contested campaign in 1970, placing
Wallace back in the Alabama statehouse in 1971.

The other Governor Wallace was touched by conditions she saw in state mental
health facilities and obtained a $15 million bond authorization from the state legislature.
It was, unfortunately, a fraction of what was needed and made virtually no difference
in the operation of the facilities. She also obtained legislation to increase the cigarette
tax, with the proceeds earmarked for development of a number of new facilities for the
mentally retarded. While those new centers were in the early development stage, the
designated tax money was used to stave off financial pressures at Bryce. The removal
of the special tax funds when construction began on the mental retardation facilities
coupled with a change in state employee pay schedules and added to the already dire
financial condition at Bryce brought about a budgetary crisis. It was the action taken to
meet that challenge that triggered the *Wyatt v. Stickney* litigation.

The Bryce Challenge

The state responded to its mental health finance disaster during the summer of 1970 by
laying off more than ninety Bryce personnel. While the employees were naturally upset
over the loss of their jobs, that was only one part of the strong reaction against the
personnel reduction. Bryce was by all accounts delapidated, overcrowded, underfunded,
and already badly understaffed. Critics associated with Bryce charged that there comes

a point at which an institution simply cannot function any longer on inadequate support. Bryce, they insisted, had now reached that point. It could no longer provide any meaningful treatment or even humane custody for its patients. The layoff was the specific event that sparked the *Wyatt v. Stickney* suit.

News of the personnel action spread quickly. Bryce was important to the University of Alabama community, which is so significant in Tuscaloosa, because the hospital was the teaching facility for mental health education at the university. Dr. Raymond Fowler, then Chairman of the Department of Psychology, joined others upset by the Bryce action at a meeting to discuss the situation.[29] He expressed his anger and frustration at home and shared it with friends who happened to be attorneys. They, in turn, were playing host to a Florida-based civil rights lawyer named George Dean. It took little time to decide what to do. Dean filed suit on behalf of former Bryce employees and patients in federal district court for the Middle District of Alabama on October 23, 1970. The case was styled *Wyatt v. Stickney* after Ricky Wyatt, a Bryce patient, and Stonewall Stickney, the state Mental Health Commissioner.

THE LIABILITY PHASE

The combination of the local impact of the changes at Bryce and the larger issue of the integrity of mental health treatment programs influenced the manner in which the suit was initially launched and then shaped as the case developed. Evidence adduced at the liability hearing led to further expansion of the litigation and an extremely important determination of the rights of mental patients in state facilities.

Shaping the Liability Case

Wyatt was a civil rights case launched not by an organized interest group but by an informal collection of concerned individuals. It was a reaction to mounting frustration with the dismal state of mental health facilities and was triggered by the layoffs. Even so, the parties involved understood some of the implications of their decision to bring suit. George Dean later remarked:

> It's hard to believe that within twenty or thirty minutes we had conceptualized that there had to be a constitutional right to treatment. Then the corollary was that you can't treat without treaters. . . . We sat there and talked that evening about the case, and everyone knew that it would have an enormous, profound effect on our lives because we just knew god-damn well, from our knowledge of Bryce, its horrible conditions, the reduction of staff, the involuntary nature of the commitment process in Alabama, that the case could be just what we could make it. . . . I never had the slightest doubts that it would be a major case.[30]

On the other hand, the claim that the employees had suffered a due process violation by virtue of their termination was not the real point. The people who launched the suit included both employees and patients as named plaintiffs because they wanted to make the argument that the terminations resulted not only in harm to the employees, but also brought about a deprivation of a right to humane care and treatment belonging to the patients. True, the litigants wanted to preserve their jobs, but that was not quite the same as a fundamental claim to a right to treatment. The essential basis for protecting the jobs was a procedural due process claim based upon Alabama law. It became clear to Dean that Judge Johnson saw that problem during an early conference on the case in chambers. Johnson's law clerk explained what took place in a later interview:

> George came in and gave the judge a fifteen or twenty-minute presentation and . . . his argument reflected that he was interested primarily, at that time, in the rights of the employees and their families. And the judge listened, then said: "I am concerned about the rights of those people, but what about the rights of the patients?" . . . Judge Johnson looked at him and said, "I'm even more interested in those rights, Mr. Dean."[31]

The employees were severed from the federal case and successfully pursued their complaint of termination without due process in state court. As presented at trial, then, *Wyatt* was a class action suit on behalf of Bryce patients and their parents or guardians, alleging that as patients involuntarily committed to Bryce Hospital they were guaranteed a right to treatment by the due process clause of the Fourteenth Amendment to the U.S. Constitution. They charged that Alabama was not providing treatment that would be judged minimally adequate by any reasonable medical standard and that the lack of staff and condition of the Bryce facilities made it impossible to provide adequate treatment.

The Liability Hearing

The suit came on for trial before Judge Johnson on January 4, 1971, and ran for two days. George Dean was joined by Jack Drake, an Alabama American Civil Liberties Union (ACLU) attorney. The charge was simple. There was no adequate treatment before the personnel reductions and, given conditions at Bryce, those cuts would exacerbate already intolerable conditions for the patients.

The defense responded that while the previous staff organization may not have been able to provide adequate care, the new approach, known as the unit system, could do so and with less personnel. Instead of using a hospital organization of medical specialty departments and patient wards in which direct decisionmaking for virtually all care rested with a mental health professional, the unit system combined professionals and paraprofessionals into teams in which all members participated in delivery of treatment and mental health professionals guided the team. What was really at issue, the state argued, was resistance to the reorganization led by mental health professionals who resented the fact that the unit system could deliver better treatment by the use of paraprofessionals to supplement a smaller professional staff. Besides, Bryce was as well staffed as Searcy, and the latter was functioning well. Moreover, there just was not any more money available to make improvements at the facilities.

The plaintiffs' witnesses were Dr. James Morris, the Acting Superintendent at Bryce, and Dr. Richard Reynolds, Bryce Staff Clinical Psychologist. Morris had served on the committee that had prepared the Alabama Mental Health Plan in 1965. Among other things, Morris had been trained at the University of Tennessee in the operation of the unit treatment system and had worked at Bryce for eight years. He provided a picture of an institution in serious trouble. The patient census was approximately fifty-two hundred, consisting roughly of the same number of men and women. Some fifteen hundred patients were geriatrics with no diagnosed psychiatric illness. Another five to six hundred patients were mentally retarded residents rather than psychiatric patients.

After the personnel cuts, Bryce had available for ward work no board certified psychiatrists, three medical doctors with some psychiatric training, one Ph.D.-level psychologist, five M.A.-level psychologists, a dozen medical doctors, thirteen day-shift and eight night-shift registered nurses (RNs), two dentists, three M.S.W. social workers, six other full-time and one halftime social workers, eleven activity therapists, and approximately 850 psychiatric aides.[32] Morris agreed with the recommended staffing standards for Alabama that had been included in the 1958 APA report. He also underscored a point made in an article by a leading defense witness, Dr. James Folsom, that the unit treatment system required more, not less, personnel.[33] From all this, Morris concluded that it would not be possible for Bryce to deliver adequate treatment to its patients based upon any medical standards of which he was aware.[34]

Joseph Phelps for the defendants pressed Morris in an attempt to demonstrate that the unit system was a valid treatment mode and, since it requires less professionals, the state would not necessarily be depriving anyone of treatment. While he accepted the validity of the unit system, Morris stuck to his argument that the unit system as implemented at Bryce would involve fewer mental health professionals who would be spread more thinly across the patient population with the result that the existing quality of treatment would decline even if more patients could technically be said to be under treatment. Under current treatment levels, he said, forty to fifty percent of patients at Bryce who needed it were not given any treatment.[35] Judge Johnson pursued that startling observation:

> THE COURT: Of those that could have benefited from psychiatric treatment and never received it?
> WITNESS: All right; I wanted to follow this up by qualifying as to what is psychiatric treatment. . . .
> THE COURT: Well, let's—let's make it a little broader; treatment from which they could have received benefit for their mental illness, put it that way; now, what percent never received any treatment?
> WITNESS: Well, all these patients were receiving supervision from a physician, from nursing staff; they were receiving psychotropic medications; they were receiving treatment in one sense of the word. But insofar as active involvement in—
> THE COURT: Well, they could receive that kind of treatment in jail; let's talk about in a mental institution. What percentage of them were not receiving treatment? . . .
> WITNESS: My figure would have to—discounting the geriatric population and the—roughly the number that I said were involved in some kind of treatment—I would say somewhere probably around two thousand.[36]

Phelps pressed Morris to admit that the hospital was understaffed before and would remain so but that this did not mean that the facilities were not serving their purpose. After listening to the argument over appropriate staffing levels with the defense asserting there is no proper standard, Johnson pressed for clarification:

> THE COURT: . . . [L]et's keep this in mind in this lawsuit, everyone, including the witness—the main thrust of the plaintiffs' case is that these patients are being

civilly committed by court order, deprived of their liberty; they are committed for treatment, and they are not receiving adequate treatment. So let's keep that in mind. Adequate treatment from an acceptable minimum standpoint; not according to Alabama standards, according to medical standards. . . .

WITNESS: That's right. I was talking about an acceptable minimum, recognizing that most hospitals do not have the ideal.

THE COURT: *We are not interested in ideals; we are interested in minimum standards. It is going to be, it looks like, incumbent upon me to determine in this case whether the constitutional rights of these parties are being deprived by being committed for treatment and not receiving treatment. . . . In doing that, if I reach that point, I am not interested in the finest treatment they can receive. . . . I will be gauging or attempting to assure the treatment that they receive according to the minimum acceptable medical standards. . . . So let's keep that in mind.*[37] *(emphasis added)*

Johnson admonished the parties that he was not going to determine whether the unit system was a good mode of treatment and asked them to address themselves to the question of what constituted minimally adequate treatment, however delivered. Dean quickly noted that the plaintiffs were not criticizing the unit system. Without saying so directly, Dean was suggesting that the state was attempting a form of sleight of hand by suggesting that through a simple reorganization, an inadequate staff could be cut and suddenly be deemed adequate.

The other key witness for the plaintiffs was Dr. Reynolds, the only Ph.D.-level psychologist remaining at Bryce after the personnel reductions. There had been four prior to the cuts. Agreeing with Morris that Bryce could not deliver minimally adequate care after the cuts, Reynolds added that another result of the changes would be that Bryce, which had served as a training hospital for University of Alabama psychology students, would no longer meet accreditation requirements.

Dean entered the *Georgetown Law Journal*'s "Right to Treatment" Symposium into evidence. It contained a thorough discussion of the *Rouse v. Cameron* right-to-treatment decision and its implications.

The leading witnesses for the defense were Dr. James Folsom, then Director of the V.A. Hospital at Tuscaloosa, and Dr. Stickney. One of the unstated tensions at play was the suspicion that Stickney was preparing Folsom to take over at Bryce. That would happen some six months after the liability decision in *Wyatt*. Folsom rejected the charge that Bryce could not provide adequate treatment, insisting that the better utilization of mental health professionals would make up for the lack of personnel. After all, Searcy was doing well with it. But Folsom's testimony broke down under cross-examination. He could hardly make comparisons about treatment levels from his experience at the V.A. hospital, Dean suggested, when Bryce had eight times more patients than the V.A. facility and while the latter enjoyed a $7 million budget against Bryce's $12 million. The V.A. funding rate was then $21 per day per patient against Bryce's $6.42. Moreover, the cross-examination indicated that Folsom did not know what the staffing levels were at Searcy and had no idea what the personnel numbers would be at Bryce after the cuts:

Q: Now, Doctor, if you don't know how many nurses they have, how many M.S.W.'s they have, how many M.D.'s deliver treatment, how can you testify that they will have enough professional staff to deliver treatment to patients?

A: Because it doesn't matter, the numbers that you have; it is whether they work.[38]

The defense followed Folsom with officials from Bryce Treatment Center 2 (known as the Jemison building) and Searcy who testified that the unit system was working well at their facilities and would work well with the staffing levels at Bryce. Under cross-examination, all admitted they did not know what the staffing levels were at Bryce. Dr. Jamie Condom, the Searcy Superintendent, went so far as to insist that Searcy was understaffed by comparison with Bryce. He, too, admitted he did not know the Bryce staffing level and was, in fact, wrong about the relative levels at the two institutions.

The defense anchored its case with its key witness, Dr. Stickney. Apart from insisting that adequate care would be provided, Stickney focused on the argument that there really was not alternative to the budget cuts at Bryce. Stickney explained that the largest cuts had to come at Bryce since it had the largest budget. Most of the temporary windfall from the cigarette tax funds that had come to Bryce had to be removed once construction on the mental retardation facility at Decatur began. His observations on how the cuts were made, however, suggested that considerations about the superiority of one treatment system over another had nothing to do with the decision:

> We found out that, with their proposed budget, right around eighty—somewhere between eighty-two and eighty-four per cent of their proposed budget was in salaries. We knew we couldn't cut medication, we couldn't cut food, we couldn't cut maintenance and, you know, utilities and all that business; so it was nowhere to cut but salaries.

Dean's cross-examination argued that Alabama's mental health budget was the lowest in the nation and that this was the principal reason for these decisions, not assumptions about quality care. Beyond that, Dean suggested, if the state were really concerned about care, there were options available to it which it had not pursued. Stickney replied:

> It was suggested, you know, that the [legislative] special session be called. I had nothing to do with calling a special session. It was suggested that we use capital outlay funds. It was suggested that we go into deficit financing. Now, the way I went into these things was to consult with my staff and my conscience and my Board. And there are several things we don't do; one is deficit financing, and the other is to use capital outlay funds for operation—so those were ruled out. The special session was not within my power to arrange. And the Governor and I did not feel that this was an emergency.

Dean reminded Stickney that he had specific statutory authority to sell some of the Mental Health Department's substantial landholdings to obtain needed revenues, but he replied that it was against Board policy to part with that property. After Dean showed him a recent newspaper article on the lands issue, Stickney admitted the Board was in the process of concluding a land swap with the University of Alabama.

The only argument the state had left was that its approach was working well at Searcy, as demonstrated by figures showing reductions in patient population and length of hospitalization. Rebuttal witnesses for the plaintiffs, however, blunted that argument by showing that the state had conveniently ignored the fact that Searcy had been closed for a time and had arranged patient exchanges with Bryce. The result was that the statistics presented showed a dramatic but fictitious decline in population and duration of treatment at Searcy.

The Liability Opinion

Judge Johnson issued his liability judgment on March 12, 1971. It was an extremely brief opinion, only six printed pages, but it was clearly just the first round in a much longer decision process for Alabama mental health policy. It established a constitutional right to treatment under the due process clause of the Fourteenth Amendment for patients involuntarily committed to state mental health facilities.

Summarizing the facts and including post trial documentation, Johnson found the patient statistics were even worse than had been suggested. There were probably between fifteen and sixteen hundred geriatric patients and another thousand mentally retarded residents at Bryce, most of whom received virtually no treatment. Given the funding and staffing levels and the testimony about the situation at Bryce before and after the cuts and reorganization, it could not be said that patients were receiving minimally adequate treatment.

Reaching the constitutional right to treatment question, Johnson held:

> The patients at Bryce Hospital, for the most part, were involuntarily committed through noncriminal procedures and without the constitutional protections that are afforded defendants in criminal proceedings. When patients are so committed for treatment purposes they unquestionably have a constitutional right to receive such individual treatments as will give each of them a realistic opportunity to be cured or to improve his or her mental condition. *Rouse v. Cameron,* . . . *Covington v. Harris.* . . . Adequate and effective treatment is constitutionally required because, absent treatment, the hospital is transformed "into a penitentiary where one could be held indefinitely for no convicted offense." *Ragsdale v. Overholser.* . . . The purpose of involuntary hospitalization for treatment purposes is *treatment* and not mere custodial care or punishment. This is the only justification, from a constitutional standpoint, that allows civil commitments to mental institutions such as Bryce. According to the evidence in this case, the failure of Bryce Hospital to supply adequate treatment is due to a lack of operating funds. The failure to provide suitable and adequate treatment to the mentally ill cannot be justified by lack of staff or facilities. *Rouse v. Cameron.* . . .
>
> There can be no legal (or moral) justification for the State of Alabama's failing to afford treatment—and adequate treatment from a medical point of view—to the several thousand patients who have been civilly committed to Bryce's [sic] for treatment purposes. To deprive any citizen of his or her liberty upon the altruistic theory that the confinement is for humane therapeutic reasons and then fail to provide adequate treatment violates the very fundamentals of due process.[39]

The plaintiffs asked Johnson to issue an order mandating standards of treatment, but he delayed doing so. He reasoned that the state should be given time to react. Stickney should have an opportunity to evaluate the unit system and his other administrative requirements in order to settle upon a course of remedial action. However, he warned that if the state did not act within six months, the court would institute remedial proceedings. The court required the state to file papers within ninety days detailing its view of the role and function of Bryce, providing an evaluation of its current posture, and stating its tentative plans for implementing patient care requirements.

The court also ordered the Department of Justice (DOJ) and HEW to enter the case as *amici curiae*

> for the purpose of assisting this Court in evaluating the treatment programs at the Bryce hospital facility and in assisting the defendants in meeting the subjective standards of the United States Department of Health, Education and Welfare as said standards pertain to adequate treatment personnel, space, equipment and facilities . . . [and] in qualifying for Social Security benefits for the approximately 1,500 to 1,600 geriatric patients who are presently housed at Bryce for custodial purposes.[40]

The events that would unfold over the course of the next year made the liability portion of the case seem simple by comparison.

THE REMEDY PHASE

The *Wyatt* ruling was of seminal importance in the national discussion on the need for mental health reform. In Alabama, though, it marked the onset of a process in which a variety of influences had to be accommodated and a plan crafted for solving the deplorable situation at all the state mental health facilities. Moreover, the implementation of the plan would have to be approached cautiously in anticipation of the outcome of the parallel appeals process. Johnson's liability ruling was, after all, a precedent-setting opinion that faced an uncertain future on appeal.

Remedy Crafting

The factors that must be understood in order to comprehend the remedy crafting process included the changing cast of characters in the litigation, the complexities of the administrative environment, and the political tensions at work both within the Mental Health Department and in the larger context. The stakes were high for the patients, the administrators, the governor, and the mental health policy interest groups around the country.

Once the liability decision was issued, the personalities and interests associated with the case underwent a dramatic change. Groups like the American Psychological Association, the American Association on Mental Deficiency, the National Legal Aid and Defenders Association, and the Center for Law and Social Policy coalesced around George Dean and Jack Drake for the remedy crafting process. It was clear that any meaningful remedy would necessarily include some statement of the standards of care that the courts would consider minimally adequate for the mentally ill and the mentally retarded. No interest group concerned with mental health could afford to be left out of that decision. Moreover, most of these political players had been working as groups or through individual lawyers to make the case for a right to treatment in several states, including neighboring Georgia and Florida. They now had an opportunity to work together to construct a defensible argument for basic standards. They brought with them their considerable legal talents and substantial expertise.

Similarly, the entry into the case of the Department of Justice through the local U.S. Attorney, Ira DeMent, brought not only the legal and policy resources of the U.S. government, but also the investigative ability of the FBI. It brought something more than that, however, since DeMent was a former undergraduate roommate of Dr. Raymond Fowler and a law school friend and classmate of George Dean.

DeMent became a key figure in the case almost immediately as a result of a surprise visit to Bryce with reporters in tow. He took the group to Bryce on Saturday, July 31, 1971, after about half the time Judge Johnson had set for state remedial action had elapsed. DeMent led the group to the Jemison building annex at Bryce, a facility state officials had said during the liability trial was an example that indicated the staffing levels at Bryce would work. As one of the reporters would later state, "That's when all hell broke loose."[41]

> Human feces were caked on the toilets and walls, urine saturated the aging oak floors, many beds lacked linen, some patients slept on floors, archaic shower stalls had cracked and spewing shower heads. One tiny shower closet served 131 male patients; the 75 women patients also had but one shower. Most of the patients at Jemison were highly tranquilized and had not been bathed in days. All appeared to lack any semblance of treatment. The stench was almost unbearable.[42]

The public outrage produced by the revelations at Jemison was met by the development of a small emergency fund for the hospital, but state officials argued that no finances were available for substantial improvement in the conditions.

Another key change in the array of parties was the appointment of Dr. James Folsom as Superintendent of Bryce Hospital and Associate Commissioner for Mental Health. Folsom took over in August 1971.

Remedy Crafting in a Complicated Administrative Environment

The two key features dominating the environment within which state administrators would have to accomplish the needed reforms were (1) inadequate finances distributed according to contentious budgetary politics and (2) the increasingly significant politics of the Alabama statehouse and the presidential contest of 1972.

Alabama was not a wealthy state. The weak revenue base was combined with an overall low tax effort and a regressive tax structure. It was a period of rapid change and complex political conflicts, none of which helped and much of which burdened the meager financial resources of the state. In an effort to respond to those difficulties, state officials made wider use of revenue bonds which only compounded the financial trouble with a rapidly increasing debt service obligation.

The state revenue picture in 1967 is explained in Table 7–1. The largest revenue source was federal assistance, making up nearly a third of the state's entire revenue base. Federal support was not to be taken for granted given the state's legal problems, its inability to meet minimum standards for some programs, and the problem of generating the state matching funds needed to qualify for other grants. The revenue estimate includes almost $52 million in "All Other Non-Tax Sources," but most of those funds were not available to the legislature since they consisted of contributions by state teachers and other employees to retirement and insurance programs.

TABLE 7–1. Alabama Revenues for 1967

Source	Amount	Per Cent
Non-Tax Receipts		
Federal Funds	$245,522,639	30.8
ABC Store Profits	19,713,030	2.5
All Other Non-Tax Sources	51,843,237	6.2
Tax Receipts		
General Sales and Use Tax	170,791,043	21.4
Gasoline Tax	92,400,821	11.6
Income Taxes	86,029,364	10.8
Tobacco Tax	23,038,734	2.9
General Property Tax	20,384,218	2.6
All Other Taxes	87,722,655	11.0

Source: Coleman B. Ransone, Jr., *Alabama Finances–Revenues and Expenditures 1957–1967* (University, AL: Univ. of Alabama, 1969), Table I. Used by permission.

The tax system was quite rigid and very regressive. The state generated only about ten percent of its revenues from income taxes, including corporate tax. That revenue was unlikely to increase since the tax rate was written into the state constitution and required voter approval for changes. The property tax situation was also weak and likely to continue that way. The state legislature set the property assessment at sixty percent of fair market value, but those legislative guidelines were not observed. In 1967 the legislation was changed to limit assessment to not more than thirty percent of fair market value, eliminating any minimum standard. In 1968 one analyst concluded, "the rates still vary and the state wide average is 15.4 per cent."[43]

Most of its remaining tax revenues were generated from consumer taxes, with sales tax leading the way at more than 20% of total revenue. Sales taxes are the most regressive forms of taxation, but Alabama's system was especially troublesome. There were sixty-four exemptions to state sales tax, covering things like auto repairs and haircuts.[44] Sales tax for automobile sales was limited to 1.5%, whereas the standard state sales tax was 4%. With all of these exemptions, however, food and prescriptions drugs were covered by the sales tax requirement. Since many of the consumer tax programs were earmarked for particular programs, the interest groups benefiting from that revenue were unlikely to support major changes in the operation of the consumer tax structure.[45]

Yet there were demands that just would not go away. The mechanism used for much of the 1960s to respond to these pressures was issuance of revenue bonds. Unlike general obligation bonds backed by the full faith and credit of the state, revenue bonds were less secure and required the state to pay a higher interest rate for the money it borrowed. While courts would rapidly apply legal limits to bonding authority for general obligation bonds, revenue bonds were treated more flexibly as special purpose levies. Consequently, the cost for debt service rose "from 1.5% of state budget in 1957 to 4.1% in 1967."[46] Perhaps more important was the fact that while the state was carrying a per capita debt of $14.27 in general obligations, it was facing a $139.23 in revenue bond debt.[47]

There was very little that could be done to alter state spending without new resources. The state's expenditures are summarized in Table 7–2 and Figure 7–1.The figures are total expenditures by the state from all available funds, including federal assistance. Some seventy-seven percent of the expenditures went for education, roads,

TABLE 7–2. Alabama Expenditures for 1967

Function	Amount	Per Cent
Schools	$382,628,187	43.6
Highways	166,138,165	19.0
Public Welfare	127,445,908	14.6
Payments to Counties	46,905,059	5.3
Debt Service	35,843,269	4.1
Protection to Persons and Property	25,323,716	3.0
Health	23,391,708	2.8
General Government	18,833,430	2.2
Conservation	13,550,597	1.6
Hospitals and Institutions	12,906,413	1.5
Payments to Cities	8,787,028	1.03
Corrections	7,901,091	0.95
All Other Expenditures	10,161,375	1.15

Source: Coleman B. Ransone, Jr., *Alabama Finances–Revenues and Expenditures 1957–1967* (University, AL: Univ. of Alabama, 1969), Table II. Used by permission.

FIGURE 7–1. Selected Alabama expenditures 1957–1967 (*Source:* Coleman B. Ransone, Jr., *Alabama Finances Revenues and Expenditures 1957–1962* [University, AL: Univ. of Alabama, 1969], Figure 3). Used by permission.

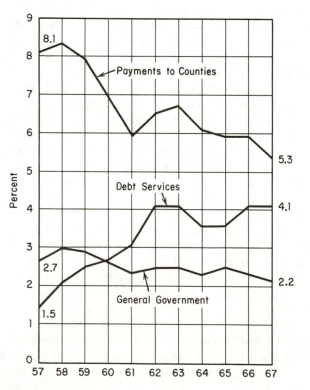

and welfare.[48] Assuming the state did not face required expenditures in particular categories, it would, nevertheless, have been difficult to reduce funding levels for leading
programs to augment mental health resources. "Even with over 40 per cent of Alabama's expenditures devoted to schools, the elementary and secondary system [then] rank[ed]
forty-ninth or fiftieth among the states in the United States in all major indices used to
judge school quality and tax effort."[49]

Alabama politics would not likely provide ways to accommodate the state's financial pressures. The constitutional and statutory structure, the general conservative ide-
ology, and the role then played by Governor Wallace in state and national politics were
all limiting factors.

The two key features of the Alabama political landscape of particular significance
for mental health reform were Wallace's political fortunes and the bureaucratic politics
of the Mental Health Board. Despite the national image of a conservative state squarely
in line behind the leadership of George Wallace, Alabama politics was fragmented.[50]
The governor's rejection of federal civil rights statutes and court decisions was not
shared by all of the state's officials. The 1970 gubernatorial campaign had been bitter
and extremely divisive for the Democratic party. It aggravated existing divisions within
the state legislature and polarized legislators into pro Brewer and pro Wallace factions.
Almost immediately, critics charged Wallace was more interested in preparing for another run for the presidency in 1972 than he was in confronting the troublesome policy
agenda facing Alabama. That was increasingly true as the campaign got under way and
Wallace scrambled to prove himself more conservative than Richard Nixon. The mere
fact of Wallace's travel schedule became an issue.

Moreover, the governor's hard line against federal authorities in Alabama was viewed
by a number of local politicos as good symbolic politics in support of his drive to lead
the political right at the national level but potentially, if not immediately, bad for the
state. For example, Wallace had used what has come to be known as financial interposition as a means to avoid compliance with civil rights law in the past.[51] He had argued
that the state could not afford to provide police protection for civil rights marchers and
assist school integration. It was clear that he was merely using the financial argument
as a tactic. Therefore, it became increasingly hard to believe Alabama officials when
they claimed, for example, that they could not provide resources to ensure minimally
adequate mental health facilities.

Further, various interest groups could use the political fragmentation of the state
legislature to protect their existing position against changes sought by the governor. For
instance, in 1971 following Judge Johnson's liability ruling in *Wyatt,* the governor
sought to divert $24 million for mental health reform from the State Teacher Retirement
Fund. When that failed, he tried to get the $24 million from the Special Education Trust
Fund. The move was beaten back under leadership of Senator Phil Smith of Talladega.[52]
Mental health may have had a dedicated group of advocates, but they were few in
number. While the Mental Health Board had a constituency of thousands, "no clientele
is worse than one whose members are not included within the American voting population."[53]

The political problems of the Alabama Mental Health Board were not merely external, concerning relationships with the state legislature, governor, and the federal court.
The Board faced equally difficult internal politics. There was a great deal of support for
a dynamic Mental Health Commissioner following the reorganization of mental health
administration in the 1960s. Stonewall Stickney brought very definite professional and

administrative values with him to that office. Resistance developed rapidly within the staffs of the state's hospitals when Stickney attempted to implement his ideas at the facilities and to make key personnel decisions. Tensions also grew between the Commissioner's office and the staff and members of the Mental Health Board as each attempted to claim the role of principal decisionmaker. During the 1970s, while the *Wyatt* case developed and a remedy was implemented, the state was served by four commissioners and suffered from rapid turnover in institutional superintendants.

In sum, the task of mental health reform would be difficult, the resources meager, and the political situation complex. These were facts that were becoming increasingly apparent as Alabama moved through the months Judge Johnson had allowed the state for voluntary compliance with the *Wyatt* ruling.

The State's Voluntary Remedy Opportunity

The Jemison exposé at the end of July made conditions at state facilities a high visibility issue. Reports circulated of conditions at other institutions that were as bad or worse than those found at Bryce. In late August, the court permitted the plaintiffs to add patients at Searcy and Partlow to the class action and make conditions at those facilities a part of the remedy proceeding.

The state filed the six month remedy report required by Johnson's March 1971 order. No significant change was suggested by the report which spoke primarily of the state's treatment philosophy and organizational concerns. Stickney later explained his rationale:

> In our first report we defined the hospital's mission and functions and set forth standards for evaluating its therapeutic effectiveness. At that point in our thinking that was *our preferred interpretation of the court request to set standards*. We were not promulgating standards of per-diem expenditure, staff-patient ratios, or physicial-plant standards for three reasons. The first was that we were still unconsciously acquiescing in the traditional poor funding of state institutions; therefore we wanted to demonstrate that by improved organization and leadership along with the change in philosophy we could provide adequate treatment for patients without a great deal of new money. I now believe this tactic was a mistake and probably wasted a lot of time. . . .
>
> The second reason was our wish to safeguard our freedom to experiment. . . .
>
> The third reason was that we were well aware that some public mental hospitals . . . have gone through periods in which they were adequately funded and staffed, had adequate physical plants, but still remained essentially static, custodial institutions. In other words, we tried to persuade the court to abandon any preoccupation with standards of effort or expenditure and to concentrate on standards of effectiveness.[54] (emphasis added)

Stickney was quite right that their approach to the compliance report was not a good tactic. The state made another such error. During the month of September, HEW offered to provide a survey team to evaluate operations at Alabama facilities, but the state ignored the offer. In addition to a general institutional evaluation, HEW was prepared to develop a minimum staffing guideline for any or all of the individual facilities.[55]

The plaintiffs and the United States, both of which entered strong criticisms to the state's report, called upon the court to initiate formal remedy proceedings at once.[56] Judge Johnson began the formal remedy crafting process by an order issued December 10, 1971.[57]

The opinion sets forth the basic elements that must be presented to ensure minimally adequate treatment. "These three fundamental conditions are: (1) a humane psychological and physical environment, (2) qualified staff in numbers sufficient to administer adequate treatment and (3) individualized treatment plans."[58] Johnson did not originate these criteria. They came from the opinion in *Rouse v. Cameron*[59] and were expanded by Judge Bazelon in his "Forward" to the *Georgetown Law Journal*'s "Right to Treatment" symposium.[60] Based upon the filings of the plaintiffs and *amici* as well as consultants hired by the state, Johnson found that Bryce failed in all of these areas:

> The psychological and physical environment problems are, in some instances interrelated. For example, the dormitories are barnlike structures with no privacy for the patients. For most patients there is not even a space provided which he can think of as his own. The toilets in the restrooms seldom have partitions between them. . . .
> Also contributing to the poor psychological environment are shoddy wearing apparel furnished to the patients, the non-therapeutic work assigned to patients (mostly compulsory, uncompensated housekeeping chores), and the degrading and humiliating admissions procedure which creates in the patient an impression of the hospital as a prison or as a "crazy house."[61]

The consultants for Bryce had found the hospital inadequately staffed in virtually all areas.[62] Finally, the records were completely inadequate to evaluate the progress of patients. There was no indication of individualized treatment plans to guide therapy. In fact, the Bryce consultant indicated that "treatment is geared primarily to housekeeping functions."[63] Preliminary submissions suggested that Searcy and Partlow were in a similar condition. While Johnson understood that the Mental Health Board may not have had funds to implement new standards in the months since the liability ruling, he insisted "the state could at least have developed the standards."[64]

Based upon his assessment that Stickney and Folsom had "demonstrated good faith and a desire to attain minimum standards," Johnson again refused to appoint a panel of masters to draft a remedy and oversee implementation. He did order formal remedy hearings for January.

Following the December 10 order, the Executive Committee of the Mental Health Board met with their defense lawyers, John Coleman and J. Jerry Wood, and Commissioner Stickney at the offices of a Birmingham law firm. The purpose was to develop a strategy for the remedy process. The core of that plan was to stipulate to standards regarding the facilities and some minimum patient care guidelines, but to contest staffing demands. The guiding principle was to try to use the court to leverage the legislature for more money without surrendering any discretion over operations.[65] Stickney, Wood, and Coleman took the negotiation plan to a meeting in the governor's office attended by Wallace, his legal advisor, financial aides, and Mental Health Board staff. After discussing the impact of the likely remedy and the situation in other states, the governor agreed to the proposal.[66]

The Formal Remedy Process

What followed was a three month series of negotiations and hearings during which lengthy, detailed remedial orders were hammered out. In years to come, Johnson would face severe criticism for the detailed manner in which the decrees addressed basic institutional facilities and services. Especially attractive to the critics would be those elements of the decrees that mandated everything from the number of toilets per patient to the temperature of the hot water in the dishwasher. In point of fact, however, Johnson wrote very little in the orders. With the exception of the staffing ratios and a few other items, virtually all of the provisions of the remedial decrees were written by the parties to the case and agreed to by all sides. Stonewall Stickney later admitted that "more than 90 per cent of the standards . . . had already been stipulated . . . by both sides before the hearings."[67]

To understand how the orders were developed and why they took their final form, it is necessary to consider the four key stages in the process. They included (1) negotiations and drafting of the Bryce/Searcy proposal, (2) the Bryce/Search hearings, (3) negotiations on Partlow, and (4) the Partlow hearings. The bifurcation of the proceedings between Bryce/Searcy and Partlow was necessary to accommodate the distinctions between minimum standards of habilitation for mentally retarded persons at Partlow and principles of treatment for the mentally ill patients at Bryce and Searcy, even though minimum requirements for safe and hygienic facilities are virtually the same. At the outset the court expected to deal with all of the institutions in one decree, but the differences between the patients served would not easily accommodate that approach.

The parties and *amici* met on January 17 in Atlanta and produced a memorandum of agreement that set forth twenty-six standards arrayed according to the essential criteria set forth in the court's December 10 opinion: humane psychological and physical environment, qualified staff to administer adequate treatment, and individualized treatment plans. For the most part, the standards set forth those principles of mental health treatment accepted by national mental health organizations. They include the right to

privacy and dignity,

the least-restrictive conditions necessary for treatment,

not be assumed legally incompetent merely by virtue of being a patient in a mental health facility,

visitation, telephone communications and mail, which specifically includes the right to communicate with legal and medical personnel,

be free of unnecessary and excessive medication,

be free of physical restraint and isolation except under limited circumstances for legitimate purposes,

be free from experimental or hazardous treatments without full knowledge and consent of the patient or guardian,

receive prompt adequate medical treatment when necessary,

maintain some private possessions and clothing unless judged dangerous by qualified mental health professionals,

have clean, serviceable clothing and laundry services,

physical exercise and to be outdoors at some interval unless medically prohibited,

be free from institutional peonage including so-called therapeutic labor which is, in fact, performance of menial maintenance and housekeeping tasks,

have a safe, humane physical environment with reasonable space, toilet and hygiene

facilities, adequate heating and ventilation, and clean kitchen and dining arrangements,

have adequate numbers of trained professional and nonprofessional staff to provide
basic treatment services,

be provided treatment according to some kind of individualized treatment program
appropriate to the patient,

have adequate records maintained,

have assistance in the transition from the institution to the community when it is time
for the release of the patient.

As they approached the hearings, the parties disagreed over only three issues. The
plaintiffs filed a reservation to the memorandum of agreement, seeking to hold medication policies to Food and Drug Administration (FDA) standards, place slightly tighter
standards on necessary uses of restraints or isolation, and add adversive reinforcement
conditioning to the list of experimental or hazardous treatments barred by the proposed
order. For its part, the state continued to contest any minimum staffing standard. The
hearing would resolve these issues and provide evidence as to why the stipulations
entered into by the parties were necessary to ensure minimum adequate treatment for
patients in state facilities.

The Bryce/Searcy remedy hearings were held February 3 and 4, 1972. Johnson
saw before him an imposing phalanx of lawyers. Dean and Drake for the plaintiffs had
been joined by Morton Birnbaum, author of the right-to-treatment thesis, and by Shelly
Mercer. Ira DeMent was jointed by Robert Johnson, David Vanderhoof, and Cleveland
Thornton for DOJ. The nongovernment *amici* were represented by Charles Halpern,
Bruce Ennis, Stanley Herr, Paul Friedman, and James Fitzpatrick, an extremely talented
and experienced civil rights team. James Jerry Wood and John Coleman represented the
state, as they had throughout the litigation.

Owing to the amount of consensus exhibited by the memorandum of agreement,
the plaintiffs kept their presentation brief. Their only tasks, after all, were to convince
the judge of the appropriate staffing standard and explain the need for fine tuning the
proposed decree to meet their reservations. The key witness was Dr. Jack Ewalt, Chairman of the Department of Psychiatry at Harvard and Superintendent of the Massachusetts Mental Health Center. Ewalt had been one of the founders of the Group for the
Advancement of Psychiatry (GAP). He served as president of GAP and, later, the APA.
Dr. Ewalt testified to the need for minimum staffing guidelines and presented a set of
standards based upon a 250 patient core hospital unit that would be able to provide
twenty-five minutes per day per patient of nursing care and one hour per week per
patient of professional psychiatric time. Such a unit would require 181 nurses (RNs,
licensed practical nurses [LPNs], and aides); 17 social workers; 10 psychologists; 10
occupational therapists; 4 rehabilitation counselors; 8 laboratory, pharmacy and x-ray
personnel; and 8 psychiatrists (5 staff and 3 for supervisory and replacement duties).
His testimony was buttressed by depositions from Doctors Harold Zwerling, Harold
Visotsky, Israel Zwerling, and Walter Fox, all distinguished professionals active in the
APA and who supported the minimum staffing principle.

Coleman's cross-examination of Ewalt sought to show that the APA and other
organizations had stopped issuing numerical staffing ratios because the types of facilities
and modes of treatment varied too widely to be held to any particular set of numbers.
In that regard, Coleman pressed for an admission that the state's unit treatment system

would be just such an approach to treatment that could manage with fewer personnel. Ewalt rejected the idea that a facility like Bryce, with no board certified psychiatrists and few psychologists, could begin to provide any kind of minimal treatment. He argued that, in any event, those facilities around the country which had been successful with the unit system had used more personnel, not less. Coleman pressed him on the fact that Ewalt did not know the details of Searcy staffing. Ewalt replied, "no hospital of thirteen hundred that has eight physicians, none psychiatrists, can be said to be giving good psychiatric care."[68]

Coleman pressed Ewalt and other witnesses on feasibility, suggesting that no other institutions met the kind of staffing standards proposed for Alabama hospitals. Moreover, given the number of mental health professionals available, it would be impossible to hire sufficient personnel to meet the demands. Later testimony showed that the experts who testified by deposition had provided numerous examples of other institutions which met the basic requirements and that some 335 mental health facilities had measured up to minimum Medicare standards while Alabama hospitals could not.

Johnson was sensitive to the feasibility considerations, noting:

> So that counsel might focus, the Court considers that this hearing not only involves the taking of testimony that will enable the Court to determine what these minimum standards should be, but the Court is concerned with the practical ability to require the defendants to effectuate these minimum standards.[69]

When George Dean called for the judge to stop all further commitments pending completion of an HEW study and implementation efforts, Judge Johnson replied, "All constitutional rights are present rights . . . but sometimes it has taken a long time to effect them."[70]

The other principal witness for the plaintiffs was Dr. F. Lewis Bartlett, a ward psychiatrist at Haverford State Hospital in Pennsylvania. Bartlett provided testimony that supported the enhanced standards associated with medication, restraint, and hazardous treatment advocated by the plaintiffs.

The case for the United States was in two parts. First, the officials who prepared and monitored Medicare regulations for mental health facilities testified as to the basis for guidelines and their bona fides as minimum requirements. Of more importance was the testimony of Dr. Courtenay Bennett, Director of the Dutchess County unit at the Hudson River State Hospital and consultant to the National Institute for Mental Health, and a number of specialized witnesses. Bennett vigorously supported the minimum staffing demands. A nutritionist from the Community Health Service addressed nutritional needs which became the basis for a subsequent set of stipulations agreed to by all parties. Donald Baker, a Public Health Service pharmacy consultant, went well beyond merely supporting the call for a tighter control on possible overmedication to explain why both the dispensing and administration of drugs required separate safeguards and properly trained personnel. His testimony would be important for all three institutions. A VA medical records consultant fleshed out the need for a comprehensive medical records system, which was lacking in existing facilities.

Amici concentrated on testimony by their key expert, Dr. Francis Tyce, Medical Director of Rochester State Hospital, Assistant Professor of Psychiatry at the Mayo Postgraduate School of the Mayo Clinic, and former President of the Association of Medical Superintendents of Mental Hospitals. Like Ewalt, Tyce presented staffing figures based upon a hypothetical treatment unit, in this case a unit intended to care for 200 patients. He called for one psychiatrist for 50 patients, one psychologist for 50 to 75 patients, one social worker to each 30 patients, one physician for 100 to 125 patients, three RNs per 50 patients, and three aides per 50 patients as the core requirement. Whatever the final standards, he said, it is possible to say that at some point a hospital is so understaffed that it cannot be said to be providing treatment.

The defendants were attempting save face professionally, obtain leverage against the legislature and governor, and, simultaneously, not yield any discretion in how the increased resources would be used. For the first purpose, the state presented none other than the renowned Karl Menninger. Folsom had studied with Menninger, whose testimony amounted to little more than a laudatory report on Folsom's qualifications and a recommendation to give Folsom the discretion to deal with the situation as he saw fit. Dr. Donald Hammersley, a psychiatrist who trained with Folsom under Menninger, supported the state's argument against numerical staffing standards. On cross-examination, though, Hammersley testified that the largest number of patients he could treat in a unit team organization would be about fifty.[71]

The key witnesses for the state, however, were Folsom and Stickney, with Folsom playing the lead as Bryce Superintendent. Stickney proposed a renovation program for Bryce, but the plaintiffs rejected it since it had not been prepared in light of the standards agreed upon prior to the hearing. Folsom had a difficult problem. He wanted to leverage the state officials, but he did not want to participate in developing specific standards that would constrain his own future actions. Judge Johnson saw what was happening and interjected:

> Gentlemen, let's keep this in mind: In this case at the termination of the original hearing, I determined that an individual who was committed through the state processes to a mental institution for treatment purposes was constitutionally entitled to treatment; otherwise it would be a violation of due process to confine him or put him in a . . . confinement status for treatment purposes and not treat him. Along with that, I held that he's not entitled to the best treatment, he is not entitled to optimum treatment; but he is constitutionally entitled to minimum treatment, and this hearing today is for the purpose of determining what these minimum standards are. *And I will not permit this Court to be used as a lever for the Legislature to get a budget for Bryce or Searcy Hospitals.*[72] (emphasis added)

Folsom continued to be evasive about minimums, arguing it was unnecessary to use such standards and rejecting the expert testimony presented by plaintiffs and *amici*. Johnson warned Folsom, "If you don't go along with them, you are going to have to give me something I can measure against what they say; and you are not doing that."[73]

Folsom did generate numbers and ultimately Johnson's opinion incorporated those figures in the final Bryce/Searcy decree. The Bryce Superintendant's argument was not helped by admissions during cross-examination that while he had not presented budget requests for what he acknowledged to be basic requirements, the request had included a raise for him. Folsom answered that the raise had not been his idea but concerned planned raises for all state facilities' superintendents. He also acknowledged that his wife was employed by Jefferson State College under a state contract to provide in-service training at Bryce for staff members.[74]

The testimony concluded with an exchange between the judge and Dr. Folsom:

THE COURT: What suggestions do you, as a—as a hospital administrator with years of experience in this field of mental health, have to make to the Court for implementing this and getting it; how are we going to get it?

WITNESS: Well, we are going to have to enter into the educational process that I talked about. . . . We will have to start with an overly large number—

THE COURT: This means I am going to have to order you to do something.

WITNESS: I am afraid so.

THE COURT: Yes.

WITNESS: I hope so.

THE COURT: And once—once I do enter this order, how are we going to enforce it? Am I going to tell you not to take any more patients until you get this staff up to a minimum?

WITNESS: I think this would be an error; I think it would—

THE COURT: Otherwise—otherwise, we are warehousing patients just for custodial purposes; we are putting them in the penitentiary; I made that finding.

WITNESS: Well, I—

THE COURT: How—how are we going to get your institution up to a bare minimum before we continue to commit them?

WITNESS: I think this is going to be a job for Dr. Stickney and the Board, and they must convince the Legislature.

THE COURT: Well, I have given them that job back in March, and that hasn't been done. They tried to do it, but they didn't convince the legislature.[75]

As the Bryce/Searcy hearing ended and the parties prepared for the Partlow remedy proceedings scheduled for the end of February, the situation was changing. The first hearing suggested that the strategy of avoiding specific recommendations on matters of staffing and the like would be unlikely to work. It was obvious that the mental health administrators wanted Johnson to take all the political heat associated with specific orders while they enjoyed the benefits of his action. It was equally clear, however, that Johnson was not going to permit that. A second factor that had changed was that the expert testimony on medications, safety and fire protection, medical records development, nutrition and the like would provide more material for negotiation. The parties held meetings in Atlanta on February 18 and Montgomery on February 24. The product was another memorandum of agreement which incorporated the fruits of the first hearing and numerical staffing ratios for Partlow State School and Hospital. This second agreement presented forty-nine separate standards as the basis for the forthcoming hearing.

There was another development that changed the tenor and lent a sense of urgency to the hearings. The state had resisted requests for inspections of Partlow by the plaintiffs and *amici*. The motions for inspection were granted in late January. The conditions revealed by the inspections and the subsequent hearings were undisputed. They were so bad that Judge Johnson issued an emergency remedial order at the conclusion of the hearings.

The Partlow hearing was quite different from the earlier proceedings. Unlike the Bryce/Searcy sessions, the Partlow hearing was not a more or less dispassionate argument over what psychiatric professionals viewed as adequate. Rather, it was a presentation in several parts of the egregious conditions at Partlow and a discussion of how to mold a remedy. Defendants' participation was minimal. The plaintiffs and *amici* concentrated on several specific tasks. First, they sought to document precisely how bad the conditions were and how they corresponded to the kinds of guidelines set down in the memorandum of agreement. Second, they argued many of the problems in the institution were a direct result of understaffing and antiquated physical plant conditions. They presented testimony contesting the claim that everything that could be done was being accomplished and argued that there were means readily available to support the necessary reforms. Finally, they presented witnesses who sketched plans for implementation of the full decree and suggested emergency guidelines to meet the health and safety threats then facing Partlow residents.

The explanation of past and present conditions was developed by two sets of witnesses. Much of the testimony came from experts in mental retardation from around the nation who had inspected conditions at Partlow prior to the hearing. Two of the experts were what might be termed local experts or at least people who could make a claim to understanding the situation in Alabama. The second group of witnesses was made up of Partlow employees, relatives of patients, and other local witnesses to some of the more extreme incidents at the facility.

Dr. Gunnar Dybwad, Professor of Human Development at Brandeis University and consultant to the President's Committee on Mental Retardation during the Johnson administration and the Kennedy administration before that, led the witnesses. Dybwad's testimony emphasized the differences between mental illness and retardation, particularly refuting the notion that some retarded persons are not entitled to habilitation because of the severity and hopelessness of their condition. He emphasized the distinction between habilitation of retarded persons and normalization, the attempt to approximate as closely as possible the noninstitutional environment, thereby reinforcing the lifestyle the person was seeking to achieve rather than the limitations and peculiarities of life in a total institution. The state could not be relieved of its responsibilities in either area.

Rejecting the term *custody,* since it "means safeguarding," Dybwad termed the situation at Partlow a mere "storage of persons."[76] He saw no habilitation taking place there and identified a range of problems undermining any progress. He found units of ninety-two and ninety-seven patients with only two and three staff members, respectively. Mattresses were spread on the floor to accommodate overcrowding. He found seclusion rooms so small that one could barely "squeeze one person through." He saw a resident with open wounds and multiple bruises sitting in the corner with nothing being done to care for him and was told by a staff member that there was no need to get the boy to a hospital.[77] Dybwad saw open drug cabinets and refrigerators for medication in unsanitary condition. He saw what he termed "cattle prods" (what Partlow personnel referred to as "training wands"), which were used in aversion therapy, laying out whether either staff or residents could use them. His examination of the records that were available indicated little concern for patient history, particularly with respect to medication. One resident he checked had been on a prescription for phenobarbitol, originally written in 1966, and continued until Dybwad's visit in 1972, with no indication that the prescription had been reviewed.[78] Residents throughout the facility, Dybwad reported, were used for institutional labor without compensation. They primarily performed the most menial tasks but also were assigned to provide direct patient services.

On cross-examination, Dybwad rejected outright the suggestion that Alabama's situation was little worse than the conditions generally encountered in the nation's mental health facilities. Dr. James Clements, Director of the Georgia Mental Retardation Center, presented testimony similar to that provided by Dybwad. He brought a unique perspective, however, since he was familiar with the situation in Alabama not only because of his location in a neighboring state, but also since he had been one of the inspectors at Partlow in the 1967 evaluation.

The most devastating testimony on the state of Partlow came from Dr. Philip Ross, Executive Director of the National Association of Retarded Children. At the administrative level, Ross found Partlow had no institutional philosophy, no formal table of organization, no policy and procedures manual, no evidence of modern financial practices, no policy statement setting forth the rights of residents, little or no employee orientation and training programs, and poor in-service training. It was understaffed, overcrowded, unsafe, and dirty. His inspection showed that at least five hundred residents were involved in institutional peonage, performing a wide variety of labor over a period of years with no compensation. "Many of them have been working in the same job for periods of twenty, thirty, and some in excess of forty years."[79] An attendant would later testify that young men who performed this kind of labor were called *working boys*. They were occasionally paid by the attendants at the rate of a penny per night for their labor. Roos was approached by several Partlow residents during his tour who expressed their displeasure with the peonage system.

There was no indication of internal evaluation procedures or participatory programs involving the community or the residents. But it was perhaps in a discussion of direct patient care that his testimony was the most powerful. One cannot truly comprehend the nature of the case after the Partlow hearing began without giving some attention to his detailed comments.

He gave a summary of the environment he saw there:

> The interior of this building—and this is true of others as well—was generally in poor shape. The paint was peeling. Some of the door panels were broken. I noticed a broken glass door—one of the interior doors. The metal screens were split with ragged edges. One resident was observed to be playing with an exposed nail sticking out from one of the benches. I also noticed it was extremely hot and humid in this as in other buildings with an unpleasant odor permeating the atmosphere. The food was slopped out unceremoniously by the working residents. There was a kind of a cake—I assume it was; I must say I didn't try it—as part of the meal, and it was handed out by the working residents using their hands and dropping it on the trays. There were no knives or forks. Many of the residents ate with their hands.[80]

Roos told of a visit to a unit for young boys where he saw no activities in progress for any of the children.

> I asked the attendant where the toys were kept and found they were firmly locked in a chest. The attendant did not possess the key to this chest and had to produce it from the supervisor. I asked to look at these toys. As soon as the chest was open, one of the young boys rushed up and tried to reach in and get a'hold of one of these implements. The box was immediately shut and locked again. I was told that because the boys were destructive, the toys would tend to be damaged.[81]

Roos was taken by the abuse of physical restraints and the lack of medical attention for patients, both of which were, in his view, directly related to shortages of staff. He found several men in one unit controlled by various forms of restraints. Some were fastened in their beds while others "were in wrist restraints and tied to benches." Dr. Roos checked one of the resident's files and found the restraint order had not been reviewed in four months. He noticed that one of the men was bleeding from the leg. "I asked the attendant about this; the attendant seemed quite unconcerned and indicated that it was common for this individual to bleed from the leg since he has a tendency to scrape his knees along the benches."[82]

He found a similar problem in a girls' ward:

> I noticed one of the residents was in a camisole tied to a bench. A camisole is a restraining device in which the hands and arms are held roughly in this position. (gestures) I asked the charge attendant about this, why it was necessary; and she explained that this was necessary because the girl sucked her hands and her fingers. And I asked the attendant how long this girl had been in a camisole; the attendant indicated as long as she, the attendant, had been on that unit, which I ascertained was the last nine years.[83]

A third example of the abuse of restraints indicated that they were used in ways that clearly prevented habilitation:

> I found one girl squatting on the floor in a sort of wooden cage-like contrivance. And I asked about this, and I was told that she spent her waking hours in this wooden cage. And I asked what happened when she is released from this thing, and I was told that she would then scoot along the floor. I was also told she could stand. And I asked the attendant what happened if this girl was given a walker, and I was told this had never been done; it had never been tried. I noticed one of the other young girls who was tied in bed by a waist restraint jumped out of bed and stood next to the bed and was promptly put back in the bed. Asked why she was tied; I was told that the doctors had mandated she be tied in bed, because when she assumed an upright position, she tended to vomit.[84]

Roos also found evidence of inappropriate institutionalization. In one case a young girl born to a patient in Bryce had been a resident in Partlow since shortly after birth. At the time Roos saw her, the girl was in the seventh grade in the local school system and doing well. The girl's chart indicated a recommendation for discharge in December 1971, but no action had been taken by the time of the Partlow hearing.

The toilets and hygiene facilities were especially upsetting. There were inadequate numbers of both kinds of facilities. Existing toilets had no toilet paper in many instances and several had broken seats. There was no soap in hygiene facilities.

Dr. Peter Blouke, Acting Superintendent at Partlow, and several present and past employees appeared as witnesses for the plaintiffs and *amici* supporting the testimony given by Roos, Clements, and Dybwad. They also testified in detail to a number of particularly sad incidents, all of which were again attributed to the lack of staff and poor facilities. An attendant discussed the case of one resident who had been kept in a seclusion room for between six and seven years primarily because the staffing situation was on the order of one attendant to eighty residents and more.[85] Another testified to seeing abuse of residents, including observing some who were punched, choked, struck with broom handles, and kicked.[86]

Blouke cooperated with the plaintiffs and *amici*. He was replaced shortly after the hearing amidst charges that the removal was a reprisal for his disloyalty. Dr. Blouke, along with supporting testimony from staff members, explained the circumstances surrounding several fatal incidents at Partlow. In one case, one of the working boys at the urging of another had inserted a hose into the rectum of a resident and ran the water until the boy died.[87] A second death resulted when an unsupervised resident who was cleaning a patient sprayed the victim with scalding water.[88] Another died when a working resident put soapy water in his mouth and inserted a hose asphyxiating him.[89] A fourth young man died from a drug overdose by gaining access to a drug cabinet while the attendant on duty had her attention diverted by other patients. She was the only aide serving forty-four patients at the time.

After these witnesses painted the dismal picture of life at Partlow, the only question was how to implement the recommendations set forth in the memorandum of agreement. The first problem was to ensure the feasibility of the proposed remedy. The second task was to design a program for beginning and monitoring implementation.

Linda Glenn, then Director of Research and Planning for the Eastern Nebraska Community Office of Retardation, supplied the feasibility analysis. Glenn specialized in programs aimed at decentralizing care for mentally retarded citizens and had participated in the development of alternatives to institutionalization at a large Nebraska facility not unlike Partlow. Community-based facilities, she said, are smaller, closer to home, and more flexible. Alternatives, such as group homes, outpatient habilitation services, and part-time assistance provide habilitation in a less restrictive and more normal environment. She explained that Alabama had the financial argument reversed. Examined closely, Glenn said, the state's contention that it could not afford some of the proposed changes was an argument against economic self-interest. She explained that services provided in total institutions are some of the most expensive that government can deliver. Moreover, a high percentage of those costs is carried by the state. Decentralized services are considerably less expensive and can be funded through a variety of means, with a far smaller percentage of the costs carried by the states and localities.

There are basically two reasons why the decentralized programs were preferable in Glenn's view. As retarded persons are placed in a less restrictive, more normalized living arrangement, they place fewer demands for care on the institution. In such a situation they can respond better to vocational and other forms of counseling and assistance. If that is successful, they can return to some kind of employment, pay their own way, and pay taxes which help to support the services they continue to seek on a part-time basis.[90] Beyond that, decentralized programs can tap more sources of support than centralized institutions.

> Q: Why the difference in the proportional cost in the community from the state and local government burden, if you can explain it?
> A: Because we are a community service agency we can utilize all the community resources and the funding mechanisms that are available to programs that are in the community—use Vocational Rehabilitation funds, we use Social Security funds, under several different titles, to fund seventy-five percent of most of our programs. There are many other programs to use through the Department of Housing and Urban Development, through the Department of Labor, et cetera.[91]

Dr. Roos laid the basis for the implementation plan. His design was supplemented by Dr. Clements. Clements focused primarily on the development of an emergency order. Roos began by suggesting that a consumer advisory group and a professional advisory group were essential to begin to develop internal information and recommendations. Several of the witnesses testified to a need for some kind of committee to oversee and respond to violations of residents' rights. Roos termed it a "committee on dehumanization," while plaintiffs called for a "Human Rights Committee." Most preferred appointment of a special master who would be independent of the State Mental Health Board and could provide support for the new Partlow administrator. Clements argued that without some protection, no professionally competent administrator would take the position because he or she would be "unlikely to survive the situation, politically or otherwise."[92] The state's only witness, Associate Mental Health Commissioner for Mental Retardation, Clopper, was asked his view of such independent professional advisory and consumer committees. He replied, "Mr. Coleman, we can't possibly make the changes we would like without such a body."[93]

In order to determine the current status of the Partlow population, Roos recommended the development of a multidisciplinary evaluation team. The team would assess the condition and needs of all patients. It would also determine whether the person should be removed to another environment.

All of the other major changes could only happen after a new Partlow Superintendent was hired. That choice had to be made at once. Given that appointment, Roos estimated deadlines for staff reorganization, staff education, development of volunteer programs, facilities improvements, and deinstitutionalization screening and release. All of these developments assumed a "massive infusion of staff."

Clements developed a plan for implementation of an emergency remedy to deal with the situation at Partlow until Roos's suggestions could be carried out. The state must immediately hire a firm to deal with fire and safety deficiencies. A consultant must survey the food services facilities to correct unsanitary and unhealthy conditions. The Medical College of Alabama should be called upon to examine every patient receiving anticonvulsive or behavior-modifying drugs for need, dosage, and records development. In conjunction with that effort, a complete immunization program should be undertaken. Finally, the acting superintendent should be authorized to immediately hire three hundred resident care workers without regard to the restrictions of the Alabama civil service requirements.

Dr. Clopper's testimony for the state, like that of Dr. Folsom in the Bryce/Searcy hearing, was puzzling. He agreed with virtually everything the plaintiff and *amici* witnesses called for, but was unwilling to indicate what he thought the court should do. After providing his support for the remedy recommendations, he simply testified that the state could not afford the cost. As he had with Folsom earlier, Johnson asked what Clopper wanted the court to do:

> THE COURT: Are saying you need the assistance of the Court in doing that; is that what you are saying?
> WITNESS: No; I don't need the assistance of the Court. . . .
> THE COURT: Why hasn't it been done if you don't need the assistance of the Court?[94]

Jack Drake had been watching this colloquy and decided to pursue it:

> Q: Dr. Clopper, I am intrigued by your testimony; what—what do you want the Court to do in this lawsuit?
> A: I feel that the Court should assist us in implementing a program that will result in bringing about the kind of normalization that is necessary and long overdue at Partlow.

TABLE 7–3. Mental Health Department Resources

	Acres	Value
I. Land Owned and Controlled by the Alabama Mental Health Board		
Land with Recent Appraisal Values		
Elmore County (Developmental Center)	100.00	$ 100,000.00
Mobile County (Developmental Center)	114.00	202,000.00
Morgan County (Developmental Center)	157.50	175,000.00
Jefferson County (Dolly Ridge Road)	254.47	763,411.00
Estimated Timber Growth		15,000.00
Tuscaloosa County (Worthington Campus)	116.00	3,000,000.00
Tuscaloosa County (Timberland—Gulf States)	2,655.00	238,418.00
Estimated Timber Growth		160,000.00
	3,396.97	$4,653,829.00
Land Without Current Appraisals (value unknown)[a]		
Bryce Hospital	1,094.00	$1,094,000.00
Bryce Farm Colony	3,624.00	1,087,200.00
Partlow State School and Hospital	130.00	130,000.00
Partlow Boys Colony	1,661.00	498,300.00
Mobile County—Searcy Hospital	125.50	37,650.00
	6,634.50	$2,847,150.00
II. Land Conditionally Owned and/or Controlled by the Alabama Mental Health Board[a]		
Land Held on Conditional Grant to State		
Searcy Hospital (Mt. Vernon Barracks)	2,563.00	$ 768,900.00
Land Owned by the Board—Controlled by the Department of Conservation (estimated)	6,800.00	680,000.00
	9,363.00	$1,448,900.00
	19,394.47	$8,949,879.00

Note: Estimates furnished by Mr. James H. Crow, Jr, Land Manager.
Source: Wyatt v. Stickney Record.

Q: And can you be specific about how the Court could give you that assistance?

A: I think that the Court might indicate certain guidelines that we could follow; perhaps suggest some revenue sources that we are not aware of—those are just two areas.

Q: You don't think of the Court as ordering you to do anything?[95]

Judge Johnson listened to debate over the financial abilities of the state, including charges that the state continued to manage large amounts of land. One member of the Mental Health Board testified that the state had indeed been trading land but not with care and sensitivity to a return on its resources. Finally, Johnson ordered the state to prepare for the next day "a list of all the assets held by the state of Alabama—by the defendant Board, capital assets, land, location, fair market value, all of it."[96] The report is reproduced in Table 7–3.

Johnson ended the hearing by entering an emergency order. He wrote:

The evidence elicited from an extensive hearing concerning the mental retardation aspect of the above-styled cause has vividly and undisputedly portrayed Partlow State

School and Hospital as a warehousing institution which, because of its atmosphere of psychological and physical deprivation, is wholly incapable of furnishing treatment to the mentally retarded and is conducive only to the deterioration and the debilitation of the residents. The evidence has reflected further that safety and sanitary conditions at Partlow are substandard to the point of endangering the health and lives of those residing there, that the wards are grossly understaffed, rendering even simple custodial care impossible, and that overcrowding remains a dangerous problem often leading to serious accidents, some of which have resulted in deaths of residents.

The remainder of the March 2 emergency order consisted of the recommendations submitted by Clements.

Shortly after the hearings, the plaintiffs and *amici* filed papers formally adding the recommendations for the Human Rights Committees (HRCs) and other implementation devices discussed at the hearings. In particular, they wanted guarantees of independence against state interference with the work of the committees. The state accepted that suggestion but insisted that it retain coordination authority for all units included in any order.

The court's decrees were issued on April 13. The Bryce/Searcy[97] and Partlow[98] orders embodied the agreements submitted by the parties and modified only by the marginal changes suggested at the hearings and later agreed to by the parties. The implementation requirements followed Roos's recommendations in substance, sequencing, and proposed timing. Johnson refused to order a special master unless and until it became clear that the state would default on its responsibilities under the remedial decrees. The HRCs would provide an independent mechanism of oversight and a vehicle for interested parties to challenge the state's actions if necessary. The HRCs, however, would be purely informational outlets unable to take any action on their own, apart from submission of reports and recommendations to the court. Selection of the members of the committees was designed to ensure that all parties to the litigation were represented.

The judge was not prepared to order sale of state land or mandate any particular financial mechanism. He did require the state to take steps toward qualifying for Medicare and Medicaid, though he recognized that the state would have to work toward compliance with federal minimum standards before it would be eligible for those programs. Johnson warned the state that "a failure by defendants to comply with this decree cannot be justified by a lack of operating funds."[99]

The Parallel Appeals Process

Initially, it appeared that the state would move to implement the orders on a cooperative basis with no mention of an appeal by state attorneys. There was no effort, for example, by Coleman or Wood to obtain stays of the court's orders pending appeal. That situation was changed dramatically.

The campaign for the presidency was already underway. One element of President Nixon's strategy was to attack federal courts for intervention in state and local matters. After Nixon's March 16 speech called for anti-busing legislation and ordered the DOJ to intervene in pending cases to block complex federal court orders, Wallace renewed his attacks on his favorite federal judicial target, Frank Johnson. Wallace denied the state had agreed to the provisions of the orders and termed the orders a search for "a utopia."[100] Critics charged that this was part of his national campaign, but Wallace rejected the allegation. He warned that taxes would have to be dramatically increased to unbearable levels to comply.

The counsel for the state during the entire *Wyatt* proceeding were caught by surprise. After the meeting with the governor's people in January and in the face of their repeated assurances of the attorneys' discretion, Wallace was now claiming they had abused their authority. In fact, Wallace retained a private attorney, Mr. Charles M. Crook, to represent him as the governor in an appeal of Johnson's orders. Crook filed notice of appeal in mid-May, followed quickly by a call for a stay. The appeal specifically denied that the governor had authorized any negotiations and stipulations. It claimed that the provisions of the orders were unlawful impositions by the court. Shortly thereafter, the Alabama Attorney General filed an appeal for the state on similar grounds.

There was no likelihood that Johnson would stay his orders, and given the conduct of the case to date by the state there was no real reason to expect the Fifth Circuit Court of Appeals to issue a stay either. Nevertheless, Johnson adopted a kind of self-imposed limited stay until the Fifth Circuit affirmed his orders in November 1974. While he did respond to requests by the parties and the HRCs for enforcement action, they were limited responses.

THE POST DECREE PHASE

The complexity of the agreements negotiated by the parties and the volatility of the political environment within which they would be implemented virtually guaranteed an ongoing interaction between the judge and state officials. These post decree developments may be divided into the HRC guided reforms, the move to receivership, and the renewed challenge to the remedial orders.

Implementation

The HRCs appointed for each of the three major mental health and retardation facilities were not, in effect, panels of special masters. They were collections of representatives of the parties rather than panels of experts. They were part-time bodies with limited authority, no staff, and virtually no resources except for minimal expense funds and meeting space at the hospitals. The HRCs were vehicles for oversight and information development. They were forums for patients and employees to raise questions about state compliance with the orders. Enforcement, however, was dependent upon the court. Nevertheless, conflict developed between institutional superintendents and HRCs early in the implementation process.

The state's response to the Partlow emergency order, accomplished before the governor's challenge to Johnson's decision, was praised by the judge for its implementation of the letter and spirit of the order. The fire and safety problems were promptly corrected with $2 million in bond revenues authorized by the state legislature. Contracts were let for the repairs that could not be made immediately. Food service facilities were dramatically reformed with one kitchen, the dairy, and a bakery closed for failure to meet health standards. Food service training began with supervision and support from three dieticians hired under the order. Two full-time pharmacists were hired, and they completely restructured the administration of medications. Surveys for general medical health, reevaluation of prescriptions, and screening for immunizations were quickly accomplished. A total of 508 staff members were employed in virtually all personnel categories except that of psychiatrist. The survey to determine proper placement under the least-restrictive environment principle found 293 residents potentially transferable to other facilities, other states, or release to families. By early April, 11 had been released, with another 59 in processing. Professional and consumer advisory boards had been appointed and a new interim superintendent, John Hottel, had been named.[101]

However, tensions grew as official state policy was transformed under the governor's leadership from negotiated cooperation to challenge of the court orders. Institutional administrators came to resent the HRCs. The firing of Partlow Acting Superintendent Peter Blouke for his cooperation with plaintiffs and *amici* during the remedy hearings did not bode well. During June, after a month of insistence by state officials that Alabama could not afford the mandated reforms, news stories broke indicating that Partlow funds and personnel were being used to redecorate administrative offices and renovate the new Acting Superintendent's state-provided house on the Partlow grounds.[102] Partlow HRC Chair, Harriet Tillman, was upset at finding hygiene and toilet facilities still dirty and in disrepair. It "was hot as hell" in Partlow buildings, she reported.

State officials countered that the funds needed to support compliance with the orders would be forthcoming from federal sources. As much as $150 million was anticipated from Social Security programs alone. That money would not be available, however, since federal budget cuts entered after the 1972 election eliminated some of the programs and curtailed eligibility for others. The HEW budget cuts meant a loss of another $16 million. The advent of revenue sharing funds allowed the state a safety valve from the financial tensions, but it was a temporary respite.

Alabama politics were complicated by the attempt on George Wallace's life, which left matters in the hands of Acting Governor Jere Beasley during the governor's recovery. The internal politics of the Mental Health Board worsened with the Commissioner, institutional administrators, and the Board regularly clashing with each other. The situation would continue to deteriorate with Governor Fob James, who succeeded Wallace, eventually arguing that the tensions between the Board and the superintendents was a principal reason for the lack of greater progress in complying with the remedial decrees.[103]

The HRCs became targets of increased opposition as soon as they began making formal reports to Judge Johnson regarding specific areas of noncompliance. The first major conflict began when the Partlow Human Rights Committee (PHRC) charged the state was not complying with the prohibition of uncompensated patient labor. The state countered by calling for a limitation on the authority of the HRCs or, as an alternative, a relaxation of the order to permit more discretion in the use of patient labor as therapy. The attempt to dismantle the HRCs was abandoned after negotiations, but the call for more discretion was answered. Johnson granted the state's request for a modification to the patient labor standard and wrote a letter clarifying HRCs authority.

Another round of conflict between state officials and HRCs was waged for much of 1973 and 1974. In March 1973 Charles Aderholt, Stickney's replacement as Commissioner, called for major funding increases from the state legislature and warned of shortfalls in anticipated revenues from the federal government. Even so, state mental health administrators assured the public that there would be no patient dumping (the release of patients who either should not have been discharged or required transition assistance and supervision before being returned to the community).[104] Shortly there-after, though, the PHRC reported that some of Partlow's progress in reducing its resident population was, in fact, the result of dumping.[105] Incidents involving some of these former patients precipitated public reaction against the court orders and state mental health officials. The Bryce HRC charged that hospital administrators had gone from one extreme to the other in moving from a complete lockdown of virtually all patients to unlocking all doors, resulting in more incidents of antisocial behavior by patients who simply wandered into the community.[106]

While progress in the first year following the April 1972 orders was very promising overall, implementation slowed thereafter. The parties pressed for compliance and the HRCs, with assistance from the U.S. Attorney's office and the FBI, produced a number of critical reports. By the summer of 1974 hospital officials were terming HRCs *harassing units*. In August, Partlow Superintendent Richard Buckley issued a "Standard Procedure Direction" that required all contacts between patients or staff and the PHRC to be authorized by his office. When the HRC informed the court and called for action, the state officials again countered with a challenge to the HRCs' legitimacy. Johnson issued an injunction against Buckley's directive.

Remedy Refinement

Two other factors affected mental health policy in Alabama during the implementation of the *Wyatt* decrees. The first concerned reports from the HRCs of excessive use of patient sterilization. The *Wyatt* plaintiffs and *amici* sued, seeking to overturn the only Alabama statute authorizing sterilization, a vague law giving administrators almost unlimited discretion in selecting treatment for patients. A three judge district court consisting of Judges Rives, Johnson, and Varner, struck the statute, declaring that sterilization of the patients "cannot be left to the unfettered discretion of any two officials or individuals."[107] The three judge panel remanded the case to Johnson to develop specific minimum standards.[108] The other element of change affecting the state's facilities involved the state's basic commitment law. It had become clear in the course of the debate over mental health in Alabama and in the *Wyatt* litigation that part of the reason for the state's difficulties was that its law governing commitment was so loose that it allowed institutionalization of many who should not have been patients in state hospitals.[109] The statute was struck down in an opinion authored by Judge Johnson for the same three judge panel.[110] The decision required that patients previously committed under the statute be provided with the essential elements of due process mandated by the order. Resources directed to implementation of the hearing requirements were, of course, not available for fulfillment of the *Wyatt* decree.

Johnson had avoided several potential confrontations with the state prior to the affirmance of his opinion, which came from the Fifth Circuit Court of Appeals in November 1974.[111] That appellate support, the growing conflict within state mental health circles and between the HRCs and hospital administrators along with the lack of continuing progress toward compliance with the 1972 orders brought the court into more direct involvement in implementation.

Specifically, Johnson had refused to rule on the requests of the HRCs for expanded staff and support pending the appeals.[112] The members of the HRCs had argued that they needed independence because of the recalcitrance shown by hospital administrators. With the added impetus of a report from an evaluation team that had visited Partlow and found serious noncompliance with the habilitation requirements, Johnson issued an order in February 1975 authorizing each HRC a full-time secretary, economic support, and a staff person who was to have complete institutional access.[113] An order followed commanding compliance with the Partlow habilitation standards. He wrote, "Positive action by defendants to effectuate these standards is now required; no longer will promises and plans suffice as an appropriate response to the mandatory injunction heretofore entered in this case."[114]

Johnson was trying to make the point, with a minimum of confrontation, that the state had to move forward on implementation. For instance, he granted the state's request to relax the standards to permit use of therapies classified as hazardous, including electroshock and aversion therapy, providing guidelines to ensure informed consent with supervision given to an Extraordinary Treatment Committee.[115] The judge delayed ruling on reports of noncompliance at Bryce because a new Chief of the Medical Staff had been recently appointed and should, in Johnson's view, have time to make changes.[116]

For a time the implementation did proceed, if at a slower pace than in the first year. Patient populations at Bryce and Searcy were dramatically reduced. The state sought and obtained a number of the grants recommended by Linda Glenn during the remedy proceedings. With completion of community mental retardation centers, more options became available to state administrators. Even though progress was slow at filling many of the mental health professional positions, general support staff numbers grew significantly. Facilities improvements were slow, but did occur.

The Move to Receivership

Two forces seemed to be inexorably moving the implementation process toward a major transition from a highly decentralized and heavily discretionary approach to a more centralized process with increased demands for accountability. The first was that while a great deal of progress had been made in some facilities and in improvements of health and sanitation, many patients were still not receiving habilitation or treatment. The politics of mental health in Alabama appeared either unwilling or unable to respond to that problem. Second, state officials were adamantly opposed to the HRCs, and it appeared those committees would not be able to accomplish anything without more direct court involvement.

The plaintiffs moved to reopen the case by launching a full evidentiary discovery process in late 1975, leading to a major challenge to state implementation efforts. This process culminated in eight days of hearings in November 1978. The plaintiffs wanted the court to order implementation under a receivership and to compel the state to appropriate funds in one way or another to support implementation.

The state called upon Johnson to dissolve the April 1972 orders. In the interim, state officials asked the judge to order the HRCs and particularly the Partlow HRC to "exercise fiscal and administrative accountability." Johnson issued a ruling in August 1978 refusing to dissolve the April 1972 orders but requiring the HRCs to practice "sound administrative and management policy."[117] Nevertheless, the state would continue to press for termination of the decrees. In April 1979, Johnson reformulated the

Partlow HRC, retaining the basic structure but changing personnel in the hope that a working accommodation could be achieved.

Finally, in October 1979, Johnson found that "seven years of failure to comply by the defendant Board mandates the appointment of a receiver."[118] The receiver was to take charge of Alabama's Mental Health system and ensure implementation of 1972 orders. *However, the person he appointed as receiver was none other than Alabama Governor Fob James.*

> As to the mental health features of the case, all defendants concede that there are many reasons for the lack of progress at Bryce Hospital, the most notable being the consistent change of superintendents during the past seven years. Defendants advise the Court that these several superintendents were given little authority and support by the central office of the Department of Mental Health in their efforts to implement the requirement of this Court's orders. These written acknowledgements concede there has been little stability in superintendents, treatment programs, employees, and patient treatment since the entry of this Court's orders in 1971 and 1972. In fact, the Court is advised by defendants that this failure to a large extent is attributable to the central office in Montgomery.
>
> In fairness and for the record, it appears that neither defendant Fob James nor defendant Commissioner Ireland is responsible for the present condition of the state's mental institutions. Defendant James did not take office until January, 1979 and defendant Ireland did not assume the position of Commissioner until September, 1979.[119]

With that, Johnson gave James until January 3, 1980, to file an implementation plan.

James filed his report on January 2. It explained a variety of implementation proposals, including fiscal considerations. The governor reported that the Mental Health Board lands were now being managed in accordance with a report produced by a Chicago-based consulting firm in order to produce their maximum financial return. An order to sell the land would be a long term loss. While cautioning that he did not know how the legislature would respond, James gave assurances regarding the levels of funding he intended to request. Johnson formally appointed James receiver by order of January 15, 1980. The HRCs were dissolved, but Lecil Gray, the former Chairman of the Bryce Human Rights Committee, was appointed as a court monitor to provide information on implementation.

Plaintiffs soon charged, however, that James had not taken the steps promised by the implementation plan and, in particular, had not moved to obtain the funds he had indicated would be requested from the legislature. Their charges were supported by a report from the court ordered monitor which found: "In the opinion of the Monitor progress toward compliance ground to a halt September 30, 1980, and will reach a crisis condition by March 1, 1981, unless additional funds are forthcoming immediately for the balance for the last 6 months of 1981."[120] In May 1981 plaintiffs launched a suit that asked for the court to mandate funding.

The Effort to Terminate the Orders

Governor James moved in two directions to terminate the April 1972 orders. He would be replaced by George Wallace in 1983, and the latter would launch the next challenge to the *Wyatt* decrees.

James formally filed in August 1981 for the termination of the receivership on grounds that the state was in compliance. While these proceedings were pending, he took advantage of the changes in litigation policy at DOJ under the Reagan administration. He put together a proposed settlement based upon a promise to comply with Title XIX and Joint Committee on Accreditation of Hospital (JCAH) standards without regard to past problems, and had it shuttled to Washington by his legal advisor. Upon securing the signature of Civil Rights Division Chief William Bradford Reynolds, the governor went public with his now presumably approved settlement.[121] Of course, the plaintiffs and other *amici* had been no part of this settlement. Jack Drake commented, "It really is kind of stupid—the whole thing is. I don't know what it means, which is to say it doesn't mean anything."[122] Actually, it did mean something. It meant that DOJ would switch sides and support the state in the proceedings then pending before the district court.

The plaintiffs sought to retain the receivership but replace James in the position. In February 1983 Judge Myron Thompson refused to terminate the receivership, rejected George Wallace's nominee for the job, and appointed David A. Harvey, the plaintiffs' choice to the position.[123] The hearings leading to this decision had contributed 27,000 pages to the record. Thompson found that "the defendants have not substantially complied with this court's 1972 standards, have not complied with the defendants James and Ireland's 1980 proposed plan of compliance, and have not even fully complied with the alternate JCAH and Title XIX standards now proposed by the defendants and the United States."[124]

Attorneys for the state had pursued the attempt to settle, promising to achieve JCAH accreditation and comply with Title XIX standards as opposed to simply insisting that the state was in compliance and that the order should therefore be terminated. They contemplated using the Supreme Court's opinion in *Romeo v. Youngberg* as a basis for an attack on the order.[125] While the Court had recognized a right to minimum acceptable institutional conditions and some form of treatment, it had cautioned lower courts to defer to the informed discretion of state mental health administrators. The defense lawyers concluded that although they might win with such an approach, it would be to the advantage of the mental health system to pursue the alternative. "We chose to go with the Title XIX and JCAH option because you've got third party funds coming in. You've got certain standards that we can argue to the legislature we have to meet. There's a certain prestige involved in gaining certification and accreditation."[126]

Judge Thompson was, however, quite right in observing that the state had a long way to go before it would have all of its programs accredited and qualified for federal funding. While all of its facilities have qualified for federal dollars, it has a number of programs that are not, at this writing, accredited under JCAH guidelines. Indeed, as a current Associate Commissioner observes, "Title XIX bailed us out two or three years in a row." Part of the problem arose because state mental health officials had difficulty convincing the governor's finance director that they really needed $65 million for capital construction projects.

Governor Wallace appealed Thompson's continuation of the receivership and the appointment of Harvey. His request for a stay pending appeal was rejected, but the Eleventh Circuit Court of appeals granted it. The appellate court did not preclude continuation of the temporary receivership under the direction of a "state official or other person agreed upon by the state." With the understanding that he was to continue with implementation, Thompson accepted the nomination of Wallace's legal advisor, Ken Wallis, as temporary receiver.[127] The Eleventh Circuit has not issued a final ruling on this appeal. According to the appellate panel, while Judge Thompson made a preliminary ruling that the receivership should be continued on a temporary basis, he did not issue final judgments on all of the issues pending before him. Since then, the Eleventh Circuit has periodically inquired about the status of the case.

Meanwhile, the state and plaintiffs have been engaged in settlement negotiations. The parties are not far apart and a resolution appears likely in the next few months. A snag has developed that threatens the negotiations. Using a combination of state revenue sharing, categorical grants, entitlement programs, community services funds, dedicated state revenues, and standard appropriations from the state's general fund, mental health expenditures increased dramatically over the decade of the seventies from $26 million in 1970–71 to current expenditures of $214 million. An essential demand made by plaintiffs in the settlement negotiations is a commitment to continued progress in mental health program development. The budget proposed by Governor Wallace for next year calls for a reduction of some $18 million below current expenditures.

Judge Thompson's options at this point would seem to favor encouragement of negotiation and avoidance of formal findings in the pending motions. The record in the case is huge. Given the nature of the case and the sunk costs of all parties, any decision would surely be appealed. Resources that might otherwise be used for improvements in Alabama could be redirected to appeals. Cooperative efforts directed at resolution of remaining practical issues could be jeopardized by efforts to preserve legal options on appeal. If budgetary issues force a breakdown in settlement talks, Thompson would be forced to move. Still, the parties are reasonably optimistic that a settlement will be reached soon.

CONCLUSION

This study indicates that the Alabama mental health litigation was no sudden surprise. The judicial findings and orders were neither startling nor totally unanticipated. The political and economic context within which the remedial orders were developed and implemented remained exceedingly problematic and difficult throughout the course of the litigation. The administrative politics of Alabama mental health was no minor factor in shaping that political context.

Contrary to the general picture painted of the crafting of the *Wyatt* remedy, Johnson did not arbitrarily decide substantive details about the operation of the state's mental facilities. Virtually all key provisions of the remedy were not only proposed, but also agreed to, by all parties. Moreover, the conditions were so bad and the state government of so little help that the judge was afforded few choices at the remedial stage.

Similarly, while it is true that the judge ultimately placed the state mental health system into receivership, that dramatic step was only taken after seven years without implementation of the core requirement of the remedy. The receiver was none other than the governor. Johnson specifically refused to order a special master to take charge. Neither did he, as it is often alleged, order sales of state lands or specific appropriations measures.

Wyatt has become a guiding example for a variety of later reform challenges in a number of states. It brought together many of the recurring issues in mental health and retardation policy. The difficulties associated with crafting and implementing a remedy are in many ways typical of similar state reform battles. The total institutional reform cases are some of the most trying disputes federal district judges are called upon to resolve.

In some ways, though, the mental health cases are easier to deal with legally and politically than the other major type of institutional reform dispute, prison conditions litigation. The next two chapters address the peculiar types of issues presented in the prison reform cases and provide a study of one of the few such cases to reach the U.S. Supreme Court, *Rhodes v. Chapman*.

NOTES

1. *Wyatt v. Stickney*, 325 F. Supp. 582 (MDAL 1971) (liability opinion); 334 F. Supp. 1341 (MDAL 1971) (remedy guideline); 344 F. Supp. 373 (MDAL 1972) (Bryce and Searcy remedy order); 344 F. Supp. 387 (MDAL 1972) (Partlow remedy order), *aff'd* 503 F.2d 1305 (5th Cir. 1974).

2. James S. Tarwater, *The Alabama State Hospitals and the Partlow State School and Hospital: A Brief History* (New York: Newcomen Society, 1964), pp. 9–10.

3. *Id.*, at 9.

4. *Id.*

5. *Id.*, at 10.

6. *Id.*, at 17.

7. *Id.*, at 16.

8. *Id.*, at 14.

9. Stonewall B. Stickney, "Problems in Implementing the Right to Treatment in Alabama: The Wyatt v. Stickney Case," 25 *Hospital and Community Psychiatry* 453 (1974).

10. Tarwater, *supra* note 2, at 12.

11. *Id.*, at 24.

12. *Id.*, at 26.

13. *Id.*, at 25.

14. *Id.*, at 27.

15. *Report of the Legislative Interim Committee on Mental Health and Retardation* 66 (1963), quoted in Comment: "Constitutional Law—Due Process—A State Mental Institution Is Constitutionally Required to Provide Adequate Mental Treatment for Patients Involuntarily Committed," 23 *Ala. L. Rev.* 642 n. 2 (1971).

16. 22 Alabama Code, Section 303.

17. Tarwater, *supra* note 2, at 28.

18. Coleman B. Ransone, Jr., *Alabama Finances: Revenues and Expenditures 1957–1967* (University, AL: Univ. of Alabama, 1969), p. 1.

19. *Id.*, at 21.

20. *Marable v. Ala. Mental Health B.*, 297 F. Supp. 291, 295–96 (MDAL 1969).

21. Tinsley E. Yarbrough, *Judge Frank M. Johnson and Human Rights in Alabama*, (University: Univ. of Alabama Press, 1981).

22. *Marable, supra* note 20, at 296.

23. *Id.*

24. This action was based upon Title VI and primarily concerned with direct aid to the mental health department, but proceedings were also launched during 1967 under the Federal Property and Administrative Services Act and the Elementary and Secondary Education Act of 1965.

25. *Marable supra* note 20, at 293.

26. "It is also clear from this submission that the medical services and facilities for care and rehabilitation of Negro patients are not only separate from but are typically inferior to those available to white patients. In contrast to the main complex at Bryce the physical facilities at Searcy are very old and crowded, have no day rooms, and have bare cement floors and seating consisting of backless wooden benches. Bryce has many recreational and occupational programs and craft shops; Searcy has a television set, dominoes and cards, if requested, and a weekly visit from the recreational department.

Negroes are also faced with inferior facilities within Bryce. While the segregated facility at Bryce Treatment Center Number Two is adequate physically, its location eight miles from the main complex denies to Negro patients several of the benefits available there. . . . Negroes are housed in the old, dimly lighted building solely to work in the laundry and certain kitchen areas at Bryce. The building is adjacent to the laundry, is set off from the rest of the complex, and has a living space comprised of one large room with approximately 87 beds in close quarters. The Lodge apparently is a converted stable and is located at the rear of the main complex. . . .

. . . Expenditures at Searcy have been proportionately lower per patient that at Bryce, and Searcy has never applied for any Public Health Service grants." *Id.*, at 294–95.

27. While *Marable* was pending, in January 1969, another suit was brought against the state involving state institutions. *Stockton v. Alabama Industrial School for Negro Children*, Ci. No. 2834–N (MDAL, filed Jan. 23, 1969) challenged conditions at the "Industrial School for Negro Children" located at Mt. Meigs, Alabama. A decree was issued in July 1971 following efforts by the state to improve the situation. *See Birmingham News*, Jan. 18, 1970, p. A–10, col. 1.

28. *Birmingham News*, Apr. 19, 1962, cited in Yarbrough, *supra* note 21, at 87.

29. The account of the events leading to the filing of the case are taken from interviews of Fowler and Dean presented in Yarbrough, *supra* note 21, at 154–58.

30. Yarbrough, *supra* note 21, at 156.

31. *Id.*, at 159.

32. *Ricky Wyatt v. Dr. Stonewall B. Stickney*, No. 3195–N, Trial Before Frank M. Johnson, January 4–5, 1971," pp. 18–19 [Hereafter "Wyatt Trial Transcript"]. *See also Wyatt v. Stickney*, *supra* note 1, at 781, 783.

33. "Wyatt Trial Transcript," at 26.

34. *Id.*, at 27.

35. *Id.*, at 39.

36. "Wyatt Trial Transcript," *supra* note 32, at 40.

37. *Id.*, at 53–54.

38. *Id.*, at 112.

39. *Wyatt v. Stickney*, *supra* note 1, at 784–85.

40. *Id.*, at 786.

41. *Tuscaloosa News*, Aug. 1, 1971, cited in Yarbrough, *supra* note 21, at 163.

42. *Id.*

43. Ransone, *supra* note 18, at 10.

44. Joseph C. Pilegge, Jr., *Taxing and Spending: Alabama's Budget in Transition* (University: Univ. of Alabama Press, 1978), p. 62.

45. *Id.*, at 63.

46. Ransone, *supra* note 18, at 29.

47. *Id.*, at 24.

48. *Id.*, at 19.

49. *Id.*, at 25.

50. *See generally* Jody Carlson, *George C. Wallace and the Politics of Powerlessness* (New Brunswick, NJ: Transaction, 1981); and Harold W. Stanely, *State vs. Governor, Ala. 1971* (University: Univ. of Alabama Press, 1980).

51. *See, e.g.*, Yarbrough, *supra* note 21, at 120.

52. Don F. Wasson, "Governor Vows Mental Health Funding," *Montgomery Advertiser*, Oct. 16, 1971.

53. Francis E. Rourke, *Bureaucracy, Politics, and Public Policy*, 3rd ed. (Boston: Little Brown, 1984), p. 99.

54. Stickney, *supra* note 9, at 453, 454–55 (1974).

55. *Wyatt v. Stickney*, Civ. No. 3195–N, Hearing Before the Honorable Frank M. Johnson, at Montgomery Alabama, Feb. 3–4, 1972 [hereafter Bryce/Searcy Hearing], at 172.

56. "Plaintiff's Objections to Defendants' Report of September 23, 1971 and Renewed Motions for Implementation of Remedies," Oct. 13, 1971.

57. *Wyatt v. Stickney*, 334 F. Supp. *supra* note 1, at 1341.

58. *Id.*, at 1343.

59. *Rouse v. Cameron*, 373 F.2d 451, 456–59 (DCC. 1966).

60. David L. Bazelon, "Foreward," 57 *Geo. L.J.* 676, 678 (1969).

61. *Wyatt v. Stickney*, 344 F. Supp., *supra* note 1, at 1343

62. *Id.*

63. *Id.*, at 1344.

64. *Id.*

65. Stickney, *supra* note 9, at 455.

66. "Affidavit of James Jerry Wood, Former Assistant Attorney General for Alabama, December 27, 1972," p. 3; reprinted in "Plaintiffs Motion for Specific Enforcement of Prior Orders on Motion to Show Cause Why Defendants Should Not Be Held in Contempt," July 5, 1972.

67. Stickney, *supra* note 9, at 456.

68. "Bryce/Searcy Hearing," *supra* note 55, at 54.

69. *Id.*, at 34.

70. *Id.*, at 176.

71. *Id.*, at 414.

72. *Id.*, at 380–81.

73. *Id.*, at 398–99.

74. *Id.*, at 364.

75. *Id.*, at 404.

76. *Wyatt v. Stickney*, Civ. No. 3195–N, "Hearing Before the Honorable Frank M. Johnson, at Montgomery, Alabama, February 28–29 and March 1, 1972" [hereafter Partlow Hearing], at 13.

77. *Id.*, at 15.

78. *Id.*, at 20.

79. *Id.*, at 277.

80. *Id.*, at 280.

81. *Id.*, at 284.

82. *Id.*, at 287.

83. *Id.*, at 291.

84. *Id.*, at 285.

85. *Id.*, at 80–82.

86. *Id.*, at 90–92.

87. *Id.*, at 101–2.

88. *Id.*, at 259.

89. *Id.*, at 128–29.

90. *Id.*, at 63.

91. *Id.*, at 64–65.

92. *Id.*, at 191.

93. *Id.*, at 418.

94. *Id.*

95. *Id.*, at 421.

96. *Id.*, at 420.

97. *Wyatt v. Stickney,* 344 F. Supp., *supra* note 1, at 373.

98. *Id.*, at 387.

99. *Id.*, at 377.

100. Stan Bailey, "Mental Order Means Tax Rise—Wallace," *Alabama Journal,* Apr. 24, 1972, p. 1.

101. "Defendants' Report on Implementation of the Court's Interim Emergency Order of March 2, 1972," Apr. 17, 1972.

102. Paul Davis, "Partlow Money Being Spent for Offices," *Tuscaloosa News,* June 18, 1972; and Wayne Greenhow, "Partlow Aid Not in Sight but Remodeling Goes On," *Alabama Journal,* June 21, 1972.

103. "Memorandum," *Wyatt v. Ireland,* Civ. No. 3195–N, Oct. 25, 1975, at 2.

104. See Claude Duncan, "Mental Health Budget Will Need Huge Boost," *Alabama Journal,* Mar. 21, 1973; and Jerry Tillotson, "Partlow Cuts, Applications in Conflict," *Montgomery Advertiser,* Mar. 23, 1973.

105. Note: "The Wyatt Case: Implementation of a Judicial Decree Ordering Institutional Change," 84 *Yale L.J.* 1338, 1355 (1975).

106. *Id.*, at 1359 n. 122.

107. *Wyatt v. Aderholt,* 368 F. Supp. 1382, 1383 (MDAL 1973).

108. *Id.*, at 1383.

109. Robert D. Segall, "Civil Commitment in Alabama," 26 *Ala. L. Rev.* 215 (1973).

110. *Lynch v. Baxley,* 386 F. Supp. 387 (MDAL 1974).

111. *Wyatt v. Aderholt,* 503 F.2d 1305 (5th Cir. 1974).

112. Note: "The Wyatt Case . . .," *supra* note 105, at 1358 n. 121.

113. *Wyatt v. Hardin,* Civ. No. 3195–N, Feb. 7, 1975.

114. *Wyatt v. Hardin,* Civ. No. 3195–N, Apr., 18, 1975.

115. *Wyatt v. Hardin,* Civ. No., 3195–N, Feb. 28, 1975.

116. *Wyatt v. Hardin,* Civ. No. 3195–N, June 29, 1975.

117. *Wyatt v. Hardin,* Civ. No. 3195–N, Aug. 30, 1978.

118. *Wyatt v. Ireland,* Civ. No. 3195–N, Oct. 25, 1979, at 14.

119. *Id.*, at 2.

120. Cited in "Motion to Require the Provision of Sufficient Funds for Compliance with the Wyatt Standards with with the Governor's Plan of Implementation," Mar. 9, 1981, at 2.

121. Duvall, "U.S. Agrees to Mental Health Pact," *Montgomery Advertiser,* Dec. 14, 1982, p. 1.

122. *Id.*

123. *Wyatt v. Ireland,* Civ. No. 3195–N, Feb. 1, 1983.

124. *Wyatt v. Ireland,* Civ. No. 3195–N, Mar. 8, 1983, at 11.

125. *Youngberg v. Romeo,* 457 U.S. 307 (1982).

126. Interview with R. Emmette Poundstone, Associate Commissioner, Department of Mental Health, Montgomery, Alabama, Apr. 24, 1986.

127. *Wyatt v. Ireland, supra* note 124.

8

Prisons: The Cruel and Unusual Punishment Controversy

The question of what a civilized democratic nation is to do with those who violate society's laws has plagued Americans for generations. On the one hand, the community seeks to protect itself from dangerous offenders, punish those who victimize others, and deter at least some of those who might contemplate crimes from giving in to their evil tendencies. Yet a society diminishes its own level of civility if it surrenders to its worst passions and subjects criminals to cruel and unusual punishments. We wish to be tough on crime but decent and humane in the process.

Our conflicting motivations are played out in a policy context in which prisoners, like mental patients, represent a generally invisible and politically unrepresented constituency housed largely in total institutions which must compete for scarce resources in increasingly difficult economic times. Beyond all that, social demands for harsher treatment of offenders have meant more prison sentences of longer duration for more criminals. These stresses have created a variety of situations in which prisoners have launched suits claiming violations of their Eighth and Fourteenth Amendment rights to protection from cruel and unusual punishments and due process of law. Like the mental health cases, the litigation in which federal judges have entered orders or authorized negotiated agreements that mandated reform of correctional institutions has been the focus of criticism and conflict.

In preparation for a consideration of the *Rhodes v. Chapman* prison case study to follow, it is useful to examine (1) the background of federal court involvement in corrections policy, (2) the law and policy issues that most frequently occupy federal courts called upon to consider prisons litigation, and (3) the political and fiscal tensions that affect the administrative and judicial responses to those issues.

THE EVOLVING CORRECTIONS POLICY DEBATE

Until the late seventeenth century, corrections policy was not particularly important since most criminal sentences involved the death penalty or some form of corporal punishment, ranging from flogging to the pillory. Jails served primarily as places to house vagrants, the poor, and defendants awaiting trial or the execution of sentences. In America, William Penn led reformers to a consideration of imprisonment as an alternative to capital and corporal punishment, creating the need to think more carefully about just how to build and operate prisons.[1]

Since that time, American corrections policy has changed in a variety of ways. In order to place contemporary issues in context, it is important to briefly consider the historical development of corrections policy, focus particularly on the mid-twentieth century reform movement, and examine the developing role of federal courts in corrections practices.

Historical Development of Corrections Policy

Penn's "Great Law" of 1682, designed to govern Pennsylvania, called for imprisonment for a variety of offenses.[2] Indeed Pennsylvania led several states in reducing the number of crimes punishable by capital or corporal sentences. In 1786 Pennsylvania adopted a reform criminal code that limited executions to two offenses. This provided an impetus for reform and development of jails and prisons that would be led by the Philadelphia Society for Alleviating the Miseries of Public Prisons.[3]

The Philadelphia efforts produced the Walnut Street Jail, still thought to be the first American penitentiary. Almost immediately, however, there emerged a disagreement as to just how to house and occupy the inmates. Should they be kept in solitary confinement at all times or would it be more constructive to house inmates in single cells at night and allow them to work and take meals together during the day? Was the object to be reform of the inmate or was the purpose of the prison primarily to make the inmate aware of his crimes and penitent? Before these questions could be answered, however, it was necessary to clarify the type of individuals who were to be housed in a prison. Misdemeanants and vagrants were separated from felons and juveniles were removed from both groups. This separation of offenders was the beginning of the system of classification under which attempts are made to grade the types of prisoners by offense and criminal background, allowing for the development of reformatories as well as minimum, medium, and maximum security prisons.

Thomas Eddy was a student of the Englishman John Howard's work and the efforts of the Philadelphia prison development project. He headed New York's first major correctional facility, the Newgate Prison, located in New York City. Eddy pressed for a system of single celling of inmates at night but congregate work in shops during the day.[4] That, he said, would reduce violence among inmates and lend itself to better order and general security within the prison. However, he was unable to implement that system in New York City. Newgate rapidly became overcrowded to the point where rioting forced construction of an additional prison. Eddy led the effort to build the new Auburn Penitentiary in upstate New York, though he was initially unsuccessful in his efforts to have the prison launched on a single-sleeping/congregate-labor pattern. There was an experiment with a prolonged solitary confinement at Auburn that failed miserably when a number of the prisoners became mentally ill and some attempted suicide.[5] Eventually, New York implemented Eddy's single cell/group labor concept.

Regardless of the basic model in use, prison discipline was stern. Auburn prisoners were required to cast their eyes downward, move and work in absolute silence, and march in lockstep from place to place. Food was often meager and of poor quality. Sanitation was generally bad. Light was extremely limited, as was fresh air. Prisons in northern climates often lacked effective heating systems, whereas southern prisons sweltered in unbearable heat. Visits were banned completely in some jurisdictions, as was communication by mail. Prisoners were often limited to one piece of reading material, the Bible.

Correctional officials determined that inmates should be occupied at useful labor. In the early period when the facilities were relatively small, handcrafts were adequate to occupy the prisoners. As the populations grew, there were increased demands to find more productive ways to employ the inmates. Coupled with that was political pressure to use inmate labor to make the correctional facilities profitable or at least self-sustaining, thus removing the financial burden from taxpayers.[6]

Three responses were attempted, with varying enthusiasm, in different states. One approach was to operate the prison as a factory, permitting a private concessionaire to operate the facility for the state. A second involved leasing inmates to entrepreneurs or operators of large farms. The latter was particularly popular in southern states after slavery was banned (except for penal servitude) by the Thirteenth Amendment.[7] Both of these approaches were terminated primarily because of reports of severe neglect and abuse of inmates.[8] The third alternative was to develop prison industries that would operate within standard government facilities and sell the manufactured goods in the marketplace. That model was attacked by business as unfair competition from government-sponsored products and by budding labor unions as an unfair labor practice that would depress wages and working conditions for free world employees. Laws were passed in several states banning completely or severely limiting the marketing of prison industry products.[9]

The Mid–Twentieth Century Reform Movement

Blake McKelvey's subtitle for his seminal history of American prisons, *A History of Good Intentions,* was most appropriate.[10] The development of corrections policy moved forward through the efforts of wave after wave of reformers, some with good ideas and others with little but good intentions. Today's American Correctional Association traces its origins back through its earlier incarnations to the Pennsylvania and New York reform groups of colonial America. The current name was given to the organization in 1954, actually a renaming of the group which had been called the American Prison Association. The substitution of "corrections" for "prison" was of major importance, for the field was entering into a significant period of reform that would occupy the post World War II decades. The central theme of the correctional movement was the need for treatment of offenders and not merely for custody.

The early reformatory movement had assumed that prisoners were bad people who could be reformed. The premise of the rehabilitation movement of the fifties and sixties, however, was that criminal offenders, in general, were suffering from social or psychological disorders that could be treated. The argument was in two parts. First, a person's environment is extremely important in influencing antisocial behavior. In a sense, the society was at least partly responsible for criminal activity because it fostered the poverty, racism, greed, and ignorance that breed crime. Related to this environmental theory was the demonstrable fact that many offenders were clearly afflicted with readily identifiable psychological disorders and educational deficiencies. Reabilitation advocates argued that what these people needed was treatment, not harsh punishment.

The second argument for rehabilitation was pragmatic. It simply is not possible to

keep more than a fraction of those convicted for criminal acts in prison for life. Therefore, the overwhelming majority of prisoners will sooner or later reenter society. The
first problem is to ensure, to the extent possible, that when they do rejoin the community, they pose no threat. The second is to help them to be productive members of
society, a condition that will reinforce the likelihood that they will not pose further
danger. Therefore, it was argued, we cannot avoid the need to provide rehabilitation. It
is not a matter of softhearted emotions or liberal philosophy, but a necessity.

The turbulent 1960s brought important changes in corrections administration. The
developing racial tensions, particularly during the latter part of the decade, were also
manifest inside prison walls where blacks, and in some parts of the country Hispanics
and Native Americans, were present in larger proportion than their minority represented
in the population as a whole. Anger and strident language as well as an insistence upon
respect by black inmates prompted anxiety among white inmates and corrections officials.

Then there was the violence flaring outside correctional institutions and within them,
"In the 1965 riot in the Watts section of Los Angeles alone, 34 persons were killed,
1,032 injured, and 3,952 arrested. Some 600 buildings were damaged . . . [and] $40
million in property was destroyed."[11] Inside the walls, prisoners reacted against conditions within the institutions and against the society that operated them. The violent
incidents continued into the seventies. In 1973 alone Menard and Stateville prisons in
Illinois, Indiana State Prison, Maryland Penitentiary, Massachusetts Correctional Facility at Walpole, the Rhode Island Correctional Institution, Vermont State Prison at Windsor, the Virginia Prison Farm, and West Virginia Penitentiary all experienced inmate
uprisings.[12] Some of these incidents were relatively limited and were quelled without
major losses. However, there were others that resulted in injuries and death, like the
Ohio Penitentiary riots of 1968,[13] the Oklahoma State Penitentiary riot at McAlester,[14]
and the tragedy of 1980 at the New Mexico State Prison in which thirty-three inmates
were killed and forty-five inmates and five guards were wounded.[15] Best known of these
sad incidents was the 1971 uprising at New York's Attica Correctional Facility in which
forty-three people were killed by inmates or by government assault forces in recapturing
the facility.[16]

There were, however, efforts to change the correctional system in the midst of the
social, racial, and political turmoil of the period. Of particular importance at the national
level were the efforts of the President's Commission on Criminal Justice and congressional attention to institutional conditions. President Johnson issued Executive Order
11236 in July 1965, which created the President's Commission on Law Enforcement
and Administration.[17] The Commission, chaired by Nicholas deB. Katzenbach, received
a broad charge, including investigation and recommendations on the causes and means
of controlling crime as well as assessment of the American criminal justice system.
Reporting in 1967, the Commission concluded:

> In sum, America's system of criminal justice is overcrowded and overworked, un-
> dermanned, underfinanced, and very often misunderstood. It needs more information
> and more knowledge. It needs more technical resources. It needs more coordination
> among its many parts. It needs more public support. It needs the help of community
> programs and institutions in dealing with offenders and potential offenders. It needs,
> above all, the willingness to reexamine old ways of doing things, to reform itself, to
> experiment, to run risks, to dare. It needs vision.[18]

Corrections was, according to the report, in particularly dire straits. The overwhelming percentage of the corrections dollar went not for rehabilitation but custody.[19] Prisoners were confined in large, aging facilities that were not conducive to any kind of treatment and were located in isolated rural settings that separated the inmate from family and community resources. These, the Commission said, should be replaced by small facilities "located close to population centers; maintaining close relations with schools, employers, and universities; housing as few as 50 inmates; serving as a classification center, as the center for various kinds of community programs and as a port of reentry to the community for those difficult and dangerous offenders who have required treatment in facilities with tighter custody."[20]

The Commission argued that the federal government should play a major role in the reform of the criminal justice system, providing expertise, training, and financial support. The president would support and the legislature adopt wide-ranging anti-crime legislation in the form of the Omnibus Crime Control and Safe Streets Act of 1968.[21] Part of the anti-crime package was a series of provisions for tougher law enforcement. Another feature was creation of the Law Enforcement Assistance Administration, intended to provide leadership in the fight against crime by dispensing grants to states and localities aimed at implementing recommendations advanced by the President's Commission.

In addition to passage of this crime control package, Congress considered a variety of conditions of confinement problems. The hearings into life in total institutions described in Chapter 6, which began with discussions of mental health facilities, also addressed minimally adequate conditions of confinement in prisons.[22] The congressional investigations took on additional poignancy as federal judges around the nation issued opinions that presented mind-numbing descriptions of conditions in prisons and jails. The congressional interest intensified reform pressures on states and localities. Despite all the activity, however, it was not politically rewarding for legislators to commit themselves too much to corrections reform when public opinion clearly favored more attention to police department operations. The public wanted offenders off the street and showed little interest in what was to be done with them afterwards. Inmates turned to the courts, particularly federal courts, to redress their grievances against the conditions of their confinement.

Federal Judges and Corrections

Prisoners, unlike mental patients, have historically been alert to legal options and have tried a variety of ways to have their cases heard in state appellate tribunals and federal courts. The tradition of the jailhouse lawyer is celebrated in books and motion pictures. Until relatively recently, however, most prisoner litigation sought writs of habeas corpus demanding the release of a particular inmate rather than presenting challenges to the general conditions of confinement, and even these were often difficult to prepare. In many states there were little or no law books available to prisoners; no assistance in preparing court papers; censorship of mail, including critical comments about prison administration; and even barriers to communication with lawyers for those few inmates who had attorneys to represent them. Like mental health patients, however, inmates began launching wider attacks on the legality of their confinement, specifically protesting prison conditions and what they argued were abusive practices by prison administrators.

Even after inmates acquired the knowledge and ability to make their claims of cruel and unusual punishment in federal courts, they still found substantial difficulties in obtaining favorable decisions. First, there was the so-called hands-off doctrine. The hands-off doctrine is a tradition of law that was widely employed in a variety of federal district courts and courts of appeals from the late 1940s to the mid-1960s that held that when inmates chose to attack the conditions of their confinement, rather than simply appeal their initial convictions, federal courts would generally refuse to take jurisdiction.[23] The Supreme Court had not mandated that doctrine and not all lower courts agreed with it. The Sixth Circuit Court of Appeals ruled as early as 1944: "A prisoner retains all the rights of an ordinary citizen except those expressly, or by necessary implication, taken from him by law. While the law does take his liberty and imposes a duty of servitude and observance of discipline for his regulation and that of other prisoners, it does not deny his right to personal security against unlawful invasion."[24] Still, other courts like the Tenth Circuit, regularly dismissed prisoners' suits, asserting, "Courts are without power to supervise prison administration or to interfere with the ordinary prison rules or regulations."[25]

The Supreme Court began reversing the hands-off doctrine cases with very brief, usually *per curiam,* opinions during the 1960s, simply stating that there is no reason for a federal court to refuse to hear a claim that prison officials have violated constitutional rights.[26] In its 1972 ruling in *Cruz v. Beto,* the Court concluded, "Federal courts sit not to supervise prisons but to enforce the constitutional rights of all 'persons,' including prisoners."[27] On the basis of that admonition, federal courts struck down racial segregation in prisons,[28] interference with religious beliefs,[29] and other unconstitutional practices.[30]

The fact that federal courts would hear prisoners' suits involving issues arising under the First, Eighth, and Fourteenth amendments did not necessarily imply that inmates would find it easy to win their cases and obtain the remedies they sought. For one thing, despite a great deal of highly charged political rhetoric by critics to the contrary, a careful reading of most of the major corrections opinions indicates that the judges involved recognized the need for deference to the administrative expertise of prison officials.[31] As Abram Chayes put it:

> In most cases, the courts have been very tough in insisting on proof. If you look at people like Judge Lasker in New York or Judge Johnson, they are not shading close cases. They're both very conservative people and they look around, and say, "What am I doing here?" But the answer they give themselves is that the violations are severe; that there is no way to avoid judicial actions.[32]

Moreover, the Burger Court, though it continued to maintain that federal courts must play a role in ensuring that constitutional protections were afforded to inmates, admonished lower courts to keep that need for deference clearly in mind. The Court's leading statement of its concern for respect of administrative authority came in a 1974 ruling:

> Traditionally, federal courts have adopted a broad hands off attitude toward problems of prison administration. In part this policy is the product of various limitations on

the scope of federal review of conditions in state penal institutions. More fundamentally, this attitude springs from complementary perceptions about the nature of the problems and the efficacy of judicial intervention. Prison administrators are responsible for maintaining internal order and discipline, for securing their institutions against unauthorized access or escape, and for rehabilitating, to the extent that human nature and inadequate resources allow, the inmates placed in their custody. The Hurculean obstacles to effective discharge of these duties are too apparent to warrant explication. Suffice it to say that the problems of prisons in America are complex and intractable, and, more to the point, they are not readily susceptible of resolution by decree. Most require expertise, comprehensive planning, and the commitment of resources, all of which are peculiarly within the province of the legislative and executive branches of government. For all of these reasons, courts are ill equipped to deal with the increasingly urgent problems of prison administration and reform. Judicial recognition of that fact reflects no more than a healthy sense of realism.

However, the Court quickly added:

But a policy of judicial restraint cannot encompass any failure to take cognizance of valid constitutional claims whether arising in a federal or state institution. When a prison regulation or practice offends a fundamental constitutional guarantee, federal courts will discharge their duty to protect constitutional rights.[33]

In particular, federal courts will not generally interfere with the determination by the state that a specific act will constitute a crime, that the crime will carry a prison term, or the length of that term.[34] In a 1980 case, for example, the Supreme Court upheld a Texas repeat offender statute under which a defendant was given a life sentence after three offenses, including fraudulent use of a credit card in the amount of $80.00 (1964), a check forgery in the amount of $28.36 (1969), and a failure to provide service promised on repair of an air conditioner (obtaining money under false pretenses) for the $120.75 fee he had received in advance (1973). Moreover, the Court has held that judges should not strike down measures taken principally to maintain order and discipline within the institution, such as searches of inmate cells.[35]

Having said all that, federal courts still found themselves facing a plethora of cases brought by inmates of state prisons and local jails that contested not merely specific corrections practices, but also the general conditions of their confinement. Most claims alleged a violation of the cruel and unusual punishment clause, a provision of the Constitution generally recognized as extremely important to a civilized democracy, yet incapable of precise definition. Nevertheless, the courts have sketched general guidelines.

The foundations of the rule against cruel and unusual punishments can be traced as far back as Magna Charta,[36] though the actual language of what would be the Eighth Amendment came from the English Bill of Rights of 1689. It provided that, "excessive Baile ought not to be required nor excessive Fines imposed nor cruell and unusuall Punishments inflicted."[37] It first came to America in the Virginia Declaration of Rights of 1776, from which the language of the Eighth Amendment was directly taken.[38] The early challenges in the U.S. Supreme Court under this provision were charges that death by shooting[39] and electrocution[40] were cruel and unusual. The Court rejected those assertions finding that cruel and unusual punishments were those involving "something inhuman and barbarous" and not "the mere extinguishing of life."[41]

The Supreme Court's ruling in *Weems v. United States* in 1910[42] established the basic principles still used to apply the cruel and unusual punishment clause. The case involved a disbursing officer who maintained a cash ledger for the Bureau of the Coast Guard and Transportation of the U.S. government then in control of the port of Manila in the Philippines. Weems was convicted of falsifying the records in the amount of 204 pesos on one occasion and 408 pesos on another. He was sentenced under a statute calling for a minimum of twelve years cadena temporal. The cadena temporal was a prison term to be served so that the prisoner "shall always carry a chain at the ankles, hanging from the wrists; they shall be employed at hard and painful labor" and receive no assistance from friends or family outside the institution.[43] There were also "certain accessory penalties imposed, which are defined to be (1) civil interdiction [deprivation of most property and family rights]; (2) perpetual absolute disqualifications [from most standard rights of citizenship]; [and] (3) subjection to surveillance during life."[44] The Court reversed the punishment as disproportionate to the offense and in violation of the cruel and unusual punishment clause.

The Court held that the Eighth Amendment is not limited to deliberate physical torture and applies as well to disproportionately severe prison sentences. In fact, the Court observed that early British precedents even struck down some fines as excessive. Moreover, the Court warned against rigid and narrow assessments of what constitutes cruel and unusual punishment. The clause "is not fastened to the obsolete, but may acquire meaning as public opinion becomes enlightened by a humane justice."[45]

In the years since, the Court has held "that the Amendment proscribes more than physically barbarous punishments. . . . The Amendment embodies 'broad and idealistic concepts of dignity, civilized standards, humanity, and decency . . .' against which we must evaluate penal measures. Thus, we have held repugnant to the Eighth Amendment punishments which are incompatible with the 'evolving standards of decency that mark the progress of a maturing society' . . . or which 'involve the unnecessary and wanton infliction of pain.'"[46] Moreover, the Amendment "bars not only those punishments that are 'barbaric' but also those that are 'excessive' in relation to the crime committed [and] . . . a punishment is 'excessive' and unconstitutional if it (1) makes no measurable contribution to acceptable goals of punishment and hence is nothing more than the purposeless and needless imposition of pain and suffering; or (2) is grossly out of proportion to the severity of the crime."[47]

When a judge is asked to assess the constitutionality of a punishment, including the treatment of a prisoner, it is against such standards that the case is to be decided. Many of the challenges to conditions of confinement have been brought not by prison inmates, but by detainees held in county or municipal jails, many of whom have not yet been convicted of any crime.[48] They are being held only to ensure appearance at trial and usually because they could not afford bail. In those situations one cannot appropriately speak of acceptable punishment, let alone punishments that are cruel and unusual. Therefore, some of the judges called upon to consider jail cases have used an additional benchmark, that "[p]re-trial detainees may not be punished and therefore must be held in conditions at least as good as if not better than those available to state prison inmates."[49]

The conditions of confinement cases came to the courts in two waves. The first, clustered around the late 1960s and into the early 1970s, dealt most often with very old institutions with the most extreme conditions one can imagine. The second round came late in the 1970s after correctional officers had been informed and prison systems warned by the first group of decisions. In some situations, this second round involved relatively new institutions with less extreme, but difficult conditions—conditions exacerbated in part by changing attitudes toward corrections that departed dramatically from the guiding principles of the 1960s.

The decisions in the Arkansas prison cases marked the first occasion on which a federal court had declared a state's entire prison system unconstitutional.[50] The conditions uncovered in the course of that suit would "shock the conscience" of many outside the litigation as well as Judge J. Smith Henley, the man called upon to decide it. Coupled with conditions revealed in parallel litigation in Alabama, the Arkansas ruling forced a recognition of the grotesque conditions found in some prisons and established constitutional boundaries which correctional institutions may not exceed. It was the leading edge of the first wave.

Challenges to Arkansas' corrections practices began in the mid-1960s when inmates charged that brutal physical punishments were administered for minor offenses. The federal court agreed, finding that there had been beatings with a "wooden handled leather strap five feet long and four inches wide" and the use of something called the "Tucker Telephone," a hand operated electrical generator used to administer shocks to "various sensitive parts of an inmates' body."[51] In 1969 Judge Henley ruled in favor of prisoners who challenged the conditions in punitive isolation at the state's maximum security facility, the Cummins Farm:[52]

> Confinement in punitive isolation was for an indefinite period of time. An average of 4, and sometimes as many as 10 or 11, prisoners were crowded into windowless $8' \times 10'$ cells containing no furniture other than a source of water and a toilet that could only be flushed from outside the cell. . . . At night the prisoners were given mattresses to spread on the floor. Although some prisoners suffered from infectious diseases such as hepatitis and venereal disease, mattresses were removed and jumbled together each morning then returned to the cells at random in the evening. . . . Prisoners in isolation received fewer than 1,000 calories a day; their meals consisted primarily of a 4-inch square of "grue," a substance created by mashing meat, potatoes, oleo, syrup, vegetables, eggs, and seasoning into a paste and baking the mixture in a pan.[53]

The state, he ruled, had a "duty to exercise ordinary care to protect [inmates'] lives and safety while in prison," a duty the state had failed to fulfill. The overcrowding, lack of guards, and inhumane conditions combined to create an intolerable situation.

The following year, Henley faced a challenge to both administrative practices and institutional conditions at the state's prisons. Summarizing the situation he found there, Henley wrote, "[A] sentence to the Arkansas Penitentiary today amounts to a banishment from civilized society to a dark and evil world completely alien to the free world, a world that is administered by criminals under unwritten rules and customs completely foreign to free world culture."[54] During the day, prisoners marched or were forced to run to the fields to work, often in extreme heat or near freezing temperatures without adequate clothing and, in some cases, without shoes. There were very few free world guards or employees. Instead the prison was run largely by "trusty" inmates who controlled virtually every aspect of inmate life. At night inmates slept in one-hundred-man open dormitories:

> At night there are one or more free world guards on duty outside the barracks proper, but they are not actually inside the sleeping area. Those areas are supposedly pa-

trolled by inmate "floorwalkers" whose duty it is to report disturbances to the guards. . . .

Since the inmates sleep together in the barracks an inmate has ready access to any other inmate sleeping in the same barracks. . . .

At times deadly feuds arise between particular inmates, and if one of them can catch his enemy asleep it is easy to crawl over and stab him. Inmates who commit such assaults are known as "crawlers" and "creepers", and other inmates live in fear of them. The Court finds that the "floorwalkers" are ineffective in preventing such assaults; they are either afraid to call the guards or, in instances, may be in league with the assailants. . . .

Sexual assaults, fights, and stabbings in the barracks put some inmates in such fear that it is not unusual for them to come to the front of the barracks and cling to the bars all night. That practice, which is of doubtful value is called "coming to the bars" or "grabbing the bars." Clearly, a man who has clung to the bars all night is in poor condition to work the next day.[55]

Examining existing case law, Henley held that the Eighth and Fourteenth amendments were violated "where the confinement is characterized by conditions and practices so bad as to be shocking to the conscience of reasonably civilized people."[56] He concluded that in order to determine whether the conditions are that bad, one must examine the totality of the conditions and not an individual problem by itself. For example, the medical care, sanitation, and food situations were all exacerbated by the fact that trusty prisoners operated them without careful supervision. The Supreme Court would latter affirm both principles in appeals of Henley's rulings. The state would have to reform its prisons.[57]

While Henley was facing the Arkansas case, Judge Frank Johnson was considering challenges to Alabama's prisons. Separate suits were launched by Alabama inmates attacking racial segregation,[58] overcrowding,[59] failure to provide medical care,[60] and, eventually, attacking the overall conditions of confinement, as in the Arkansas case.[61] Like Henley, Johnson found conditions and lack of medical treatment barbarous and shocking to the conscience. Alabama prisons lacked trained medical personnel, record-keeping systems, adequate medicine, and clinical equipment. In many cases, inmates without any meaningful training were providing what treatment was available. Care was often withheld, sometimes deliberately, from inmates known to require it, and delays in obtaining assistance for others resulted in pain and even death in a number of instances.[62] In the later *Pugh v. Locke* case that challenged conditions in the entire Alabama system, Johnson, like Henley before him, found the same kinds of problems of overcrowding, lack of security, inadequate food and sanitation, and the like. He eventually ordered major changes in the operation of the state's penal institutions.[63]

News of the conditions discovered in these cases spread through congressional hearings, news stories, and reactions from inmates and supporting interest groups around the country. The situation became all the more shocking when it was made clear that, although they protested that their facilities were not nearly so bad as those of Arkansas or Alabama, correctional officials could not and would not deny that conditions were generally very bad. Prisons litigation mushroomed. Appellate courts, including the Supreme Court, upheld most district findings with little fanfare, but things were about to change.

This wave of suits brought changes in conditions of confinement and particularly in the area of prison practices. However, the mood of the nation was moving away from the rehabilitative spirit of the 1960s and toward a more punitive disposition. Political support for prison reform declined, a fact exacerbated by the fiscal stress faced by all governments during the 1970s and 1980s. A second wave of cases moved through the courts, cases concerning new or refurbished correctional facilities that were, nevertheless, overtaxed. Confronting these suits, the Supreme Court began to signal lower courts that more deference was to be accorded prison administrators.

There was a backlash at the end of the 1960s. Some were frightened by anti-war and racial confrontations in the streets. Others saw the society changing much too rapidly. Crime increased and pundits argued there was a connection between that increase and judicial rulings protecting defendants' rights in criminal proceedings. Still others reacted against the correctional reform movement, arguing that it was undermining the basic purpose of prisons, to protect society, punish the offenders, and deter others. Richard Nixon used the crime-in-the-streets issue as a very effective theme in his 1968 presidential campaign and other candidates did the same. Legislation followed in the seventies that increased criminal sanctions at both the state and federal levels. Prison populations, which had been declining, began to rise dramatically.

At the same time economic pressures forced difficult choices for legislators concerning which programs were to receive funding in an environment of increasing fiscal stress. Given public attitudes, corrections administrators were not likely to do well in that competition, particularly when their budgets were assessed against the increasing demands on their institutions caused by the rising prison populations. By the late 1970s a number of federal programs that had previously supported corrections reform were declining. As funds shrank, administrators moved the dollars from rehabilitation programs to custody activities, often exacerbating the effects of overcrowding, since fewer programs meant more idle time in the cell blocks. Idle time and overcrowding had been two of the principal problems fought by corrections administrators from the days of the Walnut Street Jail and Newgate Prison down to the present.

The Supreme Court sent two types of signals to lower courts urging caution and increased deference to prison administrators. First, in several decisions discussed in earlier chapters, the Court generally admonished district courts to limit their use of remedial decrees and to be restrained in those cases in which equitable decrees were necessary. There was an added dimension to these warnings in cases concerning corrections reform. Nixon had declared that his appointments to the Court would go to people who were responsive to public demands to get tough on crime. There was little question that Chief Justice Burger and Justices Rehnquist, Powell, and Blackmun qualified. They were often joined on criminal justice questions by the Court's swing voters, Justices White and Stewart. President Reagan's choice of Sandra Day O'Connor to replace Stewart strengthened the conservative coalition.

The Court continued to warn states of the need to provide humane conditions and practices, but there were also directives to lower courts to avoid intervention in state corrections programs.[64] Thus, for example, while the Court held that there was a right to medical care for inmates, it added that a finding of cruel and unusual punishment for lack of medical care could only be made where the inmate proved deliberate indifference to his medical needs.[65] Though it ruled that the First Amendment prohibited a number of common prison practices, the Court warned, "In a prison context an inmate does not retain those First Amendment rights that are 'inconsistent with his status as a prisoner or with the legitimate penological objectives of the corrections system.' "[66]

While the Court upheld Judge Henley's decisions in the Arkansas litigation, it reversed lower court rulings finding unconstitutional conditions at a relatively new, but plainly overcrowded, federal jail in New York[67] and Ohio's maximum security prison (the subject of Chapter 9).[68] Justice Powell, writing for the Court in *Rhodes* insisted, "the Constitution does not mandate comfortable prisons."[69] "To the extent that such conditions are restrictive and even harsh, they are part of the penalty that criminal offenders pay for their offenses against society."[70] Powell concluded:

> In assessing claims that conditions of confinement are cruel and unusual, courts must bear in mind that their inquiries spring from constitutional requirements and that judicial answers to them must reflect that fact rather than a court's idea of how best to operate a detention facility. . . .
>
> Courts certainly have a responsibility to scrutinize claims of cruel and unusual confinement, and conditions in a number of prisons, especially older ones, have justly been described as "deplorable" and "sordid." . . . When conditions of confinement amount to cruel and unusual punishment, "federal courts will discharge their duty to protect constitutional rights." . . . In discharging their oversight responsibilities, however, courts cannot assume that state legislatures and prison officials are insensitive to the requirements of the Constitution or to the perplexing sociological problems of how best to achieve the goals of the penal function in the criminal justice system: to punish justly, to deter future crime, and to return imprisoned persons to society with an improved chance of being useful, law-abiding citizens.[71]

PRISON LAW AND POLICY ISSUES

Litigation launched by prisoners and detainees in the nation's jails has raised a variety of law and policy issues. Inmates may challenge facets of the conditions of their confinement, procedures used by prison officials, the operation of rehabilitation and release programs, or, particularly in the case of women inmates, the equality of their treatment relative to others. Judges face cases that raise individual grievances and suits that present large packages of issues. On some occasions, the broad attack across a range of conditions of confinement and prisons procedures issues is little more than a litigation tool, a sort of barrage tactic. Often, however, the prison cases present several issues that really are very much interconnected, as when severe overcrowding overtaxes available medical care.[72]

Basic Conditions of Confinement

Many of the challenges to conditions of confinement developed in older facilities that were overcrowded and operating on extremely limited finances. Not surprisingly, the issues that arose in those cases were Eighth Amendment claims concerning overcrowding, safety, sanitation and plumbing conditions, clothing and personal hygiene, nutrition and food services, climate and ventilation, insect and rodent infestation, medical care, psychiatric treatment, and opportunity for exercise and recreation.

The argument that a correctional facility is seriously overcrowded, which results in conditions that are degrading, unhealthful, and unsafe, is one of the more common charges in prison and jail suits. Since the benchmark for evaluating cruel and unusual punishments is society's "evolving standards of decency" and other similarly open textured language, the problem for the judge has generally been just how to determine whether a particular prison is unconstitutionally overcrowded. In the first wave of cases, that was not a particularly difficult task since the overcrowding was so extreme and because the other conditions existing in the institutions were so bad that there was little question for any reasonably impartial observer.[73] The second wave of cases, however, often involved new, relatively modern, or refurbished facilities. In these settings, the degree of crowding became more significant. Prison administrators point out that there may be a considerable difference between the ideal population of a prison and the point at which overcrowding is so severe as to merit the label cruel and unusual punishment. The three principal means of evaluating available space are the design capacity of the institution,[74] space standards generated by national corrections organizations or government bodies that are expressed in square feet of cell space per inmate (generally sixty to eighty square feet),[75] and studies by responsible independent evaluators.[76]

The rating information most often comes to the trial judges through introduction of expert testimony; submission of sets of recognized standards, with comparisons to the target institution; and judicial visits to the facilities, generally at the request of the plaintiffs.[77] Judges frequently employ both the design capacity and square-foot measures, often interpreting those figures in light of reports issued by state agencies or national corrections groups. The experts' standards and evaluations, though, are sometimes contested.

While the Supreme Court has, as recently as 1978, relied upon standards promulgated by professional organizations,[78] its most recent rulings have cautioned against according excessive constitutional significance to such measures. Justice Rehnquist warned in 1979, "[W]hile the recommendations of these various groups may be instructive in certain cases, they simply do not establish the constitutional minima; rather, they establish goals recommended by the organization in question."[79] He did not go on to explain what criteria trial judges ought to employ. The Court has, however, recognized that judgments about overcrowding must comprehend the nature and duration of the confinement as well as the effect of other conditions existing in the prison.[80] Housing a number of nonviolent offenders in relatively crowded conditions for short periods is not the equivalent of placing dangerous felons in overcrowded cells indefinitely with little out of cell time.

It is generally agreed that state and local governments have a duty to exercise reasonable care in protecting the safety of an inmate from physical harm at the hands of other inmates or because of institutional conditions.[81] Combining the concern for overcrowding and the duty to provide minimal safety, several lower courts have struck down the use of dormitory housing for maximum security prisoners, particularly where it was shown that the guard force was inadequate to police the facilities.[82] These decisions do not bar dormitories under all conditions, but it is extremely difficult to provide adequate security in that type of housing for the kind of inmates housed in maximum security prisons. In addition to claims of inadequate security, judges have also frequently encountered safety issues in the form of fire hazards.[83] Fire safety is a complex matter in a correctional facility given the conflicting need for secure lock down of inmates, on the one hand, and the requirement to provide rapid egress from burning cell blocks, on the other. Compliance with modern fire standards is all the more complicated in older facilities that were constructed without regard for fire safety.

Similarly, the effort to assure a stable and acceptable climate, adequate ventilation, and minimally adequate light in a secure environment has also been a major problem in older facilities. The courts that have been asked to decide conditions of confinement cases consider these as important factors in their assessment of the "totality of the circumstances." Environmental factors of this sort are particularly important when facilities are substantially overcrowded. Judge Kane described the situation in the Colorado maximum security facility:

> The heating and ventilation system are antiquated and incapable of providing minimally adequate heat and ventilation. Cellhouses 1 and 7 have open 5–6 story interiors with two four-tier islands of cells surrounded by glass windows around the entire building perimeter. This design [generally known as an Auburn-type cell block] precludes the elimination of drafts, the adequate control of temperatures, and the even circulation of air. State health inspections have consistently cited extreme temperature variations between the first and fourth tiers. Ventilation equipment is frequently not in use. During the summer months, odors, excessive heat, and humidity are unbearable on the upper tiers. The lack of adequate ventilation causes stagnant air with foul odors; the continued presence of contaminants in the air; a lack of adequate displacement of body heat; personal discomfort; health and sanitation problems and an increase in frustration, stress, and hostility among prisoners and staff.[84]

Cases attacking facilities that are old and in poor condition or severely overcrowded have often presented evidence of inadequate plumbing, poor sanitation, and limited hygiene opportunity for inmates. A lack of adequate water, toilet, and washing facilities presents the kind of "shock to the conscience" that leads to adverse rulings against prison administrators.[85] Moreover, judges have found that while these deficiencies do indeed present that kind of assault on basic human dignity, they also raise the likelihood of health threats brought on by inadequate sanitation. Where the buildings are extremely old, there may even be a threat to the structural integrity of the institution from leaking pipes. In some instances the inadequacies of the physical plant were accompanied by a refusal on the part of authorities to provide inmates with hygiene items like toothepaste[86] or clean clothing.[87] Courts facing the early conditions of confinement cases insisted on correction of these deficiencies.

Another factor frequently cited in conditions cases is nutrition and food services. Judges have generally refused to order that meals should be appetizing or that inmates are entitled to particular types and quantities of food, but they have considered whether there was food of adequate nutritional value prepared in sanitary conditions. These food service issues are often intermingled with questions of general sanitation and inmate hygiene since food is most often prepared by working prisoners. Like the personal hygiene questions, demands for adequate nutrition were answered swiftly during the first wave of conditions challenges.[88] Nevertheless, rising populations during the 1970s threatened to reinvigorate the nutrition and food preparation issue in those prisons with aging facilities and inadequate equipment or kitchens that are difficult to maintain.[89] Corrections administrators have also been called upon to deal with two added food service questions over the past decade. The first involves the need to provide medically mandated diets for ailing or aging inmates. The second demand arose when some inmates, particularly Black Muslims, asserted a religious bar to consumption of pork products, a prison staple since many facilities produce pork for internal use.

Those facilities with food service, sanitation, and hygiene deficiencies, not surprisingly, have occasionally presented serious insect and rodent infestations. Courts have considered the presence of those pests as indicators to be considered in examining other deficiencies. They have also regarded them important as potential health risks.

Prison conditions rulings uniformly insist upon the provision of basic medical care for inmates. The general principle that deprivation of basic care is cruel and unusual punishment was addressed in a series of rulings from the late 1960s on.[90] The Supreme Court issued the authoritative pronouncement on the principle in 1976 in *Estelle v. Gamble,* which held that failure to provide care to inmates who are necessarily completely dependent upon the institution for their medical needs is an infliction of unnecessary suffering that serves no penological objective and is "inconsistent with contemporary standards of decency."[91] What is not clear, as Justice Stevens observed in dissent, is precisely how lower courts are to implement the *Gamble* ruling, since the Court concluded that negligence or relative inadequacy of treatment is not sufficient to claim a constitutional violation. Rather, the inmate must "allege acts or omissions sufficiently harmful to evidence deliberate indifference to serious medical needs."[92] Stevens argued that this standard focuses upon "the subjective motivation of persons accused of violating the Eighth Amendment rather than [on] the standard of care required by the Constitution."[93]

The Court did say that it would not tolerate deliberate indifference to the medical needs of prisoners "whether the indifference is manifested by prison doctors in their response to the prisoner's needs or by prison guards in intentionally denying access to medical care or intentionally interfering with the treatment once prescribed."[94] Indeed there have been a number of studies and a variety of judicial opinions that involved cases in which doctors, nurses, or inmate medical assistants either refused to take inmates' requests for care seriously or failed to pay attention to their particular medical needs.[95] There have also been findings that medical personnel have not provided medical treatment or medicine that was prescribed for a prisoner.[96]

The most common situation, however, is not one in which there is indifference or hostility but where a facility simply lacks adequate clinical facilities, staff, trained support personnel, medical recordkeeping, and prescription services.[97] For jails and prisons lacking clinical space or equipment, the mode of treatment is often transportation to a prison medical facility or civilian hospitals near the institution. Transportation requires the availability of both vehicles and guards since such trips outside provide opportunities for escape. The inability to provide secure transportation because of personnel shortages among guards has sometimes meant lengthy delays in treatment.[98] Where correctional institutions are located in remote parts of large states, the transportation problems become particularly acute.

There are two other troublesome clinical difficulties that judges have confronted in the prisons conditions litigation. First, in some installations judges have found only token psychiatric services even though substantial numbers of inmates need intensive treatment.[99] Second, usually in jails cases but also in prisons suits, they find that though substantial numbers of inmates have severe alcohol or drug problems, the institutions often lack meaningful programs to deal first with withdrawal and later with treatment.[100]

There is one other factor often considered part of the cruel and unusual punishment calculus, the availability of exercise or recreational facilities. Prison overcrowding can tax both facilities and personnel resources. As large populations exhaust exercise facilities and equipment, those unable to exercise find themselves with more lock down time and less opportunity to vent their energies. In jails, particularly small jails, the problem is often a lack of exercise areas. Where they do exist, jail exercise facilities may be enclosed areas on the roof or in the basement. Like larger prisons, jails are also limited by personnel shortages from affording inmates adequate exercise opportunities. A number of judges have considered access to exercise as a factor in their total conditions of confinement analysis.[101] Judge E. Gordon West found "[c]onfinement for long periods of time without the opportunity for regular outdoor exercise does, as a matter of law, constitute cruel and unusual punishment."[102] West faced a challenge to conditions of confinement of prisoners on Louisiana's death row:

> They live in cells measuring approximately 6 feet by 9 feet. The building is so situated that practically no sunlight ever enters the cells. . . . During each 24 hour period the inmate is allowed out of this small cell for only 15 minutes. During that time he may go down a closed in corridor to a shower room where he must bathe, wash clothes, and supposedly exercise, all in a matter of 15 minutes. The inmates who testified in this case have been living under this condition for as long as 9 years.[103]

Challenging Corrections Procedures

In addition to challenges to the environment in which they are held, inmates frequently contest the formal and informal practices and rules enforced by corrections personnel. There are due process attacks on classification procedures, prison disciplinary practices, limitations on visits to inmates, and access to legal assistance. Equal protection charges are often lodged alleging racial discrimination. Also common are First Amendment claims concerning religious liberty and freedom of expression.

There are two important premises and one caveat underlying due process claims in prison cases. First, while a prisoner is deprived of his or her liberty to move about the community, there remains a wide range of confinement options that vary from extremely loose confinement in minimum security facilities with work release or home furlough programs to solitary confinement in maximum security prisons. Just because one has been sentenced to some sort of confinement, it is not the case that one may be made to suffer further loss of liberty as discipline without some form of due process protection, though the requisite procedures may be very informal by comparison with criminal trials. The Supreme Court has held: "[T]hough his rights may be diminished by the needs and exigencies of the institutional environment, a prisoner is not wholly stripped of constitutional protections when he is imprisoned for crime. There is no iron curtain drawn between the Constitution and the prisons of this country."[104] Second, the Supreme Court has rejected the notion that inmates possess only privileges as opposed to rights, with only rights but not privileges protected by the requirements of due process of law.[105] The question in these cases is whether corrections administrators are causing a serious injury to an inmate's life, liberty, or property. The caveat to be observed in due process cases is that the fact that inmates are entitled to minimum procedural protections and bars to arbitrary administrative action does not usually prevent corrections officials from using judgment in assigning prisoners to various facilities or punishing those who violate prison rules.

The process of classification of prisoners and detainees by type of offense and conduct has been contested. The manner in which one is classified often determines the nature of the correctional facility to which one is assigned. Higher classification means a greater loss of liberty and the increased physical risks that come from assignment to maximum security prisons with the most dangerous inmates in a penal system. However, corrections officials retain substantial interests in maintaining security, preventing escape, and rehabilitating other prisoners that justify broad discretion in the classification of offenders charged to their custody. Federal courts have not held that there is a right to a certain type of classification. The Supreme Court has rejected the assertion that inmates are entitled to due process before they can be transferred from a medium security to a maximum security institution,[106] though it has been determined that there are due process limitations on transfers of prisoners to mental hospitals.[107]

The most frequent due process questions are those concerning prison discipline. The types of prison discipline that have been used over time vary from loss of minor privileges, loss of good-time credit (credit against one's sentence earned for time served without rules violations), punitive confinement (either complete lock down with other prisoners or solitary confinement), or in an earlier day, physical punishment. Corporal punishment has been generally banned, though corrections officers retain the authority to use the force necessary to control inmates. As late as the early 1970s, some judges encountered cases in which there was direct corporal punishment administered to prisoners.[108] In others, indirect punishments like the use of mace and tear gas, chaining to the bars of one's cell, or restriction to bread and water for extended periods to physically weaken prisoners were struck down.[109]

The Supreme Court addressed the availability of due process in prison discipline in a 1974 ruling, *Wolff v. McDonnell*.[110] The Court rejected the assertion "that the procedure for disciplining prison inmates for serious misconduct is a matter of policy raising no constitutional issue."[111] Recognizing that "there must be a mutual accommodation between institutional needs and objectives and the provisions of the Constitution that are of general application," the Court observed, "[p]rison disciplinary proceedings are not part of a criminal prosecution, and the full panoply of rights due a defendant in such proceedings does not apply."[112] The Court concluded that inmates facing disciplinary action are entitled to written notice of the charges against them; to an opportunity to present evidence and make statements in their own behalf; to cross-examine witnesses, where doing so will not create a "risk of reprisal or undermine authority"; and to receive a written summary of the evidence and findings of the disciplinary board.

Apart from these core questions of prison discipline, federal courts have been asked to address three other problems. Where judges have been shown that prisoners were disciplined as a matter of retaliation, as in the case of one inmate who was sentenced to solitary confinement "in retaliation for his legal success," they have held in favor of the inmates.[113] The second set of issues concerned inmates sentenced to solitary confinement. While those sentenced to solitary or administrative confinement are entitled to procedural due process in the disciplinary action, there is no constitutional ban on the use of solitary so long as it meets minimally adequate conditions of confinement standards.[114] The third issue, and one that remains a continuing source of disagreement, is the use of rules that allow discipline for ambiguous offenses, such as "abusive language," "insolence," sarcasm," "disrespect," or being "out of order."[115] Since the first wave of litigation, most facilities have provided fairly elaborate books of institutional rules, though the conflict between the corrections officers' need for discretion and flexibility to maintain order and the inmates' demands that they not be punished for undefined and arbitrary offenses continues.

The remaining frequently raised due process complaint has to do with interference with inmates' access to federal courts. The Supreme Court has held for years that the state violates due process if it interferes with inmates' opportunities to file papers in pending litigation, including cases contesting the legality and conditions of their confinement.[116] Of course, inmates who are illiterate, cannot afford attorneys, have little knowledge of legal details, or lack access to a law library in which to do research may have a right they cannot really exercise. Jailhouse lawyers, known as writ writers, became important people in prisons because they could help others prepare their cases. Justice Fortas, writing for the Court in 1969, held that corrections administrators, at least in the absence of an adequate legal assistance program, cannot prevent writ writers from assisting other inmates.[117] Similarly, the Court has held that officials must provide adequate law libraries or assistance from persons trained in the law.[118]

The opportunity for visits from family and friends has been another difficult issue often presented as part of larger conditions and practices suits. Prisoners have a right to visitation as a protected liberty interest within the meaning of the Fourteenth Amendment and as a feature of freedom of association protected by the First Amendment. Some judges found that, at least where family members are concerned, inmates do have a constitutionally protected right to visitation.[119] The courts that have addressed the issue acknowledge corrections officials' need to regulate visitation rights to ensure security and order but note that such restrictions cannot be overly broad and must serve legitimate penological objectives. Judge Kane struck down a rule prohibiting visits by friends on that ground.[120]

Inmates have challenged a variety of prison practices on First Amendment grounds during the seventies, including claims to freedom of association, expression, and religion. The Supreme Court has upheld the claims to religious freedom within the limitations necessarily imposed by imprisonment.[121] On the other hand, the Court has ruled that "associational rights may be curtailed whenever the institution's officials, in the exercise of their informed discretion, reasonably conclude that such associations, whether through group meetings or otherwise, possess the likelihood of disruption to prison order or stability, or otherwise interfere with the legitimate penological objectives of the prison environment."[122]

The matter of freedom of expression, or perhaps more accurately communication, has been somewhat more complicated. These questions arose largely in cases concerning inmate demands to send and receive uncensored mail, press requests for interviews with prisoners, and inmate claims to a right to be able to receive books, periodicals, and newspapers. Until the first wave of prison suits, many systems had more or less complete censorship authority over incoming and outgoing mail, often limiting communications to a few people on an approved list and then only for those letters that could satisfy the censor. The purpose of the mail inspection was ostensibly to detect escape plans and catch contraband being shipped into the facility, but the practice was also employed to prevent inmates from dispatching complaints about the operation of institutions. The Supreme Court encountered the question in a case decided in 1974.[123] In prohibiting across the board inspection and censorship, the Court managed to avoid declaring that inmates had First Amendment rights to freedom of speech or press. Instead, the Court found that government could not arbitrarily interfere with the free flow of communications otherwise available to the members of society. In this case, censorship interfered with the right of the addressees to receive the inmates' correspondence, quite apart from the inmates' right to send it.[124] However, the Court left open some limited authority for officials to inspect for contraband and even to go further under carefully limited circumstances.[125] In general, though, inmates are free to correspond.

Reporters followed up on the correspondence cases and argued that they had a similar right to access to interview inmates in prisons. The Court rejected those claims in favor of assertions by prison administrators that inmates would use the notoriety of the interviews for advantage within the inmate subculture.[126] Correspondence is one thing, visits to jails with microphones and cameras might be something else. Many prisons do, however, have administrative rules which do allow on-camera and recorded interviews.

The receipt of magazines, newspapers, and books was also commonly censored on a variety of grounds, ranging from immorality for those items considered sexually explicit to radical political literature to anything administrators considered objectionable. Historically, prison libraries were often based upon donations gathered by church groups. In later times those same groups were called upon to help determine what was suitable reading material for the inmates. As lower courts began to strike down restrictions on reading material, many jurisdictions relaxed their rules.[127] The Supreme Court, in its only ruling on the matter, did uphold as a security safeguard a so-called "publisher only rule" that prohibited inmates from receiving hardcover books except for those sent directly from a publisher, book club, or bookstore.[128]

The Question of Rehabilitation and Release

Inmates have raised a variety of issues that fall generally into a category of matters of rehabilitation and release. These include questions about adequacy of prison rehabilitation, education, vocational training, psychiatric care and counseling, and parole and probation. Parole questions are of importance to prisons cases in part at least because inmates' behavior within an institution is often related to their expectations about chances for parole. From another perspective, corrections studies have have found anxiety, confusion, and frustration over the vagaries of parole decisions to be one of the inmates' leading complaints.[129]

The Supreme Court has generally concluded that while the due process clause provides procedural protection for probationers or parolees whose status is revoked,[130] it does not provide guarantees, procedural or substantive, for inmates seeking parole or commutation of their sentences.[131] It is one thing to be granted liberty and then have it removed, according to the Court, but quite another to have a possibility to obtain one's liberty and be denied.

When questions regarding rehabilitation are raised, they are most often considered as parts of the "totality of the circumstances" analysis done to determine whether there is cruel and unusual punishment. Judges have occasionally maintained that while there may not be a specific right to rehabilitation, the conditions and practices employed by state corrections officials should not prevent an inmate from rehabilitating himself.[132]

Special Problems of Women Behind Bars

The Supreme Court and other federal courts have taken a strong position insisting upon an end to racial discrimination in corrections under the equal protection clause of the

Fourteenth Amendment.[133] A less well known but very significant area of equal protection concern involves women in correctional institutions. It is in part precisely because women represent such a small percentage of inmates in a state system or county jail that they sometimes find themselves disadvantaged relative to male prisoners.[134] The total numbers of women are often low, so that the per capita cost of their incarceration appears to be disproportionately high.[135] States vary considerably in how they respond to the task of incarcerating women, ranging from contracting with other states for correctional services to incarceration in facilities adjoining men's institutions in order to take advantage of economies of scale, to the single independent state institution for women. Where the state women's prison is used, it tends to have a more diverse age group and distribution of offenses than men's institutions.[136] However women are housed, they do have special needs for health care, clothing, and other services.

In addition to complaints about a lack of special services, women inmates have charged that they have not received treatment equivalent to men. In Kentucky, for example, women alleged that their conditions of confinement, job opportunities, and vocational training and education programs were substantially inferior to the conditions in men's prisons. The federal district court agreed, ordering efforts to eliminate distinctions based solely on gender, such as vocational training only for what were considered traditionally female occupations, and not on some legitimate penological objective.[137]

THE POLITICAL AND FISCAL DILEMMAS OF PRISON REFORM

In sum, like the mental health cases, prisons are total institutions which present a variety of questions that touch on important constitutional issues and involve a wide range of state laws, regulations, and administrative practices. Like the mental health cases, the judge called upon to decide prison reform suits must operate in a complex and conflict ridden environment. Though there are similarities between the mental health and prisons cases, there are also contrasts. The politics of corrections are quite different from mental health, as are some of the fiscal pressures that must be recognized by courts and accommodated by administrators.

The Politics of Myth and Internal Instability

The question of providing fiscal resources to meet the challenges facing corrections administration in light of judicial rulings is, of course, a difficult political matter, but there are a number of other political issues apart from the budgetary questions that must be considered by those in the system. One of the most important political facts of life is the tendency of the public to respond to myth rather than knowledge about its corrections system.

The President's Commission observed that corrections "is the part of the criminal justice system that the public sees least and knows least about."[138] Perhaps as dangerous as the lack of knowledge is the belief in a number of myths about the system that simply do not comport with reality. Among the more common of these are the notion that few felons go to prison, prison sentences are getting shorter because judges are too liberal, one prisoner is more or less like any other, and it should not take much to maintain them in confinement. One of the most popular myths is the assumption that prisons are country clubs when they ought be harsh institutions and that they should be self-sufficient or profit making operations.[139] There were dramatic efforts following the first wave of prison cases to improve prison conditions and practices both through litigation and by the efforts of corrections professionals along with the elected officials they serve. However, prison populations have risen dramatically, as have the costs of confinement. As the public demands more prison sentences of longer duration, the difficulty of meeting the needs will grow. The lack of knowledge and myths are likely to continue to frustrate the efforts of prison officials to make the public understand the severity of the problems in their corrections systems.

At the same time that corrections administrators were attempting to deal with these public pressures, they faced growing human relations tensions within the system. Conflict in the system fostered increased hostility between inmates and corrections officers. At one level, staffing shortages made it difficult to meet custodial needs quite apart from efforts to provide security and support for rehabilitation programs. Reactions to low pay and a lack of public respect led to increased union organizing efforts during the 1970s, which increased stresses within the corrections system. The same pressures led to high turnover rates at both the executive level and among line corrections officers. For example, in Colorado during the mid-1970s, there were "six different Wardens at the Penitentiary, four Directors of the Division of Corrections, and four Executive Directors of the Department. As a result, policies and practices [were] constantly changed, leaving prisoners and staff in a constant state of flux."[140] Demands for affirmative action recruitment in corrections added another pressure to the complex human resource politics.

Several observers of the corrections process have noted that the 1970s witnessed the rise of increasing tensions between what they refer to as "the new inmate" and the "new corrections officer." The new inmate is more sophisticated in attacking the system, more disposed to issue those challenges, and increasingly aware of the complexities of organizational politics. The new corrections officer, it has been said, "sees himself as the victim of an unjust system—a system which is concerned more with protection of the rights of criminals, whom he may perceive as sub-human, than it is concerned with the rights of the God-fearing, upright citizens of his community. . . . He opposes prison reform as a threat to his physical security. He has organized his fellow officers in defense of his way of life."[141] The fact that large correctional facilities are generally located in rural settings and often overwhelmingly administered by Caucasions, whereas the inmate population has substantial percentages of minority inmates predominantly from urban areas adds to the conflict.[142] The rural locations often compound the difficulty of recruiting minority officers.[143]

One additional variable to be added to the mix is the conflict that arises in corrections between states and localities. In a number of states, counties house backlogs of sentenced prisoners awaiting transfer to state facilities while simultaneously holding detainees awaiting trial and misdemeanor offenders serving short sentences. When state prisons become overcrowded, sentenced felons back up at the county level, thus presenting counties with long term overcrowding coupled with increased security demands to deal with the tougher inmates. Intergovernmental complexity affects not only contests for tax dollars, but is manifest in discussions of sentencing policy and other substantive issues. County sheriffs frequently find themselves on opposite sides from state corrections officials in legislative and budgetary battles.

Meeting the Fiscal Challenge

The politics of corrections, as with mental health, are often budgetary politics. What is clear from the case law is that virtually all of the judges who have issued corrections remedial decrees recognized the hardships faced by administrators attempting to obtain adequate operating funds, let alone the further burdens posed by the need to acquire capital funds for new construction and modernization of existing facilities. On the other hand, they will not permit constitutional violations to stand on financial justifications.[144]

In addition to the obvious financial demands, corrections reform has presented two continuing controversies, First, corrections administration has had a continuing conflict between addressing costs of custody and the needs of rehabilitation programs. The internal politics of corrections have exacerbated the battles between the two sides as many administrators who have come up through the system from the ranks of guard have historically favored custody over rehabilitation. The second frustration, and one very much related to prison reform litigation, has to do with the financial demands of new construction required to replace outmoded facilities. This construction must be accomplished while simultaneously making improvements in the existing institutions needed to make them functional until the new buildings are completed. No administrator wishes to send good money into dying installations, but prisoners are legally entitled to minimally adequate conditions now, not at the end of the new construction work.

Like mental health administrators, correctional officials must assemble their budgets from a collection of state funds and federal grants. During the 1970s, at a time when financial demands were increasing because of increased prison populations and high rates of inflation, state governments fell upon financial hard times coupled with reductions in several important federal grant programs. Another similarity between mental health and corrections is the fiscal strain imposed upon the states and localities by adding bonded indebtedness to finance construction at a time of high interest rates.

One of the more common answers in corrections, as in mental health resource, discussions is to decentralize or, better, deinstitutionalize. While there is room for disagreement among corrections professionals, as there is with their mental health counterparts, over just how much decentralization saves and how much deinstitutionalization is possible, professional debate is not what drives budgetary politics at least at this time. The continued public demand is for more incarceration for longer periods. Legislators continue to heed that demand in the face of warnings by corrections administrators.

CONCLUSION

This chapter has sketched the interactions of courts and administrators in corrections policy, with particular attention to the questions of conditions of confinement and prison practices at the heart of the corrections reform movement. An examination of judicial decisions directing change in corrections operations indicates how interrelated the pieces of prison reform are. Much like the mental health cases, one of the greatest challenges to judges called upon to decide prison suits is to deal with the overlapping issues they present.

Achieving reform of institutions has been all the more complex because of a changing political atmosphere from one dominated by a spirit of reform and rehabilitation to a commitment to a more punitive corrections philosophy. The *Rhodes v. Chapman* case study to follow examines a situation confronting a state in the midst of reform efforts and facing the political and economic pressures of the 1970s.

NOTES

1. *See generally* Blake McKelvey, *American Prisons: A History of Good Intentions*, (Montclair, NJ: Patterson Smith 1977); and Ronald L. Goldfarb and Linda R. Singer, *After Conviction*, (New York: Simon and Schuster, 1973).

2. McKelvey, *supra* note 1, at 3.

3. *Id.*, at 7.

4. *Id.*, at 9.

5. *Id.*, at 14.

6. *Id.*, at 21.

7. *See, e.g.*, Georgia Advisory Committee to the U.S. Commission on Civil Rights, *Georgia Prisons* (Wash., DC: U.S. Commission on Civil Rights, 1976), at 6–7 [hereafter Georgia Advisory Committee Report]; and Louisiana Advisory Committee to the U.S. Commission on Civil Rights, *A Study of Adult Corrections in Louisiana*, (Wash., DC: U.S. Commission on Civil Rights, 1976), at 3 [hereafter Louisiana Advisory Committee Report].

8. *Georgia Advisory Committee Report, supra* note 7, at 7. *See also Holt v. Sarver*, 309 F. Supp. 362, 366 (EDAR 1970).

9. *See generally* McKelvey, *supra* note 1.

10. *Id.*

11. President's Commission on Law Enforcement and Administration of Justice, *The Challenge of Crime in a Free Society*, (Wash., DC: Government Printing Office, 1967), at 37 [hereafter President's Crime Commission Report].

12. These incidents are described in *New York Times* articles as follows: Menard State Prison, May 2, 1973, p. 50; Stateville Penitentiary, Sept. 7, 1973, p. 13; Indiana State Prison, Sept. 3, 1973, p. 25; Maryland Penitentiary, Mar. 30, 1973, p. 78; Massachusetts Correctional Facility at Walpole, May 20, 1973, p. 56; Rhode Island Correctional Institution, Apr. 3, 1973, p. 24, and June 3, 1973, p. 75; Vermont State Prison at Windsor, July 9, 1973, p. 28; Virginia Prison Farm, July 17, 1973, p. 12; and West Virginia Penitentiary, Mar. 21, 1973, p. 22.

13. The Ohio Pen riots are described in detail in Chapter 9.

14. See *New York Times* series on July 28, 1973, p. 1; July 29, p. 28; and Aug. 6, p. 14. Further descriptions of the McAlester situation are provided in *Battle v. Anderson*, 376 F. Supp. 402, 407–8 (EDOK 1974).

15. See *New York Times* series on Feb. 3, 1980, p. 1; Feb. 4, p. 1; Feb. 6, p. 12; Feb. 10, p. 51; and Mar. 22, p. 45.

16. *Inmates of Attica Correctional Facility v. Rockefeller*, 453 F.2d 12, 15 (2nd Cir. 1971). *See also* State of New York, *Attica: Official Report of the New York State Special Commission on Attica* (New York: Bantam, 1972) (also known as the McKay Commission Report).

17. The nature and responsibilities of the Commission are described in its final report. President's Crime Commission Report, *supra* note 11.

18. *Id.*, at 12.

19. *Id.*

20. *Id.*, at vii. *See also* President's Commission on Law Enforcement and Administration of Justice, *Task Force Report: Corrections*, (Wash., DC: Government Printing Office, 1967).

21. *See generally* Advisory Commission on Intergovernmental Relations, *Safe Streets Reconsidered: The Block Grant Experience, 1968–1975* (Wash., DC: ACIR, 1977), ch. 2.

22. *See, e.g.,* U.S. House of Representatives, Hearings Before the Subcommittee on Courts, Civil Liberties, and the Administration of Justice of the Committee on the Judiciary, *Civil Rights for Institutionalized Persons,* 95th Cong., 1st Sess. (1977); *id.,* Hearings Before the Subcommittee on Courts, Civil Liberties, and the Administrations of Justice of the Committee on the Judiciary, *Civil Rights of Institutionalized Persons,* 96th Cong., 1st Sess. (1979); and U.S. Senate, Hearings Before the Subcommittee on the Constitution of the Committee on the Judiciary, *Civil Rights of the Institutionalized,* 96th Cong., 1st Sess. (1979).

23. On the rise and decline of the hands-off doctrine *see,* Note: "Beyond the Ken of the Courts: A Critique of Judicial Refusal to Review the Complaints of Convicts," 72 *Yale L.J.* 506 (1963); Comment: "Constitutional Rights of Prisoners: The Developing Law," 110 *U. Pa. L. Rev.* 985 (1962); Kenneth C. Haas, "Judicial Politics and Correctional Reform: An Analysis of the Decline of the Hands-off Doctrine," 1977 *Det. C.L. Rev.* 795 (1977); and Goldfarb and Singer, *supra* note 1, ch. 7.

24. *Coffin v. Reichard,* 143 F.2d 443, 445 (6th Cir. 1944), *cert. denied,* 325 U.S. 887 (1945).

25. *Banning v. Looney,* 213 F.2d 771 (10th Cir. 1954), *cert. denied,* 348 U.S. 859 (1954). *See* other cases cited in *Ramos v. Lamm,* 485 F. Supp. 122, 130 (DCO 1979).

26. *Cooper v. Pate,* 378 U.S. 546 (1964). *See also Lee v. Washington,* 390 U.S. 333 (1968); *Younger v. Gilmore,* 404 U.S. 15 (1971); *Wilwording v. Swenson,* 404 U.S. 249 (1971); and *Haines v. Kerner,* 404 U.S. 519 (1972).

27. *Cruz v. Beto,* 405 U.S. 319, 321–22 (1972). *See also Johnson v. Avery,* 393 U.S. 483, 485 (1969).

28. *Lee v. Washington, supra* note 26.

29. *Cooper v. Pate, supra* note 26; and *Cruz v. Beto, supra* note 27.

30. *See, e.g., Johnson v. Avery, supra* note 27. *See also Younger v. Gilmore, supra* note 26.

31. *See, e.g., Bethea v. Crouse,* 417 F.2d 504, 505–6 (10th Cir. 1969); *Gates v. Collier,* 349 F. Supp. 881 893 (DMS 1972); *Gates v. Collier,* 501 F.2d 1291, 1321–22 (5th Cir. 1974); *Landman v. Royster,* 333 F. Supp. 621, 643 (EDVA 1971); *Taylor v. Sterret,* 344 F.Supp. 411, 413 (NDTX 1972); *Ramos v. Lamm, supra* note 25.

32. Testimony of Abram Chayes in *Civil Rights for Institutionalized Persons* (1977), *supra* note 22, at 167.

33. *Procunier v. Martinez,* 416 U.S. 396, 404–6 (1974).

34. *Rummel v. Estelle,* 63 L.Ed2d 382, 391 (1980). *See also Hutto v. Davis,* 70 L.Ed2d 556 (1982), upholding the sentences of two consecutive life terms plus two $10,000 fines for possession and sale of nine ounces of marijuana. *But see Solem v. Helm,* 77 L.Ed2d 637 (1983), and *Enmund v. Florida,* 458 U.S. 782 (1982), striking down penalties as disproportionate under the Eighth Amendment.

35. *Hudson v. Palmer,* 82 L.Ed2d 393 (1984). *See also Jones v. N.C. Prisoners' Labor Union,* 433 U.S. 119 (1977); and *Procunier v. Martinez, supra* note 33, at 404–5.

36. *Solem v. Helm, supra* note 34, at 645.

37. *Id.,* at 446.

38. *Id.,* n. 10. *See generally* Anthony Granucci, "Nor Cruel and Unusual Punishment Inflicted: The Original Meaning," 57 *Calif. L. Rev.* 839 (1969).

39. *Wilkerson v. Utah,* 99 U.S. 130 (1879).

40. *In re Kemmler,* 136 U.S. 436 (1890).

41. *Id.,* at 445–47.

42. *Weems v. United States,* 217 U.S. 349 (1910).

43. *Id.,* at 363–64.

44. *Id.*

45. *Id.,* at 378.

46. *Estelle v. Gamble,* 50 L.Ed2d 251 (1976).

47. *Coker v. Ga.*, 433 U.S. 584, 592 (1977).

48. *See, e.g., Hamilton v. Love*, 328 F. Supp. 1182 (EDAR 1971); *Taylor v. Sterrett, supra* note 31, at 411; and *Inmates of Suffolk County Jail v. Eisenstadt*, 360 F. Supp. 676 (DMA 1973). For a state Supreme Court ruling of the same type, *see Commonwealth v. Hendrick*, 280 A.2d 110 (PA 1971).

49. *Eisenstadt, supra* note 48, at 686; and *Hamilton v. Love, supra* note 48, at 1191. *See also Bell v. Wolfish*, 441 U.S. 520, 535–40 (1979).

50. The opinions in this lengthy case were *Holt v. Sarver*, 300 F. Supp. 825 (EDAR 1969); *Holt v. Sarver, supra* note 8, *aff'd and remanded* 442 F.2d 304 (8th Cir. 1971); *Holt v. Hutto*, 363 F. Supp. 194 (EDAR 1973), *rev'd in part and remanded sub nom. Finney v. Ark. Bd. of Correction*, 505 F.2d 194 (8th Cir. 1974); *Finney v. Hutto*, 410 F. Supp. 251 (EDAR 1976), *aff'd* 548 F.2d 740 (8th Cir. 1977), *aff'd sub. nom. Hutton v. Finney*, 437 U.S. 678 (1978).

51. *Hutto v. Finney*, 437 U.S. at 682 (1978), summarizing *Talley v. Stephens*, 247 F. Supp. 683 (EDAR 1965); and *Jackson v. Bishop*, 268 F. Supp. 804 (EDAR 1967).

52. *Holt v. Sarver*, 300 F.Supp. 825 (E.D.Ark 1969).

53. *Hutto v. Finney*, 437 U.S., at 682–83.

54. *Holt v. Sarver, supra* note 8, at 381.

55. *Id.*, at 376–77.

56. *Id.*, at 372–73.

57. For a discussion of the implementation of the Arkansas decrees, *see* M. Kay Harris and Dudley P. Spriller, Jr., *After Decision: Implementation of Judicial Decrees in Correctional Settings* (Wash., DC: National Institute of Law Enforcement and Criminal Justice, 1977).

58. *Washington v. Lee*, 263 F. Supp. 327 (MDAL 1966), *aff'd* 390 U.S. 333 (1968).

59. *McCray v. Sullivan*, 399 F. Supp. 271 (SDAL 1975).

60. *Newman v. Alabama*, 349 F. Supp. 278 (MDAL 1972).

61. Pugh v. Locke, 406 F. Supp. 318 (MDAL 1976).

62. *Newman v. Ala., supra* note 60, at 282–85.

63. For a discussion of the development of the Alabama litigation and problems of implementation of the decrees, see Tinsley Yarbrough, *Judge Frank M. Johnson and Human Rights in Alabama* (University: Univ. of Alabama Press, 1981), ch. 12.

64. *See, e.g., Pell v. Procunier*, 417 U.S. 817 (1974); *Saxbe v. Washington Post*, 417 U.S. 843 (1974); *Wolff v. McDonnell*, 418 U.S. 539 (1974); *Baxter v. Palmigiano*, 425 U.S. 308 (1976); *Meachum v. Fano*, 427 U.S. 215 (1976); *Estelle v. Gamble*, 429 U.S. 97 (1976); *Jones v. N.C. Prisoners' Union, supra* note 35; *Bell v. Wolfish, supra* note 49; *Greenholtz v. Inmates of the Neb. Penal and Correctional Complex*, 442 U.S. 1 (1979); *Rhodes v. Chapman*, 452 U.S. 337 (1981); and *Hudson v. Palmer, supra* note 35.

65. *Estelle v. Gamble, supra* note 64, at 105–6.

66. *Jones v. N.C. Prisoners' Labor Union, supra* note 35, at 129.

67. *Bell v. Wolfish, supra* note 49, at 520.

68. *Rhodes v. Chapman, supra* note 64.

69. *Id.*, at 349.

70. *Id.*, at 347.

71. *Id.*, at 351–52.

72. *See, e.g., Gates v. Collier, supra* note 31, at 1309 (1974).

73. *See, e.g., Hamilton v. Love, supra* note 48, at 1188; *Holt v. Sarver*, 410 F. Supp. 251, 254–55 (EDAR 1976); *Taylor v. Sterrett, supra* note 31, at 413; and *Pugh v. Locke, supra* note 61, at 322.

74. *See, e.g., Battle v. Anderson*, 447 F. Supp. 516, 520–21 (DOK 1977); *Pugh v. Locke, supra* note 61, at 332.

75. The most frequently cited are the "ABA Tentative Draft Statutes Relating to Standards Relating to the Legal Status of Prisoners . . . , American Correctional Association Manual of Standards for Adult Correctional Institutions . . . , National Sheriff's Association Manual on

Jail Administration . . . , National Sheriff's Association, Handbook on Jail Security, Classification and Discipline . . . , and the National Advisory Commission of Criminal Justice Standards and Goals, Report on Corrections.'' *McMurry v. Phelps,* 533 F. Supp. 742, 750 (WDLA 1982). *See McMurry, Id.,* and *Ramos v. Lammn, supra* note 25, at 154–55 (using an eighty-square-foot-per-man standard for prisoners in the cells more than ten hours per day, taken from the American Correctional Association; *Manual of Standards for Adult Correctional Institutions; Battle v. Anderson, supra* note 74, at 525 (using the American Public Health Associaiton standard of sixty square feet).

76. *See, e.g.,* Judge Garrity's discussion of the National Council on Crime and Delinquency study on the Suffolk County Prepared for the City of Boston, *supra* note 48, at 679; Judge Kane's discussion of studies done by the American Correctional Association (ACA) and the Colorado Attorney General on Canon Correctional Facility, *Ramos v. Lamm, supra* note 25, at 133, 137; and Judge Keady's consideration of the consulting committee study done for the Mississippi State Planning Agency, the Law Enforcement Assistance Administration, and the ACA on conditions at Parchman Penitentiary; *Gates v. Collier, supra* note 31, at 892.

77. Some judges, like Frank Johnson, think that one ought to avoid such judicial visits since they jeopardize one's ability to avoid emotional responses and keep the analysis focused on clear and specific rather than impressionistic evidence. Others consider it vital to see the institution themselves. Judge Garrity went so far in the cases challenging Boston's Charles Street Jail as to present himself and his law clerk unannounced for a night's stay. Inmates were not told of his presence. This experience produced some vivid impressions of conditions at the facility. He writes, ''When we spent the night there, the wall valve serving as a faucet for the sink in our cell jammed while the water was running and we narrowly averted a flood by bailing the overflowing sink into the toilet with a small paper cup while our law clerk freed the valve, after several unsuccessful attempts, by hammering on it with the heel of his shoe.'' *Eisenstadt, supra* note 48, at 680 n. 5. ''[T]he noise seemed to increase after midnight. . . . At least a dozen radios, turned to various rock music stations, seemed to be tuned up to full volume; and for hours from a nearby cell, whether above or below we couldn't tell, a deep-voiced inmate, evidently deranged, shouted an obscene, incoherent monologue, beginning, 'Ah want mah beer, you hear?'' *Id.,* at 680–81 n. 8.

78. *Hutto v. Finney,* 437 U.S. 678, 683 n. 7 (1978).

79. *Bell v. Wolfish, supra* note 49, at 543–44 n. 27.

80. *Hutto v. Finney,* 437 U.S., at 686–87.

81. *Holt v. Sarver, supra* note 50, at 827 (1969); *Palmigiano v. Garrahy,* 443 F. Supp. 956, 980 (DRI 1977); *Pugh v. Locke, supra* note 61, at 329–30; and *Ramos v. Lamm, supra* note 25, at 155.

82. *See Holt v. Sarver, supra* note 8; *Gates v. Collier, supra* note 31; *Pugh v. Locke, supra* note 61.

83. *See, e.g., Ramos v. Lamm, supra* note 25, at 135; and *Eisenstadt, supra* note 48, at 680. *See also Gates v. Collier, supra* note 31, at 887 (1972).

84. *Ramos v. Lamm, supra* note 25, at 135. *See also Hamilton v. Love, supra* note 48, at 1190; and *McMurry v. Phelps, supra* note 75, at 742.

85. *Hamilton v. Love, supra* note 48, at 1190–1.

86. *Pugh v. Locke, supra* note 61, at 323.

87. *Hamilton v. Love, supra* note 48, at 1190.

88. Judge Garrity graphically portrayed the food service inadequacies at the Charles Street Jail, *Eisenstadt, supra* note 48, at 682. *See also Pugh v. Locke, supra* note 61, at 323.

89. *See McMurry v. Phelps, supra* note 75, at 751; and *Ramos v. Lamm, supra* note 25, at 136.

90. *See, e.g., Newman v. Ala., supra* note 60; *Battle v. Anderson, supra* note 14, at 422; and cases cited in *Ramos v. Lamm, supra* note 25, at 158.

91. *Estelle v. Gamble, supra* note 46, at 259.

92. *Id.*, at 261.

93. *Id.*, at 263.

94. *Id.*, at 260.

95. *Id.*, nn. 9, 10.

96. *Id.*, n. 11. *See also Newman v. Ala.*, *supra* note 60, at 263.

97. *See generally Newman v. Ala.*, *supra* note 60; and *Battle v. Anderson*, *supra* note 14, at 422.

98. *Ramos v. Lamm*, *supra* note 25, at 143; and *Newman v. Ala.*, *supra* note 60, at 285.

99. *Newman v. Ala.*, *supra* note 98, at 285; *Ramos v. Lamm*, *supra* note 25, at 147, 159; *Eisenstadt*, *supra* note 48, at 682.

100. *Eisenstadt*, *supra* note 48, at 681.

101. *See Morris v. Travisono*, 310 F. Supp. 857, 858 (DRI 1970); *Pugh v. Locke*, *supra* note 61, at 327; and *Taylor v. Sterrett*, *supra* note 31, at 420.

102. *Sinclair v. Henderson*, 441 F. Supp. 1128, 1131 (EDLA 1971).

103. *Id.*, at 1129.

104. *Wolff v. McDonnell*, *supra* note 64, at 555–56.

105. *Morrissey v. Brewer*, 408 U.S. 471, 481 (1972).

106. *Meachum v. Fano*, *supra* note 64.

107. *Vitek v. Jones*, 445 U.S. 480 (1980).

108. *See, e.g., Gates v. Collier*, *supra* note 31, at 890 (1972).

109. *Landman v. Royster*, *supra* note 31, at 647–49; and *Battle v. Anderson*, *supra* note 14, at 411.

110. *Wolff v. McDonnell*, *supra* note 64.

111. *Id.*, at 555.

112. *Id.*, at 556.

113. *Sostre v. Rockefeller*, 312 F. Supp. 863, 869 (SDNY 1970). *See also Inmates of Attica v. Rockefeller*, *supra* note 16.

114. *Novak v. Beto*, 453 F.2d 661 (5th Cir. 1972). *See also Sostre v. Rockefeller*, *supra* note 113; and *Landman v. Royster*, *supra* note 31.

115. *Landman v. Royster*, *supra* note 31, at 632, 655. *See also* New York Advisory Committee to the U.S. Commission on Civil Rights, *Warehousing Human Beings* (Wash., DC: U.S. Commission on Civil Rights, 1974), p. 37 [hereafter *Warehousing Human Beings*].

116. *Ex parte Hull*, 312 U.S. 546 (1941).

117. *Johnson v. Avery*, *supra* note 27.

118. *Bounds v. Smith*, 430 U.S. 817, 828 (1977). *See also Younger v. Gilmore*, *supra* note 26.

119. *McMurry v. Phelps*, *supra* note 75, at 764–65; *Ramos v. Lamm*, *supra* note 25, at 161–62; and *Pugh v. Locke*, *supra* note 61, at 327.

120. *Ramos v. Lamm*, *supra* note 25, at 162.

121. *Cruz v. Beto*, *supra* note 27.

122. *Jones v. N.C. Prisoners' Union*, 53 L.Ed2d 629, 642–43 (1977).

123. *Procunier v. Martinez*, *supra* note 33.

124. *Id.*, at 408–9.

125. *Id.*, at 413.

126. *See Pell v. Procunier*, *supra* note 64; *Saxbe v. Procunier*, 417 U.S. 843 (1974); and *Houchins v. KQED*, 438 U.S. 1 (1978).

127. *See Sostre v. Rockefeller*, *supra* note 113, at 875–76; and *Taylor v. Sterrett*, *supra* note 31, at 423.

128. *Bell v. Wolfish*, *supra* note 49, at 550–52.

129. *See, e.g., Warehousing Human Beings*, *supra* note 115, at 74–78.

130. *Morrissey v. Brewer*, *supra* note 105, at 471; and *Gagnon v. Scarpelli*, 411 U.S. 778 (1973).

131. *Greenholtz v. Neb. Penal Inmates,* 442 U.S. 1 (1979); and *Conn. Bd. of Pardons v. Dumshat,* 452 U.S. 458 (1981).

132. *See Holt v. Sarver, supra* note 8, at 379. *See also Pugh v. Locke, supra* note 61, at 327; *Ramos v. Lamm, supra* note 25, at 157; *Palmigiano v. Garrahy, supra* note 81, at 989; and *Laaman v. Helgemoe,* 437 F. Supp. 269, 329–30 (DNH 1977).

133. *Lee v. Washington, supra* note 26.

134. Montana State Advisory Committee to the U.S. Commission on Civil Rights, *Corrections in Montana: A Consultation* (Wash., DC: U.S. Commission on Civil Rights, 1979), pp. 21–25.

135. Kansas State Advisory Committee to the U.S. Commission on Civil Rights, *Inmate Rights and the Kansas State Prison System,* (Wash., DC: U.S. Commission on Civil Rights, 1974), at 25.

136. *Warehousing Human Beings, supra* note 115, at 49–50.

137. *Canterino v. Wilson,* 533 F. Supp. 174 (WDKY 1982). *See also Bounds v. Smith, supra* note 118, at 821.

138. President's Crime Commission Report, *supra* note 11, at 159. *See also* Marris and Spriller, *supra* note 57, at 8.

139. *Warehousing Human Beings, supra* note 115, at 31–32. *See also Gates v. Collier, supra* note 31, at 1308.

140. *Ramos v. Lamm, supra* note 25, at 142.

141. *Warehousing Human Beings, supra* note 115, at 17–18.

142. See Pugh v. Locke, supra note 61, at 325; and *Sostre v. Rockefeller, supra* note 113, at 876–77; and *Ramos v. Lamm, supra* note 25, at 142.

143. *Georgia Prisons, supra* note 7, at 11; and *Warehousing Human Beings, supra* note 115, at 32.

144. *See, e.g., Battle v. Anderson, supra* note 24, at 526; *Gates v. Collier, supra* note 31, at 1319–20 (1974); *McMurry v. Phelps, supra* note 75, at 768–69; *Hamilton v. Love, supra* note 48, at 1194; and *Pugh v. Locke, supra* note 61, at 330–31.

9

Rhodes v. Chapman: Ohio Prisons Under Challenge

Like their counterparts in other states, Ohio prison officials approached the 1970s recognizing the need for reform of their corrections practices and with an awareness that the pressures for change were only likely to grow. At the same time, however, there was little public understanding of the increasing stress on the corrections system and virtually no support for expanding the resources available to prison administrators to meet the challenge. As in other states, prison problems meant litigation that challenged the operation of state correctional facilities. The *Rhodes v. Chapman* case was, however, a particularly important prison suit because it provided the occasion for the first direct U.S. Supreme Court pronouncement on the constitutional standards governing prison conditions.

Rhodes is an especially interesting case for examining the relationships of federal judges and state and local officials. In addition to its status as the lead decision by the Supreme Court on the subject, the Ohio prison litigation presents an institutional reform case that involves a recently constructed institution. It came after the wave of prison reform litigation of the late 1960s and early 1970s, much of which challenged nineteenth century facilities still in use. The story of Ohio's efforts to upgrade its correctional facilities is also a chronicle of the impact of the changing attitude of the public and its representatives toward how to deal with crime and criminal offenders. For during the 1970s the general trend was to disavow earlier commitments to rehabilitation and move frankly toward more punitive treatment of offenders. At the heart of this new approach was a drive to send more offenders to prison for longer periods of time for more offenses. Yet that same political shift to the right also brought resistance to growth in government budgets at the very time swelling inmate populations demanded more space and increased prison operating expenses. In this sense, the Ohio case is quite typical of the difficulties faced by most other states in the same period with greater demands for correctional services and shrinking resources.

TRIGGER PHASE

Rhodes v. Chapman was a suit brought in 1975 by inmates of the Southern Ohio Correctional Facility (SOCF) at Lucasville, Ohio.[1] The litigation attacked conditions at Ohio's maximum security penitentiary on a number of grounds, but principally on a claim that overcrowding had resulted in violations of the Eighth and Fourteenth amendment protections against cruel and unusual punishment and due process of law. Yet Lucasville was a new prison, opened in the fall of 1972, not a fast-fading old fortress from an earlier era. Understanding how this litigation came about requires a consideration of the reform pressures faced by Ohio in the early 1970s and the development of Lucasville as a state-of-the-art correctional facility in the midst of growing demands on state penal administrators.

The Stress of Reform

Ohio felt the pressures for criminal justice reform sweeping the nation in the mid-1960s. The state's 130-year-old maximum security prison, the Ohio Pen, located in downtown Columbus, was in dire need of replacement. In 1965, a bond issue provided revenues for a new maximum security prison and other corrections construction. But new prisons take time to build and staff. The awareness by many Ohio officials of the need for corrections reform went well beyond building one or two facilities. They had to come to grips with a wide range of reform demands, handle ongoing operation of the deteriorating Ohio Pen, and confront the stress placed on the state corrections system by delay in construction of the new Lucasville penitentiary.

Two major Ohio studies of the state's correctional system applied national reform priorities to the situation facing state officials. The Ohio Crime Commissions study was launched in September 1967, producing interim recommendations in June 1968 and a final report in March 1969.[2] The second project was an analysis conducted by the Ohio Citizens' Task Force on Corrections, an effort launched by Governor John Gilligan in 1971.[3] Like other critical examinations of corrections in that period, the Ohio reports chastized the public for its ignorance and apathy in the face of growing criminal justice problems, criticized the legislature for an unwillingness to appropriate funds necessary for minimally adequate operation of correctional facilities, and challenged the executive branch for a failure to organize the state's corrections offices effectively as well as for shortcomings in planning and management of correctional programs.

The studies insisted that the two key premises of reform are that sentencing more people to prison for longer terms will not stop crime and the overwhelming majority of those who are imprisoned will one day be released. Therefore, the system had better do what it can to improve the likelihood that offenders will not continue along the same path that led to crime in the first place after they are released from prison. Where it is necessary for the protection of the society to incarcerate offenders, the correctional institutions involved ought to be designed and operated in a manner that causes the least harm. Within the correctional agencies, rehabilitation programs should be given at least as high a priority as custody. Reflecting national trends, both groups urged that corrections should be decentralized as much as possible from large institutional incarceration to community-based corrections programs using small facilities:[4]

> We would urge that, as the need arises for the construction of new correctional institutions, the planning of facilities be predicated on a policy of providing small manageable units designed for specific rehabilitative functions rather than large and complex institutions of diverse purposes and costly dilution of staff capabilities.[5]

Moreover, both groups observed that correctional facilities located in remote rural areas of the state compounded the problems of incarceration and rehabilitation.[6] Opportunities for visits and communications with family members were extremely limited, exacerbating family tensions and increasing stress among inmates. From an administrative standpoint, the isolated locations of large prisons made employee recruitment even more difficult than it would otherwise be. Specifically, the chances are greater that there will be fewer minority correctional officers hired, despite the fact that a substantial portion of inmate populations is minority. The Crime Commission added:

> This committee emphasizes its opinion that sites for new institutions should be chosen for their proximity to urban centers as opposed to remote or rural locations. The institution needs to draw upon the potential of social skills and professional resources that are available in larger communities, provide for attractive living arrangements for career staff personnel and to avail itself of the local community services in pre-release programs.[7]

For the time being, both concluded that the state needed to reexamine its policies within the institutions to improve both management of services and disciplinary and other inmate control procedures. The reports urged improvements in the hiring and training of corrections officers, called for improved management capacity to deal with public employee unions, suggested reexamination of complaint procedures within the system as a whole and each individual institution, indicated a need for enhanced protections for inmate rights in such fields as religious practice, health care, mail and visitation privileges, and due process in disciplinary actions. In order to accomplish any of these goals, however, both groups urged a reorganization of the correctional agency.

Ohio's corrections administration was combined with its mental health offices. The Corrections Division was a unit within the Department of Mental Hygiene and Correction. Both study groups urged passage of legislation that would create a separate Department of Rehabilitation and Corrections.[8] That goal was accomplished with a reorganization in 1972. There remained several areas of overlap and conflict between the mental health and corrections units years after the separation officially took place.

State correctional officials began, with the cooperation of the governor, to institute a number of the suggested reforms that could be accomplished without a substantial increase in resources. Inmate councils were formed at the state's institutions to provide a vehicle for airing inmate grievances and bring issues to the attention of higher level administrators. An ombudsman, who reported directly to the Director of Rehabilitation and Corrections, was appointed to resolve complaints without recourse to formal legal proceedings. Corrections Chief Bennett J. Cooper ended inmate mail censorship, though limits remained on the types of publications that inmates could receive. Religious programs were expanded to accommodate the needs of inmates of the Black Muslim faith. Medical and food service programs were examined in response to criticisms by inmates and study groups. For a time at least, prison populations were reduced as parole and probation programs were liberalized. In fact, the total population in Ohio prisons declined from a high of over twelve thousand in 1965 to just over eight thousand by the beginning of 1973. However, major challenges remained for correctional administrators. Heading the list of trouble spots was the Ohio Pen.

Just weeks after the Crime Commission published its interim report in June 1968, the Ohio Pen exploded in the first of two inmate riots. A combination of inmate violence and labor conflicts produced serious stress on the corrections department.

At about 8:00 A.M. on the morning of June 24, 1968, inmates began the uprising, starting fires in the printing shop, the dining hall, and a number of other units of the

Ohio Pen.[9] Inmates armed with scissors, clubs, and other weapons took several hostages, though most were later released unhurt. Corrections officers, Columbus police, Ohio Highway Patrolmen, and National Guardsmen put down the uprising, but not before more than fifty people had been injured and five buildings destroyed. Almost immediately the press charged that there had been warnings of a likely explosion in advance of the June 24 incident.

The *Columbus Citizen Journal* reported that Martin Janis, Director of the Department of Mental Hygiene and Corrections, had "ignored written warnings from [Corrections Division Chief Maury] Koblentz and penitentiary Warden Ernie L. Maxwell of impending, serious trouble."[10] Some reports indicated that the conditions inside the prison had deteriorated in part because of growing racial tension and also as a result of abuses by correctional officers.[11] Others, however, argued that the violence was the product of a number of factors, including the deteriorating condition of the aging prison and staff shortages. At the time of the riot the guard staff was more than 50 men short of its normal complement of approximately 270 officers.[12]

Governor John Rhodes called for an immediate investigation of the prison system. He declared, "I want to make one thing clear. When Lucasville is completed, Ohio Penitentiary is going to be torn down. We'll move everything to Lucasville, including the electric chair."[13] But the trouble had not yet ended at the "old pen." In fact, it had only begun.

On August 20, 1968, a full-scale riot broke out involving some 185 inmates. Before it was over on the following day, ten people would be injured and five inmates shot to death.[14] Shortly after 10:00 A.M., inmates using a variety of weapons took several guards hostage, started a number of fires, and moved to control A & B and C & D blocks at the prison, threatening to kill the hostages if their demands were not met.[15] Negotiations broke down the next day, and law enforcement officials planned an assault on the cell blocks where the hostages were held. The plan to blow a hole in the wall and roof to permit police and national guardsmen access was devised by the National Guard Commander, Sylvester Del Corso, who later revealed that he had used that tactic to take the Manila City Hall in the Phillippines from the Japanese during World War II.[16] All of the prison hostages were rescued unharmed.

Whatever the precise causes of the Ohio Pen riots, it was clear that a major contributing factor was personnel disputes involving prison guards. Warden Maxwell retired shortly after the June incident and was replaced by Marion Koloski. Koloski moved quickly to solve the guard shortage that had become such an important issue in the wake of the June disorder by hiring ninety new corrections officers. But the new guards were in training and not immediately available for full-time duties. To fill the gap, Koloski called upon the Ohio National Guard, which supplied 150 troops to assist existing Ohio Pen guards.[17]

The size of the corrections staff was not the only difficulty. Negotiations had been under way for some time between the state and the public employee unions on pay for guards, which was recognized by all concerned to be unacceptably low. The inadequate salaries coupled with increased performance demands during staff shortages and a strong negative public image produced morale problems. Employee turnover at the Ohio Pen during the first six months of 1970 reached sixty-four percent.[18] There was talk of a strike. In fact, during July 1968 ninety-seven guards voted to authorize a strike if no action was taken on their pay demands.[19] The labor relations picture was complicated by the fact that several unions represented various groups of corrections employees and there was little understanding of the relationship of the bargaining units to the state. "It is uncommon to find three unions . . . representing various employees in one institution."[20] That confusion would last for some time to come.

Warden Koloski was promoted following his handling of the August riot, and Harold J. Cardwell, a Highway Patrol officer, became the new Ohio Pen chief administrator. He would operate the old institution while Lucasville was under construction. He inherited the labor tensions, the aging building, and the aftermath of the summer riots. Moreover, Cardwell would himself become the target of a variety of charges, ranging from a lack of corrections training and experience to inmate abuse.[21] While these problems were percolating, delays in the SOCF building project complicated life at the Ohio Pen even further.

Lucasville: From Promise of a Bright Future to System Overload

The specific events that gave rise to the *Rhodes v. Chapman* litigation were products of the development of Lucasville Correctional Facility and the pressures placed upon that institution almost immediately after its opening as the state's maximum security penitentiary. The critical parts of that story include the controversy over the construction of the facility, the difficult transition period during which Lucasville took over the maximum security responsibility from Ohio Pen, and the prison population explosion that gave rise to the decision to double cell inmates in the newly built prison designed for single cell operation.

There was little question that hopes for resolving Ohio's correctional crisis were pinned to the opening of SOCF at Lucasville. The facility would be of modern design, housing more than sixteen hundred prisoners in individual cells, thus improving control and simplifying the task of correctional officers by structurally enhancing security.[22] Originally planned for construction at a cost of $18 million and a 1970 occupancy date, SOCF would in the end cost more than $30 million and would not begin receiving inmates until the fall of 1972.[23] Every month of delay in the construction of SOCF meant continued operation of the Ohio Pen.

Ground was broken for the new prison in October 1968, with the sense of urgency in the project born of the summer's riots.[24] Yet the construction was plagued with delays including a five week long bricklayers' strike in May and June of 1969.[25] There were a number of labor disputes and difficulties in locating craftsmen in the rural southern Ohio community some two hours by car south of Columbus.[26]

It was not only delays and increased costs that drew fire. By the summer of 1969 a growing list of critics attacked the whole idea behind the construction of Lucasville. The chairman of an Ohio Jaycees prison study, Edward Orlett, publicly demanded legislative investigations of the new prison.[27] At hearings before the Public Improvements Inspection Committee of the legislature in September 1969, critics charged that Lucasville was "a massive, monolithic, medieval monstrosity".[28] It was the very antithesis of the small, community-based, urban-situated, treatment-oriented correctional facility called for by modern penological practice. By 1971, the Citizens' Task Force Report said of SOCF, "The Lucasville institution is archaic, already obsolete, and recognized as a testimonial to the ignorance of corrections in the 19th century, of which it is an excellent example."[29]

The new prison, situated on a plot of nearly nineteen hundred acres, with sixty-nine acres inside the fence and twenty-two acres under one roof, began receiving visitors in early 1972. Press reports indicated that most of the several thousand who toured the facility were very favorably impressed. The first superintendent (the term warden having been abandoned was an artifact of the past) W.J. Whealon, an eleven-year veteran of Ohio corrections, indicated that, while it would be a secure facility, Lucasville would apply contemporary corrections practices that permitted the best chance for rehabilitation of the offenders incarcerated there.[30]

However, the transition period during which Lucasville took over the state's maximum security custody burden from the Ohio Pen was to be difficult and violent. There was internal disorder, a lack of experienced staff, the presence of racial tension and violence. George Denton, who succeeded Bennett Cooper as Director of the Department of Rehabilitation and Corrections, finds it rather amusing to recall the optimism of those who thought it would be possible to build a new maximum security prison, transfer the hardest inmates in the system to the new facility, and that "it would be so clinically clean and safe. Everything was just fine until they began to bring in prisoners."[31]

The inmates from the Ohio Pen began to arrive at Lucasville in September 1972. Critics would later charge that labor relations problems with Ohio Pen guards and the continuing deterioration of the physical plant at the Columbus facility had caused a premature opening of SOCF.[32] Others argued that the unsettled atmosphere caused by continuing construction, efforts by prisoners to establish their subculture in the new institution, and the attempts to implement a more loose and open, treatment-oriented philosophy before the stability of the institution had been established doomed the new facility to major difficulties from the beginning.

Ronald Marshall, Superintendent of Lucasville at the time of this writing and one of the first state corrections officials to arrive on the site of what would be SOCF, recalls, "The very worst prisoners the system had to offer were here when we opened. We had chaos. There were stabbings. We couldn't get the prisoners locked up."[33]

Some observers argued that the prison should have opened only when the facility and administration were completely ready. It should have been launched under tight security, establishing a stable inmate behavior pattern. Administrators could then gradually relax conditions and allow privileges. This is the reverse of what happened at SOCF.[34] Marshall recalls, "The philosophy in those days was that you use plates, you use cups, and saucers; you give the inmates knives and forks and spoons. Treat the prisoners as gentlemen and they will conduct themselves as gentlemen. Not so. Within two days after we opened there were no knives in the dining room because the inmates were all carrying them."[35]

It would have been difficult under any circumstances to open a prison with the hardest offenders in the state prison system, but that difficulty was compounded by that fact that many of the correctional officers were inexperienced. The local recruitment of SOCF employees added to the problem. Denton observed:

> The tensions grew up around the staff in that they recruited most of the line staff from the area of the institution. Those folks were not culturally prepared for the shock of treating maximum security prisoners from Cleveland. [It was] as if they had stayed in Sunday School too long. . . . The fact that the entire [SOCF] population was 55% black was also a shock to them.[36]

Added to the instability of the transition period and the reaction of the new mostly inexperienced local staff were factors that tended to raise the level of racial tension within the institution. To begin with, the inmate population was disproportionately made up of minority offenders. Most of the minority inmates were from the state's two major urban centers, Cleveland and Cincinnati, but found themselves now confronting a correctional staff made up almost completely of rural white officers who had little experience with blacks. The rural location made it difficult to recruit minority corrections personnel. All of these factors increased the perceptions among some minority inmates that they were discriminated against in a variety of ways, ranging from job assignments to disciplinary proceedings.[37]

Corrections administrators from George Denton down resented the accusations of systemic bias, arguing that such policies would have been unprofessional and would not be tolerated.[38] Of course, the inmates were assuming bias in the system based upon their experience with guards. In any case, the perception may very well have been more important than the reality in terms of the increase in tension among inmates and between inmates and guards.

Violence among inmates was frequent and serious in the first two years of operation at Lucasville. Despite the fact that Denton and other prison officials would argue that the violence was not as bad as reported in the media nor substantially worse than comparable institutions in other states, they knew the situation was serious.[39] Then, on July 24, 1973, the killing of guard Arthur Sprouse by inmate Wayne Raney, using a gun allegedly smuggled in to Raney by another guard, coupled with the accidental shooting death of a second guard in the same incident raised the stakes considerably.

Inmates claimed that prison guards launched a program of retribution against prisoners in the days and weeks following the killing of the two guards. A task force appointed by Governor Gilligan to investigate the incident and the Ohio Civil Rights Advisory Committee argued that there was indeed evidence of misconduct.[40] Gilligan ordered correctional authorities to deal with charges of inmate abuse and confiscation of inmates' property.[41]

The Citizens' Task Force also recommended that action be taken to increase the guard staff and resolve labor relations confusion. Several unions—among others the Civil Service Employees Association; American Federation of State, County, and Municipal Employees; and the Teamsters Union—vied to represent prison employees. There was no clear designation of bargaining units and multiple unions that represented similar employees functioned at the institutions. Some of the inmates, for their part, had joined an ill-fated campaign for a prisoners' union.

Superintendent Whealon resigned in late August, to be replaced by a former federal prison administrator, Joseph H. Havener. Havener served until the end of 1974, at which time he was succeeded by Arnold Jago. Jago had been Superintendent of the Chillicothe facility. He was determined to take charge of an institution that had seemed to be out of control since the first prisoners had entered the gates.

There were two facts of life for Jago upon taking the reins at Lucasville in February 1975.[42] The first was the labor unrest. There had been several employee walkouts in 1973 and 1974.[43] Five unions continued the interunion competition for representation. After examining the situation briefly, Jago informed his superiors that

> [t]here was going to be a strike; and it's probably going to be a Lulu! And it was. We got by until May 12, 1975. We had a hell of a strike. When they walked out that left 41 of us here. Those 41 people were here from May 12 to May 18. . . . This incident made people come together. There are 41 people in corrections in Ohio today who are as close as brothers and sisters because of this incident.[44]

It was a violent walkout, with striking employees physically intimidating those who wanted to return to the job, with SOCF communications lines cut, and with an assortment of threats. Jago and his deputy (later superintendent) Ronald Marshall dispatched Highway Patrol helicopters to pick up employees who were willing to come to work from the surrounding countryside. The National Guard was called upon to provide communications and other forms of support.

In the early days of the strike, the inmate population settled down, but on May 18 things changed. Corrections officials from George Denton at the state level to those at Lucasville had been worried that inmates would attempt an escape in the midst of the turmoil brought on by the strike. Denton called Jago and asked about foot patrols around the buildings, warning that the inmates "are working someplace!"[45] Jago sent Marshall and one other man out at night in black raincoats to check the buildings. Marshall recalls, "I walked around the end of the building and they were all on their hands and knees and there was a leader. They were in a kind of V formation." Marshall notified the towers of the escape in progress. "They looked so weird in that mercury vapor sterile white light in those beige clothes."[46] The twenty-one inmates went for the fences and guards opened fire; none escaped, but two inmates were killed in the attempt. The strike finally ended on May 28.

The other major fact of life at SOCF was inmate violence. As Jago put it, "There was a lot of blood on the floor." Jago and Marshall began making charts of those inmates who were predators and those who were victims, building cases against the predators. When Jago arrived there were about 62 men in administrative control (disciplinary confinement). By the time he left, there were 342 in that status. At this writing there are approximately 500 inmates or about twenty percent of the population in lockup and segregated from the general population. Things seemed to settle down as the combination of physical security improvements, revised institutional procedures, and disciplinary policy took hold.

The Decision to Double Cell Inmates

The environment within which prison administrators were operating was not stable. Public attitudes turned away from the 1960s view of treatment-oriented criminal justice reform and toward a more punitive attitude. New state and federal criminal statutes were passed demanding longer sentences for felony offenders and imposing restrictions on the use of probation, parole, and other nonconfinement alternatives. Federal funds for criminal justice were increased, but much of that money went to police activities and relatively little to courts or corrections. The public was in no mood to pressure state legislatures for more money to build prisons. Prison populations turned sharply upward, but there was no room for the inmates. That population pressure brought about the decision to put two prisoners in most of the cells at Lucasville, cells designed for one inmate. It was that double celling which triggered *Rhodes v. Chapman.*

It was particularly frustrating to corrections administrators that neither the public nor political figures could understand what was happening to prison populations. Neither was interested in taking action to respond to the dramatically increasing prison load. Denton points to several factors that should have been recognized by those outside the corrections community in Ohio. For one thing, everyone was awaiting the opening of Lucasville, a facility designed for just over sixteen hundred inmates, to resolve the

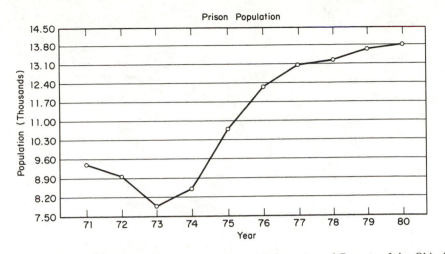

FIGURE 9–1. Ohio prison population (*Source:* Compiled from Annual Reports of the Ohio Department of Rehabilitation and Correction).

overcrowding problem. However, while Lucasville was under construction the population at the Ohio Pen rose to approximately twenty-six hundred. Since Ohio Pen was to be closed after SOCF began operation, there would be a thousand prisoners to place beyond anticipated capacity almost immediately. One answer to that concern was that the state prison population was declining as alternatives to confinement, like probation and early parole, were considered for some offenders. As Denton points out, though, those trends did not affect maximum security prisoners, the type then housed at the Ohio Pen and about to be sent to Lucasville. Finally, he said, "No one wanted to consider an age cohort chart." The children of the postwar baby boom had reached the age at which that cohort was most likely to produce criminal offenders. All these factors indicated the state would face further overcrowding quite apart from the increasingly punitive laws and sentencing practices that were a response to citizen demands to get tough on crime. As Jago puts it, "We saw it coming. The system saw it coming, but we couldn't get John Q. Public to accept it."[47]

The data quickly indicated the accuracy of the correctional officials' predictions. Figure 9–1 indicates just how dramatic the prison population rise was in Ohio beginning in 1973. The steep rise was to continue for the remainder of the decade. A comparison of the rate of prison commitments with the population curve during the same period shows that more offenders were being sentenced for longer periods, see Figure 9–2. That is why the population curve continued to rise after the commitment rate began to level off in the late 1970s.

Jago and his deputy, Marshall, kept receiving prisoners because they had no choice, but they did not know how they were going to house the new inmates. Jago would call his superiors and say, "We just [can't] handle any more. I said, 'Look I've got two in every bed now!' " He was trying to make the point that there just was no more room. "I told them. It's here. It's ready to explode. . . . We're peaked!"[48] He also knew there was nothing his superiors could really do about the situation since courts around the state continued to sentence prisoners to SOCF and other correctional facilities.

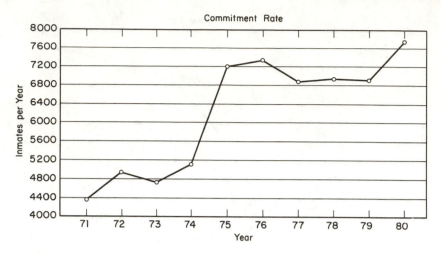

FIGURE 9–2. Commitment rate (Compiled from Annual Reports of the Ohio Department of Rehabilitation and Correction).

Jago told Marshall to try to find ways to fit more prisoners into Lucasville without compromising security, but it was an impossible task. He ordered:

Look at your industry [shops], can you make a dormitory? Look at your day rooms. How many beds can you put in there? Can you get plumbing in there? What about the center of the cell block? How many beds can you put in there, head to foot?

I'd call in Ron and he'd say, we can't do it and I'd say we have to do it.

We contemplated closing up gymnasiums and shops and making dormitories. A dormitory is the worst thing in the world for maximum security prisoners.[49]

The idea of converting shops, classrooms, or gymnasiums into dormitories was a possibility, but not one to be taken very seriously, at least not in a maximum security prison. In a dormitory arrangement, a relatively large group of prisoners is placed in an open room with beds arranged as space permits. Predatory inmates have nothing that prevents them from attacking weaker inmates for money, sex, or retribution. Policing a dormitory is extremely difficult for guards because of the lack of visibility and because there are so many people in one room at one time.

The other problem with the dormitory idea is that it would eliminate jobs in the shops, education programs in the classrooms, and physical recreation in the gymnasium at the very time officials needed to find more ways to constructively occupy inmates' time and, in particular, to increase out-of-cell time. Increased boredom and time in the cell block would exacerbate tensions. Beyond that, the loss of jobs meant a loss of the $12.00 a month inmates received from their jobs to buy personal articles in the prison store. The loss of that independence further increased tension.

The alternative for Jago was to order double celling in a facility with cells designed for one inmate. "I was forced to make that decision," he said. He anticipated "trouble with capital letters."[50] The inmates felt safe in single cells, and that is what most prisoners want from the institution. They want to feel safe, ''do their time and get out.''[51] But there is a substantial minority of the inmate population which prison officials class as predatory, and if these inmates can gain access to their prey, the result is not only harm to the victims but a general increase in stress that rises as the feeling of security among the inmates declines. Asked what he thought was going to happen when he made the decision to double cell, Jago replied, ''Riot. You could feel it. I walked back there [into the cell block areas] and you could cut the tension with a knife.''[52] Marshall added, ''The heavies said they just weren't going to put up with it.''[53]

Jago tried to buy off some of the tension by phasing the double celling in gradually. As the new arrangement was installed, Lucasville officials expanded the amount of time inmates could be out of their cells and added more privileges, like allowing inmates to watch evening sports events on television.

The problem was that there appeared to be no end in sight to the increase in population and those who entered Lucasville were likely to be there for an extended period. While Denton and others at the headquarters level were continuing efforts to obtain passage of a prison building program, institutional superintendents saw no likelihood of relief in the near term. It was a question of meeting the strain on a day-to-day basis, of buying time, but for how long and to what end?

Not long after the double celling began, inmates Kelly Chapman and Richard Jaworski filed suit on behalf of all Lucasville inmates, charging that the overcrowding meant not only an illegal confinement in an inadequate cell, but that it had burdened the overall resources of the prison to the point where essential services from medical care to food service were rendered inadequate. The conditions taken together, they argued, represented cruel and unusual punishment. The issue of overcrowding at Lucasville was about to shift to Judge Timothy Hogan's courtroom, the U.S. District Court for the Southern District of Ohio, Western Division, located in Cincinnati.

LIABILITY PHASE

Kelly Chapman knew Raymond Twohig from an earlier prison conditions suit and because Twohig was a well-known criminal defense lawyer in Columbus. Chapman sent Twohig a copy of the complaint in *Chapman v. Rhodes* and asked if the lawyer would take over the suit. He agreed. However, the litigation Judge Hogan saw was considerably more complex than this simple beginning to the suit would suggest. An understanding of the trial and liability decision in *Rhodes* requires a consideration of the organization and tactics of the plaintiffs' case, an examination of the forces driving the defendants' approach to the litigation, and a view of the trial itself as an outgrowth of these dynamics.

Fielding the Plaintiffs' Team

While the plaintiffs' side of the *Rhodes* case was considerably more complex than one lawyer and a prisoner, neither was it a piece of carefully planned litigation brought by some national interest group or the Department of Justice (DOJ). While the suit would become a purposeful litigation project, the development of the plaintiffs' legal group was almost accidental. The two leading figures in that team were Raymond Twohig and Louis Jacobs.

Twohig had been a supervising attorney at Ohio State University Law School Legal Clinic before entering private practice. Louis Jacobs had worked with Twohig on a number of cases during that period. Jacobs later returned to join the Ohio State faculty and head the legal clinic. Both attorneys were members of the National Lawyers Guild (an organization which traditionally defended minority or liberal causes), though they were not especially active in that organization at the time of the *Rhodes* litigation.[54] Jacobs and Twohig had lunch one day at which they discussed the civil liberties practicum that Jacobs was then teaching at the legal clinic. At that point Twohig said, "You know, I have a case you might be interested in."[55] From that point on the litigation would be conducted as a team effort.

Twohig and Jacobs were of the opinion that the inmates wanted to launch "a very broad-based attack on the system."[56] They wanted "as many good attorneys as they could trust" to make their case. Moreover, the team approach might present a more formidable image in court and produce, by sheer capacity for division of labor, a better case. The two called a meeting at Twohig's law office of lawyers they felt might be appropriate for such a team. The Ohio ACLU seemed a natural participant, since its lawyers already handled prisoner cases and the organization had an institutionalized persons' rights project addressing both prisoners and mental health facilities. A Cleveland attorney, Christopher Stanley, was also included. Stanley was a National Lawyers Guild member and had represented Kelly Chapman in other litigation in the past. Also added to the team were Legal Services attorneys, Bruce Friedman and Clement Pyles.

The next order of business was planning the attack. The original petition filed by Chapman asked the court to permit the case to proceed as a class action on behalf of all prisoners at Lucasville, but *pro se* plaintiffs (those bringing suit on their own behalf without attorneys) are not allowed to conduct class action suits. When the attorneys entered the case, that meant a redrafting of the complaint and a renewed application for class action status. It was during discussions of the amended complaint that the plaintiffs' team determined just what they wanted to do with the case. "The primary question raised during that period involved whether we should take on the entire prison-wide institution, all prisons in the State of Ohio, or whether we should pick the institution where Kelly Chapman was at and the one we knew something about."[57] If they attacked only SOCF, it was very likely the result would be that other institutions would be overcrowded as the state moved to reduce the Lucasville population.

There were two constraints on the plaintiffs' case. The first was a resource limitation. They lacked funds, personnel, and the means to acquire substantial numbers of experts. There was little money available to support the travel and research needed to prepare a statewide case. The second problem had to do with an attempt to avoid interfering with other institutional litigation in progress at the time. In particular, they had no desire to do anything that would create difficulties for the attorneys litigating on behalf of patients against the operations of the Lima State Hospital for the mentally ill.

The strategy adopted by the *Chapman* group was a compromise between the one-institution and systemwide approaches. "We decided that given the resource limitations and the rumors we had heard from around the state, we would strike and focus all of our energy on one institution, win there, and then follow them around the state. As each institution got worse because of the overcrowding brought on by the population ceiling on one, we would attack the worst one, forcing them to defend every suit."[58]

The Defendants and Their Defenders

The state really had two people who would carry the principal defendant role in the case, Director of the Department of Rehabilitation and Corrections, George Denton, and Superintendent of SOCF, Arnold Jago. Their defenders would be Allen Adler and Leo Conway, Ohio assistant attorneys general. For all concerned, the *Rhodes* case seemed at first no different from the hundreds of other prisoner complaints filed every year, ranging from the legitimate suit to the obviously whimsical. Consider, as an example of the latter, an actual complaint filed against the Superintendent of Lucasville that claimed guards had shot Santa Claus on his Christmas Eve rounds at the prison and asked $5,000.00 in damages for the children who did not receive their presents that year as a result.[59] Most serious complaints were, nevertheless, narrow suits, not matters to catch the sustained attention of the head of the state corrections system. The nature and timing of the *Rhodes* litigation, however, not only caught Denton's attention, but gave him an opportunity to accomplish several things he had wanted to achieve for some time.

Denton had, as he puts it, "been nursing an attitude for some time before that." That attitude was a frustration with prison conditions cases in large part based upon his dealings with Judge Young in the *Taylor v. Perini* litigation.[60] The second reason for putting up a fight was extremely practical and in some ways more important in the scheme of things than the other considerations. Put simply, it was a case the state just could not afford to lose given its financial situation and the demands on the corrections system at the time. Finally, Denton was of the opinion, as were his attorneys, Adler and Conway, that the plaintiffs had picked the wrong prison to challenge.

Denton had inherited the *Taylor v. Perini* case upon taking office. That litigation had originally been launched as a discrimination case alleging segregation of inmates at the Marion Correctional Facility, "[B]ut what the [Attorney General's Office] negotiated was a consent decree that had nine special paragraphs in it dealing with psychological training of correctional officers, psychological screening of correctional officers, inmate counseling, and other things not related to the racial issue."[61] Denton was convinced that there were major problems within the Attorney General's office in the handling of the case. In fact, there were later several key personnel changes in the law offices resulting from the furor over the *Perini* litigation. In addition, Denton was convinced that Judge Young had handled the case in an unfair and unreasonable manner, displaying little sensitivity for the problems confronting the state. Given this experience, Denton was not about to agree to a similar consent decree again if he could help it.

His "attitude" was largely based upon the *Perini* experience, but he was also convinced that the *Rhodes* case provided an opportunity to attack the involvement of the federal judiciary in the operation of correctional institutions. Denton rejected the view that judges should be welcomed by corrections administrators as allies in the prison reform struggle on the theory that their reform orders would help administrators obtain resources and administrative support from the governor and the legislature.[62]

Given the situation he saw around him, Denton felt that he could not at that point do anything to relieve overcrowding in state institutions. He needed the time a major piece of litigation would allow in order to try to move his proposed prison building project through the legislature. He recalls his fiscal situation in 1975 as crisis management:

> Prior to 1972 we were not a separate department. I was getting along pretty well with that group [mental health]. I was increasing the [corrections] program until 1973. After that, the institutions were really operated on a panic buy in. In January of 1975 we were a good $2 million in the red. All the fourth quarter of the fiscal year was gone. It was gone in January and February. We had to go and ask for emergency appropriations to finish out the fiscal year.[63]

Denton was attempting to obtain the capital budget needed to construct new facilities and renovate existing institutions at the time he faced major difficulty in obtaining adequate operating budgets:

> The first hurdle is to get your own budget through the Budget Management Office. I went in there and argued that we needed 42 million dollars. And they said we'll give you an 8.8% [increase over last year]. That's standard. You'll have to get the rest across the street [in the legislature]. I told them, "[A]fter all, we're professional and you're professional and we have some professional figures here. We're telling you that we really need this 42 million dollars." They didn't understand the critical nature of the problem. I can recall one discussion that I had with them. I said "By God when we had a riot . . . at the Ohio Pen in 1968 . . . you found 7 and ½ million dollars after that and that institution is going to be torn down." . . . But they said, we've got an order from the cabinet and Administrative Services that we're going to hold the line. That same biennium they gave mental health more increase than I got for the entire population and their population went down 4,000.[64]

Given that fiscal situation, Denton just did not know how the system would deal with a loss in the *Rhodes* case. "I had 800 extra prisoners in there and I had no place for them. They needed and required maximum security institutions."[65]

State officials also thought that this was an excellent case to fight because it targeted the state's newest and best facility. They were certain Lucasville, when viewed as a whole by a reasonable person, could not be considered to impose cruel and inhumane conditions of confinement. And they were convinced that Judge Timothy Hogan was a reasonable man. Even if they did not win at the lower court level, Denton thought, *Rhodes* might still be good for the department because the nature of the case could very well produce an appellate court precedent that limited judicial involvement in corrections.

Denton and his colleagues had confidence as well because of their high regard for the attorneys who would represent them. Leo Conway was well known, highly respected, trusted, and, beyond all that, frankly personable. It did not hurt that Conway had a long-standing acquaintanceship with Judge Hogan.

For Allen Adler, *Rhodes* would be the first major prison case. In face, he had never been inside a prison before his visit to Lucasville in preparation for the trial. Adler was to be lead counsel in the *Rhodes* case and, following Conway's retirement, the chief defense counsel for the state in prisoners' cases.

Like his predecessor, Adler enjoys the respect of Ohio correctional administrators.

He is a self-styled neoconservative who finds himself very comfortable in the role of defender of the corrections system. In general, he thinks prisoners are well treated and that courts entertain too many inmate grievances. Beyond that, Adler is a natural litigator. He enjoys a fight. It is more than a professional interest in advocacy for him, there is the flavor of a sporting challenge in his approach to the task. Given his choice, he would prefer not to settle cases at all. Not surprisingly, Adler was excited by the prospect of the *Rhodes* litigation and its possible results, though he did not consider the case itself particularly complicated. He was all the more pleased because he thought the plaintiffs had picked the wrong institution for their attack and had overreached themselves in stating their complaint. Moreover, like his colleagues, Adler thought Judge Hogan's court would be a sympathetic forum for the state's arguments.

In Judge Hogan's Court

Timothy Hogan is a Cincinnati native, sixty-nine at the time of the *Rhodes* trial. A Democrat of long standing, Hogan was appointed to the bench in 1966 by President Johnson. His party affiliation notwithstanding, however, Hogan is hardly known as a liberal.

The plaintiffs considered just how to proceed before Hogan. They sensed that they were unlikely to get both a preliminary injunction in their favor and also a prompt trial on the merits of the case in search of a permanent injunction against overcrowding at Lucasville. If they were granted a preliminary order, the case might drag on since there would be no real need for immediate relief. In the course of pretrial discussions, it became clear that they could get a relatively brief but prompt trial if they were prepared to move quickly.[66] They decided to take that option.

Twohig, Jacobs, and their colleagues had extremely limited financial resources. In fact, some of the pretrial expenses that were incurred, such as the cost of stenographic services for depositions, were defrayed by donations raised at a wine and cheese party. There was also the problem of locating and funding the expert witnesses the plaintiffs would need to testify to prison standards and conditions. Since they could not pay the experts or even provide expense money, the plaintiffs had to seek local experts and call around to other organizations in search of others who might be available free of charge. They were able to acquire the services of one such witness from New York, Adam McQuillan, with the assistance of the ACLU. The plaintiffs did not ask DOJ to enter the case, a move that could have supplied resources but might have meant loss of control to the DOJ attorneys by the plaintiffs' lawyers.[67]

The state's attorneys had no difficulty in obtaining the assistance of outside experts, including such formidable figures as the Texas Director of Corrections, W.J. Estelle. Of course, at the state level, the expertise of various Corrections Department officials and institutional superintendents was available. Marshall and other members of the Lucasville staff devoted a good deal of the time to preparation of materials on conditions at SOCF to assist Adler and Conway as they moved toward trial.

Of particular importance to the plaintiffs was the effort to get Hogan to tour the prison itself and see firsthand the size of the cells and the nature of the confinement. Hogan, though, was no stranger to Lucasville. In fact, he had previously presided over a hearing at the institution. Even so, he complied with the plaintiff's request and spent part of a day before trial at SOCF.

In the intervening period between the filing of the suit and the trial, Lucasville received a number of mixed reviews in the press. The reports cited inmate fears of increasing violence, particularly homosexual assault, racial tension, complaints about the availability of jobs, access to educational programs, and a perceived decline in the quality and quantity of food.[68] Particularly disquieting were the reports that homosexual assault increased with double celling. Interviews with Kelly Chapman figured prominently in several of these stories. On the other hand, the news items were quick to add that "the whole story is not violence and beastiality."[69] Reporters noted that despite increasing populations and fiscal stress, there were a number of notable success stories, at least on the level of the individual inmate.[70] They noted as well the concern expressed by many inmates that, "Most of us over here have families. We want to get out of the penitentiary. We don't want no trouble."[71]

Given the potential significance of the case, the trial was relatively brief, running from May 23 through May 27, 1977. It centered on the allegation made by plaintiffs that while they were not attacking double celling in all circumstances, the facts of double celling at SOCF and the relationship of that practice to institutional services meant that the totality of the circumstances at Lucasville violated the Eighth and Fourteenth amendments.

The plaintiffs' case was in three parts. The lead expert, Adam McQuillan, made the general case against double celling. Lucasville inmates indicated that the general problems McQuillan highlighted had, in fact, occurred at SOCF. Lucasville employees corroborated the inmates' story about conditions at the prison. Finally, the plaintiffs rounded out the case by emphasizing particular problems associated with the conditions at Lucasville in the wake of double celling.

McQuillan was President of the Correctional Association of New York at the time of the *Rhodes* trial. Before leaving active corrections administration, he had spent more than twenty-six years with the New York City Department of Corrections, with much of his career at Rikers Island and the Manhattan House of Detention (better known as the Tombs). McQuillan was quite impressed with his tour of SOCF. He was particularly taken by the contact visitation arrangements, found "that the institution, with very few exceptions, was remarkably clean and well kept,"[72] and considered the prison library "gorgeous."[73]

On the other hand, McQuillan found deficiencies at Lucasville as well. His examination of the prison took place on a day when exterior temperatures reached eighty-eight degrees. He found the cells hot and stuffy, with little effective air circulation. Asked about the daily food expenditures at SOCF of $1.12 per inmate per day, McQuillan replied that he had never in more than twenty-five years seen a price per inmate lower than $1.70 per day. At the core of his testimony, however, was McQuillan's attack on the practice of double celling. From an administrative standpoint, it was simply very hard for guards to monitor inmate behavior when two people were present in such a small space. Moreover, it was precisely in a double celling situation that close monitoring was necessary because it is "conducive . . . to assaultive behavior on inmates and the degree and the possibility of homosexual occurrences when you put two young males living together who are doing an awful long stretch of time."[74]

The cells at SOCF were of two basic designs with one measuring six feet by ten feet six inches by nine feet and the other six feet six inches by ten feet six inches by nine feet. Within that approximately sixty-three square foot space was a stacked bunk bed, a wall cabinet, a lavatory, and a commode. Most cell blocks have twenty cells in a range, with two upper and two lower ranges in the block. A guard operates an electronic console at one end of the cell block, which is positioned at the level of the entrance from the main corridor, slightly above the level of the lower cell ranges and below the upper ranges. At the guard's end of the block are located the shower stalls and the entrance to the dayroom, an open room with tables, chairs, and a wall-mounted television set. A guard standing at the console cannot see the interior of more than a few cells down the range. In practice, most guards remain at the consoles. Except during regular movement periods, an inmate who wishes to leave his cell to take a shower or for any other permissible reason yells out his cell number. The guard then opens the cell electronically from the console. Unless the number of guards is increased dramatically, it becomes all but impossible to monitor inmates in all parts of the cell ranges, dayrooms, showers, and cell block entrance.

Inmates testified that, after double celling, they felt a clear increase in stress. They claimed an increase in violence and in homosexual assault. Hogan heard inmate Johnny Anders testify as follows:

Q: Why did you check into P.C. or protective custody?

A: Because I had quite a few problems. They seemed to say I have to have a man protect me and stuff like that.

Q: What types of problems were these?

A: Well, a lot of these problems, mostly sex problems because I am young and everything and they were telling me I have got to have somebody bigger and he have to take care of me or have sex with me of some type. . . .[75]

Q: And what happened?

A: Well, when I was in the block, you know, I went to a dayroom one time, two guys approached me talking about they was going to do this or that to me. So I tried to take care of it, this an that.

So, one time they tried to get me and so I end up having to get a man. They threatened me, said I had to choose a guy. They said if I want to—

Q: Slow up.

A: While I was in the block the guys told me I had to choose a man. Otherwise something would happen to me or else it would be for my own good, because they would want to have sex with me or something like that, you know, at that time.

Q: Did you get a man?

A: At that time I had no choice, so I got a man, or get myself killed.

Q: Why did you get a man?

A: Because I didn't want to have anybody kill me.[76]

Anders was asked about reports that young inmates coerced into homosexual behavior were sold by other inmates:

Q: Now when you say "sell you off," what do you mean?

A: Like putting me up on a chair or table and just auction me off, lose me in a card game or some source like that.

Q: What would happen to you if you were auctioned off?

A: If a guy would have taken you, you could become his wife. That's how it is down there.

Q: Well, could you describe from your own experience what the system is of having a wife? What do you mean by that? There are no women in the prison are there?

A: No, but they say young kinds come in there, young guys, whatever you want to call it, and they figure you look good, so they are going to have a man. That's how they see it down there, you know.

They figure if he is young, he can't fight, maybe they ought to do something to him or have him around. . . .

Q: Do you know of your own personal knowledge whether people are sold in prison?

A: Yes, I have seen a few sold here and there. I was sold approximately four times to different guys.

Q: And what were the reasons you were sold for?

A: Somebody liked me. They wanted more money or something, because they usually got four or five hundred dollars off of me from the other guy that wants to have me.

Q: What happens to you when you get sold?

A: Well, the guy that is with you, they either take care of you or make you a prostitute for them or whatever, you know, something like that.

Q: What happens if he makes you a prostitute?

A: Well, you have to go to bed with somebody, have sex you know.

Q: And does the person who owns you get paid for that?

A: Some do, some don't. Some just make them give it up because they are a friend.[77]

Less significant but important to some inmates was the fact that there was no longer any place of sanctuary in which to study, read, or write relatives. Other inmate witnesses testified to increased violence and difficulty obtaining necessary services. All of the plaintiffs' contentions about double celling had been reasons that Lucasville was so enthusiastically awaited when the prison had opened as a single celled institution. At that time, the first Superintendent, Wilfred Whealon, had observed, "Single cells will make the men less susceptible to homosexual attacks, will give them more privacy, and will be more conducive to learning."[78]

Dr. Lewis Lindner, director of the receiving unit at the Lima State Hospital for the mentally ill, was an important witness for the plaintiffs. In addition to his M.D., Lindner was a specialist in forensic psychiatry and well able to testify to the characteristics of an inmate population in a maximum security prison like SOCF. It was not just the numbers that were important, he said, but the tendencies of the types of prisoners housed at Lucasville when forced into tight quarters that was particularly revealing. Lindner observed that such populations included as many as seventy-five to eighty percent of men with mental disorders.[79] In particular, he asserted that the kinds of illnesses present in maximum security prisoners would be those that caused a violent acting out, particularly when they were pressed into tight quarters as in double celling.[80] The fact that increased populations meant more idleness because there either were not enough jobs for everyone or else the necessary numbers of jobs would be obtained by watering down assignments, making them all but meaningless. That would exacerbate the worst tendencies of the inmates.[81]

Prison employees were called to corroborate the inmates' claims and to speak to the level of services provided following double celling. A former prison nurse and two guards appeared. As a part of their testimony, the guards indicated that there were actual incidents of violence that were not reported in administration records because inmates, fearing retribution, often refused to provide reports. An inmate who did report such an event could request assignment to protective custody, but that meant tighter restrictions on the inmate himself and the scorn of other inmates. An Ohio State University dentistry professor was subpoenaed to testify to the lack of dental services.

Adler pressed the inmate and employee witnesses, attempting, successfully in the end, to cast doubt upon their credibility. One of the guard witnesses had been involved in a number of altercations with SOCF administrators. A defense witness would later characterize the nurse as "a pathological liar."[82] In the end, Hogan found that the testimony of one of the guards was simply not credible and the reports of the inmates, given their unwillingness to name their attackers or provide more details on specific events, were not helpful.[83]

The defendants' case was brief, consisting chiefly of a major outside expert, one of the Lucasville architects, Arnold Jago, and the prison physician, Dr. Armin Melior. While admitting that double celling was not a technique most prison administrators would like to employ, Texas corrections chief W.J. Estelle, nevertheless, concluded that it was probably the best of the available alternatives given the "political and social reality" the state was facing at the time. The architect presented a rather unconvincing claim that he had designed cells without careful consideration of whether they would really be one-person units. That testimony simply did not square with the public claims of Ohio corrections officials dating back to the late 1960s. Particularly important to the defendants' case, however, was the testimony of SOCF Superintendent Arnold Jago and physician Armin Melior.

Jago was in a difficult spot. He was struggling within the institution to deal with a situation he knew was bad. On the other hand, the incidents of violence, while increasing, were not out of proportion to the rise in population. He felt his staff was doing extremely well in meeting the crisis and simply found it unbelievable that they could be found to be acting unconstitutionally. At the same time, he knew the Lucasville staff had been lucky and had serious doubts that the current situation could be sustained indefinitely. He recalled:

> When I was asked the question in federal court and I said I don't know what you mean by overcrowded. I was saying we're crowded but I'll never agree we're overcrowded. I was fighting for our system. I didn't want to go down there and agree that we were overcrowded. I had two tongues in my mouth. One of them said yes and the other one said no. I knew we were crowded, yes. I recognized we were crowded. Hell, [Ron] and I spent many a sleepless night or afternoon arguing about this. Where [were] we going to put these [inmates] tomorrow? We're getting a bus load tomorrow morning, Ron, where the hell are we going to put them?[84]

Dr. Melior had kept careful records on inmate medical treatments and, on that basis, argued vigorously that there simply had not been a disproportionate increase in violent incidents.

Both sides felt confident at the end of trial. The plaintiffs were sure they had more than carried the case. The defendants were equally certain that they had presented a strong case before a sympathetic judge.

The Surprising Climax

All parties were, however, surprised by Judge Hogan's liability opinion issued on June 29, 1977. The plaintiffs were jubilant at their victory but confused and disappointed by the opinion. As the defendants read the opinion they were happy to see that Hogan had ruled with them until the last page of the findings of law, when he concluded that the conditions at SOCF violated the Constitution. There is considerable speculation that Hogan had initially been prepared to rule for the defendants, but upon contemplating what he had seen of the nature and size of the cells had changed his mind. The way in which his opinion issued was particularly important for the events that were to follow.

For Hogan, the factual situation was relatively simple. Lucasville was a good, even state-of-the-art, correctional facility that was, for a variety of completely understandable reasons, thirty-eight percent over its design capacity. "Looking at it from a brick and mortar viewpoint," he said, "it is unquestionably a top-flight, first-class facility."[85] It was "new and that, of course, is a plus; as such places go it is not lacking in color and most such places surely are; generally speaking, it is quite light and airy, etc."[86] He found the library facilities good, the access to legal aid acceptable, the visitation situation more than adequate, and ventilation sufficient to provide adequate circulation and eliminate odors. Noting that "none of the inmates who testified or appeared during the trial of this case appeared in any way malnourished," Hogan found the meals "to be adequate in every respect and there is no indication whatsoever that prisoners have been underfed or that the food facilities have been taxed by the prison population."[87] Hogan concluded that while it was true that double celling had significantly affected the ability of inmates to study, there was no evidence that inmates were denied the opportunity for education.

There were problem areas, however. Judge Hogan determined that "there are not enough jobs to go around" and that many inmates assigned to jobs work only an hour or so a day."[88] Medical, dental, and psychological staff had not been increased in the move to double celling. The result, he said, was a denial of basic services in these areas, though he was quick to add that the situation "cannot be described as out of hand or the result of indifference."[89]

One of the most critical allegations made by the prisoners was that the double celling had produced a geometric increase in violence. Hogan did indeed find an increase in violence, but concluded that the rise in incidents was the result of the increase in population and that there had not been an adequate showing that the increase was caused by double celling. The basis for this conclusion was mathematical, reached by dividing the total number of incidents by population and then comparing these figures from quarter to quarter. Hogan found the guard testimony less than credible and rejected the inmate testimony on grounds that since the inmates were unwilling to risk the consequences of "snitching," they were unable to provide more than general observations which the court did not find helpful. More important, for Hogan, was Dr. Melior's reports on his records of medical treatment for violent incidents.

Hogan recognized that "[t]raditionally, federal courts have adopted a broad hands-off attitude toward problems of prison administration," but he recalled, the same Supreme Court ruling which issued that injunction to lower courts promptly added, "[A] policy of judicial restraint cannot encompass any failure to take cognizance of valid constitutional claims whether arising in a federal or state institution. When a prison . . . practice offends a fundamental constitutional guarantee, federal courts will discharge their duty to protect constitutional rights."[90] Examining the variety of lower court rulings on prison conditions to date, Hogan concluded that the "question is constantly stated as one of ascertaining the 'totality of the circumstances' of the particular case and then inquiring into whether the totality as determined is intolerant [sic] or shocking to the conscience, or barbaric or totally unreasonable in the light of the ever changing modern conscience."[91]

Despite the fact that there had been a plethora of prison and jail cases prior to *Rhodes*. Judge Hogan found that this case was somewhat different in that it was not a jail in which those awaiting trial were temporarily detained or lower grade offenders were housed for relatively brief sentences. It did not involve "jail structures which were antiquated and in which the plumbing, lighting, heating, ventilation, sanitation, and noise levels" were intolerable.[92] It did not involve the most extreme prison practices, like the use of open dormitories, or the complete deprivation of essential services, like medical care. While there were some difficulties with provision of medical care, improvements were being made. Having said all that, however, Hogan concluded "that the double celling at Lucasville is unconstitutional."

He advanced five reasons to support his judgment. First, the nature of the inmates must be considered. They are long term inmates, approximately sixty-seven percent of whom were at Lucasville on first degree felonies or facing life sentences. Of that, as many as seventy-five to eighty percent suffered from mental disorders. Perhaps as many as "15% of the inmates may be expected to be schizophrenic and that . . . type is particularly prone to violence engendered by 'close quarters'."[93]

Noting that overcrowding "necessarily involves excess limitation of general movement as well as physical and mental injury from long exposure," Hogan found that several jurisdictions had used the design or rated capacity of the prison as the benchmark against which to judge the unconstitutionality of overcrowding.[94] Based upon that standard, Lucasville was seriously overcrowded, housing more than one third more prisoners than the institution was designed to accommodate.

These features of the inmate population and the level of overcrowding were especially troublesome because the court was not evaluating a temporary emergency population problem. Recent history and general prison population trends in Ohio (and in the United States in general) indicated that the number of persons incarcerated was climbing steadily and would be unlikely to decline at any point in the foreseeable future.

Within the population, substantial numbers of inmates spent all or much of their time in cells. Even those not in some form of lock down status would be forced to share a sixty-square foot cell with cellmates most of the time.

For Hogan, a celling arrangement that allowed thirty to thirty-five square feet per inmate (including the space occupied by cell fixtures and beds) was simply inadequate when judged by any recognized standard in corrections. To that point, Hogan was unable to find a decision that had upheld a standard of less than fifty square feet per inmate. The American Correctional Institution used a standard of seventy-five square feet, the National Sheriffs Association Handbook on Jail Architecture sets a minimum of seventy to eighty square feet, the National Council on Crime and Delinquency Model Act for Protection of Rights of Prisoners set a requirement of fifty square feet, and the Report of the Special Civilian Committee for the study of the U.S. Army Confinement System "indicates that the Army standard in 1969 was 55 square feet and the Army, not known for 'coddling,' adheres to that."[95] Hogan concluded, "No one takes issue with this basic requirement for human decency and this Court holds that failure to achieve that minimal standard contravenes the Eighth Amendment prohibiting cruel and unusual punishment."[96]

Later, during the remedy hearing, Leo Conway challenged Hogan's assessment of minimum standards. Conway argued that Hogan should reconsider his decision based upon a June 1977 decision of the Fourth Circuit Court of Appeals concerning a South Carolina prison which upheld double celling. Hogan interrupted Conway and the following exchange ensued:

> THE COURT: Did you ever go out to the zoo?
> MR. CONWAY: Oh yes, your Honor.
> THE COURT: Do you know a Bengal tiger—
> MR. CONWAY: I certainly do.
> THE COURT: —has more room by far than two people in a cell up there, an animal?[97]

REMEDY PHASE

Having concluded that Lucasville was in violation of the Eighth Amendment, however, Judge Hogan was not interested in mandating a wide-ranging remedy or calling for immediate redress of the overcrowding. The plaintiffs had not even requested a detailed remedy. What they sought was an end to the overcrowding by changes within the system or release of inmates illegally confined. To these demands Hogan replied, "We rather doubt that the State is, overnight, prepared to move any substantial number of inmates from Lucasville and 'single cell' them elsewhere. . . . On the other hand, the State must proceed with reasonable dispatch to formulate, propose and carry out some plan which will terminate double celling at SOCF."[98] He gave the state ninety days to prepare a plan, with a hearing to follow for consideration of the state's proposal.

The remedy that would ultimately be fashioned to eliminate double celling at Lucasville was relatively mild and produced with little procedural complexity. Of greater long term significance was the parallel appeals process that the state would pursue, leading to reversal in the U.S. Supreme Court of Judge Hogan's liability ruling.

Remedy Crafting

The *Chapman v. Rhodes* liability decision sent Ohio correctional officials back to the drawing board. Their situation had not improved. Prison populations continued to climb, the fiscal outlook was not improving, and not one spade of dirt had been turned to begin construction of any new facilities. In fact, public demands for harsher criminal penalties had fostered legislation that would require flat term sentences that reduced judicial sentencing discretion and mandated longer sentences, thus promising continued prison population increases. There was also criticism of state parole authorities for expanding the availability of parole for serious felony offenders. Pressures to limit parole threatened to eliminate an option to long term incarceration.[99]

At Lucasville Jago and Marshall thought back to the various expansion plans Marshall had previously produced at Jago's request. Those plans had involved efforts to place beds in the center of existing cell blocks and the use of gymnasiums and shops as dormitories. Jago knew that closing these facilities would make a bad situation worse. "It would just make the pot boil" because it would further reduce the availability of jobs and recreation and result in more lock down time for inmates. Beyond that, it would create a dormitory living arrangement, which is the least secure and most dangerous way to manage maximum security inmates.[100]

The effort to meet the population crunch was not, however, limited to SOCF. The planning process was a combined effort of SOCF officials, Department of Corrections administrators, and staffs at the other state correctional facilities. The movement of the system reception center from the Chillicothe facility to the Columbus Correctional Facility, a portion of the Ohio Pen, opened up a number of beds at Chillicothe, but such small scale efforts did not begin to meet the challenge.

Correctional officials decided to submit multiple plans in response to Hogan's ruling. Denton felt that a plan with several options that showed thought and effort would impress Hogan and perhaps persuade him not to take extreme remedial action. From a legal tactics perspective, Adler felt he could hold the trial court to the least intrusive of the state's proffered remedies.

Briefly, there were five plans:

1. Modified Double Celling. Under this plan SOCF would continue to double cell inmates who had jobs or school assignments, that is, those with maximum out of cell time. It would assign single cells to inmates who were locked down for various reasons. The assumption supporting this plan was that overall prison populations would likely decline gradually in the next several years, allowing officials to phase the SOCF population down to the modified double celling goal through attrition rather than by immediate transfer of prisoners to another institution.

2. Cell Block Open Bay. This alternative would involve placement of beds in two rows on the floor in the center of the cell blocks. Administrators would have to provide more shower facilities and storage areas. The within-block plan could be implemented in two months or less without additional expenditures. The cost of this plan was in the creation of a security problem since it amounts to a dormitory arrangement.

3. Treatment Facility Conversion. The third plan called for conversion of one of the gymnasiums, the print shop, and one industrial shop into dormitories. These spaces would be subdivided to provided for fifty-man rooms. The use of such large dormitories carries well known dangers. In addition, this approach would limit further access to the gymnasium and jobs in the shops involved. Prison officials estimated that this plan would require a minimum of sixty additional guards to maintain security. Funds would be needed to cover personnel costs. There would have to be substantial construction accomplished to implement this plan, but it was estimated that the work could be finished within six months and under existing financial constraints, excluding new guard expenses.

4. New Cell Block Construction. A new cell block could be built to house 640 cells at an estimated cost of $15 million. Two years would be required for construction. An additional one hundred corrections officers would be required to patrol the new block. Decisions about that construction and necessary additional financial support were up to the legislature and the voters who were then facing a referendum on a prison construction bond issue.

5. New Prison Construction. The remaining means for resolving the overcrowding problem was to obtain passage of the proposed $280 million building program. Assuming rapid approval of the necessary funding, it would take two to four years to construct the new facilities.[101]

Table 9–1. Cost Estimates for Proposed Remedies

COMPLIANCE PLAN COSTS
CHAPMAN v. RHODES

1. No additional cost.
2. Commodes: 5 per range—11 ranges @ $65 ea. $3,575
   Sinks: 5 per range—11 ranges @ $45 ea.   2,475
   Plumbing Supplies & Materials—55 units @ $45 ea.   2,475
   Floor Modifications @ $70 per range   550
      TOTAL MATERIALS $9,075

   2 Plumbers: 176 hrs. ea. @ $8.10 + 14.3% fringe   3,259
   2 Maint. Workers: 176 hrs. ea. @ $8.20 + 14.3% fringe   3,299
   1 Maint. Supv.:   176 hrs.   @ $8.20 + 14.3% fringe   1,650
      TOTAL LABOR (at O.T. rate)   8,208
      TOTAL MODIFICATION COST $17,283

3. This alternative cannot be met due to the requirement of
   60 additional security staff; costs as follows:

   50 CO II   @ $ 8,819 + 20.5% = $10,267 $531,350
   7 CO Supv. I   @ $ 9,506 + 20.5% = $11,455   80,185
   3 CO Supv. II   @ $11,544 + 20.5% = $13,911   41,733
   Holiday and other O.T. @ 7%   45,279
      TOTAL CUSTODY LABOR   698,547

   Uniforms and Equipment @ $140 each   8,400
      TOTAL ADDITIONAL STAFF COST $706,947

   Construction Costs, utilizing the following areas—shoe
   shop, warehouse, and M—1 gym:

   38 Shower units @ $100 each $3,800
   56 Commode units @ $100 each, complete   5,600
   56 Sinks @ $80   4,200
   Security Screen in Gym   5,000
   Fencing—Roof of OPI Building   6,480
   Exhaust Fans for OPI Building   4,000
   Security Locks and Additional Doors   2,000
   Lighting and Wiring for all areas   9,000
      TOTAL MATERIALS   40,080

   Labor = 1,848 hours (8 staff) @ $63.26 hr. plus fringes   19,120
   Supplies = Lockers @ $40 × 440   17,600
      TOTAL CONSTRUCTION COSTS—base $116,880
      TOTAL FIRST-YEAR COSTS $823,827

   Loss of Income to OPI
     Shoe Shop $198,589 × 110% = $218,447 per year

   Note, Alt. No. 3:
     M-1 Gym = 110 bed spaces (8,664 sq. ft. net—110 = 78.8 sq. ft.)   15,730 sq. ft.
     Shoe Shop = 215 bed spaces (12,932 sq. ft. net—215 = 60.0 sq. ft.)   67,006 sq. ft.
     Print Shop = 174 bed spaces (10,492 sq. ft. net—174 = 60.0 sq. ft.)   total OPI

Source: *Chapman v. Rhodes*, Joint Appendix, p. 33.

Cost estimates for plans 1, 2, and 3 are provided in Table 9–1.

Hearings on the remedy proposal were held on March 7, 1978. All parties involved were cautious. The plaintiffs "did not want an order that would set up what corrections officials had to do in specific terms. Instead, we wanted an order that set goals, hard fixed goals, and they could accomplish them however they wanted. . . . It was a determination of what would sell to the court. It was a determination of how we would look best in terms of saying we did not want to run the prison; we only wanted it to be run in a constitutional way."[102] On the defendants' side, Denton's principal concern was that he did not want an order calling for an immediate reduction of population since he had no place to put the excess inmates. Neither side saw a need for a complex remedy hearing presentation. As for the Judge, Hogan had already taken the position that he did not want to order the state to appropriate funds for new prison construction, on the one hand, or to order the release of inmates, on the other.[103] Closing the hearings, Hogan said "This has gone on pretty long, and we will do something—I won't say it's going to be terribly erudite, but the time will be fast."[104]

The remedy was indeed quick in coming. On March 21 Hogan issued a memorandum on the remedy. He rejected plans 4 and 5 because they were dependent upon too many contingencies and would take too long to implement. Plans 2 and 3 both involved the use of dormitory living arrangements and Hogan concluded that "[f]rom the evidence at this hearing, as well as at the merit trial of this case, it is clear that 'dormitory' facilities are even less desirable than double celling; in other words, those cures are worse than the ailment."[105] Plan 1 would allow Ohio officials to add even more inmates to the population and would only continue the problems created by double celling and overcrowding, including reduced availability of jobs and educational programs. He concluded:

> (1) we are satisfied from the evidence that a reduction in population can be reasonably accomplished, (2) that the choice of method (reducing admissions, accelerating transfers, etc.) should be left to the defendants, (3) that a reduction in inmate population of twenty-five (25) men per month beginning in April, 1978 and continuing until the population is reduced to approximately 1700 is proper and the defendants should be ordered so to do.[106]

The judgment followed on April 7, allowing the state to reduce the population of SOCF by twenty-five men per month, by any means it chose, until it reached "the single-celled capacity of the institution." Corrections officials were relieved by Hogan's mild performance standard remedy. Jago and Marshall at SOCF were particularly happy about the order because they would have fewer people to provide for.

The Parallel Appeals Process

The fact that Hogan had delivered a mild remedy did not resolve the factors that prompted Denton and other corrections officials to fight the *Chapman* case in the first instance. Despite his relief over the type of remedy, Denton's reaction to the liability judgment was, "I will see you at another level!"[107] For that matter, the plaintiffs were also seriously contemplating a cross appeal, arguing that Hogan had made factual errors that resulted in an opinion that provided weak findings of fact to support the liability judgment and the remedy. They chose not to do so because they did not want to bring a ruling in their favor into question and because it is so difficult to prove that a trial court's findings of fact are "clearly erroneous," the legal standard for such challenges.

Hogan refused a request for a stay, as did the Sixth Circuit Court of Appeals. Adler knew early on that the state was in trouble in the first level of its appeal. He generally prepared a relatively brief set of materials for appellate oral arguments, assuming that questions posed by the court would consume most of the time available. When he presented his case in the Court of Appeals without a single question by any of the judges, he was certain the state had lost. The Sixth Circuit panel upheld Hogan's decision in a simple three paragraph opinion issued in June 1980.[108] There was never any doubt that the next move was on to the Supreme Court.

When the Court agreed in November to hear the case, Adler was convinced the appeal was already won. There were several reasons for his optimism. The first was that when the Supreme Court grants *certiorari,* four justices have concluded that a case merits serious reexamination. If they are convinced that there is a problem in the lower court ruling, an advocate need garner only one more vote to get a majority in his or her favor.

A second factor suggesting the likelihood of a state victory was the general movement of the Court to narrow district court remedial activity on federalism grounds. The factual findings in the district court ruling were not strong and a Court determined to send messages on the need for judicial restraint could easily reverse on that record.

The third, and perhaps best, indication that the Court would reverse was the *Bell v. Wolfish* ruling issued in 1979 while the *Chapman* case was pending in the Sixth Circuit.[109] The Supreme Court had issued a variety of rulings on prison practices, but prior to 1979 it had not actually addressed the question of minimally adequate conditions of confinement.[110] *Bell v. Wolfish* was a challenge to the federal government's Metropolitan Correctional Center (MCC) located adjacent to the federal courthouse at Foley Square in New York City. Opened in the mid-1970s, the principal function of MCC was to house persons awaiting trial and convicted offenders awaiting transfer to federal prison. As populations rose, MCC was double celled. The double cell arrangement was one issue in a broad challenge to conditions and practices at the institution that alleged violations of the due process clause of the Fifth Amendment. Since most of the inmates were awaiting trial, they could not be punished and were incarcerated solely to ensure their appearance at trial. Many of them remained incarcerated only because they could not afford bail. The Court, in a 6–3 ruling issued by Justice Rehnquist, reversed the lower court finding of a constitutional violation based on double celling. Justices Marshall, Stevens, and Brennan dissented.

For Jean Kamp, who had entered the case as lead counsel for plaintiffs during the remedy phase of the suit, all of these factors were troublesome. On the other hand, for all its surface similarity, the *Bell v. Wolfish* case was not the same situation as that which had confronted Hogan in Ohio. In fact, Justice Rehnquist had recognized in the *Bell* opinion that pretrial detention is not the same as long term prison incarceration.[111] The MCC was not a maximum security penitentiary with a population consisting of the hardest felons in the system incarcerated for extended periods of time under tight conditions.

Both sides attracted *amicus curiae* support. Since this would be the Court's first full consideration of overcrowding and minimum prison conditions, state governments joined Ohio. Briefs were submitted for the group under the leadership of Oregon, which was then facing a prison ruling based upon Hogan's *Chapman* decision, and Texas, which was also involved in a variety of prison litigation. The plaintiffs' side received support from the American Medical Association (AMA), which submitted a brief jointly with the American Public Health Association (APHA). The California Public Defender's office provided an additional brief. The AMA/APHA brief provided detailed argument and copious citations to support the proposition that extended crowding, particularly of certain types of people, produces very real medical and psychological results.

The journey to the Supreme Court in *Chapman* took place over an extended period during which events continued to unfold in Ohio correctional operations.

POST DECREE

While the appeals process was under way officials set about implementing Hogan's ruling. The liability and remedy judgments in *Chapman,* however, triggered another suit, *Stewart v. Rhodes,*[112] that would eventually result in the closing of the Columbus Correctional Facility (CCF), the old Ohio Pen.

Implementation

Since neither Hogan nor the Sixth Circuit Court of Appeals granted a stay pending the appeal of Hogan's rulings, implementation had to begin in April 1978. By July 1979 Ohio prison administrators had phased Lucasville down by 25 inmates per month to the design capacity of 1,645 prisoners. The overload was sent to CCF. The Columbus facility was a reopened version of the Ohio Pen. The purpose of the reopening had been to provide a central receiving and diagnostic center for all offenders bound for state correctional facilities. It was also to be a central medical facility for treatment of serious medical maladies of Ohio inmates. The old long-term detention portion of the facility had not been refurbished since no one had expected that CCF would become an operational pentitentiary again. Yet it had the basic security mechanisms to hold maximum security inmates and empty cells, both of which state corrections officials needed at the time.

Denton knew that the use of CCF would mean a lawsuit, but he was attempting to buy time.

> Oh, I absolutely knew that. But a lawsuit is twenty-six months away. We could buy some more time. Our counsel [would] keep that up in the air. You know the old story of the truck driver at the weigh station. He was banging away on the truck with a stick and a guy said what are you doing? He said well I've got two tons of chickens in a one ton truck and I have to keep half of them up in the air.[113]

For their part, the plaintiffs had fully expected that they would follow up the Lucasville ruling with an overcrowding case at another institution, but they could not believe that the state had chosen CCF, the most vulnerable facility in the state, to serve as the overflow facility. As Jacobs put it, "We expected them to go to a place like Mansfield, Chillicothe, or London and at least give us a running shot. When I heard the news I thought, well, this is it. This is wonderful. Because if we can't get this place closed after they had gone on record that it ought to be closed down, then we can't do anything!''[114]

Stewart v. Rhodes—A New Case and Another Judge

The ACLU promptly filed in federal district court in Columbus, charging violations of the Eighth and Fourteenth amendments at CCF and calling for an order to close the facility. This case brought another judge into the conflict, Judge Robert Duncan.

Duncan is a Republican appointed to the bench in 1974 by President Nixon at the suggestion of then Senator William Saxbe. Saxbe had known Duncan's family in Urbana, Ohio, where the future judge grew up. By the time Duncan came to Columbus to attend Ohio State as an undergraduate and law student, Saxbe was a state legislator. He helped Duncan obtain work in a local county government office.[115] After he was elected Attorney General in 1956, Saxbe hired Duncan and, some time and political battles later, when Saxbe returned to the Attorney General's Office, he named Duncan Chief Counsel. That visibility and his own professional efforts meant appointments first to a Municipal Court and later to the State Supreme Court. Duncan left that tribunal for a seat on the Court of Military Appeals in Washington, D.C. While there Duncan became known to a number of White House staff members and had the sponsorship of Senator Saxbe for an opening on the federal bench in Ohio.[116]

Duncan was already familiar with the implications of remedial decree cases by the time the *Stewart v. Rhodes* prison suit was brought to his courtroom. It had been Duncan who had decided the Columbus school desegregation case, a ruling that had been appealed all the way to the Supreme Court where it was affirmed.[117] In fact, while the prison and schools cases were still pending in his court, Duncan was also called upon to decide a police personnel case that alleged discrimination in hiring and promotions of minority police officers in the Columbus Police Department. On the other hand, the CCF prison case came to Duncan in a posture quite different from the kind of picture Hogan had seen in the earlier part of this litigation.

Launching the Liability Phase—Reformulating Litigation Strategy

The cast of characters changed as well on the plaintiffs' side of the bench. Jean Kamp, who had joined the ACLU Columbus office during the remedy stage of the *Chapman* case, became lead counsel in the *Stewart* litigation assisted by Clement Pyles of Legal Services. App and Friedman left the case while Jacobs, who had been away from Columbus during the remedial phase of *Chapman,* entered *Stewart* to assist Kamp. Perhaps one of the most important changes was the decision to call in the U.S. Department of Justice.

The plaintiffs asked Duncan to request that the Civil Rights Division (CRD) enter the case. The basic reason for the move to include DOJ was the need for resources.[118] The DOJ entered as a litigating *amicus curiae,* independent of the plaintiffs. Neither side felt altogether comfortable with that posture. Adler resented what he perceived to be an intrusion by the federal office.[119] The plaintiffs, who had been concerned about a loss of local control over the case if DOJ entered, saw their fears realized. It did, however, provide the experts the plaintiffs needed and had lacked in the earlier *Chapman* suit. Duncan would later say:

> I found the service that they did perform after I allowed them in the case was just outstanding. They brought in a group of reasonable lawyers. . . . They brought in great experts who had that degree of impartiality which made them quite acceptable . . . and they gained the respect of both sides. They were an extremely helpful force. If anybody really did an outstanding job, it was the Department of Justice people.[120]

The participation of the CRD became particularly complex because there was a dramatic transition while this case was pending from the Carter CRD to the Reagan DOJ. Steve Whinston, the lead DOJ lawyer in the *Stewart* case, was specifically limited as to the position he could take in the case by Reagan administration policy. In fact, Whinston resigned in protest over DOJ policy not long after this case.[121]

From Confrontation to Negotiation

The federal attorneys supported a motion for a preliminary injunction in *Stewart* to deal with two key issues without waiting for the trial on the full merits of the claim to close CCF. The first claim asserted that CCF engaged in racial segregation of inmates in double cells in the receiving section and in the area housing disciplinary problem inmates from medium security institutions, though not in other portions of the Columbus facility. The second issue arose when it became known that corrections officers at CCF were using four-way restraints as punishment for recalcitrant inmates. Duncan granted a motion for a prompt, brief hearing on the preliminary injunction request.

The defendants were caught off guard on these two points since a number of officials and, for that matter, their attorneys were not aware of the continuation of the segregation policy that had been in effect for some time or the punitive use of four-way restraints. The people involved in the restraint abuses were fired when that information came to light.[122] It was clear to Adler that the state was likely to lose on the restraints issue.

Duncan heard testimony that the limited segregation policy was intended to reduce the likelihood of racial violence among new inmates whose tendencies toward such misbehavior were not yet known and among inmates sent to CCF because of disciplinary problems at medium security facilities. There was no evidence introduced to support the likelihood of increased violence, whereas the plaintiffs presented expert testimony to the contrary. The four-way restraints complaint produced disturbing testimony about inmate abuse. Inmates testified that they had been bound spread-eagle with chains on beds for hours without an opportunity to eat or use toilet facilities. Some were left laying in their own wastes. They were provided no medical attention and there were no guidelines on the use of restraints.[123] In one case an epileptic inmate was restrained and, during that period, experienced a seizure. He complained that no medical attention was provided to him.[124]

Duncan issued a ruling granting the preliminary injunction in July 1979. Citing *Bell v. Wolfish,* he acknowledged the need to permit corrections administrators discretion to deal with a complex administrative environment without undue interference. On the other hand, Duncan noted equally clear insistence in a variety of Supreme Court rulings that prisoners do not lose all rights when they enter correction facilities and federal judges are obligated to effectuate those protections. While there may be particular cases in which an inmate's violent racially motivated behavior may justify some degree of segregation, he ruled, the general population may not be segregated in violation of the Fourteenth Amendment. As to the restraints, Duncan concluded that while "in some extreme circumstances there may be good reason to temporarily restrain an inmate, as for instance when the inmate threatens suicide or experiences a violent episode of mental instability, or needs to be completely subdued for a very short period of time after behaving violently toward another person," [125] the uncontrolled use of restraints as punishment is cruel and unusual punishment in violation of the Eighth Amendment. [126]

The preliminary injunction required desegregation within ten days and provided the state with a like period in which to submit proposed guidelines for the use of physical restraints for appropriately limited purposes. At a minimum, those restraints were not to be employed for more than three hours without a physician's approval. No inmate was to be held in restraints for more than eight hours without an examination by a physician and agreement that it was medically appropriate and necessary to continue the restraints.

After the preliminary injunction was issued, preparations began for trial on the merits of the whole case. As negotiations got under way plaintiffs began to believe a settlement might be possible, though all parties had reservations about such a resolution. Duncan presided over the negotiating sessions, which became more intense and more frequent as the trial date approached. Adler did not like negotiated settlements, and Denton, his lead client, was no more enthusiastic about such a possibility than Adler. On the other hand, Denton had no interest in maintaining CCF as a permanent correctional facility. He just wanted time to get his building program off the ground.

Denton's position at this time was that the general financial picture was deteriorating, his prison population had continued to rise, there had not been satisfactory results in his efforts to obtain resources and facilities from the Mental Health Department, and he had not yet been able to obtain full approval for his proposed construction program. Denton recalls:

> I went to the legislature and the measures were voted down. I was looking at alternatives. I cast a view of the state and I said, well, if Mental Health is getting all this money for all this [patient] release, I'm going to find some buildings. I went to talk to Mental Health. You want out of Lima and I want in Lima so I'll take it. It took about four years but we did it. . . . They rushed over and were tearing down institutions when I needed space and I said "Stop it! Stop it!" At the same time I'm still saying I'm going to get a building bill and, believe it or not, five-years later I finally got a 600 million dollar building bill. [127]

State prison expenditures were increasing but not fast enough to deal with inflation, let alone meet costs for dealing with increasing populations in facilities most of which required major refurbishing efforts. For one thing federal funds were falling off. Figure 9-3 shows total corrections expenditures for all functions, SOCF expenditures, and federal grant funds for the 1973–80 period. Day-to-day operating finance problems were handled through efforts by the central corrections office to disburse funds on a need

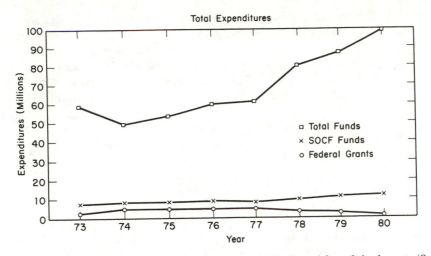

FIGURE 9–3. Expenditures for all corrections activity, SOCF funds, and from federal grants (*Source:* Compiled from Annual Reports of the Ohio Department of Rehabilitation and Correction).

basis project to project rather than in lump sum distributions of appropriated funds. The institutions themselves operated important segments of their facilities on an off-budget economy, trading foodstuffs or prison-produced goods among institutions.

In the fall of 1979 a breakthrough occurred. Governor Rhodes gave Denton an opportunity for a deal:

> The Governor said close it [CCF]. I said, but Governor I've got 1200 and some inmates over there. "Close it and leave me out of it." He said "close it." He said I'll get Merle to call you. [Merle Shoemaker, the most powerful man in the House and Rhodes's ally.] . . . Shoemaker called me and said I'm going to give you a building bill. The first requirement is that the first building has to be built in Chillicothe. I said I also need something else. I said I need to get the old Chillicothe facility from the federal government. He said fine. I said I need something else. That's when I got the Lancaster institution. He also promised me that I would get the one up at Sciota for our women because they were dedicated to a program of deinstitutionalization of juveniles and I wanted to benefit from that. I made a deal. I walked over and told the people negotiating this case, "Settle it, settle it." They said "Wait a minute!" I said, "Walk it!"[128]

The plaintiffs wanted CCF closed, and a settlement was one way to achieve that end, but they had two concerns. First, given the fact that corrections had not been successful to that point in obtaining the funds they needed, what assurance did they have that the state would deliver on a commitment to close CCF by the proposed date of December 31, 1983? The second problem was that there would be substantial numbers of inmates incarcerated in what almost everyone recognized were extremely bad conditions at CCF for a full four years before the closing date. How could they assure improvements in conditions for those inmates and maintain whatever gains they achieved as the closing date approached?

Duncan saw the situation unfolding and attempted to move the negotiations along. The last thing he needed at that time was a long complex piece of prison litigation. At one critical point in the negotiations when a settlement appeared likely, Jean Kamp hesitated, uncertain about the two critical questions. Clement Pyles recalls that, at that point, Duncan "looked down and said to no one in particular; 'You know any time there's an order either side can come back to me and ask for an extention,' but he looked around and said, 'but they would have to make a tremendous showing.' " [129] At that point, Pyles asked for a short recess during which he argued to Kamp that Duncan would not let the state evade a consent decree. She agreed.

Whatever the final impetus for settlement, the two sides did reach an agreement. Asked about his willingness to sign the decree, Duncan recalls, with a sign of relief, that he was ready to sign "just as soon as they brought it over."

Implementing the *Stewart v. Rhodes* Decree

The consent decree entered on December 4, 1979, required closure of CCF by the end of 1983 through a phased population reduction schedule: [130]

Effective Date	Maximum Population
Date of Decree	1,750
December 31, 1980	1,500
December 31, 1981	1,250
December 31, 1982	1,150

In the interim, double celling was to be phased down by limiting the maximum number of days an inmate could be kept in a doubled cell.

The remainder of the decree established improvements and set minimum guarantees in institutional procedures and conditions in the areas of exercise and recreation, rehabilitative programs, sanitation and hygiene, facility maintenance, fire safety, medical care, psychiatric care, disciplinary procedures, access to courts, mail, visitations, and religious services. The agreement included the strictures of the previous injunction concerning segregation and the use of restraints.

Compliance with the decree went well in some areas, but not in others. The supervision of the decree was vested in two special masters. The masters worked through the attorneys rather than in direct contact with corrections officials. Ronald Marshall transfered from Lucasville to CCF at the time of the decree and had responsibility for implementing much of the decree in the first few months until he transferred back to SOCF, becoming Superintendent at Lucasville following Jago's transfer to London Correctional Facility. Marshall recalls, "It was days and nights of pulling your hair out. There was vermin problems, ingress and egress problems, heating problems, ventilation problems, deterioration of the facility itself. When I went in there in September of 1979 would you believe that they were feeding continuously from six in the morning until six at night. They didn't have the facilities. They had only one dining room. Things were broken down." [131]

The plaintiff attorneys changed again during the decree implementation process. Jean Kamp had moved from the ACLU to Legal Services during the early stages of the *Stewart* case but left the area several months after the consent decree was entered. Elinor

Alger at ACLU inherited the case at that point. While Alger saw improvements in facilities, maintenance, fire safety, and recreation, there were continuing conflicts over the requirements of the consent decree with respect to medical and psychiatric care. The mental health problem was exacerbated by the fact that psychiatric services continued to be provided by the Department of Mental Health and the continuing tensions between that department and Corrections did not help implementation of the decree. The major problem was that state officials were not making much headway on the overcrowding.

Duncan was able to stay out of day-to-day problems of decree implementation by working through the special masters. He, too, was concerned about the overcrowding problem and what to do if the state could not fulfill its promises. And as the proposed closing date approached, Duncan faced requests that the state be permitted to keep the facility open.

> Obviously, I had the dilemma that all judges face when you talk about taking the ultimate act and closing it. . . . Certainly I knew in my own mind I wasn't going to let felons out. That was never a possibility. It was just a question of whether or not you're going to send them back and crowd the county jails.

> We had originally established December 31, 1983 as the closing date. As we approached that time it just looked to me like they'd never make it. The General Assembly hadn't completed its process of appropriating the money and the lead time would be enormous. They were talking about all sorts of places of temporary confinement.

> I was very nervous about that. I knew I was going to have to do one of two things. Either keep it open with a much reduced population or let them stay open under the terms they are now with more money spent in the meanwhile to make the place more habitable. . . . They never met any of the phase downs. They always had more people there because they were having more people coming into the stream all the time. They'd come in and say these people are coming in at a rate that far exceeds our expectations so give us more time. Special masters held hearings and hearings. What we tried to do was reach some acceptable compromise right down the middle. Because I just didn't see how to do otherwise. We couldn't close the place up until they got someplace else. Then suddenly out of the clear blue sky, quite unexpectedly, they said the new director took the bull by the horns and we're going to close it on X day.[132]

The Columbus Correctional Facility was closed at the end of 1984.

In the interim Adler, who had never liked the idea of a consent decree, became increasingly certain that the state never should have settled. He reasoned that Duncan probably would not have required as much of the state, even if it had lost a trial in *Stewart.* as the parties had agreed to in the consent decree. The other major factor was that on June 15, 1981, while the *Stewart* decree was in its implementation phase, the Supreme Court issued its decision in *Rhodes v. Chapman*, reversing Judge Hogan's ruling that the double celling at SOCF had been unconstitutional.

The justices who had supported Justice Rehnquist's opinion in *Bell v. Wolfish* joined Justice Powell's *Chapman* decision, concluding that the record simply did not support relief under the Eighth or Fourteenth amendments. Justice Brennan entered a concurring opinion joined by Justices Blackmun and Stevens that underscored the fact that the Court was not declaring an end to federal protection of constitutional rights but merely concluding that the record in this case did not support a finding of a constitutional violation. Marshall, who by that time had become Lucasville Superintendent, responded, "We won, but I lost. It would have been nice for me to continue on with a 1645-man institution." Following victory in *Rhodes,* state corrections officers resumed double celling at Lucasville. The total population by April 1985 had risen to 2,251.

CONCLUSION

Judges Hogan and Duncan faced a range of issues often presented in prison litigation. Yet it was an unusual case both because it found its way to the Supreme Court and involved a new prison in its initial phases and an old institution in the later stages of implementation. The administrators in the case were informed by earlier brushes with federal courts and experienced in the management of correctional facilities. At the same time, they faced severe administrative problems, pressures that the public and legislators seemed unwilling to recognize. Consequently, the administrators went into Judge Hogan's court and defended a prison system they knew was in trouble.

For their part, both Hogan and Duncan were sympathetic to the situation that confronted the corrections officials. On the other hand, both found it necessary to compel the administrators to change their existing practices. The implementation of the population reduction from Lucasville triggered the challenge to the reopening of the old Ohio Pen. Duncan, proceeding under a consent decree rather than by mandate, as in the SOCF situation, oversaw the closing of the Ohio Pen while worrying all the way that he would be faced with deadlines that the state would not be ready to meet and hoping that he would not be forced to make a dramatic final ruling.

The Supreme Court spoke to lower courts through its opinion in the *Rhodes* case, admonishing them to limit their intrusions into state penal operations unless the conditions were so bad that they could not avoid it. On the other hand, the members of the Court clearly recognized that many prison systems had severe difficulties which implicated important constitutional rights which district judges would be called upon to protect.

The distinctions between *Rhodes* and the *Wyatt* case, discussed in Chapter 7, turn on two key features of the two suits. First, *Wyatt* is one of the cases in the first wave of institutional reform litigation that involved an old physical structure and an antiquated administrative system, whereas *Rhodes* concerned a more contemporary and sophisticated problem. Second, the mental health reform case lacked the punitive dimension associated with prison operations and the public anger and fear directed at those incarcerated for criminal violations.

Litigation charging police misconduct, while not involving a total institution, is in some respects related to the prison cases at least insofar as the public attitudes and highly charged decision environment are concerned. Chapters 10 and 11 turn to that type of remedial decree litigation.

NOTES

1. *Chapman v. Rhodes,* 434 F. Supp. 1007 (SDOH 1977); *aff'd* 624 F.2d 1099 (6th Cir. 1980); *rev'd sub nom. Rhodes v. Chapman,* 452 U.S. 337 (1981).

2. Ohio Crime Commission, *Final Report of the Ohio Crime Commission*, Mar. 15, 1969 [Hereafter Crime Commission Report].

3. Ohio Citizens' Task Force on Corrections, *Final Report of the Ohio Citizens' Task Force on Corrections* (Columbus: Ohio Department of Urban Affairs, 1971) [Hereafter Corrections Task Force Report]. The Task Force had an almost completely different cast of characters from that which had staffed the Crime Commission.

4. *Corrections Task Force Report, supra* notte 3, at A8–9.

5. *Crime Commission Report, supra* note 2, at 35.

6. *Corrections Task Force Report, supra* note 3, at C19–20.

7. *Crime Commission Report, supra* note 2, at 35.

8. *Id.*, at 34. *See also Corrections Task Force Report, supra* note 3, at A16.

9. "50 Injured in Pen Rioting; Fire Destroys 5 Buildings," *Columbus Evening Dispatch,* June 24, 1968, p. 1.

10. Ed Heinke, "Governor Orders Ohio Penal Probe," *Columbus Citizen Journal*, June 28, 1968.

11. Bob Greene, Jr., "Ex-guard Tells of Inhumane Treatment at Ohio Pen," *Columbus Citizen Journal*, July 1, 1968.

12. Jack Hicks, "Officials Say Trouble Had Been Brewing," *Columbus Evening Dispatch*, June 24, 1968, p. 1. *See also* Heinke, *supra* note 10.

13. Heinke, *supra* note 10.

14. George Roberts and Stan Wyman, "Wall Blasted; Guards Freed," *Columbus Citizen Journal*, Aug. 22, 1968, p. 1.

15. Elinor Morehead, "Official Details Events of Ohio Pen Riot," *Columbus Citizen Journal*, June 16, 1970, p. B15.

16. Graydon Hambrick, "Manila Tactic," *Columbus Dispatch*, Aug. 22, 1968.

17. William Tillinghast, "Ohio Guardsmen Ordered to Pen," *Columbus Dispatch*, July 19, 1968.

18. *Corrections Task Force Report, supra* note 3, at C23.

19. Jack Hicks, "Guards' Pay Hike Board's Decision," *Columbus Dispatch*, July 19, 1968, *See also* "Guard Strength Grows at Pen," *Columbus Dispatch*, July 22, 1968.

20. *Corrections Task Force Report, supra* note 3, at B4.

21. Jack Hicks, "Pen Warden Denies Charges," *Columbus Dispatch*, Sept. 20, 1968; Elinor Morehead, "Psychologist Details Pen Sadism," *Columbus Citizen Journal*, Mar. 22, 1969; "Prisoners Petition for Cardwell Firing," *Columbus Dispatch*, Jan. 25, 1971; Stan Wyman, "Smuggled Petitions Ask Pen Warden Be Ousted," *Columbus Citizen Journal*, Jan. 25, 1971.

22. Robert Horan, "Ground Will Be Broken for New Ohio Pen," *Columbus Dispatch*, Oct. 7, 1968. *See also* Walter Johns, Jr., "Electric Chair Will Remain in New Ohio Pen," *Columbus Citizen Journal*, Feb. 25, 1972. The state later argued in the *Rhodes v. Chapman* litigation that Lucasville was never designed specifically for single celling of inmates, but all public discussion of the project prior to the decision to double cell in 1975 is absolutely clear in the expectation that the prison was designed and built to house one inmate per cell. For added evidence see the testimony of the architect during state legslative hearings on the prison in 1969. He testified to the cost per bed of the new facility with numbers that clearly indicate an intended population of 1,645.

23. Jack Hicks, "Money for New Pen Runs Short," *Columbus Dispatch*, Sept. 13, 1968.

24. Horan, *supra* note 22.

25. "Strike Likely to End at Lucasville Pen Site," *Columbus Dispatch*, June 8, 1969.

26. "Ohio Officials Unhappy Over Pen Construction," *Columbus Dispatch*, Aug. 17, 1969.

27. "New Prison Site Called Inadequate," *Columbus Citizen Journal*, June 30, 1969; Elinor Morehead, "Neew Prison Probe Opens Next Week," *Columbus Citizen Journal*, Sept. 4, 1969; "Lucasville Criticism Supported," *Columbus Citizen Journal*, Sept. 10, 1969; "Prison Specialists Slated to Testify," *Columbus Citizen Journal*, Sept. 10, 1969.

28. Elinor Morehead, "New Pen 'A Statler-Hilton,' " *Columbus Citizen Journal*, Sept. 11, 1969.

29. *Corrections Task Force Report, supra* note 3, at A2.

30. Walter Johns, Jr., "Electric Chair Will Remain in New Ohio Pen," *Columbus Citizen Journal*, Feb. 25, 1972. *See also* Don Mathews, "Pen Draws Praise," *Columbus Dispatch*, June 22, 1972.

31. Interview with George Denton, Columbus Ohio, Apr. 2, 1985 [hereafter Denton interviews].

32. George De Vault, "Ohio's Prison System Superstar Dulled by Problems," *Columbus Dispatch*, May 27, 1973, p. A–4. The Ohio Advisory Committee to the U.S. Commission on Civil Rights found in its study of Ohio prisons that while the premature opening of Lucasville was never fully explained, there was "some indication that the move was dictated by a crisis among correctional officials at the Ohio Penitentiary. . . . Senator William Bowen reported to the Advisory Committee in August 1973 that an officers' conspiracy to foment riots at the old penitentiary forced the administration to phase out that institution more quickly than originally planned in order to break up specific guard groupings. Violence had been increasing, he said, just before the move to the Lucasville prison." The Ohio Advisory Committee to the U.S. Commission on Civil Rights, *Protecting Inmate Rights: Prison Reform or Prison Replacement* (Wash., DC: U.S. Commission on Civil Rights, 1976), p. 109.

33. Interview with Ronald Marshall, Lucasville, Apr. 3, 1985 [Hereafter Marshall interview].

34. Don Mathews, "Panel Blasts Lucasville Pen," *Columbus Dispatch*, Aug. 10, 1973, p. 6A.

35. Marshall interview, *supra* note 33.

36. Denton interview, *supra* note 31.

37. *Crime Commission Report, supra* note 2, at 66–91.

38. Denton interview, *supra* note 31.

39. Interview with Arnold Jago, Lucasville, Ohio, Apr. 3, 1985 [hereafter Jago interview]; and Marshal interview, *supra* note 33.

40. Ronald B. Clark, *Akron Beacon Journal*, "Task Force Report Says Prison Crackdown 'Excessive, Unjust,' " Sept. 3, 1973. William Merriman and Nancy McVicar, "Task Force Voices Lucasville Gripes," *Columbus Citizen Journal*, Aug. 10, 1973; and Don Mathews, "Panel Blasts Lucasville Pen," *Columbus Dispatch*, Aug. 10, 1973.

41. *Crime Commission Report, supra* note 2, at 45.

42. Jago interview, *supra* note 39.

43. *Crime Commission Report, supra* note 2, at 46.

44. Jago interview, *supra* note 39.

45. Denton interview, *supra* note 31.

46. Marshal interview, *supra* note 33.

47. Jago interview, *supra* note 39.

48. *Id.*

49. *Id.*

50. *Id.*

51. *Id.*

52. *Id.*

53. Marshall interview, *supra* note 33.

54. Interview with Louis Jacobs, Columbus, Ohio, Apr. 4, 1985 [hereafter Jacobs interview].

55. *Id.*

56. *Id.*

57. *Id.*

58. *Id.*

59. Complaint in *Keaton v. Marshall et al.*, CIV–81–460, Jan. 5, 1982.

60. *Taylor v. Perini*, 413 F. Supp. 189 (NDOH 1976).

61. Denton interview, *supra* note 31.

62. Compare Norval Morris, "The Snails Pace of Prison Reform," in *Proceedings of the One Hundredth Annual Congress of Correction of the American Correctional Association* (1970).

63. Denton interview, *supra* note 31.

64. *Id.*

65. *Id.*

66. Jacobs interview, *supra* note 54.

67. *Id.*

68. David Lore, "Lucasville Prison Misses Mark as 'Shrine,' " *Columbus Dispatch*, Apr. 11, 1976, A–14; *id.*, "Unemployment Tops 40% Inside Lucasville Facility," *Columbus Dispatch*, Apr. 13, 1976, A–8.

69. Lore, "Lucasville Prison Misses Mark," *supra* note 68, at A–14.

70. David Lore, "Prison Rehabilitation Does Work," *Columbus Dispatch*, Apr. 12, 1976, A–5.

71. Lore, "Lucasville Prison Misses Mark," *supra* note 68, at A–14.

72. *Chapman v. Rhodes*, C–1–75–251, May 23, 1977, *Trial Transcript*, vol. 1, at 33–34 [hereafter *Chapman Trial Transcript*].

73. *Id.*, at 38.

74. *Id.*, at 48.

75. *Id.*, at 150.

76. *Id.*, at 154.

77. *Id.*, at 155–56.

78. Walter Johns, Jr., "Electric Chair Will Remain in New Pen," *Columbus Citizen Journal*, Feb. 25, 1972.

79. *Chapman Trial Transcript*, *supra* note 72, vol. 2, at 427.

80. *Id.*, at 430.

81. *Id.*, at 431.

82. Testimony of Dr. Armin Melior, SOCF physician, *Chapman Trial Transcript*, *supra* note 72, vol. 5, at 940.

83. *Chapman v. Rhodes*, *supra* note 1, at 1017.

84. Jago interview, *supra* note 39.

85. *Chapman v. Rhodes*, *supra* note 83.

86. *Id.*, at 1009.

87. *Id.*, at 1011.

88. *Id.*, at 1014.

89. *Id.*, at 1015.

90. *Id.*, at 1016.

91. *Id.*, at 1018, citing *Procunier v. Martinez*, 416 U.S. 396, 40–5 (1974).

92. *Id.*, at 1019.

93. *Id.*

94. *Id.*, at 1017.

95. *Id.*, at 1021.

96. *Id.*

97. *Chapman v. Rhodes*, C–1–75–251, Mar. 7, 1978, *Remedy Hearing* [hereafter *Chapman Remedy Hearing*), vol. 6, at 1242.

98. *Chapman v. Rhodes*, *supra* note 1, at 1022.

99. *Chapman Remedy Hearing*, *supra* note 97 vol. 6, at 1183.

100. Jago interview, *supra* note 39.

101. *Chapman v. Rhodes*, C–1–75–251, Nov. 11, 1977, "Alternative Plans in Compliance with This Court's Order of June 29, 1977," in *Rhodes v. Chapman*, No. 80–332, Joint Appendix Dec. 22, 1980, at JA 26–32.

102. Jacobs interview, *supra* note 54.

103. *Chapman v. Rhodes, supra* note 1, at 1022.

104. *Chapman Remedy Hearing, supra* note 97, vol. 6, at 1245.

105. *Chapman v. Rhodes*, C–1–75–251, Mar. 21, 1978, "Memo," in *Rhodes v. Chapman*, No. 80–332, Sept. 2, 1980, *Petition for Writ of Certiorari*, at A39.

106. *Id.*, at A41.

107. Denton interview, *supra* note 31.

108. *Chapman v. Rhodes*, 78–3365, 6th Circuit, June 6, 1980, in *Petition for Writ of Certiorari, supra* note 105, at A2–3. The published affirmance appeared in the case table at 624 F.2d 1099 (6th Cir. 1980).

109. *Bell v. Wolfish*, 441 U.S. 520 (1979).

110. As Justice Rehnquist pointed out in *Bell v. Wolfish*, these earlier cases included *Hutto v. Finney*, 437 U.S. 678 (1978); *Jones v. N.C. Prisoners' Labor Union*, 433 U.S. 119 (1977); *Bounds v. Smith*, 430 U.S. 817 (1977); *Meachum v. Fano*, 427 U.S. 215 (1976); *Wolff v. McDonnell*, 418 U.S. 539 (1974); *Pell v. Procunier*, 417 U.S. 817 (1974); and *Procunier v. Martinez, supra* note 91.

111. *Bell v. Wolfish, supra* note 109, at 543 n. 27.

112. *Stewart v. Rhodes*, 473 F. Supp. 1185 (SDOH 1979).

113. Denton interview, *supra* note 31.

114. Jacobs interview, *supra* note 54.

115. Adrienne Bosworth, "Robert Duncan: The Federal Court Loses a Star," *Columbus Montly*, Apr. 1985, pp. 42–50.

116. *Id.*, at 47–48.

117. *Penick v. Columbus Bd. of Ed.*, 429 F. Supp. 229 (SDOH 1977); *aff'd sub nom. Columbus Bd. of Ed. v. Penick*, 583 F.2d 787 (6th Cir. 1978); 443 U.S. 449 (1979).

118. Jacobs interview, *supra* note 54.

119. Interview with Allen Adler, Columbus, Ohio, Apr. 2, 1985 [hereafter Adler interview].

120. Interview with Judge Robert Duncan, Columbus, Ohio, Apr. 1, 1985 [hereafter Duncan interview].

121. Jacobs interview, *supra* note 54.

122. Adler interview, *supra* note 119.

123. *Stewart v. Rhodes, supra* note 112, at 1190–1.

124. *Id.*, at 1192.

125. *Id.*, at 1193.

126. *Id.*

127. Denton interview, *supra* note 31.

128. *Id.*

129. Interview with Clement Pyles, Columbus, Ohio, Apr. 2, 1985.

130. *Stewart v. Rhodes*, C2–78–220, Dec. 4, 1979, "Consent Decree," at 4.

131. Marshall interview, *supra* note 33.

132. Duncan interview, *supra* note 120.

10

Police Practices and Public
Accountability: Legal Pressures
on Local Politics

Those who deal with criminal justice at the other end of the process from prison administrators are the police. And if the problems of corrections administration are compounded because their activity has low public visibility, precisely the reverse can be
said for police officers and their supervisors. Many of the same social and political
forces that brought challenges to corrections practices during the past three decades also
prompted investigations and criticism of police performance. Since one of the most
important services delivered by local governments is police protection, the study of
police abuse controversies in the courts is a useful avenue for contemplating the class
of law and administration conflicts one might call local government management problems. This chapter, like the preceding law and policy chapters, will consider police
practices disputes in broad compass and provide a foundation for the consideration of
the *Rizzo v. Goode* case study to follow in Chapter 11.

It is difficult to discuss police/community relations precisely because, as Niederhoffer has observed, the police officer in our society is a kind of "Rorschach test in
uniform," that evokes a wide range of intense images, ranging from the fearless crime
fighter portrayed in literature, motion pictures, and television to a kind of modern Key-
stone Cops image, to a member of a brutal and corrupt occupation force.[1] One reason
for the diversity of responses to police officers is the complexity of tasks we ask them
to carry out:

> A modern policeman's tour of duty is full of radio runs which require him to correct
> the conduct of children, to mediate family quarrels, to determine the right of way
> between over-eager drivers, to care for the injured on the streets, and to protect our
> homes at night and our persons in the daytime. All of this is expected to be done
> with the concern of a social worker, the wisdom of a Solomon, and the prompt
> coverage of a combat soldier.[2]

It has been observed that the police department becomes city hall when the office doors
close at 5:00 P.M. Lipsky refers to police officers as street level bureaucrats, thus de-
scribing the sense of responsibility and demands for responsiveness that we attach to
the police.[3] When we do not know where else to turn, we call the police.

Yet we demand that police officers, the only group authorized by our society to
use deadly force, act with restraint and caution so that they do not become a tyrannical

gang rather than a peacekeeper organization. However, the difficulty of the task, the internal dynamics of police departments, the pull and haul of the political environment within which police officers serve, and the kinds of people who don the uniform have produced a variety of incidents—in some cases ongoing patterns—of police abuse, worse in some times and cities than in others. That abuse has most often taken the form of illegal use of deadly force; physical brutality; unjustified searches, arrests, and detentions; verbal abuse; racially discriminatory treatment; harassment; or failure to provide service. The victims of such misconduct have turned to the federal district courts for protection, asking for equitable relief that prohibits further illegal conduct and mandates positive steps to ensure against future abuses.

An analysis of this type of interaction between federal judges and state and local administrators requires a brief consideration of the development of police/community conflicts, a survey of the issues raised and the judicial responses, and the political dynamics of police reform.

HISTORICAL DEVELOPMENT OF POLICE/COMMUNITY RELATIONS ISSUES

The history of the police function in the United States is a story of the attempt to reconcile the need for social order with the fundamental values of individual liberty and equal justice under law. In earlier days the focal point of public discussions regarding police conduct was the problem of reconciling order and liberty. At least since the late 1950s, the emphasis has shifted to the problem of ensuring that police services are administered with an even hand to all citizens, particularly racial minorities and social or political nonconformists.

The police function in preindustrial England was primitive but provided important foundations for the more modern versions to follow. In early times order was maintained by local social groups, the families who made up the small villages and acted under what became known as the "mutual pledge" system.[4] In the thirteenth and fourteenth centuries, the Justice of the Peace was added as the local decisionmaker on matters of justice. It was also in that period that the system known as the "watch and ward," men who stood watch in the streets of the cities at night to sound the alarm in case of a disturbance and, hopefully, frighten away evildoers, was borne. The military forces available to the Crown carried the principal burden for dealing with serious offenses.

As the cities grew with industrialization, the police task became more complex. By the early nineteenth century, crime was dramatically on the rise. Sir Robert Peel, then Britain's Home Secretary, began his effort to develop a professional police force in the early 1820s. Peel laid groundwork by preparing studies of increasing crime as a means of obtaining a royal commission to consider the need for a change.[5] Among other things, the object was to ensure greater social order while reducing the abuses of power by those who had performed the police function, officials who frightened the citizenry at least as much as, if not more than, the criminals.[6] He obtained passage of his "Act for Improving the Police In and Near the Metropolis" in 1829, which created the first metropolitan police force in London.

American police practices developed with a blend of borrowed and homegrown ideas. Eastern cities copied police techniques from the British. As settlers spread out, though, American law enforcement took on a diversity beyond that seen in Europe. When America moved from the nineteenth and into the twentieth century, growing industrialization complicated the police function. Burgeoning growth of the cities meant more people in crowded and difficult circumstances. Political machines flourished, drawing on the support of immigrant groups and others to whom local politicians could provide useful services in return for political support. Police departments were extremely important elements of the patronage system undergirding the machines, both because they provided job opportunities for political supporters and because they could be used to provide services in accord with the wishes of their political masters. A police officer's pay was often very poor and the working conditions difficult. Prohibition provided fertile ground for large scale corruption in many of the nation's police departments. For those reasons and because of the patronage controls, the quality of those recruited to the force was often poor. Their behavior was widely thought to be only slightly better than some of the thugs they were supposed to control. The Wickersham Commission reported in 1931:

> [T]he people have virtually turned over their police departments to the most notorious and frequently the most dangerous persons in their communities who do not hesitate to use them for every type of oppression and intimidation. Therefore, their attempt to protect themselves from a powerful autocratic chief of police has served to place them and the government in the hands of unscrupulous cut-throats, murderers, and bootleggers.[7]

The post World War II period has been as difficult and complex in the field of police/community relations as it has in the other issue areas considered in earlier chapters. The same forces that gave impetus to, and ensured conflict around, the civil rights movement in housing and schools influenced police behavior and police criticism. In the minority community the growing tension between police and the citizens they served was the product of two very different problems. On the one hand, blacks charged, with considerable evidence, that they were not provided with adequate police services. While minority citizens clearly suffered the highest rates of victimization, they often received the poorest protection.[8] Minority residents alleged that the overwhelmingly white police forces were willing to permit criminal activity in the black communities that would never be countenanced in other parts of the city on the racist notion that such behavior was considered acceptable among minorities. On the other hand, blacks charged that police entered the black community with a combative attitude for the general purpose of controlling predominantly minority neighborhoods, not to benefit its residents but at the behest of the white community who wanted to keep minority residents in line. In so doing, critics said, the police acted arbitrarily and violently. As the nation moved into the 1960s, the metaphor often used was that of a group of shock troops sent in to occupy the minority community on behalf of whites who were afraid of the civil rights movement and wanted no change.

The extreme image may have been unfair, but that was not nearly so important as the fact that it was widely shared. The evidence was clear and virtually uncontradicted that minority residents of the nation's cities in the 1960s did not trust police or have confidence in their commitment to proper law enforcement in the minority community.[9] In police/community relations, perceptions quickly become reality in a sort of self-fulfilling prophecy. The louder minority citizens made their protests and the more some acted out against abuses, the more the white community perceived the need for tighter control to prevent disorder. Some members of the predominantly white business community seemed willing to overlook police abuses so long as they were not personally involved, treating the incidents as evidence of aggressive law enforcement.[10]

Police defenders replied that officers did not consciously apply different enforcement standards in the black community, but they simply did not have the resources to respond as they would like to the requests for action. Moreover, when they did act vigorously, minority residents provided little cooperation and in some cases interfered with the officers, focusing their anger at the establishment on the convenient symbol of authority, the police officer.

Tensions over Warren Court Rulings on Police Abuses

While the situation worsened in the nation's cities, debate arose over two related questions associated with providing remedies for misconduct by police officers. First, there was the reaction against Supreme Court rulings like the *Mapp v. Ohio* decision that mandated that police abuses in searches, seizures, and arrests would mean punishment in the form of exclusion of evidence from subsequent trials.[11] But if those rules were to be eliminated, what alternatives were available to deal with police abuses in those situations where they actually occurred? The discussions began in the early 1960s and multiplied as tensions mounted.[12]

One of the frequently cited commentators was then Judge Warren Burger of the Circuit Court of Appeals for the District of Columbia Circuit. Burger attacked the supression doctrine long practiced in the federal courts and advocated instead the development of independent civilian police review boards. He urged:

> To accomplish the objective of maintaining lawful law enforcement calls for a commission or board which is predominantly *civilian* and external rather than an internal *police* agency. The civilian members should be persons well versed by experience in the legal subtleties of arrest, search, seizure, interrogations and related matter. Although such a review body would of necessity cooperate with a police department, it must be *independent* of police administration in the same sense—and for some of the same reasons—that courts must be independent of prosecutors.[13]

Such a board, he argued, should be an independent body of five to seven members with subpoena power and access to police records in its investigations. Its members should have the same sorts of protection available to grand jury members and should have mechanisms for receiving, investigating, and processing citizen complaints, including authority to hold hearings. In cases where such a body determined that police malpractice had taken place, Burger urged that the review board should have:

   a. Power to direct or recommend suspension or dismissal of an officer; power to direct a hearing by a tribunal having disciplinary authority;

   b. Power to direct or recommend inquiry by the Police Department as to general police procedures;

   c. Power to direct or recommend reprimands short of dismissal or suspension;

  d. Power to direct or recommend specific in-job training for a particular officer;

  e. Power to direct or recommend that records be expunged, as for illegal arrest or illegal warrants.[14]

The civilian review board was to be an extremely controversial entity in its own right.

Others suggested that effective solutions to police abuses would be found in the issuance of remedial orders by federal district judges.[15] A recognition of the availability of that kind of federal court protection would provide effective remedies for violations and have the salutory fringe benefit of conveying to the community a sense that a potent independent forum would be available to protect citizens against misconduct.

The Long Hot Summers and the Struggle to Understand

Quiet contemplation gave way to violence in many communities during the second half of the 1960s and into the 1970s. The unrest of the 1960s was not a matter of one bad summer in which a few big city ghettos exploded. While some of the most serious episodes did involve racial violence—in Watts, Detroit, and Newark—the image of disorder was even greater than the reality. Overreaction to the youth counterculture and anti-war movements added to the level of conflict between police departments and their constituents. Moreover, lawful civil rights protest was often perceived as a part of a wider challenge to the status quo. While it was true that violence erupted during some of the marches led by Dr. King and others, the marchers were overwhelmingly the victims rather than the perpetrators of the attacks. But again, perceptions in such matters often mean more than reality.

As Chapter 8 indicated, the violence of the period produced a wide range of studies that had a variety of impacts, ranging from the development of new statutes and agencies to enforce them to new theories of police operations and training. The most important wide-ranging investigations included the reports of the President's Commission on Law Enforcement and Administration of Justice, the National Advisory Commission on Civil Disorders (known as the Kerner Commission), the National Commission on the Causes and Prevention of Violence, the President's Commission on Campus Unrest, and the National Advisory Commission on Criminal Justice Standards and Goals, Task Force on Police.[16]

The Kerner Commission was created by President Johnson in 1967 following the Newark and Detroit riots and some 164 other urban disturbances which had occurred in that year.[17] The Commission studied violent incidents in 23 cities. The investigators found police/community tensions present in all cities examined. Among minorities surveyed, police practices ranked in the top three complaints of twelve commonly mentioned urban problems.[18] " 'Prior' incidents, which increased tension and ultimately led to violence, were police actions in almost half the cases; police actions were 'final' incidents before the outbreak of violence in 12 of 24 surveyed disorders."[19]

The Task Force on Police focused on police operations but was a part of the larger study. The Task Force recognized that "the police did not create and cannot resolve the social conditions that stimulate crime. They did not start and cannot stop the convulsive social changes that are taking place in America. They do not enact the laws that they are required to enforce, nor do they dispose of the criminals they arrest."[20] A major focus of concern was the question of police staffing practices, particularly those which seemed to have the effect of discouraging women and minorities from careers as police officers and those which failed to identify and screen out potentially abusive or unqualified applicants. It urged more effective screening, greater recruitment of minorities, and enhancement of career opportunities for females so that women would be attracted to the service. The Task Force urged police officials to take community relations seriously, to move beyond the notion that community relations had nothing to do with real police work. The report argued that a smart police officer would see the importance of community relations if he or she really understood his or her own self-interest. Good police/community relations translate into support needed to do a difficult job in the street and the political assistance necessary in the legislature and city hall with respect to pay and personnel matters as well as substantive policy debates in which officers have a significant interest.[21] At a minimum, the Task Force argued, improvements in police/community relations require a citizen complaint process that not only is effective, but, perhaps more important, is seen to be effective by the residents of the community.[22]

State advisory committees to the U.S. Commission on Civil Rights around the nation undertook a range of investigations over more than a decade, sparked either by particularly controversial individual incidents, like shootings, or citywide problems, like the Liberty City disturbances in Miami.[23] The U.S. Commission on Civil Rights itself undertook a wider study in 1978, holding a consultation on police/community relations in Washington, D.C., followed by field studies in 1979 in Philadelphia and Houston (two cities with recurring police/community relations controversies) and concluding with the publication of its report in 1981.[24] These reports agreed with the general issue agendas established in the earlier studies, finding some improvements since the 1960s but concluding that a great deal of work remained to be accomplished before it could be said that police/community relations were generally positive.

The Professionalization of the Police

The high visibility of police/community conflicts, the findings of the various study groups and commissions, and the acceptance by the federal government of a leadership responsibility in criminal justice served as catalysts for a growing move to professionalize police services. Among other things, that drive involved efforts to insulate police departments from political interference, demands for recruitment of better educated and more carefully screened officers, improvements in police training programs, and development of new types of equipment.

The Law Enforcement Assistance Administration (LEAA), created by the Safe Streets Act of 1968, developed rapidly as a major source of resources to support this professionalization effort. Fiscal year (FY) appropriations for LEAA jumped from $63 million in 1969 to $268 million in 1970 and more than $885 million in 1975.[25] In addition, revenue sharing and block grant funds were used to augment resources for police improvements.

The calls for new studies and new types of training coupled with the availability of federal funding spawned the discipline of Criminal Justice and an entire industry concerned with providing services and training to police departments. The general quality level of police recruits did improve, more screening programs were developed, in-service training programs became more abundant, and departments were able to acquire more advanced equipment. Small police forces that had been unable to afford many of these activities were particularly well served by the federal programs.

Growing Tensions in the 1970s

At almost the same time that these reforms of the sixties were in the initial stages of implementation, there emerged countervailing pressures from outside police departments and conflict within them. The law and order backlash, the demise of LEAA, and internal tensions over personnel and financial issues were all factors that affected the tenor of police/community relations in the 1970s and 1980s.

A backlash emerged against many of the legal and social reforms of the 1960s based upon a feeling that the reformers were crafting policies that were too permissive. The courts, it was claimed, were contributing by handcuffing the police and protecting the criminal. Fear of the civil rights movement, anti-war groups, and what seemed to be a social revolution added to the general anxiety. More important, perhaps, was the fact that police and political candidates exploited those fears regardless of the factual evidence. Political campaigns hammered away at the Warren Court, the youth counter-culture, civil rights demonstrators, and anti-war protestors.

The politics of implementing the centerpiece of criminal justice efforts of the late 1960s, the Omnibus Crime Control and Safe Streets Act, turned out to be extremely complex. The LEAA, created to assist states and localities, worked through a block grant program under which much of the money appropriated by Congress was disbursed not directly by the federal agency but through state planning agencies (SPAs) and regional planning units (RPUs). Big city mayors charged that the SPAs were dominated by police officials from suburban and rural areas whose decisions failed to deal with high priority problems, particularly the severe street crime problems in the large cities. Moreover, the SPAs and RPUs were charged with a failure to take their planning role seriously by concentrating on *ad hoc* decisionmaking with a focus on individual requests from various departments. Mayor Gribbs of Detroit charged that they "perform no greater function than to assure that everybody gets something, effectively frustrating any efforts to pinpoint funds on solutions of particular problems in individual communities within the region."[26]

While the intention had been to augment financial resources to all facets of the criminal justice system, corrections and the courts received little. The great majority of the money went directly to police departments. It was alleged that by concentrating on obtaining new weapons and equipment, it was the small departments that were primarily benefiting from the politics of the SPAs, what LEAA detractors referred to as "toys for boys" programs. Some legislative challengers to the program suggested that the real beneficiaries of the block grant were the consulting firms that had sprung up around the country to provide advice and services to state agencies and local police departments.

The LEAA program presented serious difficulties of coordination and accountability. Moreover, despite all the funding, there seemed to be no clear impact on the crime problem. While part of the problem was perception, another major facet of the crime picture had to do with demographics. The baby-boom generation reached and then moved through the volatile age range in which they were most likely to commit crimes. In the end, the LEAA was dismantled to be replaced by the National Institute of Justice, which took over the research and data gathering functions of its predecessor as its major responsibility.

The LEAA was not the only federal program that provided added financial resources to state and local law enforcement bodies. Municipalities employed money from general revenue sharing, the Comprehensive Employment and Training Act (CETA), and various categorical grants to subsidize general operating budgets (even though that was a clear violation of the intent of most of the grant programs). That left flexibility to concentrate local revenues in politically popular programs, like law enforcement, though not necessarily in areas such as pay and benefits that would have pleased officers. The economic downturns of the 1970s, though, meant a squeeze on state and local budgets. Cutbacks in federal grant programs added additional pressure. In some areas, like California and Massachusetts, tax revolts forced layoffs or pay freezes.

The late 1960s and 1970s saw growing intradepartmental conflicts, some of which were characterized as labor disputes while others were simply labeled morale problems. Many police officers and their superiors were angry at the treatment they felt they were receiving at the hands of the public, the politicians, and the courts. Often not the kind of people who like change, police officers resisted what they saw as interference in departmental operations. They seemed to be caught in a squeeze between demands for attention to human relations, on the one hand, and calls to get tough on crime and restore order to society, on the other. There were other changes in progress that had important impacts upon departmental politics. Several large cities elected substantial numbers of black candidates who, in turn, appointed minority officials to positions that had historically been occupied by whites. Some cities managed the transition better than others, but it was clear that things were going to change. Affirmative action hiring and promotion was another focal point of tension. Police unions resisted the changes and minority officers formed counterorganizations. As financial pressures increased, thus limiting the availability of promotions and raises, the intradepartmental tensions rose and reached a high point in the late 1970s, when several cities were forced to make major layoff decisions. Contracts called for a last-hired, first-fired rule (sometimes referred to as the LIFO rule, last in, first out) in layoffs, but for some departments that meant losing substantial numbers of minority officers hired under affirmative action programs that were either voluntary or court ordered mechanisms to remedy past discrimination. Federal district courts prohibited LIFO layoffs in some situations where police unions insisted upon traditional seniority-based decisions.[27] The federal government had supported the minority officers in such cases until the Reagan administration changed the Department of Justice (DOJ) policy to insistance upon the LIFO principle.[28]

By the end of the seventies, as several state advisory committees for the Commission on Civil Rights noted, police/community relations were deteriorating in several areas around the country. Publicity surrounding particularly troubling violent incidents in Miami, Philadelphia, and New York City prompted renewed criticism and reexamination of police operations.

COURTS AND POLICE ISSUES

Despite the wide variation in environment and departmental characteristics, most observers who have examined the police over the past three decades have generally agreed on the most controversial issues. For a variety of reasons, federal courts have been asked to resolve some of these questions, though the sheer volume of such cases does not begin to approach that found in the housing, schools, mental health, and prisons areas examined in earlier chapters.

The Issue Agenda

The most common recurring issues raised by police critics include abuse of physical force (deadly force as well as less severe violent incidents), discriminatory behavior (in the direct sense of abusive language or conduct on the basis of race or in the more indirect sense of discriminatory patterns of police services), personnel practices that fail to ensure adequate representation of women and minorities on a police force and in all specialties within a department, inadequate supervision and oversight of police conduct, and failure to provide adequate and effective means for redress of citizen complaints. The first difficulty one confronts in addressing these issues is determining how to conceptualize them.

Are the complaints against the police issues of individual conduct or are they institutional? If, as many police officers have argued, misconduct is a matter of individual misbehavior—a question of a few bad apples, as it were—then the remedies will be quite different from those one might suggest if the abuses stemmed from departmental policy. While there was a period in which some police officials felt themselves sufficiently powerful so as to openly approve or even suggest excessive force or discriminatory action, those days have passed. Rather, the critics argue, there are many institutional norms or policies that are informal and which may, in fact, contradict the formally promulgated departmental policies prohibiting misconduct. Goldstein observed:

> A citizen's complaint alleging wrongdoing by an officer may in effect challenge a practice that is common throughout the agency. Police officers are frequently accused of having acted improperly despite the fact that their actions were in accord with their instructions from their superiors, in harmony with the actions of fellow officers, and in conformity with long-standing practice. . . .

> The situation is so serious in some agencies that the administrator who desires total compliance with a specific order has to send a special message through informal channels making it clear that he really means, in this particular case, what the formal promulgation says.[29]

In such settings remedies which are aimed at individuals not only fail to solve the problem, but may themselves be unfair to the individual officer involved.[30]

Moreover, Frank Anechiarico has warned, the presence of departmental policies cannot be determined solely on the grounds of specific rules, written or informal.[31] Rather, one must determine in any given department which patterns of behavior are rewarded and which are punished to understand what the departmental policies really are. Failure to punish officers for misconduct and rewards for aggressive action send potent signals as to the real versus the putative policies within a department.

Among the more frequent demands by police reformers is that officials close the gap between real and putative departmental policy and provide officers with reasonably detailed and realistic policy statements on as many areas of police operations as possible. One of the principal purposes of the National Advisory Commission on Criminal Justice Standards and Goals, Task Force on Police was to develop a broad range of standards that could be used as the core of departmental policies.[32] Thus, for example, most departments have attempted to develop understandable policies on the use of deadly force and many are attempting to develop clearer rules on police pursuits of fleeing vehicles. Of course, the presence of such guidelines will not prevent abuses unless they are perceived by line officers to be serious departmental requirements.

In order to deal with community fears that complaints of police misconduct will be ignored or covered-up by local politics and because departmental disciplinary proceedings are primarily designed to deal with internal matters of supervision and control rather than external complaints, police critics have insisted that there must be some way to "watch the watchman." The devices available to the citizen or group with a complaint against the police include the exclusionary rule and other procedural devices that prohibit the fruits of misconduct from being used against the citizen, criminal charges which may be brought against an officer, civil suits against the individual officer charged with police abuse, and oversight and investigations by city executive or legislative officials.

The exclusionary rule that holds that police may not use illegally obtained evidence in a criminal trial and other rulings designed to provide disincentives to officers to take shortcuts in criminal investigations are helpful only to those alleged victims of police misconduct who are tried for a crime. As one commentator put it, in order to determine what remedies are useful to citizens in different settings, one must divide complainants into three groups; "(1) those whom the police do not even consider charging with crimes because they are obviously innocent citizens; (2) those whom the police suspect of having committed crimes but either do not charge with crimes or drop the charges prior to trial; and (3) those who are charged and tried for crimes they are suspected of having committed."[33] So, even assuming that the exclusionary rule works as a deterrent in the third situation, the first two sets of complainants require some other means of pressing their claims.

If the police officer's action was serious enough, as in the case of physical violence, there may be grounds for a criminal complaint under either state or federal law. However, serious criminal charges must be filed and tried by the local prosecutor who, in turn, works closely with the police on a day-to-day basis and requires their cooperation in order to do his or her job. Prosecutors are often unwilling to damage that relationship by issuing charges against officers.[34] Even if charges are filed, they may be extraordinarily difficult to prove. Since many serious incidents occur at night and under circumstances where there may be no witnesses other than the alleged victim and the officer, evidence may not be available to prove the charge. Other officers may be unwilling to provide information about such an incident even if they possess it. This problem is often referred to as the silence of the blue curtain. Jury bias can be a major difficulty since the alleged victim may have been charged by the officer with an offense in connection with the incident that gave rise to the complaint against the officer. Historically, some officers have filed what are known as cover charges in any case in which they perceived a potential complaint against themselves. Such open-ended statutes as breach of the peace, interfering with an officer, and disorderly conduct have often been used for this purpose. The mere fact that the charge is filed places the complainant in the position of a criminal defendant who is bringing a claim against the officer to get even. It also allows police officials to trade dismissal of the charges against the complainant in return for a promise not to proceed with the police abuse claim. In any event many, if not most, complaints against police abuses do not rise to the level of criminal offenses.

It is possible to seek federal prosecution of officers for violation of the complainant's federally protected civil rights. A conspiracy to commit such an act is a felony under federal law, whereas an individual violation of one's civil rights is a misdemeanor. These charges are still very difficult to prove and jury bias is often present.[35] Moreover, federal prosecutors have little incentive, given the press of business, to entertain such a complaint unless it is of a particularly severe nature.

A third option for redress of complaints is a civil suit for monetary damages brought against the offending officer. There are two assumptions behind the idea that a civil damage remedy will be adequate to address police problems. The first is that police misconduct really is a matter of an occasional misstep by particular officers and is not institutional in character or origin. For reasons noted earlier, that may be a questionable assumption. If the officer is in reality obeying formal or informal departmental norms, as award of damages against one officer is both unfair to the officer and ineffective in terms of resolving the more fundamental institutional issues. Second, the theory behind the individual remedy is that there are two parties at issue, the complainant and the officer. The point of the dispute is to reach an accommodation between those parties by settlement or judgment and thereby satisfy all concerned. Critics argue, however, that there is a third party involved, the community, which has an independent interest in the proper operation of its police department quite apart from the particular interests of the individual officer or the specific complainant.[36] In short, the civil damages claim has too narrow a focus to comprehend or confront the problem.

There are other immediate problems associated with the civil suit against the individual officer. First, many of the same problems of proof and jury bias present in criminal cases against police officers arise in civil suits. Second, even if the suit is successful, the officer may not have sufficient resources to permit complainants to recover losses. The prosecution of such a suit is in itself an expensive undertaking, a fact that is likely to discourage many from pursuing otherwise legitimate complaints. While an individual may sue the municipality to recover, most of the same problems apply. The one difference is that juries appear to be somewhat less biased in favor of the city and there is a greater likelihood of recovery. Nevertheless, the problems of proof are enormous and individual suits do not get at the question of illegal patterns and policies of departmental officials.

Presumably, effective oversight by city councils and mayors should help resolve police misconduct issues, but there is little evidence of legislative oversight in this field. Generally, city councils do not become involved with police operations except with respect to budget battles. Legislators have little incentive to engage in such a fight for fear of being labeled as soft on crime or as a defender of criminals. Mayors face similar charges along with the added threat that they may be accused of giving in to petty politics and of refusing to defend their officers. As Goldstein observes, the effort to enhance police professionalism by protecting departments from the influence of local political machines has made it much more difficult for mayors to affect departmental operations.[37] Beyond all that, the police can be a potent political force when they perceive a common threat from an elected official.[38]

Another approach to reducing police misconduct emphasizes the use of improved personnel policies to develop the kind of force that is more likely to encourage public confidence and less likely to engender complaints. In order to do that, departments face problems of inclusion and exclusion. They must screen out the kinds of people likely to create difficulties from predispositions to violence, prejudice, or a lack of a commitment to service. They must simultaneously provide evidence that the departments are open and representative by recruitment of women and minorities to all areas of the police service.[39] Once in the department, officials are obligated to ensure that promotions are not made in a discriminatory fashion.[40] After the staffing pattern is established, the department must ensure continuing training in human relations and such specific skills as are necessary to cope with the wide range of demands on officers.

Affirmative action programs undertaken to achieve some of these ends have had three obstacles. In some departments the minority hiring programs were instituted because of proven or pending charges of discrimination. In communities where the police image was poor or where there was real or suspected discrimination by the department, minority recruitment was difficult.[41] In departments where there was discrimination in place, efforts to alter the organization's operation were often stressful. Finally, the advent of layoffs and limits on available promotions made affirmative action hiring and promotion more threatening to white men presently in the department.

While it is true that changing personnel practices in police departments since the mid-1960s have altered departments dramatically, they have not been a panacea for misconduct.[42] The remaining alternatives have been citizen complaint procedures, either through internal police-operated processes or through external so-called civilian review boards.

The "almost total lack of effective channels for redress of complaints against police conduct" was cited by the Kerner Commission as one of the principal sources of hostility toward police.[43] It is not that departments lacked any kind of means for filing complaints, but rather the perception was that it was useless to go to the trouble since little was likely to come of a grievance. The list of charges against police complaint procedures is formidable. First, because the disciplinary processes were set primarily to maintain internal discipline and not to respond to external complaints, the procedures are neither receptive nor responsive to citizen grievances. More specifically, critics charge that complaint procedures often discourage or intimidate would-be complainants. Deterrents include the use or threat of "cover charges," failure of police officials to cooperate or assist those wishing to file complaints, and, in some cases, threats that unless a complainant can prove the charges he or she will face either a libel suit by the officer or his union or a criminal charge of filing a false police report.[44] Police detractors charge that the departments simply cannot be trusted to investigate themselves since they had proven themselves to be biased against complainants. Even where they did find misconduct, some departments assessed three- to five-day suspensions for offenses which, if they had been committed outside the department, would have been treated as criminal matters, sometimes felonies. On the other hand, the treatment of officers by disciplinary boards was not evenhanded in the sense that extremely harsh penalties were invoked for relatively minor departmental infractions while very serious outside violations went nearly unpunished. The argument is that this reinforces the officer's tendency to support his department and his colleagues against any outside criticism in order to protect himself from internal attack. Critics also charge that complainants meet with lengthy delays in the resolution of complaints and are provided with little or no information about the progress of the proceeding or the disposition of the case once it is resolved.

For some time, suggestions were made that the creation of civilian review boards would solve shortcomings of complaint procedures and increase confidence that there would be impartial and independent resolution of citizen challenges to police behavior. However, external review panels faced considerable criticism both from police and the groups that had placed so much hope in them at the outset. Police charged that civilians simply lacked an understanding of the "real world" in which the police officer operates. Board members were, officers complained, inexperienced and lacking in police expertise. Moreover, officials claimed that the boards were harmful to departmental morale and discouraged aggressive law enforcement. Police reformers complained that the civilian review boards simply did not work because they lacked the leverage and resources to do their jobs properly. Furthermore, they met solid political resistance from the department and police unions.[45] Most of the boards that were created were later dismantled.

Judicial Responses

In sum, there has been a variety of principal issues and reactions to police misconduct which have met with varying success and considerable controversy. Federal courts have been asked to respond to a number of these issues with requested remedies, ranging from negative injunctions that ordered the police to cease illegal behavior to mandatory policy changes in matters from personnel to citizen complaint processing. One way to understand the role federal judges have played in misconduct controversies is to consider the contexts in which they have been asked to intervene. These include labor disputes, constitutional criminal procedures issues, civil rights activity and racial tension, antiwar protests and other demonstrations, and claims of harassment of socially stigmatized groups, including vagrants, hippies, homosexuals, and the retarded or handicapped.

Injunctions were frequently used weapons of management in the formative years of the union movement. However, unions also learned how to use injunctions, producing the first Supreme Court ruling on police abuse and an important lower court precedent in the bargain. *Hague v. Congress for Industrial Organization* is still cited as the foundation ruling for the use of federal injunctions to prohibit illegal conduct by police departments.[46] Decided in 1939, *Hague* predated the development of the so-called civil rights injunction in school desegregation cases. The case arose when a New Jersey federal district court issued an injunction barring efforts by the Mayor and Police Chief to prevent the CIO from organizing workers in Jersey City. The lower court found that the Jersey City officials had "adopted and enforced the deliberate policy of excluding and removing from Jersey City the agents of the respondents; have interfered with their right of passage upon the streets and access to the parks of the city; [and] that these ends have been accomplished by force and violence despite the fact that the persons affected were acting in an orderly and peaceful manner."[47] The Police Chief and his men had harassed union organizers entering the city, denied them parade permits, prevented distribution of union literature, interfered with organizers' attempts to communicate with workers, and, in some instances, simply ran union people out of town. The Supreme Court upheld the injunction with minor modifications.

An even broader injunction against police action was delivered by Judge Swygert of the Northern District of Indiana in 1948.[48] Violence erupted in a strike between the United Furniture Workers and the Smith Cabinet Manufacturing Company. An injunction was issued defining the boundaries of acceptable union picketing and prohibiting further violent behavior. The union began meeting in a local courthouse to plan strategy. Officials did not object and there was no indication that union members were interfering with the conduct of normal business. State police officers began attending the meetings to take notes. Swygert enjoined the officers from attending on grounds that their presence interfered with the union members' First Amendment rights.

Federal court responses to police misconduct in the area of criminal arrests, searches, and seizures, the use of illegal confessions and the like, predated even the labor relations cases.[49] While some of the rulings in this field involved injuncitons that prohibited illegal detentions and the use of the so-called third degree, most relied on the suppression doctrine to deny police the use of illegally obtained information at trial.[50] The suppression doctrine was not applied to the states in the form we now call the exclusionary rule until the 1961 ruling in *Mapp v. Ohio*.[51]

It has always been difficult to deal with a criminal suspect's demands to be treated lawfully. In some sense that discussion is at root a debate over whether we do or should maintain a real presumption of innocence for those arrested and charged with a crime. If it is not presumed that those arrested by the police are guilty, rules regarding the process of litigation are concerned with protection of the innocent against wrongful conviction. If, on the other hand, the presumption is that the police would not have arrested someone unless they were actually guilty, then procedural rules merely interfere with the proper processing of a criminal. Hence, Justice Cardozo's famous dictum that "[t]he criminal is to go free because the constable has blundered."[52]

From the police officer's vantage point, there are at least two answers. First, the officer does not accept the idea that he or she is arresting an innocent person, therefore procedural rules simply interfere with getting criminals to their proper punishment. For other officers the primary job is crime control, which is concerned with removing threatening people from the street. Whether suspects are ultimately acquitted is not nearly as significant as the fact that they were removed for at least some period. Except in those cases in which the officer takes a special interest in assuring punishment for a suspect, the procedural rules may be no more than an inconvenience.

Justice Brandeis, in his now famous dissent in the *Olmstead* case, argued vigorously that the rules of criminal procedure serve a public interest far wider than the concerns of the officer and the suspect:

> Our Government is the potent, the omnipresent teacher. For good or for ill, it teaches the whole people by its example. Crime is contagious. If the Government becomes a lawbreaker, it breeds contempt for law; it invites every man to become a law unto himself; it invites anarchy. To declare that in the administration of the criminal law the end justifies the means—to declare that the Government may commit crimes in order to secure the conviction of a private criminal—would bring terrible retribution.[53]

Writing for the majority in *Mapp*, Justice Clark recalled that while the Court had held in 1949 that the Fourth Amendment protection against unreasonable searches and seizures applied to states and localities as well as to federal authorities, it had not applied the suppression doctrine then in force in federal courts to state trials.[54] The expectation was that suits against police officers or other remedies would be adequate to discourage illegal police activity without need of an exclusion of illegally obtained evidence from the trial. Clark observed that the lesson of the experience in the states since the 1949 ruling was that "such other remedies have been worthless and futile."[55]

Despite the complex technical questions raised in the wake of Warren Court rulings on searches and seizures and the admissibility of confessions, the disputes generally involved arguments in regard to the nature of discrete events, a specific police officer's decision to seek a warrant or to search without one. Other challenges to police practices more commonly presented criticism of patterns of police conduct on a much broader scale.

While some of the challenges to police behavior based on allegations of racial bias or attempts to block civil rights activity originated in northern cities, it was the clashes of voting rights and desegregation marchers with southern police forces that provided some of the most brutal and tragic examples of police misconduct during the past several decades. The sight of outright assaults on civil rights marchers on nationwide television exacerbated the storm trooper image of police, and, unfair though it may have been, was transferred to other officers around the country. The NAACP, the Student Nonviolent Coordinating Committee, the Southern Christian Leadership Conference, and other groups asked federal courts to step in to declare their rights and enjoin police organizations from further brutality and harassment, whether conducted independently or at the direction of elected officials.

One of the most egregious such cases arose in connection with efforts by Alabama police to block voting rights drives in and around Selma, which culminated in the infamous Pettus Bridge incident on March 7, 1965. Judge Johnson summarized police conduct prior to that event:

> The evidence in this case reflects that, particularly as to Selma, Dallas County, Alabama, an almost continuous pattern of conduct has existed on the part of defendant Sheriff Clark, his deputies, and his auxiliary deputies known as "possemen" of harassment, intimidation, coercion, threatening conduct, and, sometimes, brutal mistreatment toward these plaintiffs and others of their class who were engaged in their demonstrations for the purpose of encouraging Negroes to attempt to register to vote and to protest discriminatory voter registration practices in Alabama. This harassment, intimidation and brutal treatment has ranged from mass arrests without just cause to forced marches for several miles into the countryside, with the sheriff's deputies and members of his posse herding the Negro demonstrators at a rapid pace through the use of electrical shocking devices (designed for use on cattle) and night sticks to prod them along. The Alabama State Troopers, under the command of defendant Lingo, have, upon several occasions, assisted the defendant Sheriff Clark in these activities, and the State Troopers, along with Sheriff Clark as an "invited guest," have extended the harassment and intimidating activities into Perry County, where, on February 18, 1965, when approximately 300 Negroes were engaged in a peaceful demonstration by marching from a Negro church to the Perry County Courthouse for the purpose of publicly protesting racially discriminatory voter registration practices in Perry County, Alabama, the Negro demonstrators were stopped by the State troopers under the command of the defendant Lingo, and the Negro demonstrators were at that time pushed, prodded, struck, beaten and knocked down. This action resulted in the injury of several Negroes, one of whom was shot by an Alabama State Trooper and subsequently died.[56]

The Pettus Bridge incident occurred shortly after the Perry County Courthouse disaster. Some of the same law enforcement officials, with the knowledge of Governor George Wallace, moved to block a planned peaceful and orderly protest march from Selma to the state capital at Montgomery. The officers waited for the marchers at the

Pettus Bridge on the Selma road. At that point, mounted officers and others on foot charged the marchers, leaving more than seventy-five blacks wounded in their wake. Following that incident, a number of demonstrators filed suit against the governor and state and local law enforcement officials. They sought to enjoin further illegal police conduct and court ordered protection for the rescheduled Selma-to-Montgomery march. Judge Johnson provided both the negative and the positive relief.[57]

Harassment and attacks on blacks and white demonstrators also surfaced in Jackson, Mississippi, as well as Greenville and Prattville, Alabama, producing federal court orders that barred police misconduct and required proper police respect for the exercise of constitutional rights.[58] Officials argued that there was adequate protection for the plaintiffs in state courts when charges against them were brought to trial. Judge Whitaker replied that such alternatives did not protect citizens from harassment and intimidation or the burden of defending against false or frivolous charges brought against them by abusive police officers.[59]

Requests for injunctive relief from police misconduct in civil rights matters were not, however, limited to the South. Baltimore police, in a massive manhunt for two suspects alleged to have killed one police officer and to have wounded another, moved into the black community and, over a period of nineteen days in the winter of 1964 conducted more than three hundred searches, many of which were without warrants or were based on warrants issued on the representations of anonymous informants. Heavily armed men converged on the homes of black families at all hours and, in most cases, without probable cause. With the support of the NAACP, four plaintiffs brought suit on behalf of families in the black community seeking injunctive relief against further police abuse. Judge Thomsen recognized the weight of the evidence against city officials but refused to grant the injunction, observing that he was satisfied that the officials saw the problem and would act to prevent similar occurrences in the future. The Court of Appeals reversed the trial court finding that "[this] case reveals a series of the most flagrant invasions of privacy ever to come under the scrutiny of a federal court."[60]

While the *Hague* ruling had involved a finding that the police chief had an intentional policy to drive out the union organizers, the cases decided later, including the civil rights injunction cases, relied on the existence of a pattern and practice of police abuse of a sort that a reasonable commanding officer should have known about and could have prevented.[61] Several courts found that it was not necessary for police officials to take specific actions to produce violations of citizens' rights. If there was reason to believe that police officials were aware of violations and took no action to prevent or correct them, and if there was a pattern of misconduct, the court would be prepared to intervene.[62]

Federal judges followed the same approach to suits concerning anti-war protests and demonstrations as they had in the desegregation and voting rights cases. Citing *Hague* and the Alabama precedents, the Second Circuit upheld an injunction issued by Judge Mansfield against the Port Authority of New York and New Jersey.[63] The injunction prohibited Port Authority police from excluding or harassing peaceful and orderly opponents of the Vietnam War who sought to distribute pamphlets and converse with those who would stop to talk with them about the issue. They were, in fact, put "on notice of their constitutional responsibility to protect those properly exercising rights of expression."[64]

The Seventh Circuit was confronted with a dispute in which reporters covering the 1968 Democratic National Convention and the protests surrounding that event sought an order prohibiting police from interfering with their efforts to gather news. Judge Campbell dismissed the suit, but the appeals court reversed.[65] Judge Swygert, writing for the appellate panel, underscored the police chief's obligation to take action to correct police abuse, whether it was prompted by official policy or not, concluding "From a legal standpoint, it makes no difference whether the plaintiffs' constitutional rights are violated as a result of police behavior which is the product of the active encouragement and direction of their superiors or as a result of the superiors' mere acquiescence in such behavior."[66] On the other hand, other courts held that individual incidents not apparently part of any pattern of misconduct or failure to perform would, under most circumstances, be unlikely to provide justification for injunctions against police officials.[67]

If police officers were the symbols of the white-dominated society to some racial minorities, it was equally the case that so-called hippies were symbols of the counter-culture to the police. Hippies, people with unconventional lifestyles, homosexuals, and others who were treated as somehow strange or undesirable encountered varying degrees of police harassment. There emerged a stereotype in which it was assumed that those who appeared to be hippies were drug addicts, draft evaders, irresponsible drifters, and, because of their unpredictable behavior and disrespect for authority, troublesome to have around either in the community generally or at public events.

Suits were launched in several communities that sought injunctions to ban further police abuse where there had been repeated and unjustified searches and harassment of individuals in their own home, a pattern of traffic stops with searches based on the fact that the driver had long hair, and exclusion of people appearing to be hippies from events at which political speakers were to appear.[68] Despite the fact that the judges involved often made it a point to note that their decision "was not any apology for hippiedom as a way of life," plaintiffs obtained favorable decisions in several such cases.[69]

The issue of injunctions against police abuse found its way back to the Supreme Court in 1974 and again in 1976. As the discussion of some of the cases in earlier chapters indicated, that was the transition period during which the Burger Court was modifying a variety of existing areas of law. That shift was to have important consequences for litigation challenging police misconduct, with the Court admonishing lower courts to grant greater deference to police practices.

The 1974 ruling came in *Allee v. Medrano,* a suit challenging conduct by the Texas Rangers and the Starr County Sheriff's office during an organizing effort by the United Farm Workers of America (UFA) directed at farm workers serving area growers.[70] The UFA organizers charged law enforcement officers with harassment, verbal and physical abuse, the use of vague statutes to justify arrests, and interference in a lawful labor activity on behalf of the growers. The trial record revealed beatings, threats, and false arrests. In one situation two organizers who were part of a demonstration against Missouri-Pacific trains transporting produce out of the area were arrested. "As another train passed, the Rangers held these two prisoners' bodies so that their faces were only inches from the train."[71] Sheriff's deputies delivered an anti-union newspaper throughout the confrontation. The Court concluded, "Thus, these were not a series of isolated incidents but a prevailing pattern throughout the controversy."[72]

The opinion for the sharply divided Supreme Court vacated several determinations by the lower court regarding the application of Texas statutes, but affirmed the injunction insofar as it was directed against police misconduct. Following earlier injunctions cases, the Court found a pattern of police misconduct adequate grounds for an injunction. While there were allegations of deliberate efforts by police officials to drive out the union in both the *Allee* and *Hague* cases, the Court plainly did not base its judgment on any theory of conspiracy but rather on the existence of a pattern of illegal conduct. Although Justice Douglas noted that the "complaint charged that the enjoined conduct was but one part of a single plan by the defendants, and the district court found a pervasive pattern of intimidation in which the law enforcement authorities sought to suppress appellees' constitutional rights," the remainder of the opinion makes it quite clear that it was the pattern of conduct, and not a requirement that plaintiffs prove some kind of illegal intent, that justified the injunction. The Court's actual holding came a few pages later:

> Isolated incidents of police misconduct under valid statutes would not, of course, be cause for the exercise of a federal court's equitable powers. But "[w]e have not hesitated on direct review to strike down applications of constitutional statutes which we have found to be unconstitutionally applied. . . . Where, as here, there is a pervasive pattern of police misconduct, injunctive relief is appropriate.[73]

Douglas's opinion for the Court was joined by Brennan, Stewart, Marshall, and Blackmun. Burger, writing for himself, Rehnquist, and White, concurred in part and dissented in part. Powell did not take part in the case. But since Burger and the others agreed only with that portion of the Court's decision that vacated part of the lower court ruling, it was, in reality, a dissent. Douglas would leave the Court on the very day in 1975 when the next major police injunction case came before the Court. Moreover, this time Powell would participate and it was to be the three *Allee* dissenters plus Powell who voted to grant *certiorari* in the Philadelphia police abuse case, *Rizzo v. Goode.*

Chapter 11 provides a detailed treatment of the *Rizzo* litigation. For the present, it is enough to note that the district court had found a pattern of police misconduct involving physical and verbal abuse of which police superiors were aware and in which they took virtually no action. Following the liability finding, a remedy was negotiated with city attorneys in which the court ordered police officials to implement an improved police-controlled citizen complaint review procedure. The Third Circuit Court of Appeals panel affirmed unanimously. Eight *amicus curiae* briefs were filed as the case came to hearing before the Supreme Court, with all eight briefs in support of the lower court ruling.

In an effort to be extremely deferential to police officials, Judge Fullam prepared his opinion in such a way that he found a pattern of police misconduct, but he did not find a deliberate policy of police abuse on the part of city officials. Justice Stewart found the record inadequate, on those grounds, to support a finding against the Police Department, the Commissioner, and other city leaders. Hence, the *Rizzo v. Goode* opinion was prepared by Justice Rehnquist for himself and Justices Stewart, Powell, White, and Burger. Though he saw serious procedural defects in the record, Rehnquist reached the merits of the case.[74] He reinterpreted both the *Hague* and *Allee* opinions and required "an intentional, concerted, and indeed conspiratorial effort to deprive" the plaintiffs of their rights in order to justify an injunction.[75] At a minimum, that requires that those charging police misconduct who wish anything more than an individual remedy against a particular police officer must prove direct linkages between the police authorities whom they wish to enjoin and a deliberate violation of citizen rights. He managed this reinterpretation by using selective quotations and paraphrasing of the *Allee* decision.[76] The opinion for the Court concludes with a general admonition, quite apart from any conceivable fact pattern in such a police misconduct case, that as a matter of federalism such matters just ought to be left to state officials.

Blackmun's dissent, joined by Marshall and Brennan, pointed out that the Court's effort to distinguish *Allee* and *Hague* was simply unconvincing to one who had studied those opinions and the facts of the *Rizzo* case.[77] Referring to the substantial body of case law holding that it is enough that an official had knowledge of his subordinates' illegal conduct and took no action to stop it, Blackmun observed that Rehnquist's holding was a dramatic departure from a rule of law applied around the nation in police misconduct cases.[78]

The Burger Court majority rendered other decisions that made it extremely difficult to obtain redress against institutional police misconduct. It substantially modified the exclusionary rule into what has come to be known as the rule of reasonableness, which essentially maintains that evidence obtained in violation of Fourth Amendment search and seizure rules may be admissible if the evidence was obtained in good faith by the police officer.[79] Demonstrations of that kind of state of mind are particularly difficult. Changes in the requirements to show that one has legal standing have further complicated efforts to obtain any redress apart from a suit against a particular criminal justice officer for an individual act of abuse.[80] Moreover, recent rulings on the so-called abstention doctrine, which requires federal courts to abstain from involvement in cases that may be ongoing or forthcoming in state courts, makes it difficult for complainants to shoulder the costs of litigation that arise if they are required to defend themselves in state courts and then proceed to federal courts in search of injuctive relief.[81]

As in other policy areas considered in earlier chapters, an understanding of litigation in the area of police misconduct requires a sensitivity to the political dynamics that mold policy and behavior in that field. Particularly during the 1970s and into the 1980s, police officers have faced internal changes and external scrutiny.

POLITICAL DYNAMICS OF POLICE REFORM

The police studies of the past two decades have presented several findings that are useful for understanding the politics of police reform. They concern such matters as tensions within the individual police officer as he or she goes about the job of policing, the social or organizational dynamics which guide the relationship of the officer to his fellows, and the facets of the interaction between the police department and the community it serves.

Niederhoffer, Rubenstein, and others have observed that an understanding of police behavior requires consideration of the effect of the police occupation on the individual officer.[82] The problems of isolation and alienation are two of the most commonly cited personal reactions. The person who joins the force to protect and serve friends and neighbors often finds it difficult to maintain friendships and social ties. Work schedules are unusual, making it difficult to sustain a normal lifestyle.[83] Former friends may act differently toward the officer because he or she is now a symbol of authority or thought to be too straitlaced to be comfortable company.[84] These factors plus less than munificent salaries, limited possibilities for advancement, and the element of personal danger take a high toll on sobriety and marital bliss. Niederhoffer argues that one result of these influences is anomie, "confusion, frustration, alienation, and despair."[85] These personal reactions to the job, when coupled with the types of people who choose a police career and the nature of the duty the officer performs, play important roles in the development of what Skolnick has termed the police officer's working personality.[86] The isolation officers sometimes feel is all the more ironic given the level of public contact required in their work.

Relationships within departments are also considerably more complex than the sometimes monolithic image conveyed in the popular media. On the one hand, precisely because of the tensions officers often experience in their personal lives, relationships with their colleagues in the department, both on and off the job, are all the more important. The so-called blue curtain, the tendency for officers to either protect their colleagues when criticized or to refuse to take action themselves against a fellow officer, is often attributed to this need for mutual support in an interpersonal sense and mutual protection on the street.[87] That sense of fraternity is fostered in police training and, since there is virtually no significant possibility for lateral entry into a department, all officers are exposed to a similar socialization process. Some of the factors influencing relationships among officers include the craftsman's image (the street officer's credential), role conflicts, the new school/old school tension, frustration with disciplinary inequities, labor/management tensions, and the supervisor's tenuous balancing act.

Ironically, as several commentators have noted, the community vests the greatest discretion in the police service at the lowest portion of the hierarchy. The newest and least experienced officers are the patrol officers. They are often the first on the scene of an incident and the least prepared to react given their inexperience and limited knowledge of the street.[88] Often the best of these young officers will move on to special squads or detective bureaus by the time they have achieved the status of what Skolnick refers to as the craftsman, a first rate street cop. Of course, there can be disagreement even within departments as to the characteristics of a really good officer. Indeed the reforms of the late 1960s and early 1970s added to the disagreement in what has come to be known as the debate over professionalization.[89] In some departments, tensions have mounted between younger college educated officers, intent on incorporating the lessons of sociology and political science into their jobs, and older officers who taunted these would-be professionals for their naiveté. Moreover, the reformers posed a threat to established work ways and social patterns. In some sense, these young officers were a manifestation within the departments of the pressures for change surrounding police agencies. The fact that some of these officers were able to parlay their educational credentials and political sensitivity into early promotions over more experienced colleagues did not help calm the tensions within the department. The presence of affirmative action promotion requirements and fiscal constraints that limited the availability of higher rank slots were also factors in this stress.

It is often at the point of promotion that structural fragmentation begins. Often bored by the day-to-day trivial matters that occupy their time, many officers desire a transfer or promotion to detective operations or special duty which allows them to get out of the uniform and do the interesting and exciting work they sought when they joined the department. Promotions are also important in hierarchical as well as functional divisions within the department. Lieutenants are often still considered by line officers to have street cop credentials, but captains and above are frequently thought to be too far removed from their days as patrol officers to really remember what it is like out there on the street. While discipline is maintained, the distance becomes important. One of the manifestations of the rank differentiation tension is frustration within the department over discipline. Whereas higher ranking officials are accused by their sub-ordinates of arbitrary behavior toward patrol officers because of political pressure on the department, which results in low officer morale and decreased performance, external critics charge that higher level officers are protecting their subordinates against proper accountability.[90]

On the other hand, external criticism of the department can serve as a catalyst to unite the department since it provides a common focal point for officers and their su-periors to concentrate their frustration. While it may be true that police reactions to outside critics occasionally contain a measure of hypocrisy, given the fact that police officers often know of, and tolerate, individuals within the department who ought to be disciplined, it is an oversimplification to write off police responses as dishonest.[91] As craftsmen, officers have pride in their performance and a great deal of pent up resent-ment at the way they are treated by the community.

Another area in which police administrators find themselves caught between local politics and departmental tensions is in the field of labor/management relations. The same union that attempts to work with departmental officials to obtain pay increases from city hall will challenge those administrators in matters of police discipline or sig-nificant changes in work rules.

James Q. Wilson and others have argued that local political forces play an even wider role in setting the ground rules for police operations than those described above.[92] They influence the style of policing that is likely to be adopted by any given department. Police departments are organizations, and just as individuals within organizations re-spond to the rewards and strictures imposed by their organizations, so departments re-spond to their sense of the environment within which they operate. Wilson identified three such styles: the legalistic, the watchman, and the service approach. The first of these, the legalistic, holds that the job of the police is to enforce the laws, all the laws, and to do so in an impartial and politically independent manner. That is indeed what many citizens expect of police. However, few departments have the resources to enforce more than a portion of the many laws currently in existence. Moreover, few communi-ties would like the amount of police intrusiveness into their day-to-day lives that would result if the police really enforced all the laws. The compromise is to accept the role of watchman in which the task is to maintain order by enforcing laws against serious criminal activity and holding other questionable street behavior within tolerable limits. The definition of what is tolerable and what sorts of activities shall be considered high priority matters is very much a political determination. The third style, the service de-partment, arises because some communities simply do not have enough serious crime to make that the most frequent demand on police resources. Rather, in such communi-ties, officers spend little of their actual energy on crime control and much more on performing a variety of services ranging from traffic direction to first aid.[93] The conflict between the public perception of police behavior as legalistic and the reality of service or watchman activities creates a mismatch in performance and expectations. Moreover, the level of service demands on the police officer can foster frustration on the part of officers who are criticized for inadequate crime control when they are required to expend their time and energies on providing services.[94]

It appeared in the developing years of the LEAA that the federal government would, as the study commissions of the 1960s suggested, play an active leadership role in police policy and performance. One of the principal vehicles for that federal influence was to be control over grant funds to state and local enforcement bodies. Two factors became apparent which limited the federal influence to recruitment and training issues. The first was that the federal officials never seriously attempted to employ the leverage of funding to pressure departments into meeting demands for local accountability. Several of the studies carried out by the state advisory commissions to the Commission on Civil Rights and the Commission itself pointed out that the federal government could have threatened a cutoff in funding in cases of brutality or discriminatory enforcement, but that it did not take seriously enforcement action in the fiscal area.[95] Apart from the LEAA block grant program, other sections of federal law, including Title VI of the Civil Rights Act of 1964 and the nondiscrimintion provisions of the Revenue Sharing Act, were available to federal authorities. However, there was little political incentive for federal administrators to face the pressure that would have come from a funding cutoff.

CONCLUSION

In sum, the politics of police administration must be understood as an admixture of personal tensions faced by the individual police officer, departmental politics, community demands and political conflict, national political pressures, and societal problems that range from urban blight to racism. As in most fields considered to this point in this volume, the problems of police abuse are not new, but are often manifestations of historical development. Clearly, the stresses of the contemporary environment have exacerbated some features of the continuing difficulties concerning just who shall watch the watchmen. The courts have been asked to play a role in resolving that question, a role they performed relatively actively over the years. The Supreme Court has recently admonished those courts to accept a less active role than they have in the past. In addition, it has added a number of procedural strictures on the kinds and character of cases that federal courts may even consider in this field. Nevertheless, there is no reason to believe federal judges will be spared the difficulty of addressing police misconduct disputes in one form or another. The most important ruling in the field that is to guide district judges is the opinion in *Rizzo v. Goode*. Chapter 11 investigates that interesting litigation.

NOTES

1. Arthur Niederhoffer, *Behind the Shield: The Police in Urban Society* (Garden City: Doubleday, 1967), p. 1.
2. George Edwards, "Order and Civil Liberties: A Complex Role for the Police," 64 *Mich. L. Rev.* 47, 50 (1965).
3. Michael Lipsky, *Street Level Bureaucracy* (New York: Russel Sage Foundation, 1980). *See also* William K. Muir, Jr.; *Police: Streetcorner Politicians* (Chicago: Univ. of Chicago Press, 1977).
4. President's Commission on Law Enforcement and Administration of Justice, *Task Force*

Report: The Police (Wash., DC: Government Printing Office, 1967), p. 3 [hereafter *Task Force Report*].

5. *See generally* Charles Reith, *The Police Idea: Its History and Evolution in England in the Eighteenth Century and After* (London: Oxford Univ. Press, 1938); and A.A.W. Ramsay, *Sir Robert Peel* (New York: Dodd, Mead, 1938).

6. Jerome Skolnick *Justice Without Trial: Law Enforcement in Democratic Society* (New York: Wiley, 1966), pp. 1–2.

7. National Commission on Law Observance and Enforcement, *Report on Police* (Wash., DC: Government Printing Office, 1931), p. 51, in Herman Goldstein, *Policing a Free Society* (Cambridge: Ballinger, 1977), p. 133.

8. Edwards, *supra* note 2, at 52–53. *See also* National Advisory Commission on Civil Disorders, *Report of the National Advisory Commission on Civil Disorders* (New York: Bantam, 1968), pp. 307–9 [hereafter the Kerner Commission Report].

9. *See, e.g.,* Tennessee Advisory Committee to the U.S. Commission on Civil Rights, *Civic Crisis—Civic Challenge: Police-Community Relations in Memphis* (Wash., DC: U.S. Commission on Civil Rights, 1978), p. 3; and Minnesota Advisory Committee to the U.S. Commission on Civil Rights, *Police Practices in the Twin Cities* (Wash., DC: U.S. Commission on Civil Rights, 1981), p. 83.

10. U.S. Commission on Civil Rights, *Who Is Guarding the Guardians? A Report on Police Practices* (Wash., DC: U.S. Commission on Civil Rights, 1981), pp. 3–4.

11. *Mapp v. Ohio,* 367 U.S. 643 (1961). *See also Miranda v. Arizona,* 384 U.S. 436 (1966); and *Escobedo v. Illinois,* 387 U.S. 478 (1964).

12. *See, e.g.,* Note: "The Administration of Complaints by Civilians Against the Police," 77 *Harv. L. Rev.* 499 (1964); Note: "The Federal Injunction as a Remedy for Unconstitutional Police Conduct," 78 *Yale L.J.* 143 (1968); Note "Injunctive Relief for Violations of Constitutional Rights by the Police," 45 *Colo. L. Rev.* 91 (1973); and Note: "Use of Section 1983 to Remedy Unconstitutional Police Conduct: Guarding the Guards," 5 *Harv. C.R.-C.L. L. Rev.* 104 (1970).

13. Warren Burger, "Who Will Watch the Watchman?" 14 *Am. U.L. Rev.* 1 (1964), p. 16. *See also* Wayne LaFave and Frank Remington, "Controlling the Police: The Judge's Role in Making and Reviewing Law Enforcement Decisions," 63 *Mich. L. Rev.* 987 (1965).

14. Burger, at 18.

15. *See, e.g.,* Note: "The Federal Injunction as a Remedy. . . ," *supra* note 12, at 143.

16. Goldstein, *supra* note 7, at 5; American Bar Association, *The Urban Police Function* (Chicago: ABA, 1972).

17. Kerner Commission Report, *supra* note 8, at 6.

18. *Id.,* at 8.

19. *Id.,* at 6.

20. *Task Force Report, supra* note 4, at 1.

21. *Id.,* at 144–45.

22. *Id.,* at 149.

23. Florida Advisory Committee to the U.S. Commission on Civil Rights, *Policed by the White Male Minority* (Wash., DC: U.S. Commission on Civil Rights, 1976); Arizona Advisory Committee to the U.S. Commission on Civil Rights, *Justice in Flagstaff* (Wash., DC: U.S. Commission on Civil Rights, 1977); South Dakota Advisory Committee to the U.S. Commission on Civil Rights, *Liberty and Justice for All* (1977); North Dakota Advisory Committee to the U.S. Commission on Civil Rights, *American Justice Issues in North Dakota* (1978); Kentucky Advisory Committee to the U.S. Commission on Civil Rights, *A Paper Commitment: EEO in the Kentucky Bureau of State Police* (1978); *Civic Crisis—Civic Challenge, supra* note 9; California Advisory Committee to the U.S. Commission on Civil Rights, *Police-Community Relations in San Jose* (1980); Maryland Advisory Committee to the U.S. Commission on Civil Rights, *Baltimore Police Complaint Evaluation Procedure* (1980); Kansas State Advisory Committee to the

U.S. Commission on Civil Rights, *Police-Community Relations in the City of Wichita and Sedgwick County* (1980); *Police Practices in the Twin Cities, supra* note 9; District of Columbia Advisory Committee to the U.S. Commission on Civil Rights, *Police-Community Relations in Washington, D.C.* (1981); Ohio Advisory Committee to the U.S. Commission on Civil Rights, *Policing in Cincinnati, Ohio: Official Policy vs. Civilian Reality* (1981); U.S. Commission on Civil Rights, *Confronting Racial Isolation in Miami,* (1982); Nebraska Advisory Committee to the U.S. Commission on Civil Rights, *Police-Community Relations in Omaha* (1982).

24. *Who Is Guarding the Guardians?, supra* note 10.

25. Advisory Commission on Intergovernmental Relations, *Safe Streets Reconsidered: The Block Grant Experience, 1968–1975* (Wash., DC: ACIR, 1977), p. 38.

26. *Id.,* at 19.

27. *Castro v. Beecher,* 522 F. Supp. 873 (DMA 1980), *aff'd sub nom. Boston Chapter NAACP v. Beecher,* 679 F.2d 965 (1st Cir. 1982).

28. *See, e.g., Memphis Firefighters v. Stotts,* 467 U.S. 651 (1984).

29. Goldstein, *supra* note 7, at 163–64.

30. *See Id.,* at 168–69.

31. Frank Anechiarico, "Suing the Philadelphia Police: The Case for an Institutional Approach," 6 *Law and Policy* 231 (1984).

32. National Advisory Commission on Criminal Justice Standards and Goals, *Police* (Wash., DC: Government Printing Office, 1973).

33. Note: "Injunctive Relief for Violations of Constitutional Rights by Police," 45 *U. Colo. L. Rev.* 90, 92 (1973).

34. Note: "The Administration of Complaints by Civilians. . . ," *supra* note 12, at 499, 500.

35. *Police-Community Relations in Washington, D.C. supra* Note 23, at 5.

36. "The Administration of Complaints by Civilians. . . ," *supra* note 12, at 500.

37. Goldstein, *supra* note 7, at 134–35.

38. *Id.* at 139. *See also* Algernon D. Black, *The People and the Police* (New York: McGraw-Hill, 1968); and Paul Chevigny, *Police Power, Police Abuses in New York City* (New York: Rand Institute, 1969).

39. *Police Practices in the Twin Cities, supra* note 9, at 31. *See also* Gerald Caiden, *Police Revitalization* (Lexington, MA: Lexington Books, 1977), p. 129.

40. *Who Is Guarding the Guardians, supra* note 10, at 12.

41. *Civic Crisis—Civic Challenge, supra* note 9, at 34.

42. Anechiarico, *supra* note 31, at 235.

43. Kerner Commission Report, *supra* note 8, at 310.

44. *Police Practices in the Twin Cities, supra* note 9, at 25.

45. *See generally Police-Community Relations in the City of Wichita and Sedgwick County, supra* note 23, at 42–43.

46. *Hague v. CIO,* 307 U.S. 496 (1939).

47. *Id.,* at 504–5.

48. *Local 309, United Furniture Workers of Am. v. Gates,* 75 F.Supp. 620 (NDIN 1948).

49. For earlier cases, *see Boyd v. United States,* 116 U.S. 616 (1886); *Weeks v. United States,* 232 U.S. 383 (1914); *Olmstead v. United States,* 277 U.S. 438 (1928); *Nardone v. United States,* 302 U.S. 379 (1937); and *McNabb v. United States,* 318 U.S. 332 (1943).

50. One of the more commonly cited of these injunction proceedings is *Refoule v. Ellis,* 74 F. Supp. 336 (NDGA 1947).

51. *Mapp v. Ohio, supra* note 11.

52. *People v. Defore,* 150 NE2d 585, 587 (1926).

53. *Olmstead v. United States, supra* note 49, at 485 (Brandeis, J. dissenting).

54. *Wolf v. Colorado,* 338 U.S. 25 (1949).

55. *Mapp v. Ohio, supra* note 11 at 652.

56. *Williams v. Wallace*, 240 F. Supp. 100, 104, (MDAL 1965).

57. *Id.*, at 109–11.

58. *NAACP v. Thompson*, 357 F.2d 831 (5th Cir. 1966). Federal District Judge Cox had originally refused to grant the requested injunction, but he was reversed in this opinion by the Fifth Circuit Court of Appeals. *See also Cottonreader v. Johnson*, 252 F. Supp. 492 (MDAL 1966); and *Houser v. Hill*, 278 F. Supp. 920 (MDAL 1968).

59. *NAACP v. Thompson, supra* note 58 at 838.

60. *Lankford v. Gelston*, 364 F. 2d 197, 201 (4th Cir. 1966).

61. *Id.*, at 203.

62. *Peek v. Mitchell*, 419 F. 2d 575 (6th Cir. 1970).

63. *Wolin v. Port of N.Y. Auth.*, 392 F.2d 83 (2d Cir. 1968), *affirming* 268 F. Supp. 855 (SDNY 1968).

64. *Id.*, at 94.

65. *Schnell v. City of Chicago*, 407 F.2d 1084 (7th Cir. 1969).

66. *Id.*, at 1086.

67. *See, e.g., Belknap v. Leary*, 427 F.2d 496 (2d Cir. 1970); and *Wilson v. Webster*, 315 F. Supp. 1104 (CDCA 1970), *vacated and remanded*, 467 F.2d 1282 (9th Cir. 1972).

68. *See Hughes v. Rizzo*, 282 F. Supp. 881 (EDPA 1968); *Wheeler v. Goodman*, 298 F. Supp. 935 (WDNC 1969); *Lewis v. Kugler*, 446 F.2d 1343 (3d Cir. 1971); and *Sparrow v. Goodman*, 361 F. Supp. 566 (WDNC 1973). *See also Gomez v. Wilson*, 323 F. Supp. 927 (DCCir. 1972) on vagrancy.

69. *Wheeler v. Goodman, supra* note 68 at 942.

70. *Allee v. Medrano*, 416 U.S. 802 (1974).

71. *Id.*, at 807.

72. *Id.*, at 809.

73. *Id.*, at 815.

74. *Rizzo v. Goode*, 423 U.S. 362, 371–72 (1976).

75. *Id.*, at 375.

76. *Id.*

77. *Id.*, at 382.

78. *Id.*, at 385. Blackmun provides citations to the circuit court rulings at 385 n. 2.

79. *New Jersey v. T.L.O.*, 83 L.Ed2d 720, 734 (1985).

80. *See, e.g., City of Los Angeles v. Lyons*, 75 L.Ed2d 675 (1983); and *O'Shea v. Littleton*, 414 U.S. 488 (1974).

81. *See, e.g., Hicks v. Miranda*, 422 U.S. 332 (1975), which holds that the abstention doctrine could be invoked even if the state proceeding was instituted after a federal suit had been launched.

82. Rubenstein, *City Police* (New York: Ballantine, 1973); and Niederhoffer, *supra* note 1.

83. Rubenstein, *supra* note 82, at 33.

84. Skolnick, *supra* note 6, at 51.

85. Niederhoffer, *supra* note 1, at 95.

86. Skolnick, *supra* note 6, at ch. 3.

87. Goldstein, *supra* note 7, at 165–66.

88. *Police Practices in the Twin Cities, supra* note 9, at 17. *See also* Kenneth Culp Davis, *Police Discretion* (St. Paul, MN: West, 1975).

89. One of the more interesting discussions of this conflict appears in Niederhoffer, *supra* note 1.

90. Goldstein, *supra* note 7, at 167.

91. *Id.*, at 171.

92. James Q. Wilson, *Varieties of Police Behavior* (New York: Atheneum, 1975).

93. Goldstein, *supra* note 7, at 25.

94. *Task Force Report, supra* note 4, at 13–14.

95. *See, e.g., Civic Crisis—Civic Challenge, supra* note 9, at 84 *et seq.; Police Practices in the Twin Cities, supra* note 9, at 87; *Police-Community Relations in the City of Wichita and Sedgwick County, supra* note 23, at 60.

11

Rizzo v. Goode: The Philadelphia Police Conflict

Philadelphia is a city of stately public buildings and home to some of the nation's most venerated historical monuments. It is perhaps precisely because it is the birthplace of the Constitution that Americans are particularly troubled when the City of Brotherly Love is accused of violations of civil rights and liberties. However, Philadelphia is also a large American city and, as such, has the same tensions and challenges found in other urban areas.

Controversy surrounding police practices in Philadelphia produced important and difficult interactions between federal district judges and city administrators. One of the critical elements of that conflict was the *Rizzo v. Goode* case, a complex civil suit brought against city officials that charged police abuses and asked Federal District Judge John Fullam to mandate adequate checks on departmental operations.[1] It was a dispute that would eventually find its way to the U.S. Supreme Court.

The *Rizzo* case is interesting for several reasons. Like the *Rhodes* case considered in Chapter 9, the Supreme Court decision in *Rizzo* is the prevailing high court ruling on the authority of federal district courts relative to local police management. It was one of a number of opinions admonishing district judges to limit their intervention into local administrative operations. Of equal importance, however, is the fact that while Philadelphia presents a unique set of personalities and community relationships, its police practices issues are in many respects illustrative of problems encountered across the nation.

TRIGGER PHASE

Like the other cases considered in this study, *Rizzo v. Goode* was not a test case prompted by a well developed plan to address a contemporary problem. It was produced and shaped by a variety of forces, including developing tensions in police/community relations, the politics of civilian review of police activities, the increasing conflict between federal courts and the department's leadership, the turbulence of a particular period in the nation's history, and several specific incidents.

Developing Tensions in Philadelphia Police/Community Relations

The events that triggered the *Goode* litigation in 1970 came at the end of two decades of debate among Philadelphians over the conduct of their police officers. Paul Markowitz and Walter Summerfield, Jr., in their 1952 study of Philadelphia police practices found several troublesome patterns.[2] Among other things, they determined that searches and arrests were rarely (only about three percent) based on warrants even when the circumstances would easily have allowed the officer to obtain them.[3] The department frequently used indiscriminate and unjustifiable roundups, as much to carry out street sweeps as to arrest lawbreakers for serious violations. Third, they found abuses of broad cover charges, like disorderly conduct, used to justify detention of citizens who committed no breach of law at all or whose only crime was that they challenged police authority:

> Three-quarters of the arrests for disorderly conduct appear to be illegal, in that the charge is used to cover lawful conduct of which the police disapprove. In liquor, gambling or prostitution raids, the usual police practice seems to be to charge all customers found in the establishment with disorderly conduct. No case examined showed any evidence of disorderly conduct on the part of any of these people, and invariably they were discharged by magistrates.[4]

They found that cover charge arrests were used for racial and political harassment. In particular, they concluded that police often raided racially mixed gatherings and harassed mixed couples. The study also observed that blacks who objected to police behavior were especially likely to face arrest on vague and unjustified charges.[5]

Markowitz and Summerfield determined further that there was little effective redress for the citizen who wished to challenge police conduct. Criminal prosecution of police officers required cooperation of the prosecutor, who normally maintained a continuing cooperative relationship with the police. Moreover, if a person was charged, however unfairly, with an offense and arrested by the police, the likelihood of that person obtaining a jury verdict that found criminal police abuse was slim at best. Similar factors made successful civil suits an unlikely avenue of redress. While there was a police trial board, it sat primarily to hear charges of alleged breaches of internal police discipline, usually neglect of duty or insubordination. Moreover, its findings were purely advisory, with the Commissioner having complete discretion over departmental discipline.[6]

There was pressure for reform during much of the 1950s from the NAACP, the minority press of Philadelphia, and the ACLU. These groups attacked the Police Board of Inquiry and called for some kind of external review.[7] Spencer Coxe, Philadelphia ACLU Executive Director, charged that citizen complaints were generally ignored. If they were investigated, the complaints were rarely sustained. The internal police disciplinary board was simply not designed to deal with external complaints and generally exonerated the officer.[8] The complaining citizens were not informed of the outcome even if an investigation was undertaken.[9] In any event, the fact that the police were investigating themselves simply did not provide the community, and particularly black Philadelphians, with confidence that the investigations were fair and unbiased. Coxe pointed to a 1956 case in which "there was uncontroverted and overwhelming evidence that a patrolman had beaten a civilian without provocation, cracking a rib, and had struck his commanding officer, the Board of Inquiry ignored the civilian's complaint but recommended discipline for striking the officer."[10]

The Civilian Review Board: One Attempted Solution

In June 1957 the ACLU formally called for an external civilian board parallel to the Police Board of Inquiry to resolve citizen complaints. Henry W. Sawyer III, a member of the City Council and President of the local ACLU chapter, introduced a bill to create the civilian review board later that year. Hearings held on the proposal in January 1958 received heavy publicity because of recent charges of widespread police roundups and served as a forum for NAACP and ACLU police critics. Even so, the bill died in committee.

Sawyer approached the city's reform mayor, Richard Dilworth, for executive action. Dilworth, who had previously served as District Attorney and understood the concerns expressed by civil rights groups, supported the proposal and launched the Police Review Board in October 1958. The Mayor created the Board by executive order under sections of the City Charter which provided that "[t]he executive and administrative work of the City shall be performed by . . . [s]uch advisory boards as the Mayor may appoint." Moreover, "[t]he Mayor may upon the request of the head of any department or of his own volition appoint a board of seven citizens to act in an advisory capacity to such department regarding the department's work or any specified phase of it."[11]

The Board consisted of five members who received citizen complaints against police officers.[12] It could investigate, hold hearings, and make recommendations to the Police Commissioner. The fact that the Board had been created without City Council sanction, however, meant that the Council was not obliged to provide adequate funding, and it refused to do so.[13] The Board had virtually no staff, relying on voluntary efforts in its early years. It was dependent upon the police department for investigative assistance. Even if it found wrongdoing, the Board could only recommend action to the department and could impose no penalties itself. The other implication of the Board's birth by executive decree was the fact that it could be eliminated just as easily by any future mayor.

In its first annual report, the Board praised the department for its cooperation and observed:

> We should point out that the first year's operation has revealed no general pattern whatsoever of officially condoned police brutality or discrimination based upon race, creed or national origin. The Police Department has cooperated fully in an attempt to determine whether individual policemen have exceeded the bounds of their authority or have otherwise engaged in unlawful conduct against private citizens. We have also been impressed with the investigations which have been made by the police authorities, particularly Inspector Allan Ballard. His investigations and written reports have been invaluable, not only for their perspicacity and inclusiveness, but for their fairness.[14]

It later added, however, that while there may not have been a particular policy in the department in favor of discrimination, there were problem areas, including the continuing pattern of raids on racially mixed gatherings without provocation. The Board admonished the department to accept its proper responsibility for training and supervision of the force to prevent such abuses.[15]

The members of the Board were aware of their operating difficulties but felt that they could serve a useful, if limited purpose. The lack of staff and resources, inadequate publicity, and restricted authority meant that the Board received relatively few complaints, just over two hundred in its first three years of operation. Its public image was not enhanced by the fact that the Board rarely recommended more than brief suspensions, even in the most serious cases. On the other hand, the Board claimed that its real strength was its ability to serve as a "safety valve in the community."[16] It was able to settle the overwhelming majority of cases on an informal basis since what most citizens wanted was a simple recognition that they had been wronged along with an apology and assurances that the record would be cleared. Finally, the Board argued that it was able to perform this valuable function without an adverse impact on the department's ability to fight crime:

> The four years of the Board's operation have disproved the charges of its critics that a Police Advisory Board will destroy the morale of the Police Department as the officers will become timid through constant surveillance by a civilian board. The Federal Bureau of Investigation report shows that Philadelphia has the lowest crime rate per hundred thousand population of the five major cities in the United States and that the rate of arrests for crimes committed is the highest in Philadelphia.[17]

The Demise of the External Board

Notwithstanding the extremely limited actions it had taken against the department and the cooperation of the first two police commissioners with whom the Board worked, there was substantial opposition within the department. That antagonism eventually resulted in the Board's demise. In many ways, the death of the Board was more important for its symbolic value to the police and their critics than for its actual significance as the termination of a body to remedy police abuse.

In December 1959 the Fraternal Order of Police brought a suit in Common Pleas Court that challenged the Board's validity and sought an injunction against its operation. However, the Police Commissioner and other officials testified in support of the Board. The parties finally settled out of court in February 1960. The settlement called for the name of the Board to be changed from the Police Review Board to the Police Advisory Board and included several procedural modifications in its operation.[18]

Opposition continued to grow within the department. A second suit was launched that challenged the Board's validity in 1965. Judge Leo Weinrott of the Court of Common Pleas issued an order abolishing the Board in 1967. The Board issued a strong brief in its own behalf in its Eighth Annual Report, which defined its role as a community sounding board and as an avenue for citizen redress considered by many to be more efficacious than the limited available alternatives. The city appealed Weinrott's decision and eventually prevailed in the Pennsylvania Supreme Court.[19]

It was, however, a hollow victory for the Board. By 1968 the Advisory Board was in serious trouble, viewed as intrusive by the police and ineffective by many community leaders. Though some still defended it as a safety valve, few took it seriously. The last Chairman of the Board, Mercer Tate, warned that what was needed as urban tensions mounted was reinvigoration of the Board, not its deprecation, "I feel," he said, "it is a great tragedy that your Police Advisory Board is languishing while police community relations are rapidly worsening."[20]

Tensions were indeed mounting and opposition to civilian review within the police department was headed by the new Commissioner, Frank Rizzo, a career Philadelphia police officer appointed by Mayor James H.J. Tate. In a speech to the police department on December 22, 1969, Mayor Tate announced the termination of the Board, terming it "a Christmas present to you gentlemen."[21] Speculation ran high that the real force behind eliminating external means of evaluating the police was Commissioner Rizzo, an outspoken critic of people he described as "antipolice." Rizzo warmly endorsed the Mayor's gesture, calling it "the finest Christmas present the police of this city could receive."[22]

Another avenue by which citizens could challenge police practices was effectively eliminated in 1969 as the police department halted the practice of providing the Philadelphia Commission on Human Rights with copies of departmental investigations in cases involving charges against officers. The Commission promptly ceased handling citizen complaints, referring callers to the ACLU and other similar organizations for possible legal action.[23]

The barriers to obtaining redress that had existed in earlier years persisted. It was still difficult to elicit prosecutorial support for criminal charges given the ongoing relationship between the District Attorney's office and the police. Civil suits remained doubtful alternatives both for technical reasons and because of jury bias. The department's internal review process seemed to offer little hope. Among other things, there was no guarantee that an investigation would be conducted outside the control of the officer's immediate supervisor. Complainants found it difficult and intimidating to file reports. They were often asked to submit to polygraph evaluations. They were not told that police officers were not required to take the same tests. In fact, the Fraternal Order of Police had a standing rule that it would refuse to defend any officer who did submit to a lie detector examination. Finally, the complainants were not notified of the outcome of any proceeding that was launched because of a citizen complaint.

All of this occurred during the late 1960s when urban unrest was intensifying. Friction rose as crime rates increased. Some of this tension was a result of changing lifestyles, the rise of the young counterculture. It was also a period of vigorous dissent, particularly in the areas of civil rights and anti-Vietnam protest.

Federal Courts and the Philadelphia Police

Several Philadelphia based federal judges were faced with challenges to police department practices during the late 1960s and into the 1970s in cases that stemmed from street protests, claims of harassment of hippies in city parks, and charges of First Amendment violations by the city's morals squad.

Judges Lord, Van Dusen, and Troutman sat in one such case, *Heard v. Rizzo*.[24] This litigation grew out of events surrounding a demonstration at the Philadelphia Board of Education in November 1967. The crowd was much larger than school board security personnel had anticipated. Officers of the Philadelphia Police Department's Civil Disobedience Unit, brought in to help the school board security staff, called for additional support. Commissioner Rizzo "ordered 111 men who had just been in a promotion ceremony at City Hall to the area and put in effect Riot Plan No. 3 to prevent demonstrators from moving north into a residential area of the city."[25] The police moved in to clear what the court referred to as "a howling, undisciplined and disorganized mob."

The plaintiffs charged that police used excessive force, made needless and unjustified arrests, and employed a range of vague and ambiguous statutes as grounds for arrests and detention for the purpose of interfering with the constitutional rights of those detained. They asked for a three judge district court in order to challenge as vague and overbroad the omnibus charges of disorderly conduct, rioting, breach of the peace, incitement to riot, conspiracy to do unlawful acts, corrupting the morals of a minor, loitering, sedition, obstructing an officer, revolutionary activities, and juvenile court statutes. The court upheld the laws as written but did not rule on the detailed allegations that the statutes were unconstitutionally applied. In so doing, the Court suggested that the parties involved should have avoided the broad challenge before a three judge court and gone before a single judge with the more particular complaints:

> It is most unfortunate, both for plaintiffs *and for the Philadelphia community,* that these civil rights' [sic] claims were not stated in a separate count of the complaints by plaintiffs for consideration by a one judge court, and that counsel for plaintiffs have not taken the protective action of restating them as suggested by the order of January 9, 1968, and the amendment to that order of January 19, 1968.[26] (emphasis added)

The arrests, the court found, were not without justification, and the laws on which they were based, at least as written, were not excessively vague.

Judge John Fullam confronted police abuse charges at about the same time in *Hughes v. Rizzo.*[27] As the lawyer for the city later put it, "This was the hippie case in which the police did the wrong thing. What they did was whenever they had a complaint they went down [to Rittenhouse Square] and gathered up hippies. . . . They would round them all up and take them to the station-house and keep them a couple of hours. Some judge would then come along and release all of them because the police didn't have anything against them, but it served the purpose. The city was absolutely wrong in that case."[28] The police had conducted mass arrests during June and July 1967. Fullam found no justification for the arrests, but he refused to issue an injunction against the police department, electing instead to expunge the arrest records of those involved and retain jurisdiction, at least temporarily, as a precautionary measure.

Two items of future interest are evident in Fullam's ruling. First, the judge was quite willing to recognize that some of those who demanded the protection of the court were not the most pleasant people:

> The police undoubtedly received complaints from area residents appalled by the sinister appearance of some "hippies" and the conduct ascribed to them. . . . One can almost take judicial notice of the fact that many "hippies" experiment with narcotics and dangerous drugs. And the hearings in this case were persuasive that some are promiscuous; some are overtly homosexual; and some have so completely rejected the middle-class value of cleanliness that their very presence in the courtroom was an olfactory affront. These factors may help to explain, if not to legally justify, conduct by law-enforcement personnel which would otherwise be incredible.[29]

Even so, he found that the mass arrests were clearly unjustified and carried out for purposes of harassment based on a "desire to rid Rittenhouse Square of 'hippies.' "[30] On the other hand, Fullam was not prepared to attribute the abuses that he found to a specific policy promulgated by highly placed police officials. Having granted that benefit of the doubt, however, he added that "it is not especially reassuring to suppose that under existing administrative regulations, individual police officers and park guards, or their immediate superiors, are at liberty to ignore the constitutional rights of individuals at their pleasure."[31]

Judge Fullam unwittingly anticipated his own later dilemma when he observed that federal judges ought to avoid injunctions against the police if possible:

> The cases and authorities cited above make it plain that while most of the limits beyond which police-power may not constitutionally be exercised are clearly established, the myriad factual situations in which these issues can arise are so varied, and the boundaries in some areas of the law are so nebulous, that any attempt at broad-spectrum injunctive relief should be avoided. Courts simply are not equipped to supervise the day-to-day operations of police officers by injunction. . . .
>
> Of course, mass arrests without legal justification, and similar harassment, are so clearly improper that, if there were any likelihood of further attempts in that direction, an injunction should issue. But I am satisfied that the defendants, as responsible officials, do not need to be compelled to prevent a recurrence of such violations.[32]

It would be the same Judge Fullam who, in 1973, would issue significant injunctive orders against police abuses in the *Goode v. Rizzo* case.

Judge Joseph Lord III was another of the federal jurists who presided in Philadelphia police misconduct litigation in the late 1960s. Lord found that the department had harassed the owner of a so-called head shop in violation of his due process rights under the Fourteenth Amendment and enjoined Commissioner Rizzo and the head of the Morals Squad, Inspector McCollough, from similar future activities.[33] This case developed from repeated raids of Tobin's shop by Morals Squad officers from January through March 1969. The officers charged the store operators with possession of obscene materials based upon the slogans on buttons and pictures on posters sold in the shop. The raids continued despite the fact that the store owners prevailed in the first of the trials that resulted from these sweeps. Furthermore, even though more than two hundred buttons and posters were seized as allegedly obscene items, only two were actually, and unsuccessfully, used in the effort to prosecute the store operators.

The city argued that a mere declaration of police error was all that was necessary and no injunction should be issued. If Judge Lord was to issue an order, though, the city insisted that it should be directed only to Inspector McCollough as the head of the Morals Squad. Lord rejected both claims and insisted:

> While an injunction in this case would prevent defendant McCullough from further raids without prior judicial proceedings, it would not prevent other officers not parties to this suit from pursuing such an unconstitutional course. However, the defendant Rizzo, by virtue of his office, is in a position to prevent such conduct by his subordinates. In *Schnell v. City of Chicago* . . . the court said:
>> "From a legal standpoint, it makes no difference whether the plaintiffs' constitutional rights are violated as a result of police behavior which is the product of the active encouragement and direction of their superiors or as a result of the superiors' mere acquiescence in such behavior. In either situation, if the police officials had a duty, as they admittedly had here, to prevent the officers under their direction from committing the acts which are alleged to have occurred. . . , they are proper defendants in this action."

We think, therefore, that an effective remedy here must include a mandate that defendant Rizzo prevent the officers under his command from making any future seizures of allegedly obscene material from the corporate plaintiff without a prior judicial adversary proceeding.[34]

In 1970 Judge Woods enjoined the department from cruising the streets and recruiting fill-irs for lineups without ensuring that those who were "asked" to cooperate really
fully understood their rights and obligations. This order stemmed from findings that
some citizens had felt coerced or at least did not understand the request to participate in
the lineups.[35]

By 1970, then, there was growing criticism by some Philadelphians, particularly
minorities, of the tactics employed by the police department under the direction of
Commissioner Rizzo on grounds of brutality, racial discrimination, and violations of
First and Fourteenth Amendment freedoms in street-sweep operations. At the same time,
the department and, particularly, its Commissioner were taking a harder line in responding to charges against police officers. Moreover, the alternatives for resolving these
disputes were all but gone given the demise of the Police Advisory Board, the weak-
ening of the Human Relations Commission, the limitations of criminal or civil suits,
and the restriction associated with internal departmental complaint procedures.[36] It is
against this backdrop that the events of 1970 leading to the *Rizzo v. Goode* case un-
folded.

The First of the Two-Round Main Event

Peter Hearn, then an associate, now a senior partner, with the prestigious Philadelphia
law firm of Pepper, Hamilton, and Sheetz, was riding the train to work one morning in
early December 1969 when an acquaintence who was a highly placed Deputy District
Attorney related the story of his wife's experience with some police officers on the
previous evening.[37] It seems that Ruth Rotko had participated in a program at the public
broadcasting station with three University of Pennsylvania graduate students. She had
dropped off two of the students and was taking the third, Gerald Goode, home. Mrs.
Rotko, a Caucasian, was driving and Goode, a young black man, was seated in the
right rear seat. The two stopped at Broad and Erie, a major Philadelphia intersection.
Goode spotted two white police officers frisking a black man in what he considered an
excessively rough manner. Goode rolled down the window, and without using profanity
or making personal remarks, indicated that the officers should stop abusing the man and
leave him alone. As the light changed, Rotko proceeded north on Broad Street but was
promptly overtaken by the two officers who had released the man they had been dealing
with in order to give chase. While one officer required Mrs. Rotko to produce her
identification, the other went to the passenger side of the vehicle and pulled Goode out,
striking him with a blackjack in the process. Goode objected and, after he was frisked
and handcuffed, demanded to know why he was being treated in this manner. Whereupon one of the officers struck him across the face with the blackjack. At that point,
Goode told the officer to "get your f—— hands off me."[38] Goode was taken into
custody and told that he could not use profanity on a police officer. Meanwhile, the
other officer questioned Mrs. Rotko about her relationship with Goode and threatened
to arrest her as well.

When Hearn arrived at the office, he received a telephone call from Gerald Goode's major professor at the University of Pennsylvania Graduate School of Fine Arts. "He said that standing in his office . . . was Gerald Goode, one of his students, who had just been released from jail still wearing the clothes he had on the previous night. He was covered with blood and needed a lawyer." Hearn took the case.

The first order of business was clearing Goode of the criminal charges lodged by the two arresting officers. Given the fact that the principal witness was the wife of one his chief deputies and the defendant was a graduate student at the university, the District Attorney broke the traditional pattern of support for the police department and promptly terminated the charges against the young man.

As word of the incident spread, Hearn received phone calls from other attorneys who had clients claiming to have been abused by the same police officers involved in the Goode case. It was then that Goode's lawyers determined that they were dealing with a pattern of abuse by police officers against whom virtually no disciplinary action had been taken even though there was reason to believe that police officials were aware of their conduct. They resolved to file a class action suit naming the mayor, the police commissioner, and other officers in the chain of command over Officers D'Amico and DeFazio, the two officers involved in the Goode incident.

The suit made the front page of the *Philadelphia Inquirer* on February 18, 1970.[39] Commissioner Rizzo responded immediately, terming the case part of an "insidious plot to gain community control of police" and defending the two officers involved.[40] "Rizzo was a folk hero at the time. If he said that you were doing bad things, a very considerable portion of the community would believe him."[41] Indeed, there were serious discussions within Hearn's law firm about whether to continue with the suit given the adverse publicity. Hearn lauds his colleagues for standing firm. He recalls the tension of the times:

> This was a period in which police/community relations were almost at flashpoint. On the one hand, a good part of the community felt that then Police Commissioner Rizzo had been instrumental in keeping the calm through the late sixties when Detroit and Newark and other cities had riots. We had not suffered that way. So the mentality arose that it was the Police Commissioner who was keeping the city together. . . . [On the other hand,] the activities of the police department caused a lot of hostility. . . . The manner in which police were treating citizens . . . was a matter of very intense community debate and it led to many encounters being worse than they would have in a more relaxed circumstance.[42]

Turbulent Times—1970 in Philadelphia

Commissioner Rizzo received strong public support for his aggressive approach to policing. Many whites and some minority citizens were shaken by the unrest they saw not only around the nation, but in nearby communities and in parts of their own city. Rizzo vowed to do something about it. Representatives of business and community groups later testified in U.S. Commission on Civil Rights hearings that many tacitly accepted a kind of trade-off in which they were willing to tolerate some degree of police abuse as the price for aggressive crime control.[43] Outside Philadelphia, Rizzo received favorable coverage in a segment of NBC's "First Tuesday" program which brought responses from a wide variety of viewers in support of the Commissioner. That coverage was, in turn, echoed in local news stories.[44]

Philadelphian's, including federal judges, began to receive other kinds of reports in the spring and summer of 1970. Frightening events from around the region and nation were chronicled throughout the summer. Stories of riots in Asbury Park, New Jersey, and in East Los Angeles; the Marin County Courthouse shootout in Northern California; the murder trial of Black Panther, Lonnie McLucas; and charges pending against Black Panther leaders, Huey Newton and Bobby Seale, appeared on the evening news and in daily papers.[45] Philadelphia did not escape the tensions of that summer.

In June, Mayor Tate declared a state of emergency in a nine square mile area surrounding Tasker Homes and the Lanier Playground in response to several clashes in the racially mixed neighborhood.[46] The emergency order prohibited gatherings of twelve or more persons and limited liquor sales. Press reports indicated that Commissioner Rizzo—who joined Mayor Tate for the announcement of the emergency proclamation—said "that there were some outside agitators and that 'some Black Panthers down there are trying to get things rolling.' "[47] A week later, minor clashes broke out between black high school students and area whites.[48] The students had staged a protest alleging harassment by whites in the neighborhoods surrounding their school. Two hundred police responded to restore order. The city's attorneys later characterized the summer of 1970 as "the most difficult for Philadelphians since the City was torn by urban riots in 1964."[49]

Commissioner Rizzo waded into the political fray denouncing criticism of his policemen, challenging judges, and warning that he was not going to tolerate disruption of life in Philadelphia.[50] Indeed he would ride the fear of crime and urban unrest to victory in the upcoming mayoral election. One of the civil rights lawyers who represented COPPAR (a party to the *Rizzo* litigation) recalled:

> A real division occured in the city. You had good white people scared to death of these revolutionaries. And every time you picked up the paper you saw a police statement about the efforts the police were taking to protect us from these 'black revolutionaries.' . . . You got a real schism to the point that black people couldn't even talk to white liberals about what was really going on.[51]

People tended to tie all radical black groups to the Black Panthers whether they had any connection or not.

However, it was not over yet. The events of late August brought the conflict to a climax, resulting in the launching of another major piece of police litigation in federal court which would eventually be combined with the *Goode v. Rizzo* case.

The Second Front: The Launching of the *COPPAR* Litigation

In July Mrs. Anna Hill, a black woman, moved her family into a predominantly white neighborhood in the Fairmont area. Rumors spread among some whites that she was sponsored by a militant black organization. Shortly thereafter, she experienced various types of harassment. There were flashes of anger in the neighborhood on and off over the next month as blacks came to Mrs. Hill promising protection. She firmly resisted both the offers and the harassment. Tensions were building and the police were watching. Then, on Monday evening, August 24, conflict erupted in a number of small, but ominous, violent episodes. Police moved in force to quell the unrest but scattered incidents followed over the next three evenings.

On Thursday night, with attention focused on the Fairmont situation, violence again flared at Tasker Homes. Press reports indicate that Commissioner Rizzo, operating from the Fairmont area, sent three hundred policemen into Tasker Homes with orders to "Go in and take over the project."[52]

On Friday Mayor Tate again declared a limited state of emergency to cover Tasker Homes and Fairmont, which was similar to that used earlier in the summer.[53] Commissioner Rizzo ordered that eight hundred extra officers be made available through schedule changes, overtime, and temporary reassignment from special squads. Accompanying Mayor Tate at the press briefing, Rizzo served notice that he intended to crack down.

> We've been patient and kind but some people mistake kindness for weakness. . . .
> We've been pushed, punched and bottles have been thrown at us, but now we've reached the end.
>
> We're not going to take it any more.[54]

On Saturday, Pennsylvania Governor Raymond Shafer refused to intervene to block a planned conference sponsored by the Black Panthers to be held at Temple University in early September. The Revolutionary Peoples Constitutional Convention had been granted permission to use the Temple facilities after making commitments to ensure security and bonding to cover possible damage. Since he did not receive substantial evidence of a serious likelihood of violence, Shafer felt it was important as a matter of principle to permit the conference to take place. He warned that it was particularly important to permit peaceful gatherings of the organizations considered most threatening. "This policy is not advanced without risk, (but) the risk must be run."[55]

Saturday evening someone entered the police office in Cobbs Creek Park and shot Sergeant Frank VonColln as he sat talking on the telephone at the desk.[56] Minutes later, two officers entering the park to get gasoline at the office were fired upon. Officer James Harrington was wounded by a barrage of bullets fired into the van in which he was a passenger. Rizzo rushed to the scene accompanied by some four hundred officers. They staged what police described as the most dramatic manhunt in the city's history.[57] One suspect was arrested along with weapons and four hand grenades. While the suspect was identified as a member of a radical group, he was not a member of the Black Panthers. The search for other suspects and possible bombs continued through the night and the next day. Another suspect was later taken into custody, but the strain had not yet ended.

Sunday afternoon, Commissioner Rizzo held a press briefing. Obviously exhausted from his role as line commander throughout the night at the scene of the Cobbs Creek Park shooting, Rizzo made very general and angry statements about revolutionaries, suggesting a connection among the various groups and the Black Panthers. One of his most controversial statements was a challenge for a duel. He is reported to have said, "If they [the revolutionaries] had any guts, they would call me and set up a showdown—if that's what they want. We will even give them odds on it. We'll send out fewer people with fewer weapons."[58]

Later that evening, just blocks from the location of the VonColln shooting of the night before, Officers Frank Nolen and Thomas Gibbons, Jr., were seriously wounded

when they stopped a suspected stolen car occupied by two men.[59] There was no connection between the two sets of shootings, but the combination of events added to the
tense atmosphere in the city.

At about 6:00 A.M. the next morning, Monday August 31, police officers staged
raids on three separate Black Panther offices and residences in different parts of the
city.[60] There was a brief exchange of gunfire at one location, but those in the buildings
quickly surrendered. Commissioner Rizzo later said, "I have made statements in the
past that the Black Panthers would hear form us. When they did hear from us, the
yellow dogs threw down their guns."[61] At one of the locations the men taken into
custody were lined up in the street and strip-searched. Reporters had been notified of
the raids in advance. Photos of the strip-search appeared in one of the city's newspapers
later that day.

The rhetoric, the police action, and those photographs had a profound effect on
many Philadelphians. Some found the Commissioners' outbursts an understandable reaction of anger, frustration, and exhaustion.[62] Others were appalled. Many blacks saw
the rhetoric, raids, and photographs of the searches as dehumanizing, degrading, and
disdainful of their serious complaints against the political and social system. Speaking
of the newspaper photo of the Black Panthers naked in the street, one man observed;
"It reminded a lot of us of the stories of the slave ships when they came over here and
how the slaves were examined on the docks."[63] Where some police defenders were
willing to excuse Rizzo's remarks because of the circumstances, others said this rhetoric
revealed the real mindset of the Commissioner and other city leaders who were usually
more careful not to display their true attitude toward the city's residents.[64]

Monday evening, at the request of Commissioner Rizzo and the District Attorney,
Judge Leo Weinrott of the Common Pleas Court stepped in to take over the arraignments
of the arrested Black Panthers, replacing Municipal Judge Anne Clark who was then on
the bench and ready to preside.[65] It was the same Judge Weinrott who had earlier struck
down the Police Advisory Board, a man seen by many as working hand in glove with
the police department. Weinrott set bail at $100,000 per defendant. This happened after
word circulated that Judge Thomas Reed, also of the Common Pleas Court, had agreed
to hold hearings on Tuesday morning on a petition for a writ of habeas corpus. The
expectation was that Reed would likely set a low bail. The next day, when Judge Reed
did sit in the Panther arrests, he refused the habeas corpus relief and agreed to hear only
one bail reduction request per day.[66] That would clearly have meant a longer incarceration for most of the defendants.

There was confusion among lawyers called in to represent those involved. William
Akers, one of the plaintiffs' attorneys in the case of *COPPAR v. Rizzo*, recalled the
situation as most confusing. The first thing Monday morning, Akers' telephone "began
to jump off the hook." He and the other attorneys were attempting to determine how
best to get the defendants released on bail before proceeding with any other action.
Akers, a long time civil rights lawyer, knew Harry Lore from their days together in the
mid-1960s in Mississippi, and they had been friends for some years in Philadelphia.
Lore had also received a call from Charles Garry, the Black Panthers' attorney in San
Francisco, asking for his assistance in the case.[67] Lore and Akers emerged as the lead
lawyers for the litigation arising from the raid. Akers described the situation as anything
but calm and well organized:

> You must understand that at that time there was a great deal of lawyer confusion.
> Lawyers were running around all over hell and gone. Lawyers were coming out of

the woodwork. Every lawyer had a client. Some lawyers had clients they never saw. Some people had two and three lawyers. From an administrator's point of view, it was one grand mess.[68]

It became clear that given the events that were taking place in the city and county level courts, the lawyers were unlikely to get the defendants released on reasonable bail any time soon. They decided to go to federal court in search of an injunctive remedy: first, for the immediate events surrounding the Black Panther raids and incarcerations; second, to obtain an injunction against police interference in the Black Panther sponsored conference about to begin; and, finally, by suing on behalf of Philadelphia citizens as a class, they sought wider relief on claims of systematic police violation of constitutional rights. Specifically, they decided to ask the court to find a pattern of violations of citizens' rights that was known and acquiesced in by the highest officials in the police department and the city. What they sought was an order placing the operation of the police department in the hands of a court appointed receiver until such time as a responsible city administration could assure an end to the previous abuses and provide a promise to discipline police officers in the future.

While the Black Panthers were parties to the litigation in the early stages, the principal plaintiffs were a number of named individuals and an organization known as the Council of Organizations on Philadelphia Police Accountability and Responsibility (COPPAR). A biracial organization, COPPAR was headed by Mary Rouse, a black leader of the Kensington neighborhood organization, a Floyd Platton, a white employee of the Philadelphia Water Department.

LIABILITY PHASE

The liability portion of the *Rizzo* litigation is not as complex as some of the other cases considered in this study, but the political tension, time factors, and continuing polarized environment make it somewhat difficult to follow. The *Goode* and *COPPAR* trials were conducted separately. The litigation was consolidated only later during the decision process. As in the earlier cases, it is important to try to view the pieces of the liability case as the judge saw them.

The judge drawn for the *Goode* and *COPPAR* cases was John P. Fullam. Originally from Gardenville in Bucks County, Pennsylvania, Fullam completed his undergraduate education at Villanova and his law degree at Harvard. Returning from naval duty during World War II, Fullam entered private legal practice. He began his judicial career on the Bucks County Common Pleas Court in 1960 and came to the federal bench in 1966 on an appointment by President Johnson. All of those interviewed consider him extremely bright and decisive. All but one found his demeanor as a trial judge very effective. As one of the attorneys put it, "He's a no nonsense, let's get on with it, let's get it on the record, let's move [type of person]." Like several of his colleagues, Fullam had in the past and would in the future be called upon to hear suits concerning Philadelphia police practices.

Fullam had been aware of police misconduct issues and their relationship to racial tensions since his days as a common pleas court judge. The events of the late 1960s provided everyone, and particularly federal judges, with a sensitivity to civil rights issues. Local unrest forced even more attention to these questions. Fullam recalls, "Nobody could work in Philadelphia without being aware of the racial tensions in the city."[69]

The *Goode* Trial

The trial in *Goode v. Rizzo* began in May 1970. The city's approach was "an all court press. . . . It was a brawl with no quarter given." Peter Hearn, attorney for Goode, recalls the opening day of the trail vividly:

> There were smaller rooms on the top floor . . . not originally designed as court-rooms. They were smaller than the original courtrooms which were on the second floor of the building. And I remember being in that room with something on the order of forty to forty-five uniformed police officers plus a group, obviously police officers but in civilian clothes of another ten to fifteen people. My witnesses were there. . . . With a phalanx of more than fifty police officers milling around the hall where our witnesses had to walk through this group to get into the courtroom. Then there was this army of police officers standing across the back wall. The room was too small for them to all sit down. It was a very intimidating setting.[70]

Judge Fullam observed, "It was almost as if the police had decided to put on a full dress parade."[71] At the suggestion of the plaintiffs, Fullam moved the case down to a regular courtroom to correct the situation.

The city initially argued that the actions of the two individual officers named in the *Goode* case had been reasonable and within the limits of their authority. Beyond that, they denied that senior city officials had any kind of policy or intention to suggest or permit police abuse. Ultimately, the city would switch its position. Assuming, they said, that there were a few bad police officers in the department, that certainly did not represent a policy of abuse.

The plaintiffs' case was in two parts. First, they offered witnesses to the variety of incidents involving the particular officers targeted in the *Goode* suit. Second, they attempted to demonstrate that higher level officials were aware of the problems and took no significant action; in fact, they discouraged attempts by citizens to make complaints of police abuse and by their inaction and the Police Commissioner's public statements sent clear messages to the officers in the street that there really were no limits and no sanctions.

Of the eight specific incidents charged, four involved physical assaults by one or both officers.[72] Four involved racially abusive language. In only one of the cases were charges initially lodged by the officers ultimately pressed to conviction, and that one was for interference with a police officer. In order to understand the nature of the *Goode* case it is necessary to briefly consider some of the particular incidents as recounted in the court's findings of fact.

In March 1969 Officer DeFazio in an unmarked car saw a black teenager, Roy Lee Shaw, walk out of a store and proceed down the sidewalk. The officer left the car and approached Shaw on the sidewalk calling him to halt. Shaw "asked why he was being stopped, whereupon DeFazio struck him on the head with a blackjack."[73] Shaw hit the officer on the chin and ran but stopped when DeFazio drew his revolver and called out for the teenager to halt. Shaw was struck several more times in the process of placing him in the police car, from there into the police wagon, and later at the police station. He was held for a time at the station during which his mother's requests to see her son were refused. Shaw was taken to the hospital where he received treatment, but he was then returned to the station and released. A preliminary finding of delinquency entered against him was later dropped. Fullam concluded:

> There was no basis for stopping Shaw in the first place, there was no probable cause
> to arrest him, and his arrest was illegal. He did not assault DeFazio, nor was he
> guilty of disorderly conduct; he merely made minimal efforts to defend himself and
> to protest the violation of his rights.[74]

Another of the cases concerned a blind black man who police considered a suspect
in a recent rape. The rape charges were ultimately dismissed because the victim was
unable to identify the defendant. During the initial arrest, the suspect was assaulted.
Fullam concluded that "Sisco was struck, and that the officers did not limit their use of
force to the precise amount required to 'subdue' a prisoner who was, after all, both
blind and handcuffed, and who had earlier relinquished his weapon when ordered to do
so."[75]

In one incident a white teacher at a school in a predominantly black neighborhood
who had just left a faculty meeting was stopped by one of the officers in front of the
school. The teacher got into an argument with the officer when the policeman would
not indicate the reason for stopping him. "Among other things, DeFazio told Clark to
shut up, and accused him of acting like 'the black pigs that live around here.' "[76] The
teachers came out of the school objecting to the officer's behavior, whereupon DeFazio
seemed prepared to arrest Clark but changed his mind at the urging of the school principal. Members of the faculty and staff filed complaints about the officer's conduct with
the police commissioner and the mayor.

The same officer, in another incident, "referred to a member of the public as a
'Jew bastard' in the presence of a Jewish police officer."[77]

In six of the eight incidents, the officers involved received no punishment. In the
Clark and anti-Semitic remarks cases, the officer faced the Police Board of Inquiry on
the same day for both complaints. In the Clark incident he received a two-day suspension. Fullam summarizes the second decision as follows:

> DeFazio was also tried by the Police Board of Inquiry on charges of insubordination,
> neglect of duty and disobedience of orders. He was found guilty of [the anti-Semitic
> reference]; appearing at a court hearing in improper uniform, and refusing to submit
> a memorandum to a superior officer. The Board of Inquiry recommended a 10-day
> suspension; Police Commissioner Rizzo reduced thus to three days' suspension.
>
> As a result of the two incidents. . . , DeFazio received a total suspension of five
> days. However, this was "served" by deducting five days from his accrued vacation
> time, and this did not result in any actual pecuniary loss.[78]

Officer DeFazio retired on disability before the trial ended in the *COPPAR* case in
1971.

The *COPPAR* Litigation

Whereas the *Goode* litigants presented a case focused on conduct by specific officers in
a pattern they argued was clearly known and acquiesced in by police superiors, the
COPPAR attorneys took a much wider approach and began from a very different situation. Initially they had gone into court to obtain protection for the Black Panthers who
were under arrest and to obtain an injunction preventing police interference with the

upcoming convention. Only when these goals were accomplished did they turn to their wider demand for broad remedial relief against police abuse in general.

Fullam dealt with Akers and Lore's request for an order requiring a reasonable opportunity for bail hearings for the jailed Black Panthers. Akers recalls Fullam's reaction as follows:

> The judge called us to side bar and he said, "This bail situation is really intolerable. You know we have a policy of abstention . . . and we hate to interfere with state court proceedings, but unless you find a way to hold bail hearings in the normal course, I will be forced to intervene." Whereupon he adjourned to reconvene at 2:00 pm. There was nothing in writing but the City Solicitor and the District Attorney went back to their respective offices and advised them of what the judge had said. By 2:00 pm they were in a position to advise the judge that suitable arrangements would be made.[79]

There were mixed signals concerning what the police might do regarding the forthcoming Peoples Convention. Several quite conservative community organizations took the position that the convention must be protected as a matter of free speech and assembly. Some private citizens attacked the idea and launched private suits in an unsuccessful effort to block the meeting. Police critics suggested that, like the raid on the Black Panther offices and homes, Rizzo would look for a plausible excuse to break up the convention. Rizzo denied the charges, insisting that all citizens had constitutional rights which would be protected by the police so long as they were orderly and did not break the law.

On September 4, 1970, the day before the convention was scheduled to begin, Fullam issued a temporary restraining order, which he termed "precautionary," maintaining that the meeting was entitled to legal protection and prohibiting police interference. The order was not to "be construed as limiting in any way the authority of police to enforce the law in a lawful manner and to exercise and defend their rights as citizens." Calling for calm and reason in that turbulent period, Fullam admonished:

> Nobody can justify this shooting of policemen by some madman or an idiot with a gun. But a madman out of control is not much more dangerous to the community than a policeman who loses control and goes shooting up peoples' houses and raiding them. . . .

> And every time this comes up, the court is told that this was a violation of (police) orders and no injunction is necessary because the police would not do these injustices . . . and the police can control the police.[80]

This was the same John Fullam who had refused to take action against the police on grounds that police would correct violations of citizens' rights in the Rittenhouse Square hippies case in 1968. He also had been hearing testimony in the *Goode v. Rizzo* litigation since the previous May in which the police department insisted that it could and would maintain discipline and prevent police abuses. Fullam added that his order was not based on the assumption that the police would interfere with the rights of those attending the convention but was simply intended to "reassure the plaintiffs that their rights are not being ignored . . . that they have redress with the courts."[81]

As to the wider attempt to obtain redress for police abuse, the COPPAR lawyers made two important tactical choices. The first was to press for the resolution of these claims by calling for a full hearing on their motion for a preliminary injunction, which followed on the heels of their petition for a temporary restraining order. The point of this type of procedure is that it is expedited based upon the claim that one needs the preliminary and, hopefully later, a permanent injunction because of the emergency nature of the situation. On the other hand, an expedited proceeding leaves little time to prepare a major piece of litigation, like a challenge to city police practices. Given their view that the situation was too dangerous for delay, Lore and Akers determined that there was no point in involving themselves in complex discovery and other pretrial proceedings. In any case, to them, the facts seemed so clear and the evidence so overwhelming that there really was no need to prepare for more extended litigation.

The second decision was driven by the fact that the plaintiffs had very limited financial resources. Akers and Lore had the assistance of some enthusiastic community groups and a number of law students, but not much else. They decided to prepare a substantial portion of their case by mobilizing the community activists in order to find people who had been the victims of police abuse and then follow up with interviews by the law student assistants.

The case presented by the *COPPAR* plaintiffs consisted of twenty-eight separate incidents of alleged police abuse that involved twenty-three named officers and more than fifty unidentified policemen. In at least ten of the incidents, the plaintiffs claimed physical abuse. Most of the allegations involved some mixture of abuse of authority, illegal arrests or detentions, and racial slurs. In a number of the situations, the plaintiffs presented evidence that complaints had been lodged with no later action by police officials, suggesting that the allegations made by police officers were simply cover charges. In three cases the plaintiffs argued that the victims of abuse agreed not to press complaints against police officers in exchange for dismissal of the charges against them.[82] Particularly troublesome was the claim that some of the incidents had occurred after Fullam had issued the temporary order.

The *Goode* trial was concluding just as the arguments in *COPPAR* were beginning, during the fall of 1970. The *COPPAR* hearings ran until March 1971. It was after the two trials had been concluded that Judge Fullam consolidated the cases. The *COPPAR* case presented a voluminous record containing twenty-one hearing days and nearly 250 witnesses' testimony. Because there were so many incidents involved in the litigation, "[i]t was," Fullam notes, "like deciding 30 to 40 separate civil cases."[83] The liability decision was issued in March 1973.

In the interim, the September 1970 Black Panther sponsored convention took place without any incident. In fact, Philadelphians were afforded the rare treat of reading compliments by all parties of police and citizen behavior.[84] It was, however, a brief respite.

There were other challenges for the Philadelphia police apart from the *Rizzo* and *COPPAR* cases. The Pennsylvania Advisory Committee of the U.S. Commission on Civil Rights was asked in 1969 to pursue allegations of police abuse. The Committee held hearings in 1971, in the wake of the 1970 disturbances, and issued its report in June 1972. It found that

> [t]he Philadelphia Police Department "operated as a closed system in terms of responsibility and accountability, immune to complaints of police abuse, with an attitude that the department is a law unto itself and that only the police are capable of policing themselves."

The Committee concluded that there was, in fact, no effective avenue of redress of citizen complaints. We further concluded that the role of the police, with some exceptions, in the minority community appeared to be one of containment and control, rather than protection and service.[85]

In December 1970 the Commonwealth of Pennsylvania and several named individuals brought suit against the city and several of its officers charging racial discrimination in the hiring and promotion policies of the police department. The state charged that while the city was about thirty-five percent minority residents, principally black, approximately eighteen percent of the force was minority and that that percentage was, in fact, declining. Moreover, the hiring of new minority police officers had dropped precipitously to under ten percent of new hires by 1970. Specifically, the department's written examination and background checks were named as tools used to discourage and, in some cases, block minority hiring.[86] This case, *Commonwealth v. O'Neill*, came to Judge Fullam's desk in the midst of the *Goode* and *COPPAR* litigation.[87] Fullam thought the coincidence of having the same judge assigned to both the police misconduct cases and the police discrimination suit was almost beyond belief. "I sent my law clerk down to see if it really was a result of random selection. It was."[88]

Finally, in the summer of 1970, again in the midst of the police cases, Fullam was named to preside in the Penn Central Railroad bankruptcy, a huge piece of litigation involving a host of parties and complex issues. He issued a string of orders in that case alone, quite apart from the other work pending on his calendar.

For these and other reasons, Fullam's liability finding in the *Goode* and *COPPAR* litigation was delayed for two years. That delay would be considered extremely important by some of the parties later in the appellate stage of the case.

Fullam's Liability Finding

Fullam's decision in *COPPAR v. Rizzo* found the city guilty of a pattern of police misconduct of several types, including physical abuse, illegal arrests and detentions, and discriminatory treatment of minorities. He concluded that because there were persistent violations that the department failed to correct and for which no alternative relief was available, it would be necessary for the court to order some limited form of remedy. The opinion supporting Fullam's conclusion is interesting not only for what it includes in the way of findings of fact and conclusions of law, but also for what it excludes and the foundation premises it announces as critical to resolution of police misconduct cases.

The summary of factual findings consumed all but five pages of the thirty-three page opinion, but those five pages contained several important statements about the premises that judges ought to employ in resolving this kind of case. Like all of the other judges studied, Fullam includes a deference statement that recognizes the problems and dangers encountered when federal judges issue rulings that second-guess and potentially interfere with day-to-day administrative operations. More important, however, is what he refers to as "a few general observations about the difficult problems of the police in our society, and the practical limitations upon the role of courts in resolving disputes of the kind represented by this litigation."[89] Citing key literature in the field, including Skolnick, Westley, Chevigny, Niederhoffer, the President's Commission Task Force Report on Police, and the Kerner Commission Report, Fullam suggests that any evaluation of police conduct must recognize that police are not responsible for, and cannot solve, the social problems they are called upon to confront every day. Yet police officers are the "target[s] for undifferentiated hostility generated by causes having no direct relationship to police conduct."[90] In addition, the realities of police work in the streets must be judged with a realistic understanding of the danger and complexity of the environment within which it is carried out:

> The tactics of police enforcement involve a considerable measure of naked power. Dealing so frequently with persons who have no respect for law or for the police function, the policeman cannot always rely upon peaceful and reasonable persuasion as the instrument of choice.

> The hazards of police work are very real and pervasive. The conduct of individual officers in stress-filled situations should not be judged by the standards of armchair hindsight.[91]

The recognition of these problems led Fullam to set a decision rule for himself, one that required resolution of close questions in favor of the police. "Whenever the merits were substantially in doubt, the defendants were accorded the full benefit of the presumption that the police officers acted properly."[92]

Despite that approach, however, Fullam found a pattern of police abuses that occurred "with such frequency that they cannot be dismissed as rare, isolated instances; and that little or nothing is done by the city authorities to punish such infractions, or to prevent their recurrence."[93] While he pointed out a number of examples introduced by plaintiffs that did not qualify as police abuse, others were extremely serious and could not simply be explained away as a few unusual cases. It is, he said, "the obligation of a federal court under the Civil Rights Act, to take appropriate action to prevent recurring and otherwise predictable violations of the constitutional rights of citizens":[94]

> [T]his Court has not decided that the plaintiffs and the class they represent have a constitutional right to improved departmental procedures for handling civilian complaints against police. What the Court has decided is that, under existing circumstances, violations of constitutional rights by police do occur in an unacceptably high number of instances; that, in the absence of changes in procedures, such violations are likely to continue to occur; and that revision of procedures for handling civilian complaints is a necessary first step in attempting to prevent future abuses.[95] (emphasis added)

Ultimately, the battle in *COPPAR v. Rizzo* on appeal was primarily about what Fullam did not say and the way he limited his statement of findings. Had his tone and language been less moderate and his qualifications less careful, the case may have had a different conclusion. First, he found that on the evidence it appeared that the violations of citizens' rights were committed by a relatively small percentage of the 7,500 man (at that time Philadelphia had no female patrol officers) force. He did not find that there was a conscious "Police Department policy to violate the legal and constitutional rights of citizens, nor to discriminate on the basis of race."[96] Still, the violations happened "entirely too frequently" and occurred in a pattern that tended to assure abuse for blacks under several sets of circumstances or whites if they questioned police authority or behavior. Those officers who engaged in misconduct were unlikely to be punished even where their activities were brought to the attention of their superiors. It was highly unlikely that their abuses would ever reach their superiors, however, since there was no adequate means for civilians to enter grievances and the existing mechanism was, in fact, used to block or discourage complaints.

Fullam chose not to make statements about each incident except for a few of the more egregious cases of abuse or where he wanted to make clear that there was no police misconduct at all. His opinion used very moderate language, avoiding the opportunity presented by the record to be much more critical and strident. It completely ignored Commissioner (who was by that time Mayor) Rizzo's caustic public rhetoric. Remembering his efforts in writing the opinion, Fullam notes, "I thought if there's any way that this is going to work it's got to be done carefully. If I go jumping in and lambasting the police, nothing would be accomplished."[97] In fact, it was precisely the moderate and limited nature of the opinion that the city's attorney, James Penny, chose to attack on appeal.

Another tactic that Fullam adopted that allowed him to limit the harshness and breadth of his liability decision concerned a third case against the police which had recently been settled by a consent decree. *Alexander v. Rizzo* was launched by an entirely different group of plaintiffs after the *Goode* case was in progress but before the *COPPAR* trial. The case was before Judge Higginbotham on a claim of a pattern and practice by police of illegal arrests "for investigation" and illegal detentions. That suit was resolved in December 1972 with an agreement by the police department to improve arrest for investigation procedures.[98] Though none of the attorneys involved in *Goode* or *COPPAR* were aware of the *Alexander* case, Fullam concluded that he could take judicial notice of the settlement as justification for limiting the scope of the relief he had to contend with. He wrote, "To a large extent, consideration of sweeping injunctive relief in the present cases has been obviated by the consent injunctive decree in the *Alexander* [case]. . . . [T]he entry of that decree should go far to eliminate many of the abuses complained of in the present cases."[99]

The plaintiffs' attorneys saw the judge's moderate tone as a technique used by Fullam to gain political acceptance of the opinion and the remedial order to follow. Hearn suggested:

> It certainly was moderate in tone. I think both in this case and in another case involving racial discrimination in police hiring, Fullam went out of his way to characterize the conduct of the defendants in gentle terms. . . . [T]here is a great problem in establishing the credibility of any court order that aims at establishing institutional change. My sense is that Fullam tried to lessen the rhetoric to enhance the saleability of such a court order.[100]

Lore put the matter in clear political terms:

> He [Fullam] understood . . . he was doing both a juridical act and a political juridical act. He knew from all the testimony and from his own sitting in previous cases what the situation was. What I gather that he sought to do is to find a middle road that would not constitute a challenge to the difficult job of policing the city and would afford a measure of relief that was acceptable to important litigants, though not all of the litigants, who were then before him.[101]

Crafting a remedy that would be effectively implemented would require a great deal more than a light judicial touch in the use of rhetoric.

REMEDY PHASE

Between Fullam's liability ruling of March 1973 and October 5, when the final order was issued, the parties worked with the judge to develop a process remedy for police abuse. The parties designed a civilian complaint procedure which left the decisions on police discipline within the police department. The Supreme Court ultimately reversed the liability decision, but an examination of the remedial development process in what came to be called *Rizzo v. Goode* is, nevertheless, instructive.

Crafting the Remedy

The goal of the *Goode* plaintiffs was quite different from that of the *COPPAR* attorneys with whom they were now teamed. Lore and Akers were of the opinion that since the abuses in the police department were traceable to both the actions and inaction of the city's highest officials, any remedy that left those officials with substantial discretion and final authority over police discipline was doomed from the outset. The lesson of external civilian review procedures was, in their view, that such boards generally have neither the authority nor the access to information required to be effective in policing the police. They insisted that only by placing the department under the control of a federally appointed receiver could these problems be overcome. The *Goode* plaintiffs sought only an easier means for making complaints, protection for those who did complain, guarantees that investigations and final decisions would be made by someone other than the officer's immediate supervisors, prompt resolution of complaints, and adequate information for plaintiffs on the status of their claims.

Fullam cited *Hague v. CIO, Lewis v. Kugler,* and several other lower court opinions for the proposition that the court was empowered, given the liability finding, to impose a rigorous remedy, but he concluded that "deference to the essential role of the police in our society does mandate that intrusion by the courts into this sensitive area should be limited, and should be directed toward insuring that the police themselves are encouraged to remedy the situation."[102] He adopted the approach taken by the *Goode* plaintiffs. Fullam ordered the city to revise its training manuals to clarify policies on arrests, the use of force, and other important procedures. He gave the city thirty days to produce a plan for the revision of its complaint procedures, including:

> (a) ready availability of forms for use by civilians in lodging complaints against police officers; (b) a screening procedure for eliminating frivolous complaints; (c) prompt and adequate investigations of complaints; (d) adjudication of non-frivolous complaints by an impartial individual or body, insulated so far as practicable from chain of command pressures, with a fair opportunity afforded the complainant to present his complaint, and to the police officer to present his defense; and . . . prompt notification to the concerned parties, informing them of the outcome.[103]

Unlike *Parma* and *Milliken* discussed earlier, the city of Philadelphia did produce a specific remedial plan and entered into negotiations, albeit arm's length and limited discussions, on the elements of the proposed remedy. John McNally, who represented the city in the remedy crafting, responded to Fullam's call for a plan to be submitted within a month of the liability order that would comply with the three key provisions of

Fullam's decision: revision of manuals, clarification of departmental policies and discipline procedures, and development of an adequate civilian complaint process. Though he complied with the court's order to participate in formulating a remedy, McNally was insistent from the first that the city's position was that Fullam's ruling was wrong and would be appealed.[104]

The city's proposal was a modified version of its Directive 127, "Complaints Against Police Officers," originally promulgated in 1967. The 1973 version did provide for notice to citizen complainants of the disposition of the charges against the officer concerned and specifically designated the Internal Affairs Bureau as the central body to conduct investigations, but it did not provide standards for the conduct of investigations, deadlines to ensure timeliness in processing, or protection against cases being diverted from the Internal Affairs Board back into the officer's immediate chain of command.[105]

Hearn, Akers, and Lore had a number of discussions on what to do about the remedy, agreeing in the end that Hearn would take the lead. Hearn "anticipated that the greatest attack in any appellate court on the kind of order that we were seeking would be the administrative burden."[106] For that reason, he chose to reply to the city's proposal in the form of further revisions of the "new" Directive 127 rather than proposing something entirely different or presenting arguments in a different form. A slightly modified version of Hearn's response ultimately became the court's final order.

The plaintiffs took the position that they were perfectly prepared to leave the decisionmaking on citizen complaints against police officers within the police department provided that there were clear standards to ensure a rigorous investigation process and guarantees that the process and the records developed in it would be open to public scrutiny. The proposed Directive 127, which they advanced, altered the city plan by

1. modifying the complaint form to ensure more information;

2. guaranteeing the availability of the forms around the city and prohibiting any attempt by an officer to discourage the filing of complaints including those brought by anonymous informants;

3. ensuring that investigations are not conducted by an officer's immediate supervisor but are lodged in the Internal Affairs Bureau;

4. establishing specific standards for investigations;

5. setting time limits for investigations, hearings, and final decisions; and

6. requiring hearings before the Police Board of Inquiry in disputed cases in which complainants could participate; and mandating that the records of the proceedings including the Police Commissioner's final ruling be available to the public and the news media for two years after the close of the case.[107]

While there were no formal remedy hearings as there had been in all of the other cases in this study, there were discussions and communications by documents among the parties and the judge throughout the summer and into the fall of 1973. McNally argued that police officials simply could not live with some elements of the proposal, including the required time limits on investigations and their perceived lack of discretion in separating trivial or frivolous claims from those meriting serious attention. Hearn was more than willing to cooperate in ensuring appropriate latitude on dismissal of frivolous complaints and the final order contained a very flexible provision on that subject. He was not willing to give ground on the requirement for minimum standards or time limits for investigations. The plaintiffs' proposal allowed forty-five days for investigation, recommendations to the Commissioner within five days after that, decision by the commissioner within ten days after it reached his office, another twenty days beyond that if the Commissioner determined that a hearing was needed, and up to thirty days more for the Commissioner to reach a final determination and disposition in the case. This total period of nearly four months, they argued, should be more than adequate. Beyond that, the language in the proposal was sufficiently open that special problems could be accommodated. The point was to ensure that, in the normal case, complaints would not be permitted to languish without recourse for the complainant.

There were meetings in chambers over the summer on the remedial order but little progress was made. The city stiffened its resistance and prepared for the appeals to come.

Fullam's final order was issued in October 1973. It used Hearn's recommendation as a base but included an expanded provision for termination of frivolous claims, rejected plaintiffs' call for an avenue of appeal should the Commissioner refuse to take a close case to hearing, and added protections against the use of "cover charges" to interdict the process. Under the guidelines, a refusal by a victim to provide a statement was grounds to terminate the investigation. During the trial evidence had been presented that abusive officers filed "cover charges," like breach of peace, resisting arrest, or similarly vague complaints, against their victims. The charges served to discredit a complaint since it would appear that the officer was the victim of a vindictive evildoer. The other use to which such charges were put, according to witnesses at trial, was that police officers would offer to drop the charges against the citizen in exchange for a commitment not to lodge a complaint against the officer. If, however, the citizen was facing a "cover charge," by making a statement in support of a complaint, he or she was in danger of self-incrimination. The order provided specific protections in that eventuality. Fullam observed, "I couldn't think of a less intrusive remedy. . . . I was honestly trying to come up with a solution that would solve something, not an empty declaration."[108]

While the plaintiffs had hopes that the city might agree in the end to implement what was, in fact, a very mild and quite limited remedy, it rapidly became clear that the city planned to appeal as quickly as possible.

The Appeals Process

Following the remedy order in *Rizzo,* the city gave the case to a new lawyer in the Special Litigation Section of the City Solicitor's Office, James Penny. Penny came to work for the City Solicitor as his first job after completing his degree at Villanova Law School. On arrival he found that the office, in some ways like the police, evidenced a bunker mentality, a feeling that it was under siege from a variety of directions.[109] There were federal challenges to city police hiring practices, education issues, housing disputes, and a state court challenge to conditions at the local jail all pending at once.

Penny's strategy became quickly apparent. Adopting the city's position that no federal court order was acceptable, Penny determined to use the moderate language of the opinion, the delay in its issuance, and the recognized need for deference to city officials expressed in the opinion as the cornerstones of his appeal. In essence, the idea was to use what would be considered by objective observers to be the strengths of Fullam's opinion against it. The city began by asking Fullam for a stay, claiming that anything so important as the mandating of a police complaint procedure should not be imposed before a full appellate consideration unless it was absolutely necessary. Since it had literally been two years since the case was tried and no order had as yet been imposed, surely there was no pressing need.

The city's gambit was clear to Fullam. He found the city's approach "puzzling," "unreasonable," and "unfair" to the plaintiffs:

> By referring only to the docket entries, counsel is able to ignore the numerous ne-
> gotiations, conferences and consultations which have characterized this litigation
> throughout its history. It is undoubtedly correct, as this Court acknowledged in its
> March 4, 1973 Opinion, that the decision rendered on that date was unduly delayed,
> for reasons which, for the most part, were not attributable to the parties or their
> counsel. But the earlier grant of partial preliminary relief, standing alone, would
> seem to negate the assertions in the present Motion. Moreover, it can scarcely be
> suggested that the defendants and their counsel bear no responsibility for the delays
> which have ensued since March 14, 1973, or that these delays are attributable to the
> Court.[110]

He rejected the request for a stay and the city promptly turned to the Court of Appeals for the Third Circuit for the next round.

Support in the Third Circuit

Penny added one new feature to the appeal in his argument to the circuit court. The city asserted that the effect of Fullam's decision was to provide the plaintiffs with a right to a civilian police complaint procedure. The basis for this claim was that since Fullam had not found a policy of police abuse and brutality or discrimination, there had been no violation of rights justifying a review procedure. Therefore, Penny contended, the principal problem that Fullam found was an inadequate police complaint procedure.

The Third Circuit panel rejected the city's argument and pointed out that while Fullam, in his effort to use moderate language and provide a limited and deferential approach to police problems, had not found a deliberate policy, he had found a pattern of violation of constitutional rights that was not limited to one or a few officers, was continuing and predictable, and was tolerated by high level city officials who knew of the problem. Given that, and the fact that there was no alternative redress, the complaint procedure was an appropriate remedy. "We emphasize that the district judge did not find that the plaintiffs were entitled to a change in the disciplinary procedures of the police department as a matter of constitutional right." In fact, wrote Judge Weis, "the procedure which the district court required be implemented by the police department . . . are fully in accord with the American Bar Association Standards Relating to the Urban Police Function, which were unanimously approved by the Executive Committee of the International Chiefs of Police in December, 1972."[111] Finding the record ade-quate to support the order, the court upheld Fullam's process remedy. In so doing, however, Weis wanted to make it quite clear that the appeals judges understood the problem the police faced:

> That we do not reverse the district court's conclusions, however, does not mean that
> we are unaware of the idealism and dedication of the vast majority of police officers.

Their duties are difficult and dangerous, and the work which they perform is too often unheralded and unappreciated. . . . [O]ften the most routine assignment may suddenly turn into one involving death or serious injury to the policemen. And yet, we place upon these officers the additional burdens of almost superhuman patience and forbearance in the face of hostile and provocative conduct and insist that they accord full legal protection and respect to those who would deny similar treatment to the officers. But such high standards must be maintained because of the tremendous importance of police work to the maintenance of an orderly society without which no rights can survive.[112]

The next stop would be the U.S. Supreme Court.

In the Marble Temple

The plaintiffs' attorneys had not contemplated a Supreme Court challenge, but the closer it got, the more they worried. The membership of the Court had changed. The time span between the facts and circumstances that gave rise to the litigation and the perceived calm of early 1975 suggested serious difficulties for them. When the Court granted *certiorari* in March of that year, Hearn knew the situation was looking better for the city.

The city's position in the Supreme Court was essentially the same as its argument in the Third Circuit except that Penny pressed some added arguments that the case was nonjusticiable in addition to being wrong on the merits. He raised standing and ripeness issues, contending that the claims of the plaintiffs were essentially speculative. If, however, the case was to be considered on the merits, he said, then the Court should reverse the rulings below. Even though the Supreme Court had previously upheld the use of injunctions by district courts in the *Hague v. CIO* and *Allee v. Medrano*, both police abuse cases, Penny contended that those suits involved specific findings of a deliberate policy of abuse by the administrators involved.[113] Fullam had found no such policy. The fact that the Court had agreed to hear the case augered well for the city, as did the additions to the Court of Justices Rehnquist and Powell.

Hearn was quite concerned but had taken some preliminary steps to withstand an appeal. First, there was the effort in the district court to construct a remedy that was not burdensome and was, in fact, crafted in the style of the city's own disciplinary policy, leaving the final decision on police conduct in the department. Second, he had given some thought to *amicus curiae* support as early as the remedy crafting stage:

[T]he effort was to achieve what I might call a political balance. We wanted to bring into court on our side major community institutions, conservative community institutions, which would say that this is not something that's going to blow the city wide open. It's reasoned, restrained, and appropriate to the situation. . . . I thought it would help us if they participated.[114]

Indeed, several establishment institutions, included the Philadelphia Chamber of Commerce, the Philadelphia Bar Association, the Greater Philadelphia Movement, and the Commonwealth of Pennsylvania entered the case as *amici* in addition to the more predictable participation by the NAACP Legal Defense and Education Fund, the ACLU, the Mexican American Legal Defense and Education Fund, the Northern California

Police Practices Project, and the Lawyers' Committee for Civil Rights Under Law. In fact, all of the *amici* in the case entered in support of the *Goode* and *COPPAR* plaintiffs.

The oral argument signaled the probable outcome. The first surprise for Penny was the fact that Justice Marshall, the person he anticipated would question the city's case most vigorously, was not on the bench for the argument. Moreover, as the case argued prior to *Rizzo* came to a close, Justice William O. Douglas, suffering the effects of an earlier stroke, signaled for aides to remove his wheelchair from the bench for what was to be the last time. Penny completed his comments in a scant fourteen minutes. He faced few questions and several of those were not probing but supportive, helping the city's advocate highlight the key points of his case. It was different for Hearn. He had barely spoken three short sentences before the questioning began. Questions continued in rapid fire until his time expired.

The case was actually closer than it might have appeared at the time. Justices White, Rehnquist, Powell, and Burger had voted to grant *certiorari,* while Douglas and Stewart had joined the others voting not to hear the case. Justice Douglas retired, leaving what appeared to be a tied Court. As he did so often, Justice Stewart cast the swing vote, joining Justice Rehnquist's opinion for the Court. Stewart argued in conference that Fullam simply had not made sufficiently strong findings to justify the remedy.

Justice Rehnquist's opinion suggested there may have been substance to Penny's arguments on standing and related questions, but he reached the merits of the case nevertheless.[115] Stressing the need for respect by district judges to issues of federalism, the opinion ultimately relied on the judgment that the lower court had not found sufficient linkages between the abuse by some officers and any policy supporting that abuse by leading city officials. The majority noted that there were too few incidents presented in the record and not severe enough findings of abuse to infer a policy by city officials. On reading Justice Rehnquist's opinion, Fullam found the comments about the number of incidents rather ironic. "The lawyers recognized that [the plaintiffs] could present an unlimited number of incidents. We had an informal agreement to limit the number of incidents." [116]

Justice Blackmun, joined by Marshall and Brennan, responded with a sharp dissent. The dissenters argued that the record was much stronger than the majority had recognized. Moreover, the unanimous support by a Third Circuit panel and the arguments of conservative *amici* were ignored, though they carefully underscored the thoroughness and care that went into the preparation of Fullam's opinion. Finally, in refusing to acknowledge the responsibility of city officials for the supervision of their subordinates, the Court was rejecting the rulings of ten of the nation's Circuit Courts of Appeals.[117]

POST DECREE

After the Supreme Court decision, the question was just what the city had won. It may have blocked the remedy developed in the *Rizzo* case, but it did not reduce criticism of police operations. The department faced further accusations of abuse, political pressure, and more litigation.

While the *Goode* remedy was under negotiation, Judge Huyett handed down his opinion in *Farber v. Rizzo* that found police officials, including Commissioner O'Neill, in blatant and willful contempt of court. The court had issued a temporary restraining order prohibiting police from interfering with peaceful demonstrations against a visit by President Nixon in October 1972.[118] After having been informed of the order, the Commissioner and others persisted in removing the picketers.

The *Commonwealth v. O'Neill* hiring discrimination case that had been brought before Judge Fullam was eventually resolved by consent decree. The city faced another challenge based on claims of gender based discrimination because of its policy limiting the available career options of women. In fact, when challenged by the federal government, the city argued that male gender was a bona fide occupational qualification for police patrol officers.[119] That case was eventually settled by consent decree in 1980.

The city lost another federal court fight when the U.S. Commission on Civil Rights appealed the city's refusal to produce material subpoenaed by the Commission in connection with hearings on police abuse held in 1979.[120] It did, however, win its battle when the Department of Justice (DOJ) sued the city charging massive police abuses.[121] Judge Ditter found that DOJ lacked standing to bring suit under the statute generally used in civil rights claims.

The conflict over Philadelphia police administration was not limited to the courtroom. The Philadelphia Crime Commission, the Pennsylvania Crime Commission, the city's leading newspaper, and community organizations continued to challenge police conduct.[122] Pressure mounted for reform. In December 1977 Council Members Ethel Allen and Lucien Blackwell introduced Council Bill 1063 to force action.

In January 1978 District Attorney Edward Rendell established a police brutality unit within his office. At about that time, Ian Lennox of the Philadelphia Crime Commission, Thatcher Longstreth of the Chamber of Commerce, and John Bunting of the First Pennsylvania Corporation met with Commissioner O'Neill and City Director Levinson to urge reform. In February the department implemented a modified Directive 127 that incorporated most of the key elements of the complaint procedure worked out in the *Rizzo v. Goode* case, including (1) investigation by internal affairs; (2) notice to the complainant of the disposition of a case; (3) assurances that investigations would be completed within sixty days of the complaint; and (4) use of the prenumbered complaint forms for internal control. Mayor Rizzo announced his support for the plan.[123] Critics suspected that the department was attempting to stave off serious challenges by proposing an alternative that provided no guarantee of effective implementation and oversight.

Charges against the department mounted. Some Philadelphians argued that the situation has improved dramatically. Part of the change is attributed to the administration of Mayor Green. Others suggest that times have changed and the pressures are different. Critics, like Harry Lore, remain adamant that the events surrounding the *Rizzo* decisions reinforced unprofessional attitudes within the department in a subtle but significant way. The debate over police operations in the city was recently reinvigorated by the raid on the so-called MOVE house in West Philadelphia.

CONCLUSION

The long-standing conflict over police conduct in Philadelphia presents a number of the issues that have been faced by judges in other cities around the nation. An unusual series of events crystallized opposition to police practices under Commissioners Rizzo and O'Neill and gave rise to the *Goode* and *COPPAR* cases.

Judge Fullam found a pattern of constitutional violations that was known by senior officials but in which no effective corrective action was taken. Fullam chose to present his findings in what appeared to be the least abrasive fashion, but, in so doing, prepared an opinion that did not make the most powerful record for appeal. The negotiated remedy was far from innovative. It reflected the elements of effective police complaint procedures generally approved by a variety of professional and community organizations. It left decisions on complaints of police conduct with senior police officials.

The decision was ultimately reversed by the Supreme Court, but the difficulties of police/community relations continued. Yet the *Rizzo* case provides another perspective on the operation of remedial decree litigation and the kinds of problems and choices faced by judges called upon to render judgment. This is the last of the major cases in the study. It is time now to determine what lessons we can learn from the effort.

NOTES

1. *Council of Organizations on Philadelphia Police Accountability and Responsibility [COPPAR] v. Rizzo,* 357 F. Supp. 1289 (EDPA 1974); *aff'd sub nom. Goode v. Rizzo,* 506 F.2d 542 (3rd Cir. 1974); *rev'd Rizzo v. Goode,* 423 U.S. 362 (1976).

2. Note: "Philadelphia's Police Practice and the Law of Arrest," 100 *U. Pa L. Rev.* 1182 (1952).

3. *Id.,* at 1183.

4. *Id.,* at 1201–2.

5. *Id.,* at 1202.

6. *Id.,* at 1211.

7. Spencer Coxe, "Police Advisory Board: The Philadelphia Story," 35 *Conn. B.J.* 138, 139 (1961). *See also* Comment: "Police-Philadelphia's Police Advisory Board—A New Concept in Community Relations," 7 *Vill. L. Rev.* 656 (1962).

8. Coxe, *supra* note 7, at 139–40. The author of the *Vill. L. Rev.* Comment rejected claims that police officials were "whitewashing" charges against officers, based on his finding that most of those brought before the Police Board of Inquiry from 1952 to 1959 were found guilty. Coxe's point, however, was that very few citizen abuse complaints were ever permitted to go before that body and that the internal discipline cases were generally brought by superiors against relatively junior officers, resulting in a high likelihood of conviction for the internal offenses.

9. Coxe, *supra* note 7, at 139–40.

10. *Id.,* at 140.

11. *Harrington v. Tate,* 254 A.2d 622, 624 (PA 1969).

12. The members of the Board first named by Dilworth included Thorsten Sellin, Chair of the Department of Sociology at the University of Pennsylvania; Willaim T. Coleman, Jr., an attorney; William Rose, a member of the Philadelphia Joint Board of the International Ladies Garment Workers' Union; Clarence Pickett, Executive Secretary Emeritus of the American Friends Services Committee; and Edward Reilly, Superintendent of Schools for the Archdiocese of Philadelphia. See Coxe, *supra* note 7, at 138.

13. See Coxe, *supra* note 7, at 144; and Comment, *supra* note 7, at 657–59.

14. First Annual Report of the Police Review Board of Philadelphia, Sept. 1959, p. 7.

15. Third Annual Report of the Police Advisory Board of Philadelphia, Sept. 1961, pp. 7–8.

16. *Id.,* at 4.

17. Fourth Annual Report of the Police Advisory Board of Philadelphia, Sept. 1962, p. 2.

18. Second Annual Report of the Police Advisory Board of Philadelphia, Sept. 1960, pp. 5–6.

19. *Harrington v. Tate, supra* note 11, at 622.

20. Ninth Annual Report of the Police Advisory Board of Philadelphia, Mar. 1968, p. 2.

21. John F. Clancy, "Tate Kills Advisory Board, Terms Action Gift to Police," *Philadelphia Inquirer,* Dec. 23, 1969, p. 1.

22. *Id.*

23. *COPPAR v. Rizzo,* 357 F.Supp., *supra* note 1, at 1293–94.

24. *Heard v. Rizzo,* 281 F. Supp., 720 (EDPA 1968).

25. *Id.,* at 726–27.

26. *Id.,* at 733. Emphasis added.

27. *Hughes v. Rizzo,* 282 F. Supp. 881 (EDPA 1968).

28. Interview with John McNally, Aug. 7, 1985, Philadelphia.

29. *Hughes v. Rizzo, supra* note 27, at 884.

30. *Id.*

31. *Id.,* at 884.

32. *Id.,* at 885.

33. *Leslie Tobin Imports, Inc. v. Rizzo,* 305 F. Supp. 1135 (EDPA 1969).

34. *Id.,* at 1141.

35. *Butcher v. Rizzo,* 317 F. Supp. 899 (EDPA 1970).

36. Louis B. Schwartz, "Complaints Against the Police: Experience of the Community Rights Division of the Philadelphia District Attorney's Office," 118 *U. Pa. L. Rev.* 1023 (1970).

37. Interview with Peter Hearn, Aug. 19, 1985, Philadelphia.

38. *COPPAR v. Rizzo,* 357 F.Supp., *supra* note 1 at 1296.

39. "Blacks' Suit Charges Police Brutality; Rizzo Calls It Part of 'Insidious Plot,' " *Philadelphia Inquirer,* Feb. 18, 1970, p. 1.

40. *Id.*

41. Hearn interview, *supra* note 37.

42. *Id.*

43. U.S. Commission on Civil Rights, Hearings Held in Philadelphia, Pennsylvania, February 6, 1979; April 16–17, 1979 *Police Practices and Civil Rights* (Wash., DC: Government Printing Office, 1979), pp. 102–9.

44. "Rizzo Tells U.S. How His Police Fight Crime and Demonstrations in Philadelphia," *Philadelphia Inquirer,* June 3, 1970, p. 1. *See also* Jim Nicholson, "Rizzo Enjoys Telecast, Hails 'Pro-Police Calls,' " *Philadelphia Inquirer,* June 3, 1970.

45. "Police and Fireman Battle Rioters in Asbury Park," *Philadelphia Inquirer,* July 7, 1970, p. 1; Carlo Sandella and Richard F. Casey, "At Least 75 Are Injured in Asbury Park Rioting," *Philadelphia Inquirer,* July 8, 1970, p. 1; Carol Sandella, "Did HUD Fund Denial Spark Asbury Park Riots?" *Philadelphia Inquirer,* July 9, 1970, p. 1; "Jury to Hear Testimony in Trial of Black Panther," *Philadelphia Inquirer,* July 14, 1970, p. 3; Saul Friedman, "Police Are Blamed for Panthers' Rise," *Philadelphia Inquirer,* July 25, 1970, p. 1; "Huey Newton Freed Under $50,000 Bail in Policeman's Death," *Philadelphia Inquirer,* Aug. 6, 1970, p. 1; "Judge, 3 Captors Are Slain Outside Calif. Courthouse," *Philadelphia Inquirer,* Aug. 8, 1970, p. 1.

46. Jeremy Heymsfeld, "Emergency Is Proclaimed in Tasker Area Violence: Mayor Acts in Racial Outbursts," *Philadelphia Inquirer,* June 11, 1970, p. 1.

47. *Id.,* at 4.

48. George Murray and David Umansky, "Fights Erupt Near Bartram as Blacks Stage March," *Philadelphia Inquirer,* June 13, 1970, p. 1.

49. *Rizzo v. Goode,* No. 74–942, October Term 1975, *Petition for Writ of Certiorari,* p. 8.

50. *See, e.g.,* Howard Shapiro, "Rizzo Requests Police Role in Bar's Selection of Judges," *Philadelphia Inquirer,* July 20, 1970, p. 1.

51. Interview with William Akers, Aug. 7, 1985, Philadelphia.

52. "Violence Hits Tasker Homes as Police Watch Fairmont," *Philadelphia Inquirer*, Aug. 28, 1970, p. 1.

53. Don McDonough, "Tate Declare Emergency in Tasker, Fairmont Areas," *Philadelphia Inquirer*, Aug. 29, p. 1.

54. *Id.*, at 17.

55. Vincent P. Carocci, "Shafer Declines to Call Off Temples Panther Conference," *Philadelphia Inquirer*, Aug. 30, 1970, p. 2.

56. Thomas J. Madden and James Lintz, "Park Guard Slain, Another Wounded; Police Press Hunt—Rizzo Calls Crime an 'Execution.' " *Philadelphia Inquirer*, Aug. 30, 1970, p. 1.

57. Dennis Kirkland and David Umansky, "400 Search Park Area in W. Phila.," *Philadelphia Inquirer*, Aug. 30, 1985, p. 1.

58. Thomas J. Madden and E.J. Hussie, "2 More Police Shot in West Philadelphia," *Philadelphia Inquirer*, Aug. 31, 1970, p. 3.

59. Neil K. Fischer and Fred Smigelski, " 'My Men' Are Shot, Rizzo Tells Mayor," *Philadelphia Inquirer*, Aug. 31, 1970, p. 1.

60. Robert Terry and Charles Gilbert, "14 Panthers Seized in Raid Are Held in $100,000 Bail," *Philadelphia Inquirer*, Sept. 1, 1970, p. 1.

61. *Id.*

62. *See* John F. Clancy, "The Police Say," *Philadelphia Inquirer*, Sept. 1, 1970, p. 1.

63. William J. Speers, "A Week of Violence: The Facts and the Meaning," *Philadelphia Inquirer*, Sept. 6, 1970, p. 10.

64. Akers interview, *supra* note 51; and Harry Lore interview, Aug. 8, 1985, Philadelphia. See also Charyn Sutton, "How Blacks Feel," *Philadelphia Inquirer*, Sept. 1, 1970, p. 1.

65. "14 Panthers Stand Silent as Judge Weinrott Sets Bail," *Philadelphia Inquirer*, Sept. 1, 1970.

66. "Bail Reduction Hearings Set Separately for Panthers," *Philadelphia Inquirer*, Sept. 2, 1970, p. 1.

67. Lore interview, *supra* note 64.

68. Akers interview, *supra* note 51.

69. Interview with Judge John Fullam, Sept. 4, 1985, Philadelphia.

70. Hearn interview, *supra* note 34.

71. Fullam interview, *supra* note 69.

72. There were actually ten incidents in the *Goode* case and more than thirty in *COPPAR*, but Judge Fullam consolidated several incidents in both cases. He ultimately treated *Goode* as presenting eight different incidents and *COPPAR* as alleging twenty-eight.

73. *COPPAR v. Rizzo*, 357 F. Supp., *supra* note 1, at 1295.

74. *Id.*

75. *Id.*, at 1299.

76. *Id.*, at 1300.

77. *Id.*

78. *Id.*

79. Akers interview, *supra* note 51.

80. Quoted in Edward Eisen, "Court Puts Restraints on Police: Rizzo 'Pleased' at Order Clarifying Panthers' Rights," *Philadelphia Inquirer*, Sept. 5, 1970, p. 9.

81. *Id.*

82. In the Alaberti and Whelan incident, the parties who were arrested were warned by their ward committeeman that pressing charges against police officers might result in charges against them. *COPPAR v. Rizzo*, 357 F. Supp., *supra* note 1, at 1310.

83. Fullam interview, *supra* note 69.

84. *See, e.g.*, Dennis Kirkland and Hoag Levins, "Spirit of Peace Flows Freely at Panthers' Parley," *Philadelphia Inquirer*, Sept. 7, 1970, p. 1; and Gerald McKelvey, "Rizzo's

Critics Hum Different Melody, Praise Police Handling of Convention," *Philadelphia Inquirer*, Sept. 9, 1970, p. 1.

85. Statement of Grace Alpern, Chairperson, Pennsylvania Advisory Committee, in *Police Practices and Civil Rights, supra* note 43, at 34–35.

86. Donald Janson, "A Police Ratio Set for Philadelphia," *New York Times*, May 27, 1972, p. 1.

87. *Commonwealth of Pennsylvania v. O'Neill*, 345 F. Supp. 305 (EDPA 1972).

88. Fullam interview, *supra* note 69.

89. *COPPAR v. Rizzo*, 357 F.Supp., *supra* note 1, at 1317.

90. *Id.*

91. *Id.*

92. *Id.,* at 1292.

93. *Id.,* at 1319.

94. *Id.,* at 1320.

95. *Id.,* at 1321.

96. *Id.*

97. Fullam interview, *supra* note 69.

98. *Alexander v. Rizzo,* Civ. Action No. 70–992, "Final Decree," Dec. 18, 1972.

99. *Id.,* at 1320.

100. Hearn interview, *supra* note 37.

101. Lore interview, *supra* note 64.

102. *COPPAR v. Rizzo*, 357 F.Supp., *supra* note 1, at 1320.

103. *Id.*

104. Interview with John McNally, Aug. 7, 1985, Philadelphia.

105. "Rizzo v. Goode," No. 74–942 October Term 1974, "Appendix," p. 136a [hereafter "Appendix"].

106. Hearn interview, *supra* note 37.

107. "Appendix," *supra* note 105, at 151a *et seq.*

108. Fullam interview, *supra* note 69.

109. Interview with James Penny, Aug. 7, 1985, Philadelphia.

110. *COPPAR v. Rizzo*, "Memorandum," Dec. 18, 1973, in "Appendix," *supra* note 105, at 189a.

111. *Goode v. Rizzo*, 506 F.2d, *supra* note 1, at 542, 548.

112. *Id.,* at 547.

113. See *Allee v. Medrano*, 416 U.S. 802 (1974); and *Hague v. CIO*, 307 U.S. 496 (1939).

114. Hearn interview, *supra* note 37.

115. *Rizzo v. Goode*, 423 U.S., *supra* note 1, at 362.

116. Fullam interview, *supra* note 69.

117. *Rizzo v. Goode, supra* note 1, at 385. See also Id., at 385 n. 2.

118. *Farber v. Rizzo*, 363 F. Supp. 386 (EDPA 1973).

119. *United States v. City of Philadelphia*, 499 F. Supp. 1196 (EDPA 1980).

120. *United States v. O'Neill*, 619 F.2d 222 (3rd Cir. 1980).

121. *United States v. City of Philadelphia*, 482 F. Supp. 1248 (EDPA 1979).

122. *See, e.g.,* John Guinther, "Beyond the Call of Duty," *Philadelphia Magazine,* June 1974, pp. 110; Laura Foreman, "Police Abuse Here 'Severe,' Watchdog Unit Says," *Philadelphia Inquirer*, July 17, 1974, p. A2; Kent Pollock, "How City Police Protect Each Other," *Philadelphia Inquirer*, Feb. 18, 1975, p. 4–A; Kent Pollock, "Police the Real Victims of Police Abuse," *Philadelphia Inquirer*, Mar. 23, 1975, p. G1; Gerald McKelvey, "Law Group: Complaints of Police Abuse Double," *Philadelphia Inquirer*, Mar. 19, 1976, p. A1; Connie Langland, "Parents of Man Slain by Police Sue the City," *Philadelphia Inquirer*, Dec. 23, 1978.

123. Willaim K. Marimow, "Police Complaint Plan Starts Today," *Philadelphia Inquirer*, Feb. 15, 1978.

12

The Dynamics of Remedial Litigation

The picture which emerges from this study is considerably different from most of the literature on remedial decrees. While there was no intention to argue whether judges should or should not become involved in such cases, there has emerged a kind of response. Basically, while the question may be interesting to contemplate, it does not have much to do with the reality of the situation confronting judges. They simply are not in a position to refuse to respond to proper cases instituted by appropriate parties under provisions of statutory or constitutional law. Said one judge, "If you can figure out an escape from it, I'd like to hear it. . . . If the problem is properly presented, there's no way the judge can avoid deciding it." The notion that the controversial remedial decree cases are simply manifestations of a liberal federal judiciary intent upon playing guardian without regard to the consequences of their wide ranging decisions simply does not withstand empirical analysis. Some judges are more or less favorably disposed toward decisions in public law policy cases and their attendant remedial orders. However, this study indicates that the judges in these cases were by and large more defensive in approach, more interested in resolving cases than reforming all the ills of American society. In addition, their approach was not isolated and insensitive to political forces but sought in general to mitigate rather than exacerbate conflict unless the court was provided with little or no option.

Far more interesting than such generalized discussions are the lessons that can be learned from the analysis of the cases through the use of the decree litigation model. It allows us to understand the process itself more fully, and, as Heumann and Skolnick have noted, one cannot understand law or politics without a careful study of their processes.[1] This analysis tends to confirm some positions advanced in the remedial decree literature, casts doubt on a number of others, and adds several additional proposals to the propositional inventory that is developing in this area. While the model was presented in skeletal form in Chapter 1 to provide a general conceptual framework to guide the reading of the case studies, it will be reconsidered here in greater depth for analytic purposes.

THE TRIGGER PHASE

Like most such models of the judicial process, this framework assumes environmental inputs in the form of political supports and demands aimed at, or affecting, courts. But the fact that these cases are so often multidirected conflicts that involve a number of levels of government (or differing agencies within a single level) suggests a need for enhanced sensitivity to these environmental influences. There is a tendency in remedy case studies to focus almost exclusively on local politics in establishing environmental considerations.[2]

There are indeed important local forces at work. The general open housing conflict in the greater Cleveland area clearly set the stage for the *Parma* litigation. In *Milliken*, one cannot understand how and why Act 48 developed and precipitated litigation without a sensitivity to the politics of desegregation in Detroit. In later aspects of the case local economic factors played a key role in shaping the decree eventually ordered. In *Wyatt*, the interaction of the University of Alabama community in Tuscaloosa with Bryce hospital was the starting point and a center of continuing influence in the litigation. The inability of the state to respond politically and economically to the crisis in its mental health system even though its leaders were clearly aware of the problem is critical to an understanding of the case. Commissioner Denton's conflicts with Judge Young over the Marion Correctional Facility and the unwillingness of the Ohio legislature to respond to recognized corrections needs had significant impacts on the *Rhodes* case. Philadelphia politics virtually assured litigation over police practices.

But one can miss important elements of the political environment by ignoring political system influences from the national level. In both *Parma* and *Milliken*, changes in litigation policy by the Nixon administration were important. A comparable factor entered the *Wyatt* case when the Reagan administration's Civil Rights Division Chief, William Bradford Reynolds, cooperated with Alabama's attempt to terminate the court's decree by a friendly settlement without participation of the other parties. The *Stewart v. Rhodes* case was also affected, with the Justice Department taking a limited role on the types of remedies it would seek in prison litigation. Judicial appointments at the Supreme Court level were also significant, as Judge Roth found himself in the midst of a major legal transition from one approach to remedial decree cases to another. Those appointments played significant roles in all of the policy spaces considered here and were particularly important in *Milliken*, *Rhodes*, and *Rizzo*. Statutory developments are important as well. Conflict over the shaping of the Community Development Act of 1974 led a federal district judge in Connecticut to require HUD to obtain meaningful housing need and expected-to-reside figures in block grant applications.[3] That ruling was an important element of the *Parma* case.

Viewing the development of mental health policy in national context shows that *Wyatt* was somewhat less innovative than it has been perceived. The *American Bar Association Journal* (A.B.A.J.) had already taken an editorial position in favor the right to treatment. Congress had conducted extensive hearings beginning in 1961, which led in 1964 to the enactment of a new mental health law for the District of Columbia. This law served as a model for state legislative reform efforts around the country during the sixties. The District of Columbia statute, in turn, was the basis for the *Rouse* decision that announced a right to treatment and played a key role in *Wyatt*. It provided a loose precedent for Johnson's constitutional right to treatment decision. Perhaps more important, it triggered a renewed discussion of the right to treatment issue that produced important law review literature which, in turn, played a major role in the several right to treatment cases developing around the country at the same time as *Wyatt*. The campaign of Alabama Governor George Wallace for the presidency was also a factor. In sum, environmental influences from various levels of government must be related in order to understand events triggering remedial decree litigation.

One cannot evaluate behavior in the trigger phase without paying attention to the intergovernmental as well as the government against private citizen nature of the conflicts. Wasby and others have correctly observed that some administrative organizations benefit by having their superiors lose a suit that results in a decree which provides those subordinate units with needed resources or program flexibility.[4] Even so, the literature, particularly that critical of the decrees, tends to cast the litigation as individual against government disputes, often ignoring the multidirected nature of the conflict. In *Parma*, it was a federal government unit, DOJ, preceeding against a local unit, the city. *Milliken* was a suit brought by an external group, NAACP, but it was against the state, on one set of grounds, and against the local school board, on a related but distinct basis. *Wyatt* was launched by private parties against the Mental Health Board and the state, but DOJ and HEW were invited into the case during the litigation process. *Rhodes* was a prisoner suit against the state that was litigated by lawyers from several interest groups with one private practice attorney and the instructor for Ohio State University's Law School Legal Practicum as lead counsel. The array of lawyers and groups shifted repeatedly during the case. The decision by the state to transfer prisoners to a reopened Ohio Pen triggered the *Stewart* case. *Rizzo* involved two independent pieces of litigation against city officials tried separately but decided together, with a private attorney leading one portion of the case and two civil rights lawyers arguing the other. Since, as *Milliken, Wyatt,* and *Rhodes* indicate, the position of the parties to the suit may shift dramatically in later phases of the litigation, it is important to understand the levels as well as the directions of conflict at the trigger stage.

An examination of these cases suggests that remedial decree litigation is instituted as a reaction to a combination of historic policies or practices plus some triggering event. The cases tend to arise in situations where a number of controversial actions have been taken by one or more government units over time until a trigger level is reached. At that point, one critical action will engender a challenge not only to the most recent event, but many of the past actions as well. In *Milliken* several state or local practices could have prompted a suit, but it was Act 48 that was the spark. Once launched, however, all past incidents became elements of the charge against the state and school district, thus expanding the scope of the conflict. The denial of the building permit for the apartment building in *Parma* was the trigger even though other elements in what became the pattern and practice case could have precipitated a suit earlier. In Alabama the Partlow State School and Hospital had already acquired a national reputation for egregius conditions in the late 1960s, having failed accreditation. A number of other opportunities for a legal challenge arose, but it was not until the triggering incident of personnel layoffs at Bryce Hospital that action began. Once legal action started, the other facilities of the mental health department were added to the litigation and the case grew to encompass the past events.

This study offers no evidence to indicate that most contemporary public law policy cases seeking reform orders are carefully planned. Rather, the view of reform litigation as reactive and activated by triggering incidents is far more accurate.[5] Moreover, the cases suggest—contrary to the *Brown v. Board of Education* model in which an interest group, such as NAACP, targets a jurisdiction and strategically launches a suit—that remedial decree actions are often reactive in nature. In *Milliken* the filing of the suit was a response to Act 48 which had nullified the April 7 desegregation plan, but the nature of the suit was dramatically altered by the wider charge of segregation in the entire Detroit school district. That expansion was, in turn, a reaction against the recall of the school board members who had supported the desegregation plan. But because all prior actions tend to be melded with the triggering incident, the appearance of the litigation can be confusing. Thus in *Milliken* the case was launched against the state on grounds that it was operating a segregated school system, but the primary thrust of the litigation was transformed into a challenge to the Detroit district's practices. If the NAACP had not reacted to the recall election by adding the city schools, the remedy situation might have been quite different since state officials would have been the only defendants. Similarly, the *Wyatt* suit was a reaction. Initially launched against the Mental Health Commissioner on behalf of terminated Bryce Hospital employees, the case was transformed into a challenge first to conditions at Bryce and later the problems at Partlow and Searcy hospitals. The inclusion of Partlow in the case altered the litigation dramatically since while all of the hospitals were in bad condition, the Partlow facility revealed the most dramatic examples of inhumane treatment and conditions. By the time of the trial in *Wyatt,* the employees had been removed from the case and patients at Bryce were the principal parties.

Two other aspects of the trigger phase are worth noting. First, suits may meet threshold rejection for any of a number of reasons, such as standing or an inappropriately assumed private right of action. Second, the trigger phase is conditioned by feedback from appellate rulings in terms of both calculations of potential success for those considering launching remedial litigation and in designing the form of the suit to be brought. Thus, for example, the trend toward limiting access to the federal courts procedurally, expanding requirements for proving intentional discrimination, and warnings on the appropriate nature, scope, and duration of remedies provide cautionary signals to potential litigants. The NAACP suit, for instance, begun against Parma prior to the case brought by DOJ fell victim to the standing rule.

THE LIABILITY PHASE

A case that survives pretrial disputes and comes to trial on its merits next enters the liability phase, the purpose of which is to determine the existence and define the extent of any legal violation that justifies a remedy. Much of the discussion of remedial decree cases jumps from the launching of suits to the crafting of remedies. The liability stage, however, is not merely a gatekeeping function for a remedy but a set of actions intimately connected with any future remedy proceeding.

In his discussion of remedies, Chayes asserts, "At this point, right and remedy are pretty thoroughly disconnected. The form of relief does not flow ineluctably from the liability determination but is fashioned ad hoc."[6] Insofar as one may read his comment as indicating that there is no automatic derivation of remedy from the specific nature of the acts bringing about liability, Chayes is not making a point that would differentiate remedial decree cases from other kinds of litigation. It would be unrealistic to assume that in other cases the remedy springs "ineluctably from the liability determination." A recent colloquy between Justices Brennan and Rehnquist on the subject of whether punitive damage doctrines ought to survive shows quite clearly that even in money damage tort actions, there is no inevitability of remedy given a particular statement of liability.[7] Even so, failure to establish an adequate record and opinion in the liability process will dramatically reduce the chances for an adequate decree in the remedy phase and will jeopardize that remedy in any appeal. Important features in the liability phase include that interconnection between the liability judgment and later remedy crafting, the importance of precedent, the tactics of the parties, the role of intervenors, and litigation escape techniques.

Though the presence of record evidence does not guarantee any particular remedy, a decree which orders a core remedy not at all responsive to the elements of the liability record is subject to reversal. A reading of the liability and later remedial opinions in *Parma, Milliken,* and *Wyatt* suggests that judges are well aware of that fact. If the record is carefully and logically developed in such a way as to be easily translatable into a liability opinion, a stable base for a remedy process is established. But if the defendants or others can cloud the record or if plaintiffs do not adequately construct it in the first instance, then the remedy crafting process may be considerably more difficult and the level of jeopardy of the decree is increased. Cavanagh and Sarat state more than a truism when they remind us, "Courts cannot render just decisions when they are presented with but one side of the factual situation out of which litigation arises, or when they are not fully advised of the range of applicable law."[8]

The judge, however, faces a double bind in the preparation of a liability opinion, a phenomenon that can be termed the deference paradox. Opinions written in moderate tones in an effort to reduce conflict and accord deference to decisionmakers may produce a decision which understates the gravity of the violation of law and makes the entire opinion vulnerable to reversal. Judges Fullam and Hogan found that an effort to craft an opinion that grants deference and respect to policymakers may be intended to mitigate conflict but may have very different consequences. Neither state corrections officials in *Rhodes* nor city officials in Philadelphia were impressed by the positive statements and moderate tone of the liability judgments rendered against them. Both successfully used the positive remarks and the lack of severe criticism as grounds for reversal in the Supreme Court. Though Judge Roth's liability opinion was somewhat more critical of the defendants than either Hogan's or Fullam's decisions, Roth, too, had attempted to moderate his tone and the nature of the material presented against the city in the opinion. The opinion affirming Roth in the Sixth Circuit supplied far more detailed criticism of state and local officials than Roth had employed.

There is considerable evidence of great concern by most of the jurists studied here to avoid an image of an activist, interventionist federal judge. That fear is manifest in repeated deference statements in orders and opinions at the liability stage as well as in the remedy and post decree phases. They are more than mere obligatory nods in the direction of administrative discretion. Some of those interviewed were critical of other judges whom they perceived as excessively intrusive in matters of state and local governance. Assessing their own decisions, however, they saw their responses as limited, pragmatic, and unavoidable.

Whether fashioned in response to a fear of criticism as an activist or in an attempt to prevent conflict with government defendants from intensifying in later stages of the case, preparation of liability opinions that are overly restrained seems to accomplish little. The conflict and criticism are likely in any event and the chances of reversal are increased. While it may be true that the Supreme Court (or a significant portion of it) responded to both *Rhodes* and *Rizzo* on ideological grounds, that does not minimize the point. The swing vote in *Rizzo* and concurrences in *Rhodes* may have been different with more detailed and vigorous opinions below. Second, the Court could have simply decided not to hear these cases. It had refused *certiorari* in both *Parma* and *Wyatt* earlier, cases in which the findings against the defendants had been expressed in more forceful terms.

In a number of ways, difficulties in remedial decree litigation may be more a demonstration of problems in the plaintiffs, defendants, units of government, or their attorneys than indications of inadequacies in judicial capacity. Plaintiff counsel need a number of skills and resources to develop a strong record. First, they need a solid knowledge of case law in the area in which they are operating. Wasby's observation that precedents matter is correct, but this research indicates that the point needs to be even more strongly emphasized.[9] *Parma* was a suit in which the special knowledge of developing appellate court case law was of particular importance in construction of a strong clean record. Of similar utility is knowledge of closely related lower court rulings. Battisti's opinion benefited from exposure to a number of other district court opinions in the same area. In working with other trial court rulings, the judge is not so much informed on authority as instructed by example in the art of crafting an appropriate and adequate opinion.

Another important skill for the attorneys is the ability to locate and work with expert witnesses. Two kinds of witnesses are important at the liability stage, local resident experts and national methodological and policy experts. In four of the cases the plaintiffs and supporting *amici* employed experts who could not be accused of being outsiders come to town to criticize the community. (*Rizzo* involved little expert testimony on either side.) On the other hand, these litigants employed outside experts to assess evidence from the local picture in light of national experience. Liability stage and remedy proceedings may involve the use of different types of experts. Government litigants, like their adversaries, vary markedly in their ability to develop expert resources and use them effectively. High issue salience among various government units can produce a strong spirit of cooperation among units with similar problems. Texas and Oregon provided support for the *Rhodes* litigation. The presence of Commissioner Estelle from Texas at trial and the *amicus* briefs in support of the state in the Supreme Court are specific examples. In part because of the timing of the case, virtually every state joined the Texas and Oregon submissions. Ohio has since reciprocated, responding to requests from other states based upon its experience in the *Rhodes* case.

Finally, where there are multiple parties, consensus building and case management skills on the part of lead attorneys can relieve the judge of onerous case management details and allow the court to concentrate on substantive matters. In this regard, timing is a critical factor both because of its impact on the performance by the parties and as a result of its significance for the judge. There is a risk in the assumption that good case management means a rapid disposition. The decision to move for a quick liability hearing, as in *Rhodes,* restricts preparation time for the parties. That, in turn, may limit the information made available to the judge. If justice delayed is justice denied, then justice rushed may be justice that is partial and limited.

The approach taken by plaintiffs at the liability stage may limit the judge's choices or afford them options. In *Wyatt* the plaintiffs named both the discharged state employees and patients as plaintiffs, allowing for flexibility later in the case. On the other hand, the deliberate decision by Gerald Goode's attorney not to name the specific police officers charged with misconduct as parties defendant clearly limited Fullam's choices. By naming police supervisors and city officials but not the individual officers, the litigation was intentionally and exclusively focused on the policy dimension of the case and not individual liability. There was no fallback position.

An examination of these cases suggests the use of common tactics by defendants in attempting to limit or weaken the record during liability proceedings. One approach is to deny the judge the validity check of a balanced adversary process. In *Milliken*, for example, the state filed a motion to dismiss following the plaintiffs' case and rested. Given that the state was the principal defendant, that left the judge in an awkward position. Similarly, a stipulation to facts, while in many ways helpful to the court and the plaintiffs, may weaken the record because the judge is not educated on all dimensions of the fact pattern. Refusal by the defendants in *Milliken* to stipulate to the housing discrimination claim caused Roth to be exposed to a long and detailed presentation on the nature, derivation, and impact of housing discrimination. Moreover, stipulations provide less material on which to base an inference than detailed presentation of evidence.

Still another approach used in both *Parma* and *Milliken* was to reject evidence of a pattern and practice of conduct and argue only the legality of individual incidents. Parma attorneys, for example, denied they were subject to a pattern and practice action, disputing each event in discrete terms. The corollary to that tactic is that when the case goes to appeal, the defendants can bog the appellate court down by concentrating on individual elements and ignoring the overall pattern of the liability finding.[10] An analogous approach in the institutional reform cases is the rejection of the "totality of the circumstances" standard as exemplified in *Rhodes*.

The common tendency in thinking about these cases is to concentrate on the plaintiffs and defendants, but parties who intervene can exert a considerable force. In *Milliken,* for example, Alexander Ritchie, attorney for the Concerned Citizens for Better Education, began the liability process as a vigorous supporter of the defendants, but changed positions radically following the presentation of the plaintiffs' case. In fact, it was he who moved to join all the suburban districts as defendants. *Wyatt* is a prime example. Once the liability finding has been entered, the judge called DOJ and HEW into the case, a move critical to later phases of the litigation not only because it made DOJ an active party, but also because it brought in federal government legal and subject matter resources as well as expertise. The remedy stage of *Wyatt* became an event around which a coalition of interest groups formed that ranged from professional associations, like the American Psychological Association, to public interest litigators, like the Mental Health Law Project. The leading attorneys in the field, from Morton Birnbaum—who originated the right to treatment argument—through Charles Halpern, Paul Friedman, and Stanley Herr were drawn to the case, thus presenting a phalanx of the most formidable mental health law talent in the nation. They, in turn, were able to draw on a national cadre of experts. Such groups can play key roles not only in decree formulation, but also in implementation monitoring.

The absence of intervenors may be significant as well. The plaintiffs in *Rhodes* did not solicit participation by any of the major organizations which regularly litigate prison conditions suits. If they could have interested such organizations, they might have been able to focus more expertise and resources on the case. The absence of DOJ may also be extremely important. The tradeoff in such situations is between the desire to retain control over the litigation and the need for resources. The lack of expertise and other forms of support may seriously influence the effectiveness of the adversary process, adding to the difficulty of the judge's task.

If the court finds liability, defendants may attempt to break out of the proceeding. That is generally done by attempting interlocutory appeals. Parma's attorneys worked vigorously to start an appeal to freeze the process, delay a remedy, and get to a position where they could argue detailed procedural questions that would stave off a remedy proceeding. With luck, such a process might result in a reversal of the liability finding. Judge Roth certified an appeal in *Milliken* after the remedy process was well along but before an actual desegregation plan was published. Because there was no such plan in hand, the case was argued in general terms, which was a situation helpful to defendants. They were in a position to argue against the trial court opinion on grounds of the likely injury to the government unit, but the plaintiffs could not adequately refute the assertion since there was no way to assure the appellate court that the remedy would not contain the provisions the defendants feared.

THE REMEDY PHASE

Once the liability opinion issues, the remedy phase begins. It consists of a remedy crafting stage and a parallel appeals process. The product of this remedy phase is a core remedy in the form of a decree or detailed remedy guideline. In many cases, including *Milliken* and *Wyatt,* there are later interactions between the judge and the parties over the detailed modifications to be made in the core remedy, but these are remedy refinements related to implementation activities in the post decree phase rather than part of the remedy phase.

Remedy Crafting

Remedy crafting consists of a plan development and negotiation stage and a formal decision stage. An understanding of these two facets of remedy crafting requires a consideration of a problem in existing literature highlighted by this research. Judges are often described as adopting either the role of a counterproductive interloper who intervenes rather arbitrarily in the operation of agencies or local units of government, on the one hand, or a mere negotiator who facilitates a cooperative solution between the parties, on the other. The latter picture is nearer the mark, but the role question is somewhat more complex than a simple bargaining model would suggest.

Consider Diver's thesis that remedy development is not litigation but a "bargaining process" in which the judge acts as "powerbroker" who presides over "exchange" transactions.[11] The use of the term *powerbroker* is itself troublesome. Although Diver argues that the judge is a negotiator presiding over a political exchange process, he later speaks of judges as "interventionist" actors issuing "far reaching decrees that have encompassed virtually every aspect of institutional life."[12] This ambiguity suggests the danger of ignoring the distinction between the differing roles played by the judge in the plan development and negotiation stage as compared to the later formal decision stage of remedy crafting.

Though there are elements of bargaining in the remedial process, this research suggests Diver went too far in asserting that the judge in decree litigation moves completely away from an adjudicatory role and into a purely bargaining posture. The judges in these cases, except for *Rhodes,* did invite parties to reach agreement on a remedy as a way to begin remedy crafting, but no such agreement was reached in five of the seven remedy crafting processes examined here. At least with respect to the development of the core remedy, there was no significant exchange process in the sense generally used by, for example, Hayes or Salisbury.[13] One working from an exchange perspective might very well argue that such processes exhibit several of the characteristics of political market failure, making exchange unlikely or incomplete. Plaintiffs, having carried the often heavy burden required to prevail in the liability phase, have a strong reason to resist anything less than a complete remedy. Bargaining may be difficult for defendants for other reasons. Disincentives to meaningful bargaining are particularly strong where the impact of the remedy is likely to be directly felt by the entire community, as in the cases of housing and school desegregation. Where the impact upon the community is indirect, as in the case of orders to improve prison or mental health conditions, the political penalties associated with popular resistance may be reduced. However, it is in those cases that administrators have an incentive to support more stringent remedies than their superiors in other parts of state or local government may be otherwise willing to accept and support.

Another major reason that may militate against a negotiated settlement is the troublesome nature of consent decree administration. In a period when litigation is considered an evil to be avoided and alternative dispute resolution a virtue, it is difficult to criticize a device like the consent decree. These cases and the interviews with participants who were also involved in other major policy suits indicate that consent decrees pose their own problems, which may sometimes make formal remedy crafting through litigation more attractive than consent judgments from the perspective of both the parties and the judge.

The principal advantages of the consent decree would appear to be savings of time and costs associated with protracted litigation as well as a reduction in the level of conflict which might pave the way for more positive working relations during implementation. Of course, the assumption here is that negotiated agreements can be reached relatively quickly and that the process through which such documents are hammered out produces less friction, and therefore less heat, than the alternative. These advantages may be more apparent than real. So much so that several of those interviewed indicated that in the future they would avoid consent decrees if at all possible and litigate. This study suggests an interesting change in approach by officials in remedial cases. In the late 1960s and early 1970s, there was substantial resistance to courts and limited agreements. After the defeats in the early rounds of cases, and with a recognition of opportunities to leverage legislators and governors, more defendants saw opportunities in negotiated settlements. By the late 1970s and into the 1980s, though, administrators who had had bad experiences with implementation of consent decrees and who saw greater chances for victory in court (either because their situation was defensible or because of changing Supreme Court rulings) moved toward more of a conflict model.

The presumed advantages of consent agreements may not materialize. Many consent decrees are developed after completion of the liability portion of the case rather than early enough to save substantial litigation costs. The negotiations are often complex and may drag on for an extended period. The judge's time investment may be as extensive as that consumed by adversary remedy procedures. That was certainly true in the *Stewart v. Rhodes* case. The parties in *Wyatt* agreed to virtually everything but the staffing standards; however, there were still formal processes to test the necessity and appropriateness of the proposals. A judge is, of course, not required to accept everything agreed to by the parties. Wise judges exercise caution in placing their imprimatur on decrees which may contain provisions that will return to haunt them during the implementation phase.

Discerning plaintiffs may be wary of the consent decree because of the risk of finding themselves in a false negotiation. A negotiated agreement may be false by intent or by circumstance. Government attorneys are fully aware that extended negotiations and prolonged proceedings may wear down a weak plaintiff or make the case difficult to prosecute because of changed conditions or difficulties with witnesses. The fact that one sits down at a table is no guarantee of an intention to play the kind of nonzero sum game that will lead to settlement. Second, one may bargain at the margins but not expect to produce a strong remedy on the core issues. As one of the attorneys interviewed put it, he could agree to a complicated decree but not really be committed to anything crucial, depending upon the language and enforcement mechanisms available to the other side. Most decrees contain some form of waiver provision or escape clause which can be exploited to one degree or another. A third form of false bargain is the repudiated negotiation. The parties in *Wyatt* were convinced they had agreements on almost everything. When the decrees issued, implementation began, no stays were requested, and all parties understood that the state was committed to satisfaction of the decrees. Governor Wallace repudiated the actions of the state's attorneys, instituted formal challenges to the decrees, and signaled others in the executive branch that the nature of their relationship with the court was to be adversarial and not cooperative. Furthermore, the players involved as a case moves from remedy crafting to implementation may change and later governors or agency heads may not consider agreements made by their predecessors acceptable.[14] Similarly, there is no assurance of compliance even if the executive branch does intend to conduct legitimate negotiations and expects to implement the agreement. State legislators rarely consider themselves bound by such a process. In *Stewart v. Rhodes,* the legislature refused for a lengthy period to appropriate adequate funds or provide bonding for new prisons. Even though Commissioner Denton at long last obtained authorization for a construction program, it took more than three years to acquire bonding authority. Finally, if there are difficulties encountered later in implementation, there is less of a record in a negotiation than in a formal proceeding to support further action.

From an administrator's standpoint, the consent decree may be more intrusive than what a court would have ordered in the same case.[15] While judges are not required to approve any consent order brought to court, they may not feel as constrained in accepting a remedy as they would where they knew that they would have the primary responsibility for imposing unwanted requirements on the parties involved. Moreover, as several respondents indicated, the administrators who must implement the agreement may not be allowed a role in the negotiation. Because the consent decree may be more complex than an ordinary judgment, it is likely that the implementation may involve lengthy interaction with court appointed special masters and attorneys for the parties.

Negotiation to limit and focus issues and tentative agreements on substantive policy matters may be useful in many circumstances, but they are not panaceas. The choice for careful plaintiffs, administrators, and judges is nothing so crude as an absolute judgment about whether to negotiate or not. It is more a question of decisions about how, when, and what to bargain about and when to choose adversary procedures.[16]

This study indicates that judges play different roles at different stages of a case. The judge plays a facilitator role in the first part of the remedy crafting process and a ratifier/developer role in the second. In the plan development and negotiation stage, all the judges (except Hogan) encouraged settlement or, at a minimum, a narrowing of issues. In each case (except *Stewart*), though, the judges found points at which they declared limits. When those limits were reached, the process became more formal and the judge became less a facilitator and more a validator or ratifying official who placed the court's imprimatur on specific parts of the plans submitted by the parties without regard to voluntary acceptance by other parties.

Thus, George Roumell pointed out in his *Milliken II* oral argument that DeMascio did not invent the decree elements he ordered, but ratified propositions put to him by the parties. Roth was in a similar situation in that the city board and plaintiffs supported a metropolitan remedy. The suburban districts rejected any significant change. Both judges rejected some proposals, ratified others, and enforced those accepted against the state and the suburbs. Battisti ratified most elements of the plan proposed by the plaintiffs when the community made no serious proposal and presented no substantial challenge to the plaintiff's remedy. Each of the judges (except Johnson and Duncan) went beyond mere ratification and into a developer role, adding his own features to the decree. That was particularly true of DeMascio and, to some extent, of Battisti. Hogan had no specific proposal from the plaintiffs except immediate reduction of prison design capacity and no acceptable suggestions from the state. He substituted an extremely simple performance standard, leaving administrators complete discretion as to how to achieve it. Johnson and Duncan essentially limited themselves to ratifying the stipulations submitted by the parties.

The role the judge adopts may be limited by the role options afforded the court by the parties to the case. If those involved refuse to negotiate or provide significant positive reactions to the plans that are proposed, the judge's facilitator function is extremely narrow, pressing him or her to move to the ratifier/developer role. The opposite is the case in which the parties negotiate a consent decree before a formal liability finding is issued or before required remedy crafting processes are initiated. In that case the judge is simply a facilitator. A court defender role may be played where a judge is presented with a negotiated remedy but thinks that the court is being used by the parties acting in collusion to leverage government into taking action that is not remedial but, in fact, goes far beyond what an adequate remedy would provide or the types of actions the political process would support. That was the posture Johnson assumed in the remedy hearings. He continually reminded participants that he was only concerned with changes necessary to meet minimally adequate conditions and that he would not allow the court to be used for leverage.[17] He refused requests to order a special master and to mandate state spending. Diver oversimplified the question of judicial role. Perhaps that problem stemmed from the failure to distinguish between the plan development and negotiation stage and the later formal decision stage of remedy crafting.

Common defense tactics in the plan development and negotiation stage include refusal to submit a plan at all, filing of an admittedly inadequate proposal, submission of undifferentiated multiple plans, and the use of leverage plans. Parma, of course, submitted no proposal initially, though Battisti's reaction to the two Parma experts who appeared during the remedy hearing suggests that he might have been very receptive if the city had provided a meaningful plan. Battisti was not afforded a facilitator role choice. Only when a formal decision process was imminent did Parma suggest a remedy, the Westview Apartments conversion. However, the mayor testified at the hearing that he knew that to be an inadequate remedy. The political advantage to a defendant of using such an approach is the ability to picture the judge as an arbitrary interventionist figure. The court is compelled by the defendant's actions to force all elements of the decree on the defendant community or unit of government.

The state officials in *Milliken* used the multiple plan approach. Such a tactic burdens the court with developing a process for assessing the several proposals and disrupts routine ratification/development activities. There is no focal point for the remedy hearing. It also allows the defendant to claim cooperation with the court while, in fact, avoiding any assistance to the judge. The defendants in *Rhodes* submitted five plans, in order of preference from the least to the most expensive. Only one would have resulted in a decrease in overcrowding. That option entailed construction of a new cell block and the hiring of additional guards at a high cost and an extremely lengthy delay for implementation.

The leverage plan is exemplified by the Detroit Board proposal for rather elaborate educational component programs. The city could not win a millage campaign because of existing financial difficulties and could not hope to get the state to volunteer funds for such programs. By vigorously pursuing their proposal, the Board obtained an order to implement the educational components with all the costs assessed against the state. That allowed the city to meet important needs which it would have been otherwise unable to accomplish. Similarly, representatives of the mental health board in *Wyatt* agreed with many of the standards recommended in the stipulations presented to the court, but claimed they lacked money to accomplish them. They refused to tell the judge what they wished the court to do but made it rather obvious that they wished the state to be compelled to fund their programs. This tactic gave them more resources without accepting political responsibility for the changes.

When some of these tactics, particularly the first three, result in an impasse and the judge mandates action, defendants may engage in conflict conversion. The attempt is made to suggest that the citizens or government units affected by remedies are in some sense victims suffering at the hands of the judge who is cast as the evildoer. Plaintiffs or original victims are pictured as pawns used to invoke judicial intervention. Battisti, Roth, and Fullam all faced conflict conversion pressures. Governor Wallace's use of conflict conversion tactics against Judge Johnson is well known. In sum, tactics of resistance are often employed by defendants who then accuse the judge who is forced to action of punitive intervention. These findings support Wasby as well as Cavanagh and Sarat's comments on the circularity of the interventionist judiciary charge.[18]

Plaintiffs in most of the cases studied demonstrated an ability to identify a credible lead expert to draft the basic design of the remedy proposal. They were also alert to the need to provide local experts to address detailed questions raised in the formal decision stage of a remedy crafting process. In both *Parma* and *Milliken,* the lead experts, Paul Davidoff and Gordon Foster, respectively, had substantial experience in other cases in different cities. The *Wyatt* litigation presented a slightly different situation because of the amount of negotiation involved. The other key distinction in *Wyatt* was the presence of a number of very active and able parties that led to a kind of committee proposal and presentation rather than a lead witness approach. Even so, plaintiffs and *amici* streamlined their presentation at the remedy hearings, thus providing their key expert testimony through Drs. Jack Ewalt and Francis Tyce in the mental illness phase and Drs. Gunnar Dybwad and Philip Roos in the mental retardation portion. In four of the seven proceedings, the plaintiffs made available feasibility witnesses to speak to the practicality as well as the appropriateness of their plan.

An examination of the formal decision process suggests that the judges use rather common procedures to make decisions on a core remedy. The decrees produced tend to have similar mechanics. Finally, the judges in this study approached the remedy crafting process with a very clear concern for the tension between the need for developing adequate remedies while simultaneously observing limits to judicial discretion.

The standard process for remedy decisionmaking usually centers on a remedy hearing where plans are presented and explained by the parties. Cross-examination becomes an important way of testing the boundaries of the proposed remedy. In *Parma, Milliken,* and *Rhodes* some defendants attempted, through cross-examination in the remedy hearing, to relitigate aspects of the liability question. That was particularly true of the city in *Parma* and the suburban districts in *Milliken.* The judges frequently questioned witnesses, seeing the hearing as an educational enterprise. Even so, a number of participants in Battisti, Roth, and DeMascio's hearings approached the hearing as a clearly adversary process. Duncan employed negotiations in chambers, but even these took on some of the characteristics of adversary hearings.

Feasibility witnesses were extremely important in four of the seven instances. Wasby observes that critics of the decree litigation cases charge that "courts cannot effectively make advance estimates of the magnitude or direction of the effects of their decisions." [19] These cases indicate that the feasibility facet of remedy hearings offers an important vehicle for estimating impact. Moreover, while the estimates may not be completely accurate in all respects, this study certainly belies the suggestion that judges do not know or care about the impact of their orders. The feasibility assessment seems generally to be based upon inquiries into administrative and financial feasibility. [20] A third element of a feasibility cases is technical feasibility, the ability to agree on the substance of what should be done. Though there was no critical issue in this set of case studies which presented substantive technical questions, apart from fiscal and administrative concerns, such a problem may arise in other settings, such as in reapportionment. [21] Though the opinions were rarely explicit on this point, the judges and other participants were also concerned with political feasibility. [22]

The Cavanagh and Sarat observation that "courts have reduced the impact on state treasuries by directing institutional defendants into the frequently open embrace of federal grant administrators" [23] was generally confirmed. Battisti ordered Parma to apply for Community Development Block Grant (CDBG) funds and Section 8 qualification. In *Milliken,* DeMascio ordered the defendant to continue and enhance applications for Emergency School Aid Act (ESAA) grants. Johnson directed the state of Alabama to attempt to qualify its facilities and programs for Medicare and Medicaid funds and other grant opportunities. Indeed these funds ultimately kept the state mental health establishment afloat during some of the worst financial periods of the 1970s and early 1980s. There was no such requirement in the prison litigation, though states did employ a variety of demonstration grants, block grant funds when they were available, and revenue sharing to offset some of the costs of implementation. Both Alabama and Ohio dedicated a substantial portion of their revenue sharing money to institutional reform.

Charges of anticipated excessive administrative burdens were seriously entertained whenever they were raised, though defendants rarely attempted serious challenges. Of the remedy processes examined here, it was the Detroit-only remedy hearing alone that saw a detailed administrative infeasibility case presented. In *Parma, Wyatt,* and the metropolitan remedy portion of the first *Milliken* proceeding, plan proponents were careful to build a case for both the administrative and financial efficacy of their proposals. Peter Hearn in the *Rizzo* case was convinced (and for that matter so was Judge Fullam) that crafting a remedy for minimum administrative burden was critical. Ironically, while city police officials argued in very general terms that the four-month complaint processing time in the plaintiffs proposal was infeasible, the department later imposed a sixty day limit on itself in an effort to stave off adverse city council action. The plaintiffs in the prison case did not present a strong feasibility case. The *Wyatt* plaintiffs demonstrated that beyond the fact that their proposal was feasible, the current mode of administration was both administratively and financially wasteful.

The ability to develop really effective feasibility arguments, particularly in the realm of technical and administrative feasibility, is contingent upon the willingness of high level policymakers and attorneys controlling the case to identify people at line operating levels and middle management who have the knowledge and experience to prepare feasibility positions. It also requires an effective working relationship between counsel and administrators. While the use of outside experts is valuable, it is no substitute for internal coordination. Neither is it useful to concentrate all efforts on the liability portion of the case and ignore the need for a feasibility case in the remedy portion.

The core remedies emerging from this formal decision process are structurally quite similar. They included a definition of target agencies and intended beneficiaries. Five of the seven provided procedures, of varying specificity, for further remedy refinement and implementation. Three established some form of participatory device intended to allow a forum for continuing discussion and to present a mechanism in which all parties could essentially perform a watchdog function. Four had some kind of institutional capability assessment and enhancement feature. All provided a set of substantive standards, again varying in their degree of specificity. Most provided for some mechanism of evaluation and feedback with independence from the defendant organizations, though generally supported by them. Finally, four provided for financial needs. (*Rizzo* presented no resource issues.)

Remedial Adequacy Versus Discretion Limitation

This study indicates that district judges called upon to issue remedial decrees are acutely aware of the core tension between the need to provide a remedy adequate to redress the injury suffered by the plaintiffs, on the one hand, while recognizing the appropriate limitations on judicial interference with government policy and practice on the other. Contrary to the implied criticism in the judicial capacity and role literature, there is ample evidence that the judges deciding these cases are very much aware of the dangers and difficulties, both legal and political, associated with their rulings.

A judge faced with a request for a remedial decree has several factors to consider in formulating an adequate response. These elements of adequacy include the availability, nature, scope, and duration of relief. The initial determination, of course, must be whether the alleged actions of the state or local governments are proven, and, if so, whether they amount to a violation of statutory or constitutional provisions for which equitable relief is authorized.

If a remedy is available, the judge must determine the nature of the relief to be afforded. The nature of a remedy is defined by the type of remedial action selected and the degree to which that type of remedy actually redresses the violation of legally protected rights. In most cases plaintiffs request negative relief in the form of an injunction against further illegal conduct and affirmative relief to redress the damage done to the plaintiffs. These affirmative remedies are used because money damages are often inadequate to make the victims whole again. Moreover, federal judges have experienced many situations in which negative relief was largely ignored.

Judges may select from among a range of affirmative remedy options. These include process remedies, performance standards, or specified particular actions. Process remedies include such techniques as advisory committees, citizen participation requirements, educational programs, evaluation committees, dispute resolution procedures, special masters or other devices that will operate to redress past problems without mandating the particular form of action or the specific goals the government unit must pursue. Performance standards mandate specified numbers or types of new housing, schools, staffing levels, or other targets with the means of attainment left to the discretion of the officials who are the targets of the suit. Specified remedial steps such as school busing, modified school attendance zones, required changes in the size and condition of hospital rooms or prison cells leave no flexibility with defendants concerning remedial goals or the means of attaining them.[24]

The scope of a remedy concerns the spatial dimensions of a decree. Those dimensions may be defined in terms of the programs affected, the people to be covered, or the political jurisdictions to be encompassed by the order. The duration of a remedy by comparison concerns the temporal dimension of court ordered relief. It may be defined as time limits for formulation of plans, deadlines for accomplishment of particular elements of the decree, required sequential phasing of implementation, or the duration of the district court's retention of continuing jurisdiction over an official or government unit to ensure compliance and evaluate results. Given the history of resistance to court ordered relief and the political incentives to delay or avoid compliance, the court must conduct some follow-up proceedings beyond mere announcement of an order. Taken far enough, though, unlimited duration of court involvement may place a judge in the position of administering institutions rather than remedying a legal violation.

There are, in fact, limits to the discretionary responses judges may make to demands for remedial orders. These constraints are products of doctrinal limits drawn from interpretations of the Constitution and statutes by appellate courts and self-imposed limits keyed to what might be termed *judicial policy range*. These two types of constraints pressure judges to consider problems respecting each of the elements of remedial adequacy. The Burger Court has moved to limit availability, scope, and duration of remedial orders.[25]

With respect to the availability of a remedy, the doctrinal limits require the judge to ensure that appropriate allegations and proof are offered by the plaintiffs. Appropriate allegations are the sorts of charges that properly raise a justiciable dispute for which equitable relief is available. As this study indicates, most remedial decree cases brought under the Constitution assert a violation of equal protection, due process, or cruel and unusual punishment provisions. Cases brought under federal statutes may be divided into those brought by private individuals or government officials authorized by the statute to sue and those cases brought by private parties who claim an implied right of action under a statute.[26]

The nature of the remedy which a court may impose may be limited as well.[27] The Supreme Court has come to favor a standard referred to here as incremental adverse effect.[28] In general, the nature of the remedy must reflect the nature of the violation. In some settings that means, according to the Court, that the task of a remedy is to eliminate the offending conduct and restore those injured to the condition they would have enjoyed had the violation not occurred.[29] The problem for the judge is to determine what the nature of the violation is and what sorts of process, performance, or specified particular actions will redress the harm done.[30] While some remedy cases mandate the incremental adverse effect approach, they provide no guidance on how the judge is to determine just how much of one's current plight is directly attributable to illegal action by government officials.

In addressing the permissible scope of a remedial order, the Supreme Court has reminded trial courts in several decisions that they must give due consideration to the interests of states and localities in controlling their own land-use policy, schools, and public institutions over which local control has traditionally been exercised.[31] The Court has admonished trial courts not to mandate action that will cover more than those political jurisdictions specifically implicated in illegal conduct.

The question of the appropriate duration of a remedy and judicial supervision over implementation is always a difficult matter. Some have learned that by stalling long enough they can attract broad support to end federal court involvement without having actually carried out the provisions of a decree. The history of school desegregation cases presents the classic scenario.[32] On the other hand, there must be limits. Until the mid-1970s, the Court had consistently held that judges were obliged to retain jurisdiction over implementation until the illegal conduct had been eliminated.[33] More recently, though, the Court has held that courts are to retain jurisdiction only until there is evidence of the onset of good faith implementation of an approved plan.[34] It has not explained how one is to determine when that condition has been satisfied.

There are, then, several important formal limitations on judges issuing remedial decrees. Even so, trial judges still have a great deal of latitude. That area of flexibility presents a judge with a judicial policy range. Like the doctrinal limits, one can think of judicial policy range in terms of the elements of adequacy.

The availability of a remedy and its likely success on appeal both rest upon the quality of the record as well as the inferences drawn from that record and discussed in the opinion. Since the availability, nature, scope, and duration of any remedy must be related to the nature of the violation as described in the opinion of the trial court, it is obviously critical that the findings be carefully considered and explained. In order to support the findings, in turn, one must ensure the construction of a record adequate to support the necessary determinations and inferences.

The range of discretion the judge has in selecting the nature of relief to be afforded is obviously broad. Whether he or she will employ process techniques which give the widest latitude to defendants regarding both the goals and the means of attaining them or uses specified standards offering little flexibility as to either goals or means is an open matter. The key question, at least with respect to the political feasibility of a remedy, is to what degree do judges tend to acknowledge what might be termed flexibility factors of concern to the state or local government.

The scope of a decree is related to the capacity of the judge to engage in an effective analysis of linkages. How well can the judge interrelate the activities of the various actors and political jurisdictions involved in the course of conduct alleged to be illegal? Moreover, how well can the judge articulate those relationships in an opinion? The choices the trial judge makes in crafting both the liability findings and the remedial opinion become more than mere matters of form. Similarly, the ability to understand the relationships of actions by subordinates to policy explicitly or implicitly pursued by superiors is critical to understanding whether a remedy is to be limited to a few individuals or is, in fact, a department or countywide problem. Finally, the ability to determine whether one is dealing with isolated incidents or a pattern and practice of conduct and to articulate the relationships among the elements of a pattern and practice is a determining factor in gauging the appropriate scope of a remedial decree.

Judicial policy range with respect to the duration element is significant. Judges may set time limits with respect to either the development of a decree after a finding of a violation or of the implementation and evaluation of the remedial order after it is developed. The setting of deadlines concerning negotiations or hearings conducted in an effort to craft a remedy may determine how well the plaintiffs or the defendants can prepare for, and participate in, the creation of a remedy. Further, the judge may elect time boundaries for implementation of various elements of the decree or for the evaluation of the effectiveness of the remedy or both.

In sum, to understand the kinds of problems and opportunities facing a judge called upon to issue a remedial order, one must understand the nature of the relief requested and the applicable limiting factors. Of perhaps greatest interest to students of law and politics is the matter of how judges determine and utilize their judicial policy range. However, an examination of these cases indicates that there is a much stronger interrelationship between doctrinal limitations and judicial policy range than is assumed in existing literature.

The doctrinal limits dimension was considerably more important in all phases of the cases studied here than is generally recognized. The availability of a remedy was not seriously in question in *Parma, Milliken,* or *Stewart.* The case for a remedy in *Wyatt* was strong, though not as clear. By the time of *Wyatt,* the basis for a due process based right to treatment was relatively firm and the facts of the Alabama situation seemed to provide a catalyst encouraging a constitutional ruling. In fact, the state admitted that if there were a due process right to treatment at all, the facts of the case justified a remedy for patients in Alabama facilities.[35] *Rhodes* and *Rizzo* were ultimately reversed by the Supreme Court on liability grounds, though both had received strong support in the Court of Appeals.

The nature of relief varied considerably. Battisti's decree was essentially a process remedy with one performance standard. It created a new process by which to address the housing problem in Parma, allowing Parma citizens to staff and operate the Fair Housing Committee (FHC) that was its cornerstone. The order created an Evaluation Committee as an oversight mechanism that offered a wider membership to various participants in the litigation from outside Parma. Battisti, like his Detroit colleagues, found it necessary to order several specific principally symbolic or educational elements in the decree, including an education program, an advertising requirement, and the open housing resolution to deal with the intangible dimensions of the case. At least since 1950 the Supreme Court has acknowledged that discrimination cases have important but intangible dimensions.[36]

Fullam also ordered a process remedy. In fact, it was in the form of a modification to the existing departmental complaint procedure. All substantive determinations as to the judgment and disposition of complaints were left to the Police Commissioner.

Roth employed the full panoply of remedial instruments. He used a process strategy that created a small but representative desegregation panel. The panel was given a relatively clear set of instructions and a specific time limit. The judge defined the geographical limits of the remedy area and the skeletal structure of the fifteen school clusters within that area, but left the panel with a range of techniques with which to complete the plan. He did set performance standards both as to the burden of transportation and maximum bus trip tolerances. He, like Battisti and DeMascio, worked with additional decree components to reach intangibles.

DeMascio used process techniques only for community relations and evaluation. His performance standards were not particularly flexible because they were buttressed by a number of specific particular remedial elements that left relatively few options as to how the decree's goals would be attained.

Johnson employed all three techniques, though he did not design any of them. Virtually the entire remedy were created by the participants. The only actions Johnson refused to take was the appointment of a master to supervise implementation and the call for the court to mandate particular state financial decisions. The remedy used a process technique in which Human Rights Committees (HRCs) were established at each hospital to monitor implementation and work with institutional superintendents and staff. The decree also created an expert advisory group and a consumer advisory group to make suggestions to the HRCs and hospital superintendents. The remedy crafted by the participants and ratified by Johnson presented a range of performance and specified particular standards that ranged from treatment requirements and recordkeeping to physical plant conditions and safety.

Hogan used a pure performance standard, and a modest one at that. Lucasville administrators were generally surprised and grateful that Hogan required only a reduction of twenty-five inmates per month. Duncan signed a consent decree for the other prison case modeled on agreements reached in other states. As with some other consent orders, it required specific actions and a range of prohibitions.

The scope of the decree was the principal basis for legal argument in Detroit. The Supreme Court held that Judge Roth did not respect jurisdictional boundaries and ignored the importance of individual school districts as independent units. DeMascio's problem was excessive narrowness. Given the district-wide nature of the violation, a district-wide remedy was necessary and, therefore, the core city districts had to be incorporated into the remedy. Since the *Wyatt* suit was against the operation of the entire state system, scope was not a major problem.

Though Battisti's order avoids durational requirements, the other decrees set a number of time restrictions. Roth's time limits primarily concerned development of the final plan, whereas DeMascio went beyond that to place duration limits on substantive aspects of the decree. An example is the five-year limit on transportation of any child. Johnson included a variety of timing requirements from testimony provided at the hearings. His willingness to order specific actions with specific deadlines responded to the problem of remedying conditions in a total institutions where the state controlled virtually all aspects of an incarcerated person's life. Two other factors played a role. First, the state had failed to act even though it had been aware of the problems for some time and made virtually no progress even after the liability decision. Second, the remedy hearings demonstrated that the conditions, particularly at Partlow, were clearly life threatening, thus precipitating the delivery of an interim emergency order at the close of the hearings. Timely resolution of complaints against the police was central to the *Rizzo* case, hence the time constraints in Fullam's order were critical. Both Hogan's order and Duncan's consent decree involved phased reduction in inmate populations.

The cases also reveal how judges dealt with judicial policy range considerations. Battisti's record development and opinion preparation were very strong. The fact that there was only one plaintiff, and that one was DOJ, no doubt helped. Roth had a more difficult situation. His early statements stemming from his initial antipathy toward the suit[37] and the changing positions of the parties complicated his work. DeMascio was in the interesting position of having a substantial remedy proceeding and a fully reviewed remedy opinion before him as he began his remedy crafting effort. His opinion made extensive use of expert testimony. He used his three experts to aid his understanding of the parties in the early stages. Later, he called upon two other experts to do an independent analysis of the implementation and cost problems associated with the Detroit Board's educational components proposal.[38] Similarly, Battisti asked Avery Friedman to remain in the case as *amicus curiae*. Friedman played a role that combined the capacities of an outside expert and a court ordered monitor. While the opinions in *Wyatt* were extremely brief, apart from the stipulation of standards submitted by the parties, Johnson went to considerable lengths to keep the record open and flexible.

Battisti elected substantial flexibility in selecting modes of redress. The DOJ offered a proposal which gave the defendants maximum discretion. The judge validated the plan with few modifications. Roth was concerned with flexibility, but his ability to be extremely accommodating was limited by the situation in the Detroit schools and the unwillingness of the defendants to cooperate in the crafting of details of the remedy. Hogan and Fullam both elected to moderate their opinions and provided substantial flexibility in their remedy crafting.

DeMascio provided little flexibility. He doubted very much could be accomplished by general instructions to the district given the factions within the central and regional school district administration. His remedy went so far as to instruct the board to rezone and reassign students without regard for the regions established in the city. He was responding to the fact that the ''practicalities of the situation,'' as he saw them, left him little flexibility if his remedy was to be effective.

Since the *Wyatt* and *Stewart* remedies were stipulated by the parties, Johnson and Duncan had few choices to make regarding flexibility. Despite its detailed character, the *Wyatt* decree provides discretion for the state to determine the means of achieving the necessary standards. The Mental Health Board, for example, could either increase staff dramatically to meet the staff/patient ratios or it could reduce patient loads significantly and increase staffing at a moderate pace. The order required deinstitutionalization of improperly committed patients and those who could be dealt with somewhere other than in a large state mental hospital, but it did not compel the state to use one means over another for accomplishing the goal.

Roth found himself in trouble for having exceeded his discretion with respect to scope. The problem stemmed from the fact that his early opinion did not adequately document the linkages for each of the jurisdictions in the remedy. DeMascio's second remedy established a set of remedial premises and then linked the elements of the decree to those keystones. He was able to connect the program elements to the violation rather easily even though his actions were more intrusive into local decisionmaking in some respects than Roth's. Fullam deliberately chose to avoid a full-scale discussion of the precise linkages between the conduct of the officers specifically discussed at trial and departmental and city officials. That was in part a function of the kind of evidence before the court, but it also was an effort to avoid confrontation. He perceived a need for a department-wide remedy, but he did not wish to provoke administrators with harsh and specific findings. The *Rizzo* case as well as *Rhodes* and *Milliken I* suggest that judges are caught on the horns of the deference paradox mentioned above. The specificity and unequivocal tone necessary to guarantee that the essential connections are drawn among actors, institutions, and jurisdictions is very likely to exacerbate conflict. The lesson for judges is that they can rarely have it both ways. Administrators, on the other hand, need to understand how to read and work with judicial opinions that contain extremely critical language without the kind of vehement defensive response so common in public law policy cases.

Battisti's decision to avoid deadlines established a potential tradeoff. The judge who provides clear temporal dimensions to the order makes future evaluation easier. On the other hand, hard-and-fast time constraints can increase political tension, making adjustments in the remedial implementation process difficult. While Johnson used the technical authority available to him to impose durational elements in the decree, he administered them with a relatively light hand. He and Duncan allowed substantial delays in a variety of areas of the decree.

Appeals

The appeals process is treated in this model as a parallel process within the remedy crafting stage. This study suggests that this is a far more accurate representation than descriptions that picture appellate process as something later than, and apart from, decree crafting. The principal reason is that appeals are often launched while remedy crafting is under way. Moreover, stays are often obtained just after decree crafting, which leads to changes prior to implementation. Since both liability and remedy rulings are reviewed together, the adversary character of the proceedings is both strong and important. Even where the core remedy is upheld, particular modifications required by the appeals court may substantially alter the remedy and the judge's participation in implementation. For example, the Sixth Circuit's elimination for the time being of Battisti's requirement of 133 units of housing and his special master provision expanded local discretion and promised to make Battisti's relationship with the defendants during implementation at best an arm's length interaction.

The *Wyatt* case suggests that in some situations judges may impose a kind of limited informal stay on their own rulings pending appeal. Governor Wallace filed requesting a formal stay pending appeal even though the state had previously stipulated to the negotiated decisions. Given the situation and the late entry of the governor into the process, Johnson was hardly likely to grant the request. However, he exercised considerable restraint in responding to the requests of the HRCs during the months between the April 13, 1972, order and the 1974 affirmance of his decision.

THE POST DECREE ISSUES

In a fashion rather like the relationship between remedy crafting and the appeals process, the post decree phase of a remedial decree case involves a parallel interactive relationship between remedy implementation and evaluation and remedy refinement. DeMascio's supervision of the Detroit desegregation decree and Johnson's oversight of the Alabama order are particularly instructive. After the core decree had been implemented in the winter of 1976, DeMascio found himself issuing a number of orders concerning faculty reassignment, changes in program requirements, and other rulings that did not substantially alter the core remedy but sought to resolve problems encountered during implementation.

Similarly, Johnson modified standards concerning the use of uncompensated work as patient therapy, permitted electroshock and aversion therapy under specified conditions, and altered the structure, responsibilities, and accountability of the HRCs. In fact, seven years after the original decree was ordered, the proceedings were reopened. Johnson found progress but noted remaining areas of substantial noncompliance. It was then that he eliminated the HRC plan and substituted a receiver and a court appointed monitor to report to the court on the activities of the receiver. During 1983 the state attempted to terminate the receivership in proceedings before Judge Thompson, who succeeded Johnson after the latter's elevation to the Eleventh Circuit Court of Appeals. Thompson rejected the state's motion, ordered compliance, appointed a new receiver, and clarified the responsibilities of the receiver and monitor. Where there is a master, he or she (or they as in *Stewart*) usually has sufficient authority for most minor remedy refinement tasks.

Just as parties to the case can shape the remedy crafting role of the judge by affording or denying role options, so the role played by the judge in the post decree phase is shaped by the core remedy. The basic process remedy used by Battisti left him as a policymaker with potential oversight functions, but he was not actually to be a party to the implementation if it could be avoided. Not only was the remedy structurally designed to minimize judicial involvement, but Battisti added the special master to his original remedial order, though DOJ did not ask for such a player. The purpose of the master was to be a data gatherer for the court; an information distributor for the city, DOJ, and the two remedial committees; and a remedy refiner for minor issues. The lack of such a person (owing to the Sixth Circuit's finding that selection of a master was premature) resulted during the third and fourth year of the order in more involvement by the judge and produced some of the communications difficulties Battisti had anticipated. The chairs of the two committees thus found it necessary to treat the judge's law clerk as an information center in the absence of an independent party. Duncan, like Battisti, preferred to have a special master to keep from becoming embroiled in day-to-day implementation issues. Both Battisti and Duncan had faced major school desegregation cases before and were well aware of such post decree implementation issues. Fullam's order, had it been sustained, would have virtually guaranteed little or no connection with the agency. The order merely forced police department rulemaking and adjudication within the same general form already in place.

On the other hand, DeMascio's use of a variety of specified particular steps virtually guaranteed that his office would play a major ongoing role in the implementation process. While Judge Johnson did not shape the remedy himself, the standards set by the parties in *Wyatt* promised a mixed future, with the HRCs carrying the primary burden for implementation oversight, but with the detailed specifications of the remedy suggesting likely recourse to the judge for clarification and enforcement.

In addition to the special master who is usually appointed with a delegation of decisionmaking authority, judges may choose to employ a court appointed monitor, or, under some circumstances to impose a receiver.[39] The *Wyatt* case presents examples of both. The monitor is merely an information gatherer who reports on the defendant's progress, or lack of it, in implementing the court's order, but, unlike the master, does not relieve the judge of any decisionmaking. The receiver is employed because of a failure to implement orders or because structural barriers block progress. The battles within Alabama's mental health agencies and individual facilities during the 1970s made it nearly impossible to obtain action. Johnson ordered the governor to take over as receiver, with power to disregard ordinary organizational barriers.

Several of those interviewed had participated in a number of remedial decree cases and had worked with special masters. Administrators tend to develop a resentment for masters, particularly if implementation drags on or if the master submits, as some have, substantial bills for their services.[40] It is unclear whether the reaction is really directed to the master or whether the master draws fire as the unwelcome representative of an external force.

Discussions of remedial decree implementation often ignore the fact that district judges are in no position to focus all of their time and energies on post decree matters. Their dockets are both extremely heavy and quite varied. Moreover, the longer the post decree process drags on, the greater are the incentives to disengage if at all possible since the level of antagonism which levels off after the decree is issued begins to increase and continues to build the longer the implementation process persists.

There is a facet of the deference paradox that arises in the post decree process which complicates both the attempt to implement the remedial order and attempts to evaluate the degree of compliance as well as the actual amount of improvement in the situation that gave rise to the case. Efforts made by the judge to defer to administrators in remedy crafting and post decree activities may very well undermine conditions that the policy studies literature suggests are extremely important for successful implementation and evaluation.[41] Virtually all implementation analysts agree that the clarity of a policy statement with a specification of measurable goals is extremely important.[42] A judge contemplating development of a remedial order faces two important problems in pursuit of that goal. First, like any other policymaker, a judge who specifies too much leaves little flexibility to those who must carry out the order and increases the likelihood of conflict with them.[43] The judge must also be concerned with Supreme Court admonitions to limit intervention and accord states and localities maximum flexibility. Thus, for example, the Parma order as amended by the Court of Appeals left the process remedy in place with a great deal of flexibility but few specified goals, thus leaving members of the Evaluation Committee with the problem of determining criteria against which to assess the city's performance. On the other hand, that same flexibility clearly reduced conflict among the city, the Fair Housing Committee, the Evaluation Committee, and the court.

Courts do disengage from the defendant units of government where they actually remedy the situation that gave rise to the suit. While many take years to resolve, the popular image that once judges become involved in a remedy, they never take their leave is untrue. The structure of the opinion may dictate the terms of resolution. For Duncan, the closing of the Columbus Correctional Facility (CCF) meant the end of the case. On the other hand, he found it much more difficult to determine exactly when and how to terminate the Columbus schools decree. He explained that someone had opposed termination of the order on grounds that Columbus' race relations problems had not been resolved. Duncan replied that the court sat to decide cases, not to cure the community of social ills. DeMascio left the Detroit case in 1980. Interestingly, DeMascio found in the later years of his involvement with the schools, that it was not continuing tensions and conflict that characterized the implementation of the remedy as much as it was an ending of attentive confrontation among the parties. Though the Detroit case did not end with DeMascio's departure, a termination date has been set and appears likely to be met. Duncan, too, found attorneys much more interested, effective, and helpful during the liability phase than in the remedy and post decree portions of the case. Alabama appeared for a time to be making progress that might lead to termination of federal court jurisdiction, but state politics and conflict in the Mental Health Department led to instability and indirection in mental health policy. The fact that several groups were carefully watching the post decree phase of the *Wyatt* case both ensured feedback to the judges and opposition to premature state efforts to terminate the order. As in Detroit, final resolution in *Wyatt* appears imminent. Though there is potential in Parma for protracted litigation, it would be difficult for such a thing to happen, particularly since DOJ, the plaintiff, has indicated general satisfaction with the city's progress and an unwillingness to support efforts to expand the remedy.

It is clear from those interviewed in this study that courts must learn from the literature of policy analysis about the complexities of policy termination.[44] Those who have dealt with complex cases have become acutely aware of the need to clarify the conditions for terminating jurisdiction at the time the order is crafted.

Kenneth Dolbeare described local trial courts as conversion points between local political and court systems.[45] That thesis holds for federal district courts as well. They are political pressure points. In addition to the general level of tension in the environment of the federal district court, there are particular difficulties for the judge who must craft and ensure implementation of equitable decrees. It is not enough to say that district judges are in a difficult spot. We must come to recognize and understand the dynamics of the remedial decree process and the patterns of interaction exhibited by its participants. This study has attempted to move toward that goal. It has presented a decree litigation model which guides analysis of the dynamics and tactics of the process. It suggests that while policy implementation and evaluation perspectives on district court remedies are interesting, there is another important perspective to be considered, that of the judge called upon to respond to this difficult litigation.

The hard choices involved in the cases studied here were not whether to take a case or whether there was a violation of law requiring a remedy. In most instances, the cases were clear and the violations patent. Rather, the truly hard choices come from the effort to meet the elements of remedial adequacy while balancing those demands against the need for limits to discretion, both the more formal doctrinal constraints and the less formal judgmental factors associated with a prudent sense of the court's relationship to the community and its administrative and elected officials. Proper and effective performance of the judge's task requires a facility with process and policy. Given the environment within which administrators and other policymakers operate, it is not only theoretically useful but practically necessary to understand public law policy cases not only from one's own perspective, but also from that of other participants in the governing process.

NOTES

1. See Milton Heumann, *Plea Bargaining* (Chicago: Univ. of Chicago Press, 1977), p. 12, and Jerome Skolnick, *Justice Without Trial: Law Enforcement in Democratic Society* (New York: Wiley, 1966), p. 41.

2. *See, e.g.,* Anthony Champagne, ''The Theory of Limited Judicial Impact: Reforming

the Dallas Jail as a Case Study,'' in Stuart Nagel and Erika Fairchild, eds., *The Political Science of Criminal Justice* (Springfield, IL: Charles C. Thomas Pub., 1983); and Daniel J. Monti, ''Administrative Foxes in Educational Chicken Coops: An Examination and Critique of Judicial Activism in School Desegregation Cases,'' 2 *Law and Politics Quarterly* 233 (1980).

3. *City of Hartford v. Hills,* 408 F. Supp. 889 (DCT 1976).

4. Stephen L. Wasby, ''Arrogation of Power or Accountability: 'Judicial Imperialism' Revisited,'' 65 *Judicature* 208, 213 (1981).

5. Stephen Wasby reached similar conclusions at approximately the same time in different research. *See* his ''How Planned Is 'Planned Litigation'?'' *American Bar Foundation Research Journal* 1984 (Winter 1984): 83–138.

6. Abram Chayes, ''The Role of the Judge in Public Law Litigation,'' 89 *Harv. L. Rev.* 1281, 1293–94 (1976).

7. *Smith v. Wade,* 75 L.Ed2d 623 (1983).

8. Ralph Cavanagh and Austin Sarat, ''Thinking About Courts: Toward and Beyond a Jurisprudence of Judicial Competence,'' 14 *Law and Society Review* 371, 391 (1980).

9. Wasby, *supra* note 4, at 217.

10. *See, e.g.,* ''Brief for Respondents Board of Education for the School District of the City of Detroit, et al., in No.73–434, in *Milliken v. Bradley [Milliken I],*'' in Philip B. Kurland and Gerhard Casper, eds., *Landmark Briefs and Arguments of the Supreme Court of the United States: Constitutional Law* (Arlington, VA: Univ. Publications of America, Inc., 1975), vol. 80, p. 798.

11. Colin S. Diver, ''The Judge as Powerbroker: Superintending Change in Political Institutions,'' 65 *Va. L. Rev.* 43 (1979).

12. *Id.,* at 51.

13. Michael T. Hayes, *Lobbyists and Legislators: A Theory of Political Markets* (New Brunswick: Rutgers Univ. Press, 1981); Robert Salisbury, ''An Exchange Theory of Interest Groups,'' *Midwest Journal of Political Science* 8 (1969): 1–32.

14. *But see Calhoun v. Cook,* 362 F. Supp. 1249, 1250 (NDGA 1973).

15. *Local No. 93, Int'l Ass'n of Firefighters v. Cleveland,* 54 U.S.L.W. 5005, 5009 (1986).

16. These observations, however, are not meant to go so far as to support the argument in Judith Resnick, ''Managerial Judges,'' 96 *Harv. L. Rev.* 374 (1982).

17. Johnson warned, ''Gentlemen, let's keep this in mind: In this case at the termination of the original hearing, I determined that an individual who was committed through state processes to a mental institution for treatment purposes was constitutionally entitled to treatment; otherwise, it would be a violation of due process to confine him or put him in a confinement status for treatment purpose and not treat him. Along with that, I held that he's not entitled to the best treatment, he is not entitled to optimum treatment; but he is constitutionally entitled to minimum treatment, and this hearing today is for the purpose of determining what these minimum standards are. *And I will not permit this Court to be used as a level for the Legislature to get a budget for Bryce or Searcy Hospitals.*'' *Bryce and Searcy Remedy Hearing Transcript,* at 380–81. Emphasis added.

18. Wasby, *supra* note 4, at 213. See also Cavanagh and Sarat, *supra* note 8.

19. *Wasby,* at 215.

20. See Cavanagh and Sarat, *supra* note 8, at 408.

21. This point was brought to my attention by my colleague, Roman Hedges.

21. *See generally* Arnold J. Meltsner, ''Political Feasibility and Policy Analysis,'' *Public Administration Review* 32 (Nov./Dec. 1972): 859–67.

23. Cavanagh and Sarat, *supra* note 8, at 408.

24. For a general discussion of the remedy options, *see Swann v. Charlotte-Mecklenburg Bd. of Ed.,* 402 U.S. 1 (1971).

25. See *Milliken v. Bradley,* 418 U.S. 717 (1974); *Rizzo v. Goode,* 423 U.S. 362 (1976); and *Pasadena Bd. of Ed. v. Spangler,* 427 U.S. 424 (1976).

26. These cases normally arise where government is either unwilling or unable to undertake

enforcement action. Since the Supreme Court has recently determined that enforcement discretion is presumptively unreviewable, the private attorney general suit may be the other way to enforce the law in some areas. *Heckler v. Chaney,* 84 L.Ed2d 714, 724 (1985).

27. Prior to recent decisions, once a finding of a violation of law was found with regard to, say, racial discrimination in education, the judge was charged with eliminating the problem "root and branch." *Green v. County School Bd. of New Kent County, Va.,* 391 U.S. 430 (1968).

28. See *Dayton Bd. of Ed. v. Brinkman,* 433 U.S. 406 (1977).

29. But the court has applied this with great rigidity. See *Milliken v. Bradley,* 433 U.S. 267 (1977) *(Milliken II).*

30. The Court has allowed a bit more flexibility for the remedy where the legislature had made a specific finding regarding the existence of widespread discrimination. *See, e.g., Fullilove v. Klutznick,* 488 U.S. 448 (1980).

31. *See generally San Antonio Indep. School Dist. v. Rodriguez,* 411 U.S. 1 (1973).

32. See J.W. Peltason, *Fifty-eight Lonely Men: Southern Federal Judges and School Desegregation* (Urbana: Univ. of Illinois Press, 1971).

33. See *Green v. County School Bd., supra* note 27; and *Swann v. Charlotte-Mecklenburg, supra* note 24.

34. *Pasadena Bd. of Ed. v. Spangler, supra* note 25.

35. *Wyatt v. Stickney,* 344 F. Supp. 387, 391 n. 8 (MDAL 1972).

36. *Sweatt v. Painter,* 339 U.S. 629 (1950).

37. *Milliken I,* JA, pp. IIa41, IIa44; and *Milliken I,* oral argument, at 10. Grant, reports that Roth was very open in the early stages, even holding a news conference in December 1970. William R. Grant, "The Detroit School Case: An Historical Overview," 21 *Wayne L. Rev.* 851 (1975).

38. *Bradley v. Milliken,* 402 F. Supp. 1096, 1118 (EDMI 1975).

39. *See* Note: "The Wyatt Case: Implementation of a Judicial Decree Ordering Institutional Change," 84 *Yale L.J.* 1338 (1975).

40. *See* Vincent M. Nathan, "The Use of Masters in Institutional Reform Litigation," 10 *Toledo L. Rev.* 419, 441 (1979).

41. Apart from Charles S. Bullock III and Charles M. Lamb, *Implementation of Civil Rights Policy* (Monterey, CA: Brooks/Cole, 1984), there has been little attempt to integrate the literature of policy implementation into judicial policymaking and vice versa. For a summary of that literature, see Robert K. Nakamura and Frank Smallwood, *The Politics of Policy Implementation* (New York: St. Martins, 1980); Daniel A. Maxmanian and Paul A. Sabatier, *Implementation and Public Policy* (Glenview, IL: Scott, Foresman, 1983); Gary D. Brewer and Peter DeLeon, *The Foundations of Polic Analysis* (Homewood, IL: Dorsey, 1983); Jeffrey Pressman and Aaron Wildavsky, *Implementation* (Berkeley: Univ. of California Press, 1973); and Carl Van Horn and Donald Van Meter, "The Implementation of Intergovernmental Policy," in Charles O. Jones and Robert Thomas, eds., *Public Policy Making in the Federal System* (Beverley Hills, CA: Sage, 1976).

42. Bullock and Lamb, *supra* note 41, at 5–6.

43. Brewer and DeLeon, *supra* note 41, at 268.

44. *See* Eugene Bardach, "Policy Termination as a Policy Process," *Policy Sciences* 7 (1976): 123–31.

45. Kenneth M. Dolbeare, *Trial Courts in Urban Politics* (New York: Wiley, 1967).

Bibliography

Abraham, Henry J. *Freedom and the Court,* 3rd ed. New York: Oxford Univ. Press, 1977.

Advisory Commission on Intergovernmental Relations. *Community Development: The Workings of a Federal-Local Block Grant.* Wash., DC: ACIR, 1977.

————. *Safe Streets Reconsidered: The Block Grant Experience, 1968–1975.* (Wash., DC: ACIR, 1977).

American Bar Association, *The Urban Police Function.* Chicago: ABA, 1972.

Anechiarico, Frank. "Suing the Philadelphia Police: The Case for an Institutional Approach." 6 *Law and Policy* 231 (1984).

Arizona Advisory Committee to the U.S. Commission on Civil Rights. *Justice in Flagstaff.* Wash., DC: U.S. Commission on Civil Rights, 1977.

Babcock, Richard F. *The Zoning Game.* Madison: Univ. of Wisconsin Press, 1966.

Bardach, Eugene. "Policy Termination as a Policy Process." *Policy Sciences* 7 (1976): 123–31.

Bass, Jack. *Unlikely Heroes.* New York: Simon and Schuster, 1981.

Bazelon, David L. "Foreward." 57 *Geo. L.J.* 676 (1969).

————. "Implementing the Right to Treatment." 36 *U. Chi. L. Rev.* 742 (1969).

Beer, Louis D. "The Nature of the Violation and the Scope of the Remedy: An Analysis of Milliken v. Bradley in Terms of the Evolution of the Theory of the Violation." 21 *Wayne L. Rev.* 903 (1975).

Berger, Raoul. *Government by Judiciary.* Cambridge, MA: Harvard Univ. Press, 1977.

Birnbaum, Morton. "The Right to Treatment." 46 *A.B.A. J.* 499 (1960).

Black, Algernon D. *The People and the Police.* New York: McGraw-Hill, 1968.

Bolner, James, and Robert Shanley. *Busing: The Political and Judicial Process.* New York: Praeger, 1974.

Brewer, Gary D., and Peter DeLeon. *The Foundations of Policy Analysis.* Homewood, IL: Dorsey, 1983.

Browning, R. Stephen, ed. *From Brown to Bradley: School Desegregation 1954–1974.* Cincinnati, OH: Jefferson Law Book Co., 1975.

Bullock, Charles S., III, and Charles M. Lamb, eds. *Implementation of Civil Rights Policy.* Monterey, CA: Brooks/Cole, 1984.

Burger, Warren. "Who Will Watch the Watchman?" 14 *Am. U.L. Rev.* 1 (1964).

Caiden, Gerald. *Police Revitalization.* Lexington, MA: Lexington Books, 1977.

California Advisory Committee to the U.S. Commission on Civil Rights. *Police-Community Relations in San Jose.* Wash., DC: U.S. Commission on Civil Rights, 1980.

Carlson, Jody. *George C. Wallace and the Politics of Powerlessness*. New Brunswick, NJ: Transaction, 1981.

Cavanagh, Ralph, and Austin Sarat. "Thinking About Courts: Toward and Beyond a Jurisprudence of Judicial Competence." 14 *Law and Society Review* 371 (1980).

Chafe, Robert. *Civil Liberties and Civilities*. New York: Oxford Univ. Press, 1978.

Champagne, Anthony. "The Theory of Limited Judicial Impact: Reforming the Dallas Jail as a Case Study," in Stuart Nagel and Erika Fairchild, eds., *The Political Science of Criminal Justice*. Springfield: Charles C. Thomas Pub., 1983.

Chayes, Abram. "The Role of the Judge in Public Law Litigation." 89 *Harv. L. Rev.* 1281 (1976).

Chevigny, Paul. *Police Power, Police Abuses in New York City*. New York: Rand Institute, 1969.

Comment. "Constitutional Law—Due Process—A State Mental Institution is Constitutionally Required to Provide Adequate Mental Treatment for Patients Involuntarily Committed." 23 *Ala. L. Rev.* 642 (1971).

Comment. "Constitutional Rights of Prisoners: The Developing Law." 110 *U. Pa. L. Rev.* 985 (1962).

Comment. "Equitable Remedies: An Analysis of Judicial Utilization of Neoreceiverships to Implement Larger-Scale Institutional Change." 1976 *Wis. L. Rev.* 1161.

Comment. "Police-Philadelphia's Police Advisory Board—A New Concept in Community Relations." 7 *Vill. L. Rev.* 656 (1962).

Comment. "Wyatt v. Stickney and the Right of the Civilly Committed Patients to Adequate Treatment." 86 *Harv. L. Rev.* 1282 (1973).

Council of the American Psychiatric Association. "Position Statement on the Question of Adequacy of Treatment." 123 *American Journal of Psychiatry* 1458 (1967).

Coxe, Spencer. "Police Advisory Board: The Philadelphia Story." 35 *Conn. B.J.* 138 (1961).

Cramton, Roger C. "Judicial Policy Making and Administration." *Public Administration Review* 31 (Sept./Oct. 1976): 551–54.

Danielson, Michael. *The Politics of Exclusion*. New York: Columbia Univ. Press, 1976.

Davis, Kenneth Culp. *Police Discretion*. St. Paul, MN: West, 1975.

Deutsch, Albert. *The Mentally Ill in America: A History of Their Care and Treatment from Colonial Times*, 2nd ed. New York: Columbia Univ. Press, 1949.

Developments in the Law. "Civil Commitment of the Mentally Ill." 87 *Harv. L. Rev.* 1190 (1974).

Dimond, Paul R. *Beyond Busing*. Ann Arbor: Univ. of Michigan Press, 1985.

District of Columbia Advisory Committee to the U.S. Commission on Civil Rights. *Police-Community Relations in Washington, D.C.* Wash., DC: U.S. Commission on Civil Rights, 1981.

Diver, Colin S. "The Judge as Powerbroker: Superintending Change in Political Institutions," 65 *V. L. Rev.* 43 (1979).

Dolbeare, Kenneth M. *Trial Courts in Urban Politics*. New York: Wiley, 1967.

Doudera, A. Edward, and Judith P. Swazey, eds., *Refusing Treatment in Mental Health Institutions—Values in Conflict*. Ann Arbor: MI: AUPHA Press, 1982.

Downs, Anthony. *Opening Up the Suburbs: An Urban Strategy for America*. New Haven, CT: Yale Univ. Press, 1973.

Eckstein, Harry. "Case Study and Theory in Political Science," in Fred I. Greenstein and Nelson W. Polsby, eds. *Handbook of Political Science, Volume 7*. Reading, MA: Addison-Wesley, 1975.

"Editorial: A New Right," 46 *A.B.A. J.* 516 (1960).

Edwards, George. "Order and Civil Liberties: A Complex Role for the Police." 64 *Mich. L. Rev.* 47 (1965).

Eisenberg, Theodore, and Stephen Yeazell. "The Ordinary and the Extraordinary in Institutional Litigation." 93 *Harv. L. Rev.* 465 (1980).

Fishman, Richard P., ed. *Housing for All Under Law: New Directions in Housing and Land Use Planning Law*. Cambridge, MA: Ballinger, 1978.

Friedman, Paul. "The Mentally Handicapped Citizen and Institutional Labor." 87 *Harv. L. Rev.* 567 (1975).

Fuller, Lon. "The Forms and Limits of Adjudication." 92 *Harv. L. Rev.* 353 (1978).

Georgia Advisory Committee to the U.S. Commission on Civil Rights. *Georgia Prisons*. Wash., DC: U.S. Commission on Civil Rights, 1976.

Gilmour, Robert S. "Agency Administration by Judiciary." *Southern Review of Public Administration*. 6 (Spring 1982): 26–42.

Glazer, Nathan. "Should Courts Administer Social Services?" *Public Interest* 50 (Winter 1978): 64–80.

Goldfarb, Ronald L., and Linda R. Singer. *After Conviction*. New York: Simon and Schuster, 1973.

Goldstein, Herman. *Policing a Free Society*. Cambridge, MA: Ballinger, 1977.

Grant, William. "Community Control vs. School Integration—The Case of Detroit." *Public Interest* 24 (Summer 1971): 62–79.

———. "The Detroit School Case: An Historical Overview." 21 *Wayne L. Rev.* 851 (1975).

———. "Judge Roth Dead at 66: He Ordered Area Busing." *Detroit Free Press*, Friday, July 12, 1974, p. 1A.

Granucci, Anthony. "Nor Cruel and Unusual Punishment Inflicted: The Original Meaning." 57 *Calif. L. Rev.* 839 (1969).

Guttmacher, Manfred S., and Henry Weihofen. *Psychiatry and the Law*. New York: Norton, 1952.

Haas, Kenneth C. "Judicial Politics and Correctional Reform: An Analysis of the Decline of the Hands-off Doctrine." 1977 *Det. C.L. Rev.* 795 (1977).

Halpern, Charles R. "A Practicing Lawyer Views the Right to Treatment." 57 *Geo. L.J.* 782 (1969).

Harris, M. Kay, and Dudley P. Spriller, Jr. *After Decision: Implementation of Judicial Decrees in Correctional Settings.* Wash., DC: National Institute of Law Enforcement and Criminal Justice, 1977.

Hartman, Chester W. *Housing and Social Policy.* Englewood Cliffs, NJ: Prentice-Hall, 1974.

Hayes, Michael T. *Lobbyists and Legislators: A Theory of Political Markets.* New Brunswick, NJ: Rutgers Univ. Press, 1981.

Heumann, Milton. *Plea Bargaining.* Chicago: University of Chicago Press, 1977.

Horowitz, Donald. *The Courts and Social Policy.* Wash., DC: Brookings, 1977.

Johnson, Charles A., and Bradley C. Canon. *Judicial Policies: Implementation and Impact.* Wash., DC: Congressional Quarterly, 1984.

Johnson, Frank M., Jr. "The Constitution and the Federal District Judge." 54 *Tex. L. Rev.* 903 (1976).

Kansas State Advisory Committee to the U.S. Commission on Civil Rights. *Inmate Rights and the Kansas State Prison System.* Wash., DC: U.S. Commission on Civil Rights, 1974.

————. *Police-Community Relations in the City of Wichita and Sedgwick County.* Wash., DC: U.S. Commission on Civil Rights, 1980.

Kentucky Advisory Committee to the U.S. Commission on Civil Rights. *A Paper Commitment: EEO in the Kentucky Bureau of State Police.* Wash., DC: U.S. Commission on Civil Rights, 1978.

Kirp, D.L. "School Desegregation and the Limits of Legalism." *Public Interest* 47 (Spring 1977): 101–28.

Kluger, Richard. *Simple Justice.* New York: Knopf, 1976.

Kolodner, Howard I., and James J. Fishman, eds. *Limits of Justice: The Court's Role in School Desegregation.* Cambridge, MA: Ballinger, 1978.

LaFave, Wayne, and Frank Remington. "Controlling the Police: The Judge's Role in Making and Reviewing Law Enforcement Decisions." 63 *Mich. L. Rev.* 987 (1965).

Lamb, Charles M. "Housing Discrimination and Segregation in America: Problematical Dimensions and the Federal Legal Response." 30 *Cath. U.L. Rev.* 363 (1981).

Levy, Leonard W. *The Law of the Commonwealth and Chief Justice Shaw* (Chicago: Univ. of Chicago Press, 1957.

Lijphart, Arend. "Comparative Politics and the Comparative Method." *American Political Science Review* 65 (Sept. 1971): 682–93.

Lindman, Frank T., and Donald McIntyre, Jr., eds. *The Mentally Disabled and the Law: Report of the American Bar Foundation on the Rights of the Mentally Ill.* Chicago: Univ. of Chicago Press, 1961.

Lipsky, Michael. *Street Level Bureaucracy.* New York: Russell Sage Foundation, 1980.

Louisiana Advisory Committee to the U.S. Commission on Civil Rights. *A Study of Adult Corrections in Louisiana.* Wash., DC: U.S. Commission on Civil Rights, 1976.

Lowi, Theodore. "American Business, Public Policy, Case Studies, and Political Theory." *World Politics* 16 (July 1964): 677–715.

McKelvey, Blake. *American Prisons: A History of Good Intentions.* Montclair, NJ: Patterson Smith, 1977.

Mandelker, Daniel R. *The Zoning Dilemma, a Legal Strategy for Urban Change*. Indianapolis, IN: Bobbs-Merrill, 1971.

Maryland Advisory Committee to the U.S. Commission on Civil Rights. *Baltimore Police Complaint Evaluation Procedure*. Wash., DC: U.S. Commission on Civil Rights, 1980.

Mazmanian, Daniel A., and Paul A. Sabatier. *Implementation and Public Policy*. Glenview, IL: Scott, Foresman, 1983.

Meltsner, Arnold J. "Political Feasibility and Policy Analysis." *Public Administration Review* 32 (Nov./Dec. 1972): 859–67.

Miller, Loren. *The Petitioners*. New York: Pantheon, 1966.

Minnesota Advisory Committee to the U.S. Commission on Civil Rights. *Police Practices in the Twin Cities*. Wash., DC: U.S. Commission on Civil Rights, 1981.

Montana State Advisory Committee to the U.S. Commission on Civil Rights. *Corrections in Montana: A Consultation*. (Wash., DC: U.S. Commission on Civil Rights, 1979.

Monti, Daniel J. "Administrative Foxes in Educational Chicken Coops: An Examination and Critique of Judicial Activism in School Desegregation Cases." 2 *Law and Politics Quarterly* 233 (1980).

Muir, William K., Jr. *Police: Streetcorner Politicians*. Chicago: Univ. of Chicago Press, 1977.

Nakamura, Robert K., and Frank Smallwood, *The Politics of Policy Implementation*. New York: St. Martins, 1980.

Nathan, Vincent M. "The Use of Masters in Institutional Reform Litigation." 10 *Toledo L. Rev.* 419 (1979).

National Advisory Commission on Civil Disorders. *Report of the National Advisory Commission on Civil Disorders*. New York: Bantam, 1968.

National Advisory Commission on Criminal Justice Standards and Goals. *Police*. Wash., DC: Government Printing Office, 1973.

National Commission on Law Observance and Enforcement. *Report on Police*. Wash., DC: Government Printing Office, 1931.

Nebraska Advisory Committee to the U.S. Commission on Civil Rights. *Police-Community Relations in Omaha*. (1982).

New York Advisory Committee to the U.S. Commission on Civil Rights. *Warehousing Human Beings*. Wash., DC: U.S. Commission on Civil Rights, 1974.

Niederhoffer, Arthur. *Behind the Shield: The Police in Urban Society*. Garden City, NY: Doubleday, 1967.

North Dakota Advisory Committee to the U.S. Commission on Civil Rights. *American Justice Issues in North Dakota*. Wash., DC: Government Printing Office, 1978).

Note. "The Administration of Complaints by Civilians Against the Police." 77 *Harv. L. Rev.* 499 (1964).

Note. "Beyond the Ken of the Courts: A Critique of Judicial Refusal to Review the Complaints of Convicts." 72 *Yale L.J.* 506 (1963).

Note. "Civil Restraint, Mental Illness, and the Right to Treatment." 77 *Yale L.J.* 87 (1967).

Note. "The Federal Injunction as a Remedy for Unconstitutional Police Conduct." 78 *Yale L.J.* 143 (1968).

Note. "The Implementation Problems in Institutional Reform Litigation." 91 *Harv. L. Rev.* 371 (1977).

Note. "Implementing the Right to Treatment for Involuntarily Confined Mental Patients: Wyatt v. Stickney." 3 *N.M. L. Rev.* 338 (1973).

Note. "Injunctive Relief for Violations of Constitutional Rights by the Police." 45 *Colo. L. Rev.* 91 (1973).

Note. "The Nascent Right to Treatment." 53 *Va. L. Rev.* 1134 (1967).

Note. "Philadelphia's Police Practice and the Law of Arrest." 100 *U. Pa. L. Rev.* 1182 (1952).

Note. "Rouse v. Cameron" 80 *Harv. L. Rev.* 898 (1967).

Note. "Towards a Recognition of a Constitutional Right to Housing." 42 *U. Mo. Kan. City L. Rev.* 362 (1974).

Note. "Use of Section 1983 to Remedy Unconstitutional Police Conduct: Guarding the Guards." 5 *Harv. C.R.-C.L. L. Rev.* 104 (1970).

Note. "The Wyatt Case: Implementation of a Judicial Decree Ordering Institutional Change." 84 *Yale L.J.* 1338 (1975).

Ohio Advisory Committee to the U.S. Commission on Civil Rights. *Policing in Cincinnati, Ohio: Official Policy vs. Civilian Reality.* (1981).

Ohio Advisory Committee to the U.S. Commission on Civil Rights. *Protecting Inmate Rights: Prison Reform or Prison Replacement.* Wash., DC: U.S. Commission on Civil Rights, 1976.

Ohio Citizens' Task Force on Corrections. *Final Report of the Ohio Citizens' Task Force on Corrections.* Columbus: Ohio Department of Urban Affairs, 1971.

Ohio Crime Commission, *Final Report of the Ohio Crime Commission.* Mar. 15, 1969.

Peltason, Jack W. *Fifty-eight Lonely Men: Southern Federal Judges and School Desegregation.* Urbana: Univ. of Illinois Press, 1971.

Pettigrew, Thomas F. "A Sociological View of the Post Bradley Era." 21 *Wayne L. Rev.* 813 (1975).

Pilegge, Joseph C., Jr. *Taxing and Spending: Alabama's Budget in Transition.* University: Univ. of Alabama Press, 1978.

Pindur, Wolfgang. "Legislative and Judicial Roles in the Detroit School Decentralization Controversy." 50 *Journal of Urban Law* 53 (1972).

President's Commission on Law Enforcement and Administration of Justice. *The Challenge of Crime in a Free Society.* (Wash., DC: Government Printing Office, 1967.

————. *Task Force Report: Corrections.* Wash., DC: Government Printing Office, 1967.

President's Commission on Urban Housing. *A Decent Home.* Wash., DC: Government Printing Office, 1968.

Pressman, Jeffrey, and Aaron Wildavsky. *Implementation.* Berkeley: Univ. of California Press, 1973.

Ramsay, A.A.W. *Sir Robert Peel.* New York: Dodd, Mead, 1938.

Ransone, Coleman B., Jr. *Alabama Finances: Revenues and Expenditures 1957–1967.* University: Bureau of Public Administration, Univ. of Alabama Press, 1969.

Reith, Charles. *The Police Idea: Its History and Evolution in England in the Eighteenth Century and After*. London: Oxford Univ. Press, 1938.

Resnick, Judith. "Managerial Judges." 96 *Harv. L. Rev.* 374 (1982).

Rodgers, Harrell R., Jr., and Charles S. Bullock III. *Coercion to Compliance*. Lexington, MA: Lexington Books, 1976.

Rothman, David J., and Sheila M. Rothman, *The Willowbrook Wars*. New York: Harper & Row, 1984.

Rourke, Francis E. *Bureaucracy, Politics, and Public Policy*, 3rd ed. Boston: Little, Brown, 1984.

Rubenstein, Jonathan. *City Police*. New York: Ballantine, 1973.

Salisbury, Robert. "An Exchange Theory of Interest Groups." *Midwest Journal of Political Science* 8 (1969): 1–32.

Schwartz, Bernard. *Super Chief*. New York: New York Univ. Press, 1983.

Schwartz, Louis B. "Complaints Against the Police: Experience of the Community Rights Division of the Philadelphia District Attorney's Office." 118 *U. Pa. L. Rev.* 1023 (1970).

Segall, Robert D. "Civil Commitment in Alabama." 26 *Ala. L. Rev.* 215 (1973).

Serrin, William. "The Most Hated Man in Michigan." *Saturday Review*, Aug. 26, 1972.

Skolnick, Jerome. *Justice Without Trial: Law Enforcement in Democratic Society*. New York: Wiley, 1966.

South Dakota Advisory Committee to the U.S. Commission on Civil Rights. *Liberty and Justice for All*. Wash., DC: Government Printing Office, 1977.

Special Project. "The Remedial Process in Institutional Reform Litigation." 78 *Colum. L. Rev.* 783 (1978).

Stanley, Harold W. *State vs. Governor, Alabama 1971*. University: Univ. of Alabama Press, 1980.

State of New York. *Attica: Official Report of the New York State Special Commission on Attica*. New York: Bantam, 1972.

Stickney, Stonewall B. "Problems in Implementing the Right to Treatment in Alabama: The Wyatt v. Stickney Case." 25 *Hospital and Community Psychiatry* 453 (1974).

Symposium. "The Mentally Ill and the Right to Treatment." 36 *U. Chi. L. Rev.* 742 (1969).

Symposium. "Observations on the Right to Treatment." 10 *Duq. L. Rev.* 553 (1972).

Symposium. "Observations on the Right to Treatment." 57 *Geo. L.J.* 673 (1969).

Tarwater, James S. *The Alabama State Hospitals and the Partlow State School and Hospital: A Brief History*. New York: Newcomen Society, 1964.

Task Panel on Legal and Ethical Issues of the President's Commission on Mental Health. "Mental Health and Human Rights." 20 *Ariz. L. Rev.* 49 (1978).

Taylor, Wayne. "The Supreme Court and Urban Reality." 21 *Wayne L. Rev.* 751 (1975).

Tennessee Advisory Committee to the U.S. Commission on Civil Rights. *Civic Crisis–Civic Challenge: Police-Community Relations in Memphis*. Wash., DC: U.S. Commission on Civil Rights, 1978.

U.S. Commission on Civil Rights. *Confronting Racial Isolation in Miami.* Wash., DC: Government Printing Office, 1982.

————. *The Federal Fair Housing Enforcement Effort.* Wash., DC: Government Printing Office, 1979.

————. *Hearings Before the United States Commission on Civil Rights: Hearings Held in Cleveland, Ohio, April 1–7, 1966.* Wash., DC: Government Printing Office, 1966.

————. *Hearings Held in Detroit, Michigan, December 14–15 (1960).* Wash., DC: U.S. Commission on Civil Rights, 1961.

————. Hearings Held in Philadelphia, Pennsylvania, February 6, 1979; April 16–17, 1979. *Police Practices and Civil Rights.* Wash., DC: Government Printing Office, 1979.

————. *Reviewing a Decade of School Desegregation 1966–1975.* Wash., DC: U.S. Commission on Civil Rights, 1977.

————. *School Desegregation: The Courts and Suburban Migration.* Wash., DC: U.S. Commission on Civil Rights, 1975.

————. *Twenty Years After Brown.* Wash., DC: U.S. Commission on Civil Rights, 1979.

————. *Who Is Guarding the Guardians? A Report on Police Practices.* Wash., DC: U.S. Commission on Civil Rights, 1981.

U.S. House of Representatives. Hearings Before the Subcommittee on Courts, Civil Liberties, and the Administration of Justice of the Committee on the Judiciary. *Civil Rights for Institutionalized Persons.* 95th Cong., 1st Sess. (1977).

————. Hearings Before the Subcommittee on Courts, Civil Liberties, and the Administration of Justice of the Committee on the Judiciary. *Civil Rights of Institutionalized Persons.* 96th Cong., 1st Sess. (1979).

U.S. Senate. Hearings Before the Subcommittee on the Constitution of the Committee on the Judiciary. *Civil Rights of Institutionalized Persons.* 95th Cong., 1st Sess. (1977).

————. Hearings Before the Subcommittee on the Constitution of the Committee on the Judiciary. *Civil Rights of the Institutionalized.* 96th Congress, 1st Sess. (1979).

————. Hearings Before the Subcommittee on Constitutional Rights of the Committee on the Judiciary. *Constitutional Rights of the Mentally Ill.* 87th Cong., 1st Sess. (1961), Parts I and II.

————. Hearings Before the Subcommittee on Constitutional Rights of the Committee on the Judiciary. *Constitutional Rights of the Mentally Ill.* 91st Cong., 1st and 2d Sess. (1969–70).

————. Hearings Before the Subcommittee on Constitutional Rights of the Committee on the Judiciary. *To Protect the Constitutional Rights of the Mentally Ill.* 88th Cong., 1st Sess. (1963).

Van Horn, Carl, and Donald Van Meter. "The Implementation of Intergovernmental Policy," in Charles O. Jones and Robert Thomas, eds. *Public Policy Making in the Federal System.* Beverly Hills, CA: Sage, 1976.

Verba, Sidney. "Some Dilemmas in Comparative Research." *World Politics* 20 (Oct. 1967): 111–27.

Vose, Clement. *Caucasions Only: The Supreme Court, the NAACP, and the Restrictive Covenant Cases.* Berkeley: Univ. of California Press, 1959.

Wasby, Stephen L. "Arrogation of Power or Accountability: 'Judicial Imperialism' Revisited."
     65 *Judicature* 208 (1981).

————. "How Planned is 'Planned Litigation'?" *American Bar Foundation Research Journal*
     1984 (Winter 1984): 83–138.

————. *The Impact of the United States Supreme Court.* Homewood, IL: Dorsey, 1970.

Wasby, Stephen L., Anthony A. D'Amato, and Rosemary Metrailer. *Desegregation from Brown
     to Alexander.* Carbondale: Southern Illinois Univ. Press, 1977.

Wilson, James Q. *Urban Renewal: The Record and the Controversy.* Cambridge, MA: MIT,
     1966.

————. *Varieties of Police Behavior.* New York: Atheneum, 1975.

Wolf, Eleanor P. "Social Science and the Courts: The Detroit Schools Case." *Public Interest* 4
     (Winter 1976): 102–20.

Yarbrough, Tinsley. *Judge Frank M. Johnson and Human Rights in Alabama.* University: Univ.
     of Alabama Press, 1981.

Yin, Robert K. *Case Study Research: Design and Methods.* Beverly Hills, CA: Sage, 1984.

Cases

Alexander v. Holmes County Board of Education, 396 U.S. 19 (1969).
Allee v. Medrano, 416 U.S. 802 (1974).
Banks v. Perk, 341 F. Supp. 1175 (NDOH 1972).
Banks v. Perk, 473 F.2d 910 (6th Cir. 1973).
Banning v. Looney, 213 F.2d 771 (10th Cir. 1954).
Barrows v. Jackson, 346 U.S. 249 (1953).
Battle v. Anderson, 376 F. Supp. 402 (EDOK 1974).
Battle v. Anderson, 447 F. Supp. 516 (DOK 1977).
Baxter v. Palmigiano, 425 U.S. 308 (1976).
Belknap v. Leary, 427 F.2d 496 (2d Cir. 1970).
Bell v. School City of Gary, Indiana, 324 F.2d 209 (7th Cir. 1963).
Bell v. Wolfish, 441 U.S. 520 (1979).
Benton v. Reid, 231 F.2d 780 (DCC 1956).
Berea College v. Kentucky, 211 U.S. 45 (1908).
Berman v. Parker, 348 U.S. 26 (1954).
Bethea v. Crouse, 417 F.2d 504 (10th Cir. 1969).
Blocker v. Board of Education of Manhasset, New York. 226 F. Supp. 208 (EDNY 1964).
Boston Chapter NAACP v. Beecher, 679 F.2d 965 (1st Cir. 1982).
Bounds v. Smith, 430 U.S. 817 (1977).
Boyd v. United States, 116 U.S. 616 (1886).
Bradley v. Milliken, 433 F.2d 897 (6th Cir. 1970).
Bradley v. Milliken, 338 F. Supp. 582 (EDMI 1971).
Bradley v. Milliken, 438 F.2d 945 (6th Cir. 1971).
Bradley v. Milliken, 484 F.2d 215 (6th Cir. 1973).
Bradley v. Milliken, 402 F. Supp. 1096 (EDMI 1975).
Bradley v. Milliken, 411 F. Supp. 943 (EDMI 1975).
Bradley v. Milliken, 540 F.2d 229 (6th Cir. 1976).
Bradley v. Milliken, 426 F. Supp. 929 (EDMI 1977).
Bradley v. Milliken, 460 F. Supp. 299 (EDMI 1978).
Bradley v. Milliken, 620 F.2d 1143 (6th Cir. 1980).
Bradley v. Richmond, 325 F. Supp. 828 (EDVA 1971).
Bradley v. Richmond, 462 F.2d 1058 (4th Cir. 1972).
Bradley v. Richmond, 412 U.S. 92 (1973).
Briggs v. Elliott, 132 F. Supp. 776 (EDSC 1955).
Brown v. Board of Education of Topeka, Kansas, 347 U.S. 483 (1954).
Brown v. Board of Education, 349 U.S. 294 (1955).
Buchanan v. Warley, 245 U.S. 60 (1917).
Burnham v. Department of Public Health of the State of Georgia, 349 F. Supp. 1335 (NDGA 1972).
Burnham v. Department of Public Health of the State of Georgia, 503 F.2d 1319 (5th Cir. 1974).
Butcher v. Rizzo, 317 F. Supp. 899 (EDPA 1970).
Calhoun v. Cook, 362 F. Supp. 1249 (NDGA 1973).
California v. Sierra Club, 451 U.S. 287 (1981).

Cannon v. University of Chicago, 441 U.S. 677 (1979).

Canterino v. Wilson, 533 F. Supp. 174 (WDKY 1982).

Carter v. West Feliciano Parish School Board, 396 U.S. 290 (1970).

Castro v. Beecher, 522 F. Supp. 873 (DMA 1980).

Chapman v. Rhodes, 434 F. Supp. 1007 (SDOH 1977).

Cisneros v. Corpus Christi Independent School District, 467 F.2d 142 (5th Cir. 1972).

City of Eastlake v. Forest City Enterprises, 426 U.S. 668 (1976).

City of Hartford v. Hills, 408 F. Supp. 889 (DCT 1976).

City of Hartford v. Town of Glastonburg, 561 F.2d 1032 (2d Cir. 1977).

City of Kenosha v. Bruno, 412 U.S. 507 (1973).

City of Los Angeles v. Lyons, 75 L.Ed 2d 675 (1983).

Cleburne v. Cleburne Living Center, 87 L.Ed 2d 313 (1985).

Coffin v. Reichard, 143 F.2d 443 (6th Cir. 1944).

Coker v. Georgia, 433 U.S. 584 (1977).

Columbus Board of Education v. Penick, 583 F.2d 787 (6th Cir. 1978).

Columbus Board of Education v. Penick, 443 U.S. 449 (1979).

Commonwealth v. Hendrick, 280 A.2d 110 (PA 1971).

Commonwealth v. Page, 159 NE2d 82 (MA 1959).

Commonwealth of Pennsylvania v. O'Neill, 345 F. Supp. 305 (EDPA 1972).

Connecticut Board of Pardons v. Dumshat, 452 U.S. 458 (1981).

Construction Industry Association of Sonoma County v. City of Petaluma, 522 F.2d 897 (9th Cir. 1975).

Cooper v. Aaron, 358 U.S. 1 (1958).

Cooper v. Pate, 378 U.S. 546 (1964).

Cornelius v. City of Parma, 374 F. Supp. 730 (NDOH 1974).

Corrigan v. Buckley, 271 U.S. 323 (1926).

Cottonreader v. Johnson, 252 F. Supp. 492 (MDAL 1966).

Council of Organizations on Philadelphia Police Accountability v. Rizzo, 357 F. Supp. 1289 (EDPA 1974).

Covington v. Harris, 419 F.2d 617 (DCC 1969).

Crow v. Brown, 332 F. Supp. 382 (NDGA 1971).

Crow v. Brown, 457 F.2d 788 (5th Cir. 1972).

Cruz v. Beto, 405 U.S. 319 (1972).

Cumming v. Board of Education of Richmond, 175 U.S. 528 (1899).

Daily v. City of Lawton, 425 F.2d 1037 (10th Cir. 1970).

Davis v. Board of School Commissioners of Mobile County, 402 U.S. 33 (1971).

Davis v. Hubbard, 506 F. Supp. 915 (NDOH 1980).

Davis v. School District of Pontiac, 390 F. Supp. 734 (EDMI 1970).

Davis v. United States, 160 U.S. 469 (1895).

Davis v. United States, 165 U.S. 373 (1897).

Davis v. Watkins, 384 F. Supp. 1196 (NDOH 1974).

Dayton Board of Education v. Brinkman, 433 U.S. 406 (1977).

Dayton Board of Education v. Brinkman, 433 U.S. 526 (1979).

Deal v. Cincinnati Board of Education, 369 F.2d 55 (6th Cir. 1966).

Director of Patuxent Institution v. Daniels, 221 A.2d 397 (MD 1966).

Doe v. Public Health Trust of Dade County, 696 F.2d 901 (11th Cir. 1983).

Donaldson v. O'Connor, 493 F.2d 507 (5th Cir. 1974).

Downs v. Board of Education of Kansas City, 336 F.2d 988 (10th Cir. 1964).

Edelman v. Jordan, 415 U.S. 651 (1974).

El Cortez Heights Residents and Property Owners Association v. Tucson Housing Authority, 457 F.2d 910 (6th Cir. 1973).

Enmund v. Florida, 458 U.S. 782 (1982).

Imbler v. Pachtman, 424 U.S. 409 (1976).

Inmates of Attica Correctional Facility v. Rockefeller, 453 F.2d 12 (2nd Cir. 1971).

Inmates of Suffolk County Jail v. Eisenstadt, 360 F. Supp. 676 (DMA 1973).

In re Kemmler, 136 U.S. 436 (1890).

In the Matter of Josiah Oakes, 8 Law Reporter 123 (1845–46).

In the Matter of Guardianship of Richard Roe III, 421 NE2d 40 (MA 1981).

Jackson v. Bishop, 268 F. Supp. 804 (EDAR 1967).

Jackson v. Indiana, 406 U.S. 715 (1972).

James v. Valtierra, 402 U.S. 137 (1971).

J. L. v. Parham, 412 F. Supp. 112 (MDGA 1976).

Johnson v. Avery, 393 U.S. 483 (1969).

Johnson v. San Francisco Unified School District, 339 F. Supp. 1315 (NDCA 1971).

Jones v. Alfred H. Mayer Co., 392 U.S. 409 (1968).

Jones v. North Carolina Prisoners' Labor Union, 433 U.S. 119 (1977).

Joseph Skillken and Co. v. City of Toledo, 528 F.2d 867 (6th Cir. 1975).

Keyes v. School District No. 1 Denver, 413 U.S. 189 (1973).

Kennedy Park Homes Association v. City of Lackawanna, 318 F. Supp. 669 (WDNY 1970).

Kennedy Park Homes Association v. City of Lackawanna, 436 F.2d 108 (2nd Cir. 1970).

Knecht v. Gillman, 488 F.2d 1136 (8th Cir. 1973).

Landman v. Royster, 333 F. Supp. 621 (EDVA 1971).

Lankford v. Gelston, 364 F.2d 197 (4th Cir. 1966).

Lee v. Washington, 390 U.S. 333 (1968).

Leslie Tobin Imports, Inc. v. Rizzo, 305 F. Supp. 1135 (EDPA 1969).

Lewis v. Kugler, 446 F.2d 1343 (3d Cir. 1971).

Lindsey v. Normet, 405 U.S. 56 (1972).

Local No. 93, International Association of Firefighters v. Cleveland, 54 U.S.L.W. 5005 (1986).

Local 309, United Furnitiure Workers of America v. Gates, 75 F. Supp. 620 (NDIN 1948).

Lynch v. Baxley, 386 F. Supp. 378 (MDAL 1974).

McCray v. Sullivan, 399 F. Supp. 271 (SDAL 1975).

McDaniel v. Barresi, 402 U.S. 39 (1971).

McLaurin v. Oklahoma, 339 U.S. 637 (1950).

McMurry v. Phelps, 533 F. Supp. 742 (WDLA 1982).

McNabb v. United States, 318 U.S. 332 (1943).

Mackey v. Procunier, 477 F.2d 877 (9th Cir. 1973).

Mahaley v. Cuyahoga Metropolitan Housing Authority, 355 F. Supp. 1245 (NDOH 1973).

Mahaley v. Cuyahoga Metropolitan Housing Authority, 355 F. Supp. 1257 (NDOH 1973).

Mahaley v. Cuyahoga Metropolitan Housing Authority, 500 F.2d 1087 (6th Cir. 1974).

Mapp v. Ohio, 367 U.S. 643 (1961).

Marable v. Alabama Mental Health Board, 297 F. Supp. 291 (MDAL 1969).

Meachum v. Fano, 427 U.S. 215 (1976).

Memphis v. Green, 451 U.S. 100 (1981).

Memphis Firefighters v. Stotts, 467 U.S. 651 (1984).

Metropolitan Housing Development Corporation v. Village of Arlington Heights, 373 F. Supp. 208 (NDILA 1974).

Metropolitan Housing Development Corporation v. Village of Arlington Heights, 517 F.2d 409 (7th Cir. 1975).

Metropolitan Housing Development Corporation v. Village of Arlington Heights, 558 F.2d 1283 (7th Cir. 1977).

Middlesex County Sewage Authority v. National Sea Clammers Association, 453 U.S. 1 (1981).

Milliken v. Bradley, 418 U.S. 717 (1974).

Milliken v. Bradley, 433 U.S. 267 (1977).

Mills v. Rogers, 457 U.S. 29 (1982).

Miranda v. Arizona, 384 U.S. 436 (1966).
Missouri ex rel. Gaines v. Canada, 305 U.S. 337 (1938).
Monroe v. Board of Commissioners, 391 U.S. 450 (1968).
Moore v. Charlotte-Mecklenburg Board of Education, 402 U.S. 47 (1971).
Moore v. East Cleveland, 431 U.S. 494 (1977).
Morgan v. Kerrigan, 401 F. Supp. 216 (DMA 1975).
Morris v. Travisono, 310 F. Supp. 857 (DRI 1970).
Morrissey v. Brewer, 408 U.S. 471 (1972).
NAACP v. Thompson, 357 F.2d 831 (5th Cir. 1966).
Nardone v. United States, 302 U.S. 379 (1937).
Nason v. Superintendent of Bridgewater State Hospital, 233 NE2d 908 (1968).
National League of Cities v. Usery, 426 U.S. 833 (1976).
New Jersey v. T.L.O., 83 L.Ed2d 720 (1985).
Newman v. Alabama, 349 F. Supp. 278 (MDAL 1972).
New York State Association for Retarded Children v. Carey, 393 F. Supp. 715 (EDNY 1975).
North Carolina State Board of Education v. Swann, 402 U.S. 43 (1971).
Novak v. Beto, 453 F.2d 661 (5th Cir. 1972).
O'Connor v. Donaldson, 422 U.S. 563 (1975).
Oliver v. Kalamazoo Board of Education, 368 F. Supp. 143 (WDMI 1973).
Olmstead v. United States, 277 U.S. 438 (1928).
O'Shea v. Littleton, 414 U.S. 488 (1974).
Palmigiano v. Garrahy, 443 F. Supp. 956 (DRI 1977).
Parham v. J.R., 442 U.S. 584 (1979).
Park View Heights Corporation v. City of Black Jack, 335 F. Supp. 899 (EDMO 1972).
Pasadena Board of Education v. Spangler, 427 U.S. 424 (1976).
Peek v. Mitchell, 419 F.2d 575 (6th Cir. 1970).
Pell v. Procunier, 417 U.S. 817 (1974).
Penick v. Columbus Board of Education, 429 F. Supp. 229 (SDOH 1977).
Pennhurst State School and Hospital, 612 F.2d 84 (3rd Cir. 1979).
Pennhurst State School and Hospital, 67 L.Ed2d 694 (1981).
Pennhurst State School and Hospital, 673 F.2d 647 (3rd Cir. 1982).
Pennhurst State School and Hospital, 79 L.Ed2d 67 (1984).
People v. Defore, 150 NE2d 585 (1926).
People v. Jackson, 245 NYS2d 534 (1963).
People v. Levy, 311 P.2d 897 (1st Dist. Ct. App. 1957).
Personnel Administrator v. Feeney, 442 U.S. 256 (1979).
Plessy v. Ferguson, 163 U.S. 537 (1896).
Procunier v. Martinez, 416 U.S. 396 (1974).
Pugh v. Locke, 406 F. Supp. 318 (MDAL 1976).
Pugh v. Locke, 559 F.2d 283 (5th Cir. 1977).
Ragsdale v. Overholser, 281 F.2d 943 (DCC 1960).
Ramos v. Lamm, 485 F. Supp. 122 (DCO 1979).
Raney v. Board of Education, 391 U.S. 443 (1968).
Reed v. Roe, 422 F. Supp. 706 (NDOH 1976).
Refoule v. Ellis, 74 F. Supp. 336 (NDGA 1947).
Reitman v. Mulkey, 387 U.S. 373 (1967).
Rennie v. Klein, 462 F. Supp. 1131 (DNJ 1978).
Resident Advisory Board v. Rizzo, 425 F. Supp. 987 (EDPA 1976).
Resident Advisory Board v. Rizzo, 564 F.2d 126 (3rd Cir. 1977).
Rhodes v. Chapman, 624 F.2d 1099 (6th Cir. 1980).
Rhodes v. Chapman, 452 U.S. 337 (1981).
Rizzo v. Goode, 423 U.S. 362 (1976).

Robinson v. California, 370 U.S. 660 (1962).

Robinson v. 12 Lofts Realty Inc., 610 F.2d 1032 (2nd Cir. 1979).

Rogers v. Okin, 478 F. Supp. 1342 (DMA 1979).

Rogers v. Okin, 634 F.2d 650 (1st Cir. 1980).

Rouse v. Cameron, 373 F.2d 541 (DCC 1966).

Rummel v. Estelle, 63 L.Ed2d 382 (1980).

San Antonio Independent School District v. Rodriguez, 411 U.S. 1 (1973).

Sarah C. Roberts v. City of Boston, 5 Cush. 198, 59 MA 198 (1850).

Sas v. Maryland, 334 F.2d 506 (4th Cir. 1964).

Saxbe v. Procunier, 417 U.S. 843 (1974).

Saxbe v. Washington Post, 417 U.S. 843 (1974).

Schnell v. City of Chicago, 407 F.2d 1084 (7th Cir. 1969).

Scott v. Plante, 532 F.2d 939 (3rd Cir. 1976).

Shannon v. Dept. of Housing and Urban Development, 436 F.2d 809 (3rd Cir. 1970).

Shelley v. Kraemer, 334 U.S. 1 (1948).

Shelton v. Tucker, 364 U.S. 479 (1960).

Sinclair v. Henderson, 441 F. Supp. 1123 (EDLA 1971).

Sipuel v. Oklahoma, 332 U.S. 631 (1948).

Sisters of Providence of St. Mary of the Woods v. City of Evanston, 335 F. Supp. 396 (NDIL 1971).

Smith v. Wade, 75 L.Ed2d 623 (1983).

Smuck v. Hobson, 408 F.2d 175 (DCC 1969).

Solem v. Helm, 77 L.Ed2d 637 (1983).

Soria v. Oxnard School District Board of Trustees, 328 F. Supp. 155 (CDCA 1971).

Sostre v. Rockefeller, 312 F. Supp. 863 (SDNY 1970).

Souder v. Brennan, 367 F. Supp. 808 (DDC 1973).

Southern Alameda Spanish Speaking Organization (SASSO) v. City of Union City, California, 424 F.2d 291 (9th Cir. 1970).

Southern Burlington County NAACP v. Township in Mt. Laurel, 336 A.2d 713 (NJ 1975).

Spangler v. Pasadena, 311 F. Supp. 501 (SDCA 1970).

Sparrow v. Goodman, 361 F. Supp. 566 (WDNC 1973).

Specht v. Patterson, 368 U.S. 605 (1967).

Stachulak v. Coughlin, 364 F. Supp. 686 (NDIL 1973).

Stewart v. Rhodes, 473 F. Supp. 1185 (SDOH 1979).

Stump v. Sparkman, 435 U.S. 349 (1978).

Swann v. Charlotte-Mecklenburg Board of Education, 311 F. Supp. 265 (WDNC 1970).

Swann v. Charlotte-Mecklenburg Board of Education, 402 U.S. 1 (1971).

Sweatt v. Painter, 339 U.S. 629 (1950).

Talley v. Stephens, 247 F. Supp. 683 (EDAR 1965).

Taylor v. Perini, 413 F. Supp. 189 (NDOH 1976).

Taylor v. Sterrett, 344 F. Supp. 411 (NDTX 1972).

Tenney v. Brandhove, 341 U.S. 367 (1951).

Trafficante v. Metropolitan Life Insurance Co., 409 U.S. 205 (1972).

United Farmworkers of Florida Housing Project Inc. v. City of Delray Beach, 493 F.2d 799 (5th Cir. 1974).

United States v. Board of Commissioners of Indianapolis, 332 F. Supp. 655 (SDIN 1971).

United States v. City of Black Jack, Missouri, 508 F.2d 1179 (8th Cir. 1974).

United States v. City of Parma, Ohio, 471 F. Supp. 453 (NDOH 1979).

United States v. City of Parma, Ohio, 494 F. Supp. 1049 (NDOH 1980).

United States v. City of Parma, Ohio, 504 F. Supp. 913 (NDOH 1980).

United States v. City of Parma, Ohio, 661 F.2d 562 (6th Cir. 1981).

United States v. City of Philadelphia, 482 F. Supp. 1248 (EDPA 1979).

United States v. City of Philadelphia, 499 F. Supp. 1196 (EDPA 1980).

United States v. Jefferson County Board of Education, 372 F.2d 836 (5th Cir. 1966).

United States v. O'Neill, 619 F.2d 222 (3rd Cir. 1980).

Village of Arlington Heights v. Metropolitan Housing Development Corporation, 429 U.S. 252 (1977).

Village of Belle Terre v. Boraas, 416 U.S. 1 (1974).

Vitek v. Jones, 445 U.S. 480 (1980).

Warth v. Seldin, 422 U.S. 490 (1975).

Washington v. Davis, 426 U.S. 229 (1976).

Washington v. Lee, 263 F. Supp. 327 (MDAL 1966).

Weeks v. United States, 232 U.S. 383 (1914).

Weems v. United States, 217 U.S. 349 (1910).

Wheeler v. Goodman, 298 F. Supp. 935 (WDNC 1969).

Wilkerson v. Utah, 99 U.S. 130 (1879).

Wilkliams v. Wallace, 240 F. Supp. 100 (MDAL 1965).

Wilson v. Webster, 315 F. Supp. 1104 (CDCA 1970).

Wilwording v. Swenson, 404 U.S. 249 (1971).

Wolf v. Colorado, 338 U.S. 25 (1949).

Wolff v. McDonnell, 418 U.S. 539 (1974).

Wolin v. Port of New York Authority, 392 F.2d 83 (2d Cir. 1968).

Wright v. Council of City of Emporia, 407 U.S. 451 (1972).

Wyatt v. Aderholt, 368 F. Supp. 1382 (MDAL 1973).

Wyatt v. Aderholt, 503 F.2d 1305 (5th Cir. 1974).

Wyatt v. Stickney, 325 F. Supp. 781 (MDAL 1971).

Wyatt v. Stickney, 334 F. Supp. 1341 (MDAL 1971).

Wyatt v. Stickney, 344 F. Supp. 373 (MDAL 1972).

Wyatt v. Stickney, 503 F.2d 1305 (5th Cir. 1974).

Yabarra v. Town of Los Altos Hills, 370 F. Supp. 742 (NDCA 1973).

Youngberg v. Romeo, 457 U.S. 307 (1982).

Younger v. Gilmore, 404 U.S. 15 (1971).

Index